MENNONITES AND CLASSICAL THEOLOGY

ANABAPTIST AND MENNONITE STUDIES

ANABAPTIST AND MENNONITE STUDIES

Anabaptist and Mennonite Studies is a publication series sponsored by the Institute of Anabaptist Mennonite Studies, Conrad Grebel College, University of Waterloo, published in cooperation with Pandora Press. The aim of the series is to make available significant academic works relating to Anabaptist and Mennonite history and theology.

1. A. James Reimer, *Mennonites and Classical Theology: Dogmatic Foundations for Christian Ethics*

MENNONITES AND CLASSICAL THEOLOGY
Dogmatic Foundations for Christian Ethics

A. James Reimer

Published by Pandora Press
Co-published with Herald Press

Canadian Cataloguing in Publication Data

Reimer, A. James
    Mennonites and classical theology : dogmatic foundations for Christian ethics

(Anabaptist and Mennonite studies, ISSN 1494-4081 ; 1)
Includes bibliographical references.
ISBN 0-9685543-7-7

1. Mennonites – Doctrines. 2. Theology. I. Title. II. Series.

BX8121.2.R44 2000   230'.97   C00-932149-7

MENNONITES AND CLASSICAL THEOLOGY:
DOGMATIC FOUNDATIONS FOR CHRISTIAN ETHICS
Copyright © 2001 by Pandora Press
51 Pandora Avenue North
Kitchener, Ontario, N2H 3C1
All rights reserved.

Co-published with Herald Press,
Scottdale, Pennsylvania/Waterloo, Ontario

International Standard Book Number: 0-9685543-7-7
International Standard Serial Number: 1494-4081

Cover Design: Lisa Sawatsky
Book design: Nathan Stark

Printed in Canada on acid-free paper.

10 09 08 07 06 05 04 03 02 01   12 11 10 9 8 7 6 5 4 3 2

To
Christina, Thomas and Micah

Table of Contents

Acknowledgements 11
Introduction 13

PART ONE   THE CRISIS OF MODERNITY

1. Theological Method, Modernity, and the Role of Tradition 21
2. The Ethical Implications of Gordon Kaufman's Theology 36
3. Doctrinal Renewal and the "Dialectic of Enlightenment" 54
4. Transcendence, Social Justice, and Pluralism:
   Three Competing Agendas in
   Contemporary Theology 67
5. Modern Justice and the "Oblivion of Eternity"
   The Conservatism of George Grant
   and Martin Heidegger 88

8 / TABLE OF CONTENTS

6.	Christian Theology and the Modern University	101
7.	On Bringing Forth the New Individual at the University	127
8.	Theology and Science: Response to Nancey Murphy	132
9.	Time, History, and Ethics in Gordon Kaufman	138
	Appendix: Correspondence between Kaufman and Reimer	154

PART TWO MENNONITES AND THEOLOGY

10.	The Nature and Possibility of a Mennonite Theology	161
11.	Anabaptist-Mennonite Systematic Theology	182
12.	Mennonite Systematic Theology and the Problem of Comprehensiveness	191
13.	Mennonite Theological Self-Understanding and Doctrinally Structured Systematic Theology	209
14.	Toward Christian Theology from a Diversity of Mennonite Perspectives	232
15.	Trinitarian Orthodoxy, Constantinianism, and Radical Protestant Theology	247
16.	Towards a Theocentric Christology: A Re-reading of the Bible, History, Anabaptism, and Modern Culture	272
17.	Mennonites, Christ, and Culture: The Yoder Legacy	288
18.	Theological Orthodoxy and Jewish Christianity: A Personal Tribute to John Howard Yoder	300

PART THREE THE CLASSICAL IMAGINATION

19. Lost Horizon: Whatever Happened
    to Classical Theology? ... 321

20. A Confessional Reading of the Scriptures ... 337

21. Confessions, Doctrines, and Creeds:
    Symbols and Metaphors of Ultimacy ... 355

22. Biblical and Systematic Theology:
    Two Parallel but Related Activities ... 372

23. God as Triune ... 392

24. The Two Natures of Christ:
    Reconsidering Chalcedon ... 406

25. Angels, Demons, and the Holy Spirit ... 421

26. The Grammar of Spiritual Warfare
    and Apocalypse ... 429

27. Apparitions: The Virgin Mary Appears
    in Yugoslavia ... 437

28. Chiliastic Imagination and Social Change:
    Bloch's Interpretation of Müntzer ... 443

29. Theology and the So-called "Orders of Creation":
    Nationality as an Instance ... 456

30. War as a Theological Litmus Test:
    Hirsch, Tillich, Barth, and the
    Confessing Church ... 474

31. God is Love but Not a Pacifist ... 486

32. Christians, Policing, and the Civil Order ... 493

33. Virtue, Justice and the Moral Community:
    A Critical-Appreciative Appraisal
    of Alasdair MacIntyre and the
    Narrative School of Theology   501

34. Homosexuality: A Call for
    Compassion and Moral Rigour   513

35. Christian Anthropology : The Perils
    of the Believers Church View
    of the *Humanum*   524

36. Mennonites and the Church Universal:
    Ecumenical Gifts of the Spirit   537

37. Conclusion: The Dynamic of the Classical Imagination   553

Notes   565
Index   639
The Author   649

Acknowledgements

I have numerous institutions and individuals to thank for their contributions to this volume. There are, first of all, the various institutions which provided the setting for many of the presentations here published. For the most part, these have been identified in the introductions and annotations with each essay. In particular I thank the following for permission to reprint my articles: *Canadian Mennonite*; *The Chesterton Review*; *CLIO: Interdisciplinary Journal of Literature, History, and Philosophy of History*; *The Conrad Grebel Review*; *The Ecumenist*; The Edwin Mellen Press; Herald Press; Institute of Mennonite Studies; Manitoba Historical Society; Mennonite Board of Missions; Mennonite Press; Pandora Press; University Press of America; William B. Eerdmans Publishing Co.; and Walter de Gruyter. Also, I am grateful to Gordon D. Kaufman for permission to publish his correspondence with me.

Of the many individuals who played an indispensable role in the long process of producing this book, I especially thank the following: Arnold Neufeld-Fast and Daryl Culp, who helped me begin the task of organizing and formatting the material; Michael King who, with his experienced editor's eye, read the manuscript; Joel Schmidt who began the task of indexing; Nathan Stark for formatting, copy editing, and indexing; Stephen Jones for final copy editing; and, above all, my friend and colleague, and publisher of Pandora Press, C. Arnold Snyder, who was willing to publish such a big book. I thank Lisa Sawatsky for the wonderful design work on the cover, and Gerald Loewen for permission to use the cover symbol which he created many years ago for a banner that hangs in my home. The banner features the poem by Menno Wiebe that appears with the Introduction to this volume.

Finally, I express my sincere appreciation to Conrad Grebel College for inspiring my thinking, teaching, and writing during my academic career, and for giving me research and travel grants over the years, including a grant for the preparation of this manuscript.

Introduction

> with
> one hand in the soil
> the other in the sky
> my people
> committed to the maker
> of earth and air
> maintain the balance
> of bread and belief
> *– Menno Wiebe*

The design on the front cover of this volume and the poem above that accompanies it reflect an artistic vision of a religious-ethnic community rooted in the natural world and simultaneously yearning for that which transcends nature and history. It is a vision that emerges in the history of a pilgrim people—the Mennonites—for whom human life with its toil, persecution, self-sacrifice, and love is nourished by faith in a God who commands, forgives, embraces, and sustains. Life and faith, culture and religion are here intrinsically linked.

The theology identified with such a vision is decidedly not sectarian if that term means a withdrawal from culture. Rather, it is a theology which takes *culture* seriously in all its forms, as an expression of what it means to be human, and *religion* (the yearning for the spiritual) as an inescapable part of culture. Cultural forms (customs, foods, ethnicities, languages, rituals) are the necessary means by which religious-spiritual yearnings are always mediated. If the people portrayed in the vision above and in this book are seen to be in conflict with culture, it is not a conflict with culture as such but a clash between competing cultural-religious visions.

Cultural-religious identities, whether of the dominant or the minority types, are never fixed and static. They are dynamic and constantly evolving configurations, an interweaving of older groupings (*ethnoi*) and the formation of new ones. Since human beings receive their own personal identities through such cultural, ethnic, and religious communal configurations, a certain durability over time is essential if individual life is to be nourished by them. The identity of the peoples called Mennonite has undergone significant transformation throughout its 500-year history, from its ancestral sixteenth-century origins in a diversity of Radical Reformation groups to its kaleidoscopic ethnic religious character in the modern period. And yet certain core religious and theological beliefs have endured and given a distinctive character to this group of peoples, whose historical narrative has been sustained over the centuries largely by those of North German-Dutch-Russian and South German-Swiss-French ancestry.

This book is not *a* systematic theology. The essays collected here are theological reflections on diverse themes of systematic theology, written over more than twenty years. The essays are meditations on the world in which we in the West have lived over the past centuries, on what it might mean as a Mennonite to think systematically about the Christian faith in a world of technical reason, and how the classical imagination might have relevance for us today. Most have been previously published and are here reprinted as they initially appeared, occasionally with some minor revisions. The short introductions preceding each essay are written in retrospect, identifying the original occasion for which the essay was written, and weaving together the various reflections into some kind of meaningful whole. Together the essays — some dating back two decades, some from this past year — form a kind of intellectual autobiography.

The underlying conviction of this volume is that the classical imagination (a notion which is defined below) is considerably richer than is generally recognized in contemporary thought. It is an imagination that is worth retrieving. For Christians, this means re-entering the imagination of the biblical and post-biblical "patristic" realm of thought in which the Christian doctrine of God, Christ, and the Holy Spirit evolved in the matrix of the encounter between the Jewish and the Greco-Roman world. For Mennonites, whose special gift to historic Christianity has been the call to faithful discipleship, particularly the peace witness, this entails seeing their gift as one of many gifts of the Spirit within ecumenical Christianity. I spell this out in the article, "Mennonites and the Church

Universal: Ecumenical Gifts of the Spirit" (see Chapter 36 below). It means, for Mennonites, that they should not understand themselves as developing an alternative theology which better suits their non-conformist history, but as situating themselves at the centre of classical Trinitarian and Christological orthodoxy, calling all Christians to greater faithfulness to the one creator of the universe, manifested in Jesus the Christ, and present in the church and world as Spirit. The essays below, and their introductions, are an account of how I arrived at the above convictions over a long period of thinking, preaching, writing, and teaching.

The title, *Mennonites and Classical Theology: Dogmatic Foundations for Christian Ethics*, has been carefully chosen as best describing the theological project I am articulating in this book. Although the essays vary in length, style, and systematic rigour, they all bear on this overarching theme. My concern for *dogmatics* understood ecumenically has been taken by some to be a betrayal of the historic Mennonite concern for Christian ethics, especially our peace witness. In fact, my intent has been the exact opposite — to take ethics (the principles guiding human behaviour) with utmost seriousness. To do so, however, means that ethics, particularly Christian ethics (including the Mennonite concern for peace, justice, and nonviolent love) needs a ground outside itself. An autonomous, self-grounded ethic is capricious and ultimately vulnerable to the vagaries of human convention, political correctness and false anthropologies. Only an ethic that is grounded beyond itself in the very structure of reality (what I variously call theological ontology or theological metaphysics) can give human action stability and durability in the face of temporary setbacks. I agree to a large extent with Frederick Copleston who, in his appreciative discussion of Socrates and Greek ethics, supports the Natural Law tradition with a qualifier:

> Such an ethic is indeed *insufficient*, since the Natural Law cannot acquire a morally binding force, obligatory in conscience—at least in the sense of our modern conception of 'Duty'—unless it has a metaphysical basis and is grounded in a transcendental Source, God, Whose Will for man is expressed in the Natural Law; but, although insufficient, it enshrines a most important and valuable truth which is essential to the development of a rational moral philosophy.[1]

I have used the term *foundation* in my title to distinguish the position here put forward from the anti-foundationalism (the rejection of an underlying rationality) that reigns in much contemporary theology. Reason is valued highly in these essays — not only a rationality that is intrinsic to a particular cultural-linguistic-religious tradition, but one *between* such traditions and texts. But the rationality presupposed in these essays is not the instrumental technical rationality that defines most post-Enlightenment thinking — a kind of totalizing rationality that deserves the critique put forward by zealous anti-foundationalists. Rather, the rationality espoused here is of an earlier kind, which classical thought identified with the cosmic Logos, or Wisdom, in which rational beings participate with reverence, awe, wonder, and piety.

This is the kind of reason which founds true knowledge and wisdom, that provides the foundation for Christian ethics here advocated. It is the "dogmatic" foundationalism of the early Christian apologists (particularly those of Alexandria) who sought commonalities between "Jerusalem" and "Athens," the God of Abraham, Isaac and Jacob, and the one God worshipped by the Greeks on Mars Hill (Acts 17) to which Jesus had brought shining clarity. The early apologists confessed faith not in a tribal god, but in the one God of all peoples. It is an older pre-modern rationality which takes divine wisdom, knowledge and revelation seriously — "general revelation" (Rom. 1 and 2) along with special revelation, ongoing revelation and final revelation.

The term *dogmatic* is used here as a way of talking about what Christians and the believing community (the Church) confess to be true. But it is dogmatics not narrowly defined as "church-talk" but as a defence of the faith in the biblical sense of 1 Pet. 3:15, the giving of an account to non-believers in a language they can understand; that is, an apologetics which assumes a commonality of human experience and understanding that makes communication possible. It is a dogmatics which presupposes the universal truth of Christian claims, while being fully aware of the relative and perspectival nature of all concrete expressions of that truth. Dogmatics in these essays is a linguistic genre having much in common with a family of terms that includes confessions, doctrines, and creeds. It is a way of using language that accentuates cognitive truth claims that I hold to be implicit, if not explicit, in most (if not all) forms of speech, including metaphor and narrative. I do not hold in these essays to a strict correspondence theory of truth but I do maintain that when Christians make confessional and dogmatic claims (as in the Trinitarian and Christological affirmations of the ancient creeds), they are making claims about how ultimate reality is to be understood. Creeds are more than language games and rules by which particular communities structure their behaviour — they represent "metaphors of ultimacy" which theologically ground ethics.

There are a few essays in this volume which deal specifically with ethical topics. However, the purpose of the book is to consider the theological foundations for ethics rather than systematic ethics itself. The book is divided into three parts, the first two containing nine essays each, and the third by far the longest.

Part One is my analysis and critique of modernity, to a lesser degree of postmodernity, and sets the stage for what follows. When I wrote the earliest essays in this section, I was strongly under the influence of Canadian philosopher George Grant. The criticism of modernity by theologians at the time was a trickle; it has now become a flood with 'postmodernity' and 'anti-foundationalism' being the shibboleths of mainstream contemporary thought. But I part company with most of the present critics of modernity in the solution I offer. *Part Two* represents my engagement with Mennonite thought in the light of the crisis of the modern era, with a subliminal theme that Mennonites—contrary to popular self-perception — are not so much the critics of modern culture as the anticipators and even bearers of modernity. The first essay, "The Nature and Possibility of a Mennonite Theology" spells this out most explicitly. *Part Three* constitutes my own constructive theological thinking — a way of reappropriating Classical theology. This is more than simply reiterating or translating ancient biblical and post-biblical conceptual categories but resists replacing the ancient way of looking at the world with modern and postmodern historicist thinking. The section ends with my situating myself *vis-à-vis* Thomas Oden, on the one side, and Wolfhart Pannenberg, on the other — two theologians whom I regard highly for their attempt to remain faithful to classical thought forms but who, for one reason or another, do not manage to enter the classical imagination on its most profound level. Miroslav Volf, I suggest, is perhaps the closest in spirit to the theological approach I represent. However, in the end, he falls short of consistently drawing the kind of ethical conclusions that are called for. How one manages the entry into the ancient imagination, in my view, is the key to facing the third millennium with faith, hope, and love.

PART ONE

THE CRISIS OF MODERNITY

ONE

Theological Method, Modernity, and the Role of Tradition*

This represents my first attempt to articulate for a Mennonite public the influence of Canadian philosopher George Grant on my theological thinking. It was an essay presented at the 1978 Mennonite Graduate Seminar,¹ an annual seminar for graduate students begun in the late 1950s. For the 1978 Seminar, held at Conrad Grebel College, participants were asked to consider the question: "What does your Christian faith and commitment have to offer your academic discipline by way of a critique of its assumptions, methodology, or ideology?" I chose to examine the thought of Gordon Kaufman (especially his 1975 Essay on Theological Method), *whose theological liberalism was in line with my own pre-Grant thinking. I had recently completed my Master's work in intellectual history at the University of Toronto, concentrating on Kant, Hegel, Feuerbach, and Marx, and was grappling with issues similar to Kaufman's. At the time I was enrolled in a doctoral programme in theology at the University of St. Michael's College, a Roman Catholic school which introduced me to the classics of the Christian tradition. In one of my graduate courses I was introduced to the social and political thought of George Grant, who was teaching at McMaster University at the time, and I began to devour his writings. I became involved in*

---

* Originally published in *Prophetic Vision Applied to One's Academic Discipline: 1978 Mennonite Graduate Seminar* (Elkhart, IN: Mennonite Board of Missions, 1978), 109-21. For notes on the text see the Notes section below.

conversations with Grant at a conference devoted to his thought, the proceedings of which were later published.[2] *My encounter with Grant led to a kind of intellectual conversion on my part, and started me thinking critically about the Enlightenment and the assumptions of modernity, particularly as they undergird contemporary technology. This essay, which explores critically Kaufman's (and my own) liberalism in the light of Grant's critique of the liberal tradition, ends with a conundrum: "We desperately need a more traditional concept of God, but we cannot believe in such a God." The resolution of this dilemma preoccupies me, implicitly if not explicitly, in all of the subsequent essays in this volume. It will become evident to an observant reader of the later essays how far my thinking has evolved over the years beyond this early attempt to articulate my problem with much contemporary theology.*

◆ ◆ ◆

The ineluctable drive of moderns towards a totally administered society, with the crowning of technology as the god of our modern world and as the panacea for all evils, demands a serious reconsideration of the basic presuppositions, nature, and task of theology. The most universally accepted assumption in the modern age is that we are on our own, *free to shape ourselves*, nature, and history the way we desire. The assumption lies at the heart of modernity and its belief in unlimited technological and industrial growth.[3] Theology is being used to legitimate rather than critique this prevalent belief in the freedom of human beings to determine their own destiny. What is urgently needed is first, a more rigorous approach to theology and theological method; second, a fresh look at theology's stance towards modernity, on the one hand, and tradition(s), on the other; third, a concerted effort to grasp (rather than develop) the kind of theology and God-concept demanded by every age; and, finally, an honest examination of the link between theological method and social and political ethics.[4]

Theological Method

In the past, theological orthodoxy was largely determined and preserved by the expertise of a few learned theologians, sanctioned by the church to be guardians of the true faith by means of the "queen of the sciences." Ways of doing theology were meticulously guarded by Scripture and *the* tradition. Today, the danger lies in the other extreme. The notion of theological orthodoxy has for many become defunct, the role of tradition and Scripture is under serious attack, and talk about systematic theology and theological method is suspect. The theological scene is so heterogeneous and eclectic that it is virtually impossible to speak about theology in the singular. There exists a plurality of theologies.

The extent of the confusion and the indeterminateness of modern theology is graphically illustrated in a 1975 issue of *Christianity and Crisis* entitled "Whatever Happened to Theology?"[5] Responding to the given question, leading theologians of North and Latin America almost unanimously agree that contemporary theology is in a state of disarray. Pastor Wallace Alston bemoans "the pragmatization of theology by the so-called religious 'professionals.'" Theologian Van A. Harvey laments that "the lack of serious dialogue among peers, the subsequent narcissism (the theology of autobiography) and faddism (the theologies of atheism, hope, play, revolution, and most recently, polytheism tailgating one another like automobiles on a California freeway) are all bleak testimony to a pervasive loss of vocation and the breakdown of a once noble intellectual discipline."

Catholic theologian Rosemary Ruether cites "the dramatic shift of power away from the Western world and the crisis of technological civilization" as the unmasking of traditional theologizing. Latin American liberation theologian José Míguez Bonino similarly argues that "What is happening is that the great and admirable social and cultural achievement that we call Western bourgeois culture is reaching the end of its run; and consequently, the imposing and noble theological tradition which has accompanied, at times inspired, sometimes humanized and always expressed it, is running out." "Some theologians," he continues, "have tried to latch on to the final phases of that culture: hence a theology which feeds on the ethos of technological development (theologies of secularity, of the death of God) or on the efforts to 'opt out' through imagination (theologies of game, phantasy or the new mysticisms)."

New York theologian Roger L. Shinn describes the fragmented nature of modern theology as characteristic of our age in general. "There is plenty of activity in theology," he admits, "but it is a mixture of the vital and the frenetic, the relevant and the faddish, the profound and the escapist, the pace-setting and the ephemeral." Carol Christ of Columbia University, charges that "[w]hile our experience is varied and ever-changing, theology has become at best an interpretive overlay that does not contradict what we already know and have fully articulated about self and society." According to Frederick Herzog, of Duke University, "The modern mind the theologian has been apologizing to turns out to be a monstrous misfit in more ways than one." The theologian is "being proved weak and wrong in much of that in which he seemed so strong and right: a glaring instance of virtue as splendid vice. In this tragicomedy there are no villains left for him to attack; he turns out to be his own worst enemy."

The devastating critique of theology continues. Union theologian and literary critic Tom F. Driver charges that "theology shares the decay of language in the general culture, that worship of communication which leads to the demise of understanding." For the Catholic David Tracy, what is "crucial to the elusive 'something' that 'happened' seems to be the difficulty contemporary theologians find in informing authentically public discourse and helping to transform contemporary public praxis." Finally, the Harvard systematic theologian Gordon Kaufman argues that in the sixties and the seventies theology came apart: "Theology apparently had no integrity or standards or demands of its own: its symbols could be used as a kind of decoration for and legitimation of almost any partisan position found in the culture. The once proud queen of the sciences, having lost a sense of her own meaning and integrity, had become a common prostitute." These are the judgements that respected theologians make about their own profession in this 1975 issue of *Christianity and Crisis*.

While there is general agreement on the prevalent confusion in the state of modern theology, there is no consensus on how theology as a discipline can be rescued. Serious consideration of theological method is once more necessary—a thinking through of central assumptions that will help to define theology's task in the modern world. Gordon D. Kaufman makes precisely this point in his book *An Essay On Theological Method*. While Kaufman's basic understanding of the nature of theology as "deliberate construction" is questionable at a number of points, his analysis of the contemporary scene is beyond refutation "Much current 'theological writing'," he says, "is neither very reliable as phenomenological description of experience nor clear in its theological significance or implication, because its methodological underpinnings have not been carefully thought through."[6]

The following sections of this paper will depend heavily on Kaufman's *Essay* and, at the same time, take serious issue with some of Kaufman's underlying assumptions, particularly his too strong critique of traditional theology,[7] his over-confidence in the capacity of individual theologians "deliberately" to reconstruct a more adequate concept of God,[8] and his de-emphasis of the importance of particular tradition(s) in theological construction.[9] Kaufman is committed to constructing a concept of God which will be adequate for the modern world. It is my contention, however, that his theological method is an inadequate basis for developing a theology capable of criticizing the modern age as radically as is necessary. For this, ironically, a more traditional approach may be required.

These reservations aside, Kaufman provides us with some valuable formal tools with which to proceed to develop a consistent theology. According to Kaufman, "the central problem of theological method is to discern and formulate explicit criteria and procedures for theological construction."[10] He arrives at what he considers to be three universal moments of theological construction, which can be used by theologians of widely different persuasions: 1) the construction of a concept of the world as a whole, based on a phenomenological analysis of experience; 2) the imaginative construction of a concept of God, which functions both as a limiting and a humanizing concept; 3) the re-construction of a theistic concept of the world, growing out of the second moment. These three moments in the "order of construction," according to Kaufman, "seem to underlie the generation of all theological concepts."[11] The following sections of this paper will be rather loosely fashioned after Kaufman's three moments in theological reflection: the movement from an examination of the modern world, to the need for a certain kind of theology, and a re-application of this theology to the world.[12]

Modernity and Tradition

In contrast to Kaufman, who searches for universal criteria with which to overcome the dangers inherent in sectarian particularism, George Grant sees particular traditions as a means of combating the homogenizing tendencies of the modern age. Grant, who has been referred to as "Canada's most respected philosopher," gives a profound analysis and critique of modern technological society and the assumptions on which it is based. Greatly influenced by both Heidegger's and Nietzsche's interpretation of modernity, although not accepting their historicist conclusions, Grant argues: 1) that the reality of technology, a combination of two Greek words, *techne* and *logos* (making and knowing), more than anything else defines the modern age, and 2) that this technological spirit is fundamentally rooted in the almost unanimously accepted liberal assumption that "man's essence is his freedom."[13] At the heart of the modern western view of self and world is a historicism which assumes that one belongs to oneself and that humans have an unlimited capacity, potential, and freedom to shape and control nature, history, and themselves. It is here that capitalism and communism, liberalism and Marxism, have more in common than in opposition — both are committed to the notion that technology is necessary for the improvement of the human race and the creation of an egalitarian humanistic society.[14]

While Grant's critique of modernity is harsh, it is not a simple rejection, for he recognizes his own involvement with and attachment to modern assumptions, values, and language. The point is not simply to reject modernity but "to try to understand what the coming-to-be of modernity means in terms of the whole."[15] What Grant unequivocally does reject is the modern concept of justice which follows from the presupposition that the essence of humanity is freedom. The classical notion of justice as "rendering each human being his due" is replaced with "justice as a human creation" in which in fact "some human beings have no due." It is to this modern concept of justice, based not on an eternal order of justice but on the will and creativity of humanity, that Grant responds with a resolute "No".[16]

Fully aware of his own captivity to the modern world, Grant espouses a belief in a realm of eternal values, an order of absolute justice that runs counter to all modern values and sensibilities.[17] For Grant, a classical view of justice and reason, and a traditional view of God as a transcendent being, is more true to reality than any of the modern views. His conservative view of philosophy and theology are arrived at not through any pre-modern *naïveté* but through a rejection of all the other modern options. What is needed, according to Grant, is a concept of the world and of God which will effectively *limit* humankind's arrogant faith in growth, and the will to dominate and master human and non-human nature. If it is true that theology must be in conversation with the major assumptions of the age, then, surely, Grant's biting critique of the contemporary world has something to say to modern theologians. Applied to theological method, a pessimistic appraisal of modernity, like Grant's, will determine the concept of God that is developed.

Similarly, Grant's understanding of the role of tradition(s) in the modern world has important implications for theological method. Grant defends the importance of nationalism and the rights of religious and ethnic minorities on the grounds that such social and cultural traditions counteract the ineluctable drive towards a universal and homogeneous state that characterizes technological society. This process of homogenization is "at the centre of the modern experiment . . . ."[18] While the modern age pays lip-service to the principles of liberalism—pluralism, freedom of minority groups, separation of church and state—it is deeply committed to the religion of progress and a monolithic society.[19] The symbol of this society is the computer. It is not an instrument which is value free and can simply be used for good or bad. The computer is the supreme symbol and tool of a society rushing towards a universal, homogeneous state. The computer is not neutral but itself dictates the way it must be used.[20] For Grant the important question for the modern world is "what alternative there is to the universal and the homogeneous state."[21]

It is in this light that Grant's defence of particular traditions must be seen. These traditions have a negative and a positive role to play within the modern age. On the negative side, they combat the homogenizing tendency of the technological monolith. It is in this context that Grant favours Quebec nationalism and the French separatist movement. Here there is a cultural and linguistic entity that is being determined by other than purely financial and technological interests.[22] On the positive side,

Grant considers the appreciation of family and traditional virtues as a means towards the experiencing of higher, more universal values. The universal good can only be adequately understood through the experiencing of particular goods. "On the one hand," says Grant, "love of one's own must ultimately be a means to love of the good. On the other hand, people who are deracinated, so that they have nothing which is really their own, rarely can move to the good."[23]

To understand Grant's radical critique of modern liberalism and his conservative espousal of traditional values of family, ethnicity, and nationalism, it is important to follow his intellectual development. He grew up in eastern Canada with what he calls "secular liberalism" or "English-speaking liberalism" (the American equivalent, according to Grant, is "American eastern seaboard liberalism"). He was raised "by fine and well-educated people who found themselves in the destiny of not being able to see the Christianity of their pioneering ancestors as true."[24] Grant's early writings demonstrate the strong influence this liberal upbringing had on him. At an early age, says Grant, he recognized "the barrenness of the all-pervading liberalism."[25] Gradually his disillusionment with the modern age, its belief in the religion of progress, and its commitment to technological growth convinced him that the classical traditions of Athens and Jerusalem provided a more adequate stance towards reality than modernity.

It is against this empty North American liberalism, its cosmopolitan individualism, free-floating internationalism, arrogant disregard for tradition, rampant consumerism, and decadent narcissism, that Grant's espousal of the classical tradition and particular traditions must be understood. For Grant, there is something essential that is lacking in cosmopolitan types. Contrasting the separatist Quebec premier René Lévesque to then Canadian prime minister Pierre Trudeau, Grant remarks: "Whatever Lévesque's mistakes, one does not feel that superior cosmopolitanism in him. One feels a love of his own in all its rough particularity."[26] Grant states his case even more strongly when he says that "cosmopolitanism is an appeal to a universal culture which is shallow beyond measure, and denies all the particularities of our roots."[27]

Grant's analysis of modernity, on the one hand, and the role of tradition on the other, nevertheless leaves some unanswered questions, which he himself is the first to admit. One such question is the link between the Christian tradition and modernity. Ironically, while Grant considers himself a Christian, he is fully aware that there is something inherently Christian, particularly its western interpretation, about the history-making spirit of the modern world.[28] Another question is the relationship between tradition, nationalism, and modernity. There is something ideological about nationalism itself. As one sympathetic critic put it, "If there's any insidious part of modernity it is the idea of nationalism, which goes hand in hand with technology. Nationalism is precisely the idea that produces the universal and homogeneous state."[29] A similar critique could be made of the ideological character of any tightly-knit religious, cultural, ethnic, or linguistic tradition.

These questions aside, Grant's apology for tradition in the modern world is largely justified and needs to be taken into account in developing a critical theological method. It is here that Kaufman, in my opinion, provides an inadequate account of modern culture, the important role of tradition(s), and the need for more traditional forms of theologizing.

Kaufman, who himself comes from a conservative religious and ethnic minority group, seems to embrace the kind of cosmopolitan approach to theology that Grant rejects. In actuality, Kaufman's understanding of the function of tradition in developing an adequate theological method is somewhat confusing. He stresses the importance of history and tradition as a basis for all of theology, and then proceeds to argue that modern theologians need to find other criteria than Scripture or tradition to do their constructive work.

His cosmopolitan approach is already hinted at in the introduction to his *Essay*, where Kaufman asserts that "[t]he view of theology that emerges here is one of a generally significant cultural enterprise with universal and public standards, not a parochial or idiosyncratic activity of interest only to special groups." He adds that "[i]t is my hope that the position developed here will be of help to theologians of all persuasions, liberal or conservative, Whiteheadian or existentialist or revolutionary, Protestant or Catholic or Jewish."[30] What Kaufman attempts to develop is a "formal methodological conception," free of material content, which is abstracted from any particular traditions sufficiently that it has universal application. The question of whether such a purely formal approach to theology is possible or desirable aside, one wonders whether Kaufman has in fact succeeded in freeing himself from a particular tradition. His obvious attempt to appropriate the most recent philosophical and social-scientific insights of the western world would suggest that his theology has a particularly modern, western, if not North American bent. He himself admits that the theological language which he uses to construct his theology is peculiar to western culture and not to other traditions.[31]

Kaufman argues that "there is a place for special reference to particular traditions of meaning and special communities of interpretation, but this is obviously not the place where theological reflection actually begins. Theological terms and concepts are rooted in the wide experience and history of a whole culture, or a mixture of cultures . . . ."[32] While "theological reflection must be rooted in categories and concepts and images provided by tradition and history," theology must not begin with the invocation of authority and the specific documents of a tradition.[33] It must begin with the "common language" and "ordinary uses" of words and concepts common to a whole culture. "Theology, thus," concludes Kaufman, "has a public, not private or parochial, foundation."[34]

Deeply influenced by modern linguistic philosophy, Kaufman maintains that central to the theological task is the study of how language is used. He asserts that "the distinctive and proper business of theology is neither interpretation of the vagaries of religious experience nor exposition of the particularities of Scripture or of church doctrine but analysis, interpretation and reconstruction of the concept and image of *God*, as found in the common language and tradition of the west . . . ."[35] The very notion of wanting to "re-construct" a concept of God, to fashion something radically new, suggests the extent to which Kaufman is committed to the modern view of freedom. The danger inherent in linking theological work so closely to the common language of western culture, is that, because that language has been shaped so profoundly by the values giving rise to technology, the theological construct becomes bound to those same values.

The extent to which Kaufman's methodology is a product of the history-making spirit of modernity, which Grant rejects, is illustrated even more clearly in his over-estimation of the capacity of individual theologians "deliberately" and "self-consciously" to construct concepts of God that will evoke popular piety. "But this lays upon theologians new and far-reaching responsibilities," argues Kaufman.

> We no longer can settle theological issues by appeal to the authority of Scripture or tradition. We must now undertake the much more difficult and hazardous task of deliberately and self-consciously constructing our concept of a God who is an adequate and meaningful object of devotion and center for the orientation of human life. In doing so we are free to entertain on their own merits a variety of models for constructing the concept of God, and to accept or reject them without regard to their scriptural or traditional authorization.[36]

It is my contention that theologians are in fact less free in their constructive work than they would like to think. The role of tradition, on the one hand, and the powerful influence of modern technological assumptions that seek to undermine a common tradition as well as particular traditions, on the other is in fact much more determinative than Kaufman seems to admit.

I have examined at some length two different approaches to modernity and the role of tradition(s)—that of Grant and Kaufman—in order to gain some perspective on the central issues involved. Kaufman's attempt to develop a common discipline of theology, to arrive at criteria which go beyond sectarian, parochial, and idiosyncratic traditions may be laudable. In constructing his *formal* method, however, it seems that Kaufman too readily accepts both the negative and the positive aspects of modernity.

It is this negative dimension of the modern age which Grant so powerfully explicates. While Grant tends to underestimate the positive elements in modernity, his fundamental critique remains intact. The danger in the modern world lies more with homogenization than with parochialism. With Grant, I would urge that a new interest be taken in the importance of not only the great traditions of Athens and Jerusalem but also of the role of particular traditions in combating the negativities of the modern age. One's stance towards the modern world and tradition will to a great extent determine how one goes about constructing one's theology.

Negative Theology

The negativities of the modern age demand a "negative theology" and a concept of God as "limit." That is to say, the function of theology ought to be primarily critical rather than positive if it is not to become ideological. What is needed is a concept of God who stands over against the assumptions of the modern age. Put in another way, the emphasis should be on what God *is not* rather than on what God *is*. This *via negativa* has a long tradition reaching back to Jewish iconoclasm. In the Jewish tradition the assertion "I am who I am" attributed to God illustrates the Jewish concern that no positive image, no material content should be given Jehovah. No one could see God's face, and his name could not be pronounced.[37]

The modern Frankfurt school of neo-Marxists continues this Jewish tradition in its fight against all ideology, arguing that negative dialectics is necessary. Its method of critical theory of society is based on a negation of negativities. Any positive characterization of God, truth, and the future becomes ideology.[38] Anselm's famous definition of God as "that than which nothing greater can be conceived" is a similar attempt to show what God is not rather than what he is.[39]

My contention is that, if theology is to remain critical and not be used as ideology in its legitimation of the negativities of a given ethnic group, nation, or age, there needs to be a rigorous attempt to adhere to a negative theology, to assert a concept of God as *limit*, as *unmasker*, as absolute *boundary*, as standing *over-against* the ideologies of any given age.

While Grant is a philosopher, not primarily a theologian, he stresses precisely this point. As early as 1959, Grant said in his *Philosophy In the Mass Age*:

> But the idea of limit is unavoidably the idea of God. If we say there is something that should never be done under any circumstances, we have said that something is absolutely wrong. We have said that the history making spirit has come upon that which it has no right to manipulate. The standard we have come upon is a reality we must accept, not a value we create. God is that which we cannot manipulate. He is the limit of our right to change the world. In recognition of limit, the idea of law in some form once again becomes real for us. The idea of God, having been discarded as impossible and immoral, comes back in the twentieth century as men recognize that if there is no theoretical limit there is no practical limit, and any action is permissible.[40]

Here is the crux of the matter. Grant has profoundly recognized the dilemma of the modern world. While a traditional view of God is not possible in the twentieth century because of the Enlightenment, such a concept of God is necessary if we want to assert that something is absolutely wrong. A pre-modern understanding of God is demanded to restrain the unlimited manipulation of nature, history, and humans by humans.

Kaufman also recognizes this need for a concept of God, though not as radically as Grant. According to Kaufman, the concept of God constructed by theologians must fulfill both a negative and a positive function. On the negative side, God must be conceived as the supreme relativizer of everything finite, preventing *hubris* and idolatry. God is one who restricts, restrains, and "impinges" on our existence.[41] On the positive side, God is conceived as the supreme humanizer, as an "adequate and meaningful object of devotion and center for the orientation of human life."[42] Kaufman convincingly argues that "it is impossible to worship, to order one's life by, or even to think clearly a completely bare and empty 'X.'"[43] To give this "X" any content, therefore, it is necessary to draw on human experience for models of the divine. An adequate concept of God's positive dimension, consequently, demands first of all that a theologian is a good anthropologist who knows what it means to be truly human. He will then relate these insights to God somehow. An acceptable concept of God will, for instance, relate to the moral, intellectual, and cultural dimensions and needs of humans.[44] To keep us from "legitimating the mundane interests, class structures, or revolutionary movements," in our putting content into the God-concept, we need both the relativizing and the humanizing aspect of the concept of God.

The problem inherent in Kaufman's understanding of theological method as deliberate and imaginative construction is precisely the fact that the concept of God and other secondary theological concepts *are known* to be deliberate human constructions. The notion of limit is built into the concept of God because of its pragmatic necessity, not because of any objective over-againstness, which would imply a "correspondence" theory of reality.[45]

Kaufman's methodology illustrates profoundly the dilemma of modern theology. He sees the necessity of God as limit and transcendent, but rejects the pre-modern notions that make belief in the truth of such a concept possible. Kaufman rejects the traditional theologies which presuppose "the acceptance of a model concerning God and God's Truth which is based on the objectivity and overagainstness of the object of perception."[46] The importance of Kant, for Kaufman, is his discovery "that the concepts or images of God and the world are imaginative constructs, created by the mind for certain intra-mental functions . . . ."[47] He rejects the old subject-object split between the self and God because of its unacceptability after the Kantian turn in philosophy; yet Kaufman wants to admit a facsimile of this concept into the notion of God through the back door because it is necessary. The problem of modern theology is exactly this, that a concept of God as radically standing over against human history-making arrogance is necessary, but the theologian cannot believe in such a reality, because he or she knows that the very notion of God as limit is a theological construction. My contention is that, for the radical critique which is demanded by the modern age, a traditional approach to theology may, ironically, once more be necessary. A negative theology, a radical concept of God as transcendent, as standing outside and over against history, judging that history, is once again required.

Social and Political Ethics

The radical discontinuity that is sometimes espoused between theological method and social and political ethics is to be seriously questioned. One's moral stance within the world surely follows logically from one's presuppositions in theological method. A particular concept of God, for instance, will determine a certain approach to ethical activity within society. A strong emphasis on God as willing, becoming, creating, and dynamic would seem to imply a revolutionary, evolutionary, or progressive understanding of history and society. An emphasis on God as being, as absolute limit, as boundary, can be used more readily to support a more conservative social and political ethics.

In Kaufman's three moments of theological reflection, morality and ethical concerns fall into the third moment of theological construction "so as to 'fit' intelligibly with the God who is thought to be its (the world's) ultimate ground and limit."[48] The problem with much contemporary theology, in Kaufman's opinion, is that it starts or dwells with this third moment of theological activity without an adequate consideration of the first two moments of construction, and thus results in confusion and triviality. The concern for "urgent social issues such as racism, poverty, and problems of the 'under-developed nations'" are an important part of theological constructions but need to be seen in their proper place.[49]

We do not get a clear picture of Kaufman's own political stance within the modern world, except that, contrary to Grant, he seems to be on the side of the modern project: "The most a theologian can do," he remarks, "is attempt to show that the interpretation of the facts of experience and life, which he or she has set forth, holds within it greater likelihood than any other for opening up the future into which humankind is moving—making available new possibilities, raising new hopes, enabling men and women to new levels of humanness and humaneness, instead of closing off options and restricting or inhibiting growth into a fuller humanity."[50] Kaufman's rhetoric sounds thoroughly modern in its future orientation and negative appraisal of "closing off options" and "restricting or inhibiting growth."

Grant's position in regard to the modern project is much more pessimistic. His early writings betray a passionate optimism about the perfectibility of humanity and a belief in human progress. By 1959, however, he has serious questions about the modern liberal drive into the future for humanitarian reasons. He begins to argue for a balance between conservatism and radicalism. The "truth of conservatism" is its emphasis on order and limit. "The truth of radicalism" is its dogged belief that evil is not necessary and can be overcome. The unique fusion of conservativism and radicalism in Grant has sometimes been referred to as "red toryism." There has always been a socialist tinge in Grant's writings. This was illustrated in his pro-left sympathies during the sixties. His disillusionment with modern socialism, however, is that, like liberal capitalism it is committed to the religion of progress with its will to mastery and growth.[51]

His intellectual development and critique of the assumptions of the modern world lead Grant ultimately to a profound conservatism, which cannot be reduced to any of the modern political options—liberal, socialist, or conservative—for all three have capitulated to the modern obsession with making history. The very notion of "political activism" is rooted in this assumption that humans can shape their destiny, and tends simply to harden the direction in which society is already going. Grant ends up espousing a type of meta-political stance which "calls us to account for what we have done to the world, in the biblical terms of good and evil."[52] He concludes by asserting that we need once more to remember the classical understanding of reality as represented by Athens and Jerusalem, Greek philosophy and the Christian religion. Ironically, it may be that Grant's radical denial of modern politics and modernity has more social and political potency than all the other directly political options of the modern world.

All this is to say that one's political stance with respect to the modern world largely determines one's way of doing theology. A remarkable example of this link between social and political ethics and theological method is the theology of Karl Barth, perhaps the greatest theologian of the twentieth century. Only recently has a good case been made for interpreting Barth's so-called "conservative" theology from the perspective of Barth's radical view of politics and unequivocal critique of liberal thought.[53] It was when a group of ninety-three German intellectuals, including some well-known liberal theologians, signed a document supporting the Kaiser's war policy in 1914, that Barth — together with many of his contemporaries — became disillusioned with his own liberalism and convinced of the bankruptcy of modern liberal bourgeois culture.[54] It was then that Barth began developing a theology based on a concept of God as "totally other" and totally transcendent, a concept of God which was not a human construction but stood over against modern liberal culture. Here we see how a radical political stance directly influenced a theological method.

This link between theology and social and political ethics is also implicit in Kaufman and Grant. Kaufman's rejection of Barth's theology in favour of modern philosophical and anthropological assumptions is at the root of his method. Unlike Barth, he de-emphasizes the priority of traditional theological concepts, the authority of Scripture and tradition, and challenges theologians to "deliberately" and "self-consciously" construct a *new, more adequate* theology. While Grant is not concerned with theological method, his pessimistic analysis of the modern world, and his preference for the ancient view of reality implicitly suggest a much more conservative approach towards theology, one with a greater appreciation for tradition(s), traditional documents, and the importance of community. At the heart of Grant's world view is the belief that we are not our own (or on our own). He describes his conversion experience, which came during the Second World War, as follows:

> I went to work at five o'clock in the morning on a bicycle, I got off the bicycle to open a gate and when I got back on I accepted

God. Obviously, there is much to think about in such experiences. All the Freudian and Marxian questions (indeed, most: the Nietzschian questions) can be asked. But I have never finally doubted the truth of that experience since that moment thirty-six years ago. If I try to put it into words, I would say it was the recognition that I am not my own. In more academic terms, if modern liberalism is the affirmation that our essence is our freedom, then this experience was the denial of that definition, before the fact that we are not our own.[55]

The liberal assumptions at the basis of modern technology—namely, that we are on our own and free to shape our destiny—are in fact leading to a homogeneous, technocratic, and totally administered society. Modern "developmental" theologies grow out of the same assumptions that have given rise to the technological age and tend merely to legitimate this mastery and domination of the future. What is needed is the recovery of a more traditional approach to theological concepts, which can unmask and combat these prevalent assumptions.

The dilemma of moderns, however, is precisely the following: while a more dualistic world view seems necessary — a more traditional belief in a transcendent God who stands above history and judges, restricts, and limits human *hubris* — such a world view is impossible in the modern age after the philosophical (Kant), psychological (Freud), social (Marx), and scientific (Einstein) enlightenments. In short, we desperately need a more traditional concept of God, but we cannot believe in such a God. And to deliberately and self-consciously fashion such a concept for pragmatic and humanistic reasons begs the question. This is the dilemma confronting the modern theologian.

TWO

The Ethical Implications of Gordon Kaufman's Theology

Having identified the cul-de-sac *in which modern theology finds itself—the conundrum of needing a more classical theology but not being able to believe in a traditional, transcendent God—in the essay below I probed more deeply into the inadequacy of the modern, liberal agenda by studying in greater depth the thought of Gordon Kaufman. This previously unpublished essay was presented for discussion to the Conrad Grebel College faculty in the early 1980s. In it I pose the dilemma somewhat differently: we are all (including Mennonites) captive to the assumptions of modernity; the question is: do we embrace modernity joyfully and thereby reinforce it with our theologizing, or do we accept our fate with an "uneasy conscience," attempting to unmask its dominant assumptions? My own inclination here was clearly in the direction of the latter, having become persuaded that the positive gains of the Enlightenment in humanizing life are outweighed by the losses and dangers to human civilization. Evident is my growing conviction that classical theology, with all its difficulties, is in general more profound (and more adequate) in its understanding of reality than the liberal world view represented by Kaufman. I use David Tracy's five approaches to contemporary theology in his then recently- published* Blessed Rage for Order *(1975) to situate Kaufman's project. By examining Kaufman's* Nonresistance and Responsibility and Other Mennonite Essays *(1979)in the light of his* Relativism, Knowledge and Faith *(1960), and* The Context of Decision *(1961), I try to show how his historicism relativizes the traditional Mennonite ethic of nonviolence. The essay ends rather abruptly without suggesting how one might formulate an alternative theology more adequate to Christian-Mennonite ethics, something that preoccupies me in later essays.*

Introduction: Some Underlying Assumptions

Before examining Kaufman's theology, particularly the ethical implications of his theological method, I want to reflect on a few of my own underlying assumptions. It seems to me that the way one engages in the theological enterprise today depends to a large extent on how one views the analytic, technical, and scientific achievements and assumptions that grow out of the Enlightenment and define the modern age. If one is fundamentally in sympathy with these achievements and assumptions, then one will make every attempt to embrace modernity and try to synthesize one's views as a theologian with the general insights of modern thought. If, on the other hand, one has some serious doubts about the modern project itself—its view of the dominance of technical reason, for instance, if one is overwhelmed by the negativities of the modern age, then one's theology will inevitably move in a different direction. One will be inclined to espouse a theology that does not easily reconcile itself to modernity, but finds itself committed to questioning, unmasking, and criticizing basic contemporary assumptions, and espousing either a postmodern or a more traditional-classical form of theology.

This latter stance is not grounded in a dogmatic notion that the church and the world must be separated as such, but is rather a strong conviction that the modern assumption that we are on our own and that our human essence is constituted by the freedom to shape nature, ourselves, and history without reference to universal, possibly even "eternal" norms of justice, does not provide an adequate view of what humans are fitted for.[1] This rather "pessimistic" view of moderns and their way of looking at the world is also not blind to the obvious contributions of the modern liberal, humanitarian tradition to the betterment of humankind—literacy, democratic and economic freedoms, the struggle against class and economic injustice and various older forms of heteronomical oppression, eradication of certain diseases, elimination of infant mortality, lengthening of average life expectancy, the potential decrease or even eradication of starvation through modern means of production and distribution, and so on.

The fact that this so-called human progress has benefited only a small fraction of humanity up to this point aside, this stance simply finds the negative side and threat of modern impulses—military and nuclear proliferation, industrial and technological dominance, domination and exploitation of human beings and nature, intoxication with consumerism, genetic experimentation, uniquely modern forms of totalitarianism and tyranny, atrocities and genocides of an unparalleled nature, to name a few— outweigh by far the positive aspects. The losses seem greater than

---

For notes on the text see the Notes section below.

the gains. Ironically, it is precisely the positive vision at the heart of the modern project—that is, the humanitarian improvement of humankind—which seems to have turned into its very opposite, into a kind of tyranny. This has sometimes been referred to as the "negative dialectic" or the "dialectics of Enlightenment."[2]

There is, to be sure, the historical fact that we all partake of the modern world. We are a part of it. Whether we like it or not, whether we are Mennonites who want to withdraw from the mainstream of society or not, we live in and are products of the modern age. Not only are we shaped by technological assumptions, for instance, but our very language and means of conceptualizing reality is technical, or, as George Grant puts it, "technique is ourselves."[3] We cannot but perceive ourselves and time as historical. Therefore, simply to reject or criticize modern society, as though we could distance ourselves from it, or isolate ourselves from its negative or "sinful" aspects, is impossible. The least we can do, it seems to me, is to try to understand our captivity and unmask some of the prevailing assumptions by which we live and make decisions. It is one thing to embrace joyfully and unambiguously the fundamental presuppositions of the modern scientific and intellectual world. It is another thing to admit one's own captivity to these assumptions but attempt to maintain an "uneasy conscience" within the situation.

Thus, it seems to me that, in trying to come to terms with any given theological model, one must first of all ask how it perceives itself in relation to the modern world and its assumptions. That is, does this particular theology perceive its primary task as the reconciliation or synthesis of "traditional biblical and historical Christianity" with the "historicist assumptions of the modern age" at all costs, or does it find itself in a profound dilemma with respect to the modern world? Does it see the classical traditions of Jerusalem and Athens in sharp conflict with the presuppositions of the modern age, while at the same time recognizing that the very language, concepts and values available to it are inescapably modern? It is in the light of these remarks that I examine and evaluate Kaufman's theology as it pertains to ethics.

The Context: Kaufman as a Post-Liberal "Revisionist" Theologian

In his book *Blessed Rage For Order* (1975), published in the same year as Kaufman's *An Essay on Theological Method*, the well-known Catholic theologian David Tracy places Kaufman alongside a line of what he calls postmodern or post-liberal "revisionist" theologians, including himself, Leslie Dewart, Gregory Baum, Michael Novak, Langdon Gilkey, and Van A. Harvey.[4] Tracy argues that we need to see theology not as literal descriptions of reality but as "models" with which to interpret reality. He calls them "'disclosure (or analogue) models'" as distinct from "'picture (or scale) models.'"[5] That is, theologies dare not "claim to provide pictures of the realities they describe—God, humanity, and world." Rather, they can only "disclose such realities with varying degrees of adequacy."[6] Tracy then lists five basic contemporary models for theological work.

The first model is that of *orthodox theology*, as represented by the Catholicism of the First Vatican Council for instance, in which a theologian sees his or her task as "to express an adequate understanding of the beliefs of his particular church tradition," for which the claims of modernity are not understood to have any inner-theological relevance. The main weakness of this model, according to Tracy, "lies in [its] theological inability to come to terms with the cognitive, ethical, and existential counter-claims of modernity" as expressed in other scholarly disciplines.[7]

The second model is that of *liberal theology*, or modernist theology as it is more appropriately called when applied to liberal Catholic theologians. It finds expression in a long line of nineteenth-century thinkers such as Hegel, Schleiermacher, Blondel, Ritschl, Wieman, Harnack, Troeltsch, Loisy and so on. There is here an "explicit commitment of the Christian theologian to the basic cognitive claims and ethical values of the modern secular period." The liberal theologian is "committed not marginally but fundamentally to the values of the modern experiment" such as "free and open inquiry, autonomous judgment, critical investigation of all claims to scientific, historical, philosophical, and religious truth." He or she takes seriously the challenge against the traditional view of truth and value that arises out of these modern views. While there are some inadequacies in the "specific material conclusions" of liberal theology, still this model sets the new agenda for post-modern or post-liberal theologians, Tracy argues.[8]

Neo-orthodoxy is the third model, and is most prominently represented by Karl Barth, but includes others such as Brunner, Bultmann, Tillich, the Niebuhrs, and neo-Thomists such as Karl Rahner. Tracy makes the important point, that neo-orthodoxy is deeply indebted to its liberal predecessor and must therefore be considered a post-modern model. The neo-orthodox theologians, however, were deeply aware of the inadequacies of liberalism and modernism—particularly evolutionary optimism and autonomous rationality—as were many of their secular counter parts such as Marx, Freud, and Nietzsche. They were especially critical of the inability of liberalism to account for the radical nature of human tragedy, sin and guilt, and regarded the liberal explication of major tenets of the Christian faith as shallow and inadequate. The weakness of this model, in Tracy's opinion, is its unwillingness to face up to some of the difficulties that the concepts of God, Christ, and revelation present to the modern mind, relegating such difficulties to the realm of the paradoxical, mysterious, and scandalous.[9]

The fourth model is *radical theology*, which radically affirms secularity and negates theism. It is espoused by "Death of God" theologians such as Paul van Buren, William Hamilton, and Thomas J.J. Altizer. Informed by both neo-orthodoxy and liberalism, but committed to a reformulated Christianity in which the central tenet—belief in a theistic God—is perceived as alienating and therefore rejected, it affirms at the same time Jesus as a paradigm for true liberated and unalienated humanity. The strength of radical theology is its pin-pointing of the problematic nature of the traditional concept of God. This is also its weakness, for it is hard to imagine carrying on the task of Christian theology without an affirmation of this central reality (i.e., belief in God).[10]

Finally, the *revisionist model*, or a theology committed to the critical correlation between the meaning of contemporary human experience and the meaning of traditional Christianity, is espoused by Tracy himself, Gordon Kaufman, and other contemporary theologians engaged in continuing "the critical task of classical liberals and modernists in a genuinely post-liberal situation" while at the same time taking seriously the neo-orthodox critique of the liberal tradition. It sees the main task of theology as being "the dramatic confrontation, the mutual illuminations and corrections, the possible basic reconciliation between the principal values, cognitive claims, and existential faith of both a reinterpreted postmodern consciousness and a reinterpreted Christianity."

While together with its secular colleagues is aware of the disillusionment with some of the oppressive consequences of the Enlightenment, this model refuses to return to a form of mystification. Instead, the revisionist theologian "believes that only a radical continuation of critical theory, symbolic reinterpretation, and responsible social and personal *praxis*, can provide the hope for a fundamental revision of both the modern and the traditional Christian self-understanding." "For the post-liberal theologian," says Tracy, "both secularity and traditional Christianity should be challenged in accordance with publicly available criteria for meaning, meaningfulness, and truth."[11] The important aspect of Tracy's fifth model is that it is basically a continuation of the liberal program: it is an attempt to synthesize modern secular thought with traditional Christianity.

This brings us back once more to Gordon Kaufman's theology. I find Tracy's models helpful in understanding not only modern theology in general, but Kaufman's thought in particular. I agree with Tracy's identification of Kaufman as a postmodern or post-liberal theologian who, while aware of the recent disillusionment with the consequences of

Enlightenment thought, is still basically committed to the so-called liberal task of correlating modern cognitive and ethical claims with traditional Christianity using publicly available criteria.

I became convinced of this view of Kaufman upon first reading his *Essay on Theological Method*, prior to my reading Tracy's appraisal. In that book, Kaufman's allegiance to modern phenomenological, linguistic, cognitive, and ethical presuppositions becomes quite clear. For instance, he identifies the three moments of all theological construction as: 1) the construction of a concept of the world as a whole, arising out of a phenomenological analysis of our experience; 2) the deliberate imaginative construction of a concept of God, which is adequate to the modern mind and modern piety, and operates both as a limiting and a humanizing concept; and 3) the re-construction of a theistic concept of the world, based on the second moment.[12] In effect, all theological construction is ultimately grounded in experience.

I find myself attracted to Kaufman's theology and Tracy's fifth model (postmodern model) revisionist. At the same time my encounter with certain other modern thinkers, particularly Canadian philosopher George Grant, has forced me—despite strong resistance—to look at the poverty of the modern project itself and to wonder whether a traditional, classical theology may not provide us with a more adequate understanding of human experience and ethical concepts such as justice.

In an earlier essay I have examined at length Kaufman's *Essay on Theological Method* in light of Grant's critique of modernity.[13] I contrast Kaufman's commitment to the assumptions of the modern age with Grant's unhappiness with those assumptions, particularly the notion that "our human essence is our freedom," a presupposition which Grant thinks defines the "liberal" view of humanity, nature and the world, and which he considers to be at the heart of modern technology.

While I am somewhat unhappy with Grant's undialectical view of modern technology, in that essay I side with Grant against Kaufman, arguing that Kaufman is too critical of traditional theology, overly optimistic concerning the ability of individual theologians to "deliberately" construct a more adequate concept of God for moderns— a concept which will aid lay people in their piety, and that he tends to de-emphasize the importance of particular tradition(s) (parochialism as he calls it) in theological construction. While Kaufman stresses the importance of history and tradition in general for theological construction as a whole (he titles his major work *Systematic Theology: A Historicist Perspective*), I argue in that essay that Kaufman rides roughshod over the idiosyncrasies of *particular* traditions in an attempt to arrive at *universal*, formal methodological concepts.

Grant provides a valuable counter-claim. For him, it is only through the love of one's own particular good that one can learn to love the universal good. "It is not the element of possession or of extension of self, which makes one's 'own' so important; but rather its availability for being known by us, and known as good."[14] Kaufman wants to detour around the particular good of his own (the conservative ethnic minority group of which he was and is a part) to arrive at the universal good.

I contend in that essay that Kaufman's "theological method is an inadequate basis for developing a theology capable of criticizing the modern age as radically as is necessary" and suggest that "[f]or this, ironically, a more traditional approach may in fact be required."[15] I am not advocating a reactionary adulation of a golden age in the past, nor defending heteronomous and authoritarian political, economic, and ecclesiastical structures of the past. Rather, I attempt to guard against all romantic enthusiasm about the present direction of our western society and a dangerous utopianism about our future. The dilemma of the modern theologian is precisely that while a more traditional view of God as totally transcendent, as one who limits and stands over against human *hubris* and arrogant history-shaping activity is necessary, she finds it impossible to defend such a dualistic concept of reality; that is, the Kantian, Freudian, Marxian, and Einsteinian enlightenments have destroyed the very possibility of the contemporary theologian to know (maybe even believe in) a God who stands above and external to human historical consciousness.

We now turn to a more detailed examination of three books by Gordon Kaufman that have a direct bearing on his ethical thought: *Relativism, Knowledge, and Faith* (1960), *The Context of Decision: The Theological Basis of Christian Ethics* (1961), and *Nonresistance and Responsibility and Other Mennonite Essays* (1979). The first book lays out the theoretical foundation for his approach to ethics, and the second and third address the question of ethics more directly within the context of a Mennonite audience.

Relativity: Truth and the Evolution of Consciousness

Kaufman's *Relativism, Knowledge, and Faith* is probably his most important book, growing out of his doctoral dissertation at Yale University on the problem of relativism and metaphysics, and laying the foundation for all of his later thought. His indebtedness to Immanuel Kant, Wilhelm Dilthey, R. G. Collingwood, Paul Tillich and modern linguistic and analytic philosophy is evident throughout. What Kaufman proposes to do is to attempt "an analysis of our thought processes which will enable us to understand why it is that our thought is relative and inadequate and subject to radical doubt, coupled with a careful assessment of the metaphysical and theological significance of this fact."[16] He acknowledges the "rootlessness" and "aimlessness" of our modern western culture and its concomitant dangers (fascism and communism). He acknowledges, furthermore, the disillusionment that has set in concerning much of the liberal humanitarian tradition that lies at the heart of the modern western world. Thus, for example, for Barth "the central problem is precisely the modern problem arising from our awareness of being cut off from our roots." But says Kaufman, "[h]and-wringing and nostalgia for the good old days before this insistent doubt had cut so deeply can do nothing but increase the anxieties of which we are already sufficiently conscious."[17]

Kaufman, therefore, wants to explain the modern problem of doubt and scepticism by examining the cognitive processes of the human self and show why it is a phenomenological fact that our knowledge is relative. He does not want to impose any dogmatic conclusions, prior theological commitments to tradition and so on, onto the analysis but rather seeks to examine "the problem of the relativity of truth *in its own terms*."[18] The validity of the argument, he says, must be determined solely on "anthropological" not "theological" grounds. We can suppose, therefore, that if his conclusions about the human self and human "cognitive processes" do not corroborate traditional theological concepts (sin, creation, redemption, and others), then Kaufman is ready to reject the traditional stance, or at least to change it substantially so that it will correspond with modern assumptions about reality. Kaufman's agenda seems to be dictated by prevalent understandings of the human self, and traditional views of God and humankind must bow to these modern discoveries and insights. It is clear that some kind of dialectical relationship between "tradition" and "modernity" is necessary. But the danger in Kaufman's thought, in my estimation, is a too easy accommodation to modernity.

Kaufman's case for relativism rests on a lengthy examination of the evolution of individual and group consciousness. In his phenomenological analysis of the various stages of consciousness, Kaufman is not alone but joins a large company of modern thinkers beginning with Hegel, whose *Phenomenology of Mind* was also a tracing of the different levels of consciousness—though for Hegel, who was a German Idealist, consciousness was the expression or actualization of Absolute Spirit.[19] Kaufman is more interested in the evolution of the self from its early pre-cognitive stages through various levels or "orders" of consciousness. At the lowest level is pure experience (*Erleben*), at which point there is no distinction between subject and object, and no differentiation between the real and the unreal, reality and illusion, truth and error. These distinctions come much later in the development of consciousness and depend on the exercise of "creative freedom" in sifting out and selecting various aspects of *Erleben*, the criteria for which "vary from culture to culture and from individual to individual."[20] In this most primitive stage of pure undifferentiated *Erleben*, the individual human organism experiences a form of "givenness" in its continual encounter with restricting wills and forces which stays with it throughout its life and is reinterpreted in various ways.

There are at least three general orders of consciousness, each with many sub-levels or stages. First-order consciousness is "mere 'consciousness'" and engages primarily in synthesizing and unifying experiences and contents of consciousness. Second-order consciousness is "thought," and reflects on the degree of success in the synthesizing activity of the first order. Third-order consciousness reflects on the second order—namely, on our thought and our knowledge—and through this third order "we discover the fallibility of our knowledge . . . ."[21] We thus arrive at a stage of self-critical thought: "we eventually arrive at a set of basic convictions—or first principles or self-evident truths or innate ideas or absolute presuppositions—which appear to be self-justifying and in terms of which we always find that we are justifying and explicating all other truth."[22] Thus our norms and criteria by which we distinguish between truth and error gradually emerge together with the development of the structure of the self and its world.

Probably the most important aspect of this development of the self is language, which defines us as member of a community of selves, and guides us in selecting and choosing between various dimensions of *Erleben*. Kaufman's view of language, in which he again is part of a growing number of modern linguists, is that language and thought are intrinsically linked. Language "structures and defines the world which the individual comes to know."[23] While Kaufman agrees with Kant that concepts and knowledge are constructs of the human mind, unlike Kant he does not believe that these linguistic-conceptual structures are universal; rather, they gradually evolve within history and time, and change as the historical situation changes. For a particular individual these linguistic structures may be *a priori*, but for the culture as a whole they are *a posteriori*.[24]

Therefore, according to Kaufman, truth and knowledge are in a very real sense evolutionary, or "historical," the term that he prefers. This view of knowledge stands in marked contrast to the classical notion that knowledge is "the grasping of the eternal forms (Greek) or laws of nature (modern)—factors which are forever constant, however much the situation of the subject may alter in time and history."[25] The dilemma which Kaufman faces, however, is that while he sets out to defend the relativity of all knowledge, he wants at the same time to explicate the need for the "objective validity" of knowledge, for "the search for truth demands of us that we go beyond any and all parochial interests, and the claim of truth is that it somehow has gone beyond the particular and the arbitrary to the universal and the valid."²⁶ The success of Kaufman's whole book depends on his ability to demonstrate both the "relativity" and the "objective validity" of truth and knowledge.

Kaufman attempts to explain the notion of validity through a phenomenological analysis of the self. There are three roots of the validity of thought: 1) "givenness" (which the human self experiences from the time of its earliest pre-cognitive level, and which expresses the "unconditionality of the demand upon thought to grasp being perfectly");²⁷ 2) that of "universality" (which is the drive of thought to move beyond all parochiality in an attempt to unify all our experience and thought);²⁸ and 3) "logical interconnectedness" (logic consisting not of purely formal principles of thought but abstractions of "concrete historico-linguistic" situations).²⁹ Thus "[t]he final standard or criterion of thought, which stands behind every particular act, is the ideal of the complete unification of all the contents of consciousness."³⁰

We are in a very real sense "prisoners of our own thought." We do not have access to "universally valid" truth. This does not mean that truth and error are not meaningful or real, or that we are imprisoned in "undiscriminating solipsism." Our memory extends through our individual and corporate history, and even into the future through imagination. It is this history which provides us with criteria, or norms by which to evaluate our knowledge and our actions. These absolutes are not eternal, however; they are absolutes only in the functional or pragmatic sense.

Despite the relativity and historicity of our knowledge and our thought, we have the profound conviction "that our knowledge somehow participates in that which transcends the relativities of our situation," that these functional absolutes are "somehow rooted in what is ultimately real, beyond all illusion."³¹ Metaphysics and theology deal with this realm of the "Ultimately Real," and address questions concerning the "riddle of life: Where have I come from? What is my destiny? What will I become? What does human existence mean?"³² But, since all our metaphysical and theological concepts are historically and psychologically relative, our talk about the nature of the ultimate reality which we "constantly presuppose as the final support of [our] existence" must remain symbolic or metaphorical, never literal.³³ It is at this point that Kaufman introduces his discussion of myth.

What Kaufman says about ancient and modern myths and the breakdown and replacing of myths is highly significant for our discussion:

> This, of course, does not mean that modern man must heteronomously accept some ancient myths which do this job but which seem to him to be absurd. What it does mean is that he has in fact already accepted certain modern myths—e.g., the

> notions of progress, will to power, scientific method, American destiny, the democratic way of life—in which this hidden gap between destiny and freedom is bridged and in which the faith of modern man in his relationship to a ground adequate to sustain his existence through the vicissitudes of history is expressed. The truth of these modern myths is now doubted in many quarters, and the current feeling of the meaninglessness of life to which all of the arts, and philosophy as well, bear witness, is no merely accidental corollary of this breakdown in the modern mythic consciousness. For this widespread doubt does not mean that man is at last transcending the necessity to live in myths; rather, it indicates a transition now in process to new myths which will give us (or perhaps already are giving us) a different relationship in faith to some transcendent ground of meaning—or else it points to the complete breakdown of Western civilization.[34]

I agree wholeheartedly with Kaufman's claim that moderns, like the ancients, are involved in myth-making, and that there is, further, little evidence that this myth-making will come to an end in the near future. I also agree that many of us doubt the adequacy of much of the modern western mythic consciousness. Yet I find myself disagreeing with the totally "historicist" means by which Kaufman suggests the adequacy of myths are tested and new ones created. For him the course of history itself is the ultimate test of the adequacy of a myth in its "interaction with reality."[35] Only the *eschaton*, the end of history, can be the final judge. Thus our present stance with respect to the Ultimate Reality, our present myth, may in fact be a totally wrong one. Thus also, the tests of coherence and pragmatic verification may lead us only farther along the path of error, as for example, "the success of *laissez-faire* economics" and "the success of modern technical thinking." It may be that only a historical disaster or catastrophe will demonstrate the error of our ways.[36]

It seems to me that ultimately there must be a non-historical criterion by which we judge the adequacy of our faith, of our myths, of our morality. While this supra-historical reality or norm can be perceived only historically, within a mythical or symbolic framework, nevertheless, for the Christian, the biblical myth if you like, stands as a judge and criterion of all other myths.

Kaufman continually refers to the Ultimate Reality (for the Christian, the Judeo-Christian God as revealed through Jesus Christ) "which stands behind, pervades, and guides the whole process . . . ." But Kaufman juxtaposes this with statements like "[w]e never overcome our historicity—

and even in this statement our historicity has not been overcome—for we do not know what are the relativities which limit us . . . ."[37] It appears that for Kaufman the Ultimate Reality which stands behind or above history can be only a formal or abstract concept without concreteness and particularity. "The burden of this essay," says Kaufman, "has been directed to showing that such a non-historical understanding of truth is inadequate and misleading. The very conception of what truth is and the criteria in terms of which truth is measured have varied with different historical situations in the past, and there is no reason to suppose they will not continue to vary and change."[38] "This work of ours," he adds, "stands under canons of truth, error, validity, and the like (themselves changing in history), just as thought in other presents has known itself to be standing under such norms."[39] It is this total "historicity" and "relativity" of norms, especially when applied to ethics, that I find unacceptable.

In this regard, Kaufman's remarks about Paul Tillich, the man who greatly influenced his own thought, are enlightening: "It is regrettable," says Kaufman, "that the tendencies, evident early in Tillich's thinking, to think through the significance of the *historical* foundations of human existence and thought, have given way to absolutistic principles and concepts. Many of Tillich's notions start out as historical conceptions (e.g., Kairos, the Protestant principle) but seem to go over too easily into eternally valid ideas . . . . This is typical of Tillich's thought as a whole: though it is very suggestive in its philosophical use of historical ideas, in the end it does not make *history* a category of decisive philosophical significance."[40] This is precisely where my own thought tends to move with Tillich rather than with Kaufman. Tillich's development of the "Kairos" category (that appropriate moment at which God acts within or reveals himself within history) was developed in the context of his own attempt as a religious socialist in the years between the wars, to reconcile Christianity and Marxism. It was in his conflict with National Socialism and the supporters of that movement, such as his friend Emanuel Hirsch, that he became convinced of the weaknesses of this category, and that he put a new emphasis on an "absolute" norm which transcends history and judges history as "revelation." Thus Kairos must always be seen in terms of a "Revelation-Kairos" correlation.[41]

While I find Kaufman's explication of the relativity and historicism of all human knowledge—namely, relativity as far as epistemology is concerned—illuminating and partially persuasive, I find it inadequate as far as its implications for ethics are concerned. In the following pages we see how Kaufman applies his assumptions about relativity, truth and faith to ethics more specifically.

Nonresistance and Responsibility

In Kaufman's *The Context of Decision: The Theological Basis of Christian Ethics* (1961), which grew out of his Menno Simons Lectures at Bethel College (Kansas) in 1959, and his much later publication *Nonresistance and Responsibility and Other Mennonite Essays* (1979), which consists of previously unpublished and published essays on a wide range of ethical questions written between 1958 and 1978, we see how Kaufman applies his theoretical presuppositions concerning relativity, knowledge and faith to concrete ethical issues facing the Mennonite tradition.

Kaufman begins his "Preface" to *Nonresistance and Responsibility* with the statement that "[f]or some time it has seemed to me desirable that there be available to Mennonites a more liberal and open interpretation of Christian faith and life than customarily appears under Mennonite auspices."[42] He uses the term "more liberal" to mean "an interpretation of the Mennonite perspective which breathes more freely the atmosphere of the contemporary life and culture in which they (i.e., Mennonites) are so deeply involved."[43] Kaufman has a strong distaste for any kind of narrow parochialism, biblicism, traditionalism, and authoritarianism. While he is not blind to the negativities of modern culture—exploitation, injustices, gas chambers, brainwashing, atomic bombs[44]—these are not intrinsic products of modernity, but must be overcome with the tools of Enlightenment. This is clear when Kaufman says:

> It will be observed that I do not agree with Yoder . . . that I have rejected the all-too-great authority of the church in the Anabaptist tradition in the name of the mass-church tradition; it would be more correct to say I am rejecting the common authoritarianism of both these lines in the name of "liberal" traditions rooted in the Enlightenment and modern democratic experience. The character and the theological significance of the relativism emergent from these more recent traditions, I have sketched in my book on *Relativism, Knowledge and Faith.*[45]

While Kaufman says his views have changed significantly over the years within which these essays were written, these changes, he adds, are primarily of a technical nature. Thus, "I now would not interpret the Christian life as founded so arbitrarily on an authoritarianism of revelation, as some of the chapters of the book written a good many years ago suggest but would be inclined to argue the value of a posture of redemptive love as intrinsically right and good for humans."[46] I assume that by "authoritarian revelation" Kaufman is referring to a form of absolute transcendent normativity which stands external to and above human history and judges that history. I presume, also, that by "redemptive love"

Kaufman is, in contrast, referring to an immanent and historical criterion, which is defined within the human situation and according to which we shape our actions.

Below I examine in detail what Kaufman means by "redemptive love" or "nonresistant love"—concepts which link Kaufman's concerns with his own Mennonite background. While most other features of early Anabaptist thought (such as the separation of Church and State) which in the sixteenth century distinguished them from the rest of society, are no longer unique to Mennonites, the tenet of radical discipleship in the form of nonresistant love remains quite distinctive and is not widely accepted in our society.[47] We ought, as modern Mennonites, according to Kaufman, to decide whether this doctrine still remains a valid part of Christianity in the modern world. If not, we might as well cease to be Mennonite. If so, then we must consider it our task to represent this particular part of the Christian tradition. We should, however, never claim to have the only right or true interpretation of the gospel, for such a claim would be idolatrous.[48] We need to see the Christian tradition as pluralistic—various groups having different tasks in the modern world.

Furthermore, says Kaufman, our commitment to nonresistant love has too often been based on a simplistic and naïve biblicism which ignores the vast gulf that separates the "three-story cosmology characteristic of ancient humankind," as expressed within the Bible itself, and the "modern scientific mind with its belief that the earth is really but a second-rate planet revolving around a third-rate sun somewhere in one of the millions of galaxies which make up the universe . . . ."[49] The authority of the Bible rests not in the document itself but in the actual historical events which lie beyond the document.[50] The Christian believes that God has created this world for the purposes of establishing the kingdom of love, and God is now acting to transform this world of hate and evil into his perfect kingdom through self-sacrificial love. Thus, "the Christian ethic makes . . . sense, not to any pragmatic or prudential or rational analysis of experience, but only in light of the Christian eschatological hope for the actual coming of God's perfect kingdom."[51] The crucifixion is ultimately the source for all norms of Christian ethics, for here the "underlying movement of the historical process becomes visible and decisively effective in the actual transformation of history."[52] We can, therefore, as Christians "look forward to that grand and glorious future in which God's kingdom shall finally be realized."[53] Our Mennonite ethic of nonresistant love, therefore, one must assume, is one interpretation of this process of transformation and through it we in fact participate in bringing about that glorious perfect kingdom.

Probably the clearest outline of Kaufman's argument concerning the actual concrete social and political implications of Christian pacifism and nonresistant love appears in his essay "Nonresistance and Responsibility" (1958). While it is a very early essay, I assume from Kaufman's 1979 Preface to the volume of the same name that his basic position remains intact. We will conclude our study of Kaufman with an examination of his argument in this essay.

According to Kaufman, modern Christian pacifists and non-pacifists seem to agree that "nonresistant love leads us inevitably to withdrawal from and failure to take responsibility for the social order...."[54] It is this assumption that Kaufman sees as problematic and wants to reject. It implies that "the basic orientation of Christian ethics removes it from concern with the deepest problem of society."[55] It implies that to be responsible means to take as one's norm some standard outside of revelation—orders of creation, natural law. But this negates the very essence of love as expressed in the Sermon on the Mount and in Philippians 2, where love is seen as never withdrawing from an evil situation but advancing into it. "Love," says Kaufman, "is precisely that which goes into the very heart of an evil situation and attempts to rectify it.... All the more sinful the situation, the greater is the imperative that love enter it."[56] The Christian ethic is one of "absurdity" and "imprudence" in its entering and taking personal responsibility for the sinful situation. While Mennonites have seen clearly one side of this paradox—the sinfulness of the "power struggles, where self-centered and selfish individuals and groups attempt to dominate others and subject them,"[57] they have ignored the other side—the demand of love to enter the fray and take responsibility for it.

Christian responsibility entails a witness to individuals and society to God's redemptive love, but this witness must always be an expression of love for our neighbours which does not impose itself or its own views on others "as though I were God with absolute truth in my hand."[58] We should not condemn others for their ideas or actions, but must "understand his situation as he himself understands it, and thus to try to appreciate his own efforts to see the truth and the right and to live by them."[59] The non-Christian cannot be expected to have a Christian ethic, nor can every Christian be expected to have the same ethic as we ourselves have.

Our approach to modern society must be similar for it has its own standards and morals by which it acts. Let me quote Kaufman at length here, because it illustrates how far he is willing to go, not only to take responsibility for modern society, but in supporting it and shaping it:

> For example, we must not, as too often pacifists have, simply witness against every military bill that comes before Congress. This is indeed part of our obligation, our obligation to witness. But we who know well that it is folly to expect non-Christians

to act as Christians, and to expect Christians whose understanding of the faith is of one sort to act as Christians whose understanding of the faith is different, ought to know that it is folly to expect our nation to demilitarize completely. We ought, therefore, to be prepared, along with our negative witness, to *support* the military bill most in accord with the highest ideals and best moral insights of the total American society. Americans as a whole do not believe in defenselessness or nonresistance, and to demand that they act as if they did is not only folly, it is positively immoral; for this is to demand that others in our nation live by our faith, our understanding of the will of God, rather than their own.[60]

What then is the task of Christians given, a commitment to "redemptive love"? The following is Kaufman's answer:

If we would truly be disciples who would love, we must go beyond merely witnessing to our faith. We must concern ourselves with attempting to help our nation come to a deeper understanding of her own faith, her own convictions, the moral insights which are the context in terms of which she lives and acts. And we must attempt to help her come to a decision and work out a course of action in terms of her faith, rather than our own, however much we might desire her to follow what we believe to be the right.[61]

Love itself demands, therefore, that we enter the evil situation and help society make decisions in the light of its own, rather than our own, best insights and values. This will involve us in shaping and formulating policy with which we do not agree and even in implementing it:

As Christians, then, we have no right to withdraw from even the most horribly unchristian (as it seems to us) decisions which our nation finds itself facing, and we have no right to withdraw from support of the course of action to which it is led, if that action is in accord with the nation's best insights. Instead, we must constantly be attempting to help our nation come to the very best decision of which it is capable (and this will no doubt not be a pacifist decision in the case of war), through not only witnessing to our own understanding of the demands God lays upon us and the nation, but also through helping our nation become more clearly aware of its own highest convictions. This will involve our participating in the actual formulation of policy, for without such participation, our help is only abstract and unreal. The policy which we must help to formulate will not be the kind of policy we might formulate were we acting as members of a Mennonite society; it will be a policy in line with the ideals of the nation in which we are working.... Having aided in the formulation of policy, we must not shy away from also helping to implement it. For this would be to refuse to help our nation stand by its convictions; it would be backing out at just the moment when the greatest support is necessary.[62]

We will in effect be required to support bills and actions of our society with which we personally as pacifists do not agree. This, according to Kaufman, does not mean compromising the Christian ethic of love, "if compromise is interpreted as sacrificing voluntarily the demands of love."[63] Love must adapt itself to the needs of every new situation for "[l]ove thus never becomes a rigid absolute, the ethical implications of which are clearly and absolutely defined for every situation."[64] Therefore, despite the seeming contradiction, the pacifist Christian could theoretically hold the highest office in the land during wartime, "for his obligation out of love is to act responsibly in the situation in which he finds God has actually placed him."[65] Like Yoder, Kaufman accepts the real duality between the world and the church, the Christian and the non-Christian ethic, but unlike Yoder, he does not conclude thereby that the Christian must withdraw from assuming responsibility for the "moral structure of non-Christian society."[66] The dichotomy is not an objective one but a subjective one in the "consciousness of the Christian."[67] It is not a "dichotomy of condemnation" which leads to pride and to a "false division of human nature" and a "destruction of the very unity of God," but a "dichotomy of understanding" which leads to humility and acceptance of God's placing us as agents here upon the earth.[68]

It is interesting that Kaufman's defence of relativism, as we saw earlier, and of Christians understood as agents of God helping to bring about God's kingdom of perfect love in transforming the world, and of taking "absolute responsibility for the moral structures and activity of all the world," is made with the belief that prevents the kind of self-righteousness, arrogance, and idolatry of more traditional formulations. It could be argued, on the contrary, that the whole argument for "relativism" and human "responsibility for shaping the world"[69] is arrogance and idolatry of the highest sort, because it rejects any kind of absolute supra-historical norm which stands in judgment over all human activity and history, and places an absolute limit on the human will to shape our destiny.

Ultimately, in my opinion, Kaufman's ethics ought to be evaluated in light of the larger theological and philosophical assumptions lying behind his moral stance on nonresistance, pacifism, and so on. It seems that Kaufman wants to embrace a "redemptive form of individual and human love" without absolute norms by which this love is pre-defined, without reference to a supra- or non-historical realm, and in this he is accepting the assumptions of the modern age. He repeatedly stresses relativity and historicism of truth and creative historical freedom as the essence of being human. He notes:

> It is no longer possible for us simply to take over the view of biblical writers, or the Anabaptists, or, for that matter, earlier twentieth-century Mennonites; and it is a serious and highly constricting mistake to regard any of these as "authoritative" in the sense that we must 'believe' them true ... To live in freedom is to be open to what God is doing here and now, in this world and in this society in which we find ourselves, and to live in response to that activity of God. But that requires us to have the courage to think through afresh, from the perspective of our lives and our world, where God is and what God requires of us.[70]

For Kaufman, the criteria and canons by which we judge God's activity in the world are themselves historically determined. They are, in effect, shaped by us. It is this assumption — namely, that the very criteria and norms by which we judge our actions are created by ourselves or by humans more generally (throughout history to be sure)—that is at the heart of modern ethics and Kaufman's ethics as well. We cannot escape this conclusion if we breathe the atmosphere of the modern world as we all do. The dilemma is that this starting point is not adequately rigorous in saying "NO" to the negativities of the twentieth century. The horrors of Hiroshima, Nagasaki, Auschwitz, and the distinct possibility of limited or even total nuclear destruction of western civilization demand a much more radical critique than Kaufman's theology can provide. These horrors are not mistakes that modern western civilization has made along the way toward a utopian classless society; rather, they have grown out of and are intrinsically linked to our view of nature, science, and the human as a creative agent with unlimited freedom as a historical being to shape his or her destiny without reference to some absolute realm of justice or limit.

THREE

Doctrinal Renewal and the "Dialectic of Enlightenment"*

In the late 1970s I was introduced to the thought of the so-called "Frankfurt School of Critical Theory" by two of my theological and philosophical mentors, Gregory Baum and Rudolf J. Siebert. Baum was my doctoral advisor, and Siebert is a Catholic thinker from the University of Western Michigan, Kalamazoo who founded the "Future of Religion" course in Dubrovnik, Croatia (then still Yugoslavia) in 1976-77. I attended that first course at the Inter-University Centre for Postgraduate Studies in 1977 and was captivated by Siebert's passionate interest in Critical Theory. The following essay was presented in 1984 at a conference at Renison College, University of Waterloo,[1] on the recently published book by British theologian Stephen Sykes, The Integrity of Anglicanism. *The essay reflects both my reading of Frankfurt Critical Theorists and my growing interest in the possibility of doctrinal renewal within contemporary systematic theology. Sykes's book called for clearer theological reflection within the Anglican communion, but touched on a variety of issues which I thought were relevant for all denominations, including the Mennonite church. Mennonites too were*

---

* Originally published as "Doctrinal Renewal: An Adequate Alternative to Theological Liberalism?" in *The Future of Anglican Theology*, ed. M. Darrol Bryant (Lewiston, NY/Toronto, ON: The Edwin Mellen Press, 1984), 73-86. For notes on the text see the Notes section below.

suspicious of doctrine and had historically emphasized freedom of religious thought (at least theoretically) with its concomitant diversity and plurality. Like Sykes within Anglicanism, I was becoming increasingly convinced that Mennonites needed rigorous doctrinal thinking. I also was grappling with the pros and cons of modern liberal thought, certain that liberalism could not be rejected as such. Doctrinal thinking was not an alternative to liberalism, but would need to take the Enlightenment seriously and to take place within a liberal framework. It could not presume simply to restate, without reinterpreting, classical thought. In the end, however, I found Sykes unsatisfying. He was not sufficiently conscious of the extent of his liberalism. Through the influence of George Grant, Max Horkheimer and Theodor Adorno I had been persuaded that liberal assumptions were far more pernicious than Sykes realized, and needed to be much more self-critically appropriated within theology, even though I still had no constructive proposal of my own.

◆ ◆ ◆

> The dilemma that faced us in our work proved to be the first phenomenon for investigation: the self-destruction of the Enlightenment. We are wholly convinced—and therein lies our *petitio principii*—that our social freedom is inseparable from enlightened thought. Nevertheless, we believe that we have just as clearly recognized that the notion of this very way of thinking, no less than the actual historic forms—the social institutions—with which it is interwoven, already contains the seed of the reversal universally apparent today. If enlightenment does not accommodate reflection on this recidivist element, then it seals its own fate. If consideration of the destructive aspect of progress is left to its enemies, blindly pragmatized thought loses its transcending quality and its relation to truth. In the enigmatic readiness of the technologically educated masses to fall under the sway of any despotism, in its self-destructive affinity to popular paranoia, and in all uncomprehended absurdity, the weakness of the modern theoretical faculty is apparent.[2]

These words were written in 1944 by the neo-Marxists Max Horkheimer and Theodor W. Adorno in their classic study of modern culture, *Dialectic of Enlightenment*. In this important work Horkheimer and Adorno, founding members of the Institute for Social Research in Frankfurt, show their own ambiguous relation to modern liberalism. On the one hand, they are deeply committed to the fundamental assumptions and aims of the enlightenment tradition, particularly in their use of critical reason to examine and unmask contradictions in Western society and to work toward a more just and humane social order. On the other hand, they are profoundly aware of the almost inevitable tendency of the Enlightenment to destroy itself by converting into "positivism"—the reduction of all metaphysics to physics, transcendence to immanence, spirit into matter, subjectivity into objectivity. On this critical issue they and the other proponents of Frankfurt Critical Theory continue the tradition of German Idealism.[3]

"The program of the enlightenment was the disenchantment of the world; the dissolution of myths and the substitution of knowledge for fancy."[4] Ironically, however, in its very rejection of mythology, mystery, and superstition, enlightened thought itself turns into a totalitarian mythology, manipulating humanity, nature and history as objects to be controlled, mastered, and shaped. "Enlightenment becomes toward things as a dictator toward men. He knows them in so far as he can manipulate them."[5] Horkheimer and Adorno call for the Enlightenment to become self-conscious: "The point is rather that the Enlightenment *must consider itself*, if men are not to be wholly betrayed. The task to be accomplished is not the conservation of the past, but the redemption of the hopes of the past."[6] The problem that faces the Frankfurt social critics is this: how is it possible to criticize the *negativities* of modern Western culture, which has its roots in the Enlightenment, as radically as is necessary without abandoning the *positive* elements of that same tradition?

While Horkheimer's and Adorno's analysis and critique of the consequences of the liberal Enlightenment are directed primarily at culture in general and not at religion in particular, their insights have a direct bearing on the nature and poverty of *theological* liberalism. Theological liberalism, with its commitment to applying the historical and scientific method to theological questions, is not a totally separate phenomenon, but an outgrowth and particular expression of the more general cultural assumptions growing out of the Enlightenment. My presupposition in this paper is that a rather thorough critique of modern liberal culture and its assumptions is necessary both outside of and inside the church, but that it cannot be accomplished by using pre-Enlightenment categories in their purity, or by recovering and conserving the past in its pristine form. A recovery of classical categories from antiquity is necessary for the purpose of judging and transcending our own culture as a church, but these concepts must first go through the crucible of the Enlightenment before they can be effectively appropriated by the Christian church today.

I turn now to an examination of Stephen Sykes's view of theological liberalism as articulated in his book, *The Integrity of Anglicanism*.[7] Sykes's primary concern is not with liberalism *per se* but rather with the sorry state of affairs within Anglican theology: a prevalent view within Anglicanism that it is devoid of doctrinal commitment. Only in a secondary sense is Sykes concerned with liberalism, seeing it as largely responsible for the present situation within the Anglican communion. Not being a member of the Anglican church, nor being a specialist in Anglican church or theological history, I must for the moment assume that Sykes's analysis of the situation is largely correct and that his proposals are to be taken seriously.

I find myself in fundamental agreement with Sykes's views. I agree with his call for a recovery and renewal of clear thinking, of systematic theology, for the purposes of clarifying for oneself *what one believes to be true*, of articulating for oneself criteria with which to distinguish between the negative and the positive elements of modern culture and with which to check "institutional drift," of establishing for oneself some kind of standpoint from which rational discussion, self-criticism and ecumenical conversation are possible. If anything, it seems that Sykes does not go far enough in appealing for a strong position from which to judge modern liberal assumptions.

However, I find myself asking some critical questions of the author. Among them is this: By characterizing liberalism primarily as a "negative" phenomenon, merely as a reaction and a protest against other theological types, something essentially "parasitic," can Sykes take the categories and assumptions of modern liberalism as seriously as he needs to in order to carry through his own program? My second question is related to the first: Is Sykes fully aware of how far his own stance, particularly in the last chapter, is dependent upon liberal Enlightenment categories? With these opening observations I turn now to a discussion of themes arising out of Sykes's book: the nature of theological liberalism, criticisms of theological liberalism, alternatives to theological liberalism, and our inescapable indebtedness to the liberal tradition.

The Nature of Theological Liberalism

The terms "modernist" and "liberal" tend to take on distorted meanings and conjure up ugly memories of theological disputes between religion and science in the early part of this century. They are often used loosely and in an ill-defined manner to dismiss theological opponents without taking them seriously. It seems especially important, therefore, to begin with a consideration of various uses of the term "liberal," and particularly Sykes's own understanding of it.

Canadian philosopher George Grant argues that the basic assumption of modern liberalism is the notion that freedom is the essence of humanity and that this "freedom lies at the heart of technology."[8] Central to modern liberalism, for Grant, is the idea that human beings are ultimately on their own, free to shape human and non-human nature in an unprescribed and unlimited way. For Catholic theologian David Tracy, "[t]he liberal and modernist theologian accepts the distinctively modern commitment to the values of free and open inquiry, autonomous judgement, critical investigation of all claims to scientific, historical, philosophical, and religious truth." According to Tracy, the liberal theologian is "committed not marginally but fundamentally to the values of the modern experiment. He cannot but find himself open to the challenge which these values, when applied by modern cognitive disciplines, pose for the classical claims of traditional Christianity."[9]

Grant is committed primarily to illuminating the poverty of modern liberal and technological culture, to unmasking the prevalence of the liberal illusion of unlimited freedom, and to calling western humanity to the contemplation of a higher good, a good more adequately grasped by ancient Athens and Jerusalem than by moderns. Tracy is much less disillusioned by the modern project than is Grant, and is devoted to developing a post-liberal, "revisionist" model for theology, which in effect adopts the liberal agenda for the modern world. He is concerned with bridging the gap between "common human experience" and the "central motifs of the Christian tradition" more adequately than did orthodoxy, classical liberalism, neo-orthodoxy and radical theology.[10] Despite their differences, both Grant and Tracy view liberalism as having quite specific and substantive tenets which have a certain integrity of their own and must be taken seriously in the theological and philosophical enterprise.

Sykes, unlike both Grant and Tracy, argues that liberalism does not have a positive set of assumptions, does not exist as a positive entity in its own right, but is rather a negative phenomenon. Modern liberalism, according to Sykes, is a "cuckoo in the Anglican nest."[11] It is a parasite feeding on other forms of theology. The view that nineteenth century liberalism was a party in the church with a positive program is a myth, he claims. Unlike the evangelical or Anglo-Catholic parties within Anglicanism, liberalism is not a party at all and has no doctrinal or philosophical viewpoint. It is a "negative phenomenon," and like conservatism is a "habit of mind" without any positive content. "Liberalism in Christian theology can only operate by challenging the familiar authorities, whatever they may happen to be. But it does not itself stand for or profess any one philosophy or set of doctrines, other than the doctrine that theological proposals are not true because they are traditional."[12] Thus, to ascribe positive content such as "self-sufficiency of reason" or a necessary anthropocentricity to liberalism is extremely unfair. Theological liberalism can never stand by itself—it always depends upon what it rejects. One can only be a liberal in the camp of some other form of theology, such as liberal evangelical or liberal Catholic. This is why one can never reject liberals *en masse* but must consider each particular case.

Although it may be true that liberalism does not have a doctrinal platform such as that of the evangelical or Anglo-Catholic wing of the church, Sykes implicitly ascribes to more than simply a "parasitic" role in Anglicanism. For Sykes the "tolerance of diversity" is itself the principle *par excellence* of liberalism. The defence of a thorough-going pluralism within theology is itself the product of liberalism. This is in fact stated explicitly by Sykes: "The Anglican church, which has developed, under the impact of modern liberal theology, a breadth of doctrinal tolerance of doubt and internal contradiction unparalleled by that of other episcopal churches, has an urgent responsibility to articulate what it stands for as an institution in its liturgy and canon law, and to subject that content to rigorous criticism."[13]

Comprehensiveness, complementarity, and *via media* are all to varying degrees expressions of this fundamental principle of tolerance of diversity within Anglicanism. But the extent of that tolerance underwent a major change with the coming of modern liberalism in the nineteenth century. It is this shift, according to Sykes, which William Temple, in his 1925 statement that modern liberalism stands in continuity with the Latitudinarian tradition, has not adequately taken into account. Temple does not distinguish between the pre-critical and the post-critical stage. In the earlier latitudinarian phase, diversity could be defended against the sterility of dogmatic orthodoxy on the basis of the diversity of Scripture itself. Modern Biblical scholarship, though, subjected the documents themselves to criticism.[14] In the earlier period there was always an assumed distinction between essentials and non-essentials in which only the non-essentials were subjected to scrutiny. With modern liberalism this distinction becomes unclear, and the fundamentals themselves come under attack.[15] All limits to theological diversity now cease to exist.

Nevertheless, the seed of modern Anglican liberalism is already present in the sixteenth- century Elizabethan Settlement, an attempt by the bishops to create a *modus vivendi* between warring factions within their dioceses. With the notion of comprehensiveness in the hands of men like F. D. Maurice, this seed has grown into a confusing and "bogus theory ... which for far too long has lain like a fog over the Anglican mind."[16] It is a form of confusion because it disguises the true nature of Anglican diversity and identity. Sykes claims that militant Tractarianism (the Anglo-Catholic wing) and militant Protestantism (the evangelical wing) have been more accurate in their appraisal of the situation than liberalism, for they have recognized their fundamental differences and learned to co-exist without trying to unite the opposites. Sykes is to a large extent correct in claiming that tolerance is of the very essence of liberalism. Liberalism supports a rather superficial pluralism within the church rather than come to terms with fundamental contradictions and passionately held convictions. The weakness of Maurice's liberalism, according to Sykes, is that it equates onesidedness with disloyalty to Anglicanism. This is a misunderstanding of Anglicanism. Maurice's concept of the church was "a paper church, a figment of the imagination and not the Church of England, where men had the right to call contradiction by its proper name."[17]

Liberalism is, therefore, not the principle of diversity itself, but rather a superficial tolerance of diversity, a white-washing of contradiction. Sykes is quite ready to admit the existence of diversity and conflict within the Anglican Church, the inclusion of both Protestant and Catholic elements, "elements regarded as mutually exclusive in other communions."[18] But they must learn to co-exist within a framework that has a solidly rational and theological basis. It is a watered-down notion of *via media*, a vague concept of the complementarity or union of opposites, which seeks to define Anglicanism as an undefined middle position that Sykes wants to reject.

The Poverty of Theological Liberalism

Because Sykes defines liberalism mainly as a negative phenomenon without giving it any positive content, he does not adequately expose the extent to which certain liberal assumptions shape today's church in particular and modern technological culture in general. He considers the poverty of liberalism too narrowly in terms of doctrinal questions.

Modern so-called post-liberal, "revisionist" theologians such as David Tracy and Gordon Kaufman are attempting to incorporate "limit language" into their theological models precisely because they recognize the weakness in the classical liberal position.[19] Sykes is right, therefore, when he argues that one of the critical problems of modern liberalism is its incapacity to set limits to human freedom and to the amount of tolerance that the modern church can allow. There must be some kind of standard by which the church can determine, for example, what aspect of modern culture is consistent with the Christian tradition and what it must reject. Gross forms of syncretism were unacceptable to primitive Christianity and must be rejected by the modern church.[20] In this context Sykes asks the valid question: "Are there then no boundaries to the degree to which the Church of England is prepared to tolerate diversity of doctrinal conviction?"[21] He is also right to say that "it is perfectly conceivable that under certain conditions, such as when a totalitarian regime requires that the church abandon or distort essential features of the gospel, it might be necessary to distinguish between a true and a false church, in order to preserve the integrity of the faith."[22] With the painful memory of most recent history still present, I cannot see how this can be denied. It seems true that liberalism in its defence of tolerance and pluralism tends to become impotent at a time of crisis.

This is because liberalism does not have a clear vision of what it believes to be doctrinally true. Like nineteenth century Anglican liberalism, which did not constitute a cohesive party but was a variant of German liberal Protestantism, so today liberalism is not a well-defined entity. It has no doctrinal base because the essentials for such a base—Scripture, the Catholic creeds, the Thirty-nine Articles, and other historical formulations of the Anglican Church—are all subject to doubt and private interpretation. It has not always been so. "It is simply not historically correct to suppose that the present wide doctrinal freedom has always been characteristic of Anglicanism. The case is rather that in response to the pressures initially of controversy and subsequently (and decisively) of biblical and historical criticism, the Anglican church has progressively shed its distinctive confessional commitment, relatively broad though that always was."[23] Liberalism, Sykes implies, is in the end to blame for the loss of doctrinal and confessional distinctiveness in the Anglican church and for what Sykes sees as its inability to make a decisive contribution to ecumenical conversation at the present. In his opinion, the Anglican confession would cease to exist if the majority of its adherents were as unclear about their views as are its most liberal members.

It is interesting that, in contrast to some modern theologians who see a certain intellectual rigour as essential to the liberal cognitive method, Sykes views liberalism as having induced "intellectual laziness and self-deception" in the Anglican church.[24] This is due to the Maurician view that Anglicanism must ultimately be defined in terms of what is "practically effective" rather than what is "theoretically true." This is an implicit assumption behind the 1948 and 1968 Lambeth Conference statements. "Might it not be the case," asks Sykes, "that Anglican theologians have for too long been complacent and lazy, and that their reluctance to formulate and defend Anglican theology is a serious disservice not only to their own communion, but also to the universal Church of Christ?"[25] Because the Anglican church has defined itself almost exclusively on practical rather than theoretical grounds, there has been, to Sykes's dismay, an almost total disregard for systematic theology. Historical theology, modern theology, and the history of doctrine have been taught to the exclusion of any systematic theology in the theological faculties of the universities. It is at this point that Sykes suggests his own alternative to theological liberalism. There must be a recovery of systematic doctrinal theology.

An Alternative to Theological Liberalism?

In order not to misrepresent Sykes's position, it is important to emphasize that Sykes is not committed to attacking liberalism as such but is bemoaning the lack of theological and doctrinal clarity within Anglicanism. This is clear when he states unequivocally:

> It seems, in fact, that there will always be doctrinal conflict. But because liberal theologians do not constitute a party there should never be any attempt either to assimilate or to reject them *en masse*. To accept the inevitability of some liberals, does not necessitate the toleration of all. Views are neither right nor wrong by being liberal in character. Only a church which had despaired of the possibility of rational argument about theology altogether could adopt such a stance.[26]

It is precisely rational argument about theology and doctrinal issues which Sykes wants to engender. However, by linking the present alleged dearth of theological commitment in the Anglican church directly to the triumph of liberal views of unlimited tolerance, Sykes's proposal for a recovery of doctrinal theology is in effect intended as a critique and an alternative to theological liberalism. The question is whether a renewal of doctrinal theology is an adequate response or alternative to theological liberalism, or whether doctrinal theology as Sykes envisions it may not itself be dependent upon and even part of the liberal vision.

Sykes is *not* calling for a new form of reactionary theology which will attempt to turn the clock back to pre-critical times. He is not appealing for "what was once, and still may be, called 'definite teaching' (that is, dogmatic views on all the subjects which have, in the course of time, been matters of theological discussion)." Neither is he calling for a type of theological uniformity. Sykes wants the Anglican church not necessarily to eradicate liberalism or eliminate diversity within its ranks, but "to offer a definite reason for doing so (that is, tolerating diversity) and to justify that reason in the face of objection." As Sykes puts it, "'[t]oleration of diversity' itself needs to be justified theologically."[27]

If the agenda of modern liberalism is to engage the church in active conversation with common human experience within the modern cultural context, then Sykes himself must be seen as having liberal sympathies. He does not defend the idea of a static and uncritical church, a church that withdraws into an intellectual and cultural ghetto. The church that claims that it has undergone no changes is no better than the church that uncritically adapts itself to its cultural environment. "If the Christian Church proposes faithfully to preach the gospel it has no alternative but to launch out into the ambiguities of interaction with its environment, an interaction in which it must keep itself open to criticism, and ready to change its ways."[28] It must maintain at the same time both "respect for traditional standards and sensitivity towards the danger of turning the church into a cultural ghetto."[29] Sykes wants the Anglican church "to articulate the characteristics of the matrix it provides for the growth of Christian character, and to subject that self-understanding to criticism."[30] He calls for criticism, argument, and mature judgement for bringing to consciousness that which is already implicit, that already exists in the Anglican liturgy and canon law. Sykes is not calling for a rigidly held "corpus of dogma." Systematic theology does not necessarily entail the acceptance of a body of dogma or an explicit set of doctrines.

Sykes's argument is confusing. Sykes does not want to be accused of defending a specific "corpus of dogma," yet he claims that the distinctiveness of Anglicanism is more than methodological; it has doctrinal content. While he strongly emphasizes that method and content cannot be separated, he appears to favour method over content, the rational and consistent argument *per se* more than the actual set of beliefs that might arise out of such inquiry. Here he betrays his fundamental kinship with the rationalism and pluralism that characterizes the modern liberal spirit. Sykes is not calling for *one single* theology but a group of theologies which bear the mark of Anglicanism: "Once it becomes obvious that there is no one Anglican systematic theology, any more than there is one Lutheran or Calvinist, one Greek Orthodox, or even one Roman Catholic, then nothing is lost if non-Anglicans discover that Anglicans do, as a matter of fact, bring a rather distinctive approach or group of approaches to questions of theological discussion."[31]

Sykes seems to argue that Anglicanism has a specific theological content arising particularly out of its worship, liturgy, and canon law, but that the nature of this content is not at all clear and can be interpreted in many different and conflicting ways. Systematicians themselves will not agree. "My position," he says, "is that Anglicanism has a specific content, and that it ought to expose that content to examination and criticism; it ought also to encourage specific individuals to write systematic theologies or extended treatments of Christian doctrine." "There ought," he continues, "to be Anglican systematic theologies, that is, theologies of high standards of internal consistency written by Anglicans of conviction" without considering them to be the exclusive Anglican systematics.[32] What exactly the bond that links these various theologies together will be (other than their rootedness in a common worship) never becomes clear. The only hint Sykes gives is that it may have something to do with the principle of the Incarnation.[33]

On the one hand Sykes assumes that his proposal of doctrinal renewal through systematic theology is an alternative to theological liberalism in the church, a necessary correction for gross forms of syncretism. On the other hand, his doctrinal proposal is not really an alternative to theological liberalism, but is itself quite dependent on the liberal Enlightenment.

Our Indebtedness to the Liberal Tradition

Sykes's own relation to liberalism within the Anglican communion is thus ambiguous. He lays the blame for what he considers to be the chaotic state of theological affairs in Anglicanism at the feet of modern liberalism and its indiscriminate tolerance of diversity. At the same time Sykes is greatly indebted to certain assumptions of modern liberalism. Part of the problem is that he defines liberalism too onesidedly as simply a reaction to the past. In this regard thinkers such as Max Horkheimer, Theodor Adorno, George Grant, Gordon Kaufman, David Tracy and Paul Tillich have a more adequate view of liberalism, seeing it as a more substantive movement in the modern world. They see liberalism as having some quite specific assumptions that have shaped the modern mind in a way that Sykes's purely negative appraisal does not sufficiently take into account.

I am not convinced by Sykes that the "self-sufficiency of reason" or a "necessary anthropocentricity" are not products of the modern liberal spirit. The liberal tradition as it grows out of the Renaissance, Reformation, and more forcefully out of the Enlightenment does have certain distinctive marks. One is the concept of "autonomous reason" with its emphasis on human subjectivity and its protest against all forms of "heteronomy (the uncritical acceptance of an external law)," as represented in Scripture, church dogma, or church hierarchy. In the words of Tillich, "[i]n the eighteenth and nineteenth centuries, in spite of some heteronomous remnants' reactions, autonomy won an almost complete victory. Orthodoxy and fundamentalism were pushed into the corners of cultural life, sterile and ineffective."[34] Liberalism was a rejection not simply of the past but of particular aspects of that past, namely, heteronomous authority in favour of subjective autonomy which acts, I would argue, as a substantive principle. Sykes reveals his indebtedness to the liberal tradition most profoundly in his last chapter where he deals with "Authority in Anglicanism."

There Sykes says he comes to the heart of the matter, the question of authority. This question lies at the centre of the liberals' concern, and it seems that they and Sykes come out more or less on the same side. First, Sykes rejects traditional heteronomous authority, adding that "by the recognition of the significance of personal responsibility, the Council (i.e.,

Vatican II) has liberated the Roman Church from a long tradition of reactionary rejection of the European enlightenment and initiated a development which can only lead in due course to a similar dispersal of the elements of authority."[35] Sykes defends the idea of "dispersed authority" over against the traditional notion of "embodied authority."[36]

Second, Sykes argues implicitly for a "spiritual" (if not actual) democratization of the church. While he admits that in fact the Anglican church structures are not democratized, it does accept the principle that individual members of the laity themselves must possess the means of judging the truths of Scripture, that "Christians to whom Scriptures are read in their own language are able to judge of the essentials of the faith."[37] Third, Sykes assumes the fundamental reality and even necessity of conflict within the church. This assumption—that there will be and should be conflict between members of a particular communion and between different communions in the search for a higher more unified concept of truth—lies at the bottom of Sykes's whole essay and his call for systematic theologies. Although it is true that conflict is central to early Christianity itself, in my view the nature of the conflict takes on a different and more fundamental character in post-enlightenment thought. Conflict in the modern world is based on the presupposition of a basic pluralism as a positive principle within the Christian tradition which was not present earlier. It is this pluralism that Sykes accepts throughout his essay. "The conclusion must be," he says, "that authentic Christian preaching and living can only be achieved in the midst of ambiguity and with attendant controversy, in which it is the Christian's duty to exercise careful discernment, if he is not to go (or be led) astray."[38]

While the traditional Anglican criteria of authority—Scripture, tradition, and reason—continue to have normative value, there is ultimately only one source of authority "which is freedom and love of the Triune God."[39] Here Sykes appears to give his final tribute to the liberal notions of freedom and love as the central criteria by which one worships God.

In conclusion, I restate my agreement with Sykes's call for a renewal of systematic theology, his appeal to the church (of whatever communion) to formulate a doctrinal position from which it can more adequately enter into ecumenical conversation, and from which it can judge the self-destructive aspects of the modern world. I also agree with Sykes that we cannot isolate ourselves and disengage ourselves from our modern pluralistic environment. Doctrinal renewal in isolation is inadequate, and ought not to take the form of a simple recovery of ancient sources in their pure simplicity without imaginative reinterpretation. In this sense we are deeply indebted to the assumptions of the Enlightenment in the very theological and doctrinal task in which we are engaged.

Yet Sykes does not go far enough in spelling out how that enlightened thought must become critical of itself within this theological task. In Tillich's words:

> The double fight against an empty autonomy and a destructive heteronomy makes the quest for a new theonomy as urgent today as it was at the end of the ancient world. The catastrophe of autonomous reason is complete. Neither autonomy nor heteronomy, isolated and in conflict, can give the answer.[40]

With reference to theology's struggle against "empty autonomy" and "destructive heteronomy," Tillich stands in the tradition of Horkheimer and Adorno. Tillich was professor of philosophy in Frankfurt during the early years of the Institute for Social Research—in fact, he assisted Horkheimer in obtaining a position at the University of Frankfurt, and Adorno wrote his habilitation thesis on existentialism under Tillich's supervision. Tillich joins them in their fight against the self-destructive aspects of modern liberal thought. Any attempt at systematic and doctrinal renewal written by the church in the modern era must penetrate more deeply into this self-destructive tendency within liberal-enlightened thought (what Horkheimer and Adorno call the "dialectic of the Enlightenment") than Sykes's otherwise laudable proposal achieves.

FOUR

Transcendence, Social Justice, and Pluralism: Three Competing Agendas in Contemporary Theology*

My reading of neo-conservative, socialist, and liberal theology had by the late 1980s convinced me that there are really three major agendas in contemporary theology, each premised on a different analysis of modern and postmodern culture, and each one proposing quite different solutions to the problems facing modern societies. Neo-conservatives like George Grant, Jacques Ellul and Hans Jonas believe the major problem facing us has to do with technology and the loss of transcendence and metaphysics. Socialists like Gregory Baum and Rudolf Siebert see the fundamental problem as economic oppression, the growing disparity between rich and poor nations, and the need for social justice. Liberals like David Tracy and Hans Küng are preoccupied with the fragmentation and pluralism of postmodernity, the problem of truth, and the need for inter-religious encounter. It seemed to me that each of these analyses and proposed solutions had their own legitimacy but tended to compete with each other. Theologians found themselves in one camp or another. I was interested in finding a way of developing a coherent theological framework within which to give each their due. In the following essay, presented for a conference in Winnipeg

---

*Originally published as "How Modern Should Theology Be? The Nature and Agenda of Contemporary Theology"in *The Church as Theological Community: Essays in Honour of David Schroeder*, ed. Harry Huebner (Winnipeg: CMBC Publications, 1990), 171-98. For notes on the text see the Notes section below.

in 1989 under the title "How Modern Should Theology Be? The Nature and Agenda of Contemporary Theology," I consider each of these three agendas as legitimate challenges.[1] I propose that a consideration of the three articles of the creed can help us in addressing all three agendas: the first article (God as Creator) speaks to the issue of transcendence; the second article (God as Christ) speaks particularly to the issue of liberation and social justice; and the third (God as Spirit) to pluralism, truth and the religions. More clearly expressed than before is my growing conviction that the classical Trinitarian imagination offers a creative way of dealing with a variety of contemporary issues which is more adequate than other less traditional approaches. The three agendas of contemporary theology identified above do not receive equal treatment. The major part of the essay is devoted to the first agenda — a critique of modern technology and the search for transcendence. I find myself drawn to the Jewish philosopher Hans Jonas whose critical analysis of modern historicist, utopian thinking and apparent "lament" for earlier thought forms (although, unlike myself, he denies the possibility of retrieving the Classical heritage) provides support for my own attraction to Platonic thought. A suspicion of all utopian, historicist, progressivist, and future-oriented or "directional" theology pervades many of the essays in this volume. For a Mennonite, for whom ethics and the struggle for historical peace and social justice is at the heart of the Gospel, the question then becomes: Is it possible to ground the motivation for human action in a theology that does not reduce everything to pure history-making?*

◆ ◆ ◆

One of the difficulties in speaking about "modernity" is the variety of ways the term is used in contemporary discussions. It cannot be assumed that the term means the same thing for scientists, sociologists, historians, philosophers, poets, and theologians. What is "modern" for many signifies whatever is current: the latest idea, invention, movement, or event. The term "modern" is used below more technically to refer to a certain historical epoch with particular assumptions about freedom (individual autonomy), reason (technical and analytical rationality), and history (the chronological sequence of time from past to present to future). In this essay I will concentrate on the agenda(s) of contemporary theology in light of the "historical" understanding of the term "modern," answering only indirectly the question of how modern contemporary theology should be.

In some literary circles the modern figure (referring to writers such as James Joyce, D.H. Lawrence, T. S. Eliot, and Virginia Woolf) is someone who "is acutely conscious of the contemporary scene, but . . . does not accept its values." In the words of literary critic Stephen Spender, it is the modern person to whom "it seems that the world of unprecedented phenomena has cut us off from the life of the past, and in doing so from traditional consciousness."² For the nineteenth-century philosopher Friedrich Nietzsche and his twentieth-century interpreter Martin Heidegger—the two thinkers the late Canadian philosopher George Grant considers to be moderns *par excellence*—the modern age begins with the loss of God as an eternal horizon for all human endeavour and experience.³ In a similar vein sociologists frequently talk about modernity in terms of secularity, disenchantment, individualism, and the loss of social cohesion provided in the past by the great religious traditions.

Grant, greatly influenced by Nietzsche and Heidegger, views moderns as those who have accepted the liberal assumption of freedom from all external restraints (or limits) that lies behind the rise of modern technology. Technology in Grant's thought presupposes a view of nature as devoid of value and at our own disposal, of humans as free to dispose of nature the way they see fit, and of reason as a means of controlling nature and history as cumulative progress. Liberalism is for him that "set of beliefs which proceed from the central assumption that . . . [the human] essence is . . . [human] freedom and therefore that what chiefly concerns . . . [humans] in this life is to shape the world as we want it."⁴ Although Grant thinks Heidegger, following Nietzsche, has correctly described the "oblivion of the eternal" which characterizes the modern age, he objects to Heidegger's happy acquiescence, and believes that we are finally not fitted for this modern view of reality. After much reflection he concludes that the classical way of looking at things (including the views of both Jesus and Plato) is more adequate than our own. Grant avows that despite the deprived nature of our technological language, it is possible through imagining, remembering, desiring, thinking, and contemplating to experience, momentarily at least (presumably as individuals), the eternal verities which transcend our and every historical period.⁵ The Eternal, he thinks, can take care of itself and break through even our age. In fact, nature is already revolting against human control and domination. In doing so the inadequacy of the modern historicist and anthropocentric project is unmasked. Grant considers himself both a Christian and a Platonist. It is here where he parts company with Heidegger and Nietzsche.

Behind the philosophical analysis of Nietzsche, Heidegger, Grant, and others, is the assumption that the great watershed in western intellectual history is the Enlightenment: that constellation of factors accompanying the rise of modern science, reason, freedom and time as history (in contrast to the classical conception of time as enfolded within eternity).⁶ It was the German theologian Ernst Troeltsch (1865-1923) who identified these intellectual currents of the Enlightenment, rather than the theological and ecclesiastical motifs of the Reformation, as the true birth of the modern world.⁷ While there may be room to debate this basic assumption—there might be reason, for example, to argue that the modern as it emerged with the seventeenth and eighteenth centuries is not as novel as these philosophers have made it out to be—it is this understanding of the modern which shapes my own thinking on the subject of "How modern should theology be?" I believe with Grant that the Enlightenment and its effects has virtually cut us off from a reverence for the past, and that the Eternal enframes the temporal. In affirming this I am saying that ancient Christianity, as portrayed in the biblical text and understood in classical theology, continues to be more adequate to human existence and self-understanding than theologies based on historicist perceptions of reality.

What has become increasingly transparent in the twentieth century—more so than it was for Troeltsch—is that the so-called "modern paradigm" is losing its explanatory, symbolic, and moral power in light of the crises that are facing contemporaries. This has given rise to talk about the "post-modern" world; a world where Enlightenment assumptions about science, reason, freedom, and history are no longer uncritically accepted, but are frequently seen to be part of the problem, leading to our present *aporias* ("dead ends"). "How modern should theology be?" when put in this light takes on entirely new dimensions.

Theology, in my opinion, does not have the freedom to be or not to be "modern," or "non-modern" for that matter, as if its practitioners sit above the historical flow of things making such choices. It has been shaped by modern scientific, rational, and historical assumptions. We participate in the age of which we are a part. The fact is that new paradigms cannot arbitrarily be created or chosen; they emerge gradually replacing older paradigms that have lost their power. The urgent question for theology, therefore, is whether, on one level, it is willing to release itself from some of the assumptions of the previous historical (the modern) epoch and open itself to the emergence of a new paradigm. It dare not absolutize any historical moment—either the pre-modern, the modern, or now apparently the postmodern. On a more important level, however, the question for theology is whether it has the capacity to receive an Eternal Word from outside, yet within, a given paradigm and then to address the challenges of a postmodern world with this historically-cloaked Eternal Word.

While there is growing consensus that the previous paradigm is finished, or at least seriously inadequate, and that something has to be done to save this planet, for example, there are competing analyses of the problem and its solution. The dilemma which seems to characterize the emerging paradigm is a sense of urgency that some kind of common front, including shared values, will be necessary if we are to find global solutions to the various crises facing us, realizing all the while that the contemporary global scene is defined by an increasing fragmentation of life and loss of corporate identity (the apparent impossibility of a common front).⁸ It is to these competing motifs and analyses of the crises in current theology that I want to turn my attention here.

There appear to be at least three conflicting sets of theological agendas arising out of different diagnoses of the present global situation in contemporary theology: 1) the total triumph of modern technology (including its threat to our planet) and the need for a new metaphysically or transcendentally based ethic in a disenchanted universe; 2) increasing economic disparity and political oppression and the struggle for social justice; and 3) growing diversity, pluralism, fragmentation, and loss of social cohesion with the accompanying concern for identity, tolerance, dialogue, and ecumenicity. A proliferation of theological literature is appearing in each of these three areas, and individual theologians, schools and even denominations frequently identify with one or other of these camps. One could, with some justification, characterize these three fronts as neo-conservative, left-wing, and liberal causes, respectively.

My own work has taken me into all three spheres of theological concern. In the remainder of this essay I will consider in greater detail the first of these (the technological), then comment briefly on the second (social justice) and third (inter-Christian and interreligious discourse) theological agendas in light of the first. I suggest that all three are legitimate theological concerns challenging us to serious reflection in the light of the three articles of the *Credo*. Incidentally, I understand *Credo* not as alternative to *Canon* but as personal and corporate appropriation and confession of *Canon*; as affirmation of the mysteries of faith which are as well (perhaps even better) chanted, sung, poeticized, even painted as logically argued and rationally analyzed.

The Technological Crisis and the Search for Transcendence

Technology raises questions for us as Christians concerning the nature of God's transcendence and relationship to the created order (nature), issues especially appropriate for consideration under the first article of the Creed: belief in God as Creator and Sustainer (or Ground). There is growing literature on the nuclear, environmental, and bio-medical dangers resulting from the global triumph of technical rationality. As I read this material I detect quite a different diagnosis of the current situation, a different critique of modern assumptions, and different solutions, than I find in literature where the overriding concern is emancipation and social justice, for instance. Rather than attempting a comprehensive survey of this literature I want to concentrate on the thought of one particularly significant contemporary Jewish philosopher of technology, Hans Jonas, and draw some conclusions for theology. I choose Jonas not only because of his profound insights into the contemporary technological situation, but also because I am fascinated with his critique of all eschatological-utopian thinking and his philosophical attempt as a non-Christian to articulate a responsible ethic for our age.

Jonas was born in Germany in 1903, fled Nazi Germany to England in 1933, spent 1935 to 1948 in Palestine, taught at McGill University (Montreal) and Carleton University (Ottawa) during 1949 to 1954, and since 1955 has been associated with the New School for Social Research in New York. He describes himself as having gone through three academic stages: a pre-war preoccupation with existentialist philosophy and ancient gnosticism, a post-war turn of interest to the natural sciences and the philosophy of organicism (he found himself sympathetic to Whiteheadian process philosophy, but in the end could not go along with it); and, in the last part of his career, a concern with practical philosophy or ethics, growing out of his fear of what was happening to our planet because of modern technology.[9]

Before his emigration to England in 1933 he studied with the philosopher Martin Heidegger and the Protestant theologian Rudolf Bultmann. While he pays great compliments to Heidegger as a teacher, he observes that Heidegger failed to connect his philosophy of Being to the physical and organic ground of Being, to nature itself. The German philosophers did not take the natural sciences seriously, he notes.[10] It was this growing conviction—that our own being, our very transcendence over nature, our freedom and our morality (*Sittlichkeit*) are themselves grounded in nature—that becomes a dominant theme in Jonas's second and third stages. It becomes especially crucial for his very influential environmentally concerned work in the area of ethics and technology. The almost inevitable cumulative effects of our daily peacetime use and application of technology, he comes to realize, is a much greater threat to us and our future than the danger of a nuclear disaster.[11] In "Technik, Freiheit und Pflicht" (Technique, Freedom and Responsibility), an address delivered in Frankfurt October 11, 1987 on the occasion of his receiving the German Book Publishers Peace Prize, he masterfully elaborates on how we as humans have become *the* danger to nature.[12] Technique is the product of our own human freedom and this freedom now calls us to responsibility. Our responsibility is to limit, to set boundaries to our own freedom, premised on the notion that "[l]ife is a good or a 'value in itself.'"[13] It is a collective duty and therefore a political one. Jonas, himself a fugitive from modern tyranny, is fully aware of the great temptation of fascism for the twentieth-century, and thinks the challenge is to walk the precarious line between preserving fundamental rights and freedoms and limiting, coercively if necessary, those individual freedoms that threaten the survival of human and nonhuman nature. There are no clear blueprints for the future—the technological reality in which we live is much too complex—and there is no possibility of stepping out of it. There can be no more talk of utopia (such thinking being itself partly responsible for the threat facing us) or of an earthly paradise, but only of a world which continues to be habitable (*Weiterwohnlichkeit der Welt*). "This means that for our whole future we will probably have to live in the shadow of the threat of calamity."[14]

In a remarkably personal essay written in 1976, "Im Kampf um die Möglichkeit des Glaubens" (The Struggle for the Possibility of Faith), Jonas reflects on personal memories of his teacher Rudolf Bultmann and on some of the philosophical aspects of the latter's work.[15] Jonas, together with Hannah Arendt, both Jewish students of Heidegger, attended Bultmann's New Testament seminar in 1924. What is particularly significant about his essay for our purposes—there are some highly interesting details about his personal relationship with Bultmann as a Jew prior to emigration in 1933 and immediately after the war which we cannot go into—is Jonas's critical evaluation, as a non-Christian, of Bultmann's perception of the scientific worldview and the possibility of belief in the modern world. While he agrees with Bultmann that the Enlightenment has put religion on the defensive, he thinks Bultmann concedes too much to modern science when the latter says that "modern science does not believe that the process of nature can be interrupted by supernatural powers . . . ."[16] Science, says Jonas, holds only to a methodological precept, not a metaphysical one. Bultmann solves the problem by arguing that God does not break into natural processes in any external sense but that behind all immanent-external necessity stands inner-transcendent personal and divine freedom.[17]

It is at this point where Jonas offers his own unique contribution to the debate about the possibility of metaphysics in the modern world. The example he uses is free human agency that does not violate the canons of modern science and history. Jonas shows how every time humans act there is, in effect, a nonphysical (one might say metaphysical) intervention in the physical realm. Every time we as human beings act with conscious decision in the face of a number of alternatives, the physical course of events is altered, caused to move in a direction that it would not have moved had no such nonphysical intervention taken place.[18] Jonas provides us with a philosophical defence of metaphysical freedom; a freedom that is rooted in the physical realm of nature but is nevertheless distinct from it, transcends it, and intervenes in it. Applied to theology this would mean for the believer, according to Jonas, that what can be attributed to human action surely cannot be denied of God; that is, God also has the capacity to intervene in a nonphysical way with the physical world while preserving the integrity of that physical world.[19]

One of the agendas for contemporary theology in the face of the rationalistic, historicist, and technological legacy of the Enlightenment is to reflect on how transcendence might be understood in the post-modern context. Jonas's example of free human action as a form of non-physical intervention in the course of the physical world, can provide theology with a phenomenological analogy for understanding divine transcendence, freedom and intervention in nature and in history.

Having introduced some of the main themes of Jonas's life and thought, I turn now to his more sustained treatment of the novel nature of modern technology and the need for a new metaphysically-based ethic of responsibility, as he offers it in his book *The Imperative of Responsibility*.[20] I concentrate on three aspects of his argument which have important implications for the contemporary theological agenda: his view of the modern versus the classical worldview, his proposal for an ethic of responsibility that is grounded in Being itself, and his critique of all eschatological-utopian thinking.

1.*Classical versus Modern Ontology* To read Jonas carefully is to find that he is torn between the classical and the modern view of reality. He feels we are trapped in the modern and need to take responsibility in the modern sense but his proposal draws on important classical motifs. The classical world viewed nature as essentially immutable and "given once for all." Human control was insignificant in the face of "abiding nature." Responsibility for nature was not a prominent theme. Nature could take care of itself. Ethics was defined in terms of the good or the virtuous; what was good for human beings in the present would be good for them in the future. The ancients thought "vertically" (in terms of the eternal) not "horizontally" (the prolongation of the temporal). In classical ethics "the drive is upward, not forward, toward being, not into becoming" (*The Imprative of Responsibility*,125).

This has changed in the modern period. What dominates modern existence is dynamism, that is, historical change. Our ontology is not one of eternity but of time. At the basis of this novelty is a new view of nature and human action. Nature, including "the whole biosphere of the planet," has become vulnerable to the intervention of human science and technology. It can no longer take care of itself. Nature can no longer carry the freight of human exploitation. It thus has acquired a "moral claim on us." The irony is that this novel situation comes exactly at the point where nature has become disenchanted, reduced "to the indifference of necessity" and "divested ... of any dignity of ends," a result of "the dominant, scientific view of Nature." Nature has become desacralized stuff at our disposal. According to Jonas, "the very same movement which puts us in possession of the powers that have now to be regulated by norms—the movement of modern knowledge called science—has by a necessary complementarity eroded the foundations from which norms could be derived, it has destroyed the very idea of norm as such" (22).

2. *An Ethic of Responsibility* The challenge Jonas faces is to establish a modern (or post-modern) ethic which is grounded in norms outside of human willing; that is, outside the historical dynamism which has created the technological threat in the first place. He faces it by developing a view of nature which is neither supernaturalistic (what he considers traditional religious dualism) or naturalistic (modern evolutionary and deterministic materialism). His basic moral axiom is "act so that the effects of your action are compatible with the permanence of genuine human life" (11), or to put it differently, "never must the existence or the essence of . . . [humanity] as a whole be made a stake in the hazards of action" (37). This contradicts an eschatological or utopian-progressivist ethic which considers "everything past as a stepping-stone to the future" (16) and insists on continually improving "what has already been achieved, in other words, for progress, which at its most ambitious aims at bringing about an earthly paradise" (36).

Implicit in this call for a non-utopian ethic is the need for ontology, the idea of humanity as such, an "ought" which stands above all present or future particular human beings; the idea that there ought to be human beings generically speaking. In other words, " . . . it follows that the principle of an 'ethic of futurity' does not itself lie within ethics as a doctrine of action . . . but within metaphysics as a doctrine of Being, of which the idea of . . . [humanity] is a part" (44). This, however, runs headlong against one of the central dogmas of our time: that there is no metaphysical truth; that Being is neutral, value free; that one cannot derive an "ought" from an "is." This, nevertheless, is precisely what Jonas sets out to argue persuasively for in this book: "the metaphysical *grounds* of obligation" (44-45); that "value, or the 'good'" is intrinsic to Being itself. We cannot here go into the details of Jonas's sophisticated attempt to show how nature in its most primitive form has a *telos* in the Aristotelian sense, an "aiming" or "directional" quality. According to Jonas, "already in the 'simplest' true *organism* . . . horizons of selfhood, world and time . . . are silhouetted in a premental form" (75). This "purposiveness" within nature itself is the basis for value, the ought, the good. Human beings, themselves rooted in nature, stand out from nature and, unlike the rest of nature, have the metaphysical freedom to say yes or no to nature. This is the source of human obligation. Human nature is obligated to say yes to nature and to limit its own arbitrary will and inclinations, obligated by the good of Being itself. Our duty is to say "No to Not-Being"; caring for the future of all nature is a type of "metaphysical responsibility," based not on self-interest or utilitarian calculation but on the goodness of Being as such.

3. *A Non-Eschatological Basis for Justice* At times Jonas appears to lament the loss of the Eternal found in traditional religions and in Platonic thought. It may be, he reflects, that sometime in the future "Plato's way" will once again become "eligible." In fact, "we must leave it open whether it may not be more adequate to the truth of being than ours." He even admits that "the abolition of transcendence may have been the most colossal mistake in history...." Nevertheless, for the moment we cannot extricate ourselves from our situation; "responsibility for what has been set aside and is kept moving by ourselves, takes precedence before everything else" (129). The novel view of nature and human action characterizing the modern era requires a novel ethic of responsibility if Being is to survive. This means, however, that one of the central aspects of the modern will have to be rejected: eschatological and utopian thinking as found particularly in Marxist and neo-Marxist thought.

Although Jonas is highly sceptical of the possibilities of limiting human freedom in the "capitalistic-liberal-democratic complex" (147) and considers the publicly controlled economy of Marxist countries as offering greater hope in this regard, he is sharply critical of the Promethean dream of an earthly paradise (a classless society) and of faith in the omnipotence of technology as a means to material well-being present in socialism (155). Contraction rather than the expansion of productivity will be necessary. This contradicts eschatological thinking. Our hope lies in recovering

> ... absolute *presence* in itself—no past, no future, no promise, no succession, whether better or worse, not a prefiguration of anything, but rather timeless shining in itself. *That* is the "utopia" beyond every "not yet," scattered moments of eternity in the flux of time.... The basic error of the ontology of "not yet" and its eschatological hope is repudiated by the plain truth—ground for neither jubilation nor dejection—that genuine man is always already there and was there throughout known history: in his heights and his depths, his greatness and wretchedness, his bliss and torment, his justice and his guilt—in short, in all the *ambiguity* that is inseparable from his humanity (200).

What is required for our world to survive, to be able to bear the burden of human activity, is "to *unhook the demands of justice, charity and reason from the bait of utopia*" (201).

Theological Implications

My intent here is not to give a thoroughgoing and much needed biblically and theologically based response to technology. Carl Mitcham and Jim Grote have made a valiant attempt to begin such a project in their anthology, *Theology and Technology*.[21] My purpose is rather to show how in contemporary theology there are a variety of preoccupations. Three examples are technology, social justice, and inter-Christian and inter-religious dialogue. Each of these have their distinctive agendas and their respective diagnoses of the modern situation. Their theological answers differ remarkably from, and frequently conflict, with each other.

I have spent considerable time examining Jonas's philosophical analysis of technology and its challenges for modern ethics because I believe it raises crucial questions for contemporary theology, including Mennonite theology. I want to reflect briefly on three of these: our view of history, our view of God and nature, and our view of human action.

1. *History* Jonas's critique of eschatological and utopian thought, including the whole genre of "already/not-yet" thinking needs to be taken seriously. In Jonas's mind this kind of thinking simply legitimates the forward directionality and progressivism that lies behind the modern misconception that true humanity lies in the future; that there is not authentically experienced humanity in the present; that every past and present event and moment is simply a stepping-stone for that which is still to come. This poses a valid challenge to all the future-oriented theologies that have become so prevalent in recent decades, including various forms of political, liberation, and hope theologies.

All Christian theologies which emphasize the importance of history (becoming) over ontology (being) are vulnerable to Jonas's critique. This applies even to the *Heilsgeschichte* (salvation history) tradition. George Grant, according to Joan E. O'Donovan, identifies the *Heilsgeschichte* approach with liberal historicism,

> ... as sharing above all a common understanding of time as a finite, irreversible process in which individual events have ultimate and unique importance. They both portray events as actions, springing from the will of a universal agent (God or Mankind), of which individual agents are instruments, to carry out a plan, purpose, or program for the world.... Both

Heilsgeschichte and liberal historicism recognize history as the realm of a sovereign will to whom all things are possible, because the end of history springs from it, so that evil (negativity) is not finally necessary.[22]

There is no doubt that eschatology is central to a Christian view of history. Modern secularized eschatologies like Marxism are profoundly indebted to the Judeo-Christian tradition in this regard. The danger arises at the point where this eschatological vision is no longer embraced by an eternal divine reality, contains no eternal content, and is defined exclusively in terms of the chronological movement from past to present to future. For moderns it is virtually impossible to think of eschatology in anything but historicist terms. For the classical Christian, however, history and all historical willing took on relative meaning before an eternal truth: the eternal reality of God and God's historical revelation in Christ mediated by the Holy Spirit. Another way of expressing this is to say that Christian truth is both *foundational* (it grounds the tradition and the created order) and *eschatological* (it is incomplete and awaits final redemption).

I partially agree with O'Donovan's gentle chiding of Grant for his almost total avoidance of eschatology in favour of tradition as foundation. O'Donovan argues that

> The Truth ... has a double presence among us: Christ is present in the unified testimony of the Spirit and of Scripture. And in his double presence, the Truth is present as present and future as well as past: his presence is *eschatological* rather than *foundational*. He is the Truth of the End pre-eminently, and the Beginning under the sway of the End. The revelation of Christ in Scripture is foundational in only one sense: it is the foundation of an ongoing community of believers, a temporal community of faith, hope and charity.[23]

For O'Donovan past, present, and future are placed within the embrace of eternal truth. The eschatological end is more than historical culmination. It is proleptically present in the beginning. I would, however, put more emphasis on the foundational nature of the truth of Christ (as in some sense distinct from eschatology) than O'Donovan appears to do. The truth of Christ is both eschatological and foundational; that is, foundational not only to tradition but to the created order itself. The Anabaptists' notion of "the Christ of all Creation" or "the Gospel of all Creatures" would be worth exploring in this regard.[24]

2. *God and Nature* A second challenge Jonas's analysis throws at Christian theology concerns our view of God and nature. Classical ontology, Jonas argues, viewed nature as eternal and abiding, not vulnerable to human historical action. This has changed. Nature after Francis Bacon has been divested of value, disenchanted; it has become stuff to be controlled and exploited for human purposes. Jonas's solution is to "re-enchant" nature (although he does not use this term), to show how there is a purposive quality within even lower forms of nature—the root that becomes genuine subjectivity in higher nature (human beings)—that provides us with an ontological basis for obligation; that is, Being has value in itself and it falls on us as humans to preserve Being. What is the challenge here for Christian theology? I believe we, particularly Protestants, need to reexamine our understanding of nature and its relation to the divine. Protestants traditionally, and I would include Mennonites here, have tended to emphasize God as acting agent over (if not to the exclusion of) God as ground of Being. God is understood primarily as "personal willing," the One who acts; human beings are seen as those who are called to will God's will, to fulfill divine purposes within history. In Mennonite theology, this frequently takes the form of emphasizing moral and ethical obedience (discipleship) as the determining factor for Christian theology.

There is no denying that fundamental to the Old and New Testament is the concept of God as One who acts within history and calls God's chosen people to obedient action. However, there are also other more feminine metaphors for God as the ground, sustainer and bearer of life and nature which are closer to the ontological imagery that Jonas calls for. The environmental crisis brought about by arbitrary historical willing, now demands of us to retrieve what I would call "sacramental" or "ontological" metaphors for describing the relation of God to nature; the notion that God is graciously present within the natural order; God grounds, sustains and bears nature. In short, the continuities between lower and higher forms of nature (including humanity itself) need to be retrieved. Here Protestants can learn something from the Catholic notion of *analogia entis* (the analogy of being), in which all being in some sense participates in the being of God. In the Thomistic tradition God is defined as "Being Itself" (*ipsum esse*); to the extent that anything has being it is contingent upon and participates in God, the Ground of Being. The danger in this more ontological tradition is that the personality of God tends to be lost in an abstract notion of Being; that sin, evil, and the fallenness of the created order—the radical discontinuity between God and the world—are not emphasized strongly enough; and that the concern for religious and moral conversion is weakened. This is why the ontological tradition needs to be combined with the Barthian dialectical tradition of *analogia fidei* (analogy of faith) and *analogia Christi* (analogy of Christ). Both of these theological traditions—the analogical and the dialectical—are important for Christian theology today.

3. *Human Action* The main point Jonas makes as far as responsible ethics in our technological age is concerned, and I fully agree with him here, is that norm(s) for ethics must have an objective basis outside of historical action itself. Jonas as a philosopher makes the case for this objective ground as the "value, or the 'good'" that is intrinsic to Being itself. Christians can learn from Jonas's revivification of nature. No longer can we afford to think of nature as dead stuff. We need in our theology to retrieve the value that is intrinsic to nature, including human nature, all the while recognizing that for us the source of obligation is ultimately not nature itself (nature is not self-sufficient) but God as the creator and sustainer of nature. For the Christian, this objective ground is God in God's threefold being: Creator, Christ, Spirit. Ethics, in short, is anchored in the three-fold divine reality and revelation. The demands of historical justice are rooted in God's own justice and righteousness, not necessarily in what liberal democracies, social democracies or Marxists label justice. This is where Jonas makes what is perhaps his most provocative statement for contemporary theology: What is required for our world to survive, to be able to bear the burden of human activity, is to "*unhook the demands of justice, charity and reason from the bait of utopia*" (201).

Exploitation, Oppression, and the Struggle for Social Justice

This brings me to what I consider to be the second major stream of thought in contemporary theology: a preoccupation with questions of economic disparity between rich and poor, political oppression and the struggle for social justice. By devoting the amount of space I have to technology and its challenges for modern theology, I am suggesting that this is where the most pressing agenda for modern and post-modern theology lies. I believe this to be so, although I fully support the urgent need for theology to engage itself with questions of social, political and economic justice. It seems to me, however, and here I agree with Jonas, that our fight for justice must be reconceived in less historicist language than is frequently the case if we are to survive as human beings and remain faithful as Christian believers. Our view of justice will need to be framed within a more classical understanding of eternal justice and righteousness.

My treatment of this agenda will be considerably shorter than the first. I will again restrict myself primarily to looking at one representative, Gregory Baum and his theology as reflected in his collection of essays,

Theology and Society.[25] Baum grew up in a family of Jewish origin, he emigrated to England, then to Canada during World War II as a sixteen-year-old boy. Here he converted to Catholic Christianity and became a priest. In the 1970s his theology, which had been deeply influenced by what he calls the "soft liberation" theology of Vatican II (in contrast to the "hard liberation" of the more radical theology he now espouses, in which reality is viewed as conflictual rather than harmonious) and by the liberating insights of modern psychology, underwent a shift to the left. This change came about largely through his studies of sociology and social philosophy at the New School for Social Research, the academic home of Hans Jonas and other German intellectuals.

In the past two decades Baum has become, without doubt, the best-known Canadian theologian, giving voice to social criticism in a wide range of journals and books, most consistently in his own periodical *The Ecumenist*. Evident throughout his writings are the influences of Critical Social Theory and recent left-wing movements within the Roman Catholic Church, notably in Latin America, Canada and the United States—movements that are committed to Christian solidarity with the poor and the struggle for social justice around the world.

Underlying all his recent work is the assumption which he takes from Latin American liberation theology, namely that ideas must

> ... be evaluated by their effect on people's lives. The ultimate norm of truth ... is the transformation and emancipation of the human family. If a scholar, a social scientist, a thinker, a theologian is not committed to the emancipation of humankind, the knowledge which he or she generates will, no matter how brilliant the mind and how convincing the arguments, lead to the alienation of people (121).

The passion for theology as a transforming power comes through on every page of *Theology and Society*, which is divided into three parts: the first dealing with social teaching as it is evolving in the Catholic church; the second concerned with theology and various movements of emancipation around the globe; and the third treating a variety of critical social issues facing the church.

Baum traces what he considers to be a remarkable shift to the left by a "significant minority" in the Catholic church in many parts of the world since the early 1970s. What is emerging in the Roman Catholic Church of Canada, he says, is a "minority deeply marked by a new religious experience, Christians for whom faith and justice are inextricably intertwined, who read Scripture and ecclesiastical doctrine in a new light, who discover in them the

82 / MENNONITES AND CLASSICAL THEOLOGY

transformative power of Jesus Christ, and who for this reason find themselves in solidarity with the poor and marginalized" (21).

Baum considers Pope John II's call for "the priority of labour over capital," "the solidarity *of* and *with* the poor," to be a clear indication that the church at the highest level has adopted a more radical form of social analysis and has in effect, blessed liberation theology. This new social gospel is, however, to be clearly distinguished from Marxist and neo-Marxist Critical Theory. For one thing, its call for solidarity grows out of theological and ethical thought in the context of "religious experience, tradition and community" (225). It is a call for social justice based on a "transformist" Christology which assumes that "Divine Revelation illumines and transforms the world" (91, 92). The transcendence of God is important but not in the individualistic and pietistic sense. Transcendence rather functions theologically as a source and inspiration for social criticism; "encounter with the transcendent" means "being overwhelmed by the divine call to justice, being turned inside out by the revelation of a new light on reality" (126).

The most fascinating aspect of Baum's book, especially pertinent for our consideration here, is his conversation with the great classical social thinkers on two issues related to the Enlightenment: modern science and technology. Baum is fully aware of the dangers of historical reductionism and the negative side of the Enlightenment: the triumph of positivism or instrumental rationality, the total mechanization of life and the consequent loss of precisely that freedom which the modern era intended to secure. The basic Enlightenment commitment to emancipation, Baum thinks, needs to be affirmed but under the rubric of the Christian view of salvation: "Without the Christian doctrine of salvation, the emancipatory struggles against domination appear as a Promethean project, as humans saving themselves" (139). Salvation includes emancipation, but it is an emancipation grounded in what Christians believe to be God's revelation in Christ: "that God enlightens and empowers people . . . to become the subject of their history" (139).

What is significant about Baum's social vision is his view ,much more optimistic than Jonas's, of modern technology in the struggle for social justice. He is harshly critical of Jacques Ellul and neo-conservative sociologists like Peter Berger for being overly pessimistic and deterministic in their analysis of modern technology. Although Ellul and Berger differ in important ways, they have, Baum believes, a misplaced diagnosis of the modern problem. Each of them erroneously identifies the primary form of contemporary degradation as being technocracy and bureaucracy, and lament the concomitant loss of transcendence. They see socialist alternatives as simply increasing technocracy and bureaucracy, and end up with little more than offering solutions for isolated individuals or small mediating groups (211, 297).

In contrast, Baum sees the dominant form of alienation in the modern world as being economic and political rather than technological. He credits critical theorist Jürgen Habermas with convincing him that technocratic theories of alienation are exaggerated and disregard certain humanizing trends in modern society (166). Baum urges Christians to remain suspicious of a technocratic theory of alienation because of its inherent determinism; that is, of not recognizing the genuine freedom of human beings to continue the struggle. It also relativizes the condition of the poor and the marginalized. Baum's greater optimism concerning technology and its possibilities is in keeping with Pope John Paul II's own stance. Modern technological development is not to be despised in itself but affirmed as a gift from God if it is to be properly understood and used. Such a positive view, however, is conditional upon the acceptance of the priority of labour and workers over capital and large corporations, protecting worker's jobs, decentralizing capital, struggling for greater worker management and community ownership and preserving the environment (54, 80-81, 93, 100). In short, technology's positive potential for human emancipation ought to be recognized and its negative consequences repudiated.

While Baum would probably agree with most of what Jonas says about the danger of technology to our environment, and although he would most certainly agree that we must limit our freedom to shape and control nature, and to develop a responsible ethic if we are to survive, there is a different spirit at work in Baum's theology, as in most left-wing political and liberation theologies. The primary devotion is to historical and social justice; everything else is defined with reference to this passion. Fundamental to the emancipatory project is a commitment to historical becoming, to prophetic-eschatological thinking, and a suspicion of metaphysical and ontological language as espoused by Jonas. Baum's softer interpretation of technology and the modern scientific enterprise generally is a natural part of his struggle for historical freedom. The question is whether it is possible to combine Jonas's quest for an ethic based on ontology (Being) and Baum's struggle for social justice in the context of history (Becoming). This is the urgent challenge for contemporary theology within the emerging paradigm. In my view both are absolutely essential and urgent.

A longtime friend of Baum's, another German intellectual emigré, Rudolf Siebert, is keenly aware of the danger which is present in political and liberation theologies, of reducing theology to historical action. In his own work he combines metaphysics and the historical struggle for social justice through a Hegelian synthesis. Siebert, professor of sociology and religion at the University of Western Michigan, has directed the annual

"Future of Religion" course at the Inter-University Centre of Postgraduate Studies, Dubrovnik, Yugoslavia, since 1977. Scholars from socialist and non-socialist countries gather there to talk about the nature and future of religion in the modern/post-modern world. In his book, *The Critical Theory of Religion: The Frankfurt School,* Siebert examines the critical thought of various members of the Frankfurt School of Critical Theory, particularly its most recent member, Jürgen Habermas. He also analyzes German political theologians Johann Baptist Metz, Helmut Peukert and Edmund Arens.[26] Siebert himself, like Baum, is a strong advocate of political and liberation theology. He finds that many political and liberation theologians are too optimistic and deal unsatisfactorily with the "theodicy" problem (God and the problem of evil). He criticizes them for tending to reduce theology to communicative praxis and for not dealing adequately with sin, evil and suffering.

Siebert's own solution is to call these critical philosophers and political theologians back to Hegel, who he considers to be the last great Christian philosopher to attempt a bridging of the classical and modern world. Siebert feels that much more can be rescued from traditional religious-metaphysical systems of meaning than these thinkers, especially Habermas, assume. For Hegel the transcendent and objective reality of God, the Absolute, still remained the central starting point. Human intersubjectivity was still grounded beyond itself, mirroring the communicative intersubjectivity within the Absolute itself (God as Trinity). Human suffering and death were still seen as reflecting the tragedy within God. The crucifixion and resurrection of Jesus took on meaning only in relation to God's own crucifixion and resurrection. Human action and historical justice were grounded in absolute divine justice.

For those of us in a strong biblically-oriented and confessional-theological tradition, Siebert's Hegelian starting point sounds strange; too philosophical. Why not go back in an unmediated way to the biblical narrative itself? But there is no unmediated access to the ancient texts. We read the biblical story from within the modern and now emerging postmodern context. Hegel is one of the giant transitional figures between the pre-modern and modern eras who attempted to bridge the two worlds. Central to his whole enterprise was a trinitarian philosophical-theological schema. In my own theological work I also have tried to retrieve some form of classical trinitarian theology as an onto-metaphysical framework for ethics in the contemporary world, as a way of combining concerns like those of Jonas and Baum.

Pluralism and the Concern for Inter-Religious and Inter-Christian Discourse

A third agenda item for theology today—one that appears to be producing more literature currently than the other two combined, particularly in North America—is religious pluralism and the search for both identity and unity while respecting genuine diversity.[27] What is interesting about this stream is that, in contrast to the technological and the social justice agendas, it perceives the most obvious fact of the modern world to be diversity and pluralism. For some this is seen negatively, as fragmentation and the loss of cohesion. For others it is viewed positively, as an opportunity for developing greater tolerance and understanding others' points of view, thereby enriching one's own. Nevertheless, what we have here is quite a different diagnosis of the contemporary situation than that given by the other two groups. The first school of theology—that concerned with technology and its threat to our world—sees the world becoming ever more the same, overrun by the technological monolith, with diversity being merely a surface phenomenon. The second group—that devoted to the cause of social justice—tends to divide the world into the oppressor and the oppressed, and to suspect that the "liberal" concern with pluralism and interreligious dialogue is a North American concern that ideologically avoids the most pressing issue of our time.

This is not the place to examine in detail the daily increasing volume of literature on this subject by David Tracy, Hans Küng, John Hick, George Lindbeck, and many others. What I find intriguing about this genre, however, is what appears to be a renaissance of interest in the doctrines of religious communities as a way of identifying oneself and one's differences from, and commonalities with, other groups. Liberal theology appears suddenly to have rediscovered the importance of the dogmatic and creedal tradition after its long eclipse in the post-Protestant-Scholastic period. "Church doctrines," says Lindbeck, "are communally authoritative teachings regarding beliefs and practices that are considered essential to the identity or welfare of the group in question." There is no such thing as a creedless Christian community. "A religious body cannot exist as a recognizably distinctive collectivity unless it has some beliefs and/or practices by which it can be identified."[28]

Not only are doctrinal categories seen as a useful way of organizing Christian belief; they are also a way of accommodating interreligious understanding. This is what William A. Christian sets out to do in his philosophical study, *Doctrines of Religious Communities*: "If we think of religion as a kind of human activity about which something can be learned, and survey the scene from that point of view, a striking fact is the existence of a number of massive and enduring communities with non-overlapping memberships, each with its own body of doctrines." William Christian divides the doctrines of religious communities into *primary doctrines* ("for example . . . their teachings about the constitution of the world in general and about human nature in particular") and *doctrines about doctrines* ("principles and rules to govern the formation and development of their body of doctrines").[29] He concentrates on the latter, showing how there are some governing principles that are common to the various religious communities.

There is something quite new about the way doctrines are treated here, different from the traditional dogmatic tradition. This is particularly evident in Lindbeck's understanding of doctrines as self-sufficient intrasystematic "cultural-linguistic" models (borrowing heavily from Wittgenstein's notion of "language-games") in contrast both to what he calls the "classical cognitivism" of traditional orthodoxy where doctrines represent propositional truths, and to "experiential-expressivism" where a common, universal "experiential core" among all religions is assumed. In Lindbeck's cultural-linguistic approach, "religions are thought of primarily as different idioms for construing reality, expressing experience, and ordering life."[30] No common propositional or experiential framework is assumed. Even within a single religious community, doctrines in the cultural-linguistic model cannot be assumed to correspond to a common foundational experience or cognitive truth.

It is not my intent to evaluate the adequacy of this new retrieval of doctrinal thinking within contemporary "liberal" (or perhaps more accurately, "post-liberal") theology. Rather, I will point out that doctrinal language is being given a lot of attention but in a significantly new way. One critical question I have about this post-liberal doctrinal thinking is this: Is the cultural-linguistic model, which in my view inevitably leads to religious relativism (that is, there can be no universal truth claims that transcend any particular cultural-linguistic-doctrinal complex) adequate to meet the challenges of our age? I think not. There is a growing sense that the ethical issues raised by the technological and the social justice agendas of contemporary theology are universal and global ones which require a united front. The ethical urgencies raised by the technological crisis, for instance, call for a non-relativistic metaphysics and ontology.

This conviction has inspired my interest in classical theology. I would like to conclude by suggesting, as I have in a number of articles in the past few years,[31] that for Christians, including Mennonites, classical trinitarian and christological doctrinal categories are richer in potential for interpreting God, human and nonhuman nature, and historical action than are the alternatives. These doctrines are more than "regulatory rules" for Christian communities; they are archetypal truths, "metaphors of ultimacy."[32] J. Denny Weaver misunderstands me when he caricatures my proposal as follows: "Mennonite theology would look like classic Protestantism with some additional points lower down in the outline for a few doctrines or practices—such as adult baptism, feetwashing, pacifism, community—to exist alongside but not central to classic theology shared by all Christian traditions."[33] What I do hold is that central to the Christian faith is an affirmation of the threefoldness of God and the twofoldness of Christ, as classically formulated in the creeds, and that this holds for all Christians, including Anabaptists and Mennonites. Further, I hold, as I try to show at some length in my article on the doctrine of God in the fifth volume of the *Mennonite Encyclopedia*,[34] that in the sixteenth century most Anabaptists accepted the standard trinitarian creedal pattern but interpreted the Trinity itself with a heightened ethical consciousness, bringing in ethical concerns not at the end of a list but right at the start in their interpretation of the first article of the creed. The point I try to emphasize, however, is that Christian theology, including Anabaptist-Mennonite theology, dare not start with ethics (that is, with human action), but must begin and end with God in God's threefoldness: Creator, Christ, Spirit.

All three of the agenda items discussed in this essay will no doubt receive even greater attention in contemporary theology in the future than they have up to now. All three are legitimate concerns and need serious reflection by Christian theology in the context of the Christian community. I would suggest that these three very different streams would be fruitfully brought together and thought of in terms of the threefoldness of God. The issues raised by modern technology might fruitfully be reflected upon in light of a Christian doctrine of creation, a doctrine that has unfortunately not received nearly the attention it deserves by Mennonites. The second, that of dealing with economic and political oppression and the need for social justice, could appropriately be considered under Christology—a Christology, however, that receives its true meaning only as a trinitarian Christology, not a Jesus-monism. A doctrine of the Holy Spirit offers provocative possibilities for the third set of issues—religious pluralism and interreligious understanding—for the work of the Holy Spirit defies easily-definable human-religious and denominational boundaries while remaining the very Spirit of Christ and of God.

FIVE

Modern Justice and the "Oblivion of Eternity": The Conservatism of George Grant and Martin Heidegger*

My fascination with the thought of George Grant and his particular type of philosophical and political conservatism ("red toryism"), combined with my continuing research into the theology of the Hitler period, with special interest in the conservative-nationalist thinking of the "German Christian" Emanuel Hirsch, provide the backdrop for the following essay, published in 1990 under the title "Do George Grant and Martin Heidegger Share a Common Conservatism?"¹ What worried me at the time were the similarities between Grant's arguments in support of the conservative values of ethnicity and nationality against the liberal assumptions of freedom at the basis of modern technology, and some of the views of Hirsch and Heidegger, both Nazi sympathizers. I was worried because I found aspects of their reasoning persuasive (e.g., the love of one's own). This worry led me some time in the late 1970s or

---

* Originally published in *The Chesterton Review: George Grant Special Issue* 11.2 (May 1985): 183-98; republished in *Two Theological Languages by George Grant and other Essays in Honour of his Work*, ed. Wayne Whillier (Lewiston, NY: The Edwin Mellen Press, 1990), 105-20. For notes on the text see the Notes section below.

early 1980s (at the time I was writing my doctoral dissertation), to join the New Democratic Party, as a symbol of my political allegiance to the left. I would later withdraw from the Party in protest over its stand on abortion on demand as a "right."[2]

The essay was written for a special issue of The Chesterton Review *in honour of George Grant, and focuses on an intellectual comparison of Grant and Martin Heidegger, who is known to have had strong pro-Nazi sympathies especially in the early years of National Socialism. Was there something in the conservative thought of great thinkers like Hirsch and Heidegger that made them susceptible to "fascistic" politics? And what might be the political dangers of Grant's conservative social thought? These were questions in my mind as I wrote the essay, although I did not attempt to answer them directly. What I did was show how Grant's thinking is significantly different from that of Heidegger's at a crucial point—namely, the concept of Being. They share a common, conservative critique of modern deracinated culture, and of the technological preoccupation with domination and mastery. They each lament the loss of national identity ("the love of one's own") and long for thinking and contemplation as a way of opening ourselves up to that which reveals itself (or is given) to us. For Grant that which reveals itself is "eternal Being," whereas for Heidegger the Being that reveals itself is "historical becoming." This historicity of Being makes Heidegger less pessimistic than Grant regarding the modern project; for it is through technology that Being can make itself known in the modern period.*

This radical historicism, with its accompanying oblivion of an "eternal" normative-ethical horizon, I would suggest (although I did not do so in the 1990 essay), makes the modern project so vulnerable to the "will to power" at the heart of modern tyranny. The nihilistic tendencies of some forms of postmodernism and deconstruction, in my view, heighten the danger of tyranny and the capricious excercise of power by those who happen to have the means to do so at a given historical moment and location. In contrast, Grant's older concept of justice, based on some form of natural and divine law, makes rights and freedoms more secure than modern, historicist notions of justice. The inclination of contemporary theologians who emphasize God's futurity (including hope theologians of various stripes) is to interpret Being primarily as Becoming and justice consequently, as an aspect of this becoming. My debate with Wolfhart Pannenberg's complex understanding of this issue comes exactly at this point. His theology ultimately hinges on his view of the relation between the Immanent Trinity (Being) and the Economic Trinity (Becoming), the subject of the last essay of this volume.

◆ ◆ ◆

The entire corpus of George Grant's thought is essentially a musing, a meditation on what it means to partake of the assumptions, values and language of the modern era rather than those of the age of Athens and Jerusalem. As Grant so frequently reminds his readers, however, his is no simple rejection of "modernity" in favour of "antiquity."[3] The task of the philosopher is not to make such simple choices but rather to consider deeply the meaning of the whole. Grant's philosophical stance *vis-à-vis* the modern world is highly nuanced. He recognises the strengths of the Enlightenment tradition, the extent of our captivity to the assumptions of an all-pervasive scientific-technological culture, and our need to transcend those assumptions if we are to avoid disaster and find what "we are fitted for."[4] It is precisely the complexity of Grant's perspective on modernity that precludes any easy caricature of his conservatism as a romantic or even reactionary lament for the lost world of the past. The depth of his struggle with and appropriation of Friedrich Nietzsche and Martin Heidegger, the two interpreters of modernity *par excellence*, is ample reason for discarding any lingering suspicion that there is in Grant an incipient anti-modern obscurantism.

In order to arrive at some clarity about Grant's attitude toward modernity and about the nature of his conservatism, we must note that Grant gives the term *modern* a specific meaning which differs from that of certain other intellectual traditions.[5] For him modernity describes the post-Enlightenment age and the triumph of scientific and instrumental reason which lies at the heart of today's technological monolith. Moderns are those who have accepted the liberal assumptions of freedom behind the rise of modern technology. *Liberalism* is that "set of beliefs which proceed from the central assumption that [human] essence is . . . freedom and therefore that what chiefly concerns [us] in this life is to shape the world as we want it."[6] While Grant's definition of modernity and its inherent liberalism is not universally accepted, it does represent the understanding of a respected circle of thinkers on the subject, including that of Nietzsche and Heidegger.

The issue here is not the problem of semantics but the nature of Grant's thinking about modernity. What is Grant's stance in the face of modernity? In what sense is he a conservative? If he does not simply reject modernity, then how does he propose to transcend it? Grant admits that his great mentor in coming to understand the nature and meaning of modernity is Heidegger, who, together with Nietzsche, he says, is one of "those who have thought most clearly what is happening in modernity, and thought it within the acceptance of the basic assumptions of that modernity."[7] It is, therefore, to Heidegger and to Grant's perception of Heidegger that I want to turn in order to try to comprehend Grant's meditation, his "questioning" concerning our being in the world as moderns.

Grant on Heidegger

Grant makes relatively few overt references to Heidegger and at no point does he embark on a lengthy explicit analysis of Heidegger's thought as he does, for example, with that of Nietzsche.[8] But much of his work clearly bears the imprint of Heidegger's ideas and the few references which he does make are highly illuminating. Grant appears to have come under the strong influence of Heidegger's philosophy relatively late in his intellectual development and largely by accident in connection with his reading of Nietzsche. The two thinkers he feels belong together in their unmasking of the assumption of the modern epoch. Heidegger, he says, is unthinkable without Nietzsche. These two thinkers, he maintains, "have most completely thought through the modern project within it . . . they are the modern project conscious of itself."[9] In a 1977 conversation concerning the influence of Heidegger on his thought, Grant pays the following tribute to the German philosopher:

> As it seems to me that the great task of philosophy now is to think through the modern project to its fundamental assumptions, then we must study those thinkers who can help us. Simply at the level of academic philosophy, what is breathtaking about Heidegger is the way he shows us what is going on in the philosophers and scientists who originated the modern project.[10]

So the first thing that can be said about Grant's stance toward modernity is that it needs to be thought through to its underlying assumptions. Throughout his work we see him following in the footsteps of his mentor in trying to think through what is going on in the modern project without making premature judgments.

More specifically, however, it is Heidegger's analysis of modern technology itself that shines through most clearly in Grant's writings. Especially Heidegger's book on Leibniz, *Der Satz vom Grund* has most illumined his own understanding of the nature of technology. "In his book on Leibniz," Grant says, "he just lays down what technology is, as I have never read elsewhere."[11] It is not so much for an understanding of technology *per se* that Grant thanks Heidegger, as well as Nietzsche, but for unmasking for him the connection between technological assumptions and a new modern notion of justice. Thus, according to Grant,

> . . . the greatest book for understanding Heidegger is in my opinion his first volume on Nietzsche—an amazing book. What he declares about justice in that volume is, it seems to me, the modern view of justice taken much further than what

we find in American liberalism or Marxism. It is a turning away from what is given about justice in Platonism or in Christianity and Judaism, a turning away which in my opinion bodes ill for the future.[12]

With modern technology, then, comes a new modern notion of justice. What is this new view? It has to do with historicism—the comprehension of time as history: "What seems to me true is the connection between this new view of justice and historicism. It seems to me that Heidegger is the most perfectly thought historicist that I have ever read.... And that historicism is, above anything else, responsible for the undermining of the older tradition of justice."[13] Historicism, the concept of time as history—the movement from past to present to future—has to do with the primacy of the will as understood in western Christianity and culminating in the thought of Immanuel Kant.[14] It is linked to the rejection of the ancient Platonic perception of "eternal justice"—where justice is defined not as something we create but as a rendering to each human being his due.[15] With the "new conception of justice some human beings have no due."[16]

This is where Grant sees himself parting company with both Nietzsche and Heidegger. He accepts their analysis of modern technology, historicism, the primacy of the will, and the ensuing concept of relative justice as an accurate diagnosis of the modern situation, but he believes that this is not what is best for humans: "I think this is both the greatness and the terror of Nietzsche and Heidegger; they recognize that the new affirmation of reality in technology brings a new account of justice. I think the English-speaking world is only beginning to see this; namely, that the new affirmation of reality in technology means a new conception of justice. This will be a terrible realization in the English-speaking world. It is to this new account of justice as a human creation that I fundamentally say no."[17]

Grant's "no" to Nietzsche and Heidegger represents his "no" to modernity. Grant does not reject all of the insights of the western liberal tradition. In fact, I have argued in another context that there continues to be a strong residue of his early liberalism in his later thought.[18] What Grant says "no" to is the loss of the eternal in modernity, the loss of what was dear to both classical Christianity and to Platonism:

> As I have said, Nietzsche and Heidegger are those who have thought through most clearly what is happening in modernity, and thought it within the acceptance of the basic assumptions of that modernity. The negative side of that thinking-through is their assessment of what is wrong about Christianity and Platonism—why human beings thought they were true in the

past, but why no sane person should do so now. Somebody such as myself, inescapably bound to Christianity, must try to understand what it is to think at a superlative level, with Christianity put aside root and branch.[19]

So Grant says "no" to them at the point where they reject the world as seen by early Christianity and Platonism. He states this even more explicitly when he says, "Seeing modern assumptions laid before me at their most lucid and profound in Nietzsche and Heidegger has allowed me (indeed only slightly) to be able to partake in the alternative assumptions of Plato. It is by looking at modernity in its greatest power that one is perhaps able even slightly to escape its powers."[20] For Grant, then, through one's delving into and savouring of modernity one is given the chance to move beyond it.

For an interpreter of Grant's thought, however, his statements about the Christian-Platonic tradition, on the one hand, and the Nietzschean-Heideggerian modern project, on the other, are somewhat problematic. If we are to take seriously Grant's own frequent declarations about his refusal simply to reject modernity out of hand, and about the indebtedness of modern assumptions to the ancient tradition (assertions with which I agree), then the above unequivocal no to Nietzsche and Heidegger does not adequately reflect even Grant's own declared position.[21] Nor, for that matter, does it do justice to Heidegger's ambivalent attitude toward both modernity and Christianity. Both Heidegger and Grant, as we shall see, while parting company on a number of important issues, nevertheless share in a common conservativism. Both have a more nuanced attitude towards modernity and Christianity and Platonism than the above assertions by Grant seem to indicate.[22]

Heidegger and Grant on Modernity

In his provocative essay, "The Uses of Philosophy in George Grant," Laurence Lampert isolates some of the key areas in which Grant is indebted to Heidegger: technology, language, the nature of thinking and the role of the thinker, and the way of being in the modern world.[23] From Heidegger, Grant learns that with modernity comes not so much a rejection of metaphysics and ontology but a new historicist ontology:

> No longer is the modern simply a way of thinking about time and nature that differs from the classical. It is that, but more pervasively and overwhelmingly it is a way of being, and consequently a way of taking beings. It is a particular vision of the nature of things, of the being of beings, and as such it is much more than simply a matter of intellectual assent to a

new set of propositions about man and the world. It is an unquestioned predisposition to a new form of what Heidegger calls the "presencing" of things.[24]

Almost in the same breath, however, Lampert goes on to say:

It should be added immediately that for all of this Grant is still no Heideggerian. To mention only the three most important matters: regarding history, Grant is not committed to the historicity of being itself; regarding the philosophical task, he is not committed to awaiting a new beginning in man's way of taking being; regarding the ancients, he is not committed to the view that Plato and Aristotle are the forerunners of our present technological way of taking the being of beings.[25]

I agree with most of Lampert's analysis but do not think that he adequately reflects first upon the extent to which Grant himself considers the modern view to be rooted in the classical Christian tradition, and secondly upon the points at which Heidegger also turns away from the modern project and draws upon the Greek view of reality for his view of the "unconcealment of Being" and, therefore, to a conservative perception of the nature of things. These factors bring Grant and Heidegger closer together in their stance concerning modernity than Lampert suggests.

In order to identify where Grant and Heidegger share a common turning away from modernity and where they differ in their attitude toward modern assumptions, we must now turn our attention to their respective reflections on Nietzsche and modern technology. Grant's inspired treatment of Nietzsche (in his 1969 Massey Lectures, *Time as History*) is breathtaking in its persuasive portrayal of this great thinker's exposition of modernity. It is true that in the end Grant turns away from Nietzsche's conclusion, but the language of his turning away pales in comparison with his powerful elucidation of the thought of this modern. This has something to do with what he describes in other contexts as the overwhelming "darkness" of the modern age—a darkness which robs us of the language to describe the eternal, the good, the beautiful, the excellent, and the true.[26] Occasionally, one fears that in his profound sense of the darkness, Grant himself has capitulated to the modern eclipse of hope and belief.

Nietzsche, says Grant, "thought the conception of time as history more comprehensively than any other modern thinker before or since" and "did not turn away from what he thought."[27] While most previous philosophers have presumed the existence of "something permanent in human beings," Nietzsche was the first to think through historicity to its logical conclusion as "the finality of becoming."[28] He realised that "horizons . . . are not true statements about actuality" but "man-made perspectives by which the charismatic impose their will to power."[29] To view God himself as horizon is in fact to have killed God. The death of God is for Nietzsche "the end of all horizons."[30] This loss of God, through perceiving him as horizon, is the loss of a sense of purpose, of the very possibility of all definition: "To have been told that man is the creature of Trinity was to know that our highest activity was loving. To say that man has a history and, therefore, cannot be defined is to say that we can know nothing about what we are fitted for. We make ourselves as we go along."[31]

With the recognition that "horizons are only horizons," we are left only with human mastery. For Nietzsche, the only question remaining is who deserves to be master on this planet. He rejects the option of the decadent "lastmen"—the products of a secularised Christianity who make up the majority in a technological age. He also rejects the option of the "nihilists" who are fully conscious of their historicity and the relativity of all values, and will for willing's sake alone. Nietzsche favours a third option—that of the "overmen" (*Übermenschen*), those who love fate, who know their historicity and the relativity of all things, but who nevertheless courageously assert a joy of life in their willing, in their desire to overcome *ressentiment* and the spirit of revenge.[32]

Grant is patently shaken to the core by Nietzsche's enucleation of the modern crisis and even tempted by his conclusion but ultimately refuses to bow to the "oblivion of eternity." Grant's refusal is expressed with the full recognition of the power of Nietzsche's stance:

> In this sense, the thought of Nietzsche is a fate for modern men. In partaking in it, we can come to make judgements about the modern project—that enormous enterprise that came out of western Europe in the last centuries and has now become worldwide. Nevertheless, . . . the conception of time as history is not one in which I think life can be lived properly. It is not a conception we are fitted for. Therefore I turn away from Nietzsche and in so turning express my suspicion of the assumptions of the modern project.[33]

Grant cannot understand how Nietzsche can assert the "love of fate" and the "finality of becoming" without an intimation of "perfection (call it if you will, God) in which our desires for good find their rest and their fulfillment."[34]

It is clear to Grant that we cannot "turn away from our fate." What then is left for us to do? He rejects Nietzsche's conclusion about the finality of becoming and loudly proclaims that the "absurdities of history" are "enfolded in an unchanging meaning, which is untouched by potentiality or change."[35] For Grant the "core of our lives is the desire for perfection."[36]

But how can we face our fate in the modern world and at the same time assert that our fate is "enfolded in a timeless eternity"?[37] This is the question! In some of his writings, Grant seems to suggest that all we can do is to "lament" for a lost vision of the good.[38] In other places he urges his readers to listen to "intimations of deprival."[39] In yet other contexts, he calls for "irony."[40] Here, at the end of *Time as History*, he calls for "remembering," "loving," and "thinking": remembering a "tradition of reverence," when people still thought something beyond time as history; but also loving and thinking of that very reverence for the good, the beautiful, and the perfect.[41] This, admits Grant, is to say very little in the face of the modern oblivion of the eternal.

In turning to "thought" Grant turns away from the modern obsession with "dynamic political doing". Here Grant comes remarkably close to Heidegger's own apparent turning away from the frenzied self-willing of modern technology. Heidegger, too, after powerfully elucidating the thought of Nietzsche and the essence of modern technology, calls for art, poetry, and thought in the face of the danger inherent in technology.[42] When we read Heidegger's essay, "The Word of Nietzsche: 'God is Dead'," it becomes clear that Heidegger and Nietzsche cannot simply be identified in their attitude toward modernity as Grant identifies them. In Nietzsche, Heidegger claims:

> The suprasensory is transformed into an unstable product of the sensory. And with such a debasement of its antithesis, the sensory denies its own essence. The deposing of the suprasensory does away with the merely sensory and thus with the difference between the two. . . . It culminates in the meaninglessness.[43]

The sensory is de-essentialised. Grant's simple lumping together of Heidegger and Nietzsche as "accentors" of the modern will not do. A more nuanced view of Heidegger's own ambivalence toward modernity is required. Throughout this whole essay on Nietzsche, Heidegger finds himself torn (as does Grant) between being persuaded by Nietzsche's conviction that the suprasensory has been lost in the modern world, and protesting against Nietzsche's "nihilism," the emptying out of the sensory, and the deification of the will to power. For Heidegger, the central challenge to human beings in the modern world is to listen to, to ponder, to question and to think about what is happening to Being itself in the modern epoch.

Everything hinges, however, on Heidegger's notion of *Being*, a concept which, despite its centrality for Heidegger's thought, defies clear definition. *Being* encounters us like the lighted clearing in a forest. With Nietzsche, Heidegger appears to reject the classical Christian and Platonic metaphysics where Being is thought of as something or someone (God) objectified, distant, transcendent, immutable and eternal. For Heidegger,

> What is given to thinking to think is not some deeply hidden underlying meaning, but rather something lying near, that which lies nearest, which, because it is only this, we have therefore constantly already passed over. Through this passing over we are, without noticing it, constantly accomplishing the killing in relation to the Being of whatever is in being.[44]

The problem with all of western metaphysics, beginning with Plato, is that "[n]*owhere do we find such experiencing of Being itself.* Nowhere are we confronted by a thinking that thinks the truth of Being itself and therewith thinking truth itself as Being."[45] The essence of genuine thought for Heidegger is "preparatory thinking"—that is, "[lighting] up that space within which Being itself might again be able to take man, with respect to his essence, into a primal relationship."[46] For Heidegger this kind of thinking would be a kind of homecoming.[47]

What Nietzsche does not recognize, according to Heidegger, is that the ultimate blow in the killing of God is his own striking of Being down to a new value. By debasing Being into a value, Being is not acknowledged as Being but as unconditional will to power.[48] Being itself is thus done away with.[49] The history of western metaphysics is the history of the "oblivion of Being" and the final step of modern self-consciousness, epitomised by Nietzsche, is the debasing of Being to the will to power and mastery, the willing of will for its own sake. In this new consciousness,

> [t]he world changes into object. . . . The earth itself can show itself only as the object of assault, an assault that, in human willing, establishes itself as unconditional objectification. Nature appears everywhere—because willed from out of the essence of Being—as the object of technology.[50]

Like Grant, Heidegger turns away from this total objectification of everything that comes about with the death of the suprasensory and the triumph of self-will in modern technology. But, unlike Grant, he thinks of Being itself as historical, and consequently he is more open than is Grant to the possibility of Being revealing itself in a new way through technology. It is, in fact, Being itself—the being of whatever is—that is manifesting itself in a novel way in the modern will to mastery. The problem is that human beings forget this and presume to be the masters of the earth. The flaw in Nietzsche's philosophy is that he also does not think modernity from within Being itself. In this sense he is still within, albeit at the end of, the western metaphysical tradition. The challenge is not to reject, but to think the truth of Being which is coming to be in beings in the modern epoch.

Heidegger is, therefore, fundamentally ambivalent toward modern technology; Grant is not. For Heidegger technology holds within itself both a danger and a saving power. The danger is that human beings exalt themselves as lords of the earth assuming that everywhere they encounter only themselves and what they construct.[51] The potentially saving power is that human beings may ponder, recollect, watch over and safeguard "the coming to presence of truth" that is taking place within technology.[52] Human beings are the privileged guardians of Being, the shepherds of all coming to presence of Being on this earth.[53]

Having looked in some detail at both Grant's and Heidegger's exposition of Nietzsche and modernity, we can now venture some tentative judgments about their common and distinctive attitudes toward the modern world. There is, we have seen, a striking similarity in their common protest against the modern illusion that human beings are the constructors, masters, and lords of the earth. Both reject that concept of truth and Being which is seen to be the historical creation and construction of human beings. Both yearn for a rootedness in a more primal truth. Where they differ is in their understanding of the nature of that primal truth.

Do They Share a Common Conservatism?

Grant has come to believe that the ancient Judeo-Christian and Platonic notion of truth is a more adequate account of reality, justice, and what human beings are fitted for than the modern historicist conception. Heidegger, in contrast, espouses a dynamic truth of Being which is in effect the truth of becoming. Grant is right to say that Heidegger is ultimately a historicist. For Heidegger, the primal truth of Being is intrinsically historical:

> The history of Being is neither the history of man and of humanity, nor the history of the human relation to beings and to Being. The history of Being is Being itself, and only Being. However, since Being claims human being for grounding its truth in beings, man is drawn into the history of Being, but always with regard to the manner in which he takes his essence from the relation of Being to himself and, in accordance with this relation, loses his essence, neglects it, gives it up, grounds it, or squanders it.[54]

Even here, however, Heidegger's historicism is mitigated by a protest against "historically calculated time" and a positive use of the language of Origin. According to Heidegger, "that time span when Being gives itself to openness can never be found in historically calculated time or with its measures."[55] The future of Being is in some sense a return to the Origin. "Recollection in the history of Being," he says, "is a thinking ahead to the Origin, and belongs to Being itself."[56] What we have in Heidegger is a strange mixture of conservatism with its concern for rootedness, contemplation, and the myth of origin, and of modern liberalism with its drive to break out of the myth of origin into a free and open future.

This unique combination of a commitment to modernity and a basic conservatism—the desire to bring together technology and soil—is what attracted Heidegger to National Socialism. This is why Heidegger could refer in 1935 to "the inner truth and greatness" of the National Socialist movement.[57] Herein lies the answer to Grant's provocative statement and question concerning Heidegger's relation to National Socialism:

> The modern era is extraordinarily strange, but this is one of the strangest facts. This consummate thinker welcomed Hitlerianism, in the early years of its power. Some silly academics have seen this as a kind of regrettable foolishness, as if Heidegger could be interpreted as a political innocent who simply did not know the score in practical matters. But that is a childish view, which makes out that philosophic questions are just games played in useless ivory towers. In the last ten years this fact has become a symbol of what I want to think about. How could this amazing unfolder of the nature of modernity, this person who can illuminate the philosophic past, how could he opt for National Socialism at the political level? This is much more than an historical question about Europe in the 1930s. If one uses it as an oyster knife to open up his brilliance, the whole question of the destiny of modernity can be revealed.[58]

Heidegger's stance toward Hitler and National Socialism is a highly debated and controversial question for which the evidence is not nearly all in. There is no doubt, however, that Heidegger was initially attracted to something in National Socialism which was not simply a matter of political *naïveté* but due to his own philosophical orientation. He says as much in his now famous 1966 interview for *Der Spiegel*, in which he recalls his Nietzsche lectures of 1936 as having been an implicit critique of National Socialism. Nevertheless, he does admit that he saw something positive in the movement at its inception, something new, a political awakening which tried to come to terms with modern technology. National Socialism went in the direction of developing an adequate modern human response to the essence of modern technology, but its adherents were intellectually too poverty stricken to think profoundly enough about their relation to the modern epoch.[59]

Technology, Heidegger goes on to say in this posthumously published interview, uproots us from the earth and leaves us with purely technical relationships. "According to our human experience and history," he says, "I know that everything that is essential and great has arisen from the fact that man has a home and was rooted in a tradition."[60] Technology leaves us homeless. Through human effort we cannot turn around the movement of modern history:

> Only God can help us at this point. For us there remains only one possibility, through thinking and poetizing to prepare a readiness for the appearance of God or for the absence of God and go to ruin; that we go to ruin [*Untergang*] in the face of the absence of God.[61]

Do Grant and Heidegger share a common conservatism? The answer must be a qualified yes. Their common conservatism rests in the fact that they both turn away from the modern obsession with the objectification of everything, from the assault upon human and non-human nature, from the reduction of the essence of human life to purely technical relations and instrumental reason. They both turn away from the modern preoccupation with radical political doing and human construction to thought and contemplation of that which is granted to human beings to think. They both share a disdain for a shallow deracinating cosmopolitan culture and yearn for the "love of one's own" including one's body, family, nation, and tradition.[62] But there is one fundamental difference. For Heidegger, as for Grant, "*Only what is granted endures. That which endures primally out of the earliest beginning is what grants.*"[63] But for Heidegger, in contrast to Grant, that which grants and that which is granted itself changes temporally and historically. For Grant that which grants and is granted is permanent, immutable and eternal as envisioned most adequately within classical Platonism and Christian theism. For him the love of one's own particular good is only a means to the experiencing of what is universally and eternally good.[64] Only such a suprahistorical anchor can secure true justice for the weak and the strong alike and limit our arrogant human drive into a tyrannical future. The eternal is the standard by which the temporal scientific and political ideologies of history can be measured and judged.

SIX

Christian Theology and the Modern University*

Under the influence of the Enlightenment the modern university has squandered its rich Greek and medieval European legacy and fragmented into a multiversity. The search for truth, synthetic knowledge, meaning, and "the good" has been replaced by the quest for positivistic analytical skills in the service of technological progress. In this essay, presented as the annual Eby Lecture at Conrad Grebel College in 1990, I discuss the history of the university, the critiques of the modern university by philosophers like Allan Bloom and George Grant, and recent debates about the teaching of religion in the university, and I explore the positive role which Christian theology might play in pushing the academy to debate and discuss different perceptions of "the good" and "the human" in the university.[1] I begin with my own commitments as an academic, Christian, and Mennonite, and seek to show how I can remain faithful to each of these while playing fairly by the rules of the university. My thesis is that, given the university's own stated dedication to free and open debate (a positive inheritance from the Enlightenment), religion departments in particular bear a responsibility to foster discourse on the nature of the ends for which we are striving in contemporary

---

* Originally published as "Christian Theology and the University: Methodological Issues Reconsidered," *The Conrad Grebel Review* 9. 3 (Fall 1991): 223-41. For notes on the text see the Notes section below.

academic culture. Unfortunately, religious studies faculties have largely relinquished this obligation in favour of a dated "scientific methodology" which defends "neutrality" in a way which other departments of the university have long discarded, for fear of being labelled "confessional." I suggest that Christian theology might fruitfully think of itself as engaged in post-modern apologetics in the university, self-critically giving account of itself and its perception of the true and the good in the face of multiple, alternative claims.

◆ ◆ ◆

Introduction

My thoughts on what is involved in teaching Christian theology at the modern university are organized around three basic assertions. First, I am an academic. I am devoted to teaching and scholarship, a member of the scholarly community at large but more specifically at the University of Waterloo. This implies that I have something in common with other people who teach and do research in the academy: the physicists, engineers, chemists, biologists, mathematicians, psychologists, sociologists, anthropologists, artists, linguists, musicians, dancers, historians, philosophers, religiologists, optometrists, environmentalists, and so on. It is difficult to imagine that all of us specialists have something in common with each other. But surely there must be some common justification for our teaching in the university. There must be some rules by which this institution plays. And if so, then I have some responsibility to play by the rules of this community. If at some point I find that I can no longer in good conscience abide by those rules, I ought either to seek to convince the community to change those rules for better ones or leave.

What are those rules? How do teachers of religion abide by these rules? These are the issues addressed in the first part of this essay. There is a common assumption that the modern university operates or at least ought to operate under rules of scientific or academic "objectivity," and "neutrality," or "distance" from one's subject matter. I want to examine whether this is in fact, or ought to be, the rule by which academics play.

Second, I am a Christian. I am a believing member of the Christian community. This means that when I teach Christian theology in the university I do not teach it from a neutral vantage point; I teach the subject matter from the perspective of a commitment to its doctrines as true. This raises questions about what theology is, how it ought to be taught in a university classroom, and how the discipline of Christian theology relates to the study of other religions, for it is commonly assumed that in a university religion department all religions should be dealt with equally and fairly in line with the rules of scientific detachment mentioned above, on "a level playing field" as one religious studies professor put it recently.[2] Am I playing by the rules of the game when I believe in what I teach? These issues will be dealt with in the second part.

Third, I am a Mennonite. I am an active member of a Mennonite church—I worship, I preach, I teach catechism to potential baptismal candidates. When I teach Christian theology in the university classroom, not only do I teach Christian faith generally from the perspective of a believer, I teach it from the perspective of a small confessional group within the larger tradition. I hold to the basic doctrines of the Mennonite tradition, where, nonconformity to the "world", a pacifist or non-violent commitment to peace and social justice, a personal confession of faith, and a life commensurate with that confession is assumed to be a condition for church membership. Mennonites have historically been suspicious of theologizing in any explicit, systematic sense for fear that it will not only undermine faith but divorce faith from real life, and from upright moral living. This raises for me the question of how I as a Mennonite can pursue and teach academic theology on a so-called "secular" university campus, supported and subsidized by the state. In the third short concluding part I will deal with this latter question and propose what I consider to be a responsible way of teaching Christian theology as a believing Mennonite Christian in the academy, abiding by what I consider to be the rules of the university.

University or Multiversity? Religion Within the Academy

A. The Study of Religion in the Context of Modern Pluralism

1. *What is the University?* It is easy to be critical of the university as an institution. Such criticism rings just a bit hollow, however, when it comes from those of us who most benefit from the university, who have spent most of our lives in its embrace. On the other hand, maybe we who are a part of it have earned the right to be critical. I for one owe the university a great deal and consider it to be a great privilege to be identified with the academy. So I hope that my criticisms are seen only as a serious struggle with the nature of the community that I consider my own. It is an exercise in self-understanding and self-criticism.

In preparation for this lecture I looked more carefully than I had before at the University of Waterloo 1990-91 *Undergraduate Calendar*. I had never really gone through it faculty by faculty to see what each says about its intent. It proved quite illuminating. The first thing that caught my attention was the description of the symbolism of the university mace. We are told that "the fundamental concept is unity amid diversity and tension in the creative intellectual process that strives to bring forth a new individual. The design of the mace interprets this theme in the idiom of the life process: from the seeds at the base of the stave the mace grows in unity and strength until it differentiates by a four-fold separation into diverse elements." The four-foldness represents the four faculties existing at the time the mace was designed and the four church-related colleges affiliated with the university. What is clear is that from the beginning this university was not committed simply to a static, neutral, objective search for factual knowledge, but to the creative process, to the bringing forth of a new individual.

One finds interesting gems of philosophical intent at a variety of places in the calendar. The main objective of the Faculty of Arts, we are told, "is to provide a liberal arts education which is designed to acquaint the student with some of the major ideas and forces that shape our civilization and other civilizations, to develop the ability to think clearly, critically and creatively, and to make a contribution to living a full life." The purpose of the Faculty of Applied Health Sciences "is the development of knowledge and programs related to health and well-being," "fostering [an] enhanced quality of life." The interdisciplinary program "Society, Technology and Values" seeks to address the questions "How can people guide technology so that it will contribute to human betterment? What values shape, or should shape, the direction and pace of technological change?" It is the pure and natural sciences which offer the least in the way of philosophical reasons behind their disciplines. The sixty-four-thousand-dollar question is of course what the new individual, health and well-being, human betterment is to look like. This is not answered. I want to propose that this is precisely one of the primary roles of the university: not to give unilateral answers to the question (which, incidently, it appears inadvertently to do in the advancement of modern technology) but to provide a genuine forum for vigorous debate amongst a multiplicity of positions concerning the question: What does it mean to be authentically human and moral in any society? Here the religions, with their classical texts, the historical experience and wisdom of the ages, have an incredible contribution to make.

Interestingly, the University of Waterloo in its Policy Document No. 53, on "Faculty Appointments—Tenure" invites such free and committed debate about fundamental issues of truth and value when it says:

> The University supports academic freedom, which means the freedom to study, teach, publish and debate, independent of current opinion, subject to commonly accepted scholarly standards. The right to academic freedom carries with it the

duty to use that freedom in a responsible and ethical way . . . . Specifically, and without limiting the generality of the above, academic freedom entitles all faculty members to freedom in carrying out their activities, in pursuing research and scholarship and publishing or making public the results thereof, and freedom from institutional censorship. Academic freedom does not require neutrality on the part of the individual. Academic freedom makes commitment possible, and carries with it the duty to use that freedom in a manner consistent with the scholarly obligation to base scholarship and teaching on an honest search for knowledge.

This I would argue is the credo of the academy (in its modern form) at its best, one which I can live with, one which we need again and again to hold up as a mirror before the academic institution. It guarantees the freedom to be committed, and to teach not from a neutral standpoint, but from the perspective of one who is sincerely interested in the truth and the good, one who teaches and does research from the perspective of truth as she sees it, always willing to listen to others and debate with others in the search for truth. It is doubtful whether the contemporary university, including the University of Waterloo, with its a priori commitment to High Tech, is in the end committed to the kind of serious debate about underlying assumptions concerning the true and the good called for by the above *Credo*. There are some critics of the modern university who are convinced that a genuine debate about ultimate questions of truth, knowledge, the good, the beautiful, and the virtuous no longer takes place and may not even be possible.

2. **Medieval Origins** Where do universities come from? Modern universities, says Charles Homer Haskins in his little classic, *The Rise of the Universities*, are the direct descendants of the universities of the Middle Ages, particularly those of Bologna and Paris.[3] It was with the revival of learning, known as the twelfth-century Renaissance, that there emerged what we call the university. Education in the early Middle Ages, in monasteries and cathedral schools, had consisted of the seven liberal arts: the *trivium* (grammar, rhetoric, and logic) and the *quadrivium* (arithmetic, geometry, astronomy, and music). In the twelfth century Arab scholars of Spain introduced a whole new horizon of learning including the writings of Aristotle, Euclid, Ptolemy, Greek medical knowledge, new arithmetic, Roman law, and so on. Bologna and Paris quickly established themselves as the first organized university centres of learning, drawing to them hundreds of youths from various parts of Europe. Haskins has given us an engaging account of student and professorial life in these early universities.

The term "university" was not connected "with the universe or the universality of learning" but referred quite simply to the total group of individuals coming together for a certain purpose. The beginning of the university was the uniting of hundreds of students in Bologna "for mutual protection and assistance" against the rent and food prices of the townspeople, who were inclined to take financial advantage of the newcomers.[4] The students also organized in self-defence against the professors, who lived entirely from the fees of the students, to make certain they got their money's worth. The professor could not be absent even for one day, without official leave, and to leave town he had to make a deposit. If the professor drew less than five students to his lecture he was fined. He had to stop within a minute of the bell, and was not permitted to postpone a problem to the end of class.

By 1231 Paris had four faculties, each under a separate dean: arts, canon law, medicine, and theology. No history, no social sciences, no environmental studies, no society, technology and values, no peace and conflict studies. Arts consisted chiefly of Aristotelian logic and philosophy. According to Haskins "logic was not only a major subject of study itself, it pervaded every other subject as a method and gave tone and character to the medieval mind. Syllogism, disputation, the orderly marshalling of arguments for and against specific theses, these became the intellectual habit of the age in law and medicine as well as in philosophy and theology."[5] Abelard's *sic et non* (yes and no) method of teaching was the model. Paris in the Middle Ages became the pre-eminent university, largely because it was the most important school of theology, the supreme subject of medieval study—even though there were relatively few theological students in the Middle Ages, because of the high admission requirements, the costliness of the books, and the length of training required. Grammar, rhetoric, and literary form were subordinated to logic.

The most important characteristic of the medieval university and university curriculum, however, at least as it bears on our topic here, was the issue of academic freedom and the role of authority. According to Haskins, how we regard the question of academic freedom depends on how we view truth:

> If it is something to be discovered by search, the search must be free and untrammelled. If, however, truth is something which has already been revealed to us by authority, then it has only to be expounded, and the expositor must be faithful to the authoritative doctrine. Needless to say, the latter was the medieval conception of truth and its teaching. "Faith," it was held, "precedes science, fixes its boundaries, and prescribes its

conditions." "I believe in order that I may know, I do not know in order to believe," said Anselm. If reason has its bounds thus set, it befits reason to be humble.[6]

Outside of philosophy and theology (in law, medicine, grammar, mathematics) there was general academic freedom to teach what one pleased. It was only in questions related to theological orthodoxy that freedom was restricted, and even here few found themselves cramped. "Accepting the principle of authority as their starting point, men [academics] did not feel its limitations as we should feel them now," says Haskins. "A fence is no obstacle to those who do not desire to go outside, and many barriers that would seem intolerable to a more sceptical age were not felt as barriers by the schoolmen. He is free who feels himself free."[7]

3. *The Enlightenment* This all changed with the eighteenth-century Enlightenment. No longer was "the principle" of external authority (either in the form of bishop, prince, Scriptures, tradition, dogma, or revelation) accepted as a legitimate starting point for intellectual work on the university campus. What separates us from the medieval university is not so much the Reformation as the Enlightenment and a certain view of reason and freedom. Probably the most concise statement of what the Enlightenment is in this regard can be found in Immanuel Kant's "An Answer to the Question: What is Enlightenment?"[8] Enlightenment, Kant says, is "the [human] emergence from self-imposed immaturity." Immaturity is "the inability to use one's understanding without guidance from another." It is self-imposed in that the cause of this immaturity "lies not in lack of understanding, but in lack of resolve and courage to use it without guidance from another." So the motto of Enlightenment is "*Sapere Aude!*" That is, "Have courage!" "Have courage to use your own understanding!"[9] Kant comes at the end of the so-called age of Enlightenment, the eighteenth century (he died in 1804), and is a rationalist who has become aware of the limits of reason. In his most important book, *Critique of Pure Reason*, he says, "I have therefore found it necessary to deny *knowledge*, in order to make room for *faith*."[10] What he really intends is not to deny knowledge at all but to limit it to the empirical sphere, against traditional Christian dogmatics which thought it could have knowledge of eternal supernatural matters. The Enlightenment threw off the shackles of external authorities, whether pope, prince, church, dogma, or Bible. Its rallying cry was individual autonomy (the word literally means "self-law") against all forms of heteronomy (or "external law"), where judgments concerning truth and what one believed to be true would no longer be made on the basis of outside authorities but on the basis of critical reason, that is, a reason

which was unwilling to accept any assumption without critical examination.

This Enlightenment view of free, critical, rational inquiry is frequently touted as the model for all university curricula including, in the past three decades, for the study of religion. I would argue that this eighteenth-century vision of free, critical reason, were one to espouse it as an ideal, has all but vanished and been replaced by a close relative, technical and progressive reason. Kant still believed that universal truth could be known, and that reason must ultimately serve the highest good, virtue. In the modern university, the very notion of universal truths in relation to moral goodness no longer undergirds the search for knowledge. The modern university reflects what some have called the crisis of modernity—that total fragmentation, loss of cohesion, and absence of a set of shared values and assumptions concerning the common good. What we are left with is fragments, a smorgasbord of faculties, departments, options, and courses with no intrinsic link to each other, a multiversity rather than a university.

4. *A Critique of the Contemporary University* Allan Bloom is one of the severest recent critics of the contemporary university. He knows the contemporary university from the inside, better than most. In his best seller, *The Closing of the American Mind*, he claims that the democracy of disciplines is really an anarchy, leaving the university with no shared vision, not even "a set of competing visions, of what an educated human being is.... The student gets no intimation that great mysteries might be revealed to him [or her], that new and higher motives of action might be discovered within him [or her], that a different and more human way of life can be harmoniously constructed by what he [she] is going to learn."[11] Gone is the old concept of the university, in which each part saw itself as "incomplete, only parts of an unexamined and undiscovered whole."[12] He refers to this as the "decomposition of the university" and sees it evident in all faculties: the sciences, social sciences, and the humanities. The state of the humanities, now the only caretakers of the great books, the classics, is particularly lamentable. Even the humanities where larger questions of meaning were traditionally addressed, and to which the sciences look for guidance in such matters, no longer "presuppose the being of the noble and the beautiful" and therefore no longer attend to "questions that children ask: Is there a God? Is there freedom? Is there punishment of evil deeds? Is there certain knowledge? What is a good society?"[13]

How the Bible is studied in the university is for Bloom a paradigm for the sad state of affairs in all study of classical literature. Anyone who teaches it as true, as "Word," stands in danger of being charged with *naïveté*, "scientific incompetence and lack of sophistication." Here, says

Bloom, "one sees the traces of the Enlightenment's political project, which wanted precisely to render the Bible, and other old books, undangerous. This project is one of the underlying causes of the impotence of the humanities. The best that can be done, it appears, is to teach 'The Bible as Literature' as opposed to 'as Revelation,' which it claims to be."[14] Bloom does not call for an authoritarian imposition of one understanding of the true and the good on all who darken the doors of the university. What he calls for is that the university truly become a "community of those who seek the truth," a community after the model of Plato and Aristotle, who disagreed about the nature of the good but "[t]heir common concern for the good linked them; their disagreement about it proved they needed one another to understand it."[15] I cannot go along with Bloom's underlying intellectual elitism and anti-democratic, egalitarian sentiments, but I find convincing this latter vision of what the university should be.

Another critic of the same ilk as Bloom is the late George Grant. Grant might be ranked as one of the most distinguished and controversial philosophers and religious thinkers that Canada has produced. He was a prophet who preached unrelentingly against the dehumanizing aspects of our so-called enlightened, liberal western technological culture. He, like Ernst Troeltsch, the great German social philosopher and theologian, identifies the eighteenth-century Enlightenment as the watershed in western history. Liberal assumptions about freedom, history, and reason replaced the ancient understanding of knowledge as the grasping of eternal truth(s). Unlike Troeltsch, however, Grant laments the loss of the ancient openness to the eternal.

Grant calls our universities "multiversities."[16] He is particularly critical of the multiversity for having made the scientific method the standard for all knowledge. At its heart, says Grant, science is the "project of reason to gain objective knowledge."[17] "Reason as project... is the summonsing of something before us and the putting of questions to it, so that it is forced to give its reasons for being the way it is as an object."[18] Everything we study at the university is objectified first, made into an object standing over against us, there for our analytical examination, the animate as well as the inanimate world.

The three main faculties in the modern universities—natural science, social science, and humanities—are divided on the basis of the classification of objects to be studied. Even in religion departments, the classical texts, the diverse religious movements, and religious experience itself are studied as objects that have to give us their reasons. The term "multiversity" best describes the growing specialization and fragmentation of such objective knowledge, the division of scientific research into departments and sub-departments. Grant is, of course, highly critical of the way this scientific paradigm has taken over completely on all levels of the multiversity, and robbed the academy of its more traditional concern for the meaning behind the universe (the university), faith, understanding a genuine love of the true, the good, the beautiful, the universal community, the whole. "The good of a being," he says "is what it is distinctively fitted for. Human beings are fitted to live well together in communities and to try to think openly about the nature of the whole."[19]

I have read most of what Grant has written and must confess that over the past fifteen years he has profoundly shaped my thinking about God and the world. I can only describe my first encounter with Grant's thought as a kind of conversion. But I think his analysis of modern science is one-sided. Behind much scientific research there is a reverence, awe and genuine love of nature—a yearning for true knowledge, a longing for nature to reveal its mysteries to us. It is when scientific methodology is taken to be the only legitimate approach to knowledge, and when it becomes an all-embracing worldview (scientism), in which no true knowledge is possible outside that which is empirically observable, that it threatens the true nature of the university. Have we truly come to that, as Bloom and Grant think? I hope not. Maybe a look at how religion is being studied in the contemporary university will shed some light on this question.

B. The Search for Method in the Study of Religion

What is religion anyway? All attempts at giving a universally valid definition of the essence of religion (the feeling of absolute dependence; ultimate concern; concern with transcendence, ultimate reality, divine reality, or the beyond; or simply cultic rituals of some kind) have floundered, so I will not even attempt here to offer and defend my own version, although I do have one —religion is ultimate concern expressed in ritual. There has been a general consensus in the past few decades that there is no such thing as a generic essential religion (a common denominator that binds all religions together) but that what we have is a variety of religions, each with their idiosyncrasies which need to be respected. Any talk of religion in general is purely for convenience.

The fragmentation of knowledge, specialties, disciplines, and fields of study has given birth to a whole new preoccupation with method. This is particularly the case in the field of religious studies, which is a relative newcomer to the university, and as such a bit overly obsessed with establishing its own credentials among the so-called other sciences. Method is not the actual doing of something, but the attempt to figure out what we are doing when we are doing it. So of special interest to those working in this area is whether behind all the different sciences, social sciences, and humanities there may be some common way of thinking, doing, or going about things that unites us despite our different subject matters.

The concern by religious studies to establish itself as a legitimate member of the liberal arts curriculum on the modern university campus has led to a preoccupation with method in religion departments as well. This is evident in the just published "Report of the Task Force on Study in Depth in Religion," part of a national review of arts and sciences majors initiated by the Association of American Colleges and cosponsored by the American Academy of Religion.[20] I summarize briefly here the findings of this report, because it fairly well reveals to us where the university religious establishment stands. Until the 1960s, it says, American undergraduate religious studies programmes were sectarian in nature, fashioned after Catholic and Protestant seminaries. A major shift came in the 1960s with faculty designing "cross-cultural, interdisciplinary studies in religion, without sectarian bias."[21] New faculty, trained in phenomenological studies, the history of religions, or the social sciences, were recruited for teaching Jewish studies, Asian religion studies, and the "religions of non-literate peoples." The study of religion was now to be "free of sectarian purpose." The methods used were to be "appropriate to the modern university" and "differ markedly from the various venerable practices of textual study, self-interpretation, catechesis, and spiritual reflection that have developed within many of the religious communities themselves."[22] Thus, academic religious studies has become a legitimate discipline within the university. The most serious problem is the disparity between the undergraduate programmes fashioned along these new lines and the more traditionally oriented graduate programmes which are the resource for new faculty.

The new non-sectarian approach to the study of religion, the report suggests, might be characterized in the following ways. First, it is multicultural, reflecting the pluralism of modern society. Students should study more than one of the historic religious traditions (Buddhism, Christianity, Hinduism, Islam, Judaism, Native Spirituality, and so on), using a variety of different methods.

> The academic study of religion is not ethnocentric, much less Christocentric, or even theocentric. It is directed to the cultural specificities of each religious tradition under study. It brings no preconceived definition of generic "religion" to its study, but interrogates the tradition itself to discover what is "religious" in it, on its own terms. It proceeds inductively, suiting the methods of study to the specific contours of a common life in its own time and place.[23]

I find the emphasis on the study of a variety of religions, as fairly and as much on their own terms as possible, entirely laudable. Preferably we should learn from the mouths and writings of devotees. What I find incomprehensible is the suggestion that one come to the study of religions bracketing one's own Christocentricism and Theocentricism, without prior conceptions of what God, religion, or culture are. This is neither possible nor desirable. I hold with Hans-Georg Gadamer that "[w]hat is necessary is a fundamental rehabilitation of the concept of prejudice and recognition of the fact that there are legitimate prejudices, if we want to do justice to man's finite, historical mode of being."[24] To have prejudice in the sense of prior commitments is to be human. Through our own prejudices (prejudice not as in bigotry or "closedness" but in the sense of unabashed orientation or "position-taking") that we learn to understand the prejudices of others.

Second, the report tells us that while it has much in common with other humanities, what differentiates the study of religion from other disciplines, is the subject matter: religion and religious experience. The "study of religion is a meditation on cultural difference, the deep differences in what is ultimately valued."[25] Religion, therefore, has to do with what is "ultimately valued" and "ultimately serious," and the study of religions is always pluralistic in that it is the study of differences in beliefs concerning what is of ultimate importance. What this new approach to religious studies cannot tolerate is the preconceived notion by a student of religion that her own religion is the true one, or superior to another being studied. Such prejudice, if it exists, needs to be suppressed if one is to understand fairly the other point of view. This is the methodological point that I want to dispute. I would like to argue that it is precisely in the apologetic defence of one's religious faith in the forum of public debate with others, a forum which has certain rules of fairness to hearing each other, wherein lies the best possibility for the gaining of knowledge and truth. But this presupposes a whole totality exists behind or beneath the parts, to which the fragments point.

Third, the report states that religious study must be "an empathetic study of the 'other'" to guard against the "moral and cultural superiority of the critic." Empathy entails an appreciation for and a distance from the object of one's study, including texts, rituals, icons, hymns, practices, sayings, rules, and so on. It is truly regarding the objects of one's study as an other which talks back to us, and eludes easy categorizations and "reductive 'explanations'." These objects of study "challenge our own ways of life, they contradict our wisdom, they pose severe tests of self-examination. They teach us. Some of them represent traditions of learning as rigorous as ours and far more ancient."[26] I found this particular section of the report most attractive, in stressing that religion is more than an artifact to study objectively. Nothing outrages me more than the almost unquestioned assumption in our society and particularly in our institutions of learning that we in the twentieth century are smarter than the ancients, and that the ancients (intellectual pygmies because of their pre-modern and pre-scientific cosmologies) have little to teach us of eternal things, other than how we got to where we are. Here in the report there is the sense that great and ancient traditions are worth listening to and have some truth(s) to teach us from other centuries and other worlds. Empathy and love for the truly other is a requisite for our common search for truth and goodness, and does not conflict with a prior commitment.

Fourth, we are told "the academic study of religion is conducted on the premisses of the modern non-sectarian university." "The premisses on which we conduct our study," the report openly admits, "are located institutionally and intellectually in centers of learning that have their origins in the medieval European university and have been methodologically informed by critical traditions that have developed since the European Enlightenment."[27] The very notion of "religion" in a generic sense is a product of the modern university, and while there may be no such thing as a "religious essence," to talk about "religion" generally is a useful academic heuristic device by which to study critically the variety of religions. "It makes a text or an institutional structure an object of specific modes of investigation, conducted on terms that have evolved in academic study since the Enlightenment." And now comes the underlying presupposition behind the whole document, and also the predominant paradigm of much current religious studies:

> Criticism of religion is not hostile, but it is independent and suspicious. It does not accept at face value the apologetic self-presentations of religious devotees, or, for that matter, the popular polemics of their opponents. Academic critics do not, like missionaries, argue the superior truth of one tradition or the falsehood of others. But the posture of suspicion is the legacy of post-Enlightenment academic study.[28]

It is with this "hermeneutics of suspicion" that, according to the study above, the critical student of religion must approach all religious movements, texts, rituals, and beliefs, including her own.

This section, in my opinion the heart of the whole document, brings out clearly the dilemma, paradox, even impossibility of the modern study of religion. On the one hand, it wants to deal empathetically with other religions as "other" and to allow ancient texts to speak back and teach us. On the other, it wants to subject these great traditions to the critical scrutiny of Enlightened reason, premised on suspicion. It identifies this approach as standing in continuity with the medieval university and the Enlightenment. To some extent this is true, but, as we have seen, the medieval university presupposed external authorities, and the Kantian version of Enlightenment reason presumed universal truths and the highest good, both of which are missing in the contemporary discussion. The internal dilemma of the new non-apologetic approach to religious studies is most visibly present in the document when it accepts feminist criticism in the study of religion as a unquestioned given. "But the modern rise of feminism in the academy," it states, "has been virtually coterminous with the emergence and maturation of our discipline, and the number of gifted feminist critics attracted to the academic study of religion has achieved an influential critical mass."[29] I am a great supporter of feminist criticism. This is not at issue. What is at issue is the fact that once one accepts the feminist hermeneutic, one brings to bear on objects of study an ideological preconception of truth—just as prejudiced as Christocentricism, ethnocentricism, or theocentricism. Liberation and emancipation movements of all kinds have a dialectical relationship to the Enlightenment. They emerge out of the modern impetus toward freedom. But they contradict that very vision in that they are based not on a position of neutrality but presuppose a much needed position of prejudice and ideological bias within the university. They, like religious movements, need to be heard in terms of what they are: *apologists* for truth as they see and experience it. These liberation movements need to be listened to and debated rationally for the truth claims they make, and religious traditions must be examined in light of them.

One of the better things I have read recently on the study of religion is Darrol Bryant's unpublished paper, "Religion in a New Key: Notes Towards the Symphony of Living Faith."[30] What I find especially attractive about Bryant's approach to other religions is his emphasis on "the priority of the lived experience of religious life over its study."[31] He is highly critical of the overly rationalist and historicist paradigm that has predominated in the study of other religions in the past, and believes that this has distorted our understanding of how religious people actually live and experience divine reality. Consequently, he gives a much greater role to imagination and intuition—what he refers to as "disciplined imagination"—to the study of religious experience. He believes that art and music offer us better methodologies for understanding religious experience and religious movements than technical reason. In the end, however, Bryant in my opinion does not do justice to the apologetic element in the encounter between religions.

I love the university; I love research, writing, teaching, ideas, interacting, debating, and reflecting with colleagues and students about ideas and about truths as I see them. The university plays by certain rules. These rules have increasingly been described in the terms of the methodology of the natural sciences with its commitment to "objective" observation of empirical information. While there is a place for this approach even in the social sciences and humanities, including religion (certain aspects of religious movements can be studied in this manner), I do not consider this to be the only or even dominant method that should be employed in the university. It is questionable whether even within the natural sciences the observation, description, theorizing, and explanation of data remains objective and free of value assumptions. I would say that the paradigm of the ancient academy and schools of learning (both in the Hebraic and Greek traditions), as well as the medieval centres of learning, have something to teach us in the contemporary university setting. The university should be a forum for rational debate and argument between opposing points of view, free of external coercion. It should, in short, be a place where truth is defended from a variety of positions, governed by a common understanding of fairness. Fairness would mean that opposing points of view get a fair hearing and personal faith and value assumptions are critically examined.

Alasdair MacIntyre, in his just published Gifford Lectures, holds a similar point of view. He comments on the great shortcomings of the liberal university and calls for a recovery of true debate between conflicting points of view in line with my own comments above, although a bit more stridently than I would make them. He asks provocatively:

> ... can we now realize, within the forms imposed by the contemporary university, the kind of and the degree of antagonistic dialogue between fundamentally conflicting and incommensurable standpoints which moral and theological enquiry may be held to require from within one or more of the contending standpoints? Or can fundamental debate on moral and theological questions now only be carried on outside the constraints of the conventional academic system, in the waging of a kind of guerilla warfare against that system?[32]

I hope and believe, and so does MacIntyre, that the contemporary university can make room for serious, albeit constrained intellectual, moral and theological debate between conflicting positions, where the rules are not defined solely by the method of the empirical and technical sciences. Having said this I fear that I may be perceived to be defending pure rational debate alone. While I hold rational discourse in high regard, I believe the university classroom is also a place for inspiration: literary, artistic, and musical masterpieces ought to inspire students to greatness, excellence and moral goodness as much as rational debate. I turn now more specifically to a discussion of Christian theology in the university.

Christian Theology as a Legitimate Field of Study in the University

A. Religion, Theology and the Other Disciplines: How are they Related?

The narrow definition of theology is "thinking about or studying the subject of God." In this definition any religion that believes in God or gods or some kind of divine reality can theologize. I define *Christian* theology more specifically as the human act of reflecting (using fallible human language and concepts) on God, Christian experience, and the contents of Christian faith in the light of God's revelation in Christ as witnessed to by the Holy Scriptures and understood throughout history. I still find Anselm's famous dictum the most adequate: theology is "faith seeking understanding." In other words, the experience of and encounter with God is primary and the reflection on that experience is secondary. I deliberately say "reflection" because it better includes within itself the contemplative, even intuitive, aspects of insight as well as the rational—or in today's parlance, the right brain as well as the left brain. I say "contents" because there are cognitive aspects to be rightly reflected upon—beliefs, doctrines, dogmas. My definition clearly betrays my confessional understanding of theology. My position is theocentric and Christocentric and colours my whole intellectual life. How can I hold these preconceptions about truth and teach with integrity at the university? Because I believe that the university is a place where diverse, even conflicting, commitments to truth should be freely expressed and taught, in a spirit of fairness and openness to conversion by the other's position.

Here my position bears some resemblance to Rodney Sawatsky's, as argued in his essay "In Defence of Proselytizing: A Contribution Towards Interfaith Dialogue."[33] I take Sawatsky to mean the best approach to genuine dialogue is to take the other side seriously enough to try to convert that person to the truth of your position without compromising the dignity of the other or impinging on the other's freedom to choose. This is close to my position, although I do not see Sawatsky making a distinction between what happens in the classroom and what happens outside. It seems to me that the university is a special place where greater attention is paid to the "reflective/rational" mode of apologetics. Theology is precisely the reflective moment of Christian life, faith and experience. While it is most properly done in the context of the church community it also has a legitimate place within the academic community. Here it is forced more rigorously than in other contexts to examine critically its own ground and assumptions, to challenge and listen to others, and to be open to interpret, reinterpret and change its self-understanding.

The place of theology in a university takes on immediate significance for us at Conrad Grebel College and in the University of Waterloo Religious Studies Department because of a proposal to incorporate our present Master of Theological Studies programme into a university M.A. programme as one of three fields or options, alongside Education Studies and Interreligious Studies. The proposal has raised once again thorny issues surrounding what religious studies is, what theology is, and how they are related to each other and other disciplines methodologically.

The nature of the academic study of religion and its relation to Christian theology has been hotly debated in this country over the past two decades in issues of the major Canadian religion journal, *Studies in Religion*. I want to spend some time looking at the shape of this debate, because it sharpens the issues considerably. The controversy quickly turned into a heated interchange between Charles Davis, well-known Canadian theologian and now Professor of Religious Studies at Concordia University, Montreal, and Donald Wiebe, Professor of Religious Studies at Trinity College and the University of Toronto. Other religiologists and theologians joined the fray on one side or the other.

1. *Charles Davis: The Reconvergence of Theology and Religious Studies*
The debate began with a major article by Charles Davis entitled "The Reconvergence of Theology and Religious Studies."[34] His basic point is that, in the past, when theology was still subject to external ecclesiastical authorities, the distinction between theology and religious studies was useful. But now that theology is free from all external authority there is no longer a need to distinguish the two. Theology, freed from its rootedness in a specific confessional tradition, should now rightfully take its place beside the academic study of religion in the university. His whole argument rests on the distinction between "religion" (the common sense, pre-reflective, pre-cognitive, "world of common meaning as lived and shared in day-to day community experience"[35]) and "studying religion," which is reflecting and theorising about religion. In this latter sense, the "science of religion" and "theology" are partners. Such theology should be distinguished from "preaching theology," "praying theology," and "kerygmatic theology." Theology, in both its historical and its systematic sense should not be bound confessionally to a certain tradition but follow the procedures and methods that apply to any religion. Foundational and systematic theologies, like philosophies, cannot restrict themselves to one confessional tradition, but

must reflect and ground themselves in the universal structures of human consciousness.[36] Davis claims there are three related levels to the study of religion in the university: the history of religions or historical theology which, like all historical sciences, seeks to investigate particular historical religious data; the science of religion like systematic theology which "deals with what is general or at least recurrent in religious experience and expression"—its aim is not simply to describe and classify but also to explain and theorize about the data provided by history; and the philosophy of religion and foundational theology which "probes and thematizes the grounds of religion and theology."[37]

Out of the five respondents to Davis in the same issue of *Studies in Religion*, Gregory Baum and William Fennell had the best criticisms of Davis's position. Baum found completely unacceptable Davis's "proposal that the disciplined and scholarly reflection of various Christian churches on their tradition and their present experience is not theology but something else" and concluded that "a theologian, even when he is teaching in a religious studies department, reflects out of a critical responsibility for a religious community an orientation which the student of religion does not have or at least need not have."[38] In short, Baum argues, theology is most properly done, even in the university, in the context of a believing community and this distinguishes it from religious studies.

Fennell argues that a Confessional theology need not be under ecclesiastical control or limited to a particular religious tradition to have as its basis "a revealed or encountered truth." Such a theology is independent from religious studies and has a continued place in the university. This is so, provided it is

> ... willing to give a reasoned account of its foundations, of the methods appropriate to the apprehension and articulation of the reality and truth it asserts, and of their application to a human existence that seeks and promises good for man—and provided that in all these procedures theology proves willing to be addressed by the critical questioning of persons with another, perhaps contrary, understanding, and to answer that questioning seriously, and as best it can, out of its own understanding of truth."[39]

The position I am espousing is in most ways closest to that of Fennell, although I would defend more strongly than he does the legitimacy of a diversity of religious studies and theological methodologies in religion departments, and the link of Confessional theologies to specific religious communities.

2. *Don Wiebe: The Failure of Nerve in the Academic Study of Religion.*
Donald Wiebe occupies the opposite end of the spectrum from Charles
Davis and elucidates his position most clearly in an article entitled "The
Failure of Nerve in the Academic Study of Religion."[40] He defends
passionately the original Enlightenment vision for "an objective, detached,
scientific understanding of religion" in the tradition of the "International
Association for the History of Religions." This association came up with
five minimum presuppositions for the academic religion, among them the
following: that the "experience of transcendence" is "to be studied like all
human facts, by appropriate method," that the science of religion "rejects
the claim that religion is a *sui generis* phenomenon," that "the Association
must keep itself free of all ideological commitments."[41] Early on there
emerged agreement, which Wiebe supports, "that the truth-question not
be raised in religious studies. The academic study of religion was to forego
the philosophical/metaphysical task of determining the truth or falsity of
the various historical religious traditions which had thus far been an
unsuccessful and divisive theological exercise."[42] Wiebe shows how, despite
the lip service religious studies in this country has paid to the Enlightenment
vision of a scientific approach to religious studies free of ideological
commitments, confessional-theological commitments have remained just
beneath the surface and are now coming out of the closet with people like
Davis. He calls this "the disturbing trend in religious studies that would
jettison the gains it has inherited from and since the Enlightenment."[43]
"The *a priori* acceptance of (or belief in) the reality and existence of the
Ultimate ('God, the gods, the Transcendent, the Ultimate Reality, etc.')" is,
according to Wiebe, "a species of religious thinking and, if it is to be called
theology at all, ought to be referred to as 'confessional theology.'"[44] Wiebe
considers such theologizing incompatible with the academic study of
religion on a university campus. "Consequently," he adds, "to avoid any
further ambiguity, I reiterate here that theology, when it commits itself to
the existence of the Ultimate (that is, without being open to the possibility
of a 'reductionist explanation') constitutes a form of religious thought that
can only 'infect' the academic study of religion and not complement it."[45]
I dare not take the time here to consider all the other related essays in the
Fall 1984 issue of *Studies in Religion*, including Davis's strident response to
Wiebe, with the charge that Wiebe's "scientific rationalism" is a form of
"sectarian Protestantism," "a fundamentalist idolatry."[46] The Wiebe-Davis
controversy was taken up again in the Spring, 1986 issue of *Studies in
Religion*,[47] with further clarification on both sides, but no essential changes
of position.

I find myself in a different position than either Davis or Wiebe. I agree
with Davis, against Wiebe, that theology and the academic study of religion

both have their place in the university. But with Wiebe, against Davis, I hold that they must be distinguished. The so-called study of religion which uses a scientific methodology to compare and contrast religions, to study aspects of religious cultic life and experience as empirical facts, using a wide range of disciplines to do so (including sociology, anthropology, psychology and so on), as free as possible from ideological bias, is in my view a necessary component of religious studies in a university. Theology, even in its theoretical mode, is something else, but also has a legitimate place in the academy. My basic disagreement with Wiebe is not over his espousal of a scientific methodology in the study of religion, although I am much less enthusiastic about the Enlightenment project than he appears to be, but rather with his argument that the scientific approach must be the sole methodology in the search for true knowledge. This is the kind of scientific triumphalism most severely criticized by Grant and Bloom. When I read these debates between religion specialists and theologians in their scholarly journals, it frequently seems that we in the religion departments are completely out of touch with what is really happening out there in the other disciplines on the university campus. Very few departments of the university employ the kind of scientific methodology that Wiebe espouses. Here it seems religious studies in its paranoia about being accepted as a legitimate science in the university beside other disciplines adopts a method no longer recognized as normative in most other departments, except maybe the natural sciences. I agree with John W. Dixon, Jr. when he says:

> This is the paradox of the study of religion. It studies the faith of other people but, in fidelity to the university, cannot participate in faith. Departments of religion are the only departments forbidden to be committed to their own subject, compelled to act as though it did not exist. We can do anything we want to do with the study of religion except for one thing: we cannot, professionally, take it seriously, believe that it is true, or act on that belief.[48]

Confessional theology, even in its theoretical mode, is quite different from the scientific study of religion—here I part company with Davis—but it is in my view as legitimate if not more legitimate in the search for truth and goodness on the university campus as is a methodological approach borrowed from the natural sciences. However, Confessional theology must be willing to give account of itself publicly. Here I find myself much closer to William O. Fennell.

B. Alternatives in Method

Implicit in what I have said so far is that the university has not only different disciplines, different fields of studies but different ways of going about looking for knowledge. In a healthy academic environment a diversity of methodologies ought not only to be recognized or tolerated, but encouraged; for it breaks the debilitating grip of methodological triumphalism. I am an apologist for a polymethodology as over against a monomethodology. There are different types of truths and different ways to look for and discover truths. Confessional theology, as I have been using the term here, begins with certain faith assumptions about ultimate reality (God) and seeks critically and self-critically to understand and give account of that faith in the public forum of the university, and to draw out the implications for a moral life. This is different from the approach natural scientists take to examine nature, and social scientists take to study psychic and social phenomena, and comparative religiologists take to study the empirical aspects of religious movements. Each of these, of course, also begin with faith assumptions and ideological commitments. Scientists are, for example, themselves committed ideologically to their particular "objectifying" method of exploring data. Theology, like philosophy, is interested in examining self-critically those faith assumptions and ideological commitments, and to defend them publicly in the search for truth and virtue. Within theology itself, there is a great diversity of methodologies. There is no one theology and one theological method even within Christian theology.

That is why Christian theology has seen a mushrooming of literature on methodology in recent years. Names like Paul Tillich, Bernard Lonergan, David Tracy, Gordon Kaufman, Schubert Ogden, and George Lindbeck come to mind. Within our own Master of Theological Studies programme at Conrad Grebel College, we have a required course called, "Methods and Issues in Theological Studies," in which we introduce students not only to the various faculty members but to the different disciplines and methodologies they represent: philosophy, history, sociology, literature, Scriptures, theology, and so on. I have now taught this course a number of times and each time find it amazing how diverse the approaches of each discipline are, and how possessive each is of its own domain. While we are all engaged in the common task of theological studies, we think and approach our materials quite differently, quite suspicious of the other.

For the second year now I have used as one of my textbooks for this Methods course Bernard Lonergan's *Method in Theology*. Both times I faced a near revolt by students. It is not only that the text is difficult; it is what Lonergan is trying to do that provokes such resistance. Lonergan argues that it is precisely in the modern world, where culture and theology are no longer seen as static but rather as dynamic and an "ongoing process" that one turns to method—a scientific model modified for theological purposes—as the one rock upon which to stand. He defines method "as a normative pattern of recurrent and related operations yielding cumulative and progressive results."[49] Lonergan, through an analysis of human consciousness and human knowing, is intent on identifying one common method for all disciplines within which, however, there are different tasks or functions.

The rock upon which we can stand in the modern world of flux and change is the universal structure of human consciousness and knowing, what Lonergan calls conscious intentionality. Human consciousness moves through four levels towards authentic knowledge: from experiencing to understanding to reasoning to acting responsibly. These he calls the transcendentals (the experiential, the intelligible, the rational, and the responsible). They apply to all academic pursuit of knowledge: natural sciences, social sciences, and humanities. He comes up with what he calls eight functional specialties for theology: research, interpretation (or hermeneutics), history, dialectic (or philosophy), foundations, doctrines, systematics, and communications.

Lonergan argues that we need clear distinctions between these functional specialties, each of which build upon the other and need each other, for the following reasons: 1) "to distinguish different tasks and to prevent them from being confused"; 2) to "have clear and distinct ideas" about what exactly each task is and how it contributes to the whole process; 3) most important, "to curb one-sided totalitarian ambitions. Each of the eight has its proper excellence. None can stand without the other seven. But the man with the blindspot is fond of concluding that his specialty is to be pursued because of its excellence and the other seven are to be derided because by themselves they are insufficient." "From such one-sidedness," says Lonergan, "theology has suffered gravely from the middle ages to the present day"; 4) the division of specialties is required "to resist excessive demands" on any given specialist. Important for Lonergan is conversion: intellectual, moral, and religious conversion, which is the progressive move towards authentic self-transcendence on each level.[50] In Lonergan we have one attempt to deal with the fragmentation of specialties that exists in the theological field.

Although I am not persuaded by Lonergan's apology for one scientifically-oriented methodology for all, I do find his divisions within this one methodology helpful in identifying the different but related tasks within Christian theology. Further, I have problems with his grounding of these divisions within human consciousness itself. Behind it there is a

Catholic neo-Thomist understanding of the continuity between being, thought, and God as divine mystery of the world. My Protestant students object to what seems to them an overly rational approach to theology and the divine-human encounter. They believe that Christian theology is ultimately grounded in a more radical encounter with the divine as coming from the outside. One of my students argued consistently for an anti-methodological approach to theology, which he called "fragmentalism." "Fragmentalism," he argued, "reflects the human experience of God and life: it contains the recognition that faith is inconsistent and yet the most powerful force in the universe."[51] There may be a way of combining the Catholic analogy of being and the Protestant analogy of faith. I hope so.

Even within the restricted field of Christian theology there is a diversity of positions and viewpoints and methodologies (or anti-methodologies) that can be legitimately defended. It is precisely in the university classroom where the debate between such opposing points of view needs to take place to see if there is some common ground or need of conversion. The Anabaptist-Mennonite tradition brings what I consider a distinctive contribution to such debate. This brings me to my third and concluding section.

A "Postmodern" Apologetics: A Proposal

My basic view of what ought to happen at the university, upon which I rest my case on the legitimacy of teaching Christian theology on the university campus, has already been alluded to a number of times in this essay. The university ought to be a place where free public debate occurs on the nature and meaning of human and nonhuman existence, on the good, on the beautiful, on the virtuous, and so on. Christian theology, with its classical texts, has a long and venerable tradition of insight which it offers on these and other issues and therefore deserves its rightful place in the academy. Many of our public Canadian centres of higher learning initially emerged in institutions of the Christian church. What is new in the modern and postmodern context is the recognition that these institutions can no longer represent monolithically one religious—let alone Christian—tradition. The university must truly be a public institution in which a variety of religious and other worldviews and perspectives are allowed to find expression. This contribution of the Enlightenment needs to be welcomed. I propose that Christian theology might most fruitfully perceive its role in the university apologetically, that is, reflecting critically upon itself, seeking to determine the truth about itself and its responsibilities in the contemporary world, and giving rational account of itself in the public arena of intellectual debate—a postmodern apologetics.

One could do worse than look once again at the classical model of apologetics for guidance on how this might be done in the postmodern situation.

During the second and third centuries, the classical period of Christian theology, Christian thought was directed increasingly to a new audience—the Greco-Roman world, a task for which it had only a few precedents, as reported in passages like Acts 14:15-17, 17:22-31, and Romans 1:19-2:16.[52] Christianity came on the scene with its dramatic claims exactly at the point where, according to Jaroslav Pelikan, the leaders of Greek thought had emancipated themselves from "the crude anthropomorphism" of their own mythological traditions. So the early Church Fathers set about to examine the truth of their own claims and to defend these claims in the public intellectual arena. They did this nonviolently with pure force of argument, persuasion, and confession. They were willing to suffer persecution and martyrdom and frequently did so. They walked the fine line between remaining faithful to their triadic experience (their encounter with the one God Yahweh of the Old Testament, the Christ as the risen Messiah, and the Holy Spirit who had given birth to the church) and articulating this three-way religious encounter with God in terms that might be understood by the intellectual leaders of the time and perhaps persuade them. The credal tradition, with seeds in the Hebrew and Christian Scriptures developed into its full form at Nicea, Constantinople, and Chalcedon, precisely as the attempt by faith to seek understanding and truth about its own experience, and to defend that truth in the face of distortion at a time when the movement was being threatened inside and out.

The context in which Christian theology finds itself in modern culture and the modern university is in some regards like that in ancient culture. It is one of pluralism: a diversity of religious and other truth claims being made within a pantheon of public gods. It is of course true, as John Meagher has recently pointed out, that Christianity was from the beginning "founded on exclusive claims to definitive truth and treated the faith and beliefs of others as falsities from which they should be converted."[53] Meagher considers this "an intolerant triumphalism," and alludes to "the fairly unremitting hostility of the Fathers of the Church to all forms of non-Christian religious life, Judaism not least."[54] I would argue with Meagher that the word "triumphalist" does not accurately describe the earliest truth claims of Christians. The word ought best be reserved for the period in which Christianity became a privileged worldview in which its exclusive truth-claims were combined with political state power in the fourth century. Intolerance is not the making of exclusive truth-claims, which everyone makes explicitly or implicitly, but arisies from making truth-claims which become ideologically linked to political power and in effect muzzle true diversity and debate.

As in the Roman Empire and in modern technological culture, what appears on the surface to be genuine diversity is in fact threatened by monolithic and homogenizing forces and values. The university does not escape this phenomenon of modern culture. The university ought, however, to be the place where authentic diversity and plurality survives to challenge any imperialistic claims. The project of the second-century apologists was thwarted when it accommodated itself to the imperial powers of the day. What occurred in effect was a *Gleichschaltung* or co-ordination; for some theologians like Eusebius of Caesarea, the apologetic task became that of providing the emperor Constantine with a theological ideology for the defence of the empire. This coordination of state and church, imperial politics and theology, has sometimes been referred to as the Constantinian shift or synthesis. The church, instead of being a critical creative force within the ancient world, became a privileged arm of the state.

Mennonites have historically seen this Constantinian shift as a sign of widespread Christian apostasy, as the "fall of the church." This negative evaluation of the Constantinian period, which gave the Christian church privileged status within Roman imperial society, has commonly spilled over into a suspicion of the Patristic period and especially historical ecumenical creeds, seen as intrinsically linked to and legitimating a growing ecclesiastical hierarchy and political power, rather than as faithfully expressing biblical truth. In another context I have discussed the Anabaptist-Mennonite view of the fourth century, and argued that theological orthodoxy and Constantinianism are not intrinsically linked, as is so often assumed by Mennonites, but are in fact in tension with each other. I propose that classical trinitarian orthodoxy needs to be retrieved in contemporary Christian theology after having eroded in the eighteenth and nineteenth centuries, to serve as a basis for taking a stand against various forms of twentieth-century Constantinianism.[55] Here I propose that a form of classical apologetics be similarly retrieved.

Constantinianism need not be restricted to the fourth-century phenomenon of state-church alliance; but, as John Howard Yoder so frequently reminds fellow Mennonites, it is a symbol for any era in which Christianity unreservedly aligns itself with the establishment and thus loses its critical power.[56] I have serious difficulty with much of the Mennonite critique of that century, including Yoder's: it tends to view the fourth century and so-called Constantinianism, not to mention "establishment" generally, too monolithically. The Constantinian period was much more differentiated than it is often made out to be, with numerous theologies of culture competing with each other. It was a rich period of

Christian self-reflection about the nature of its changing role within the Greco-Roman world, and Mennonites would do well to re-examine that era in an attempt to address contemporary cultural questions. I do, however, find myself sympathetic to the Anabaptist-Mennonite suspicion of an establishment ideology which accepts uncritically the dominant assumptions of an age and rides roughshod over minority and nonconformist viewpoints. This is, I believe, where Christian theology taught from the Anabaptist-Mennonite perspective has a place on the university campus. It does not withdraw self-righteously from the university into its own sectarian, ghetto enclaves judging all establishment as demonic; but neither does it accept without question the reigning methodological paradigms of modern culture and the modern university.

A postmodern Christian apologetics taught from a Mennonite perspective would 1) give public and rational account of the Christian faith in the arena of public debate—a faith which does not rest on reason but on a personal encounter with the divine; 2) engage itself critically with modern culture including modern intellectual life without allowing itself to be coordinated by imperial designs and false syntheses. It is not the giving up of exclusive truth claims that defines the postmodern situation; but rather the allowance of a genuine diversity of such claims to truth and authentic openness to conversion by the other, that is, the breaking up of an ideological truth-claim hegemony in the public sphere, which—especially when combined with political power—eliminates true debate and true apologetics, and consequently robs the opposing truth-claimant of his or her human dignity.

My Mennonite ancestors never tired of quoting 1 Peter 3:15: "Always be prepared to make a defence to anyone who calls you to account for the hope that is in you, yet do it with gentleness and reverence; and keep your conscience clear, so that, when you are abused, those who revile your good behaviour in Christ may be put to shame." Our apologetics, our vigorous intellectual debate in the public arena of the academy, must ultimately not be a game we play, but a genuine search for truth and virtue in which the other is respected and granted the dignity we ourselves desire, that is, reason informed by love for the other. Years ago my teacher, Gregory Baum, told me that we Mennonites had a certain intellectual advantage. Because we had historically been a religious and ethnic minority and frequently persecuted, we tended to think more dialectically than majority-traditions; that is, we looked at issues from more than one side. I like to think that Baum is right, and that the cultural and religious nonconformity that has characterized so much of our history might somehow also influence our academic life.

SEVEN

On Bringing Forth the New Individual at the University*

The first part of this essay was presented at a conference on "Market Values and Christian Values: Christian Identity at the University of Waterloo Colleges," at St. Jerome's University College on the University of Waterloo campus on April 8, 1998, and was subsequently published in the UW Gazette.[1] *The whole essay was presented to the South West Ontario Regional Chaplains Conference at Wilfrid Laurier University, on November 20, 1998 on the topic "Religion and the Public University: An Uneasy Alliance?" It was extensively reported on in the Laurier student paper. The views articulated in this piece stand in continuity with those in the earlier article on "Christian Theology and the Modern University," but go further, particularly in the second part. I have been charged by students upon reading the first article of having too optimistic a view of the academy and reason. Although it is true that a high view of reason pervades my essays of the past twenty years, I do not consider myself a rationalist in the modern sense. In fact, I am critical of a modern reductionist view of reason, in which instrumental or technical reason replaces older forms of reason, knowledge, and wisdom. In these reflections, I hope for*

---

* Originally published as "On Bringing Forth 'the New Individual' at the University: A Call to the Church Colleges," UW *Gazette* (June 3, 1998), 2. For notes on the text see the Notes section below.

the retrieval of the medieval monastic approach to learning, which is a more contemplative openness to divine knowledge. Here, thinking is a form of piety including more than simply the cognitive, let alone purely positivistic reason, and takes in all forms of human yearning after the divine.

◆ ◆ ◆

A. What New individual is to be Brought Forth?

Our 1998-99 University of Waterloo Undergraduate Calendar cites the University's official motto as *Concordia Cum Veritate* — "In Harmony with Truth." The design of the University Mace highlights the separation into the four faculties that existed at the beginning of the University, as well as the four federated and affiliated colleges. The symbolic meaning of this Mace, according to the Calendar, is as follows: "The fundamental concept is unity amidst diversity and tension in the creative intellectual process that strives to bring forth a new individual." It further states: "This creative process is focused not on the traditional spherical orb of static perfection but rather on an elliptical silver ovum—the egg-shaped symbol of creativity—the marvellous potential of a new individual life." Since this appears in the general introduction to the University, I assume that the philosophy of education expressed in these words applies to all the faculties.

To satisfy my curiosity I checked the prolegomena to the various faculty course offerings in the Calendar. Here is what I found. Applied Health Sciences claims that "The major theme of the Faculty is the development of knowledge and programs related to health and well-being . . . . the well-being of groups and individuals" (8.2). The Faculty of Arts says its main objective is "to develop the ability to think clearly, critically and creatively, and to make a contribution to living a full life." In the Engineering section I had to do a bit searching, but did find the following: ". . . most first-year Engineering courses are organized to promote the study of skills and work habits which will lead to academic and professional success." Later, under "Complementary Studies Requirements," the Calendar states: "Further objectives are that the engineering student develop a broader intellectual outlook, a broader understanding of moral, ethical and social values, and an improved ability to communicate." Environmental Studies says of itself: "As a whole . . . the Faculty concentrates on using diverse knowledge and methods from different disciplines to understand human relationships with both built and natural environments." Central to Independent Studies is "The ability to ask a meaningful question, obtain information related to that question, synthesize that information, and communicate conclusions. Applied Mathematics "reflects the belief that there exists a basic order and harmony in the universe which may be described by the logical structure of mathematics." Under the Faculty of Science I was unable to find any statement of general philosophy or purpose.

In response to my findings, particularly as this response relates to the purpose of today's colloquium, I make one simple point: It is the task of the four Church-related Colleges to take seriously the University's stated motto: "In Harmony with Truth." Further, it is the responsibility of these Colleges to challenge the University community to address the meaning of its explicitly stated goal: to further "the creative intellectual process that strives to bring forth a new individual."

Ontario Premier Michael Harris's remarks at the "Scotiabank Summit on the Future of Ontario Universities" (November 19, 1997) make clear the "new individual" which the government expects a university to bring forth is the one that will serve the economic market values of our society as efficiently as possible. From statements that have been made by University administrators in recent years, it is evident that the University of Waterloo is dedicated to that purpose as well. The Church Colleges have the faculty resources and supporting constituencies to challenge that definition of the "new individual" we are to bring forth. If we can take the University of Waterloo "Policies, Procedures and Committees" handbook seriously then we, as those who are committed to Christian values in the University, have every right to take a committed stand and publicly debate the issue of fundamental values. Policy 53 states:

> The University supports academic freedom, which means the freedom to study, teach, publish and *debate*, independent of current opinion, subject to commonly accepted scholarly standards. The right to academic freedom carries with it the duty to use that freedom in a responsible and ethical way.... Specifically, and without limiting the generality of the above, academic freedom entitles all faculty members to freedom in carrying out their activities, in pursuing research and scholarship and in publishing or making public the results thereof, and freedom from institutional censorship. *Academic freedom does not require neutrality on the part of the individual. Academic freedom makes commitment possible*, and carries with it the duty to use that freedom in a manner consistent with the scholarly obligation to base scholarship and teaching on an honest search for knowledge. (Emphases mine)

Religious groups on the campus, including those affiliated with, administering, and teaching at the four Church Colleges, do not have the right to impose ideological and confessional standards on the whole University community. They do have the right, on the basis of Policy 53, to be committed to certain values, and to try to further those values in a responsible and ethically sensitive way, respecting the values of others. The most important contribution that Church Colleges can make is to be catalysts for open and public debate on the meaning of the "new individual" we are seeking to bring forth on this campus.

The Church Colleges and the rest of us as Christians engaged in teaching or some other activity at the University should take up the challenge of the University's own policy and express as persuasively as possible our understanding of the human and the true. In the apologetic defence of our faith in the forum of public debate, we can make our most important contribution to the search for knowledge and truth at the university. The more intense the debate the better, always remembering, however, the good advice of the Apostle Peter: "Always be prepared to make a defence to anyone who calls you to account for the hope that is in you, yet do it with gentleness and reverence; and keep your conscience clear, so that, when you are abused, those who revile your good behaviour in Christ may be put to shame"(I Peter 3:15). The university is a place where diverse, even conflicting, commitments to truth should be freely expressed and taught, while respecting the spirit of fairness and openness to conversion by the other's position.

B. The Monastic Model of Learning and Character Formation

The medieval university had its origin in two centres of learning: 1) the monasteries (the various religious orders), and 2) the Cathedrals (e.g., University of Paris).[2] The first took the mystical and contemplative approach to knowledge and was more Platonic. The second was more rational and analytical, more Aristotelian in nature. Both presupposed the need for religious piety in the search for truth and knowledge. Reason, also in the Cathedral schools, was only a means to the religious end.

The modern university has taken as its model a secularized version of the Cathedral schools approach to learning. The university as "Cathedral" school is no longer the place for worshipping the transcendent reality but for worshipping at the altar of instrumental/technical reason. The University of Berlin, founded in 1809, is perhaps the best prototype of the modern university, with its strict separation of the disciplines, all allegedly devoted to free scientific and rational inquiry.[3] Theology and philosophy had their important function in the early modern university like Berlin—they were to ask the large questions unfettered by ecclesiastical control. But as we move into the twentieth century, both philosophy and theology reinvent themselves to survive with the other scientific disciplines in the academy: philosophy turns into positivism and theology into the scientific study of religion.

In the postmodern university all coherence—even the universality of rational principles that was still operative at the Berlin University—is in question. Faculties and disciplines are more and more isolated "language games"—ghettos of learning which may be internally coherent but have nothing in common with each other. There is silence between the disciplines and fields of study.[4] The sole unifying factor, ironically, is the computer, ironic because deconstructionists would have us believe there is no unifying principle in a postmodern society. In this situation, and we experience it particularly at the University of Waterloo, the "MIT of the North," the humanities in general and religion in particular get pushed to the periphery of relevance. Their language is foreign to the university. They try desperately to learn the other languages and the meta-language of technology but in doing so they give up their own true voice.

I propose that in these circumstances the Colleges and para-religious groups on the university campus see themselves as the guardians of the humanities, and within the humanities especially of religion (i.e., those disciplines that address what it means to be human in relation to the whole); and that they do this by retrieving for themselves the Medieval monastic model of learning. The Church Colleges and other religious groups would become para-academic *collegia* (in the medieval sense of master and student guilds) devoted to formation of human character and reverent scholarship.

My special challenges to the chaplains on the university campuses include the following: 1) Do not allow yourselves to be co-opted by the university into individualizing and privatizing faith in your personal counselling. Attach yourselves to communities of formation; 2) Select the communities you identify with carefully. My daughter, who is in Religion and Psychology, tells me how susceptible lonely, isolated students are to various forms of 'cultic' belonging; 3) While I believe para-church and para-religious groups should be encouraged on campus, I also believe that there are both good and bad (healthy and unhealthy) forms of community experience. How to distinguish them requires careful discernment; 4) The English practice of establishing Halls or Church Colleges on university campuses is a rich tradition in this regard—it puts learning and character formation into the context of long-standing religious traditions. Let's not sell our birthright.

EIGHT

Theology and Science: Response to Nancey Murphy

My interest in the relationship of theology to science has come primarily by way of the philosophical assumptions behind the rise of modern science, culminating in modern technology; and the methodological similarities and differences between the sciences (abstract, natural, social) and the humanities (history, philosophy, religion, literature, fine arts, theology). My reading of George Grant has been particularly determinative in my orientation on the first of these ways, and my reading of Paul Tillich on the second. It is this background that I brought to my reading of Nancey Murphy's book Reconciling Theology and Science: A Radical Reformation Perspective.[1] I had been asked to respond to Murphy's book at the Mennonite Scholars Meeting, as part of the American Academy of Religion and Society of Biblical Literature meetings in San Francisco, November 22, 1997, a response to which Murphy replied at some length. My two main difficulties with Murphy's proposal for the interactive model between science and theology are 1) that she sees theology at the top of a scientific pyramid built up from the particular sciences to ever more abstract, generalized sciences in which theology addresses the most general, overarching, conceptual cosmological issues; and 2) she proposes a problematic reading of biological evolution from the underside—i.e., rather than reading nature in the light of Hobbes and

Tennyson (nature "red in tooth and claw"), it can just as well be read from the side of the victims who give their lives for the survival of the species. In such a reading, she proposes, the Anabaptist notion of redemption through nonviolent love and suffering can be interpreted as the ultimate origin and goal of the natural order—God and the cosmos are on the side of the prey rather than the predator. First, Murphy's schema lacks a recognition of the humanities as a radically different approach to knowledge than the sciences. Theology, it might be argued, has more in common with the humanities than the sciences. Second, to base the Christian ethic of nonviolent love and redemption on the natural law(s) of evolutionary processes, rather than revelation, poses serious difficulties. The fact of "tooth and claw" in nature cannot so simply be dismissed.

◆ ◆ ◆

I appreciate this opportunity to respond to Nancey Murphy's fine book *Reconciling Theology and Science: A Radical Reformation Perspective.* I have been teaching a course on "Methods and Issues in Theological Studies" in our Master of Theological Studies programme at Conrad Grebel College for a number of years, and Murphy's attempt to reconcile religion, theology and science addresses some of the very questions that I have been struggling with in that course. Ours is an interdisciplinary theology programme on the University of Waterloo campus, known best for its technical offerings, especially computer engineering. So in the course we look at how the different disciplines and fields (natural sciences, social sciences, humanities, including biblical studies, history, philosophy, literature, religion, systematic theology, practical theology) all with their different methodologies, contribute to theological studies. So I come to the Murphy book with a special interest in how the different disciplines relate to each other.

Murphy comes to theology from the philosophy of science, and as a convert to the "Radical Reformation perspective" from a Catholic perspective, a tradition she continues to love. I come to the sciences from a life-long study in the humanities and this obviously colours my approach to the subject matter of her book. I also come as someone having grown up in a Mennonite community both in its German-ethnic and its religious sense, and although I have not converted to the Catholic church, I have come to love its tradition and believe Mennonites have a lot to learn from it theologically. With this background, I pose a few questions to Murphy.

Murphy distinguishes her own position from two other common approaches: the "conflict model" in which science and theology are seen

---

For notes on the text see the Notes section below.

to be in opposition and the "two-worlds model" which sees them as addressing completely different dimensions of reality—one dealing with the empirical world of 'facts' and the other the world of 'meaning and interpretation of those facts.' Her own proposal is what she calls the "interaction model" in which science and theology, while different, interact with each other. She gives an interesting example of the Mars Rock which has traces of extinct life in it, a fact that raises important questions for theology. On this general level, I have no difficulty with Murphy's proposal. It is when she begins spelling out how it is that theology and science interact and where theology fits in the hierarchy of sciences that I begin to squirm.

Let me comment briefly on the two models Murphy rejects. First, the conflict model. On a popular level there has been throughout Christian history a lot of rhetoric pitting science and theology against each other. But is it not the case, on the more serious level, that the conflict has not been between theology and science in general, but between a theology wedded to one particular scientific model against a theology wedded to another? For instance, the Catholic church supported Ptolemaic science over against Copernican science, twentieth-century fundamentalism premised its theology on a Newtonian system against liberals' Darwinian science, and so on. The issue has been not so much a conflict between science and theology as between different theologies wedded to different sciences.

Second, the two-worlds model. Is it really the case that the prominent proponents of this position have argued there is *no interaction* between theology and the sciences? Have they not argued that, while they have overlapping spheres of interest, the primary subject matter of science and theology, and therefore their methodology, is different? Even someone like Paul Tillich, who is usually cited as an instance of this approach, wrote a book in 1923 on the *System of the Sciences*, in which he shows how the pure sciences, the natural sciences, the social sciences, and the human sciences (which he calls *Geisteswissenschaften*) might be seen as relating to each other. For Tillich, on a purely formal level one could make comparisons between theology and the sciences—they all had specific subject matter and appropriate methods of dealing with their subject matter. On a substantive level, however, he made a clear distinction between the *Naturwissenschaften* and the *Geisteswissenschaften*, those disciplines having to do with the Spirit (what we might call the humanities). The social sciences were divided between two worlds: the natural sciences and the humanities. Tillich put theology at the extreme end of the *Geisteswissenschaften*. Karl Barth also thought of theology as a science in the purely formal sense—it had a particular subject matter (the Word of God) and it had a method appropriate to the subject matter. But his separation between theology and all the other sciences was much more radical than Tillich's. Barth was against putting theology on any kind of continuum, both formally and substantively. This distinguishes him both from Tillich and, I believe, also from Murphy. There is, in Barth's theology, a radical discontinuity between a) God's Spirit and nature (natural sciences), and b) Spirit and spirit (social and human sciences). Murphy rejects any form of spirit-nature dualism. Tillich is closer to Barth than to Murphy on this issue, although Tillich rejects Barth's dualism between "Supernatural Spirit" and "spirit." For Tillich, as a so-called proponent of the two-worlds model, the humanities, and especially religion and theology, address the meaning or ultimate concern question at the bottom of every other discipline. Because, as a good Lutheran, he believed that anything in the finite, created world can potentially mediate the Spirit to us sacramentally (or symbolically), theology and the sciences have a bearing on each other for him, even though their subject matter is different at the most fundamental level.

This brings me back to Nancey Murphy and her own "interaction" model. The model is rightly premised on the most recent scientific knowledge but, *supposedly*, not wedded to a fixed scientific system, as in the conflict model. A future Einstein may come along and bring dramatic revisions to previous scientific knowledge. But does Murphy not wed her theology to a new non-fixed scientific model? Science itself has changed, she says, from a static Newtonian approach to an open post-Einsteinian, post-quantum-physics model. It is this new, more dynamic scientific model that Murphy reconciles with her theology.

Murphy argues that both modern science and theology work with a "hypothetico-deductive" approach to knowledge—that is, they make hypotheses on the basis of empirical evidence and then make inferences and deductions on the basis of these hypotheses. In cases of competing hypotheses for explaining the same phenomena there are ways for reaching a provisional decision in theology, just as in the sciences. For instance, there may be competing hypotheses about whether it was really the Holy Spirit or just psychological suggestion at work at a prayer group meeting. She calls her approach a "non-reductive physicalism"—premised on a hierarchy model of the sciences beginning with physics (basic material building blocks of the world), moving up to chemistry, then to biology, after which there is a branching out into cosmology on the left and the social sciences on the right. On the top, overarching both sides, is theology which asks the questions with the most complexity. Theology is a form of physicalism because it begins with the stuff of reality. It is non-reductive because it does not reduce everything to the stuff of nature but as it goes up in the hierarchy moves into levels of complexity having to do with organization and interaction with environment. Each level is confronted with "boundary issues" which it is incapable of fully explaining within its own parameters and for which it needs the next level. At the topmost level we have theology which has as its subject matter "God," a hypothesis which addresses the boundary question of cosmology on the one side and the social sciences on the other. Theology is different from the other sciences comparable to the way they differ from each other, but it nevertheless stands in some continuity with the hierarchy as it goes up to ever more general categories of subject matter. The non-reductive nature of Murphy's model also rests in her claim that there can be a "top-down" movement and not only a "bottom-up." But it is a top-down/bottom-up dialectic that is similar to the relation of epiphenomena to phenomena.

Here I have my greatest difficulty with Murphy's intriguing proposal. There is no place in her system for the humanistic approach to theology. It may be that Murphy has simply decided to limit her discussion in this particular instance. She may have addressed the issue elsewhere. Nevertheless, this absence seriously skews the whole schema. Only at a few points does she make fleeting references to the arts. On page 19 she says, "It would make no sense to count theology as the topmost science in the hierarchy of the sciences were theology itself not a science in any sense or at least very much like a science. That is, we would not think of adding art or music, for instance, to the hierarchy, or even art history." I find this a telling comment. Theology is placed within the sphere of the sciences rather than the arts. This begs the question: Where does Murphy place the humanities in what Tillich would call the system of the sciences? If the arts and the humanities are something completely outside Murphy's schema, where do they belong, and what are the ultimate questions they address? Are we to consign them to the realm of rhetoric and form? I would argue that the humanities address dimensions of reality which cannot be understood under the category of physicalism—hate, love, fear, hope, guilt, redemption, and so on. These are the very questions theology addresses.

This brings me to Murphy's most poignant chapters—the ones dealing with her conversion to Anabaptism and the ethic of love and nonviolence. From my vantage point, this is theologically the most interesting part of her proposal. She places "ethics" on the right side on top of the social sciences, leading up to theology. The social sciences lead us to the boundary questions of psychological and social reality, dealing with issues of freedom and moral responsibility, which can ultimately only be satisfactorily addressed by theology "top-down"— that is, presupposing God. At this point she makes a remarkable suggestion: that rather than reading nature in the light of Hobbes and Tennyson, we read it in the light of the Sermon on the Mount as interpreted by the Anabaptists—

that the ultimate origin and goal of the natural order is redemption through non-violent love and suffering. God and the cosmos are on the side of the prey rather than the predator.

At this point the model fails to work. I do not see how one can derive the ethic of nonviolence from a theological approach that is built on a non-reductive physicalism and hypothetico-deductivism. Nature is simply too ambiguous on this question. The Christian ethic of nonviolence can finally be grounded only on God's revelation in Christ. It may be that at the end of her book Murphy does move to a revelatory model which does not stand in continuity with the rest of her schema. Here I am with Barth. The whole issue of "Spirit-Nature" dualism needs, in my view, to be re-opened in contemporary theological discussion.

NINE

Time, History, and Ethics in Gordon Kaufman*

The transition from a pre-modern to a modern to a postmodern cosmology brings with it changes in our understanding of time. The ancients (pre-moderns) had a notion of historical time as but a shadow of eternal time; that is, chronological time, as the sequence from past to present to future, took its meaning from an eternal cosmic order. This holds true both for the Jews and the Greeks, although they conceptualized time in somewhat different ways. In modern thought the eternal horizon within which historical time receives its significance collapses into historical time. This absolutization of historical time at the expense of eternity is the essence of historicism. Gordon Kaufman's theological project is premised on the modern historicist understanding of time as directional. His earlier anthropocentric historicism has now been enlarged to include a cosmic historicism—in his recent work, In Face of Mystery, *the historicist model is applied to all of creation. For many postmoderns, however, there is a deep suspicion of all linearity and directionality, not to mention a total rejection of*

---

*Originally published in Alain Epp Weaver ed., *Mennonite Theology in Face of Modernity: Essays in Honor of Gordon Kaufman* (North Newton, KS: Bethel College, 1996), 227-43. For notes on the text see the Notes section below.

the classical metaphysical-ontological model. What these postmoderns are left with is an affirmation of incoherence, discontinuity, fragmentation, and struggle. Some Christian theological anti-foundationalists have adopted this postmodern view by disavowing all underlying unity in favour of separate systems of intra-textual coherence only. The most pressing issue facing contemporary theology in postmodern culture is the question of time. The possibility of Christians confessing faith in transcendent divine reality, in ultimate meaning and coherence, and in the truth of norms for human behaviour within history, rests on this issue. Kaufman argues that the ancient view of time is no longer credible; only historical time is worthy of consideration. He does however defend historical continuity against the postmodernists. In this sense he remains firmly within the modernist paradigm.

In the following essay[1] I argue that his proposal is not adequate for understanding the full range of human experience and that classical notions of time have creative possibilities for the future of theology in a postmodern era. Postmodernist cosmology is ultimately self-contradictory and incoherent (it makes the absolute claim that there is no underlying unity or foundation to reality, thereby contradicting its own disavowal of all absolute claims), driving us to a new postmodern metaphysic in which historical time needs to be supplemented with non-directional, nonlinear notions of time. No, more than merely supplementing such a view, I would hold that historical time needs to be relativized and grounded in a non-historical view of reality. This would bring us back virtually full-circle to a modified version of ancient cosmology.

In this essay I suggest that one need not choose, as Kaufman does, between the two views of time that he identifies — i.e., the modern cosmic evolutionary-historical view and the ancient eternal structural view. Neither is it a matter of identifying one with a literalist understanding and the other as metaphorical or symbolic. Both use language metaphorically or analogically — in fact, the modern, historicist view tends to be more literalistic than the ancient one. It is a question of which model is the most true to our experience. Here I disagree with Kaufman. I argue that ancient Trinitarianism is a way of combining both views of time within a more comprehensive, classical Christian vision that more adequately envisions reality than either of the two taken separately. It is an imagination in which transcendence, historicity and immanence are dynamically held together within a Christian understanding of God. In the last essay of this book I elaborate further on how we might creatively enter and retrieve this classical imagination in a postmodern world.

In 1996 Kaufman wrote me a letter in which he responded to some of the issues I raise in the essay. After a lengthy delay I responded in return. These letters appear as an appendix at the end of this chapter. In a subsequent letter by Kaufman, written to me on January 19, 2000 he continues the discussion. This third letter does not appear here but I paraphrase a few of his points: a) he agrees with my view that the political-hope theologies of Metz, Moltmann, and Pannenberg are too directional and naively teleological — his own notion of directionality (as trajectory) being quite different: it is an evolutionary movement into an open future not toward a specific goal; b) he also thinks that the value, meaning, and symbols of our traditions have to be taken seriously but holds that any particular formulation of these is fallible and subject to critical reconsideration by each new generation; c) we apparently disagree on our views of the Trinity — his being more Christocentric than mine (an insight he may have gained from Barth and Mennonites); he suggests that I presume to know too much about the hidden purposes of God, whom he prefers to describe as the ultimate mystery. In response to the three points of this letter, my suggestion of the scrabble game as a model for how I view directionality, the greater weight I put on the role of tradition in my work, and my more theocentric approach to the Trinity (without thereby presuming to know too much about the Immanent Trinity) distinguishes my theological project significantly from Kaufman's.

Gordon Kaufman, unlike some of his Mennonite contemporaries with whom he might be compared, has evolved and changed considerably in his thinking over the years.[2] This is most evident in his later discomfort with the traditional notions of authority and revelation that he used in his earlier theological work.[3] There is one aspect of his theology, however, which has remained central from the start. It is his view of "time as history," and his rejection of the pre-modern understanding of time as taking on significance only in relation to the Eternal.[4] The Eternal, in the classical understanding, is that which is not temporal but is beyond time, and provides the context for time and history. In the traditional Christian (including the biblical) perspective, time and history are themselves part of the finite, created order. God is the creator of this order and interacts dynamically with it, but is clearly to be distinguished from it. Whether it is still possible to think the "ancient" vision of God, time, and history, or whether it may again become possible, is something I consider toward the end of this essay.

A Personal Tribute

I have read Kaufman with great interest for many years. He, like Paul Tillich, has the capacity to put old things in a new light. It is this creative imagination, which is unafraid to tackle the most difficult challenges of modern thought for Christianity, that has always inspired me. Tillich introduced me to the possibilities of mediation between the old and the new much earlier than did Kaufman, but the special significance of Kaufman for me was his Mennonite connection. He was the only

Mennonite systematic theologian I knew who was seriously attempting to mediate between the tradition and contemporary experience and thought. For me, too, the Mennonite-Christian tradition as it had been passed on to me by home, church, and some other Mennonite thinkers, needed critical evaluation and reformulation in light of the modern world.

By the time I came to Kaufman I had become somewhat disillusioned with the modern liberal project. Earlier, I had accepted rather uncritically the deconstruction of the tradition in Western intellectual history from Kant onwards. My master's research was on Ludwig Feuerbach, whom I criticized for not following through consistently enough his own theories in his life and practice. Even more important for me personally were the liberating insights of Freud and modern psychology.

In the mid-1970s, however, I came under the influence of the Canadian philosopher George Grant.[5] I experienced a kind of "intellectual conversion." Here was a thinker who opened my eyes to the assumptions lying behind the modern enterprise, particularly technology, from a Canadian perspective. For the first time I began seriously to question the direction in which the modern scientific and intellectual heritage has taken us.

The influence of Grant, combined with my studying at a Catholic university, which introduced me to the early Christian and medieval classics, moved me to a reconsideration of the classical imagination for the modern and postmodern period. During this period I began studying Kaufman intensively. It seemed to me that Kaufman had bought into the modern liberal project too uncritically. He had gone beyond mediation to deconstruction and reconstruction. In this he was much more radical than Tillich ever was—Kaufman, in fact, criticizes Tillich for not being historicist enough, especially in his (Tillich's) later thinking. I began writing articles critical of Kaufman's theology.[6]

My basic disagreements with Kaufman were outlined in a 1978 essay, "Theological Method, Modernity and the Role of Tradition," in which I contrast Kaufman's and Grant's views. Although not rejecting everything Kaufman says, I take Grant's side and criticize Kaufman for writing off the classical tradition too easily, for not taking individual traditions (e.g., the Mennonite) seriously enough in constructive work (traditions which he tends to write off as parochial), and for presuming that individual theologians can "deliberately" construct more adequate concepts of God.

I identify Kaufman's theology as a legitimation of the modern spirit committed to "opening up the future into which humankind is moving." Although arguing that his theology is not adequate for our age, I acknowledge the many problems with traditional notions of God and end my essay with a *cul de sac*: "In short, we desperately need a more traditional concept of God, but we cannot believe in such a God. And to deliberately and self-consciously fashion such a concept for pragmatic and human reasons begs the question. This is the dilemma confronting the modern theologians." Ironically, it was a new appreciation for the doctrine of the Trinity, partly inspired by Kaufman's own interpretation of it, that later helped me to move beyond this dead end in my thinking.

This is the background to the present essay, to which I come, however, with a new appreciation for Kaufman's theology. For one, I have now lived intellectually with Grant for a while, and my enthusiasm for his powerful critique of modern thought has been qualified on a number of accounts.[7] For another, through some recent, personal experiences with Kaufman as a conversation partner, as a gracious participant in my Pastors' Theology Seminar (discussing his recent book *In Face of Mystery*[8]), and as a public lecturer in our university, I have encountered the unexpected in him.

First, his break with the tradition(s) can easily be over-emphasized. This holds for his method of doing theology, as well as for his concept of God as "serendipitous creativity" and "mystery" of the world. It also holds for his Christology in which the emphasis is not exclusively on the "Jesus of Nazareth" (a liberal temptation) but on the whole Christ-event, finding its fullest expression in the "community of reconciliation" (traditionally defined as the "body of Christ").

Second, Kaufman's self-perceived connection with the Mennonite tradition is much stronger than I had earlier realized. The late Hans Frei, a fellow student of Kaufman at Yale University, portrays him as someone engaged in pure academic theology abstracted from any commitment to a particular church context or religious tradition.[9] Kaufman tells me that this is a false appraisal of him and his theology. He grew up in a Mennonite home and community, is an ordained Mennonite minister and continues actively not only to participate but periodically to lead a Mennonite congregation in the Boston area. Furthermore, he explicitly identifies some of his central theological concerns as rooted in the Mennonite tradition—particularly the concern for the practical and ethical implications of his theology, rather than abstract dogmatic speculation. His view of the church as the "community of reconciliation," characterized by nonviolent love, is the Mennonite in him. What struck me more forcefully than it had earlier was his nuanced understanding of freedom in *In Face of Mystery*. It is possible to read his constructive theology as premised on the radical autonomy of the individual—his repeated critique of all forms of external authority (heteronomy) can easily be interpreted this way. This is to do an injustice, however, to his anthropology, which sees the individual not as isolated, but as historically shaped by the community of which he or she is a part. It is also to ignore passages like the following where he explicitly rejects individualism:

> It is to the *community of selves in interaction* that we must look for the actual locus of the human, not the individual self, the ego. No individual selves could exist without a community which gave birth to them and continued to sustain them.... Human existence is fundamentally social in character, not individual, and the complexities to which "we," "they," and "you" point cannot be understood as simply the consequence of putting a number of autonomous ego-selves together in various combinations (*Mystery*, 151).

What Kaufman objects to is this community exercising authoritarian power over its members, robbing individuals of personal responsibility to act morally in the world.

Third, what surprised me was Kaufman's pastoral concern and appeal. I invited Kaufman to visit my Pastors' Theology Seminar, where we were reading *In Face of Mystery*. It was interesting to hear pastors ask questions of the Harvard theologian, sometimes thought of as removed in his theology from the life of the believing, practising, worshipping community. There was a remarkable openness on the part of many of the pastors to Kaufman's ideas. He was attempting to meet the challenges of modern life squarely, something the pastors in their own congregations are called upon to do, especially with young people. He drew our attention to his lengthy footnote directed especially to pastors. Their primary task, he says, is not to do the constructive and analytic work concerning God that he is doing in his book. Rather, it consists of dealing with the problems of people, taking care of administrative matters, leading in worship, and, most important, "using the language and symbolism of faith" in their liturgical and counselling activities. To take apart (deconstruct) the symbols of faith in the context of the congregation would be counterproductive. In educational settings, or in their own studies, however, it is appropriate for ministers to become theologians engaged in analytical, interpretive and reconstructive work (*Mystery*, 356).

Finally, it was his gracious, humanitarian spirit, and respect for religious experience and worship—also the recognition of the need for piety—that impressed me about Kaufman. He is profoundly aware that faith is not purely an intellectual exercise. It involves a reverent attitude to the mystery of life and a commitment to a world view which, if it is to orient our whole life, must evoke religious devotion. This is evident throughout *In Face of Mystery*, beginning with the preface, which says: "in the theology set out in this book I attempt to express both my piety toward and my gratitude to the ultimate mystery which we daily confront." He is aware, as well, of the difficulty of, but the need for, deliberately constructing new theological concepts which will take on the symbolic power presupposed by religious devotion (*Mystery*, 232). He maintains that the metaphysical task with which he is occupied—namely, constructing a more adequate concept of God than the traditional one, a concept that is responsible ecologically and in every other way—points to "the real God who is in fact our creator, sustainer, and redeemer, and thus the God whom we today can and should worship and serve with unqualified devotion, respect, and love" (*Mystery*, 249). This is close to a traditional understanding of the God whom no one has seen and of whom no images can be made, the God behind all our own projections, the ineffable in the face of whom all our language is inadequate, the mystery which evokes astonishment and reverence.

In the light of this, what I have always found enigmatic in Kaufman is why he considers it necessary to dwell on the discontinuities between his work and the tradition. Why not labour more imaginatively from within the tradition, nurturing creatively the continuities in an age so ahistorically prone to reject the past? I find his use of the metaphors of "deconstruction" and "construction" jarring. In his concept of "imaginative construction" he oddly juxtaposes what to me suggest quite different activities—imagination and construction. There is little doubt that imagination is central to theological thinking—it has been central to Christian theology and popular piety from the start. Good theologians have always recognized this. Imagination suggests openness to influence and inspiration from the outside. The artist (musician, poet, painter) is moved to create (or "grasped," to use Tillichian language). Mozart is, for me, an example of a composer whose creativity cannot be adequately accounted for purely in terms of his own learned skills. The term "construction," taken from the building trade, suggests the techniques of the craftsman, who uses materials at hand to build a product from bottom up. There is, to be sure, a craft-like activity to theological work, but by itself, the term "construction" is too impoverished to do justice to the creative, inspirational dimension of theological work that Kaufman wants to emphasize.

A Constructive Theological Anthropology

Two passions drive Kaufman's theology. One is intellectual integrity. The modern Christian and theologian must, if he or she is to have integrity, come to terms with contemporary thought—philosophical, psychological and scientific. Insights from all the disciplines must be allowed to shape one's understanding of the Christian faith if it is to be adequate for our age. The other passion is moral and ethical passion. This is a legacy of his Mennonite heritage. Kaufman is convinced that the traditional concept of God is at least partially responsible for many of the inhumanities and evils of modern history, and inadequate to meet the crises facing us. If we are to survive as a species we will need consciously and deliberately to construct a new concept of God for our age.

To construct a concept of God which has both intellectual integrity and can serve as a metaphysical grounding for a responsible ethic for today, Kaufman begins not with authoritative revelation but with cosmic and human origins and evolution, developing what he calls his "constructive theological anthropology" (*Mystery*, 141). Taking the natural and social sciences as his starting point, he traces the evolution of the human species in the context of cosmic evolution, and constructs a theology compatible with this. Here is the bare outline of his theological anthropology.

We are "biohistorical" beings: 1) biological beings (animals) who along with everything else have evolved over millennia into our present form, and 2) historical beings in that at some point in the evolutionary process we have developed consciousness. He calls this the "threshold" of consciousness (*Mystery*, 172). We are nature become conscious of itself, or spirit. Here Kaufman's thought has significant affinities with Hegel and other philosophers of consciousness (without Hegel's notion of spirit as Absolute). The "bio" part connects us with nature; the "historical" part distinguishes us from nature, reflecting our freedom over nature and our culture- and religion-creating capacity. Human life and consciousness is but one of the many evolutionary trajectories that emerge serendipitously out of this process.

This bio-historical evolutionary process has given rise to diverse cultural and religious expressions in human history. Various religious world views have been created by human beings as ways to understand the world in which they live, and to deal with the existential questions having to do with their own mortality, as well as with the moral and ethical questions about how to exercise their freedom responsibly. Christianity is but one of these many religious world views. It has no intrinsic, self-evident or revealed superiority over other religions. Any preference given to Christian symbols (God, Christ, etc.) is purely functional—that is, they happen to be available to us and, as Kaufman tries to show in his book, they continue to be more adequate than others in focusing and orienting our lives, and providing a metaphysical grounding for our ethics.

The crucial factor for Kaufman is the recent (modern) realization that these religious beliefs are world views, interpretive schemes, flames of orientation, that humans have created, and not revelations or descriptions of things as they really are. Kaufman calls this "imaginative construction." As a crafter of a material object builds his artifact, so the theologian carefully, step by step, constructs his or her theology. It has always been so. Christians through the centuries have constructed their religious belief systems and doctrines this way. It is only in the modern period, however, that we acknowledge that our theological concepts are our own constructions. This makes all the difference.

To recognize that these are our own constructs 1) gives us the freedom to own this imaginative enterprise, makes us humble about our assertions, thus preventing idolatry; and 2) gives us the freedom more deliberately and consciously to set about to create new ones when necessary. The time has come, says Kaufman, to develop a more adequate Christian world view as a way of dealing with the contemporary ecological, economic, political, and social crises facing us. Our world view remains Christian in the sense that "God" and "Christ" continue to be useful images for us, but there is nothing of essential value in these particular symbols over others. If others can be found which are more adequate, we should abandon these.

Something which is frequently overlooked is that Kaufman is not denying the existence of a divine reality outside of our concepts. I found it surprising—something I had not noticed in earlier writings—how strongly Kaufman believes that we are not on our own (*Mystery*, 358) and that divine reality needs in some sense to be seen as outside ourselves and our own constructions: our symbol "God" points beyond us, thus avoiding the "narcissism of individual egos" and the "curved-in character of human existence" (*Mystery*, 313). The divine reality behind or beyond our concept is "the ultimate mystery of things and the serendipitous creativity at work in the world" (*Mystery*, 320). Here we run up against a difficulty.

To be consistent, Kaufman must recognize his own conceptualization, including his understanding of the bio-historical evolution of the human species and culture, to be a historical construct, and not a description of the way things really are. Despite his good intentions, one does get the impression that he does think his theological construct is more adequate than all others (particularly classical ones) because it is consistent with our understanding of the physical world and its historical evolution *the way it really is* (see, for instance, *Mystery*, 267). Consequently, he rules out more traditional, dogmatic interpretive schemes, despite his genuine desire to include all voices as conversation partners in the theological enterprise (*Mystery*, 305, 455).

Two Views of Time

Kaufman's key for understanding reality is historical time — that is, the movement from past to present to future—a sequential, linear, forward directionality. It is true that cosmic evolution and the development of different forms of life within the cosmos is, according to Kaufman, no simple straight line. There are whirls and eddies, the emergence of life forms and their demise, the possibility of human self-destruction. He calls these emergences of life forms "trajectories," "time's arrows," the very language Cambridge physicist Stephen Hawking uses to talk about cosmic processes.[10]

Kaufman consciously rejects the concept of a simple, straight line evolutionary development, and distinguishes his concept of historical time from nineteenth-century views of progress and historical relativism. Yet he finds a "forward directionality" in the universe, and even talks about the "inexorable conveyor belt" (*Mystery*, 167) and the "great evolutionary march upward" that we are on (280). Human beings have transcended blind evolutionary movement (106); nevertheless, even they with their freedom from necessity are caught in the forward flow of history from which they cannot escape—they are condemned to be free and historical beings (131-33). The cosmos is a unified whole which is evolving, and the fact that bio-historical beings, who have purposes, have emerged within this cosmic evolution justifies us talking about cosmic teleology, a kind of "proto-teleology" leading up to human life. It is a teleology and purposefulness that is evident only retrospectively.

Kaufman is quick, however, to distance himself from traditional notions of teleology and time. We cannot turn the clock back to a previous unhistorical way of existing (131). We have passed the point of no return. Early (parochial) conceptualizations of the world, which assumed the existence of unchanging truths, eternal values, natural rights, and universal human essences are outmoded (136). While Kaufman sees the need for a universal, global ethic—one which calls on people to take full responsibility for their historical freedom—he does not by this mean to turn to some traditional notion of universal, self-evident or rational principles of what is right, good, just, beautiful (198-99). To act morally is to act in such a way as to further the cause of human historicity and freedom. Earlier trans-historical pictures of existence contain absurdities and incoherences which make them incredible for today (222). The choice, for Kaufman, is between two ways of viewing time:

> Should we conceive the evolutionary-historical development here on earth (which has given rise to human existence) (a) as transpiring within *an eternal structure* of things which follows

essentially the same patterns forever, that is, as set within parameters or limits determined by some eternal, unchanging order? or (b) as a part, and expression of, a *cosmic evolutionary-historical process* that characterizes or pervades all reality? (251)

According to Kaufman, there is a great division among civilizations, between those who have emphasized the primacy of structure, order, and being (Greeks and oriental world views), and those which have taken history, change, process, and development to be primary (Judaism, Christianity, Islam, Marxism). Ancient Israel already moved toward a more historical-evolutionary understanding in which "the structures and cycles of the cosmos are not permanent or eternal; they come into being through God's creative activity in time" (*Mystery*, 252). In my own thinking, this sharp division between the Greek (ontological) and the Judeo-Christian (historical) that is implicit in Kaufman's portrayal of the classical tradition needs to be seriously questioned. I continue to believe that "Athens" and "Jerusalem" have more in common with each other than either one has with our modern and postmodern historicism. Both presuppose a reality (an eternal order or a transcendent God) which is to be differentiated from linear time and history.

Having introduced us to this great division, Kaufman says we are unable to choose between these two world views on the basis of empirical evidence because we are never in a position to see the universe as a whole (254). These are two imaginative constructs, and there continue to be those who hold on to the earlier understanding of time. So we choose between them on the basis of other than objective or empirical grounds—namely on the basis of which one most adequately "facilitate[s] and promote[s] human existence within the actual ecosystem within which we live" (257) and "most adequately interprets all the wideness and richness of human life in our ecologically ordered world" (258). In the end, therefore, Kaufman unequivocally opts for the evolutionary-historical model. He remains convinced that people who continue to think of reality in terms of more classical understandings of time are out of touch with modern scientific and philosophical insights. No longer can we legitimately postulate a reality "outside of" the one interconnected world ("this world") of which we all are a part (325-26).

Questions of Kaufman

I challenge Kaufman in three areas: 1) Adequacy: Is the evolutionary-historical model alone truly adequate to account for the full spectrum of human experience? 2) Credibility: Is it necessary to choose between the two views of time, the way Kaufman does, in order to offer a credible imagination for today? 3) Fidelity: Are there not resources in the classical tradition which might inspire the theological imagination for today and tomorrow?

1. Adequacy One of Kaufman's criteria for determining the acceptability of a theological model is its adequacy for grounding ethics and accounting for the full range of human experience. He defends "moral and personal values such as loyalty, honesty, integrity, freedom, self-sacrifice, love, responsible action" (347), and the treating of human beings as ends in themselves and not as means to an end (198-99). Is this not a deontological ethic; and if so, does it not contradict an evolutionary-historical ethic, in which the survival of the human species, the balance of the ecosystem, and the prolongation of the historical future as goals are the primary determinants of right or wrong? Must one not finally hold to the rightness of promoting freedom, justice, equality, human dignity, nonviolent love, loyalty, and regard for all of God's creation on other than pragmatic-historical grounds (the continuation of history)? And are these other grounds not something akin to what the tradition has called, for lack of a better term, "revealed truths?" Also, if we talk about ethics this way, aren't we saying that not everything in human life can be explained in terms of the historical-evolutionary model?

The most dramatic illustration for me of the inadequacy of viewing both the basis and the goal of ethics solely as the prolongation of life and history was the television movie some years ago (during the cold war era) that depicted the morning after a hypothetical nuclear holocaust. There were some survivors but they were all dying, and it was a matter of hours before the entire human race would be wiped out. A doctor was still going about trying to save lives and applying healing medicines. Why was he doing this? Because there was a commitment to the intrinsic duty of mitigating suffering and caring for people, independent of historical time. He was treating human beings as ends in themselves. Each moment and life had an "absolute" quality to it. Kaufman could say this illustration supports his point: namely the intrinsic value of prolonging lives. But does this argument not leave us with the absurd situation in which one's reason for ethical action is grounded in nothing else but the history that is about to come to an end? In other words, the basis for the action is gone. It strikes me that both Kaufman and the doctor in their commitment to the prolongation of life are drawing on an older tradition than the evolutionary-historical one. Luther's famous dictum that "should the world end tomorrow I would still plant an apple tree today," is similarly premised on a view of time different than the historical one.

Especially in the birth of my children I experience that their lives appear *from some realm beyond historical time or the evolutionary process*. There appears an individual personality not fully explainable with reference to parental genes and sexual intercourse. Here, in some metaphorical sense, is an "absolutely" new beginning (the entry of the eternal into the temporal). Similarly, in the face of death, one senses the end of history for a particular life. Kierkegaard and the existentialists understood this finality of the moment before God in a way that is missing in Kaufman's evolutionary-historical model. The possibility of freedom and novelty, so highly regarded by Kaufman, is more adequately preserved in a non-evolutionary picture of reality.

2. Credibility But is such a non-evolutionary model of time credible today? I find myself restless with the criterion of credibility. Credible to whom? To the academic elite (scientists, philosophers, theologians), or to artists, the general populace? There seems to be little consensus within any of these groups as to what is credible and what isn't. I will propose below that we need not choose between the two views of time described by Kaufman, but can combine them in a creative and imaginative way that is both credible today and faithful to the tradition.

There are those (e.g., George Grant and Hans Jonas) who have thought deeply about these matters and given a penetrating analysis of modern technology and the liberal assumptions behind it, who struggle with the same issues that Kaufman does and offer viable alternatives. They do not deny that we are historical beings, that we cannot escape our historicity, that we cannot turn the clock back, and that we have historical responsibility to overcome evil and injustice. What they say is 1) that historicism (interpreting all of reality in terms of historical willing and dynamics—the evolutionary movement from past to present to future, or forward directionality) does not adequately account for everything; 2) that, in fact, the modern crisis in the ecosystem, among other things, is not to be solved by, but is largely the consequence of, the human-history-making obsession in the modern period; and 3) that some imagination beyond the purely historical will need to be found not only for the sake of our survival but for its intrinsic truthfulness.

Hans Jonas, a Jewish philosopher concerned with ethical responsibility in a technological age, deals with the same issues Kaufman does but rejects the evolutionary, forward directional model. Like Kaufman he is convinced that we cannot go back to the ancients. They thought "vertically (in terms of the eternal)" not "horizontally (the prolongation of the temporal)."[11] In classical ethics "the drive is upward, not forward, toward being, not into becoming" (Jonas, 125). This has changed in the modern period. What dominates modern existence is dynamism, that is, historical change. Our ontology is not one of eternity but of time. At the basis of this change is a new view of nature and human action.

Nature can no longer take care of itself; it has become vulnerable to intervention by human science and technology, and needs rather to be taken care of. It can no longer carry the freight of post-Enlightenment human exploitation and thus has acquired a "moral claim on us." The irony is that "the very same movement which puts us in possession of the powers that have now to be regulated by norms—the movement of modern knowledge called science—has by a necessary complementarity eroded the foundations from which norms could be derived, it has destroyed the very idea of norm as such" (22).

Jonas seeks to establish a contemporary ethic which is grounded in norms outside of human willing; that is, outside the historical dynamic which has created the technological threat in the first place. His conclusions bear some similarity to Kaufman's. He develops a view of nature which is neither supernaturalistic (what he considers to be traditional religious dualism) nor naturalistic (modern evolutionary and deterministic materialism). His basic moral axiom is: "Act so that the effects of your action are compatible with the permanence of genuine human life" (Jonas, 11), or "Never must the existence or the essence of . . . [humanity] as a whole be made a stake in the hazards of action" (37). So far he is in agreement with Kaufman. But then he makes a crucial move which distinguishes him from Kaufman.

He rejects evolutionary, "becoming" world views which consider "everything past as a stepping-stone to the future" (16). Instead, he develops an ontological ethic—a metaphysics of being rather than becoming. The source of human obligation is the goodness of Being itself (of which human and non-human natures are a part). Although, like Kaufman, Jonas does not think we can go back to the eternal truths of a bygone age, he is more pensive and tentative about it. He even appears to lament the loss of the Eternal found in traditional religions and in Platonic thought. It may be, he reflects, that sometime in the future "Plato's way" will once again become "eligible." In fact, "we must leave it open whether it may not be more adequate to the truth than ours." He even ponders whether "the abolition of transcendence may [not] have been the most colossal mistake in history." Nevertheless, for the moment, we cannot extricate ourselves from our situation; "responsibility for what has been set aside and is kept moving by ourselves, takes precedence before everything else" (Jonas, 129).

The novel view of nature and human action required in the modern era makes imperative a moral ethic of responsibility, premised on the intrinsic goodness of Being itself. This new ethic of responsibility must be radically different than modern eschatological-utopian thinking. Our hope lies in recovery of "absolute *presence* in itself—no past, no future, no promise, no succession, whether better or worse, not a prefiguration of anything, but rather timeless shining itself. *That* is the 'utopia' beyond every 'not yet,' scattered moments of eternity in the flux of time" (200). What is required for our world to survive, to be able to bear the burden of human activity, is "to *unhook the demands of justice, charity and reason from the bait of utopia*" (201). Kaufman's theology cannot be said to be utopian, but he does, it would appear, hook justice, charity and reason to forward directionality.

There is no question that when one talks about the cosmos, the world as a whole, that which transcends the biological and material, one is no longer describing literally the ways things are but using metaphorical and analogical language. Early Christian theologians knew this. So the issue is not whether one chooses a literal approach over a metaphorical one, but which picture one thinks more adequate, credible and faithful. It seems to me just as credible to interpret the modern, post-Enlightenment approach to history and history-making as largely responsible for the crises of the modern period as to view this same commitment as a solution to them. Further, if this is the case, then it would appear credible to search for an imagination which grounds a responsible ethic more adequately and more fully accounts for the full range of human experience.

3. Fidelity There is something to be said for maintaining a fidelity to the tradition, particularly if one appropriates for oneself the name and central symbols of that tradition. To call oneself a Christian theologian, rather than something else, is to make a decision to interpret the world within certain parameters given by the sacred texts and historical confessions of Christianity. At what point one's reinterpretation and reimagining of that tradition in new situations becomes a transition to a new religious world view is not self-evident. That there is such a point I do not doubt. How far can one "deconstruct" and "reconstruct" the symbols of the Judeo-Christian tradition and still remain a *Christian* theologian? The answer may have to be left to the individual theologian and the Christian community of which she or he is a part, but it is worth asking. Fidelity to the tradition(s) has to do with intellectual, personal, and moral integrity just as much as do the criteria of adequacy and credibility.

I would say that the central affirmations of faith, as expressed in the historical confessions and creeds of the Christian church, are relevant to the question of fidelity. Of these the Christian doctrine of God, in which 1) the Jewish-Christian notion of the one transcendent

God, of whom no images can be made; 2) the Christ in whom this God is confessed to be revealed historically; and 3) the Holy Spirit through whom this God is experienced as dynamically present in the world, generally, and in the church as the community of reconciliation particularly, are indispensable. This is the language of faith and experience, not of abstract philosophical speculation, a language passed on from generation to generation. These central Christian affirmations together with the other historical doctrines related to them are not literal descriptions of reality but are truly "symbols" of the faith (as the ancients called them) by which we orient our lives.

I do not believe, as Kaufman apparently does, that one needs to choose between the two views of time he identifies—the "ontological-eternal" and the "evolutionary-historical." It is precisely the trinitarian doctrine of God that allows us to hold these together: the eternal dimension, the historical dimension, and the dynamic-evolutionary interaction of the two. Kaufman's own interpretation of the Trinity can help us to combine the two, thereby avoiding a "deism" on the one side and a "pantheism" on the other (*Mystery*, 412-25, 492-94).

Kaufman uses the evocative model of conversation to illustrate serendipitous creativity (God) at work, combining both determinacy and indeterminacy: "Often the interchange comes to have 'a life of its own' (as we say), and it may well go in directions no one had anticipated and lead to new insights and ideas which none of the participants had thought of before" (*Mystery*, 275). Although I find this model attractive, it does not adequately capture the "structure," "durability," and "givenness" that I believe the Christian confesses as present in human experience and reality as a whole.

After all, even Einstein's theory of relativity is premised on the fixed speed of light, and physicist Stephen Hawking talks about boundary conditions and underlying order when referring to the cosmos: "The whole history of science has been the gradual realization that events do not happen in an arbitrary manner, but that they reflect a certain underlying order, which may or may not be divinely inspired. It would be only natural to suppose that this order should apply not only to the laws, but also to the conditions at the boundary of space-time that specify the initial state of the universe."[12]

An analogy that I have used is that of the scrabble game in contrast to a jigsaw puzzle. In a jigsaw puzzle the outcome (final design) is predetermined. There is virtually no freedom involved. People "play the game" only to find the right piece for the right spot in order to complete the picture. It is true that some traditional theologians have seen God's activity in this way, but it does not adequately represent the classical Christian tradition. The scrabble game is a more appropriate metaphor. With the scrabble game there are a number of invariables: the limits of the board, the alphabet, the values of the letters, the rules by which the game is played. These represent the structure and givenness of the game. The variables include the luck (chance) involved in picking the letters, the intelligence (rationality) of the player's knowledge of vocabulary, the skill of the playing itself. The game also depends on the interaction and interdependence of the various players without which it could not be played. The most interesting factor is the extent of the individual player's freedom in relation to the fixed limits of the game. There is no predetermined design; the design emerges gradually with the playing, and is fully evident only at the end—no two games are identical in their design. Can it be said that the players construct the outcome? In some sense this is true; but there are too many variables (including chance, intelligence, creativity, the moves of other players) to say that what is happening is pure construction. A mysterious quality behind the playing of the game moves it towards its final, unique end, weaving together all the factors mentioned.

Theologically speaking, this metaphor is not perfect. It does, however, suggest what I mean when I think of divine presence unifying the various diverse factors in the movement toward an emerging pattern. This pattern emerges within the framework of cosmic structure, boundaries, and laws. Human construction is only one of the variables involved.

Appendix

Correspondence between Kaufman and Reimer

6 Longfellow Road
Cambridge, MA 02138

July 16, 1996

Professor A. James Reimer
Conrad Grebel College
Waterloo, ON N2L 3G6
CANADA

Dear Jim:

I recently received a copy of my new Mennonite *Festschrift*, and I want you to know that the first article I decided to read was yours. I have felt for sometime that you, better than many Mennonites, seem to understand what I am about, and I wanted to see just how you articulated yourself on my work. Naturally, I was very pleased with what you had to say–both about me personally and about my work– and I want to thank you right away for the article. It clearly deals with important issues, especially the matter of "two views of time," and it raises responsible questions about my theological program. With respect to the latter, I might just make a few remarks here.

You pose the question whether I am not really employing a deontological ethic (237), and if so, whether this does not contradict the evolutionary-historical ethic that I also seem to advocate. You are right that both emphases are there, but I have tried to present them in a way that avoids contradiction. Throughout (as you know) I stress what I call "humaneness" as a moral standard, and this clearly has deontological roots (as my using Kant as a principal point of departure in ch. 14 is intended to emphasize). But in my interpretation of moral acts, moral persons, and moral societies, I give the Kantian point of departure a slight twist, attempting to show that, though Kant did not himself make this point about moral duty, "*righteousness* . . . , the principle underlying our moral rules, virtues, social ideals, et cetera . . . is whatever supports and enhances the web of action, making possible its fecundity for further action" (IFOM, 198f.). Kant was unable to make the move that I do, because he had no way to get together cosmological issues (1st critique) with moral action (2nd critique). By treating cosmological issues as essentially matters of *faith* rather than of speculative knowledge (IFOM, Pt. III), as Kant treats them, I am able to connect these up in a way that he cannot (though he also makes God, immortality, etc. "postulates" of action – a move which partially inspires my own cosmological approach). And thus I do not need to leave the moral sphere just hanging in the air autonomously, as he does, but can bring it together with the cosmological vision I articulate with no inconsistencies. Thus morality is no longer simply anthropocentric (as in Kant), but can be placed in a wider cosmocentric (ecological) and theocentric context, thus modifying the deontology. I think your criticisms of my ethics depend on your reading it too much as an *unqualified* Kantian (i.e., deontological) program.

I do not want to be understood as disagreeing at all with your claim (along with Grant and Jonas) that "the modern crisis in the ecosystem . . . is largely the consequence of the human-history-making obsession in the modern period" (239). Of course, it is–that is, our *historicity* has itself become badly corrupted (see IFOM, ch. 15). But, as you also seem to admit, we cannot effectively address this problem by attempting to go back to a kind of *pre*-historical mode of human existence; we must move forward with some sort of newly transformed and transforming historical action that will acknowledge the *limits* within which human historicity must live. It is an outline of precisely that move which I attempt to give in my chapter on "an ecological ethic." I don't think we are as far apart here as you might suppose. But you want to frame these issues in non-historicist terms, whereas I, of course, am trying to set them in a more historicist frame. I do not find your (and Jonas') hopes for a recovery of some kind of "absolute *presence* in itself" (241) very plausible, perhaps not even really intelligible.

You suggest that a specifically *Christian* theologian must "make a decision to interpret the world within *certain parameters given by the sacred texts and historical confessions of Christianity*" (241, my emphasis). Here, of course, we disagree very sharply. I do not regard theologians as bound to the verbal formulations of *any* particular doctrines or texts (all of these always being decisively historically conditioned, and thus subject to critical reformulation); to accept constraints of this sort seems to me a form of henotheistic idolatry. I prefer to define the parameters of Christian theology in this way. A *theo*logian who wishes to be *Christ*ian must, of course, organize his/her thinking and writing in a way that gives centrality to these two defining symbols of Christian faith: God and *Christ*. But nothing can be foreclosed ahead of time about how these symbols *must* be interpreted. This always remains an open and debatable question in each new historical situation; and an argument, therefore, must be given for every interpretation proposed–an argument that, in every case, will probably seem persuasive to some, incredible to others. So the theological conversation–and the new imaginative construction–continues, as long as there are those interested in making what they regard as Christian commitments. I have the impression that you are in agreement with much of this, but if so, I don't understand your use of the clause quoted above.

I must bring this to a close. I hope, Jim, we can have the opportunity to discuss some of these matters sometime. Let me say again how much I appreciate your article, and the important questions it raises; and I thank you for it. I hope my comments go some distance in closing the gap between us. My very best wishes to you.

Sincerely,
Gordon D. Kaufman

P. S. Perhaps I ought to call to your attention the curious typo (if that's what it is–perhaps it is some kind of joke?) that keeps recurring in your text. You have repeatedly used the word "trajectile" (which I never use) to refer to what I call a "trajectory"; the meanings of these two words, as you will be aware, are really quite different, and your use of "trajectile" significantly changes the sense of the text.

January 7, 2000

Prof. Gordon D. Kaufman
Harvard University
The Divinity School
45 Francis Avenue
Cambridge, Massachusetts 02138

Dear Gordon:

It was good to see you, albeit briefly, at the AAR/SBL meetings in Boston. Someone just recently informed me that Mrs. Kaufman (Dorothy, I believe) passed away some time ago. I was sorry to hear that. I remember her from the time you invited me to dinner at your house a number of years ago.

I recently came across the July 16, 1996 letter you wrote to me in response to my article in the *Festschrift* for you. I never did respond in return, so I thought I'd drop you a few lines re. your observations in that letter, especially in the second and third paragraphs. Thank you, by the way, for your careful reading of my article and your generous comments.

First, it is true that I am attracted to the ancient (Platonic but also biblical in my view) notion that time and history as we know them take on their ultimate 'meaning' from a reality which is beyond history–that is, history (as the movement from past to present to future) is not grounded in itself, is not to [sic] be itself absolutized. I like very much the idea that finite time is the moving shadow of eternity. Virtually all contemporary theology including the political-hope theologies of Metz, Moltmann and Pannenberg are too directional for me. Somehow the assumption behind this future-oriented theology is that one gradually gets closer to God, which I reject passionately: all historical moments are equidistant from the divine, because the divine is by definition beyond time and space. Pannenberg tries to have it both ways through his complex understanding of the relationship between the 'economic' and 'immanent' Trinity, but in the end it seems he collapses the immanent Trinity into the economic Trinity (I may be wrong). It just seems to me the ancients had this right and we have it wrong. The way one thinks about these things has serious implications for Christian ethics, also the way Mennonites think of the relation of church to society. I'm enclosing two popular articles I recently wrote on this: "God is not a Pacifist" and "Christians and the Civil Order" (I'm sending two versions of . . . this second piece, the other entitled "Christians and the use of force"). I would love to hear your response to them.

Second (re. the points you make in your 3rd paragraph), I am in full agreement with you that every statement we make theologically, every claim to truth we make, every appropriation of ancient confessional/doctrinal/dogmatic symbols, are interpretations within historical situations. Christian theological language is never univocal, nor equivocal, but always analogical. When I say a theologian needs to "make a decision to interpret the world within certain parameters given by sacred texts and historical confessions of Christianity," I mean to say that: just as in marriage when one finally chooses to commit oneself to a particular person from the myriad of possibilities, so in committing oneself to a particular "religion" (like Christianity) one finally takes a leap that is not entirely rational but that is existential. At that point one commits oneself to live by the confessional belief system of that worldview. One can get to the universal only through the particular (one's own), and to truly experience the religious one ultimately has to live with one's whole heart, soul and mind within some particular religious home. When one does this, one decides to allow the wisdom of the ages (the tradition, the texts, the dogmas) that has historically been mediated through the lenses of that particular religious community a relative (not absolute) priority over one's own individual reason and judgment. Not that one does this uncritically, but the "burden of proof" is on departure from the tradition. In other words, as you yourself in your system frequently suggest, one never begins tabula rasa. I think the difference between you and me is not an absolute one but the degree to which one weights the priority of the tradition over one's own individual judgment . . . .

Sincerely,

Jim

PART TWO

MENNONITES AND THEOLOGY

TEN

The Nature and Possibility of a Mennonite Theology*

Part One of this book deals broadly with the crisis of modernity and the liberal assumptions of the Enlightenment. In Part Two I reflect on the consequences of this crisis for Mennonite theology—or, more accurately, a theology from a Mennonite perspective. Mennonites ought not to develop their own separate theology. We should be engaged in Christian theological reflection. Our being Mennonite, however, needs to self-consciously colour the way we think theologically.

In the following essays I seek to show how our being Mennonite might shape our self-understanding as Christians and our conversation with other Christians. The first essay, "The Nature and Possibility of a Mennonite Theology," was published in 1983, in the initial issue of a then-new Canadian Mennonite theological journal, The Conrad Grebel Review.[1] *In it I look critically at twentieth-century Mennonite self-interpretation in the light of my growing unease with the liberal assumptions about history and freedom that dominate modern technological culture.*

---

* Originally published in *The Conrad Grebel Review* 1.1 (Winter 1983): 33-55. Howard John Loewen responded to this article in the subsequent issue (*CGR* 1.2 [Spring 1983]: 56-8), and my rebuttal appeared in *CGR* 1.3 (Fall 1983): 51-54. For notes on the text see the Notes section below.

In this essay I take four influential Mennonite thinkers—Harold S. Bender, Robert Friedmann, John H. Yoder, and Gordon D. Kaufman—and put them on a theological continuum, suggesting that all have more in common with each other than in distinction. Although on one level there are serious differences, for example, between Yoder and his teacher Bender, and between Kaufman and Yoder, common assumptions tie them together. What all of them share to a greater or lesser degree is an anti-metaphysical and anti-ontological world view, in which human freedom and ethics are more important for theological thinking than eternal divine truths as in classical theology. By carefully examining primary texts by each thinker, I show how Kaufman's historicism is really the logical extension of Bender's "Anabaptist vision," Friedmann's "existential" Anabaptism, and Yoder's "political" Anabaptism.

Rather than twentieth-century Mennonite self-understanding being a radical critique of modern liberal culture, I suggest it reinforces the basic assumptions of modernity. In their anti-sacramentalism the early Anabaptists participate in and perhaps contibute to the emergence of the modern world. I propose that Mennonites begin to theologize more systematically, and do so by revisiting classical creedal theology, trinitarian thought in particular. To be Christian and Mennonite in our theology would be to build our christocentric ethic on trinitarian foundations. Since 1983 I have come to realize that some early Anabaptists were in fact more trinitarian and dogmatic in their ethical convictions than I realized at the time. This is clearly demonstrated in the most recent archival research of my colleague Arnold Snyder.[2] I have also come to think that the so-called "Bender school" of theology was probably more classical in its theological orientation than I give it credit for in this article.

◆ ◆ ◆

Introduction

This essay on the nature and possibility of a Mennonite theology in the modern world is written from the strong conviction that some of the fundamental Enlightenment assumptions about history (historicism)[3] and human freedom (that humans are on their own)[4]—presuppositions which have long been accepted without question and have largely shaped modern theology—need to be critically re-examined and a more traditional-classical view of God, human nature, history, and moral accountability given another hearing. This conviction arises not out of a romantic nostalgia for some golden age of the past, nor out of the hope that a classical world view can be transported into the modern world in its full pristine purity. It is not rooted in a reactionary rejection of the important emancipatory insights of the Enlightenment tradition nor a simplistic denial of humanity's historical nature. It grows out of a strong belief that the atrocities of the modern age (including the imminent threat of nuclear self-annihilation) are, ironically, in some sense intrinsically linked to the Enlightenment and the triumph of technical reason, and call for a more radical critique than Enlightenment assumptions can offer. It may yet be the case, paradoxically, despite modern humanity's almost total incapacity to believe in a radically transcendent God whose essence cannot be defined historically, that the classical biblical and patristic-creedal trinitarian view of God can provide a more adequate understanding of reality and human ethical accountability than the modern historicist perception.

What is called for is not a simple rejection of modernity—that would be to misunderstand how profoundly we have all been shaped historically, philosophically, theologically, and linguistically by the presuppositions of the modern age—but rather a critique of the Enlightenment from within the Enlightenment.[5] Somehow, traditional theological doctrines and creedal formulations concerning God and his creation must be recovered and reaffirmed, by taking them through the prism of the Enlightenment without simply accommodating them to the modern age and thus divesting them of their critical power over us. Rather than deliberately setting out to "construct" a new concept of God on the basis of modern historicism, we ought to recover the profundity of the classical trinitarian view and put fresh meaning into it in the context of our age.[6]

These are the basic concerns at the heart of my reflections in the following pages. My interest here is primarily systematic, not historical—that is, I am not first and foremost concerned with a "right" interpretation of sixteenth-century Anabaptism, nor with "the recovery of the Anabaptist vision," nor, for that matter, with a defence of an Anabaptist-Mennonite theology over against that of other theological traditions. I am also not interested in determining how accurately our Reformation ancestors interpreted or embodied the essence of the gospel. Neither do I want to debunk the ethnic and theological tradition of which by fate and by choice I am a part. I want, rather, first to engage in a conversation with four recent and contemporary Mennonite theologians—Harold S. Bender, Robert Friedmann, John H. Yoder, and Gordon D. Kaufman—about the nature of Mennonite theology in the modern context; and, second, to suggest a few possibilities for a Mennonite theology which would take seriously its historical *particularity* and integrity and address, in an ecumenical spirit some pressing issues facing the *universal* Christian body in the post-Enlightenment world.

Bender's Anabaptist Vision

The contribution to general historical-theological scholarship and to Mennonite self-understanding of Bender's 1943 classic *The Anabaptist Vision* is well known and beyond dispute. Of special interest are two remarkable aspects of this manifesto of Mennonite theology. First, Bender defends Anabaptism against its traditional defamers by drawing attention to the fact that the left wing of the Reformation was ahead of its time and pioneered some basic modern assumptions. For him, the fundamental democratic assumptions of the modern world—freedom of conscience, separation of church and state, voluntarism in religion—presuppositions "so basic in American Protestantism and so essential to democracy," are ultimately "derived from the Anabaptists of the Reformation period, who for the first time clearly enunciated them and challenged the Christian world to follow them in practice."[7]

Much can be said in favour of such an interpretation. The Protestant Reformation in general and the Radical Reformation in particular must surely be seen—especially in their voluntarism and emphasis on personal-individual freedom and choice—as harbingers of modernity. As long as one is generally happy with the basic presuppositions of the modern project, such a connection could of course be greeted with enthusiasm. The more disillusioned one becomes with modernity, however, and the more one questions some of its central assumptions, the more one is driven to re-examine critically this strange and alleged alliance between one's tradition and the modern world. Ironically, the very principles which pushed sixteenth-century Anabaptism to the periphery of late medieval heteronomous society today have become common stock and put us at the centre. An important question that must be asked, therefore, if Bender's interpretation is correct, is this: To what extent must the Radical Reformation and the Free Church tradition in general be seen as representing not a fundamental critique of the Enlightenment but as both a product and an ally of the modern western spirit?[8]

The second noteworthy aspect of Bender's essay is its understanding of the substance of Anabaptism. The essence of Anabaptism, Bender says, is threefold: "first, a new conception of the essence of Christianity as discipleship; second, a new conception of the church as brotherhood; and third, a new ethic of love and nonresistance."[9] He goes on to explicate all three essentials in more or less ethical terms. He distinguishes Anabaptist theology from the sacramental-sacerdotal theology of Catholicism, on the one hand, and forensic justification and the inner subjective experience of God's grace, on the other. The early Anabaptists emphasized not primarily intellectual understanding, doctrinal belief, or subjective experience, but rather a regenerate life best described by the term *Nachfolge Christi*. In contrast to Lutheranism, for the Anabaptists there could be no compromise with the evil of the world but only a withdrawal from the worldly system in favour of a new Christian social order in the context of the fellowship of believers: "extension of this Christian order by the conversion of individuals and their transfer out of the world into the church is the only way by which progress can be made in Christianizing the social order."[10] While the Anabaptists were realistic—they had no illusions about the imminent transformation of the world—they did understand the kingdom of God in historical terms: "The Anabaptist vision was not a detailed blueprint for the reconstruction of human society, but the Brethren did believe that Jesus intended that the kingdom of God should be set up amid earth, here and now, and this they proposed to do forthwith."[11]

While early Anabaptists, as interpreted by Bender, cannot be charged with espousing an illusory optimism about gradual human progress so characteristic of the eighteenth and nineteenth-century enterprise, there is implicit in it an anthropological and historical optimism nevertheless—an optimism which distinguishes it dramatically from Lutheranism. According to some of its modern interpreters, Anabaptists believed that finite, sinful human beings could be radically regenerated, their basic nature transformed, and their egoism theoretically overcome by the grace of God in the context of the visible church. The essence of Christianity is in some cases radically historical and ethical, and the kingdom of God is seen as having a measure of continuity with the empirical visible church of regenerated believers. In this "anthropological optimism" and "historicalist" understanding of the kingdom of God, early Anabaptism has a profound affinity with the modern project. The crucial difference is that early Anabaptist views of humanity and the kingdom of God were anchored in an inherent recognition of God's transcendence—a recognition lost to the modern world.

Friedmann's "Existential" Theology

The emphasis on the historical-ethical nature of Anabaptism becomes even more pronounced in Robert Friedmann's 1973 book *The Theology of Anabaptism*.[12] Here the high regard for the ethical nature of Anabaptist Christianity is combined with a strong anti-doctrinal, anti-creedal, and anti-systematic bias. Friedmann, who has been called "one of the foremost experts of Anabaptism," argues that Anabaptist theology is *intrinsically* non-systematic. He uses the problematic term "existential" as distinct from "systematic" to describe the nature of Anabaptist theology.[13] The early Anabaptists, he maintains, espoused an existential or *lived* theology.

They had an implicit rather than an explicit theology. This implicit theology is suspicious of systematizing theological ideas and doctrines. It stresses, rather, as Jesus and the gospel writers do, "the expectation of the imminent breaking-in of the kingdom of God."[14] It calls for a concrete human response to the Christian message, little concerned with the organized intellectual coherence of doctrinal categories. With Paul there begins an explicit and doctrinal theology which was not present earlier, and which later, with the church fathers, particularly Augustine, becomes a full-fledged rational and systematic theology.

While, according to Friedmann, the Reformation spawned an abundance of theological systems, the Anabaptists were unique in their rejection of such systems of thought and in their adherence to an unsystematic and in some cases non-rational theology. Their creedal formulations consisted of "semi-conscious theological insights and ideas concerning God and man and their mutual relationship, eventually expressed in confessional statements."[15] The reason for this lack of systematic theology among early Anabaptists, says Friedmann, was not historically *accidental* but *essential* to their view of Christianity. Systematic theology was essentially contrary to the very spirit of early Anabaptism itself: "Theology *as a system* they considered rather a stumbling block to discipleship and no real help in man's earthly predicament."[16] For Friedmann, therefore, there can, *in principle* be no explicit or systematic Anabaptist theology. He makes the rather presumptuous claim that "[e]ver since the days of the apostolic church, Anabaptism is the only example in church history of an 'existential Christianity' where there existed no basic split between faith and life . . . . "[17] He also makes the astounding claim that for Anabaptists there was no such thing as post-conversion doubt and anxiety in the Lutheran sense. Anabaptism, he claims, "does not experience an ongoing *Anfechtung* (inner doubt), no feeling of despair or, worse, of perdition, but rather the exact opposite: *the certainty* of resting in God's gracious hands, of being called and able to respond to this call."[18] It rejected Luther's famous dictum *simul justus et peccator* (at the same time justified and sinner)—Luther's profound sense that even after the experience of forgiveness and justification one continues to be plagued and tempted by sin and inner doubt.

Despite this rejection of Luther's "inward" theology, Friedmann claims Anabaptist theology was subjective rather than objective. What he means is not the kind of subjectivity of Luther's inner doubt but an emphasis on existence and historical actuality—a regenerate life which expresses itself in historical concreteness. "The Anabaptists were always willing `to give account of the hope that is in you' (1 Pet. 3:15), but they were not willing, nor even able, to construct a systematic theology, a rational edifice of thought. It would be foreign to them and inadequate to the `subjectivity' of the new birth."[19] Friedmann reveals a remarkable lack of understanding for the nature of and need for *systematic* thinking about the Christian faith, the importance of which—precisely for Mennonites today—I will allude to in the last part of this article. Ironically, in Parts Two and Three of his book Friedmann goes on systematically to discuss Anabaptist views of the two kingdoms, the Trinity, anthropology, soteriology, eschatology, and ecclesiology.

Friedmann makes the significant point that the Anabaptist vision must be clearly distinguished from the mainstream of modern thought:

> It is almost a truism to say that most of the values of Western civilization—aesthetic, scientific, and philosophic—do not fit into this dualistic vision and the implicit hope for the kingdom. The Renaissance, Baroque, Enlightenment, Rationalism, and the philosophy behind the Scientific Revolution—in brief, the entire history of 'Modern Man'—remained outside the Anabaptist realm. All these movements were to them secular happenings which had no bearing on the kingdom of God.[20]

This is where I think Friedmann seriously misinterprets the nature of modernity and therefore misunderstands the fundamental connection between the radical left wing of the Reformation and the modern spirit. It is precisely the yearning for the kingdom of God on earth and the assumption that humans have the freedom to create such a kingdom that lies at the heart of modern political projects. While it is true that the modern vision is largely a secular one—divested of its transcendent ground—and that Anabaptism cannot be reduced to such a secular Enlightenment vision, still the basic notion of "freedom" (the rejection of predestination is a case in point) and the expectation of an earthly historical realization of God's kingdom and its proleptic realization in the empirical church appears to be at the heart of Anabaptism.

Friedmann states that, while the Anabaptists did not equate the brotherhood with an ideal as sublime as the kingdom of God, still *"Theirs was always a visible church* (in contrast to Augustine's and Luther's invisible church), the living brotherhood-congregation which they regarded, at least in part, as the nucleus of God's kingdom on earth [in] its attempted realization."[21] Of primary interest here is not the accuracy of Friedmann's interpretation of Anabaptist theology, nor even of Anabaptist fidelity to the biblical view, but rather the affinity of these views with the modern Enlightenment vision of humanity and history.

Yoder's "Political" Theology

In the case of John Howard Yoder, no doubt one of the foremost contemporary interpreters and exponents of Anabaptist-Mennonite theology, we have a peculiar combination of biblical, historical, and systematic theology at work. For Yoder the hermeneutical key by which to understand and unlock the whole of the Bible is clearly the normative New Testament christocentric ethic of non-resistant love and "revolutionary subordination," best captured historically by sixteenth-century Anabaptists. We cannot enter into conversation with Yoder on the impressive list of topics which he addresses, all basically from this theological starting point. Nor can we do justice to the nuances of Yoder's theological position. All we can hope to do is to illustrate how Yoder, like Bender and Friedmann, interprets Christianity essentially in historical and ethical terms, betraying in the process a noteworthy anti-metaphysical and anti-ontological bias. To put it differently, using a classification sometimes employed in recent theological debates, Yoder shows a clear preference for a prophetic-eschatological theology over a sacramental-priestly one.[22]

In what is probably his most widely-known book, *The Politics of Jesus*, Yoder is concerned from beginning to end with demonstrating the social and political nature of Christ's message.[23] Acutely critical of most modern ethical theories which reject the relevance of Jesus' message for the modern world and construct an ethical position from this side of the bridge, based on common sense fittingness, adequacy, relevance, and effectiveness, Yoder is committed to the task of demonstrating the political-ethical "relevance" of Jesus' message for today.

Yoder calls his stance "biblical realism." What this means is that the "biblical vision of reality" has direct relevance for our age in that it stands "in creative tension with the cultural function of our age or perhaps of any age" without being collapsed into any one contemporary view.[24] It is this normativeness of Jesus' message and the New Testament for all ages, including our own, which is most attractive in Yoder's position. What is less convincing is his politicization of that message at the expense of other dimensions of the biblical message which can better be described in metaphysical and ontological language than with modern political language. In an anti-metaphysical and anti-ontological age like ours, which has, it appears, almost totally lost a concept of radical transcendence—a belief in the first article of the creed—to emphasize the historical-political essence of the *kerygma* is not a radical critique of the fundamental assumptions of the modern world (as Yoder intends it to be) but a tacit acknowledgement of modern historicist assumptions.[25]

Yoder's hypothesis in *The Politics of Jesus* is "that the ministry and the claim of Jesus are best understood as presenting to hearers and readers not the avoidance of political options, but one particular social-political-ethical option."[26] So, although Yoder's argument is that the political option of Jesus is radically different from that espoused by most contemporary ethicists, it is still a "social-political" option—a social-political alternative based on non-violent love. It is evident throughout the book that Yoder is engaged in a polemic, as were Bender and Friedmann, against individualistic, existentialistic, and "spiritualistic" interpretations of biblical texts and, consequently, also of later subjective expressions of Christianity.

Largely through an exegesis of Luke, Yoder shows that the kingdom of God, which John the Baptist and Jesus proclaimed as imminent, must not be understood primarily as a spiritual reality, but as a historical reality, a "visible socio-political, economic restructuring of relations among people of God, achieved by his [God's] intervention in the person of Jesus as the one anointed and endued with the Spirit."[27] This "new social reality" is not a quietistic, mystical, spiritualized kingdom but a messianic-prophetic vision: "The cross is beginning to loom not as a ritually prescribed instrument of propitiation but as the political alternative to both insurrection and quietism."[28] The alternative Jesus is offering to earthly, kingly rule is "not `spirituality' but servanthood."[29] It is "not a cultic or ritual separation, but rather a non-conformed quality of (`secular') involvement in the life of the world. It thereby constitutes an unavoidable challenge to the powers that be and the beginning of a new set of social alternatives."[30] This strong urge in Yoder to *de-spiritualize* the *kerygma* and to de-emphasize the cultic and the ritual (the priestly sacramental) dimension of the early Christian message and religious experience in general fails to adequately meet the crisis of the modern age in which this mystical, contemplative, sacramental quality of life has lost out to technical and historical reason.

Jesus' message and vocabulary, according to Yoder, was not "existential" but "political." Jesus was not primarily a moral teacher with political implications, nor a teacher of spirituality who was misinterpreted politically, nor a sacrificial lamb for the purpose of atonement, but rather, in his prophethood, priesthood, and kingship, someone who bore the possibility of a new social and political order. Christendom, says Yoder, has by and large remained unaware of this political-social dimension of Jesus' message and has given a mystical interpretation to being "in Christ" and "dying with Christ." In fact ". . . the apostles had and taught at least a core memory of their Lord's earthly ministry in its blunt historicity"— namely, a social, political stance within the world.[31] The cross of Calvary "was the politically, legally to be expected result of a moral clash with the powers ruling his society," not "an inward experience of the self" (as in

Müntzer, Zinzendorf, revivalism, and Christian existentialism).[32] Yoder's treatment of Christ and power, revolutionary subordination as expressed in Romans 13 and the authority of the state, his reinterpretation of the Pauline notion of justification by grace, and finally his discussion of the apocalyptic image of the war of the lamb are all seen as further bearing out his central thesis:

> A social style characterized by the creation of a new community and the rejection of violence of any kind is the theme of the New Testament proclamation from beginning to end, from right to left. The cross of Christ is the model of Christian social efficacy, the power of God for those who believe.[33]

Yoder's emphasis on the social-political-ethical significance of the New Testament message is rooted in a theological method that is fundamentally historical-eschatological (horizontal) in nature and entails a tacit bias against a metaphysical and ontological (vertical) understanding of the Christ event. This is perhaps most clearly evident in his *Preface to Theology: Christology and Theological Method*, a compilation of lecture notes given in systematic theology over a period of almost twenty years.[34]

While the first part of the book is an explicitly historical examination of the development of theology from the New Testament to Chalcedon and the second part deals more systematically with the theological discipline and doctrines as such, both are fundamentally historical in approach. Metaphysical interpretations of the Christ event must be seen as accretions—historically understandable and quite likely legitimate and necessary for given periods of history, but nevertheless, additions—which are superimposed upon, move beyond and possibly depart from the original claims of Christ and the earliest disciples. Yoder is quite ready to defend systematic thinking about Christianity and allows for the development of Christian doctrine to meet the exigencies of given historical periods: "The New Testament Church," he says, "did not assume that the truth was all there in the teachings of Jesus or in the teachings about Jesus. It is assumed that truth will keep coming, that new revelation of a kind, new workings of the Spirit, will continue."[35] He treats the early development of the Logos doctrine of Christ and the trinitarian and christological creedal formulations with remarkable sympathy. Nevertheless, an underlying bias against metaphysical and ontological understandings of Christ surfaces repeatedly.

The earliest claims concerning Jesus did not give him metaphysical status but were simply "Jesus Christ is Lord."[36] While using the Hebraic and Greco-Roman language of deity, these earliest claims were not metaphysical in the sense of the theological synthesis that came after the first two centuries. Thus, in his interpretation of Philippians 2, Yoder expunges any metaphysical sense from what is probably one of the earliest creedal and hymn-like affirmations of Christ's nature and work: "So then the humiliation is not a metaphysical humiliation, ceasing to [become] [sic.] absolute and becoming finite—but a moral humility of staying in one's place; of doing what Adam didn't do—accepting the position of creatureliness."[37] Yoder in effect reinterprets many passages as well as the creeds—traditionally understood in a metaphysical sense—ethically and morally. What distinguishes the Judeo-Christian tradition from the Platonic worldview is precisely the former's historical-moral-prophetic-eschatological view of reality as distinct from the more metaphysical and ontological perceptions of the latter. The biblical view emphasizes primarily the meaningfulness of time as an ongoing historical process in distinction from a Platonic non-temporal and non-historical hope.

The assumption that biblical, historical Christianity and Greek Platonic philosophy cannot truly be reconciled hovers in the background of Yoder's thought and becomes much more explicit in the theology of Gordon Kaufman, as we shall see below. Even in Yoder, however, this assumption becomes quite distinct, at points bordering on an alliance with modern historicist thought. Following his explication and critique of various atonement theories, and in an attempt to search for new ways of describing the work of Christ on the cross which is both more faithful to his perception of the biblical view and to modern thought, Yoder makes this telling comment:

> We are aware of history as a process. This awareness is characteristic of our age as it was not of earlier ages. We are learning to discern a more Hebraic view of things, which differs from the Hellenistic and later Greco-Roman world view. We think of the church as a concrete group of people and not first as an institution or an organization or a body of doctrine. We think of reality as going on in the awareness of people in groups. History is the only reality we know, we do not think about realities "out there" having their being in themselves. We think of reality as happening in personal relationships, in institutional relationships, in the passage of time. So if we would take historicism as a philosophical stance that is congruent with the Bible, in reading the Bible—we might have a new resource for developing an understanding of the need for the work of Christ.[38]

Here Yoder shows his true colours. His "Hebraic view" of biblical Christianity is quite explicitly linked to modern historicist thought. His emphasis on the social-political-ethical nature of the New Testament message is in fact deeply rooted in and influenced by modern Enlightenment thought.[39] All of us—including Mennonite theologians—are in a sense captive to Enlightenment assumptions. We cannot— even if we wanted to — extricate ourselves from modern views of history and freedom. Nevertheless, a profound critique of the modern perceptions of reality which have shaped us is surely called for.

On what basis can such a critique take place? Simply to say that the historical Jesus is normative begs the question. The point is: What kind of theological and historical interpretation do we give Jesus? To interpret Jesus primarily from a moral, ethical, and political perspective is itself a modern stance. I think it could be argued quite persuasively that Athens and Jerusalem, the Greek view of things and the Hebraic view of reality (that is, the classical perspective, whether Hebrew or Greco-Roman), have more in common with each other than either has with the modern world in which a metaphysical and ontological understanding of God's transcendence and interaction with the world is almost completely lost. If this is the case, then it seems that some kind of recovery of transcendence in its classical form—a recovery of metaphysics and a notion of "eternal verities" whose essence cannot be defined in historical-political terms but stand as points of reference limiting and judging history and politics—may be the basis upon which a critique of modern assumptions can take place.

This metaphysical or transcendent sense of God's reality and presence has historically been expressed through creedal and doctrinal formulations, sacraments, cult, worship, prayer, and corporate and private spirituality. My objection to Yoder's interpretation of primitive Christianity is not ultimately an objection to his emphasis on the relevance and normativity of Jesus' claims for Christians in the modern world (with this I heartily agree), nor with his emphasis on the social-political-historical dimensions of the Christian message (which, I agree, is *one* fundamental aspect of Jesus' life, teaching, death, and resurrection), but with his inadequate recognition of the ritualistic, cultic, mystical, and sacramental aspects of the religious experience, both in the corporate-communal sense and in the personal, existential, individual, and private-inward sense. It is the communal and individual-personal, *sacramental-priestly* dimension of human existence and religious experience that is inadequately allowed for by Yoder, who tends to emphasize the *prophetic-eschatological* above all else.

It may be that in this respect Anabaptist-Mennonite theology has been truncated all along. We idealize our Anabaptist ancestors in terms of their prophetic-eschatological power and tend to view historical periods in which the cultic and ritualistic on the one hand, or the inward "spiritualistic" on the other, predominate, as periods of departure from the original ideal (an assimilation to mainline Protestantism). I contend that both the sacramental-priestly and the prophetic-eschatological—or to put it differently, both the metaphysical-ontological (the vertical) and the historical-ethical (the horizontal)—are implicit in the Christian experience from the beginning and that both are ineradicable dimensions of religious experience. The prophetic eschatological understanding of the Christian message has often been associated with the capacity to critique that which "is" in the light of that which "ought to be." The sacramental-priestly emphasis, in contrast, has sometimes been seen as "sanctifying" the present at the expense of the ethical imperative. I would argue, however, that stressing the sacramental-priestly dimension of religious experience *today* may itself be a powerful left-handed critique of an age that no longer recognizes the importance of contemplating a universal good which transcends and intersects with the historical and the temporal plane.

Gordon Kaufman's "Historicist" Theology

Gordon Kaufman's theology draws us into the very centre of modern liberal and post-liberal theological concerns. David Tracy places Kaufman in a long line of what he calls postmodern or post-liberal "revisionist" theologians.[40] Kaufman, in his major theological work—not including some essays where he deals specifically with the nature, distinctiveness, and task of Mennonite theology[41]—makes few explicit references to the Anabaptist-Mennonite tradition. His basic historicist approach I maintain, is the echo of his own heritage and in some sense stands in continuity with Bender's, Friedmann's, and Yoder's emphasis on a historical, ethical, and eschatological interpretation of New Testament and Anabaptist theology. In short, it seems to me that, while Kaufman's historicism is much more explicit and radical than the "historicality" of Bender, Friedmann, and Yoder, there is still a continuity among the four which harks back to the left wing of the Reformation with its voluntarism, protest against all forms of human heteronomy, and emphasis on the historical, ethical, and eschatological kingdom of God.

In *Relativism, Knowledge, and Faith*, probably the most important of Kaufman's books, at least for understanding his underlying philosophical assumptions, he tries to show why all human thought is relative and subject to radical doubt. The book is basically a phenomenological analysis of the evolution of the human self from its early pre-cognitive stages through various levels or "orders" of consciousness. The norms and criteria by which we distinguish between truth and error gradually emerge together with the development of the structure of the self and the world. Truth and knowledge is in a genuine sense evolutionary or "historical," the term Kaufman prefers.

This view of knowledge stands in marked contrast to the notion that knowledge is "the grasping of the eternal forms (Greek) or laws of nature (modern)—factors which are forever constant, however much the situation of the subject may alter in time and history."[42] In a very real sense we are prisoners of our own thought, captives to history, and do not have access to universally valid truth(s). On a philosophical level, the book is an impressive attempt to address the epistemological problems that have so bedevilled modern thought ever since the Enlightenment. The problem with modern historicism, however, of which I take Kaufman's stance to be a good example, is not only that it is an inadequate view of human experience,[43] but that it ultimately leaves one without an adequate basis for ethics. Having accepted the fundamental Enlightenment assumptions of historicism and freedom, it cannot critique the negativities of the modern age as radically as is necessary. In Kaufman's case, this is particularly evident in his ethical relativism, perhaps best expressed in his essay "Nonresistance and Responsibility," one of a number of essays in his book by that title.[44]

We cannot here do justice to Kaufman's serious struggle with the assumptions of modern thought and the problems inherent in his attempt to deliberately construct a more adequate concept of God for modern humanity on a post-Kantian basis.[45] We must look briefly, however, at how he applies his historicism to systematic theology in his most substantive theological book to date, *Systematic Theology: A Historicist Perspective*.[46] What does Kaufman mean by "a historicist approach" to theology? It entails the fundamental affirmation that human beings are "intrinsically historical like God Himself," that one "has been created in the on-going movement of history (as has all other finite reality) and been shaped into a being intrinsically historical, one whose distinguishing characteristic is his historicity. . . . "[47] It is the profound conviction that in a genuine sense humans create themselves, each other, and the human species. In his historicity man is truly created in the image of God, who is the "primordial historical being."[48]

In the light of this profound conviction of human historicity Kaufman shapes his major theological categories around the trinitarian understanding of God rooted in the historical Christ, and radically distinct from Greek ontological dualism with which, according to Kaufman, the biblical view of God and humanity has little affinity.[49] Indebted to Barth's view of the Trinity, but, unlike

Barth, interpreting the Trinity from his own historicist perspective, Kaufman understands God as having three "modes" or "masks" of being: God as Father is God as historically transcendent, God as Son is God as seen historically in the event of Jesus Christ, and God as Holy Spirit is God as historically present in, to, and with us.[50]

What does Kaufman mean by "systematic theology"? Systematic theology is concerned with comprehensiveness, inclusiveness, and inner consistency and coherence. Each of the various Christian doctrines expresses a sphere of experience in relation to God, and together they give us a comprehensive picture of the world as a whole. The whole of human experience and knowledge must be illuminated through theological thinking.

Systematic theology has a double reference point: a historical norm (the Christ-event) and present experience. It is the attempt to show not so much the historical connectedness between past and present but the universal significance of the Christ-event for *all* of life; it tries "to develop a special conceptuality making it possible to grasp and understand the entire world of our experience as under the sovereign lordship of the God-defined-by Christ: built into the very logical structure of Christian theological language is reference to the historical Christ as normative."[51] Systematic theology is concerned with showing the different Christian doctrines in their essential unity and interconnectedness, as a way of illuminating all of human experience in a balanced way, to avoid one-sidedness and self-contradiction.

In his general theological enterprise—his concern with the linguistic and epistemological presuppositions of all theology, his preoccupation with the problem and meaning of God in the modern world, and his attempt to illumine all aspects of contemporary human experience in a *balanced* way—Kaufman differs from Yoder's more critical-prophetic-eschatological approach to theology. In his emphasis on the *normativity of the historical Christ* and the ethic of self-giving non-resistant love as central to an understanding of the Trinity and the biblical message as a whole, Kaufman has much in common with Yoder.

Kaufman's comprehensive theological approach—his attempt to develop a theological perspective which takes seriously Christian doctrines as well as insights from all spheres of modern thought and life—is impressive and persuasive. What I find less convincing is his too-quick rejection of the traditional, classical, and orthodox (conservative, if you like) understanding of the Christian faith.[52] While I am fully aware of the dangers of obscurantism, of the problems of certain forms of rigid orthodoxy and classical dualism, I am not at all convinced that the modern post-Enlightenment historicist view of reality is more adequate or truer than the classical non-historicist Christian and Greek view.

I have in another essay tried to show to what an extent Kaufman's theological method is grounded in the Enlightenment protest in favour of the individual theologian's capacity "deliberately" and "self-consciously" to construct concepts of God which will evoke popular piety.[53] In his *An Essay on Theological Method*, Kaufman explicitly states:

> We no longer can settle theological issues by appeal to the authority of Scripture or tradition. We must now undertake the much more difficult and hazardous task of deliberately and self-consciously constructing our concept of a God who is an adequate and meaningful object of devotion and centre of the orientation of human life. In doing so we are free to entertain on their own merits a variety of models for constructing the concept of God, and to accept or reject them without regard to their scriptural authorization.[54]

It is in how they view the normativity of biblical and ecclesiastical authority *vis à vis* Enlightenment views of freedom that Kaufman and Yoder differ. Kaufman himself states this difference perhaps most clearly in his 1963 essay, "The Christian in Church and World," when he says:

> It will be observed here that I do not agree with Yoder . . . that I have rejected the all-too-great authority of the church in the Anabaptist tradition in the name of the mass-church tradition; it would be more correct to say I am rejecting the common authoritarianism of both these lines in the name of 'liberal' traditions rooted in the Enlightenment and modern experience. The character and the theological significance of the relativism emergent from these more recent traditions, I have sketched in my book on *Relativism, Knowledge and Faith*.[55]

The basic Enlightenment project of emancipation from heteronomous finite authorities cannot be disregarded without becoming reactionary and obscurantist. Nevertheless, the Enlightenment protest is profoundly ambiguous: the modern triumph of human freedom and technical reason (a direct consequence of the Enlightenment) makes possible a technological monolith and the tyranny of a totally administered society which is more heteronomous than any of the traditional authorities.

While Kaufman understands some of the ambiguities and negativities of modernity and partly for this reason develops a concept of God as "Limit," his confidence in the Enlightenment assumptions of historicism and freedom remains relatively unscathed. In fact, in some of his later comments this confidence seems to have increased rather than lessened. In his 1979 Preface to *Nonresistance and Responsibility*, he says:

> I now would not interpret the Christian life as founded so arbitrarily on an authoritarianism of revelation, as some of the chapters of this book written a good many years ago suggest, but would be inclined to argue the value of a posture of redemptive love as intrinsically right and good for humans ... thus the heavy appeal to supposedly authoritative biblical texts would not find such a prominent place were I to rewrite these chapters today.[56]

In a similar vein, in his 1977 Preface to *Systematic Theology*, Kaufman states:

> It is now clear to me, therefore, that a properly conceived systematic theology should not begin with simple acceptance of the givenness of "revelation" (as in the present work). This simply perpetuates the authoritarian structure of theology and makes it difficult to see at what points the tradition is to be seriously criticized and reconceived. On the contrary, a theology should begin in a careful analysis of the way in which, and the reasons why, the human mind finds it appropriate, and even necessary, to create and use the concept of God.... [57]

What I find questionable in Kaufman's analysis is not his rejection of arbitrary and destructive authoritarianism and heteronomy, but rather his increasing confidence in a modern historical alternative to a traditional, classical understanding of reality. I am fully aware of the epistemological problems and the dangers of heteronomy inherent in the classical view of God, but I am not convinced that the modern-historicist model has fewer problems and frees us from heteronomy.

In an age faced with total self-annihilation on the one hand, or total administration on the other (all under the guise of freedom, science and reason), the traditional view and formulation of God, human nature, and history calls for a new hearing. In this view human beings see themselves not as the masters and creators of themselves, the human species, and the future, but as accountable to a radically transcendent being. The point is not that this view can be transplanted into the modern world in its pristine purity—it necessarily must be taken through the prism of the Enlightenment which has profoundly shaped us all—but at least its fundamental affirmations should be openly reconsidered.

The Possibility of a Mennonite Theology

Is there a Mennonite theology? I have tried to show in my examination of Bender's Anabaptist vision, Friedmann's "existential" theology, Yoder's "political" theology, and Kaufman's "historicist" theology that there is a continuity here, a common thread that runs through all of these modern representatives of Mennonite thought. The thread is an emphasis on the historical-ethical. All four have a deep suspicion of a more classical emphasis on that part of human experience which one might variously call the vertical, mystical, ontological, sacramental, or ahistorical dimension of reality. While Kaufman, more than the other three, is interested in metaphysical-epistemological problems and allows for the aesthetic-sacramental dimension of the Christian experience in the context of a systematic theology which attempts to illumine all aspects of life, in the end he defends the most radical historicism of all. Thus Kaufman can say, "*We are our histories*"[58] or "Man is pre-eminently an historical being because he is both made by his history and he himself makes history; thus man makes and remakes himself. All of nature is created in the historical process; man alone takes an active part in his own creation in history."[59] Kaufman, I would suggest, is simply drawing the more radical conclusion to what is already seminally present in the other three.

So, in answer to the question: Is there a Mennonite theology? I would say, *Yes*, there is an implicit Anabaptist-Mennonite theology which has evolved over the years and, particularly recently, has expressed itself as a "historicalist" theology suspicious of classical doctrine, sacramentalism, and cult. All four thinkers we have examined ultimately stress the actual, concrete, prophetic, and ethical side of the Christian faith at the expense of the mystical, "spiritual," and sacramental side. In this, I would suggest, all four are fundamentally modern, for to be modern is to see time as history, as movement from past to present to future, to see human nature as defined primarily in terms of history, ethics, and politics rather than ontological being. Such historicalist thinking can be traced back to the left wing of the Reformation, which in turn, can be linked with the rise of the modern spirit.

This historicalist Mennonite theology has some particular strengths; it, possibly better than some other theological traditions, can translate traditional theological categories into historical-ethical terms understandable to the modern world. But in its over-preoccupation with ethics to the exclusion of other-than ethical dimensions, it is in danger of becoming truncated and needs serious reassessment. While all human experience can take place only within history (this is self-evident), there are experiences which are in themselves *not intrinsically or essentially historical and ethical*. This must be loudly affirmed if our social-political-ethical-commitment as Mennonites is not to become a form of human ideology and positivism. Mennonite theology must break its unquestioned alliance with some of the dominant assumptions of the modern age if it is to maintain the critical stance that has historically characterized it. To do this it must develop a systematic theology which is larger than prophetic-eschatological-ethical theology.

Is it possible to develop a Mennonite systematic theology? Can there be a way of theological thinking which has a distinctively Anabaptist-Mennonite mark, context, or methodology, different from the way Catholics and Lutherans and Calvinists think and engage in theology? Can such a distinctiveness be built into a system? Friedmann says there is such a distinctive Anabaptist-Mennonite theology, but it is unique precisely in its *not* being a system. It is rather a concrete, historical, lived faith based on discipleship, the way of the cross, a theology of the kingdom of God. There is an *implicit* Mennonite theology, but there can be no distinctive Mennonite *explicit* or *systematic* theology that is faithful to the Anabaptist heritage, for such a theology would in principle not be a lived "existential" theology.

This is where I must strongly disagree with Friedmann. I can see nothing intrinsically contradictory between a *systematic or explicit theology* and an *implicit, existential or prophetic-eschatological theology*. I strongly believe Mennonites must develop an explicit theology which will reflect the implicit theology they have had all along, and that exactly such an explicit systematic theology will push them to place their strong historical-ethical concerns within a larger and sounder theological context. In a sense, Gordon Kaufman has attempted to do just that, but because of his radical historicism his theology, in my opinion, does not provide an adequate basis upon which one is able *both* to illumine all of human experience *and* to critique the modern age as seriously as is demanded.

Why should we have a systematic theology? First, we need it because for some of us there is no other option. For some of us it is absolutely imperative, if we want to remain both Mennonite and Christian, that we systematically bring together our inherited Christian beliefs with the critical questions and insights we encounter in the various disciplines and in the cultural matrix of the modern world.

Second, we need a systematic theology (here I agree with Kaufman) to help prevent us from becoming one-sided and truncated in our Christianity and our humanity; to guard us from reducing the whole of the gospel to one of its parts (ethics or the historical Jesus of Nazareth).

Third, we need it for the sake of ecumenical conversation. I stress *conversation and not only critique and witness*. We need to recover as Mennonites the concept of the universal catholic church, of which we are only a small fragment. Only through systematic theological thinking, in which we identify our distinctiveness theologically in the context of the whole, can we both learn from and make a contribution to the universal Christian community.

Fourth, we need a systematic theology for catechetical reasons, so that we have tools by which not only to teach younger generations the accumulated wisdom of the ages but also to guide ministers in their preaching and teaching ministry. In an age when the tyranny of common values and assumptions is rapidly eroding any kind of traditional distinctiveness, we need an explicit theology which will give us an identity and integrity, a continuity with our own past, while at the same time accounting for the diverse cultural and religious traditions that have in the past century claimed the name Anabaptist-Mennonite for themselves without identifying with a Swiss or Dutch stream. We must develop a theology which is larger than what most of us have traditionally understood as Anabaptist-Mennonite without sacrificing the central tenets we hold dear.

What more specifically might such a systematic Mennonite theology look like in the light of what has been said up to this point? First, there would need to be in such a theology a *universal* element; namely, that which makes it not uniquely Mennonite theology but *Christian* theology. This universal element would link it not only with the biblical text and the earliest Christian creeds, but with the Christian church as it has developed through the ages—with believers past, present, and future. It would attempt to express the eternal verities of the Christian faith.

What are these eternal truths of the Christian faith which the church affirms? They have been expressed in the earliest creeds: "I believe in God, the Father almighty, maker of heaven and earth," "And in Jesus Christ his only Son our Lord . . .," and "I believe in the Holy Spirit. . . ." The universal element of Christian faith which binds together all Christians of whatever tradition is the affirmation of faith in the trinitarian God: God as transcendent Creator, God as revealed in the historical Christ and Redeemer, and God as immanent Spirit, dynamically active and present within history and his creation. A trinitarian affirmation is important, not only because it is implicit in the biblical text, or because it is expressed in the early creeds of the church, but also because it prevents us from a heretical one-sided emphasis only on the transcendence of God, the historicity of God, or the immanent-experiential presence of God. Our Mennonite christological theology—in which the *historical Christ* plays such a primary role—should be systematically woven into a trinitarian theology to keep it from becoming a form of theological reductionism.

In his emphasis on a christocentric trinitarianism, Kaufman provides us, I believe, with a possible paradigm of how one might go about "constructing" a Mennonite systematic theology. It would include a *particular* element, which would constitute a distinctively Anabaptist-Mennonite colour to the whole theological enterprise without becoming solipsistic as a church. This element would consist of a strong *christocentric-ethical* component which would find its place not at the end of the theology, but would run as a thread through the whole "system."

All the classical theological categories would be interpreted from the perspective of the Mennonite historical-ethical emphasis on nonviolent love without reducing theology to ethics. This eschatological and ethical concern should not be perceived as the starting point for theology (only an affirmation of faith in the trinitarian God can be the basis of theological thinking), but rather as the tone of the entire enterprise.

The strength of the Anabaptist-Mennonite tradition has always been its prophetic-eschatological capacity to stand over against and critique radically the negativities of violent contemporary culture. The possibility for such a critical stance should be preserved in such a systematic theology without isolating the Anabaptist-Mennonite community from other Christian traditions, and without sacrificing what I have in this essay called the cultic, sacramental, and mystical dimension of the Christian faith.

ELEVEN

Anabaptist-Mennonite Systematic Theology*

This essay continues the inquiry into the possibility, desirability, and nature of a Mennonite systematic theology. It is written in a popular style, as a report on a conference on the subject sponsored by the Institute of Mennonite Studies, and appeared in The Ecumenist, *a Catholic journal promoting Christian unity, edited by Canadian theologian Gregory Baum.[1] Having surveyed the Mennonite theological scene—the views of J. Lawrence Burkholder, J. C. Wenger, Harold S. Bender, Robert Friedmann, John H. Yoder, and Gordon D. Kaufman—I argue that there should be no one systematic theology but a plurality of systematic theologies, in fidelity to the polygenetic nature of our origins, drawing on an unlikely source for support: the Anglican theologian Stephen Sykes.*

Despite this plurality (which, incidentally, is not to be understood as a form of pluralism or relativism, but rather as diversity, something quite different), these diverse theologies would have certain features in common—most important, a christocentric commitment to non-violent love. The essay dates from a period when I was under the influence of Catholic theologian David Tracy, and I apply his dual emphasis on the "prophetic-ethical" and "mystical-aesthetical" (Tillich

---

* Originally published as "Anabaptist-Mennonite Systematic Theology," *The Ecumenist* 21:4 (May-June, 1983), 21:5 (July-August, 1983): 68-72. For notes on the text see the Notes section below.

employs a similar duality: the "prophetic-eschatological" and the "priestly-sacramental") to Mennonite theology.

Throughout all my theological thinking, I have sensed a danger in Mennonite thought of reducing theology to the ethical, and have consequently strived to balance this heightened ethical consciousness with a weighting of the mystical, sacramental, priestly, and aesthetical. Without any awareness before this conference of the work of Thomas Finger, I had, under the influence of Neo-Marxist thinking in the Frankfurt School of Critical Theory and Liberation Theology, concluded that an eschatological approach to theology might be a way of combining all these various elements. Finger, as it turned out, presented his own eschatological vision of a systematic theology (strongly influenced by Jürgen Moltmann) at the Elkhart conference, part of a two-volume work which had grown out of many years of lectures on the subject.[2] What bothered me, however, about most Western eschatological approaches, was their inevitable linear historicism—despite their caveats to the contrary. Even someone like Wolfhart Pannenberg, for whom eschatology is the central organizing principle, falls prey to this in my view, as I will analyze in the final essay of this volume. The issue for me was and continues to be: How is it possible to take eschatology and history seriously without absolutizing the linear movement from past to present to future? At stake is the confession of God being beyond time and space, and consequently equidistant from all temporal moments.

◆ ◆ ◆

Is it possible to develop a systematic theology from an Anabaptist-Mennonite perspective, from the vantage point of "radical Protestantism" or the "left wing of the Reformation?" If so, should there be such a theology, and what might it look like? If there ought to be Mennonite systematic theology, should there be one definitive theological model or a variety of systematic theologies done by Mennonites?

These were some of the central questions addressed recently by a small group of Mennonite theologians interested in the state of systematic theology in the Mennonite Church, meeting under the sponsorship of the Institute of Mennonite Studies, in Elkhart Indiana, June 23-25, 1983. They represent a small but growing movement within the Mennonite communion of individuals who are becoming increasingly persuaded that a self-conscious systematic theology from an Anabaptist-Mennonite perspective is necessary for a number of reasons: to preserve the integrity of the Mennonite communion in the face of the pluralism of modern culture, to provide the basis upon which to become self-critical and move beyond a "sectarian" stance into the wider public ecumenical arena of discussion and debate, and to make a positive contribution theologically to the universal Christian church.

Historical Resistance

In his "Impressionistic Survey of Theology in the Mennonite Church: 1900-1970," J. Lawrence Burkholder, former professor of theology at Harvard Divinity School and later president of Goshen College, pointed to some of the unhappy consequences of the lack of sound systematic theological reflection among Mennonites. "It [Mennonite theology] cut its baby-teeth in the orthodontic framework of the Fundamentalist debates of this century," he mused. While this Fundamentalist aberration of certain segments of the Mennonite Church in the early part of this century has been largely superseded through critical biblical and historical theology in Mennonite seminaries, Mennonites have produced few systematic theologians, let alone a distinctive Anabaptist-Mennonite systematic theology.

Historically, Mennonites have not had what might be considered a distinctive and explicit systematic theology for a number of reasons. One reason is that by and large Mennonites have perceived their distinctiveness not to be in the area of doctrinal questions but in the consistent application of belief and faith to life.

Thus John C. Wenger, one of the few contemporary Mennonite systematic theologians, wrote in 1950: "A number of monographs on Anabaptists have been written and several books on biblical doctrine have been issued by Mennonite publishers, but the definitive Anabaptist-Mennonite theology is yet to appear."[3] Wenger represents a rather widespread Mennonite self-perception when he interprets Anabaptism as basically orthodox in its Protestant orientation but pushing the Reformation to its logical conclusion: "It was not an unbalanced movement," he writes. "It was rather *a more earnest effort than the other Protestant groups made to break with religious and ecclesiastical tradition to render absolute obedience to the text of Scripture.* This point of view was regarded as revolutionary in the sixteenth century—as it is in modern Christendom" (Wenger, 2).

In matters of doctrine, says Wenger, Anabaptists were generally orthodox, not differing essentially from the views of other Reformers: "On the great doctrines of God, Christ, the Holy Spirit, the Trinity, depravity and sin, regeneration, holiness of life, grace, and eschatology, the Brethren held common views with the Protestant bodies" (Wenger, 23). It was in the area of individual and social ethics, in the framework of a new ecclesiology, that they became distinct from the mainline Reformers. Individual regeneration was intrinsically linked to a new corporate life: *"They also thought of the Church as a corporate body achieving the will of God for society."* This doctrine distinguished them more sharply than any other from the large Protestant groups. They held that the state had to live its life on a sub-Christian level, restraining unregenerate men by the employment of police force and the magistry. But when a person became a Christian and accepted baptism he was lifted up into the society of the redeemed, a body of people who loved one another and were mutually concerned for the welfare of their fellow believers and for the corporate witness of the brotherhood, a society in which there was no need of force and coercion (Wenger, 56).

This visible corporate model of Christian existence here and now stood in some kind of relationship of continuity to the anticipated Kingdom of God: "It was the Anabaptists who sought earnestly to build Christ's *kingdom* here and now. And that kingdom was not a theoretical concept for Anabaptists, but a glorious reality, composed, at it was, of their fellow believers, the members of their congregations" (Wenger, 56).

Wenger's interpretation of early Anabaptism and general Mennonite self-perception is not an isolated one but bears the marks of the so-called "Bender school of Anabaptist thought." In his classic 1943 essay, *The Anabaptist Vision*, delivered as a presidential address before the American Society of Church History, Harold S. Bender expressed a very similar conception of early Anabaptism: "However, there is another line of interpretation, now almost one hundred years old, which is being increasingly accepted and which is probably destined to dominate the field. It is the one which holds that Anabaptism is the culmination of the Reformation, the fulfilment of the original vision of Luther and Zwingli, and thus makes it a consistent evangelical Protestantism seeking to recreate without compromise the original New Testament church, the vision of Christ and the apostles."[4] Bender views Anabaptism as orthodox Protestantism but as more consistent in its carrying through of the Reformation ideal than the other Reformers. What is new in Anabaptism, for Bender, is not a new intellectual or doctrinal theology but the inner and outward transformation of life—repentance evidenced by new behavior. Anabaptist distinctiveness, therefore, is defined largely in ethical terms: "first, a new conception of the essence of Christianity as discipleship; second, a new conception of the church as a brotherhood; and third, a new ethic of love and non-resistance" (Bender, 20).

Bender's Anabaptists are neither institutionalists (as in the Catholic sacramental-sacerdotal system of dispensing objective divine grace) nor mystics and pietists (as in the Lutheran emphasis on the inner experience of God's grace through faith) but regenerated believers who put the emphasis on following Christ in life. Bender's passionate interest in the recovery and rehabilitation of the Anabaptist vision through a return to sixteenth-century sources contributed to the renaissance of left-wing Reformation studies and helped to free Reformation historiography from its traditional caricature of Anabaptists as simple fanatics and enthusiasts.

Nevertheless, there are problems with Bender's vision, the most important perhaps being the tendency to view the origins of *authentic* Anabaptism too monogenetically, freed from any significant links with the Peasants' War, and revolutionary impulses such as that of Thomas Müntzer and the Munsterites. I have also argued in a recent essay that there is in this school of Anabaptist self-perception and interpretation, with its somewhat exaggerated emphasis on the ethical distinctiveness of Anabaptism, a danger of theological reductionism marked by an anti-sacramental, anti-doctrinal, and anti-mystical bias, which may be rooted in the Anabaptist movement itself.[5]

While there has been a flurry of interest in Anabaptist historical studies since Bender's essay, there has been relatively little work in the area of modern Anabaptist theology, due partly to this emphasis on ethical rather than doctrinal distinctiveness. One of the few exceptions is the work of John H. Yoder, who continues to be one of the most articulate spokesmen of contemporary Anabaptism in his attempt to interpret and reinterpret theologically the meaning of the Anabaptist vision in the context of the modern world. Nevertheless, there remains a dearth of work in the area of Mennonite systematic theology *per se*. Mennonite historian and theologian Robert Friedmann, in his 1972 book *The Theology of Anabaptism*, has suggested a more fundamental reason for the historical resistance of Mennonites to systematic theology. According to Friedmann, there is something intrinsically contradictory in Mennonites doing systematic theology.

Friedmann maintains that the Anabaptists had an *implicit* theology but not an *explicit* one. Every religious movement, in his opinion, has an implicit theology—that is, it has certain ideas about God and humanity, and God's relationship to humanity. Sixteenth-century Anabaptism too has such an implicit theology, anthropology, soteriology, eschatology, and ecclesiology.

But Anabaptists did not have, nor should Mennonites today have, an explicit or overt systematic theology. In fact "systems are obnoxious to those who hold to such an implicit theology."[6] While numerous creedal statements and confessional formulations appear in Anabaptist-Mennonite history, there is an intrinsic resistance to developing rational systems of thought. Friedmann strongly asserts that there can *in principle* be no explicit Anabaptist theology. He rests this claim on the assumption that sixteenth-century Anabaptists, like the early apostolic Church, espoused an "existential" Christianity, which refused to split apart faith and life. A theological system, a "rational edifice of thought," would contradict the very nature of such a "lived Christianity." It would undermine the unity of faith and life, the subjectivity of the new birth, the Anabaptist emphasis on the cross, the "bitter Christ," discipleship, and the prophetic-eschatological witness of the visible Church to the kingdom of God.

Despite the weaknesses of the Wenger-Bender-Friedmann interpretation of early Anabaptism, there is a profundity to the historical resistance of Mennonites to systematic theology as perceived by these modern interpreters. The *raison d'etre* of all systematic theology is a passion for illuminating *all* dimensions of human existence from a particular theological vantage point or key category. Systematic theology has by nature an almost totalitarian ambition to order and control all data of human experience. While there is a legitimacy to this desire for comprehensiveness—it guards against fanaticism, one-sidedness, and theological reductionism—all systematic theology also posesses the danger of losing the dangerous memory of the historical and prophetic Christ. In its emphasis on the universal, systematic theology does an injustice to the particular. In its stress on understanding, illuminating, and clarifying all sides of human experience, it is of necessity involved in a balancing act which does not adequately account for a particular side of tradition. In the words of the political and liberation theologians, a concern with universality and wholeness ignores the prior claim of the oppressed, marginalized, and victimized in any given society. The systematician too readily locates synthesis and harmony where there is antagonism, contradiction, and suffering.

Although I do not see the intellectual discipline of doing systematic-doctrinal theology as necessarily leading to a split between faith and life, belief and lived Christianity (as Friedmann seems to), one cannot ignore the *de facto* historical tendency of rational systems to lead to the divorce of theory and practice. Here the Marxist critique of ideology and the political-liberation critique of traditional orthodoxy in favour of orthopraxis express something similar to the Anabaptist-Mennonite concern with the unity of thought and behavior.

Need for Systematic Theology

In the light of the historical resistance by Mennonites to developing a systematic theology, the Elkhart meeting of older and younger Mennonite theologians interested specifically in the need for a self-conscious Mennonite systematic theology is highly significant. There are a number of factors at the basis of this new interest among Mennonite theologians. One is the increasing conviction that Mennonites need more aggressively to enter the ecumenical theological forum, not only because the Anabaptist-Mennonite tradition has an important contribution to make but also because it needs to supplement its own particular understanding of the

Christian tradition with the insights from other communions. Another is the growing concern for a more comprehensive understanding both of the contents of the Christian faith as passed on *and* of all levels of the modern situation. It is this latter concern that, in my view, is especially important.

Despite the legitimate concern of the Anabaptist-Mennonite tradition with the dangers of all-encompassing systematic and speculative systems of theological thought, the need for a comprehensive theology simply cannot be ignored by any church tradition if reductionism and one-sidedness is to be avoided. Here I agree with Gordon K. Kaufman, Mennonite minister and professor of theology at Harvard Divinity School, when he says: "Theology must attend to and be prepared to analyze political and economic developments, scientific and philosophic theory, communal and religious practices, works of art and literature, everyday personal and social experience—everything that contributes to the stuff of human existence must be brought under the revelatory light. Since the Christian Gospel is good news about the human situation as such, and thus about every dimension of life, no aspect of existence is too insignificant or too remote to be of theological interest."[7]

Though the Anabaptist-Mennonite tradition has too often been falsely accused of a sectarian type of withdrawal from society, economics, and politics, of espousing a simple "Christ against culture" model, there is some truth to the Troeltschian claim that "sects" are to be distinguished from the "church-type" by their non- or even anti-universalism. Troeltsch holds that

> The Church is that type of organization which is overwhelmingly conservative, which to a certain extent accepts the secular order, and dominates the masses; in principle, therefore, it is universal, i.e., it desires to cover the whole life of humanity.
>
> The sects, on the other hand, are comparatively small groups, they aspire after personal inward perfection, and they aim at a direct personal fellowship between the members of each group. From the very beginning, therefore, they are forced to organize themselves in small groups, and to renounce the idea of dominating the world. Their attitude toward the world, the State, and society may be indifferent, tolerant, or hostile, since they have no desire to control and to avoid them; their aim is usually to replace these social institutions by their own society.[8]

Sectarian theology is non- or even anti-comprehensive in favour of smallness, non-conformity, separation, a theology of the critical remnant of "pilgrim church," a theology of faithful "messianic community." The burden, therefore, for Mennonite theologians like myself and an anti-comprehensive attitude is no longer satisfying, for whom a comprehensive systematic theology seems imperative but who want to remain faithful to their own rich prophetic and radical Protestant tradition, is to find a way of bringing together these two seemingly contradictory impulses.

The question facing a Mennonite systematic theologian is this: Is there a way of developing a systematic theology which is both comprehensive *and* preserves the genius of the radical Protestant tradition—namely, the historic tradition of social non-conformity and radical prophetic critique of the negativities of dominant culture? I think a possible way is hinted at by Troeltsch himself when he observes: "Insofar as the sect-type maintains Christian universalism at all, like the gospel, the only form it knows is that of eschatology; this is the reason why it always finally revives the eschatology of the Bible" (Troeltsch, 339).

One way in which a Mennonite theologian could, therefore, quite consistently develop a comprehensive systematic theology and still remain faithful to his or her prophetic-critical tradition would be from an eschatological vantage point. The key category or organizing principle would be eschatology. The perspective from which all traditional loci of theology would be interpreted would be the eschatological future, the "universal ideal", the "Kingdom of God as the real universal end of all things," to use Troeltsch's terms (Troeltsch, 335). Such a systematic theology would find itself in the company of some of the major contemporary theological movements—the orthopraxis theologies of hope, political theology, and liberation theology. These, it seems to me, would become its primary ecumenical conversation partners.

This prophetic-eschatological approach to a comprehensive Mennonite systematic theology has much to say for itself. There are, however, some serious difficulties with this model that have to do with the way eschatology is perceived in the historicist framework in which much modern theology is done. In this historicist context, the eschatological future is viewed primarily in terms of the culmination of time as history—namely, the temporal end of the movement from past to present to future. It is almost impossible to think that some radical transcendent reality could break into and shatter actual or imagined historical realities. A historicist eschatology tends to legitimate an ideology of either right or left. To discuss this problem in any greater detail is beyond the scope of this essay.

There is, however, another lesser problem with the eschatological model which is particularly relevant for the Mennonite tradition. It has to do with the anti-sacramental and anti-mystical bias in much of Anabaptist-Mennonite theology. The prophetic-eschatological model might very well accentuate this bias rather than modify it. A theology which truly sought to be comprehensive would need to take into account the "sacramental" dimension of all religious experience. Here David Tracy is surely right when he asserts that the "prophetic-ethical" and the "mystical-aesthetical" both together constitute human religious experience and that the notion that "any religion is really *only* mystical-metaphysical or only ethical-political seems an illusion produced by some partial vision of the complexity of the whole."[9]

A systematic theology in which an eschatological-prophetic-ethical vantage point would function as the key organizing principle would need, first, to rethink eschatology and place it within less of a historicist framework, and, second, to supplement its primary emphasis on the radical critique of the negativities of the present in the light of the kingdom of God, with a significant emphasis on sacrament, liturgy, worship, and confession. It would have to find a place for what Tracy calls the "manifestation" dimension of human experience which affirms the graciousness of the present.

Finally, in his recent book *The Integrity of Anglicanism*, Stephen Sykes calls similarly for an Anglican systematic or doctrinal theology, and proposes that there be not one universally accepted definitive Anglican systematic theology but numerous ones. "There *ought*," Sykes suggests, "to be Anglican systematic theologies, that is, theologies of high standards of internal consistency written by Anglicans of conviction. No one will expect such theologies to be awarded the accolade of being *the* Anglican systematics, any more than the work of Karl Rahner or of Karl Barth is spoken of as *the* Catholic systematics or *the* Reformed systematics."[10]

Sykes's suggestion is especially appropriate for Mennonites in light of the polygenetic and heterogeneous nature of their origins and history. There would be something inauthentic about attempting to write one definitive Mennonite systematic theology. A plurality of systematic theologies written by Mennonites intent on remaining faithful to the tradition would reflect more genuinely the diversity of the movement. There would of course be commonly held assumptions and values, as there were also in the sixteenth century. One such common orientation would need to be the commitment to the christocentric norm of nonviolent love, the tenacious espousal of which might very well continue to place the Anabaptist-Mennonite theological position, despite its comprehensiveness, in the camp of the non-conformist and critical minority.

TWELVE

Mennonite Systematic Theology and the Problem of Comprehensiveness*

The dilemma for Mennonites thinking systematically about the Christian faith is: 1) theology is the comprehensive understanding of the Christian faith as disclosed to us in the biblical tradition and as handed on to us, and the critical illumination of all of reality and human experience in the light of this; but 2) a "sectarian" (non-foundationalist?) theology is non-comprehensive by its very nature. Such theology tends to fragment and reduce reality to a very narrow slice of the whole. It is not a question of how seriously one takes the particular—all theology is done from a particularist vantage point—it is a matter of being concerned with the particular as a part of the universal, or as a window onto it.

In this essay, prepared for a 1983 consultation on "Hermeneutics and Systematic Theology" convened by the Institute of Mennonite Studies in Elkhart, Indiana,[1] I address this dilemma. I explore ways of being comprehensive in theology while remaining faithful to our particular Mennonite tradition, especially to the premium it places on nonresistant love. I applaud Gordon Kaufman's call for a comprehensive systematic theology which considers all of reality, but I reject his

---

* Originally published in *Explorations of Systematic Theology: From Mennonite Perspectives*, Occasional Papers No. 7, ed. Willard Swartley (Elkhart, IN: Institute of Mennonite Studies, 1984). For all subsequent notes see the Notes section below.

deconstruction-of-the tradition approach. I find myself closer to Bernard Lonergan's and David Tracy's greater appreciation for the disclosure and revelatory nature of the classics of the Christian tradition, although I have difficulty with Lonergan's form of progressivism.

One possibility would be an eschatological approach in which universality is anticipated in a fragmentary way but waits for completion at the end. This is the way taken by many contemporary theologians—such as the European political-hope theologians Jürgen Moltmann and Johann Baptist Metz, and including the Mennonite Thomas Finger, and Latin American liberation theologians. The problem with the contemporary eschatological approach is that no matter how stringent its critique of "progressivist" thinking, there is a linear "directionality" involved that does not do justice to the ontological and metaphysical dimensions of classical thought.

Even someone like Wolfhart Pannenberg falls prey to this forward directionality in his three-volume Systematic Theology.[2] *He never quite manages to reconcile the tension between his historicist view of the economic Trinity with his non-historicist explication of the immanent Trinity. Critical to classical eschatology is the equidistance of all historical moments to God. The end of history is no closer to God than the beginning or the middle, because God is beyond time, non-temporal, and transtemporal. Only in this classical model can the ultimate dignity and value of every historical moment and creature under the providence of God be safeguarded.*

The danger of "already-not-yet" thinking is a type of forward directionality which sees the present as a stage, phase, or stepping stone for the future, and as not having intrinsic dignity before the Absolute. Mennonite theological thinking needs to find a way of "sacramentally" experiencing universality and timelessness within the present without losing its "prophetic" charism. It can do this only by grounding its witness to the Jesus love ethic of the cross in a trinitarian christology of cosmic proportions.

My probings into the possibility of a self-conscious Anabaptist-Mennonite systematic theology in this essay are of a highly methodological type. They represent a relatively early stage in my speculations about a potential Mennonite theology and therefore do not deal with the actual substance or content of such a theology, although I am fully aware that method and content are intrinsically related. Nor for that matter am I engaged in the actual method of a theological "system" for Mennonites, but I am making observations about a possible method. At this point, therefore, mine is a kind of "meta-methodological" stance. I am not yet doing Mennonite systematic theology proper, nor am I fully convinced that we should as a Mennonite communion have one definitive systematic theology, although I am persuaded that Mennonites ought to do systematic theology.

◆ ◆ ◆

The Problem: Comprehensiveness and Sectarianism

The *raison d'être* of all systematic theology is the passion for comprehensiveness. Systematic theology, much like traditional philosophy, is by definition concerned with questions concerning the whole, with a compulsion to bring some kind of order into *all* of human experience. It has an almost totalitarian obsession to illumine all of human existence and reality from a particular key vantage point. In the words of Episcopalian theologian Owen C. Thomas:

> Systematic or dogmatic theology is the methodological investigation and interpretation of the content of the Christian faith. It is the orderly clarification and explanation of what is affirmed in the Christian message. Theology is an activity or function of the Christian church carried out by members of the church. It is the church reflecting on the basis of its existence and the content of its message.[3]

Thomas's thesis is that

> theology and philosophy are parallel enterprises, the same kind of thing. More specifically, Christian theology is a species of the genus philosophy. Philosophy in its constructive function is the attempt to organize and interpret the data of human experience in the light of some key-category or organizing principle, such as matter in motion, nature, life, organism, process, mind or spirit. The key-category or organizing principle is chosen by a decision which is analogous to the decision of faith, and the first task of the constructive philosopher is to analyze and clarify this key-category.[4]

Christian theology, therefore, in Thomas's view,

> is the analysis and clarification of the key-category or organizing principle of Christian faith, namely, God as he is manifest in the events of the Bible. Then the larger task of theology, usually called Christian philosophy, is the interpretation of the data of human experience in the light of the Christian key-category.[5]

Thomas identifies theology too exclusively with philosophy and does not give critical social theory a sufficient place in the theological enterprise.[6] Nevertheless, his notion of the "key-category"—arrived at not by deduction or induction but by means analogous to faith—by which the systematic theologian organizes in a comprehensive way the contents of the Christian faith and the data of human experience— is essentially correct.

Further, while the key-category of Christian theology in general may be "God as he is manifest in the events of the Bible," to use Thomas's terms, I would argue that any given systematic theology done in the service of a distinct ecclesiastical tradition will have a more particular key-category or vantage point from which it reads and interprets the biblical tradition and its own understanding of that tradition. One of my questions in this essay is consequently: What is the *particular* key-category by which Mennonites do or ought to read, interpret, and organize the contents of the Christian faith in such a way that it illumines all levels of human experience?

On one level, systematic theology is committed to a critical and comprehensive understanding of the contents of the Christian faith as passed on to us in the biblical and ecclesiastical tradition. On another level, systematic theology is dedicated to a critical and comprehensive understanding of *all* of human existence and the illumination of *all* of reality in light of the contents of the Christian faith *as passed on to us.* In the words of David Tracy, "Systematic theologians cannot simply repeat, they must critically interpret the tradition mediating the event. Theologians cannot collapse into, they must critically interpret the situation in the light of the event."[7]

I find myself in basic agreement with Tracy's interpretation of this dialectical relationship between revelatory event and the situation. I also think Tracy is right when he emphasizes the important role of tradition in the hermeneutical enterprise. It is for this reason that I emphasize here the notion of the "Christian faith as passed on to us," because I believe the only access we have to the Christian faith is as it has been mediated to us, first, by the biblical tradition, second, by the Christian church in general and, third, by the particular ecclesiastical and theological tradition in which we find ourselves. In short, we have no simple access to the Bible in a *sola scriptura* sense, which is not in some sense mediated by the various traditions which have shaped us and our reading of the Bible.

Returning to the notion of theological comprehensiveness, Gordon Kaufman is right when he says:

> *Systematic theology* is the attempt thus to see each doctrine in its relation to the whole Christian faith, and to see the whole with all the fullness and richness which the several doctrines collectively disclose. Such critical systematic study is essential for anyone seriously interested in understanding and appropriating God's action, since we easily fall into extravagant overemphasis and onesidedness, often falling into self-contradiction.[8]

Kaufman is also correct to assert that:

> Theology must attend to and be prepared to analyze political and economic developments, scientific and philosophic theory, communal and religious practices, works of art and literature, everyday personal and social experience— everything that contributes to the stuff of human existence must be brought under the revelatory light. Since the Christian gospel is good news about the human situation as such, and thus about every dimension of life, no aspect of existence is too insignificant or too remote to be of theological interest.[9]

I agree with Kaufman's emphasis on the comprehensiveness of systematic theology, both in regards to the internal unity, coherence, and consistency of the contents of the Christian faith and with respect to the totality of reality as we experience it—politics, economics, science, philosophy, art, literature, and culture.

Where I part company with Kaufman is in my understanding of the ongoing role of tradition in theological work. Kaufman's "constructionist view of the theological task" is too individual and autonomous, freed from the *restraints of the revelatory tradition as passed on to us*. This becomes especially evident in his 1983 presidential address to the American Academy of Religion, "Nuclear Eschatology and the Study of Religion," in which Kaufman in effect concludes that the Christian faith as passed on to us has little or no relevance for "the utterly new historical situation into which the possibility of all-out nuclear warfare has brought humanity."[10] He makes his point of view unmistakably clear:

> Instead of assuming that we already know from revelation or authoritative tradition the correct values and standards—the faith-orientation—in terms of which life is to be understood, and decisions and actions formulated, we must recognize and acknowledge that humankind has moved into a historical situation unanticipated by biblical writers and subsequent theological commentators alike, a situation of much greater human knowledge, power, and responsibility than our religious traditions had ever imagined possible. In consequence, instead of understanding ourselves largely as hangers-on of these traditions, as having a task simply of interpretation, we must be prepared to enter into the most radical kind of deconstruction and reconstruction of the traditions we have inherited, including especially their most central and precious symbols, *God* and *Jesus Christ* and *Torah*.[11]

While I agree with Kaufman that the technical and theoretical possibility of total self-annihilation, that "that fact-which-is-not-yet-a-reality," as he puts it, exists, that this is the most crucial moral issue facing human civilization since its inception, that the situation is radically and qualitatively novel in human history and that it places an inescapable burden upon our shoulders to prevent this fact from becoming a reality, I do not share his conclusion that traditional classical symbols of the Christian tradition as passed on to us, like the sovereignty of God over the cosmos and human history, no longer have "disclosive" and "revelatory" relevance for us today.

This "pessimistic" conclusion could only be arrived at on the basis of a radical historicism. In his conclusion, Kaufman is fully consistent with the position he had held all along, first expressed philosophically in his *Relativism, Knowledge and Faith* and more fully articulated theologically in his *Systematic Theology: A Historicist Perspective*.[12] My own stance is that only the recovery of a more classical view of transcendence and the sovereignty of God gives us any hope for averting the nuclear and environmental catastrophes which loom ahead of us. Only some notion of radical transcendence can give us grounds for meaning, even in the face of a potential or actual end of human history as we know it.[13]

It is precisely the loss of a sense of accountability to such a transcendent reality through a modern obsession with unlimited freedom, autonomy, and historicism that has brought us to the abyss of the imminent end of life on this planet. In that sense, Kaufman's call for a radical deconstruction and reconstruction on the basis of historicism is simply compounding the problem which he wants to solve and hardening the direction in which we are already heading.

I find myself in much closer agreement here with David Tracy. While Tracy sees the agenda of modern theology in much the same way as Kaufman, he, like Bernard Lonergan, has a much greater appreciation for the mediating role of the church and the tradition, as well as the revelatory and disclosive nature of the "classic."[14] "'Truth' in systematics," Tracy says,

> ordinarily functions in some form of "disclosure" model implied in all good interpretation. With that working model for the universality of the hermeneutical task as the task of all disciplined reflection, a fidelity to and involvement in a classical religious tradition ("faith" or "belief in") can function as an appropriate theological stance.

It follows that the main reference group of the systematic theologian will be the church as the primary mediator of the tradition. "It does not follow," he continues,

> that this will render systematic work private for either society or academy—provided the case for the authentic publicness of the real disclosure truth that is always present in every cultural classic, and some disclosure of the reality of God present in every theological classic, is recognized.[15]

Although Tracy and Kaufman agree on the publicness of theology—that is, theologians must argue their position on the basis of criteria available to the public—Tracy has a much greater recognition of the "disclosure" and "revelatory" nature of tradition and traditional classics than does Kaufman. Tracy realizes this difference between himself and Kaufman:

> The failure even to consider this option—indeed to assume, not argue, that church-traditions are by definition particularist—seriously mars the argument of Gordon Kaufman's *An Essay on Theological Method*.[16]

Tracy sees the systematic theologian's task as primarily hermeneutical, as "the reinterpretation of the tradition for the present situation. All serious interpretation of the tradition for the situation is called systematic theology."[17] Tracy is much readier than Kaufman to accept the "truth disclosure" possibility of the classics of tradition—texts, events, images, persons, rituals, and symbols—for the present situation. His definition of the "classic" bears this out:

> My thesis is that what we mean in naming certain texts, events, images, rituals, symbols and persons "classics" is that here we recognize nothing less than the disclosure of a reality we cannot but name truth. With Whitehead, here we find something valuable, something "important"; some disclosure of reality in a moment that must be called one of "recognition" which surprises, provokes, challenges, shocks and eventually transforms us; an experience that upsets conventional opinions and expands the sense of the possible; indeed a realized experience of that which is essential, that which endures.[18]

For the Christian, the religious classic event is "the spirit of the risen Lord who is the crucified Jesus of Nazareth."[19] The achievement of David Tracy is that besides giving us a virtual encyclopedia of information about the diverse trends in modern theology, he is able, from within his particular Catholic vantage point, to make a credible case for a commitment to a

Christian theology within the context of modern cultural pluralism without each religious tradition either "dissolving into some lowest common denominator" or "accepting a marginalized existence as one interesting but purely private option."[20]

My basic point in all of this is that the task of systematic theology is not a radical deconstruction and reconstruction in Kaufman's terms, but a critical and comprehensive understanding of the contents of the Christian faith as disclosed or revealed to us in the biblical tradition and *as handed on to us*, and the critical illumination of *all* of reality and human experience in the light of that tradition, including the nuclear threat and our responsibility in the face of it. How one interprets the classical biblical and doctrinal tradition will of course be determined to a great extent by how one perceives the modern situation. If one is generally optimistic about the modern project, with its Enlightenment assumptions of autonomous reason and the unlimited freedom to shape and master human and non-human nature through scientific and technological means, if one is basically committed to the ineluctable drive forward toward some future *telos* which stands in continuity with the present, then the classical tradition will be interpreted and reinterpreted in such a way as to give credence and legitimacy to this drive into the future.

If one is less enthusiastic about the assumptions of technical reason and freedom that undergird the modern historicist project (as I am), then one will interpret and appropriate the classical traditions of Jerusalem and Athens differently. I view the central crisis of the *modern age* to be *the loss of accountability* to a transcendent reality. This fact must shape our diagnosis of the present situation, and our theological interpretation and appropriation of the Christian tradition even as Mennonites. The Anabaptist-Mennonite emphasis on an ethic of nonresistant love formulated simply in terms of a historicist view of time and reality is just not adequate to meet the present crisis. It must be rooted in an affirmation of Jesus as somehow transcendentally and metaphysically grounded— the way classical trinitarian and christological formulations attempted to do—so that our faithfulness to the normativity of Jesus is not one of pragmatism or a legitimizing of the modern project but one of obedience to Jesus as the *Cosmic Lord*, because what he is, does and teaches is eternally true or intrinsically right. Once this kind of metaphysical and transcendent normativity is asserted of Jesus, then we once more enter a classicist orientation that needs somehow to be thought again amid the current crisis.

I have in this first part of the essay defended the necessary desire on the part of the systematic theologian for comprehensiveness. This necessary and legitimate desire however, presents those in the free church tradition, particularly the Anabaptist-Mennonite tradition, with a serious problem. Those of us in the so-called "sectarian" tradition of the Christian church are opposed almost by definition to universalism and comprehensiveness in favour of smallness, nonconformity, separation; a theology of the critical remnant or "pilgrim church," a theology of the faithful "messianic community." Ernst Troeltsch is still basically right, despite his rather reductionist contrast of the church-sect type, when he writes:

> The Church is that type of organization which is overwhelmingly conservative ("liberal" if one thinks of its much greater toleration of diversity within itself than the sect-type), which to a certain extent accepts the secular order, and dominates the masses; in principle, therefore, it is universal, i.e. it desires to cover the whole life of humanity. The sects, on the other hand, are comparatively small groups; they aspire after personal inward perfection, and they aim at a direct personal fellowship between the members of each group. From the very beginning, therefore, they are forced to organize themselves in small groups, and to renounce the idea of dominating the world. Their attitude toward the world, the State, the Society may be indifferent, tolerant, or hostile, since they have no desire to control and to avoid them; their aim is usually to replace these social institutions by their own society.[21]

Sectarian theology is non-comprehensive by its very nature. The burden, therefore, for those who are convinced that some kind of comprehensive Mennonite systematic theology—which remains essentially faithful to Radical Protestantism—is necessary, is to find a way of solving this seeming contradiction or dilemma.

One Possible Solution: The Prophetic-Eschatological Model

One way of solving the dilemma is suggested by Troeltsch himself; namely, comprehensiveness viewed *eschatologically*:

> In so far as the sect-type maintains Christian universalism at all, like the gospel, the only form it knows is that of eschatology; this is the reason why it always finally revives the eschatology of the Bible. That also naturally explains the greater tendency of the sect toward "ascetic" life and thought, even though the original ideal of the New Testament had not pointed in that direction. The final activity of the group and of the individual consists precisely in the practical austerity of a purely religious attitude toward life which is not affected by cultural influences.[22]

One possible basis upon which a Mennonite theologian, therefore, could consistently develop a comprehensive systematic theology and still remain faithful to his or her sectarian tradition would, according to this view, be on the basis of an eschatological vision. The key-category or organizing principle of Christian faith would be eschatology. The vantage point from which all the traditional *loci* of theology (God, creation, reconciliation, redemption) would be understood would be the eschatological future, the "universal ideal," the "Kingdom of God as the real universal end of all things."[23]

Such a systematic theology would find itself in the company of some of the major contemporary theological movements—orthopraxis theologies such as theology of hope, political theology, and liberation theology. These would be its ecumenical conversation partners. The strength of such an eschatological vantage point for a self-conscious Anabaptist-Mennonite theology would allegedly be that the possibility for critique, for standing prophetically over-against the negativities of modern culture, would be imbedded in the very systematic theology itself. In this it would supposedly be in line with the great Jewish prophetic tradition and to some extent with the apocalyptic traditions throughout western history. It could appropriate for itself some of the best in Marxist and neo-Marxist analyses of history and critique of ideology without collapsing into crass or metaphysical materialism. It could, for instance, benefit greatly from the insights of the Critical Theory of the Frankfurt School.[24]

The Anabaptist-Mennonite tradition has a natural predisposition to develop a systematic theology oriented toward the victimized, marginalized, oppressed, and exploited elements in any given society in a way which the church-type would find it difficult to do. Recent political and liberation theologians are just now discovering what Anabaptists have consciously or unconsciously known all along: that the Christian church is a critical and voluntary community of believers, a messianic community for whom theory and practice are intrinsically connected. One option for a Mennonite systematic theology could quite justifiably, therefore, be a whole theology written from a prophetic-eschatological perspective in which the anticipated and promised kingdom of God is the ordering principle; individual and social ethics based on a christology of non-violent, self-giving love would be the kind of hermeneutical key that justification by grace through faith is for the Lutherans.

There are some serious problems, however, with this prophetic-eschatological model as perceived and proposed by much modern theology. Aside from the danger of reducing Christian faith and life to individual and social ethics and activism, which is inherent in such a model, there is a more serious danger.[25] It has to do with the radical historicist context in which all modern thinking about eschatology takes place, bringing with it the rejection of what I call the classical world view with its ontological and metaphysical assumptions about reality. To think eschatologically and apocalyptically from within the classical framework is dramatically different from thinking eschatologically and apocalyptically in the modern post-Enlightenment context. In the *former* (the classical) there is the possibility of a breaking into human history of a transcendent non-historical reality—a reality which is itself not defined essentially in terms of history. To put it differently, in the classical model not all of reality is thought of in terms of "time as history," the chronological movement from past to present to future. In the *latter* (the modern historicist model) reality is seen almost exclusively in linear terms and the eschaton is viewed primarily as the future culmination or fulfillment of the past and the present. One participates in that eschatological future, consequently, only in terms of hope and anticipation of that fulfilled future, the "already" of the "not yet," a rather shallow comfort for the suffering and dying and disenfranchized at any given moment.

The classical view does not negate the importance of time as history, the movement of past to present to future, but puts historical reality in the context of a much larger ontological, metaphysical and cosmic framework. Human freedom and action within history is not considered autonomous and unlimited in what it can do and achieve— it is not on its own— but is perceived as restrained by and held accountable to that larger theological, ontological, and metaphysical foundation. Ethics and human responsibility in this framework are not based exclusively on freedom but have a theological, metaphysical, and ontological ground. Here reality is perceived in larger than purely historical terms. Here myth, ritual, cult, liturgy, art, and sacrament are important means of experiencing "timelessness" within history.[26]

This emphasis on the non-historicist dimensions of religious experience runs counter not only to much in the Free Church tradition but also to major currents in modern theology and philosophy, with their anti-doctrinal, anti-creedal, and anti-sacramental tendencies. I do not share the conviction of some that the Hebraic-Christian view as expressed in the biblical tradition stands sharply over against the more ontological-metaphysical view of the Greek philosophical tradition and that one must reject the latter and align oneself unequivocally with the former to be faithful to the truth of the gospel.

On the contrary, I share the conviction of those, like the Catholic theologian Bernard Lonergan, who believe that the synthesis of these two worlds in the first few centuries of church history was a positive and a "necessary" development.[27] I think it could quite convincingly be argued, in fact, that the classical Judeo-Christian world view (Jerusalem) and the classical Hellenistic world view (Athens) have much more in common with each other than either of them have with the modern historicist world view. What they had in common was the notion that human history is not the only or even primary level of reality but that it is significant only in the context of an eternal plan or order: for the Jews represented by a more personal and sovereign creator God who had a purpose for history, acted upon and within history, but remained uncontingent; the Greeks signified by a less personal cosmic and eternal ideal, an order of truth and justice.

I expressed some of these same themes somewhat differently in an essay entitled "The Nature and Possibility of a Mennonite Theology," (Chapter 10 above), through the heuristic device of entering into conversation with four Mennonite thinkers, Harold S. Bender, Robert Friedmann, John H. Yoder and Gordon Kaufman. My particular interest there was the relationship of Anabaptist-Mennonite theology to modernity and the basic assumptions of the modern age—especially the assumptions of "freedom" and "historicism."[28] I am not interested in reviving the old modernist debates nor am I concerned with the "slippery slope to modernism," but I am interested in trying seriously to understand the nature of the Enlightenment and the post-Enlightenment world and its presuppositions, the extent to which we have all been shaped by those presuppositions, and whether the crises we are facing in the modern world (particularly the environmental and nuclear crisis) are not in some sense linked intrinsically to those assumptions. At no point in that essay do I suggest, nor do I want to suggest now, that the emancipatory insights of the Enlightenment, the importance of scientific reason and a scholarly commitment to free inquiry and a critical study of the Christian tradition as passed on to us, should be forfeited. But what I am suggesting is that we need to take a serious and critical look at some of the negative aspects of the predominant assumptions of the western post-Enlightenment world and not reject the classical model too quickly.

I was pleased when Howard Loewen, in his response to the above essay, refers to my "classicist orientation."[29] If labelled at all, I would prefer the label "neo-classicist," since what I am interested in is not a simple return to some past age but in looking at new alternatives to the predominantly historicist models of the present. Is it not possible, for instance, "to think in a new way" the radical transcendence of God which is *both* faithful to the classical Christian and doctrinal tradition as passed on to us *and* takes history and historical responsibility seriously? For must not historical action—to be truly responsible—have some ontological and dogmatic basis? Is the biblical confession that "Jesus is Lord" itself not implicitly a metaphysical and ontological statement of some kind?

If this is the case, then the door is open once more to taking seriously the philosophical and theological debates leading up to and including the trinitarian and christological formulations of the first few centuries, for here metaphysical and theological-biblical language were combined in the confrontation between Christianity and pagan culture. Here we have a horizon and a worldview which is not hopelessly out of date— this could be maintained only within a radically historicist perspective in which a past age is seen to have nothing significant to teach us other than showing us how we got from there to here— but one in which battles were fought and concepts formulated that offer alternative models to our present ones in our very similar battle with a "pagan" culture.

The consequence of thinking via the prophetic-eschatological model within the modern historicist context is that it does not adequately illumine the entire realm of human experience, especially what I would call the priestly-sacramental dimension of life, or what David Tracy refers to as the "manifestation" or "disclosure" dimension of religious experience. This means that the eschatological model can by itself never be completely comprehensive. It does not have the power to illumine the "mystical-priestly/metaphysical-aesthetic" aspects of life, to use Tracy's terms.[30] Tracy believes, as I do, that the "prophetic-ethical" and "mystical-aesthetical" both together constitute human religious experience: "That any religion is really *only* mystical-metaphysical or *only* ethical-political seems an illusion produced by some partial vision of the complexity of the whole," he rightly observes.[31] Tracy prefers to use the terms "manifestation" and "proclamation" to express this same polarity. Manifestation is "world-affirming" and proclamation is "world-shattering."[32] Both belong dialectically together: "Manifestation is always the enveloping presupposition of the emergence and, at the limit, the eruption of the defamiliarizing word of proclamation."[33] Manifestation gives us a sense of sacramental participation in the whole. Proclamation is rooted in the sense of alienation from the whole and is committed to the eschatological transformation of reality. In a most important passage, Tracy explains his stance rather persuasively:

> Where the kerygmatic power of the word in sacrament is lost, the distinctively Christian paradigmatic power of proclamation is soon spent and sacrament becomes magic, aesthetics or even mechanics. Yet the opposite danger is equally debilitating to Christianity. If the cosmic and symbolic reality is disallowed, if the paradigmatic power of real manifestation is allowed to slip away quietly under the defamiliarized blows of the paradigmatic power of the proclaimed word, then the

deepest needs of our hearts and imagination are themselves discarded and Christianity eventually retreats into a righteous rigorism of duty and obligation. We are in nature. We are embodied. However ethical our consciences, however committed to time and history our spirits, we rob ourselves and history of their roots when we dare to strip away the power of religious manifestation.[34]

This latter danger is precisely the danger of the radical modern historicist vision and project, and it is also the danger of the non-sacramental and prophetic-ethical tradition of which we Anabaptist-Mennonites are perhaps the leading historical representatives.[35]

In Conversation with the Sacramental Traditions

My proposal, in light of the above, is, therefore, that in trying to develop a self-conscious Mennonite systematic theology, which is both comprehensive and faithful to the critical-prophetic tradition of the left wing of the Reformation, one could take as the key-category or organizing principle eschatology and the kingdom of God, but an eschatology and a view of the kingdom of God freed at least partly from the prevailing historicist perspective of modern theology; an eschatological perspective which is rethought more in classical terms and where there is the possibility of a radical breaking in of transcendent reality, not only socially and corporately but also for the individual in the face of aloneness, suffering, and death.[36] In such a theology there would also be a greater appreciation for that dimension of life and religious experience which I call sacramental, or which Tracy calls "manifestation"—namely, the gracious and "world affirming" aspects of experience.

In an Anabaptist-Mennonite systematic theology the prophetic-eschatological emphasis would be the primary one, and as such the primary conversation partners might legitimately be the so-called theological and political left—the orthopraxis theologians of hope, politics, and liberation; namely, those modern theologians which have been largely influenced by a Marxist or neo-Marxist analysis of society and the critique of ideology. While recognizing that no theology can ever be apolitical or politically neutral, and every theology has an ethical obligation to speak for the oppressed, such a theology would not identify itself *per se* with a particular political party or option.[37] Such a theology would also in its search for comprehensiveness enter into a secondary conversation with the great sacramental traditions represented by the Catholics and Anglicans in the West and the Orthodox in the East. Mennonites can no longer afford the luxury of building *ipso facto* a common front together with one side of the Christian church over against the other side. They can no longer restrict themselves to a conversation with the so-called Free Church or Believers Church tradition to the neglect of the great religious insights of the Catholics, Anglicans, and the Orthodox.

It is interesting that the Anglican theologian Stephen W. Sykes, in his recent book *The Integrity of Anglicanism*, urges Anglicans to develop a self conscious systematic theology, similar in many ways to what I have been proposing here. He uses "systematic theology" and "doctrinal theology" interchangeably and argues that such a discipline would "contribute to a deeper self-understanding and to a more rigorous self-criticism."[38] By "systematic theology," Sykes means "that constructive discipline which presents the substance of the Christian faith with a claim on the minds of men." While it is "only part of the Christian's offering of himself to God," it still is a necessary "intellectual discipline" which ought not to be avoided if the Anglican communion is to overcome its reputation of being "tolerantly receptive to every passing opinion."[39] Sykes asks some pointed questions of the Anglican communion—questions which are the very questions we must ask ourselves as a Mennonite communion:

> Is there an Anglican theology, a proposal which many have denied? Is there an Anglican method in theology, which some have affirmed while denying that there is an Anglican theology? And what in any case is the present state of Anglican study of the doctrine of the church, and why is there so little deliberate cultivation of doctrinal or systematic theology?[40]

Sykes admits that the traditional strength of the Anglican Church has been its latitudinarianism, its comprehensiveness, and the theory of complementarity where tractarians, liberals, and evangelicals could belong to the same communion, bonded together through a common liturgy and the Book of Common Prayer. But he argues that this very comprehensiveness and complementarity must be justified systematically, theologically, and doctrinally.

Sykes is not calling for a return to what once was, nor for a "doctrinaire rigidity" and "intransigent dogmatism,"[41] but for a rational and coherent approach to the theological basis of Anglicanism and to a confessional commitment which has been progressively shed first through controversy between tractarianism, liberalism, and evangelicalism and subsequently more decisively through biblical and historical criticism.[42] Only by means of such a confessional commitment on the part of the laity and the clergy, says Sykes, can Anglicanism recover its integrity and the possibility of self-criticism essential for the health of the church. Self-criticism is truly possible only from within such a confessional and doctrinal commitment.

In Sykes's view, a church must be continually open to reform since "no church is immune from the insidious processions of adaptation to an environment." Further,

> if the Christian church proposes faithfully to preach the gospel, it has no alternative but to launch out into the ambiguities of interaction with its environment, an interaction in which it must keep itself open to criticism, and be ready to change its ways.[43]

Sykes's suggestion that there be not one universally accepted rigid Anglican theological system but rather a plurality of Anglican systematic theologies is particularly appropriate for us as Mennonites. "There *ought*," he says,

> to be Anglican systematic theologies, that is, theologies of high standards of internal consistency written by Anglicans of conviction. No one will expect such theologies to be awarded the accolade of being *the* Anglican systematics, any more than the work of Karl Rahner or of Karl Barth is spoken of as *the* Catholic systematics or *the* Reformed systematics.[44]

This does not mean, in Sykes's view, that there are not some commonly held and generally shared theological values in Anglicanism which give it an integrity and distinguish it from other theological traditions. These include an emphasis on the centrality of the incarnation, a common liturgy and canon law, and particularly the espousal of "dispersed authority," in which it is and should be "maintained in principle that the means of judging matters concerning the faith are in the hands of the whole people of God by reason of their access to the Scripture . . . ."[45] These shared theological beliefs would implicitly find their way into the various systematic theologies within Anglicanism and would provide a common theological, doctrinal, and confessional basis between them.

Much of what Sykes says about Anglicanism applies equally well to Mennonites in the present situation—the need for a coherent and cogently argued systematic and doctrinal theology as an intellectual discipline, the need for a clearer and stronger confessional commitment to give us a rock upon which to stand as we enter into ecumenical conversation and on the basis of which we can become more self-critical, and maintain an internal integrity and consistency in the face of some of the insidious assumptions of the modern age. In another essay, "Doctrinal Renewal and the "Dialectic of Enlightenment'" (Chapter 3 above), I have gone into a much more substantive analysis of Sykes's proposal for Anglican theology and pointed out my fundamental agreement with his call for a recovery and renewal of clear thinking, traditional, if you like, systematic theology for the purpose of clarifying for oneself *what one believes to be true*, of articulating for oneself criteria with which to distinguish between the negative and positive elements of modern culture and check 'institutional drift', of establishing some kind of standpoint from which rational discussion, self-criticism and ecumenical conversation is possible.[46]

I also point out in that essay some of the problem areas in Sykes's proposal, particularly his inadequate understanding of so-called modern "liberalism," his not fully recognized indebtedness to modern Enlightenment assumptions, and his inability to critique the negativities of modern culture as strongly as is necessary. Here, in this context, I simply suggest that as Mennonites seeking to formulate our own systematic theology, Sykes's proposals deserve some serious consideration and can give us fruitful ideas.

One of these fruitful ideas is his suggestion that there be a plurality of systematic theologies coherently, consistently, and comprehensively thought in the service of the particular church tradition of which we are a part as well as the universal church of which we are also a part. Because of the heterogeneous and polygenetic nature of sixteenth-century Anabaptism and of 450 years of Mennonitism, and especially in light of the multiplicity of ethnic, cultural and religious emphases in the contemporary Mennonite church, it seems perfectly in order that we would encourage a variety of comprehensively conceived Anabaptist-Mennonite systematic theologies.

I would also argue, however, that there are some commonly held assumptions that bonded sixteenth-century Anabaptists together and that have bonded Mennonites together since. What these shared elements were and continue to be could be expressed in a variety of ways, but a certain form of ecclesiology, eschatology, and ethics would figure strongly. If, for instance, a distinctive ecclesiology with a distinctive view of baptism, church order, and decision-making procedure were to become a shared principle of a given Mennonite systematic theology, it would, to fulfill the requirement of comprehensiveness, need to view the church not only in terms of the future-oriented and eschatologically conceived community of faith but also as a sacramental community of faith emphasizing the graciousness of the present world and remembering the importance of the past.

The most distinctive trait bonding together these various Mennonite systematic theologies might well be the normative claim of Jesus' ethic of nonviolent love and the "dangerous memory of the historical Jesus."[47] That this would become a shared commitment in all such Mennonite theologies I would welcome. That it become the organizing principle upon which a definitive Mennonite systematic theology be conceived, I would strongly question and even resist, for I am not at all convinced that the moral, ethical, social, and political claims of Jesus of Nazareth, although intrinsic to the gospel, are in themselves an adequate basis or starting point from which to construct a whole systematic theology, one that comprehensively illumines all levels of human religious experience.

My strong conviction is that the three-fold Credo—the trinitarian and christological affirmations of the early church—need to be the basis of all sound comprehensive theological work, whether Mennonite or non-Mennonite. How classical trinitarian thinking remains faithful to the biblical witness and how it can be theologically significant in the modern post-Enlightenment pluralistic context must remain the topic of another essay. All I want to suggest here is that the particular vantage point of Mennonite systematic theology or theologies ought not to be such that it replaces the trinitarian-christological framework of classical theology with some other key-organizing principle, but one which builds upon it and provides a particular reading of the Credo.

THIRTEEN

Mennonite Theological Self-Understanding and Doctrinally Structured Systematic Theology*

A frequently identified aspect of modernity is its anthropocentric turn: the shift from a pre-modern theo-cosmo-centric worldview to a historico-human centred one. Anabaptist-Mennonite theology, in its voluntarism and ethics-centredness, falls prey to this anthropocentric turn when its dogmatic foundations are replaced by psycho-experiential, historicist and political languages.

In this essay, prepared for a conference on "Mennonite Identity" at Conrad Grebel College, May 28-31, 1986, I make the case for a doctrinally structured systematic theology which safeguards a theocentric approach to Mennonite belief and ethics.[1] The social-historical school of Anabaptist studies, which has replaced the Bender "normative vision," is limited methodologically to describing the diversity of Anabaptist origins and Mennonite history. Theology's task, however, is to go beyond pure description to making value judgments between various historical positions.

---

*Originally published as "Mennonite Theological Self-Understanding, the Crisis of Modern Anthropocentricity and the Challenge of the Third Millennium" in *Mennonite Identity: Historical and Contemporary Perspectives*, eds. Calvin Wall Redekop and Samuel J. Steiner (Lanham, MD: University Press of America, 1988), 13-38. For notes on the text see the Notes section below.

Using the insights of social historians like Hans-Jürgen Goertz and historical theologians such as Howard John Loewen, I ask which direction Mennonite theology ought to go in the future. Loewen, in his analysis of Mennonite confessions of faith, has shown how important doctrines have been to the Mennonite community, what these confessions have in common with historical ecumenical creeds, and how they are distinct. What is distinctive is their emphasis on free will, conversion, church discipline, non-resistance and non-conformity; but these distinctives are incorporated into a theologically orthodox, confessional framework. Where Goertz and Loewen agree, despite their very different methodologies, is in identifying the "ethicization of the faith" (Goertz's phrase) that all Anabaptists had in common.

This overriding concern with ethics has continued in the historical Mennonite community, although Goertz laments what he considers the Mennonite compromise of its early Anabaptist ethical radicalism. I argue that this ethical consciousness needs to be preserved but grounded in a classical confessional orthodoxy. In this approach "doctrines" would not be considered as static, literalistic propositions (as in twentieth-century Fundamentalism), but as a dynamic genre mediating between the diversity of biblical texts and the tradition, and the complexity of the contemporary situation. Creation, redemption and consummation would be seen more like theological archetypes based on a trinitarian structure in which the transcendence, historicity, and immanence of God are all preserved.

In this way ethics would be theocentrically grounded, and theology be safeguarded from becoming pure anthropology. Methodologically, systematic theology, unlike the descriptive disciplines (sciences) and other prescriptive disciplines (some social sciences and the humanities), would quite unapologetically presuppose the existence and activity of a transcendent divine reality working within human and cosmic history.

◆ ◆ ◆

What might it mean for Mennonites to think theologically about themselves and the issues facing them within the context of the universal Christian church, as they near the end of the twentieth century and look toward the third millennium? That is the underlying question of this paper. The general anthropocentricity of modern thought and life, beginning with the Renaissance and on through the Reformation and the eighteenth-century Enlightenment to the present, is widely recognized. Also clear is the complexity of the phenomenon called "modernity" and the diversity of opinion about what exactly modernity consists of. There are those who view the modern primarily in terms of the process of secularization (Max Weber et al.). Others argue for the universality and permanence of religion, seeing it as having continuing significance in the modern and postmodern era albeit in altered form

(Emile Durkheim et al.).² This latter position holds that occidental post-Enlightenment developments stand in fundamental continuity with the ancient Christian religious tradition. In both cases, however, there is agreement that what distinguishes the modern from the traditional is the turn from a theocentric way of looking at the world and reality to an anthropocentric orientation.³ My interest here is not in entering that debate but in exploring the possibility of articulating a theocentric theology in an age when "God Himself has become the decisive problem."⁴ This problem is compounded for the Mennonite church which in some sense may itself—especially in its underlying voluntarism, its defence of religious liberty, and the radical autonomy of the secular sphere from the religious realm—have contributed to modernity and thus be strangely linked historically to the demise of more traditional ways of speaking about God and the world.⁵

The modern anthropocentric turn is grounded in certain important views of history and human freedom, the positive significance of which cannot be dismissed by the Christian church without dire consequences for its thought and life.⁶ Nevertheless, the universal Christian community, of which the Mennonite church is admittedly only a small fragment, is today facing serious religious, moral, and social-ethical issues which, while not calling for a simple return to the golden age of the classical past, signify a need for retrieving from the past a theocentric-theological framework for modern anthropology.⁷ The question for us as Mennonites in particular is this: How can we be faithful to our biblical foundations and to our origins in the "radical" left-wing of the Reformation, and at the same time face openly, honestly and realistically our relatively novel present historical situation? In short, how are we to seek creative solutions to the urgent issues that face us now and will no doubt confront us with increasing intensity in the imminent future? My own systematic-theological orientation will become evident as I proceed with an analysis of the so-called "demise of the normative vision," examine two approaches to our historical origins and ongoing Mennonite identity (social-historical and confessional-theological), and offer my own theological proposal in the final section of this paper.

The Demise of the Normative Vision

Any attempt to make synthetic generalizations about Mennonite origins in the sixteenth century, especially by a theologian interested in confessional distinctiveness, in the face of the abundance and diversity of present-day theories about the historical nature and beginnings of Anabaptism, is destined to be discarded as an "ideological distortion" of the past for polemical purposes. This state of affairs has to do with what Werner Packull in a 1979 article called "the demise of a normative vision," referring to the end of a monogenesis understanding of Anabaptism characteristic of the Harold S. Bender school of historiography.[8] Interestingly enough, Bender's own revisionist understanding of the past has itself been seen as replacing an earlier more "doctrinal" perspective. Leonard Gross in his 1986 article, "The Doctrinal Era of the Mennonite Church," for instance, makes the case that the doctrinal period of the (Old) Mennonite church flourished between 1898 and 1928 and came to an end with the death of Daniel Kauffman in 1944.

This doctrinal orientation of Kauffman and friends Gross describes as "ahistorical" and "propositional" in character, having little to do with the integration of "faith and history" and the "warm, traditional...piety" of earlier Mennonite self-understanding.[9] Gross does not hide the fact that he believes the reorientation of Mennonite thinking under Harold S. Bender and his colleagues was a returning "to the way of history and faith as the sum and substance of Christianity...."[10] For Gross doctrinal thinking is a thing of the past: "The concept of 'Doctrine' in the mid-1980s continues to be in descendence, and the traditional Mennonite view of Christianity as faith and history in ascendance."[11]

The weaknesses of a rigid and inflexible doctrinal propositionalism and a one-sided Anabaptist monogenesis understanding of our faith and history need not to be recounted here. There are, however, explicitly recognized assumptions of normativity which distinguish both of these approaches from the more recent social-historical method, which prides itself on attempting to look more honestly at what really happened. The fact is that the social-historical method of studying our past has gained the upper hand. This is attested to by Packull in the above article. According to him, perhaps the most important reason for the demise of Bender's normative concept of mainstream Anabaptism "has been a disenchantment with intellectual history, and the resurgence of liberal, secular interest in the social history of the period.... Although few have forgotten the importance of religious motivation of sixteenth-century phenomena, interest has shifted from theological conceptions and their intellectual or spiritual pedigree to the socio-political function of religious ideas."[12] Packull is fully aware of the "hidden commitments" behind every social-historian's attempt to understand what really happened, and is not as ready as some to deny the validity of 's normative vision or of intellectual history in general, but nevertheless in his own methodology leans to the side of social history.[13]

The thorny question as to what ultimately moves history (ideas or social-historical forces, or a dialectical combination of both) aside, my own discipline as a systematic theologian compels me to ask the normative questions arising out of any study of historical events; namely, how can one move from an honest and fair study of historical facts (the "is") to making moral and religious judgments (the "ought")? The social historian is methodologically committed to a *descriptive* analysis of past and present events. At the points where one attempts to make normative or *prescriptive* judgments as a social historian one ventures out of one's own methodology into another, such as theology or philosophy. To be responsible within the modern matrix one dare not avoid the awesome task of addressing these "ought" questions. Normative positions in the contemporary situation need themselves, however, to be grounded not only in careful biblical exegesis but also in thorough historical analysis both of the Mennonite past and of the present state of affairs. This bridging of the descriptive and prescriptive disciplines seems to me to be the task of systematic theology. How to combine these two methodologies with integrity is of course the difficult task.

In the following pages I examine two approaches to Mennonite origins and ongoing Mennonite existence, both of which are necessary and legitimate if we are to arrive at a sound understanding of sixteenth-century Anabaptism(s) and the historical continuity of the Mennonite tradition(s) in its relation to modernity and in its relation to the universal Christian church. These two approaches I will call the social-historical and the confessional-theological. In both cases I am particularly interested in the relationship between our Mennonite origins and the rise of the modern anthropocentric spirit. In the final section of the paper, I will propose a way of looking at "doctrinal" or "confessional" theological thinking which is not rigid and inflexible but which might be considered afresh as a way of dealing creatively with some of the issues facing us.

Hans-Jürgen Goertz: A Social-Historical Perspective

The essay I will take as representative of the social-historical approach to the study of Mennonite origins is Hans-Jürgen Goertz's recent article "Das Täufertum—ein Weg in die Moderne?" As the title suggests, Goertz is interested primarily in the historical link between Anabaptism and modernity. After giving a brief survey of the question as addressed by a variety of modern historians and theologians, Goertz proceeds to offer his own analysis and proposal. He begins by reviewing the main points at which the traditional picture of Anabaptism has undergone revision. First, Anabaptism has come to be seen as a heterogeneous movement differentiated geographically, socially, and theologically. Second, Anabaptism has come to be recognized not only or even primarily as an ecclesiastical-religious phenomenon but as a social-political one which in both its militant-revolutionary and its peaceful variety was linked to the concerns of the "common person" (*des gemeinen Mannes*). Third, the Anabaptist vision of reform was not clearly defined from the start but evolved gradually within the context of the changing fate of peasant social unrest. Initially, for instance, the Swiss radicals envisioned some kind of "folk-church" (or "territorial Anabaptism" as it is occasionally referred to) and only in time did it evolve into a separatist peaceful-church-concept as represented most clearly by the Schleitheim consensus. Finally, while there were without a doubt some common elements uniting the various groups—particularly the espousal of confessional or believers' baptism—the theological grounds for these common aspects were so diverse that "the picture of diversity is greater than that of unity."[14] It is this diversity which makes the question concerning the relation of Anabaptism to modernity so difficult to answer.

What complicates the issue even more are the different perspectives on "modernity." Modernity can be understood from the perspective of the *history of ideas* (the rise of modern subjectivity during and after the Enlightenment), *political history* (the rise of capitalism, the republic, civil society, and social-political equality), *theological history* (the changing role of the institutional church in modern society with respect to confessional pluralism, secularization, and the separation of church and state).[15] Problematic also is "the way" in which Anabaptism might be seen to be linked to modernity. Did Anabaptism simply contain certain elements which anticipated the modern spirit but which were then later taken over and actualized by more powerful modern movements? Or did Anabaptism itself actually contribute to the rise of modernity in the sense of some historical continuity?

Despite the complexities involved, Goertz does think a positive link can be demonstrated to exist between sixteenth-century Anabaptism and modernity, and he proposes to show it by using the social-historical method. Only through this method, he thinks, can we derive one general concept of the movement without denying its heterogeneous nature. The key for Goertz is to understand all the different forms of early Anabaptism in the light not primarily of their theological distinctiveness *vis-à-vis* other Reformation groups (as for example in their deviation from Luther's doctrine of justification) but in terms of the general anti-clericalism of the period in which they participated, and in their identification with the concerns of the "common person" and the Peasants' Struggle against feudal hierarchical society. In fact, he suggests that the more traditional understanding that "Anabaptism arose 'in, with, and under the Reformation'" might be reformulated as "Anabaptism arose 'in, with, and under the Peasants'

War.'"¹⁶ This social-historical hermeneutical key, Goertz thinks, aids us in unlocking the common impulse behind the mystical-apocalyptical piety of Hans Hut, the territorial reform vision of the earliest Swiss radicals, the dualistic separatism of the Schleitheim group, and the distinctive Anabaptism of the Dutch Brethren in both its Melchiorite-Münster and later peaceful varieties. At the heart of all early Anabaptist groups was this anti-clerical energy of the laity. It is in its identification with the rising consciousness of the general population, that Anabaptism can be seen as having something to do with the rise of modernity.

Goertz is careful not to disregard the theological framework within which the anti-clericalism of Anabaptism found its expression, but clearly for him the social forces at work are the determinative ones. In his concluding section he emphasizes how intimately the theological and social-historical factors were connected in the Anabaptist struggle on behalf of the "common person" and as such for the modern. In their anti-clericalism the Anabaptists stood firmly on the side of modern egalitarian society over against the old feudal tiered society. While the contours of modern civil society took definite shape only a century later, the Anabaptists contributed to the coming society through their non-conformity to their contemporary society, and their search for communities faithful to God and primitive Christianity. To what an extent Anabaptist anti-clericalism sided with the process of secularization itself—or the laicization of cultural and political life—is debatable, since amongst some early Anabaptists the protest against priests took the form not of secularization but of the "clericalization of the laity," while amongst others (Swiss separatists) the process of secularization, although not hindered by this dualism, would have been perceived as a demonic rather than a desirable development.

Theologically, the Anabaptists did not share Luther's pessimism concerning human nature and believed in the possibility of a genuine life of discipleship in which the rule of sin could be progressively overcome, something akin to the Enlightenment notion of human perfectibility and the modern notions of religious and moral individuality. In short, the Anabaptist espoused the "ethicization of faith" rather than the Lutheran dialectic of *"simul justus et peccator."* This ethicization of faith, which admittedly took on different forms in Anabaptism, humanistic piety, Calvinism, English Puritanism, eighteenth-century pietism, and the moral perception of religion in the Enlightenment, ended historically with the "separation of Christianity from general morality ... an essential mark of the modern spirit."¹⁷ Even more important, however, Anabaptism played a significant role in the struggle against territorial feudalism through its unique concept of the communal church or congregation as the locus for the full and free participation of the "common person." The diversity of forms by which the different Anabaptist groups expressed this religious communalism itself testifies to their link with modern pluralism.

Although the Anabaptists may not have had a clearly defined goal in their struggle for the modern, and while their communalism which they identified with primitive Christianity may not have been adhered to consistently, on the whole one can in retrospect, according to Goertz, judge the Anabaptists to have moved significantly in the direction of modern republican and democratic communities. The groups that survived—the Swiss Brethren, the Hutterian Brotherhoods, and the Dutch Mennonite congregations—were those which were able to give the communalistic ideal its strictest organizational structure. But it is this very separate institutional consolidation that Goertz suggests led to the betrayal of the movement's initial potency: "And yet the more these communities distanced themselves from their origin in the anticlerical communal struggle of the early Reformation period, the more they lost their connection with the complicated developmental process of the modern and shrivelled up into an anachronism."[18] In its tendency toward the community of goods Anabaptism contained within itself an element that functioned as a bulwark against the possessive individualism of modern civil society which could have contributed to moving modern bourgeois society self-critically toward a more radical-democratic human community—that is, presumably, if it had not become a sectarian institutional anachronism.

Here we have a social-historian's perspective on Anabaptism origins. I have taken considerable space outlining Goertz's analysis and conclusions because 1) I believe his to be the kind of social history of the sixteenth century that has prevailed in recent decades replacing not only the normative Anabaptist history of the Bender type (with which, incidentally, it may have more in common than might first appear),[19] but a much longer tradition of intellectual and theological history; and 2) this essay summarizes some of the best and most recent insights into the social, cultural, and political undercurrents of sixteenth-century Anabaptism, insights which can no longer be ignored by the theologian who is serious about connecting ideas with real life and is aware of the importance of the "sociology of knowledge" for one's discipline. Of particular importance in my view is the honest recognition of the heterogeneity of early Anabaptism (socially and theologically), its developing self-identity, and its fundamental connection with the modern egalitarian and voluntaristic spirit.

Nevertheless, the social-historical approach is but one means of understanding historical events and not necessarily the most definitive one. It cannot adequately address from within its own discipline the normative questions of history. A diversity of methods, including other-than-social-scientific approaches, must be employed if one is to take seriously human freedom and moral responsibility, and not reduce history to some form of causal necessity. Underneath Goertz's descriptive analysis there is *also* a normative assumption—namely, the rightness or desirability of the modern egalitarian-democratic-communal vision. But on what grounds is this assumption to be defended? I am not denying the preferability of this vision over others at this point, even though it may very well be asked whether the anthropocentricism, which has accompanied the egalitarian and Enlightenment assumptions of modern thought and life, is one which we can afford to continue to legitimate without some major modifications in respect of the modern historicist and scientific crisis.[20]

At the point where one encounters the normative and "truth-claim" questions of history the social-historian, despite the indispensability of his descriptive analysis, comes up against the limitations of his own discipline. Here he must come to terms with the theologian as representative of another more prescriptive discipline, one which is concerned with making value judgments about historical events, human beliefs, and actions. Some notion of the division of labour and the diversity of tasks between the sociologist, the historian, and the theologian even as applied to the study of our historical origins, is necessary.

The Mennonite theologian, for instance, is interested not only in the fact of diversity within early Anabaptism but in making a judgment about which of these various groups had the "right" or "better" or "truer" understanding of the essence of Christianity and the nature of the Christian church, and whether or not it found ongoing Mennonite institutional expression. For that a careful *theological* analysis of the theological differences between various Reformation groups and figures, as recently exemplified by J. Denny Weaver in his comparison of the theologies of Martin Bucer, Michael Sattler, and Hans Denck, is invaluable.[21] But an historical-theological methodology is also not adequate in itself. The Mennonite systematic theologian is concerned with the imperatives of the present situation and how some kind of "ought" can be recognized within the diversity of the past as having relevance for the present and future.

These are *systematic theological* questions which call for more than what a purely historical analysis can offer. What is required is a "normative sensitivity" to our past, present, and future which is fully appreciative of critical historical insights but also dares to make moral, religious, and theological judgments. The doctrinal and confessional genre of theological thinking and church life and piety is not a foreign element that temporarily distorted our Mennonite view of faith and history, as Leonard Gross appears to suggest, but is a long-standing and integral part of our heritage. A look at our past from such a doctrinal-confessional perspective, as illustrated by Howard J. Loewen in his recent book, *One Lord, One Church, One Hope, and One God: Mennonite Confessions of Faith*,[22] can aid the Mennonite systematic theologian and the Mennonite church in general in addressing the normative questions of today.

Howard J. Loewen: A Theological-Confessional Approach

Much has been made of the "non-creedal" nature of the Believers Church tradition, including the Anabaptists of the sixteenth century and the Mennonite church up to the present. While there is a fundamental truth to this observation about our "low church" heritage, it tends to overlook the definite confessional, catechetical, doctrinal, and even creedal elements in our past which in many ways resemble the classical model of the creeds. It is in fact these elements which give us as a Mennonite community a continuity throughout our own history and with the universal Christian church through the centuries. In the final section of this paper I argue for the necessity of a continuing confessional-doctrinal orientation. Here I look at how the doctrinal dimension has always been historically a part of our thought and life from the beginning, a dimension that can all too easily be under-valued by the social historian. To see this doctrinal side of our past as significant and as a window through which certain aspects of our distinctiveness and commonality with other Reformation groups can be understood, not to mention our link with modern assumptions about God and the world, is to recognize the importance of intellectual history in the movement of history.

In his introduction to *Three Reformation Catechisms: Catholic, Anabaptism, Lutheran*, Denis Janz, fully recognizing the complexity facing the modern student of the Reformation period, especially in regard to the relation of religious ideas to religious movements, argues that "catechisms also are windows through which one can view lay religious consciousness of an age" and the "[c]atechisms mediate, as it were, between the religious consciousness of the masses and the theological speculation of the elite ... documents which tend to bridge the gap between religion as it is practised and religion as it is speculated upon by theologians."[23] According to Janz, "[t]he catechisms of this era help us to understand why, in a relatively short period of time, masses of people cast aside religious values and practices sanctioned by centuries of tradition in favour of new ones."[24]

One may fault Janz for not taking seriously enough the social factors at work in determining religious ideas. Nevertheless, in his comparison of three Reformation catechisms he does provide a persuasive additional method of studying religious movements which has relevance for us today. Kolde's late medieval Catholic catechism of 1470, which "went through nineteen editions before 1500 and at least twenty-eight more editions thereafter . . . [and was] translated into various European vernaculars," Balthasar Hubmaier's 1527 catechism, which in its "question and answer format makes his work more recognizable as a catechism in the modern sense," and Luther's *Small Catechism* of 1529, which "is often seen as the beginning of catechism in the modern sense because of the enormous influence it had on all subsequent catechisms, both Protestant and Catholic," in their differences "reflect the fragmentation of Christianity and the birth of the modern world," and in "their common elements can perhaps today, after centuries of strife, be seen as a basis for increasing unity among Christians."[25]

These catechisms are windows not only into the lay piety of a fixed period of time but also into the Reformation as a transitional moment in Western intellectual history. Confessional and catechetical statements represent the movement and development of ideas within history, and all three of the above catechisms reflect to a greater or lesser degree the transition from a classical to a modern theology and anthropology. Most striking is the movement from the late medieval Catholic preoccupation with sin and confession, the sacrament of penance and the anxiety over "perfect confession" and eternal salvation, to the emphasis in both Hubmaier's and Luther's catechism on *certitude*. For Hubmaier this certitude is rooted in the possibility of a "living faith" in which the rule of sin is progressively overcome, producing "works of mercy," whereas for Luther certainty is grounded in a humble trust in God's objective and gracious work in Christ.

With this emphasis on individual certitude and morality, ethics and the freedom of the human will to strive toward relative perfection in this life, the Anabaptist Hubmaier reflects general Anabaptist assumptions and anticipates the modern preoccupation with self-confident human action. At the same time the obvious respect for the Apostolic creedal tradition which is implicit even in Hubmaier's catechism prevents his theology from becoming anthropocentric in the modern sense.[26] Other Anabaptist writers—particularly Menno Simons and Peter Riedemann—similarly see the call for genuine repentance, moral regeneration, and the new life in Christ within a trinitarian-confessional framework.[27]

On the whole, therefore, it is largely accurate to say with John C. Wenger that "[o]n the great doctrines of God, Christ, the Holy Spirit, the Trinity, depravity and sin, regeneration, holiness of life, grace, and eschatology, the Brethren held common views with the Protestant bodies."[28] It was in their ethical interpretation of each of these, however, that they helped move Western theology in a new direction.[29] This led in time to a reinterpretation of classical doctrines more in line with modern anthropocentric orientations. One might go so far as to suggest that the Anabaptists contributed to the de-hellenization of classical Christian doctrines.

This doctrinal-confessional framework for Mennonite thought and life has existed with few interruptions until recently, a fact which has been well documented by Howard J. Loewen's valuable study, *One Lord, One Church, One Hope, and One God: Mennonite Confessions of Faith*. In the words of Loewen, "Mennonite theology today cannot be done only in light of the twentieth-century Anabaptist vision of the origins of our tradition; it must also be done in the light of the twentieth-century Anabaptist vision of the ongoing confessional and theological development of a common tradition."[30] Loewen is right when he claims that because of the importance both of the study of origins and the ongoing development "one is not necessarily forced to choose between a monogenesis or a polygenesis approach to Anabaptist studies but to transcend it and to affirm a genuine diversity of visions within a real unity that exists in Mennonite origins as well as in the development of this tradition."[31] This approach, he rightly states, can give us a starting point for working toward a theological position in the present which takes ecumenicity seriously both within the Mennonite community and between Mennonites and other Christian traditions.

What is surprising is the number and diversity of confessions that have been produced by Mennonites throughout their history, and the fact that despite this diversity there is an underlying unity bearing some remarkable similarities to the classical ecumenical creeds. In his foreword to Loewen's book, C. J. Dyck distinguishes between "creeds" and "confessions"—the former tending to "denote timeless, classic and universal statements" and the latter being "more particularistic, personal, and occasional, that is, written for a specific purpose at a particular time and place."[32] According to Dyck, "[i]t is generally true that the Anabaptists and later Mennonites have been and are non-creedal." For this reason it comes somewhat as a surprise "to find that the Anabaptists and especially the Dutch Mennonites wrote many confessions . . . probably more than any of the other three Reformation traditions."[33]

What makes Mennonite confessions unique is their diversity within a common tradition. Noteworthy is that Loewen accounts for both the heterogeneity and the unity of the Mennonite tradition through a theological-confessional analysis as well as Goertz does through his social-historical approach. All of the North American confessions—conservative, progressive, and independent—belong to a single family tree rooted in the Dutch Mennonite tradition. The Dordrecht Confession of 1632 functions as "[t]he mother among Mennonite confessions" of North America.[34] Further, the Mennonite confessions of North America grew out of two distinct cultures—North America and Europe. The European confessions on which the North American confessions depend are characterized by "deep Anabaptist roots and a clear Anabaptist orientation in their theology...."[35] Out of this one family tree and these two cultures grow three separate traditions: "the hegemony of the Dordrecht-MC [Mennonite Church] tradition," "the diversity of the Ris-GC [General Conference Mennonite] tradition," and "the stability of the Russian-MB [Mennonite Brethren] tradition."[36] A group of independent confessions by other small Mennonite groups or individuals makes up a fourth branch. Finally, Loewen examines the rich diversity of Mennonite confessions in terms of four periods: "The Confessional Period: The Period of European Origination (1600s-1800s); The Transitional Period: The Period of North American Transition (1700s-1900s); The Ideological Period: The Period of Fundamentalist Tension (1920s-50s);" and what he calls "The Ecumenical Period: The Period of Anabaptist Reorientation (1960s-80s)."[37] Although one wishes that Loewen could have provided readers with a more extensive introduction to and analysis of the historical matrix which gave rise to each of the confessions he deals with— a task which remains to be done, it becomes clear from his brief historical categorization that the various confessions within the Mennonite community cannot be abstracted from their social-historical contexts.[38]

Most significant is Loewen's theological analysis of the North American confessions, in which he compares them structurally, doctrinally, and confessionally. Of structural importance is the unusually high view of Scripture that is evident throughout all the confessions, particularly of certain New Testament texts, pointing, in the words of Loewen, "to commonality among the various confessions and to something like a canon within the canon in the way the Mennonite confessions use Scripture."[39] In general, Matthew is the most preferred book, with Matthew 5 (the Sermon on the Mount) receiving the most attention, and within this chapter the section dealing with loving one's enemies (vv. 43-48) being emphasized by a margin of nearly three to one.[40] This ethical core that Loewen finds in all of North American Mennonite confessions clearly links the ongoing confessional thinking of Mennonites with what Goertz in his social-historical analysis calls the "ethicization of faith" characterizing all sixteenth-century Anabaptist groups, and what Denny Weaver sees as the *intrinsic* connection between faith and ethics that defined both Hans Denck's and Michael Sattler's theology.[41]

This ethical centre is evident also in some of the distinctive doctrines emphasized in the Mennonite confessions of North America. While there is, according to Loewen, a rather uniform progression of doctrines following largely the classical model of theology, there are certain distinctive emphases not present in the classical creeds and confessions: "free will, conversion, footwashing, church discipline, Christian life and nonconformity, integrity and oaths, nonresistance and revenge, and the Christian state."[42] This ethical orientation, however, is placed within the framework of the natural progression of articles largely following the classical model of theology: Triune God and Creation, Word of God and Revelation, Jesus Christ and Redemption, Holy Spirit and Transformation, Human Nature and Salvation, Church of Christ and Missions, Eternal Hope and Resurrection.

Collectively, North American confessions revolve around four axes, each with a common focus: Creator, Christ, Church, and Consummation. What distinguishes the Mennonite confessional statements from the classical model is that, generally speaking, the christology implicit in the various doctrinal formulations is more soteriologically than metaphysically oriented, the doctrine of the Holy Spirit is not pronounced, and free will receives special attention in at least seven confessions. "This [latter] distinction of Mennonite confessions stresses the importance of the limited but real freedom of wo/man after the fall. Wo/man is accountable for both the fall into sin and the faithfulness in redemption."[43] In light of the fact that the issue of the freedom and bondage of the human will was of central importance in the theological debates of the Reformation period, this Anabaptist-Mennonite confessional espousal of "free will" is highly significant, and once again, in my view, links the Mennonite tradition to modern assumptions about human freedom. What distinguishes the Mennonite confessional anthropology from modern anthropocentricism is the theological framework within which it is couched. When this theological-confessional framework is given up, the ethical core loses its theocentric ground. According to Loewen,

> ... the confessional and consistent centre of these confessions revolves most singularly around ecclesiology and mission, with the focus on the inner life of the church's mission (its marks, membership, offices, mission, ordinances, marriage, and discipline) and the outer life of the Christian's discipleship (nonconformity and discipleship, integrity and oath, nonresistance and revenge, Christian and the state, and the Lord's day).[44]

Only a strong theocentric context along classical lines—assumed, I believe, in all traditional Mennonite confessions—keeps this ethical core that is undeniably present in the Mennonite concept of the church from being autonomous historical human action.

Unfortunately, Loewen's book does not give us any of the Anabaptist confessions of the sixteenth century (except the Schleitheim Confession of 1527) that might aid us in seeing the development of doctrine and beliefs that occurred within the first century of the movement. Nevertheless, it is rather remarkable how well Goertz's social-historical analysis and conclusions (particularly his emphasis on the diversity and unity of Anabaptist origins, the "ethicization of faith" common to early Anabaptists, and the fundamental link between the Anabaptist identification with the "common person" and modern egalitarian-democratic principles) dove-tail with the conclusions one can draw from an examination of the various Mennonite confessions through the centuries from a theological and intellectual-history approach.

A Proposal: Doctrinal Thinking as a Theocentric Genre of Theological Thinking

Having examined two approaches to a study of our origins and ongoing historical existence as a Mennonite church—the social-historical and the theological-confessional—I now look at what might be termed theology proper, usually referred to as systematic theology as distinct from biblical theology, historical theology, and practical theology. While systematic theology has more in common methodologically with Loewen's historical-theological study of Mennonite confessions than with Goertz's social-historical analysis, the task of the systematic theologian is to build on the *descriptive* and *analytical* insights of both approaches and then to go from there to address synthetically the *prescriptive* and *normative* questions facing us today.

To think theologically is methodologically distinct although by no means isolated from thinking sociologically, psychologically, politically, and socio-historically. What is distinctive about a Christian-theological approach is that it methodologically presupposes the existence and dynamic activity of a transcendent God upon and within human and cosmic history. How this existence and dynamic presence of God is to be understood in the contemporary situation requires an ongoing conversation with a) the biblical sources, b) the church "fathers," c) the Christian tradition(s) of the past two millennia, and d) the various disciplines that shed light on the human situation. Of course, no single theologian can engage in a comprehensive conversation with all of these spheres. Some division of labour is required.[45] Further, this theological thinking cannot be done adequately by single theologians, but in order for it truly to reflect the broad range of human experience and insight it needs to take place within the community of faith. This is especially important for the Mennonite church, which stands in the Believers

Church tradition in placing a high (possibly too high) value on a "congregational hermeneutic."[46]

When attempting to answer the question of what it might mean to think theologically as distinct from other forms of thinking, it is important to remember the principle of *diversity* and *unity* that characterizes both our sixteenth-century origins, as we have looked at them through Goertz's eyes, and our ongoing historical, theological-confessional existence as we have examined it through Loewen's study.

For Goertz the unifying factor in the otherwise heterogeneous movement of sixteenth-century Anabaptism is the common identification with the "common person" and the "ethicization of faith," characteristics which intrinsically link our origins to the spirit of the modern world. For Loewen, Mennonite confessions throughout the ages, despite their diversity, are united in their unusually high view of Scripture, more specifically their espousal of a "canon within a canon" which gives all the confessions an ethical core reflected especially in their common ecclesiological centre.

Noteworthy in Loewen's study is the fact that the strong ethical orientation of Mennonite confessions does not overshadow or replace the classical doctrines of the Christian church but is incorporated into the classical model. It is precisely this larger classical-doctrinal framework for our ethical distinctives as a Mennonite church which needs to be retained in the present situation if we are to see ourselves as remaining faithful to our own ongoing tradition and part of the universal Christian church.

This doctrinal-type of thinking has, however, for various reasons suffered a serious decline in the Mennonite church in recent decades. Leonard Gross is therefore correct when he says that, "[t]he concept of 'Doctrine' in the mid-1980s continues to be in descendence, and the traditional Mennonite view of Christianity as faith and history, in ascendance."[47] I disagree, however, with Gross's implicit negative valuation of doctrinal thinking as such and with his assertion that "[t]he doctrinal era in the history of the (Old) Mennonite church was a unique epoch of almost a half century, 1898 to 1944."[48]

Although the particular understanding and exposition of doctrine by Kauffman and his colleagues in the first quarter of the twentieth century may have been unique, especially as it was shaped by the Fundamentalist-Modernist debates, doctrinal thinking as such has not been alien at all to the Mennonite confessions. That recently there has been a decline in doctrinal-type thinking, however, cannot be denied. In my own initiation into the Altona Bergthaler Mennonite Church I was still systematically taken through the Catechism first published in 1783, at Elbing, Prussia, a German-English version which was printed by the Evangelical Mennonite Church (*Kleine Gemeinde*) in 1954.[49] My baptism into the Mennonite church was premised at least partly on a clear knowledge of the essential classical doctrines of the Christian faith. To my knowledge, this particular form of catechetical instruction has been largely replaced by other types of preparatory theological education for baptismal candidates. What this transition from a doctrinal-catechetical orientation to other modes of theological education in the churches means for us needs serious scrutiny.

What are these newer modes of thinking and understanding that have replaced the doctrinal orientation? It is not my purpose here to scrutinize these various new modes shaping our theological identity, other than to mention what I consider to be four distinct non-doctrinal orientations prevalent in the Mennonite church today: the clinical-pastoral, the social-political, the historical-developmental, and the literal-propositional. This rather simplistic classification can be no more than a caricature, and is not meant to stereotype unfairly any individual movement, let alone branch of the Mennonite church as it exists in the present situation. I am using these categories simply as "ideal types" which I think help to illuminate four distinctive groupings, all of which have a substantial following and accompanying literature within the contemporary Mennonite community.

The *clinical-pastoral* orientation, employing insights and techniques from the various schools of psychology and therapy, concentrates on addressing the *existential-priestly* dimensions of religious experience and the Christian gospel.[50] The *social-political* orientation is quite distinct from the clinical-pastoral approach, in that rather than concentrating on individual existential concerns (anger, anxiety, doubt, despair, guilt, forgiveness, acceptance, self-worth, human potential, etc.) it focuses on the *prophetic-eschatological* aspects of the Christian proclamation in its concern for social, economic, and political justice.[51] The third and fourth types, which I have called here the *historical-developmental* and the *literal-propositional* orientations respectively, have perhaps become most clearly manifest in a series of conferences in the General Conference Mennonite Church at Camp Wonderland, Camp Lake, Wisconsin, and in the Mennonite Church at Laurelville, Pennsylvania, on biblical hermeneutics and related topics.[52] The *historical-developmental* orientation, using all the most recent tools of the historical-critical and historical-contextual methods of biblical interpretation, tends to emphasize the *historical, temporal, changing,* and *this-worldly* nature of God's revelation in Christ as interpreted in ever new and creative ways by the people of God.[53] The *literal-propositional* orientation, highly suspicious of the historical-critical and scientific method of contextualizing the biblical revelation, is concerned to safeguard the *eternal, unchanging truths* of Scripture, which it says must be directly and literally accepted as applying to all ages and all issues the church faces in the contemporary situation.[54] One could perhaps add a fifth type of orientation, the *mystical-pious*, which is content to read the Bible devotionally and live out the Christian life faithfully and prayerfully to the best of one's ability without any deliberate or conscious analytical, historical, political, or psychological reflection.

Remembering the diversity of our origins and our history, this diversity of orientations within the Mennonite community needs to be welcomed, each one of them embodying essential aspects of the Christian faith and offering important contributions to our understanding of the Christian church in the modern world. Nevertheless, there is one obvious deficiency in all of these orientations, with the possible exception of the fourth one; namely, their inattention to the doctrinal, confessional and creedal aspect of the New Testament witness and the Christian heritage. It is this doctrinal orientation which acts as a bulwark against the reduction of the Christian *kerygma* to psychological-existential, social-political, historical-developmental, literal-propositional, or intuitive-mystical understandings. This is where the so-called "conservative" wing of the Mennonite church, in its emphasis on "sound doctrine," has a particularly valuable contribution to make. The inadequacy of the literal-propositional orientation is that doctrine is too narrowly and rigidly conceived as standing over against the other orientations and does not fully recognize the universality and creative-dynamic quality of the early creedal-confessional tradition.[55]

It is noteworthy how in certain periods of church history the interest in creedal, doctrinal, and confessional formulations is revived. One thinks here not only of the Patristic period of classical orthodoxy (Nicea, Constantinople, and Chalcedon), and of sixteenth and seventeenth-century Protestant orthodoxy, but also more recently of the early period of the German Church Struggle and the Barmen Declaration of 1934, in which the Confessing Church declared a position of orthodoxy over against the "heresies" of the so-called "German Christians" who supported Hitler and the National Socialist revolution from within the newly established German Evangelical Church, and who wanted to apply Nazi state policies to the church. In each of these periods the church or parts of the church were moved to consolidate their views on what they perceived to be true or "right" belief over against distortions of the faith. Some Christians feel that we are today again living in a state of crisis calling for new confessions of faith [*status confessionis*]. It is significant that certain segments of the Mennonite church as well are expressing renewed interest in confessional and doctrinal thinking.

Within the Dutch Mennonite church, sometimes considered to be representative of the most liberal and non-dogmatic wing of the historical Mennonite tradition, Sjouke Voolstra, professor at the Mennonite Seminary in Amsterdam, has recently called for a new confession of faith among Dutch Mennonites. Describing the initial non-conformist and persecuted Mennonites of the Netherlands as a confessional people for whom "the written confessions of faith originally served as a way of giving account of one's faith before the government, the state church and each other, with the purpose of settling differences," he decries the "aversion to confessions of faith" that began "in the second half of the eighteenth century and is elevated to a virtue after the institutionalization of the United Brotherhood (*Algemene Doopsgezinde Sociëteit* in 1911), in a gradual process of coordination with liberal Protestantism to this day." According to Voolstra,

> Now is the time to formulate a policy with an eye to the future, using all the available sources. And the starting point for that policy can be none other than a new confession of faith. Not a confession of faith that takes the place of Scripture itself, but which invites a constant scrutiny of our practice on the basis of intensive reading and interpretation of Scripture. No stick to beat with, but a staff to walk with. Not formulation with an eternal value, but a program with the points of faith upon which the Mennonites want to concentrate. Not separated from ecumenism, but precisely to strengthen our particular contribution in the cooperation of churches.[56]

Voolstra's urgent appeal to Mennonites to once again formulate confessions of faith in the modern context has much to say for itself, and my own proposal stands in line with Voolstra's concerns at many points. However, to keep Voolstra's and my appeal from falling on deaf ears, it is imperative that we take seriously the reasons for the modern eclipse of doctrine in favour of non-doctrinally oriented modes of expressing the Christian faith. Rightly or wrongly, doctrinal thinking has been perceived as the abstract and doctrinaire petrification of certain dogmas with little sensitivity to changing times and the concrete, existential, social-political, and historical realities of human existence. In order for doctrinal thinking to have any meaning whatever in the modern "historicist" and "anthropocentric" context, the very notion of doctrine as such must be not so much reconceived as understood as it originally functioned and ought to function today.

What is particularly significant about the early ecumenical creeds is not so much the specific terminology and formulations with which they attempted to express Christian belief (although these also are remarkable for their enduring power and truth) but the very notion of the development of doctrine or belief itself. This developmental nature of belief within the New Testament church and the Patristic period is intrinsic to a genuine doctrinal way of dealing with the ongoing exigencies of the life of the church in the world. Doctrine in the early period of Christian history is precisely a way of handling new issues as they confronted second, third, fourth, and subsequent generations of Christians in new social and historical situations.

I am proposing that "doctrinal-confessional-creedal" thinking be considered a *genre* which, while having parallels in other disciplines, has some unique attributes in Christian thought and life. As a genre it is a *way* or *mode* of expressing the essentials of the Christian faith in a creative and dynamic way rather than a set of petrified dogmas. Thus, the confessional formulas of the New Testament, the creedal statements of the early church, as well as the post-Reformation confessions of the various Protestant groups and denominations need to be taken seriously not only for the specific "dogmas" they express but their fundamental structures, affirmations and negations. The obvious *lacunae* in the early creedal tradition, as pointed to again most recently by Thomas Finger, do not therefore speak against creedal-doctrinal thinking as such but against the verbal absolutizing of the particular doctrinal expression at a given historical moment in the life of the church.[57]

Doctrines ought to be conceived as "mediating principles" somewhat akin to the "middle axioms" espoused by John Howard Yoder in his still highly important book, *The Christian Witness to the State*.[58] But instead of mediating simply between church and state, doctrines help us mediate between the multiplicity of texts within the canon, on the one hand, and between the manifold biblical material and the complexity of the contemporary situation, on the other.

As Mennonites who have tendencies toward biblicism—that is, the desire to be literally faithful to the biblical texts as such—we run into severe difficulties when new situations arise in the life of the church and when we are confronted either with a set of seemingly conflicting biblical texts on a given subject or find no texts at all which speak directly to the issues facing us. What we need are mediating principles, like doctrines, which help us find some overarching unity in the biblical material and enable us to move beyond the biblical text in the particulars while still remaining faithful to the biblical narrative as a whole.

This is precisely what doctrines are meant to do. Doctrines are theological archetypes, not that dissimilar from the literary archetypes used in literary criticism (prominent especially in the works of Northrop Frye),[59] that seek through analogical language to express the universal truths of the Christian faith while at the same time recognizing the fact of the meaningfulness of historical process.

What are these universal Christian truths? Along the lines of Henry Vander Goot's proposal outlined in his book, *Interpreting the Bible in Theology and the Church*, I would suggest that the underlying schema of the biblical narrative from Genesis to Revelation is that of creation, fall-redemption, and consummation.[60] These are the fundamental doctrines which serve as a kind of umbrella for all the other doctrines. It is within this—what in effect represents the "trinitarian" structure of the biblical materials as viewed from the Christian perspective—that the earliest New Testament confession "Jesus is Lord" takes on its universal meaning. It is this three-fold emphasis which gives shape to the three articles of the classical ecumenical creeds and which, I would argue, also lies at the heart of the four-fold axes of European and North American Mennonite confessions as identified by Howard Loewen. This trinitarian framework is not simply a human construct imposed arbitrarily on the biblical narrative, but grows inductively out of the canon when viewed as a whole. While not explicitly and formally expressed in the New Testament as it was to occur later at Nicea and Constantinople, it is still implicitly present in the earliest New Testament *kerygma* as evident particularly in the first sermon of Peter in Acts 2.[61] Further, this trinitarian schema is not purely an abstract intellectual formula but is confessional in nature, part of the corporate worship, liturgy, prayer, and daily life of the early Christian community.

What is distinctive about such a trinitarian-doctrinal approach is that it is fundamentally theocentric. The anthropology implicit in this way of looking at reality—namely, our view of human origins, human nature and "human potential (salvation, happiness, and fulfilment)"—is understood in the light of God's own three-fold way of being and action in relation to the world. The doctrines of creation, providence, and preservation of the world are interpreted in the light of God's unconditional *freedom* and *transcendence*. The doctrines of incarnation, atonement, and redemption are viewed in light of God's definitive *historical* revelation in and action through a particular person, Jesus of Nazareth, seen as the Christ. The doctrines of the church and eschatology are explicated in terms of God's *immanent presence* and dynamic activity within the ongoing life of the world as it moves toward its consummation in the future. It is this three-fold analogical way of speaking about God—transcendence, historicity, and immanence—that is reflected in the early doctrinal-creedal formulations and that needs once more to be thought and believed and acted upon in the modern world, which tends either to push God deistically out of this world altogether (thus secularizing the world), or historically to bind God to a one-dimensional historical expression of himself (a form of idolatry), or pantheistically to reduce God to the life-forces and immanent processes of the natural world (thereby sacralizing the natural world). Within this trinitarian understanding of God, the classical ontological truths, the Enlightenment historical-anthropological truths, and the modern evolutionary-developmental truths can be brought together. While taking seriously the historical, anthropological and developmental insights of Enlightenment and post-Enlightenment thought, this trinitarian perspective enables us to place these contemporary insights into a theocentric and christological framework, and thus saves us from the crassly reductionist tendencies of modern anthropocentrism. We thus reject the cry "Let God be God" and "Let the world be the world," and affirm that both God and the world are intimately and dynamically related to each other within the Christian vision.

What does all of this mean for the life of the Mennonite church as it faces urgent issues in the present? As alluded to above, from the numerous special conferences, study documents, and position papers produced by various segments of the Mennonite community, it would appear that we are at present seriously struggling with a wide range of pressing issues. The doctrinal approach as I have been proposing it here ought not to be seen as usurping other approaches but might be considered as a foundational orientation for the other perspectives. This would have some decisive implications for how we attempt to develop our positions on important religious, moral, ethical, and social-political questions.

On the question of leadership and authority in the life of the church, for instance, matters of church polity, leadership, authority, and ordination (both of men and women) would be addressed not in isolation, nor simply on the basis of a selection of biblical texts literally or historically interpreted, nor merely to meet present needs. Rather one would develop a *doctrine of the church* in relation to the other doctrines of the Christian faith.[62] How the other doctrines would be interpreted by Mennonites and where the doctrine of the church might be placed (in terms of sequence and importance) would have a profound bearing on one's stance on the particulars. Women ministries in the church, for example—especially the ordination of women to the role of bishop, elder, or pastor—would be determined not only by exegeting specific texts but also on how one perceives from the canon as a whole the movement of God's ways with the world from creation to redemption to consummation.[63] Seen in this way Galatians 3:27ff. (which stresses unequivocally the full equality of men and women in Christ) would appear to take precedence in determining God's intent in creation, redemption, and consummation over passages like 1 Corinthians 14:34, which limit the role of women in the church, and others like 1 Corinthians 11 and Ephesians 5 where some kind of subordinate role of women is assumed.

For a variety of other issues, including human sexuality, artificial means of reproduction, marriage-separation-divorce-remarriage, and so on, one would need to seek answers not purely on the basis of the psychological well-being of individuals involved, nor on the basis of some rigid and inflexible adherence to isolated biblical texts, but in accordance with clear doctrinal formulations concerning what we as a church believe about created nature, fallen nature, and redeemed nature (both in its present penultimate and in its ultimate consummated sense).[64] The strength of the doctrinal method properly understood is that it recognizes 1) the need for religious and moral-ethical rigour in distinguishing between heterodoxy and orthodoxy, and "right" action from "wrong" behavior, and at the same time 2) the reality of a fallen world in which knowledge and faithfulness is limited by natural and social evil and human sinfulness, and 3) that regeneration and reconciliation are possible in the present but only in a relative sense, final perfection being anticipated as a future reality when creation as a whole will be redeemed at the end of time and history. Further, a doctrinal approach takes seriously both the unchanging *ontological* truths to which the Christian proclamation points and the *historical* and *developmental* nature of human understanding as it is shaped by the exigencies of time. The doctrinal method would be anchored in the biblical revelation but take seriously church history and the ongoing development of belief under the guidance of the Holy Spirit as we try to unfold the meaning of the biblical revelation for us in every new age without yielding to "the temptation to keep traditions which fall short of the biblical vision and the temptation to accept uncritically trends of today's society."[65]

FOURTEEN

Toward Christian Theology from a Diversity of Mennonite Perspectives*

The diversity of theological perspectives among Mennonites is not to be lamented but to be embraced as consistent with the heterogeneity (polygenesis) of Anabaptist origins. I identify at least fourteen different Mennonite "theologies" in this essay, which was presented at a conference on "Beyond Pluralism: What Mennonites Believe Today!" at Laurelville Mennonite Church Center in Laurelville, PA, March 11-13, 1988.

I had been asked to address the theme: "Toward a Mennonite Theology," but reformulated it as "Toward Christian Theology." This was because I do not believe we ought to do Mennonite theology; our task is to do Christian theology as Mennonites.[1] Diversity is to be welcomed; however, where pluralism descends into historical relativism, ethics has lost its metaphysical and ontological ground and becomes capricious. This is the case in much so-called postmodern thought that rejects the very notion of foundational coherences. Ethics, as a consequence, is little more than manipulation and the arbitrary exercise of power.

By metaphysical-ontological grounding I mean a dogmatic framework for belief and action, emerging out of a trinitarian doctrine of God. This would be a theocentric-theological foundation for Christian ethics which guards against

---

* Originally published as "Toward Christian Theology From a Diversity of Mennonite Perspectives," *The Conrad Grebel Review* 6.2 (Spring 1988): 147-59. For notes on the text see the Notes section below.

anthropocentric reductionism. First, God as creator of the world ex nihilo *is the irreducible and transcendent source of all that is; second, God as redeemer in Christ is irreducible either to docetism (which errs on the side of spirituality), on the one hand, or Arianism (which errs on the side of materiality), on the other— the two-nature christology of Chalcedon seeks the balance of these two; third, God as Spirit empowers the church as the "body of Christ" to continue the divine work of reconciliation, where perfection is understood eschatologically. Spiritual discipline and moral formation, discipleship, and vocational responsibilities in family, economics, politics, culture, and society would all be premised on all three theological affirmations. This would help to modify the Mennonite propensity to deal with all ethical matters within the rubric of the church narrowly understood. This trinitarian-dogmatic foundation—understood more as a gravitational-magnetic centre than as a means for rigid boundary maintenance—allows for diversity within an underlying unity, a unity which is itself both one and three. What is touted as contemporary pluralism is, after all, a diversity only of a very superficial sort. The homogeneity of modern and postmodern civilization is symbolized by the omnipotent computer.*

◆ ◆ ◆

Introduction

Ever since the appearance of its first issue (Winter 1983) there has been in *The Conrad Grebel Review* a vigorous and ongoing debate about what a "Mennonite theology" might look like. In this article, I pull together some of the themes of this debate by looking, first, at the diversity of viewpoints in the present Mennonite theological landscape; second, at the confessional-doctrinal approach to theology as I have been articulating it in various contexts; and, finally, at what we as Mennonites do believe and ought to believe as we look to the future.

Before I launch into the substance of what I have to say, I want to comment on the notion of "a Mennonite theology." This phrase does not adequately describe how we ought to think systematically about what we believe. First, there is no *one* homogeneous Mennonite theology. The debate in the *Review* alone reflects the heterogeneity of the theological thinking within the Mennonite community, a phenomenon which brings with it certain problems for church polity, but needs to be welcomed as consistent with our history.

Second, our intent ought not to be to develop a "Mennonite" or "Believers Church" theology as though this were an enterprise distinct from the ecumenical-Christian theological task. We are first and foremost Christians engaged in Christian theological reflection. Since, however, none of us can do this in abstraction, removed from our particular historical context and tradition, we seek to understand what it means to be Christian from a particular point of view. For us this point of view happens to be a Mennonite one, with certain central theological accents which I spell out below. This is why I have chosen the title "Toward Christian Theology from a Diversity of Mennonite Perspectives," a phrase reflecting both the primacy of our common Christian project, itself characterized by plurality, and the particular and diverse vantage points from which we approach our universal task.

Noteworthy in this regard is the statement made by Gordon D. Kaufman: "For much too long Mennonites have presented themselves as somehow set apart from the rest of the Christian world in a little self-sufficient enclave of their own." His challenge to us is "to transcend narrow and short-sighted Mennonite provincialisms—and to transcend as well the parochialisms and prejudices of traditional Christian speech and of modern Western culture—as we seek to participate in the emerging community which includes in its circle of conversation partners all of humankind."[2]

I basically agree with Kaufman that we need to move beyond our sectarian past and think in larger terms. I believe, however, that we are (and ought to be) perspectively more bound to our own tradition(s) as Mennonites and to the past generally than Kaufman seems to think. The important role the theological formulations of the past play in my own attempt as a Mennonite Christian to think theologically today will become clear as I make my own proposals below.

Postmodernity and the Fact of Theological Diversity

One of the facts of modern theology is the plurality and diversity of theological positions and viewpoints that vie with each other for recognition and prominence in the public arena. The number of recent books with "postmodern," "postliberal," "plurality," or "pluralism" somewhere in their title bears out the importance which contemporary theologians give to the fact that we are entering a new age characterized by fundamental diversity of perspectives. In the so-called "liberalism" of the preceding epoch diversity was also recognized, but underneath this plurality there was assumed to be a harmonious unity binding everyone together. Toleration of other viewpoints was possible because of this underlying optimism. The postmodern era recognizes a much more thoroughgoing and conflictual heterogeneity which calls not for harmonious toleration but fair and tough-minded theological and political discourse.

We have in contemporary theology various forms of process theology, political theology, liberation theology (including Latin American liberation theology, black liberation theology, feminist liberation theology, gay liberation theology), dialectical theology, existentialist theology, evangelical theology, narrative theology, and so on. The American Catholic theologian David Tracy, in his book *Plurality and Ambiguity*, notes:

> We find ourselves, therefore, with a plurality of interpretations and methods. We find ourselves with diverse religious classics among many religious traditions. We find ourselves glimpsing the plurality within each tradition while also admitting the ambiguity of every religion: liberating possibilities to be retrieved, errors to be criticized, unconscious distortions to be unmasked.[3]

This means that the term "orthodoxy" (or neo-orthodoxy for that matter), as though there were behind all this diversity still a commonly accepted core of "right belief," no longer appears to many to have descriptive or prescriptive power.

My problem with much of this current literature about the diversity and plurality of our age is that it does not deal satisfactorily with a countervailing phenomenon not only in our own society but in all societies. Beneath this real diversity there is a more substantial homogeneity: not a beautiful harmonious core in the nineteenth-century liberal sense but a sameness that arises out of the tyranny of modern technology. Computers, for example, particularly the assumptions behind computers, do not encourage diversity but its very opposite: sameness. These two phenomena combined—the conflicting diversity of theological options which tends to relativize each and the absolutizing technological monolith which tends to make us all the same—have a way of blocking out any faith in and experience of that which is eternal and transcendent.

For the moment, however, let me stay on the superficial level of diversity. One needs only to look at the theological writings by different Mennonite authors in the various Mennonite periodicals to realize that a significant plurality of theological viewpoints or schools of thought exists right within our own community. Let me briefly allude to a few of them. There is the evolutionary or process theology of a Carl Keener, in which truth is viewed not as a "timeless given" but dynamic and changing. Time is understood historically and as linear. The challenge for Mennonites in this model is to develop a theology in conversation with Darwinian science and Whiteheadian process philosophy. The Anabaptist understanding of freedom, according to Keener, fits nicely with the "modern worldview of cosmic organicism." In this view orthodoxy with its notion of "God as omnipotent, timeless, omniscient, complete, immutable, impassable, and simple, is incommensurable with the Anabaptist vision of human freedom of choice within Christ's body." The traditional orthodox view of God cannot be reconciled "with the modern view that chance and freedom are built into the very fabric of a contingent and evolving universe."[4]

There is the *shalom* theology of a Perry Yoder, which stresses the need for a biblical theology that uses the historical critical method and acknowledges the surface diversities within the biblical materials while at the same time recognizing in the Bible a common core or deep structure. Central to the gospel is *shalom* or peace, "an element from which the rest makes sense and without which the rest is less than the gospel."[5] *Shalom* in the Hebrew world signified not simply the absence of war but connoted peace and justice in the positive sense. It included justice not only between individuals but within economic and political structures as well. What is called for, according to Yoder, is an explicit Mennonite biblical theology in which this more comprehensive notion of *shalom* becomes not something added on to other theological doctrines but intrinsic to the whole of theology from creation to consummation.

Those like Arnold Snyder, who urge us to develop a theology in conversation with Latin American liberation theology, make up another school of thought. Snyder thinks there are remarkable similarities between the Peasants' War of 1525 and the recent Nicaraguan Revolution, on the one hand, and sixteenth-century Anabaptism and twentieth-century liberation theology, on the other. What Anabaptism and liberation theology have in common is their shift of emphasis from "individual belief to social practice," from orthodoxy to orthopraxis. "The primary emphasis in post-Constantinian Christianity has been orthodoxy, or right teaching and belief."[6] For the Anabaptists and the liberation theologians, however, "it is orthopraxis, or right action, which makes Christianity genuine, rather than mere orthodoxy, or right teaching."[7]

J. Denny Weaver represents another theological model, a theological approach that is in vogue in contemporary North American theological circles: narrative theology. Here, similar to the theological proposals of Carl Keener, truth depends ultimately on process and "the locus of authority resides more with the ongoing people of God as a whole than in a particular institution or law code or absolutized biblical proposition."[8] Authority is not static but "a dynamic process which maintains and preserves truth through the interaction of God's people and their perpetual seeking."[9] Taking issue especially with my own theological position, Weaver says: "To entertain the reality of God in our world, it is not necessary to add a 'vertical mystical, ontological, sacramental, or a-historical dimension' to an apparently meaningless horizontal world."[10]

According to Weaver, a narrative christology which stresses the teachings and life of Jesus rather than an orthodox, sacramental, mystical, and ontological christology is more appropriate to Mennonites. The Hebraic emphasis on "the ultimate significance of time or horizontal movement" is more relevant to Mennonite theology and the contemporary situation than the Greek vertical-horizontal dichotomy. The transcendent ought not to be conceived of as breaking into the plane of history from the outside in a vertical, ontological, sacramental, or cultic fashion, but rather as a dimension within the historical stream itself.[11] Mennonites ought to develop a theology which begins with a Mennonite agenda: peace, discipleship, community, visible church and so on, not with something that is foreign to Mennonite theology such as the Trinity.

In a recent issue of *The Conrad Grebel Review* Gayle Gerber Koontz develops what might be considered a Mennonite feminist theology. She proposes to take seriously both the traditional Mennonite reverence for the authority of the Scriptures, in which the Bible in some sense stands in judgment over us, our assumptions, and our experience, and important insights of secular feminism, particularly equality in legal, social, economic, and familial matters.[12] Her approach is not so much to take specific texts or particular theologies in the biblical materials as authoritative, but rather to look for a "movement or a trajectory within Scripture which would be consistent with or supportive of feminist conviction and which we might receive as divine intention."[13] She finds in the Bible a trajectory which calls for "mutual submission" and "reciprocal servanthood," themes which support equality between men and women with a vision for eventual reciprocity of men and women."[14] In the same issue Mitchell Brown strongly urges us to accept an adoptionist christology which he thinks is much more appropriate to Mennonite theology than traditional trinitarian orthodoxy.[15]

These are some of the major theological points of view that have been represented in *The Conrad Grebel Review* over the past five years. One could go on to list other approaches to Mennonite theology: the Anabaptist Vision theology of Harold S. Bender, existentialist theology of Robert Friedmann, political theology of John Howard Yoder, historicist theology of Gordon Kaufman, eschatological theology of Thomas Finger, so-called "Evangelical-Anabaptist" theology of George R. Brunk II and Ted VanderEnde, therapeutic theology of David Augsburger, and even a kind of ethnic-cultural theology evident in the Winnipeg periodical, *Mennonite Mirror*. Some of these writers would likely not think of their approaches as theologies, particularly not systematic theologies. Nevertheless, they do represent distinctive emphases, perspectives, or approaches to Mennonite theological thinking. One ought not, of course, to limit the issue of diversity to theological pluralism. We have other forms of diversity in our Mennonite community which affect our theology, particularly ethnic plurality: Black, Hispanic, Russian, Swiss, Dutch, Chinese ethnicities and so on.

There are a number of inferences one can draw from the above. First of all, there is the phenomenon of *diversity* itself. I have named fourteen distinct theological approaches and there are others. Even if in the past we had semblances of a common theological core, we can today no longer assume a united theological position. We, like other Christian communions, reflect the diversity and pluralism of the modern age.

We should embrace genuine diversity. We ought to welcome the opportunity to engage openly in public discourse about differences and commonalities not only among ourselves but also between ourselves and other Christian bodies and religious traditions. In fact, what distinguished the early Anabaptists was precisely their heterogeneity and diversity. The polygenesis theory of Anabaptist-Mennonite origins and the confessional diversity of Mennonites throughout their history would suggest that fidelity to our own tradition entails and calls exactly for the kind of theological pluralism that we have seen above.

A Doctrinal-Confessional Approach to Theology

There is, of course, a significant difference between the diversity of our own twentieth-century theological landscape and that of our ecclesial ancestors in the sixteenth century. The pre-moderns still always assumed the existence of eternal and transcendent truth. What was believed to be true was for them of ultimate significance and worth dying for. The conflicting Reformation positions, and the call for religious toleration by our pre-modern forebears, did not presuppose the historical and religious relativism of the post-Enlightenment period but precisely the opposite: an unbending commitment to absolutes though diversely expressed.

Sometimes I think we make too much of the differences between the various sixteenth-century groups: Catholics, Lutherans, Reformed, Anabaptists, Anglicans. This suits us as we try to preserve our denominational distinctiveness. But did not all of these have more in common with each other than any of them have with us? They lived in a pre-modern context in which it was still assumed that historical events were ultimately to be explained theologically and confessionally; that is, the contemporary distinction between sacred and secular (or profane) history did not exist. Behind all historical phenomena there was perceived to be the transcendent reality of God. This is why theological thinking was taken with utmost seriousness. It is this theological presupposition (the reality of God) as the backdrop for all human action and historical action that is in question today.

This brings me to the second inference. The surface diversity of Mennonite theological positions is somewhat deceptive. If one looks at the whole spectrum of theological viewpoints above, one notes that there is in fact a *common element* running through many of them. This common thread has to do with certain prevalent assumptions of the modern period: an emphasis on history, becoming, process, development, narrative, dynamic truth, and orthopraxis, and a discomfort with the language of ontology (or structures of being), eternal truths, transcendence as the vertical intersection with time as history, and orthodoxy. This discomfort is most clearly illustrated by the general absence of interest in recent Mennonite theology (with a few exceptions) in the whole genre of confession and doctrine. The reasons for this *lacuna* are not difficult to find. Confessions, doctrines, creeds, and dogma, while different from each other in some ways, are all part of one family or theological genre. They entail a common concern for fidelity to *right belief* and have in their classical-orthodox model the tendency to pass over ethics and the Christian life.

There is some truth to the claim that Mennonites and the Believers Church generally are a non-creedal tradition having historically emphasized practice, life, and ethics more than speculative thought and right belief. In this Mennonites simply anticipated and shared in the general modern suspicion of dogma, so prevalent in post-scholastic theology which saw dogma as the mark of dogma*tism* and intolerance.

But one can easily overstate the case, as C. J. Dyck implicitly acknowledges when he says in his foreword to Howard J. Loewen's book on Mennonite confessions of faith: "It is generally true that the Anabaptists and later Mennonites have been and are non-creedal. . . . It is surprising, therefore, to find that the Anabaptists and especially the Dutch Mennonites wrote many confessions, as this volume demonstrates, probably more than any of the other three Reformation traditions."[16] To explain this, as Dyck does, solely by saying that while "[c]reeds tend to denote timeless, classic, and universal statements . . . confessions tend to be more particularistic, personal, and occasional, that is, written for a specific purpose at a particular time and place," is not entirely convincing. Confessions, doctrines, creeds, and dogmas have in fact much in common with each other. One of the things they all assume is that right belief is important. And, I would argue, Mennonites have in the past taken "right belief (orthodoxy)" as being the basis and theological framework for "right action (orthopraxis)."

I have in my writings over the past few years urged us as Mennonites not only to recover our own confessional heritage but also to take a serious look at classical orthodoxy, especially as expressed in the early ecumenical creeds. I am thinking here particularly of the trinitarian formulations of the Apostolic Creed and the Nicene Creed, and the christological formulation of Chalcedon. I have seen this as my particular contribution to the theological discussion within Mennonite circles. If there is a softness in our historical-theological point of view as Mennonites, I think it is located here. We have not taken seriously enough the classical or Patristic period of the early church. My intent has not been to urge us to go back to a previous age and a previous formulation in any absolute sense. That would be to betray the intent even of those who formulated the early confessions and creeds. Nor has it been my desire to reject the other approaches mentioned above, replacing them with a classical confessional-creedal approach, for I believe diversity is here to stay and genuine diversity is in fact to be encouraged.

The reasons I have suggested that we take a fresh look at these classical symbols of the faith include the following: a) the dogmatic and creedal approach has unfortunately been largely missing in the Believers Church tradition and especially in recent Mennonite theological reflection; b) although the so-called Believers Church (of which Mennonites are a part) has been historically suspicious of the classical creeds for some legitimate reasons, our tradition has in actual fact until quite recently been theologically and catechetically dependent on doctrinal and confessional statements with classical elements; c) finally, a doctrinal approach to theological and ethical issues has some distinct advantages over some of the alternate approaches that have replaced the confessional genre.

One of these advantages is that the articles of a confession serve as a very general framework for a variety of theological interpretations and approaches, including both ontological and historical-developmental ones. These doctrinal categories represent the bare-bones frame of our theological house, reflecting what we hold in common while allowing for a considerable amount of diversity in the particular contents. In my view, doctrines provide a larger umbrella or framework for discourse concerning our differences than any one of the different options cited above, which usually assume an implicit doctrinal structure.

This doctrinal interest is not an idiosyncratic concern of mine, for there appears to be a renaissance of interest in doctrinal questions in theology in unexpected circles. The number of books dealing with the meaning of the Trinity in the context of modern pluralism is really quite remarkable. Jürgen Moltmann's trilogy is one example. George Lindbeck's *The Nature of Doctrine* is another, having received an amazingly sympathetic hearing even among biblical scholars who have in the past been rather sceptical of the doctrinal approach.[17] Yale University Press has published a work by William A. Christian, Sr. entitled *Doctrines of Religious Communities*.[18] I am proposing that we join others in re-examining a confessional and creedal way of thinking that takes doctrinal language as a way, not of moving beyond pluralism, but as moving toward a unity which allows for substantial diversity within itself.

What Do We and Ought We to Believe? Some Specific Proposals

How ought we to go about doing this? We might begin by looking at the confessions that have played an important role in our past. Here Howard J. Loewen's book, *One Lord, One Church, One Hope, And One God* is a helpful guide. Let me summarize some of the central insights about our own confessional tradition as Mennonites in North America that Loewen arrives at. According to him, Dordrecht is the mother of all the later confessions. There is a great variety of emphases in the many subsequent confessions, often reflecting the larger social and religious context in which they were drawn up. For example, the 1921 Mennonite Church confession, "The Christian Fundamentals," clearly mirrors the concerns of fundamentalism in its debate with modernism.

Despite this variety Loewen identifies a common four-fold axis around which most of them are ordered: Theology (doctrine of God), Christology (doctrine of Christ), Ecclesiology (doctrine of the church), and Eschatology (doctrine of the future). This order interestingly bears a remarkable resemblance to the classical orthodox model. Further, Loewen finds seven major accents: Triune God and Creation, Word of God and Revelation, Jesus Christ and Redemption, Holy Spirit and Transformation, Human Nature and Salvation, Church of Christ and Mission, and Eternal Hope and Resurrection.[19] Loewen's study demonstrates that in our tradition there is a basis for broad agreement on some very general doctrinal categories, not only among ourselves but also between us and other Christian churches.

There are, however, also some distinctive elements in these confessions which have distinguished us from the mainline Christian traditions; these have largely to do with our view of the church and ethics, giving our whole theology a unique flavour. What Loewen has found in comparing the confessions is that there is a consistently high view of Scripture and a common theological centre—ecclesiology and mission—confirmed by the prominence of references to Matthew, Acts, and Ephesians. Of these three, Matthew is the most important, within which chapter five (the Sermon on the Mount) is by far the most popular, and the passage on loving one's enemies (vv. 43-48) receives the most attention.

One further observation is of interest. What distinguishes the Mennonite confessions from classical models are specific emphases and articles not usually found in other confessional statements: "free will, conversion, footwashing, church discipline, Christian life and nonconformity, integrity and oaths, nonresistance and revenge, the Christian and the state."[20] This latter list is highly significant for any systematic theological thinking we want to do today and in the future as Mennonites, for it defines who we are. These items are not simply a litany of additions to the other doctrines but shape the very way we think about God, Christ, church, and consummation.

Free will, for instance, is a highly significant doctrine for early Anabaptists and for later Mennonites. With this doctrine our sixteenth-century ancestors clearly rejected Luther's and Calvin's doctrine of predestination and the particular view of grace and the sovereignty of God that gave rise to it. These distinctives reflect a concern for moral and ethical perfection premised on a rather optimistic view of the possibility of human transformation within the context of the church. It may be that we will want to modify some of these accents in the context of the modern world in which free will has come to mean unlimited and unrestrained human autonomy to shape and dominate the world of nature and values. The first step, however, is to recover the language of doctrine itself.

We need to take a fresh look at these older confessions, to study them, to preach about them, to use them for catechesis, to write theological commentaries on them, to translate them into contemporary idioms, to modify them as we learn from other traditions and adapt them to the contemporary situation. Before we too quickly write new confessions, ought we not to acquaint ourselves with our own classics, to engage ourselves with them, to reinterpret them for our day? We need to develop doctrinal categories that stand in substantial continuity with the classical past and our own Mennonite past, and at the same time deal creatively with the present. As a bare minimum we need to recover the four basic traditional theological *foci* for our creative theological thinking as a Mennonite community.

For a comprehensive theology we need, first of all, to have *doctrine of God and creation*. I would argue very strongly, against Mitchell Brown, that we need a trinitarian view of God if we are to remain nonreductionist in our theology and faithful not only to the early Christian tradition but also to our own tradition(s). I agree wholeheartedly with Krister Stendahl when he says: "Perhaps that same suspicion of mine explains why I am so fond of the Trinity, a most daring attempt at not sacrificing richness and diversity on the altars of theoretical monisms of various kinds."[21]

I see trinitarian language not as foreign to the New Testament but as growing directly out of it. Trinitarian language needs of course to be translated into meaningful contemporary terms. While historically this doctrine may not have played as significant a role in our theological thinking as it might have, it nevertheless was on the whole taken with great seriousness. The twelve affirmations, including the three primary articles, of the Apostles' Creed are intrinsic to Hubmaier's 1527 catechism. Menno repeatedly affirmed a faith in the triune God, most directly in his "A Solemn Confession of the Triune, Eternal, and True God, Father, Son, and Holy Ghost" (1550). The first half of Peter Riedemann's 1545 Confession of Faith follows closely the articles of the Apostles' Creed with a careful defence of the doctrines of God, Christ, and the Holy Spirit.

As the high church traditions are tempted by a one-sided emphasis on God's transcendence, and the low churches, particularly the holiness and charismatic movements, by a one-sided preoccupation with the immanence of God, so Mennonites tend in my view to reduce God to the lordship of the historical Christ. The doctrine of the Trinity is an expression of the one God having three modes of being: God as wholly other, transcendent mystery, of whom no finite images can be made; God as historically revealed in the person of Jesus Christ, including his birth, life, teaching, death, resurrection, and ascension; God as immanently present to us and in us as individuals, the church, the world, and the cosmos.

The doctrine of the Trinity has specific implications for our ethics. Take our position on peace and non-violence. Basing our peace position too exclusively on the life and teachings of Jesus of Nazareth, frequently referred to as the "lordship of Christ," without a profound trinitarian christology, threatens to weaken not only our stance on nonviolence but our attitude toward sin and evil generally. The simple fact is that the problem of innocent suffering, death, evil, including violence, cannot be rationally understood and adequately addressed exclusively with reference to human action and the Sermon on the Mount. Ultimately, we need a doctrine of God in which God himself is allowed to be radically free from our systems of morality and our vision of what God ought to be. In other words, there are dimensions of reality which are not covered by our particular understanding of the nonviolent Jesus, even though we are called to be faithful to that christocentric ethic.

We need, further, *a doctrine of Christ and redemption*. This, of course, gets us to the heart of the Mennonite theological ethos. Mennonites have always tended either toward Docetism or Arianism. With the one we fail to recognize the humanness of Christ, resulting also in a failure to acknowledge the humanness of the redeemed community (the visible church). With the other we tend to lose the mystical and divine element of Christ. The consequence is that we also lose the mystical and sacramental nature of the church. Christ becomes little more than a historical figure that we struggle to imitate, and the ordinances formal signs lacking in mystical and gracious substance.

I would defend with many (although not all) of our ancestors that the two-natures formula of Chalcedon, despite its inadequacies, still remains an essential guide for developing a contemporary christology with profound implications for our ethics both inside and outside the church. Our view of salvation, regeneration, and atonement ought to be interpreted and reinterpreted in conversation with the Chalcedonian formula. There is in that two-natures Christology a carefully considered and balanced anthropology (having to do with the relation of the divine and the human in all those who participate in the nature of Christ) which we ought to ponder deeply before deviating from it.

We need a more developed *doctrine of the Holy Spirit and the church* in which mission, service, and social action are taken seriously and the Spirit is truly seen as capable of transforming and empowering us. Too often, however, we as Mennonites have limited the reality and work of the Holy Spirit to the church as the visible body of Christ and not recognized the Spirit when it is working outside the church, in other Christian traditions, in other religions, in the world of politics and economics, in the realm of culture and the fine arts. Further, it is in the light of this third way of speaking of God's reality that many of the recent Mennonite theological emphases on process, development, dynamic truth, narrative and so on, ought to be evaluated. The dynamic, immanent, developmental way of talking about divine reality is a legitimate way of speaking about God, but not to the exclusion of God's radical transcendence and God's historical particularity.

According to Loewen it is this doctrine (ecclesiology and mission) where we find the "most consistent uniformity" among Mennonite confessions in North America. Here the truly distinctive elements of Mennonite theology are situated: its view of the marks of the church, membership, offices, ordinances, marriage, discipline, nonconformity, discipleship, integrity and oaths, nonresistance, the Christian and the state, and the Lord's day and work. Here in the context of the church our Christian life and ethics are most fully expressed. This doctrine needs, therefore, special attention. The urgent issues we have been recently facing concerning leadership and authority, ordination of women, sexuality, marriage-divorce-remarriage, and so on need to be developed quite consciously and deliberately in the context of our doctrine of the church.

It is not a matter of slavishly following what we have said in the past but of framing the question theologically and doctrinally. Essential to doctrinal thinking as it was first employed in the early church was its developmental character. Doctrines were meant to help the church mediate between the biblical teachings and new situations to which the Bible did not speak directly. Thus doctrines in effect helped the early Christians to move beyond the Bible. It is when doctrines become static and ossified that they lose their value. In regard to the above issues, we may well need to move beyond what we have said before. Particularly we may need to modify our historical tendency toward a Docetic or overly perfectionist view of the church which ignores the reality of sin and therefore also of forgiveness and acceptance among its members.

Finally, we need a *doctrine of eschatology and consummation* which speaks both to the personal-existential aspects of death, judgment, and the resurrection and to the corporate-social vision of a new heaven and a new earth. With the political and liberation theologians among us there is always the temptation to identify the eschatological future (frequently described in terms of the kingdom of God) with the historical ideal of social justice, freedom, and equality. With the more evangelically-oriented among us there is the temptation to identify the kingdom of God with a totally non-historical, non-political and inward realm (sometimes referred to as eternal life). We need an eschatology which includes both dimensions and reserves perfection and consummation truly for the end of time. Neither individuals nor the church can reach perfection until that day when the whole context will be perfected by God himself.

In conclusion, the most important and the most problematic doctrine for modern theology generally, and also for us as Mennonites today, is the doctrine of God. All the other doctrines hinge on this starting point. It is a well-recognized historical fact that what characterizes the modern age is its anthropocentric turn. That is, with the Enlightenment there was quite understandably a turn from a theocentric worldview to an anthropocentric or human-centred one. I have posited in a number of my articles that the Anabaptists, and we Mennonites as their progeny, in some indirect ways anticipated (possibly even helped to create the mood for) this important turn to the human subject as the focal point for historical action. In particular our emphasis on free will and preoccupation with ethics and practical Christianity held within it the seeds of modernity. What saved us theologically in the past was, I have argued, the confessional and doctrinal framework within which we couched our anthropological and ethical concerns. God remained the alpha and omega of our human striving for perfection.

As we partake ever more in the assumptions of the modern age, especially the assumptions behind modern technology, and the eclipse of the eternal and the transcendent, our ethics and our social and political programs often become little more than temporary human ideologies of the right, centre, or left. Personal morality, human perfection, social and political action, while intrinsic to our whole theology, dare not become the starting point, the hermeneutical key, for our whole theology. God as wholly transcendent creator, God as historically incarnated in human flesh, and God as powerfully present in us as individuals, in the church, and in the course of history ought to be the beginning and end of our theology even as Mennonites. The challenge of working on a theocentric theology for today—one that takes human agency seriously—calls for clear-thinking public discourse. All theocentric claims must themselves be recognized as finite and subject to human fallibility. This is the positive insight of modern anthropocentric theology: that all our language about God is ultimately human language pointing to transcendent mystery.

FIFTEEN

Trinitarian Orthodoxy, Constantinianism, and Radical Protestant Theology*

My 1983 essay, "The Nature and Possibility of a Mennonite Theology," and subsequent essays on my vision of a Christian theology for Mennonites sparked strong critical response, especially from those in the John Howard Yoder tradition, like J. Denny Weaver, who considered my classical, ecumenical approach to Christian theology as a sell-out of Anabaptist-Mennonite and Believers Church non-conformity to mainstream thinking.¹ Weaver was inclined to see our two

---

The Conrad Grebel Review became one of the forums for an ongoing debate about the role of the classical creeds in Mennonite theologizing: cf. Reimer, "The Nature and Possibility of a Mennonite Theology," *CGR* 1.1 (Winter 1983), 33-55; Howard John Loewen, "Reader Response [to Reimer]," *CGR* 1.2 (Spring 1983), 56-8; Reimer, "Reader Response [to Loewen]," *CGR* 1.3 (Fall 1983), 51-4; J. Denny Weaver, "Perspectives on a Mennonite Theology," *CGR* 2.3 (Fall 1984), 189-210; Darrol Bryant, "Reader Response [to Weaver]," *CGR* 3.2 (Spring 1985), 189-93; Thomas N. Finger, "The Way to Nicea: Reflections from a Mennonite Perspective," *CGR* 3.3 (Fall 1985), 231-49.

* Originally published as "Trinitarian Orthodoxy, Constantinianism and Theology from a Radical Protestant Perspective," in *Faith to Creed: Ecumenical Perspectives on the Affirmation of the Apostolic Faith in the Fourth Century*, ed. S. Mark Heim (Grand Rapids: Eerdmans, 1991), 129-61.

approaches as the two opposing theological options open to Mennonites in the future, one (his) remaining faithful to the Jesus narrative in which an ethic of nonviolent love is the core, the other (mine) buying into a mainstream Constantinian theology which spells the end of the Mennonite peace witness. He proposed that we jointly author a book with the title Mennonite Theology at the Crossroads, *in which we would outline our divergent approaches to the future of Mennonite theology.*

Herald Press expressed interest in the project but it never got off the ground, partly because of my own resistance to being painted with Weaver's brush. I never saw my position as a polar opposite to Weaver's. I always considered Yoder's and Weaver's ethical concerns essential for Mennonites, but was wary of what seemed to me to be their (particularly Weaver's) ethical reductionism. I sought not to compromise the Mennonite peace witness but searched for ways to ground it theologically. I remain convinced that ethics devoid of metaphysical-theological foundations is like building a house upon the sand.

In this essay, which was in part a response to Weaver's insistence that I more directly respond to his critique of my theology, I offer my theological and political reading of the so-called "Constantinian Shift." It was occasioned by an invitation to represent the believers church tradition at an ecumenical conference, sponsored by the Faith and Order Commission of the National Council of Churches in Boston, Mass., in October, 1989.[2] I argue that trinitarian orthodoxy cannot be equated with Constantinianism, but is in fact the best theological defence against all Constantinian-type political theologies (whether of the left, right, or centre) that make political and ethical correctness the criterion for good theology. It is the Christian doctrine of God that is the foundation for good ethics, not good ethics which is the norm for our view of God.

◆ ◆ ◆

Introduction

I have been asked to reflect on fourth-century theological developments from a Mennonite-theological perspective. It is well known that the so-called "Believers' Church" tradition (a rather presumptuous title for those Christian groups, like the Mennonites, who adhere to a certain "visible church" ecclesiology that marks them off from other, mainline Christian groups)[3] has historically seen the fourth century as the sign of widespread Christian apostasy, the "fall of the Church." This negative evaluation of the Constantinian period, which gave the Christian church privileged status within Roman imperial society, has commonly spilt over into a suspicion of the historical ecumenical creeds, seen to be intrinsically linked to and legitimating growing ecclesiastical hierarchy and political power rather than faithfully expressing biblical truth.

In the following pages I first outline what I consider to be the representative position for a significant number of contemporary Mennonite thinkers. I survey not all the contemporary literature, nor look at Anabaptist sources, but focus on the thought of one of our foremost contemporary theologians and ethicists, John Howard Yoder. After having outlined Yoder's views, and that of a younger interpreter of Yoder, J. Denny Weaver, I make my own proposal. I argue that theological orthodoxy and Constantinianism are not intrinsically linked, as so often assumed, but are in tension with each other. I propose that classical orthodoxy needs to be retrieved in contemporary Christian theology, after its erosion in the eighteenth and nineteenth century, as a way of taking a stand against various forms of twentieth-century Constantinianism. Nicene orthodoxy needs to be retrieved by the Christian church in general and by the Mennonite Church in particular as a way of remaining faithful to the Bible, as a way of preserving the essential tenets of the Christian faith within a post-biblical context, and as a theological framework for contemporary ethics.

In emphasizing so strongly the relevance of Nicea and Constantinople for contemporary Christian theology, I am admittedly departing from much recent Mennonite thinking, but not from what I consider to be the central conviction of our historical Anabaptist beginnings—a trinitarian orthodoxy with a heightened ethical fidelity to the Jesus narrative as offering an alternative to Nicea, Constantinople and Chalcedon— as a position that needs to be incorporated into the framework of classical theological orthodoxy. In this process of retrieval, I believe we need to enter vigorously into conversation with other theological traditions like Eastern Orthodoxy, which can teach us much in this regard. These other traditions, however, may also be able to learn something in turn from the Radical Protestant emphasis on personal and social ethics based on a particular reading of the Gospels—especially political non-conformity and a view of the church as a visible, prophetic minority within society.

The Constantinian Shift

As an ethicist and historical theologian (rather than as a systematic theologian), John Howard Yoder has in the last three decades become the leading interpreter of Anabaptist-Mennonite theology both for the Mennonite communion itself and for the larger ecumenical Christian community. He has in his writings, more than any other person, except perhaps for Harold S. Bender (largely responsible for the twentieth-century renaissance of Mennonite interest in its Anabaptist sources), shaped Mennonite self-understanding in the second half of this century.[4]

Yoder's primary preoccupation has been with the social and political relevance of the biblical Jesus (a position he calls "biblical realism") for our age, and the accompanying understanding of the church's relation to the world. He has been outspoken in his prophetic critique of the wrong direction taken by the established churches ever since the time of Constantine in the fourth century. Many of his writings deal either explicitly or implicitly with the ethical implications of what he calls the "Constantinian shift," represented by the imperial decree of toleration toward Christianity in 311, the "conversion" and later baptism of Constantine, and the crucial role Constantine played in the formulation of theological orthodoxy, especially at Nicea in 325, as the great negative watershed in Christian history. While, according to Yoder, the shift occurred gradually,[5] Constantine's person and period symbolize a "great reversal" in the relation of the church to the larger society, which can only be considered an apostasy. No longer is the church a critical, prophetic, and suffering minority within a hostile pagan world; it takes on a privileged role as legitimator of power, wealth, and hierarchy. In a series of three essays, "Radical Reformation Ethics in Ecumenical Perspective," "Anabaptism and History," and "The Constantinian Sources of Western Social Ethics" Yoder's position is consistently articulated.

In "Radical Reformation Ethics in Ecumenical Perspective," initially presented in 1978, Yoder offers what for him is the heart of the matter—a doctrine of the church. What happened in the Constantinian era was a reversal of the New Testament doctrine of the church. The three criteria for a sound doctrine of the church are 1) disestablishment (that is, a church neither governed nor supported by civil government), 2) voluntary adult membership (church membership based not on infant baptism but on an adult confession of faith), and 3) renunciation of all violence, wealth, and imperial office.

These characteristics of the true church were assumed by the New Testament Christian community, the early church before the fourth century, sixteenth-century Swiss Anabaptists, and seventeenth-century Quakers. The mainline churches, however, fell from faithfulness when they changed from a critical prophetic minority into a privileged minority and gradually into a majority from the fourth-century onward. With the medieval synthesis of church and state, clergy and sword, ecclesiastical hierarchy and wealth Christianity came to be identified with "violence, money, and social stratification."

Jesus as revelatory norm for social ethics was gradually overshadowed by common sense, natural reason, and a sense of responsibility for society and history as sources for ethics. Yoder in this essay does not address the theological agenda as such, although he suggests that "A different ethic obviously involves the possibility of a different doctrine of humanity or Christology, or of nature, of sin or grace or law."⁶ He also states that for the Radical Reformers "the humanity of Jesus of Nazareth" and "human obedience" were the primary grounds for Christian ethical decision-making. His primary concern, however, is not with a systematic treatment of Christian doctrine but an analysis of Christian social ethics.

In "Anabaptism and History," Yoder outlines the three basic characteristics of the "restitutionist" pattern of historical thinking as espoused by Anabaptism: a past normative state of the church, a radical fall of the church, and a radical renewal. The *normative state* is the incarnation as related in the canon, more exactly "a very particular story of the New Testament," the story and claims of Christ. This is a historical norm with "historical objectivity and distance," equally accessible to all.

The *fall* occurred in the Constantinian era with the strategic church-state alliance, the development of the just war approach to violence, and the repression of dissent. For the Anabaptists the fourth century was wrong in the light of the New Testament not "because it was later than the New Testament, but because wrong fourth-century options were chosen rather than right fourth-century options."⁷ According to Yoder, Anabaptists viewed the pre-Constantinian fathers and "over two centuries of fallible, divided, confused church life" favourably because the official teaching remained basically sound. He adds: "If twentieth-century restitutionism needs correction or refinement at this point, it would be to look for still earlier or deeper pre-dispositions toward the Constantinian shift (anti-Judaism? Neoplatonism? creeping empire loyalism despite the commitment to pacifism?)."⁸ Radical *renewal* requires offering a social alternative to fallen Christendom, finding a normative stance within Scripture, and locating the authoritative interpretation of Scripture outside the establishment—as in the congregation or with the prophet.

In the third essay, "The Constantinian Sources of Western Ethics," Yoder spells out the conceptual and ethical implications of the "Constantinian shift" especially in regard to the church's attitude toward war and peace. Before Constantine violence was considered to be morally wrong; after Constantine there was a growing acceptance of imperial violence as a Christian duty. What is presupposed is a new ecclesiology, a new eschatology, and a new metaphysics, among other things. The *new ecclesiology* is reflected in the shift from the church as a persecuted minority to the church as everybody, with paganism now becoming the minority, and with heresies now being officially repressed. The *new eschatology* has to do with a new view of providence and history. Before God's way with the world and history as a whole was ambiguous and a matter of faith; only where the church was God's way.

After Constantine this is reversed. Now the true church is invisible and God's working within history and through the empire is beyond dispute. Imperial values and culture, legal tradition, and social structures are identified with Christianity. One's duties of station, office, and vocation within the civil government replaces Jesus and his teachings as the ethical standard. With the "Constantinian wedding of piety with power" efficacy and utility replace the principles of "revelation," "nature," and "`received' standards" as sources for the ethical principles.⁹ At the bottom of this is a *new metaphysics,* a neoplatonic dualism between invisible spirituality and visible worldliness. Christianity becomes interiorized and individualized with a growing distance between Jesus and worldly authorities.

This perceived gap between ourselves and the Bible, in which the New Testament is perceived to be irrelevant to the pressing duties of the historical moment constitutes apostasy. What is called for is radical "disestablishment" and "deconstantinianization." Yoder puts it unequivocally: "What the churches accepted in the Constantinian shift is what Jesus had rejected, seizing godlikeness, moving *in hoc signo* from Golgotha to the battlefield. If this diagnosis is correct, then the cure is not to update the fourth-century mistake by adding another 'neo-' [as in neo-Constantinianism] but to repent of the whole 'where it's at' style and to begin again with *kenosis.*"¹⁰

Yoder's position as articulated in these published essays is the product of years of writing and teaching on Christian pacifism. His lecture notes on the subject have been collected and informally published under the title *Christian Attitudes to War, Peace, and Revolution.* In the first few chapters of this volume Yoder traces the gradual shift that occurs within the early church from an initial total rejection of soldiering to a slow acculturation by the church to the Greco-Roman world; an accommodation also to the military requirements of the Empire, with the church becoming less and less rigorous in its ethical requirements. Two levels of Christians with different ethical obligations come to exist: the religious monastics for whom the high moral claims of Jesus especially in regard to nonviolence continue to apply, and the average Christian for whom a lower, common sense approach to life suffices. Constantine represents this basic reorientation and the lowering of standards for the ordinary believers. The "Just War" as articulated by Ambrose and Augustine, a moral theory not based on Jesus' teachings but dependent on an extra-biblical common sense epistemology, is the ethical outworking of this reorientation.

What is suggested but not demonstrated in detail by Yoder is that theologically this shift gets legitimated by the council of Nicea and its theological formulation of trinitarian orthodoxy. Constantine, intent on unifying the church as a means of uniting the empire, plays a decisive role at Nicea, calling the council, chairing it, and providing the crucial terminology. As the theological formulation of trinitarian orthodoxy is completed only by 381, so the political and legal consequences of the shift gradually but ineluctably become visible: by 390-392 pagan temples are closed, by 420 dissenting Christians are officially repressed and persecuted, by 436 non-Christians are not allowed to be in the army.[11] This is a long way from New Testament Christianity.

Trinitarian Orthodoxy

It is not entirely clear whether Yoder considers the "Constantinian Shift" and "Trinitarian Orthodoxy" as defined at Nicea and Constantinople as part of the same movement; that is, whether the two are intrinsically linked. There are times when Yoder seems to suggest that the two are thus connected— that theological orthodoxy, as assisted (if not dictated) in its official definition by Constantine, is little more than a theological reflection and legitimation of Constantinianism (and therefore also a sign of apostasy). On other occasions Yoder offers a more sympathetic reading of the theological development of doctrine that these councils and resulting creeds represent. The most significant work by Yoder in this regard is his *Preface to Theology: Christology and Theological Method*.[12] We summarize here briefly his analysis of the development of doctrine in the post-biblical period as reflected in the Apostles' Creed and the Nicene Creed.

The Apostles' Creed, which was basically in place by the third and fourth centuries, according to Yoder, retains the christological emphasis of the first New Testament confessions: "Jesus Christ is Lord." The second article is the longest, and is in narrative form as is the New Testament *kerygma*, with the first article a kind of prologue and the third an epilogue. Nevertheless, there is already a deviation from the biblical narrative. There is no reference to the Old Testament narrative, nor is there any allusion to the life and teachings of Jesus. What we have in the second article is a leap from birth to crucifixion. More noteworthy than this is the lack of any sense of urgency concerning repentance. As Yoder puts it, "By this time we have had Constantine. The pagan world is moving under the control of the church. So the concept of the minority church calling people to listen, to repent, to believe, to receive forgiveness, does not quite fit."[13] Instead there is reflected in the Creed the beginnings of the sacramentalism and metaphysical speculation so prevalent in the medieval church, with the Catholic church itself becoming an object of belief.

The fourth-century debates around the question of the Trinity are a further expansion of the tendency already present in the Apostles' Creed. What we see in effect is the triumph of Alexandrian intellectual, philosophical, and systematic thinking over the simple, exegetical, historical, narrative, and more unphilosophical Hebraic approach of Antioch. Yoder concedes the partial similarity between the wisdom (*sophia*) tradition of the Scriptures and Greek notions of cosmic rationality (*logos*). He is, consequently, sympathetic to what the theologians in the Patristic period were trying to do with the concept of Jesus as Logos being both equal to and distinct from God.[14] He appears also to support the attempt by the church to define an orthodox position against various heresies, particularly Arianism; that is, the desire to maintain both the diversity and unity of God.

What is clear, however, is that Yoder understands the fourth-century theological debates primarily within a socio-political framework (both ecclesiastical and imperial), and this makes him suspicious of them. This is the age of accommodation to the Greco-Roman culture. A radical conversion is no longer required. Neither is there a strong sense of sin. The pressure to stress the uniqueness and deity of Jesus, as a necessary means of God's breaking in to save the world from sin is weaker, replaced rather with a preoccupation with the dignity and transcendence of God. The growing strength of Arianism mirrors this kind of accommodation to a Hellenistic and imperialistic culture, and theological deviation from the New Testament.[15]

Yoder's treatment of the political context and implications of the Arian-Alexander/Athanasius debates behind the Nicene formulation is particularly noteworthy. Yoder admits that Arius' theology fits imperial aims better than Athanasius' theology: "If you lower the concept of who Christ was, then you raise your vision of the emperor, because the logos was in both Jesus and the empire.... If Jesus is a little smaller, the king will be a little higher, and that is just what Constantine and his advisors wanted."[16] This is why Arius had more friends in the imperial court. In contrast, Athanasius had more popular support. The Athanasian-orthodox position did in fact safeguard the christological content of the New Testament ("that Jesus, the Word in Jesus, is genuinely of the character of deity and genuinely human, and that his work is the work of God and yet the work of a man"[17]) relatively well, even though it employed non-biblical concepts and language. Nevertheless, there is a serious change of mood and style; a deviation from the biblical centre.

For Yoder what is this biblical centre that is departed from at Nicea? It is the "Gospel story." And what is the "Gospel story?" This is how he puts it: "The form of the confession is still used but it has been so padded out with the statements about the essence of Christ that you don't recognize any narrative to it anymore. One is not driven to think of the movement of time, of God doing something among men in a given time and place, as being crucial."[18] Yoder concedes that one finds in the Bible references to the existence of God the Father, the Son, and the Spirit, and the assumption that they are the same. This is not, however, given in the Bible as revealed information. The doctrine of the Trinity as later formulated does not appear in the Bible but "is the solution of an intellectual difficulty which arises if we accept the statement of the Bible."[19] It itself is not revealed. What is revealed is the revelation in Jesus and ongoing revelation in the Holy Spirit. "The doctrine of the Trinity is a test of whether your commitment to Jesus and to God are biblical enough that you have the problem which the doctrine of the Trinity solves."[20]

In other words, the trinitarian formulation is itself secondary in importance; it tries to solve an intellectual problem which follows logically from asserting both Jewish monotheism, on the one hand, and God's revelation in Christ and the Holy Spirit, on the other. Other words and solutions, possibly better ones, could potentially be found. What is important is the commitment "to the man Jesus, and . . . to the unique God" manifested in Jesus behind the trinitarian struggle of the fourth century. If we do not possess the same commitment as the early church Fathers who debated the trinitarian question, we have departed from the Christian family. Yoder is, in short, distinguishing between 1) revelation (and commitment to that revelation), and 2) intellectual reflection upon that revelation (Nicea-Constantinople).

Yoder is struck by the fact that many Christians who reject the teaching of "anything above the Bible or beyond the Bible" continue to give equal authoritative status to the Nicene Creed and the doctrine of the Trinity. Despite this positive and empathetic portrayal of the Patristic controversies of the first four centuries, in the end Yoder is highly dubious about the political motivations behind the final statement:

> If we look back at the politics that were played between 325 and 381, the methods these men used, some of their motives, at the personal quality of Constantine, or if we ask in what sense he was a Christian when he dictated this dogma, then we have to be pretty dubious about giving to this movement any authority. If we call into question the acceptance of *Hellenistic* thought forms which are foreign to the way the Bible thinks, which don't fit with the *Hebrew* mind, or with the *modern* mind either for that matter, then again we have to challenge whether it does us much good.[21]

Yoder can understand why the high church tradition would give the Nicene Creed and the later creeds a certain kind of hermeneutic authority which in practice stands above the Bible even if it does not do so theoretically. After all, orthodoxy becomes the official kingly position. For the "Believers Church" tradition (and the modern reader), however, the only authority is the claims of Jesus, creating the intellectual problem to which the Nicene statement tries to find an answer. "The doctrine is not supernatural truth, supernaturally communicated for its information value. It is not learning which the Holy Spirit gave to the Council Fathers of Nicea because these were bishops assembled from the whole world at the invitation from the Roman Emperor. It is valid because it reflects the serious struggle of men, within their language and their culture, with their commitment to an absolute God and to a normative Jesus."[22]

J. Denny Weaver, a younger Mennonite theologian, is heavily indebted to Yoder's general theological orientation and follows Yoder's critique of the Constantinian-shift almost word- for-word, drawing even more radical conclusions than does Yoder (that is, he is less sympathetic to trinitarian orthodoxy) in his critique of the theological developments that occurred between the Gospels and the fourth and fifth century. This is especially evident in his recently published essay, "Christology in Historical Perspective," in which he argues that Mennonites as "charter members" of the Believers Church tradition—that is, as descendants of the radical wing of the Reformation who are "neither Catholic nor Protestant"—have a unique contribution to make to contemporary christological discussions. He believes there is a "true theology which does not, or need not, pass through the Constantinian church" and believes there is a clear choice between reading the Bible through Believers Church eyes or Constantinian church eyes.

What are Constantinian church eyes? They are the eyes of the established church throughout the ages, most graphically represented by Constantine, but a temptation already present in the Old Testament and always present to the church. It is the temptation "to affirm the status quo" that is already apparent "in the Old Testament in the tension between prophet and priest or king, so that Constantinianism has always tempted God's people."[23] It boils down to the loss of Jesus' nonresistant love ethic (discipleship) as normative for Christian life, and replacing it presumably with a societal norm premised on the need for coercion (although in this essay Weaver nowhere spells out what this Constantinian norm is, only what it is not).

Weaver is concerned to show how the theological changes that occur in the development from the Gospels to Nicea/Chalcedon are to be seen as part of the gradual Constantinian shift that is taking place. The underlying theological shift is from the use of narrative to ontological (or generic) categories in defining Jesus. "Jesus is identified in terms of essential (generic) categories to which he belongs—humanity and deity—rather than in terms of the unique way he was a human being or how he specifically made God's presence known."[24] Jesus' particularity—his concrete life, deeds, and teachings—gets lost. Further, there is a narrowing down of christological images. From a diversity of New Testament christological images, the one from the Prologue of John's Gospel is selected as the only legitimate way of talking about Jesus. Related to this is the fact that certain titles, like "Son of God," change their meaning. Whereas initially it was a reference to God's relation to the world, it now designates "a relationship entirely within the heavenly realm, a relationship within the Godhead itself."[25]

As an alternative to Weaver's portrayal of early church theological development, I would like to suggest that what happened was not a narrowing of christology, or a selection of one of many christologies in the New Testament, but the development of a distinctively Christian doctrine of God out of the diversity of the Scriptures, a broad theological framework large enough to hold within itself a variety of theological emphases. It was the "heresies" that narrowed down the gospel, and it was for the purpose of protecting the Christian view of God from such a narrowing that orthodoxy was formulated. Further, Aloys Grillmeier, in his definitive study of this period, has concluded that the Nicene theologians did not change the meaning of the "Son of God":

> Without having thought through all the implications and problems, the Fathers of Nicea had the courage to maintain the tradition of the "Son of God" to be found in Bible and church in all its strictness, in part with unbiblical words.... So much did the Fathers of Nicea wish to remain within the framework of the baptismal *kerygma*, that they did not add any explanation of the way in which they themselves wanted the *homoousios* to be understood.[26]

Behind both Yoder's and Weaver's critique of the theological changes that took place in the first five centuries of the Christian church lies their legitimate concern for ethics. What occurs, as they correctly see it, is an ethical watering down of the Christian message. According to Weaver, Anabaptists take discipleship (shorthand for saying that Jesus—his life and teaching—are normative for the Christian life) to be at the heart of the gospel narratives. The formulations of Nicea and Chalcedon are devoid of this ethical-discipleship dimension: "That fact should help us to understand that Nicea-Chalcedon is not a lens through which to read the New Testament, nor can Nicea-Chalcedon alone serve as the norm which tells us whether we have read the New Testament correctly."[27]

Neither is there in these definitions of orthodoxy any reference to the manner of the atoning work of Christ.

Since, however, Mennonites and others consider the nonviolent and nonresistant manner of Jesus' death crucial for people who claim Jesus as authoritative for their lives, these definitions are suspect. I share Yoder's and Weaver's concern to retrieve the ethical normativity of Jesus for Christian theology, and lament the loss of this narrative, historical, and ethical dimension in the first few centuries. Nevertheless, I see the theological development that occurred as the needed creation of a barebones theological substructure which is required as the framework for or ground of ethics; not as something that contradicts the ethical claims of the New Testament.

The reasons for these theological shifts away from the New Testament are for Weaver intrinsically linked to the gradual Constantinian shift that occurred over the centuries and reached its symbolic climax with the person of Constantine himself. Jesus is no longer taken to be normative for the life of average Christians, nor is the church thought of as a critical, prophetic minority. Now the emperor and responsibility for the state is authoritative. The Nicene council, called by Constantine and helped in its theological formulations by him, "was a matter of political expedience as well as a search for theological truth."[28]

The slight hint by Weaver that there may have also been at work among the bishops of the fourth century a search for theological truth is overshadowed by the general tenor of suspicion throughout that ultimately political expedience determined the entire project of so-called orthodoxy. While alluding to the fact that Arius gained the upperhand after the Council in 325, that Constantine later threw his support behind Arius, that Athanasius (the defender of orthodoxy) was banned five times, and that in the end an Arian baptized Constantine, Weaver does not draw the obvious conclusion: that it was Arian theology rather than orthodoxy which lent itself more readily to Constantinianism. Here Weaver is less nuanced than Yoder, who acknowledges, as we have seen above, that Arianism and the erosion of the claims regarding the exclusive deity of Christ, were less faithful to the New Testament and could more easily be adapted to political idolatry than the claims of orthodoxy.

Weaver's conclusion is that, while Nicea and Chalcedon have provided the church with a time-honoured answer to the christological issue, it is only one, and not necessarily the best, answer. The answers given at Nicea and Chalcedon, according to Weaver, are the products of a conference of people gathered together, similar to a conference of Mennonites meeting today to discuss christology. What Mennonites need to do in their contemporary search for christological clarity, is to remain faithful to their sixteenth-century spiritual ancestors. Hans Denk's mystical christology, Pilgram Marpeck's external christology, and Menno Simon's suspect "un-Chalcedonian" christology differed in substantive ways but they had one thing in common: they considered Jesus' life, deeds, and teachings normative for Christian life. The established (or mainline) church has given up this normativity of Jesus since Constantine, and the Believers Church needs to offer an alternative christology based on the normativity of the earthly, historical Jesus. In short, we have the choice of reading the Bible through Constantinian-establishment (which includes trinitarian orthodox) eyes or Believers Church eyes.

Both Yoder and Weaver reflect in good part the historic Radical Protestant position: the identification of the fall of the church with the Constantinian synthesis of church and state, and an accompanying suspicion of the metaphysical, sacramental, and ontological language of the historic creeds.[29] There are many other contemporaries who could be cited to illustrate the same point of view. John E. Toews, for instance, has recently argued that the creeds and confessions do not help us in developing a sound doctrine of the church:

> The Christology of the creeds represents the thought and language of a particular time in history. Their theological affirmations served the churches of their era. *But the language is neither biblical nor modern, let alone postmodern*. Furthermore, as scholars have pointed out, the creeds do not offer good Christologies, nor were they intended to. The ecumenical creeds were never designed as Christologies. Instead, they answered specific and narrow Christological questions of their time, e.g. was Jesus both human and divine? They outline rules for doing Christology but not Christology itself.[30]

A devaluation of the classical creedal tradition is evident here. Toews implies that the creeds and Scripture are mutually exclusive categories, and that the New Testament is the only acceptable "starting point for Mennonite theological reflection" on the nature of christology and the church. Also, interestingly, there is the implication that one reason why the creeds cannot be taken seriously is that they are alien to modern and postmodern thinking. I would argue that it is precisely in the modern and postmodern context, which has seen the consequences and collapse of strictly historicist and empiricist modes of perceiving the world, that the ontological and metaphysical presuppositions behind the classical creeds offer an appealing alternative way of viewing reality.

A Proposal: Trinitarian Orthodoxy Without Constantinianism

There are, however, new voices being heard within Mennonite circles, voices which are taking a second look not only at the importance of post-biblical Patristic theological development but also at the Constantinian and post-Constantinian church. One of the most outspoken has been Dennis Martin, who has taught at Associated Mennonite Biblical Seminaries in Elkhart, Indiana. In a provocative 1987 article, Martin distinguished between the modern linear view of history and the premodern multidimensional, multitemporal view. The former subordinates "the timeless, transcendent, traditional past to the present and future," and "rejects traditional premodern history to restore `true history'," locating "`true history' not in tradition or the mystery of the church but in a lost yet supposedly recoverable body of `facts'."[31]

This fallacious view of history, Martin says, lies behind the Anabaptist-Mennonite *restitutionist* model of church renewal, in which a traditional, sacramental approach to history as characterized by the Catholic Church between A.D. 300 and 1500 was rejected in favour of what was perceived to be a more New Testament view of the church. "They [Anabaptist-Mennonites] believed that they could restore, recreate, or reconstruct that original Christian community rather than represent, or re-call (anamnesis) it. In the process they read back into the first three Christian centuries elements of their own situation."[32]

In effect, says Martin, it is "discontinuity" rather than "continuity" that characterizes history in the restitutionist model. In this view most everything post-biblical is seen to be discontinuous with the Gospel. The fourth century and the Constantinianization of the church is most frequently identified as the place where the "fall of the church" occurred. John H. Yoder suffers the brunt of Martin's critique. "Yoder," says Martin, "distorts ‚Constantinianism' by reading the `established churches' of the post-Reformation era back into the fourth century. Nearly all the characteristics of 'Constantinianism' that Yoder adduces are more recognizable in the modern world than in the ancient or medieval world (dualism, establishment power, utilitarianism). He makes little distinction between the 'Constantinianism' of Eusebius in the early fourth century and that of Augustine."[33]

Martin defends what he calls the *reform* view of history: "It is the way the ancients understood history. It is the attitude toward history that predominated in the world of the Bible, in the world of the Greeks and Romans, and in the world of medieval Christianity. The traditional way of reform accepts the past all the way down to the present while at the same time calling for reform of institutions where they have become deformed. .... It is an attitude that accepts institutions and has a basic attitude of trust toward the handing down (tradition) of institutions, even when it recognizes that institutions are deformed, and need reform."[34] Although Martin does not go into what this might mean in the way of understanding the theological formulations of the fourth and fifth centuries, his analysis and critique of the Anabaptist-Mennonite restitutionist approach to history prepares the way for a much more sympathetic appropriation of classical trinitarian and christological formulations within Mennonite theology.

There are other voices that do indicate precisely such a new, more positive interest among Mennonites in the classical formulations of the ancient creeds. This is reflected in recent essays by Ben C. Ollenburger, Cornelius J. Dyck, and Marlin E. Miller.[35] The 1985 publication of Howard Loewen's *One Lord, One Church, One Hope, and One God: Mennonite Confessions of Faith,* has contributed significantly to this renaissance of interest in the fourth and fifth-century formulations.[36] What Loewen's study suddenly brought to the attention of Mennonite readers, who had presumed that Mennonites like other Radical Protestant groups were non-creedal, was that the various Mennonite groups have produced probably more confessions in their 465 years than any other Christian tradition. Many of these confessions, in their general structure (theology, christology, ecclesiology, eschatology) bear some remarkable similarities in their organization to classical creeds. What distinguishes them from the classical formulations and other mainline post-Reformation confessions is a heightened ethical-consciousness. This concern for personal and social ethics, obedience to the life and teachings of Jesus, colours all of the articles of these confessions from beginning to end.

The Radical Protestant suspicion of creedal development during the Patristic period is rooted, as we have seen, in its rejection of the Constantinian synthesis of Christianity and classical culture, and in its restitutionist view of church renewal, its legitimate objection to the loss of the ethical. There are certainly valid grounds for this historic suspicion of Constantinianism and its theological legitimation. The insights of Radical Protestantism in this regard ought, in my opinion, to be in the forefront of ecumenical discussion.

Nevertheless, I want as a self-critical Mennonite to propose in the final section of this essay 1) that theological orthodoxy as it developed in the first five centuries after Christ stands in fundamental continuity with the Scriptures, 2) that orthodoxy necessarily went beyond the Scriptures in developing a uniquely Christian doctrine of God, and 3) not only that classical, trinitarian orthodoxy need not be identified with social-political Constantinianism (it is more able than alternative theologies to function as a critique of all forms of Constantinianism) but that it actually provides a necessary framework for Christian ethics.

Orthodoxy Stands in Continuity with the Scriptures

While the full-blown trinitarian formulation of Nicea-Constantinople is not explicitly present in the Scriptures, it is there implicitly in the form of a question. The New Testament writers asked how they as early Christians could (1) remain faithful to the Jewish monotheism of the Old Testament (the one God, Yahweh, creator of everything visible and invisible, whom no one has seen, of whom no images are to be made, and who has repeatedly acted in the history of His people); and at the same time (2) acknowledge or account for the fact that this God has communicated Himself to us, has been with us (Immanuel) in the birth, life, teachings, death, resurrection and ascension of Jesus of Nazareth, in an absolute sense with the power to forgive sins and restore all things; and (3) acknowledge or account for the fact the Holy Spirit, who descended upon the early followers of Jesus at Pentecost, is in fact the very presence and reality of God, and of Jesus, giving birth to the church and uniting all believers with God, Christ, and each other.

Behind the trinitarian debates of the first few centuries lies the need to express these three separate convictions, while asserting simultaneously the unity of God.

What is one to make of the claim by both Yoder and Weaver that between the Gospels and the Creeds a major shift has occurred? Both (Weaver even more so than Yoder) stress the discontinuity between the fourth-century theological definitions and the New Testament. They talk about the shift from the narrative mode of the Gospels to the ontological mode of the Creeds as though this were a deviation from the biblical text.

This fails adequately to recognize the "ontological-metaphysical" presuppositions behind biblical narrative itself. The biblical *kerygma* is distorted if narrative (historical chronology or story telling) and ontology (generic being-language) are torn asunder the way Yoder and particularly Weaver tend to do. Not only are both modes present within the biblical texts, but narrative as we have it in the Synoptics (not to mention the Pauline epistles which were written earlier), takes place within an ontological framework (another way of saying this would be: the Bible does not absolutize history but places historical events within the context of ultimate reality or the way things are). The ontology of the relatively late prologue to the gospel of John is not unlike the confessional ontology of Philippians 2, one of the earliest hymns to be found in the Christian Scriptures (likely sung or chanted well before the retrospective and narrative setting-in-order of events as we have them in the Synoptics). Only in the modern context does narrative become pure historicism—that is, freed from cosmic and ontological moorings.

Yoder seems to equivocate in this regard. At some points, he draws direct links between the wisdom literature of the Hebrew Scriptures, the Logos traditions of the Christian Scriptures as imbedded in Colossians 1, Hebrews 1, John 1, Philippians 2, and 1 Corinthians 8, and the Greek concept of Logos as cosmic rationality.[37] At other times, he talks about the shift from narrative to ontological language as a form of discontinuity, as a "moving away from the biblical centre in mood, in style, in content."[38] There is, of course, a good deal of truth to Yoder's critical observation that with the passage of time, as we get closer to the fourth and fifth centuries, there appears to be less and less historical narrative present within the ontological framework of the creeds. The ethical gets lost. The alternative is not, however, as Weaver seems to suggest, to find a christological alternative to Nicea and Chalcedon but to retrieve the historical, narrative, and ethical content of trinitarian christology.

The basic point to be made here is that the ontological language of Nicea/Constantinople stands in fundamental continuity with the Scriptures. The numerous binitarian (Rom. 8:11, 2 Cor. 4:14, Gal.1:1, Eph. 1:20, 1 Tim. 1:2, 1 Pet. 1:21, and 2 John 3) and triadic references (Matt. 28:19, Acts 2:32-33, 1 Cor. 6:11, 12:4ff, Gal. 3:11-14, Heb.10:29, and 1 Pet. 1:2) simply confirm this basic continuity. In the words of William G. Rusch, "No doctrine of the Trinity in the Nicene sense is present in the New Testament. However, the threefold pattern is evident throughout, despite the fact that there is usually nothing in the context to demand it. The conclusion seems obvious; the idea of the triadic manifestation of the Godhead was present from the earliest period as part of Christian piety and thinking."[39]

The pressure of heretical groups (who threatened the truth of the biblical *kerygma*), the missionary impulse to explain the truth of the *kerygma* to the pagans, and the simple desire to know the truth of the matter propelled the church in the first five centuries to formulate what she took to be true. In the process a Christian world view developed which was distinct from strict Jewish monotheism, on the one side and Greco-Roman dualism on the other. What unfolded was a doctrine of God as three in one, and one in three, with profound implications for the Christian view not only of God but of the whole created universe and of human history. God was seen as having three modes of being: *transcendent* creator of all things visible and invisible, *historically* incarnated in human flesh in the person of Jesus of Nazareth, and *immanently and dynamically* present in all of creation but particularly in the church through the Spirit.

The specific heresy which brought the issue to a head was Arianism. The upshot of Arias' theology was that Christ was not fully divine, shorthand for saying that the power of God in Jesus was not really the eternal divine power itself but a lesser power (that is, in Jesus God was not fully with us as humans).[40] Both the christological debates leading up to Chalcedon and the Trinitarian debates leading up to Nicea and Constantinople have finally to do with the nature of our salvation, and are, consequently, deeply concerned with God's relation to the world of human experience. To question the full deity of Christ is to call into question the fullness of our salvation. A trinitarian christology is essential for soteriology. This is especially relevant for Mennonites and their concern for regenerate life. The Anabaptists repeatedly spoke of regeneration as not only becoming Christ-like but actually taking on or participating in the divine nature itself. In this they have something in common with the Eastern theological tradition. It was, they believed, through the Holy Spirit that we become Christ-like; and through being Christ-like that we partake of the divine nature itself.

The Creed of Nicea-Constantinople is the culmination of a development which begins in the New Testament itself. What occurred was not a corruption of the original message, but an unfolding and development of the ontological implications of that message. It was not one possible line of development; one of numerous other lines which might have been taken just as legitimately. Nor was it a formulation necessary for only one historical moment. The orthodoxy that was defined, and the distortions of the truth that were identified, continue to have universal significance for the Christian church. Creedalization took place more or less at the same time that canonization took place and for more or less the same reasons: to establish norms by which to determine what was true and what was false. The primary importance of the Nicene formulation is not each literal word (no plenary or verbal inspiration) but the basic trinitarian structure which becomes theologically normative for the church. By it the church defined the Christian doctrine of God: the one God having three modes of being: Father, Son, Holy Spirit.

Classical Orthodoxy is a Necessary Doctrinal Development Beyond the Scriptures

No one disputes the fact that the language of Nicea, Constantinople, and Chalcedon is not pure biblical language; and that the doctrine of the Trinity as articulated in 381 cannot be found as such in the New Testament. I propose, however, that Nicea and Constantinople represent a required development of doctrine beyond the Scriptures, retaining a faithful continuity with Scriptures as far as its formal christological claims are concerned but unfortunately losing sight of the existential component of the *kerygma* and the ethical claims of Jesus without which all dogma becomes abstract formalism. The point I make at the end of this essay is that classical dogmatic formulations are essential for assuring an ontological-metaphysical grounding for ethics; relevant especially in an age when ethics is defined primarily if not exclusively in terms of free human agency, without reference to a transcendent ground. Here I concentrate on what Hanson, in his recent book *Studies in Christian Antiquity*, describes as the development of a uniquely Christian doctrine of God that occurs during the Patristic period.

Hanson distinguishes between the "immediate occasion" of the Trinitarian development (the Arian controversy) and the "original urge or need or dynamism" which gave rise to it. The latter is more important and has to do with the development of a specifically Christian doctrine of God distinct from the Jewish doctrine of God. The New Testament just hinted at such a doctrine. "It was when Christianity emerged during the second century into a non-Jewish largely Gentile milieu that the pressure to produce a specifically Christian doctrine of God became unavoidable."[41] Why was a Christian doctrine of God so necessary? I find Hanson's answer to this question persuasive: "If Christianity was to be more than an enthusiastic or moralizing sect making no pretensions to intellectual respectability, more than an ethnic religion . . . it was bound to produce a specifically Christian doctrine of God."[42] It was necessary "if Christianity was to be a missionary religion, a religion capable of sustaining the daring claim that it was a faith for all races and all classes and all minds, a religion for the whole world."[43] In other words, what Hanson appears to be saying is that in the first few centuries after Jesus of Nazareth came and went a new religion was born, the Christian religion with a new doctrine of God profoundly indebted to but ultimately different from the Jewish doctrine of God. According to Hanson, Christianity was more than a "subvariety of Judaism."

The noteworthy fact is that the fourth-century development destroyed "the tradition of Christ as a convenient philosophical device, of Christ, as the Cappadocian fathers put it, existing for the sake of us instead of our existing for his sake."[44] It was the Arians who (influenced by Middle Platonist cosmology[45]) Hellenized the gospel and tended to see Christ as a "demi-god" philosophically understood. The trinitarian faith of Nicea/Constantinople, as shaped finally by the Cappadocians, was in fact much truer to the biblical Christ ("the monotheism that is part of the inner nature of Christianity and that also did justice to the ancient practice of worshipping Christ"[46]) than had been the theological positions as articulated by most of the leading theologians from the second century onward. What Hanson is arguing is that the fourth-century doctrine of God is in fact a return to biblical origins.

It is, however, a return characterized by new language and new imagery. Hanson makes the lucid point that "One of the lessons learnt by the bitter experience of the Arian Controversy was that you cannot interpret the Bible simply in biblical terms. If your intention is to explain the Bible's meaning, then on crucial points you must draw your explanation from some other vocabulary apart from that of the Bible. Otherwise you will be left with the old question in another form still unanswered."[47] It may be the case, as he states, that pro-Nicene theologians found it difficult to deal with a transtemporal God acting in temporal history, with the Word taking on human flesh, with "the full force of the dynamic, eschatological language which the N.T. uses of Christ and the Holy Spirit." In Hanson's words , "They flatten and blunt this language, transposing it into ontological categories. For Athanasius, as has frequently been observed, the divinity of Christ means his ontological stability."[48]

This charge (that the dynamic element is lost in the fourth and fifth centuries) is in my view, however, open to further debate. Already in 1940 the great classicist Charles Norris Cochrane, in his definitive work *Christianity and Classical Culture*, argued persuasively that it was precisely the dynamic nature of the fourth-century trinitarian schema, particularly as later formulated by Augustine, that overcame static Greek dualism and helped shape western views of dynamic history.[49] Hanson, I would say, here slips into a Yoderian kind of argument which he does not sustain consistently. Further on, he qualifies the above comments and talks about the fact that the fourth-century Fathers remained with non-philosophical language when talking about the bodily resurrection, creation of matter *ex nihilo*, and the incarnation. He concludes that "[p]erhaps the best way to express the situation would be to say that in all their theology there is a tension between the ideas of Greek philosophy and those of the tradition of Christian truth which they inherited . . . ."[50] The point I am arguing, more strongly than Hanson does, is that the two (the biblical and the philosophical, the historical-Hebraic and the ontological-Hellenistic) ought not to be torn asunder. They belong together in the formation of primitive Christianity, and in the theological development that occurs in the first four centuries, and ought to be held together.

One could say that the nature of theological language itself evolved during these first four centuries as the uniquely Christian doctrine of God unfolded. Hanson traces the changing use of trinitarian imagery in the first four centuries (Logos, Father and Son, icon, ray or reflection, character as impression or stamp, stream, branch, sunbeam and so on).

Arians, interestingly, tended to be more literalistic in their use of such imagery. They argued, for example, that since sons come after fathers, therefore the Son of God must have been produced after and be inferior to God the Father.[51]

The important point here is that the Church Fathers and particularly the Nicene theologians (Athanasius and the Cappadocians) fully recognized the inadequacy of human language to talk about God. They were less concerned with precise literal wording and formulae than later generations and than we are, and more concerned with the meaning and content of what was expressed.[52] In the end Basil and the two Gregories reduced their use of images and analogies to a minimum because they disagreed with the way these images had been used by previous generations of theologians. In particular they objected to the use of "the pre-existent *Logos* as a convenient *philosophical* device" to preserve the "impassability of God."[53] They went back to the New Testament *theological* notion of Christ as Logos, as found in John 1. "The interesting and almost startling repudiation of tradition," says Hanson, "should remind us further that a process of development of doctrine can very well include a movement of pruning, almost reformation, as well as a positive evolution into something new."[54] They insisted that the Christ as *Logos* was both incarnate and pre-existent, and that it was in this way that the transcendent God had involved Himself with human existence and experience.

Although it is unfortunately true that the historical, narrative, ethical Jesus largely got lost in this theological development, it is not true that the God whom the Nicene theologians envisaged was solely a transcendent distant God who was removed from the world of human experience. The whole point of the trinitarian formulation was to express as adequately as possible that God is transcendent and impassable, that God did take on human flesh in the incarnation, and that God remains with us historically in some way. It is within the framework of these three claims that a contemporary ethic can be theologically retrieved.

Trinitarian Orthodoxy as a Necessary Framework for Ethics

We come now, finally, to the most difficult and most important aspect of our discussion: the relation of the theological developments of the fourth century to Constantinianism and to ethics in general. It is the agenda that has been set for us in this essay particularly, by Yoder and Weaver. I want to support the Radical Protestant suspicion of all forms of Constantinianism and its theological legitimation, but dispute the frequent assumption made by Radical Protestant theologians that theological orthodoxy is necessarily always a hand-maiden of Constantinianism.

Even the fourth-century connection between Constantine's political ambitions and the bishops' theological concerns at Nicea and post-Nicea is more ambiguous than some claim. Aloys Grillmeier gives us a penetrating historical analysis of Constantine's role at Nicea. Grillmeier acknowledges that Constantine's personal intervention in religious politics after his conversion in 312, and more actively in 324, "was the most momentous decision on the way toward the imperial church.[55] It was Eusebius of Caesarea, however, with his Arian tendencies, who truly espoused a political theology: "A historico-political theology emerges: the appearance of the Messiah and the imperial peace, Christianity and the empire, are bound together in an indissoluble unity by the idea of providence."[56] The Roman monarchy comes to represent the heavenly monarchy. The divine *Logos* is seen by Eusebius and some of the bishops he influenced as embodied within the Constantinian monarchy.

This is not a uniformly held opinion, however, and Augustine decisively breaks through such a view of history and the world in his *City of God*. It is this diversity of views concerning the role of the emperor in church affairs that Grillmeier emphasizes. According to Eusebius, the Emperor is the sovereign even in deciding matters of orthodoxy. Others, including Constantine himself, did not view it this way. Constantine is, of course, convinced that "the well-being of the state and the unity of the church" belong indissolubly together. But Constantine, according to Grillmeier, believed that this bond "had been created by experience of the power of the God of the Christians and his grace."[57] He had sleepless nights over the Arian controversy, and his calling of and participation in the Nicene Council was to help bring unity, end heresy, and search for truth.

According to his own correspondence he saw himself not as one who dictated a solution but as a "fellow servant" of the bishops. He thinks of his own intervention as "subsidiary"; the final norms being the church's own canons and tradition: "In his own documents he does not claim to have directed the synod. On the contrary, the decisions were worked out by the bishops themselves, under the guidance of the Holy Spirit, in search of the will of God. The ultimate norm for the decision of the council is to be sought here, as in the apostolic traditions and the canons of the church."[58] In short, Eusebius makes much higher claims for the Emperor than does Constantine himself. It is Eusebius' sacralization of the Emperor as "the interpreter of God and of the Logos-Christ," as someone at "the supreme summit of the visible world understood in religious terms" that accompanies later Byzantine history. According to Grillmeier, the imperial documents between 325-335 suggest that Constantine did not really influence the council's theological statements significantly; that Constantine was not even up to the theological debates going on at the time, although in time his advisors, especially the Eusebian party, seem to have increasingly found his ear.

Hanson makes the point in a slightly different but complementary way. He argues that, while most of those involved in the Arian controversy (with some rare exceptions) thought of the Emperor as having final authority, and while several Emperors attempted to play such an authoritative role but failed because they did not have sufficient support of the church, in the end Theodosius succeeded because he was backed by the general assent of the church.[59] It was the Eusebian-type of political theology in which Constantine takes on divine status, becomes a Logos figure, an Arian-like demigod, that must be seen as the prototype of a fallen church, not the era as a whole or theological orthodoxy in particular.

Where does this leave us as far as our immediate proposal is concerned? The particular contribution that the theology of Radical Protestantism can make to any ecumenical discussion of the fourth century resides in its suspicion of all forms of "Constantinianism;" that is, in its critique of all political theology in which theology and politics are fused, or worse, where theology functions as an instrument of political ideology. In such political theology, theology loses its own ground; it no longer witnesses to transcendent revelatory norms by which critically to evaluate political society — thereby sanctifying finite, historical empires, nations, parties, movements, groups, or figures.

That this happened during the time of Constantine and subsequent emperors cannot be denied. In fact, that this has happened throughout most of Christian history cannot be disputed. Constantinianism and so-called "Caesaropapism" must from the Radical Protestant perspective be severely judged. Here Yoder and Weaver are surely right. The question is whether classical orthodoxy, as articulated in the ecumenical creeds of the fourth and fifth centuries, is contingent upon Constantinianization (or the other way around). We have attempted, using Hanson's and Grillmeier's historical analysis of the period, to distinguish between the two, and to say that the theological development cannot be explained comprehensively with reference solely to the socio-political milieu in which it occurred.

It is true that the Emperor Constantine called the Nicene Council, chaired the meetings and doctrinal discussions, and allegedly contributed some of the crucial terminology. It is also possible that Constantine's own conversion and interest in creating ecclesiastical unity during the Arian controversy was motivated largely by political expediency, the desire for political unity. It does not follow, however, that the theological formulations coming out of this and subsequent councils are therefore to be rejected. The formulations of Nicea, Constantinople, and Chalcedon cannot be accounted for exclusively in terms of their socio-political context. If one looks carefully at the historical events surrounding the trinitarian and christological debates one comes to the following conclusions:

1. Nicea itself was the culmination of a long process that began in the New Testament (as a question to be answered); a process that gave birth to a uniquely Christian doctrine of God. It so happened that Constantine was the catalyst who brought the various groups together and played a crucial role in moving the theological development forward for whatever reasons.

2. The alleged wording that Constantine provided ("of the same essence") was in fact quite ambiguous and began a heated round of debate that was only solved at Constantinople, largely through the influence of three biblically minded theologians, the Cappadocians.

3. Athanasius, one of the chief early architects of Nicea, was a political *persona non grata* during the Constantinian period.

4. The emperors and their immediate circle of advisors (e.g., Eusebius) appear to have been more inclined toward Arianism than orthodoxy. Theologically, as Yoder so astutely observes, Arianism, which allowed for demi-gods was much more congenial to Constantinianism than orthodoxy.

In conclusion, I give three reasons why I believe an orthodox trinitarian theology is important for a contemporary Christian ethic. First, it provides us with the best conceptual critique of all political theology that legitimates a civil religion—that is, one in which religion or theology functions primarily as a conservative force in society, a glue which holds things together, usually sanctifying the dominant culture of an age.[60] A trinitarianism in which the one God is believed to be genuinely *transcendent* (Yahweh, of whom no graven images can be made, alongside whom there are no other gods), *historically* uniquely present in Jesus Christ (who is not one more demi-god who can be incarnated in numerous forms, political figures, historical movements, but is truly God with us), and *immanently* present within the cosmos, nature, history, and particularly the church as the Holy Spirit (not as the human spirit, but as the Spirit that proceeds from God the "Father" and God the "Son"), is the surest way of guarding against all forms of political and national idolatry (Constantinianism). This is the basis of Karl Barth's own twentieth-century defence of a christocentric trinitarianism in the face of the "Aryan" heresies of the pro-Hitler German Christians in the 1930s.

Second, the mystery of the Trinity has throughout history inspired mystical thought and spiritual formation. In fact, as Roberta C. Bondi has so persuasively shown in her contribution to this colloquium,[61] many of the bishops who played leading roles in creedal development in the fourth century themselves came from the monastic tradition and were shaped by the moral and spiritual formation at the heart of monasticism. There has been a growing recognition amongst Christians engaged in the struggle for social justice that if the contemporary ethical agenda is not to be reduced to human action pure and simple, and if the struggle is to have staying power, it will need to be rooted in spirituality. I would hold that the kind of spirituality that provides a distinctively Christian basis for moral and ethical action in the world is a trinitarian spirituality. Classical trinitarianism is not merely an abstract philosophical construct but is concerned precisely with what *God* is doing in the world in and through *Christ* and the *Spirit*. For Mennonites who are especially concerned with the ethical dimensions of Christ's message (a non-violent love ethic in particular), it is doubly important to ground the moral claims of Jesus and the regenerative power of the Holy Spirit in the very nature and person of God, without thereby claiming to have said everything about the mystery of God that can be said.

Finally, trinitarian thinking about God is urgently needed in the face of the contemporary environmental crisis. This threat of ecological disaster has its origin in modern assumptions about historical progress, unlimited human freedom, nature as "dead stuff" to be subdued in whatever ways we see fit, and the loss of a sense of moral responsibility to a transcendent reality for what we are doing with and on the earth. A trinitarian doctrine of God provides us with three necessary ways of perceiving divine reality in relation to this world and our moral responsibility: as transcendent creator to whom we are accountable and who is ultimately in charge of the cosmos despite what we do; as historically self-disclosed in the being and nature of Christ (therein giving us a quite specific moral and ethical agenda); and as Spirit immediately present to us in the church but also in all of creation. No longer can the created order be seen as dead stuff at our disposal. All of creation is in some sense grounded in the very being of God.

SIXTEEN

Towards a Theocentric Christology: A Re-reading of the Bible, History, Anabaptism, and Modern Culture*

Some contemporary christology, including some Mennonite theology, would be better described as "Jesusology." It makes "Jesus Christ" into a proper noun, so that the human, historical "Jesus of Nazareth" is understood to be the sum total of God. When Jesus of Nazareth is worshipped in this sense, believers are in danger of idolatry. When an ethic of discipleship and nonviolence is premised on an imitation of this Jesus of Nazareth, ethics becomes little more than historical, human action.

Christ is the honorary title given to Jesus of Nazareth by early Christians, thereby confessing that in the phenomena of the conception, birth, life, ministry, teaching, crucifixion, death, resurrection, and ascension of Jesus of Nazareth the God of the Jews (Yahweh) was fully present—salvation occurred, the kingdom of God came near. Furthermore, in the coming of the Spirit upon the believers at Pentecost, the same Spirit of God that was at work at the creation of the World, throughout Jewish history, and in the life and resurrection of Christ was now also

---

* Originally published in *The Limits of Perfection: A Conversation with J. Lawrence Burkholder*, edited by Rodney J. Sawatsky and Scott Holland (Conrad Grebel College: Institute of Anabaptist and Mennonite Studies, 1993; 2nd ed., Kitchener, ON: Pandora Press, 1996), 95-109. For all notes on the text see the Notes section below.

at work in the Christian community and in all of creation, reconciling it to God. Unless our christology is understood in relation to the larger trinitarian life of God, our Jesus ethic will be Promethean and idolatrous. The only adequate basis for a Christian ethic is a "theocentric christology," in which love of neighbour and enemy derives from a personal faith in and relationship with Jesus the Christ, what Wolfhart Pannenberg calls our "participation in the filial relation of Jesus to the father."[1]

The following essay was first delivered as a paper in 1992 at a conference on the thought of J. Lawrence Burkholder hosted by the Laurelville Mennonite Church Center. It has been published under the title "Towards a Theocentric Christology: Christ for the World."[2] In it I examine sympathetically the ethical thought of Burkholder in relation to John H. Yoder and Gordon D. Kaufman. I suggest that Burkholder is helpful in identifying the dilemmas we as Mennonites face in trying to follow the teachings of Jesus in the modern world, but that he doesn't really help us in shaping a constructive way of moving into the future.

I propose that for this we need to theologically ground our love ethic in a theocentric christology which goes beyond the Sermon on the Mount, that we read the history of the early Church (including the Constantinian period) in a more empathetic and nuanced way, that we re-examine the diverse options within early Anabaptism as well as other traditions that we may have rejected too quickly, and that we explore imaginative ways of reappropriating classical trinitarian thought in the postmodern era.

◆ ◆ ◆

Yoder, Kaufman, and Burkholder

John Howard Yoder, Gordon Kaufman, and J. Lawrence Burkholder are three contemporaries, all influenced by the Bender historical and theological renaissance of Anabaptist idealism yet each finding a very different way of attempting to bridge Anabaptist-Mennonite idealism and modernity. Yoder's *The Christian Witness to the State* (1964), Kaufman's *The Context of Decision* (1961), and Burkholder's *The Problem of Social Responsibility from the Perspective of the Mennonite Church* (completed as a doctoral thesis in 1958 but not published until 1989), all conceived and written more or less during the same period, offer distinctive models of how Mennonites ought to relate to modern culture.

Yoder's theology in *The Christian Witness to the State* is essentially a contemporary hermeneutic of Schleitheim, in which the church and the larger society/culture/state represent a dualism of response to the Christian message of nonviolence: "We need to distinguish between the ethics of discipleship which are laid upon every Christian believer by virtue of his very confession of faith, and an ethic of justice within the limits of 'relative prudence and self-preservation, which is all one can ask of the larger society.'"[3] The dualism between the church (made up of those "inside the perfection of Christ," and governed by nonresistance as laid out in Rom. 12:9-21) and the world (made up of those "outside the perfection of Christ" and governed by the violence of the state as outlined in Rom. 13:4), are both "ways of God's acting in the world." These are not two different realms but two different responses to God's way in Christ: one of obedience and the other of disobedience and sin.

There is no place for compromise on the part of the Christian in his or her relation to society. The only options for Christians are to witness to individuals in the world in the hope that they will be converted to the perfection of Christ (*agape*, or self-sacrificial love) or to use "middle axioms" (the "pagan" language of justice, liberty, equality, fraternity, democracy, human rights) to communicate to the world in the hope that the world's behavior can be raised to a higher level. But in no sense can the Christian enter the world of political compromise. It appears that Yoder has remained largely consistent in drawing out the logical implications of the schema articulated in this early work.

Kaufman, on the other hand, no longer accepts the strict dualism of response between church and world that characterizes Yoder's thought. Unlike Yoder's, Kaufman's theological position has evolved and changed substantially over the years. He explicitly states in later works that he was earlier much more ready to use the language of authority and revelation when talking about God and Christ. So when we look at his early book, *The Context of Decision*, we must remember that it no longer adequately represents his present thought. Having said this, however, it is still interesting to look at how even then his thought was quite different from Yoder's and contains hints of later themes. Kaufman, like Yoder, starts with the Anabaptist *à la* Bender view that "the radical sayings of Jesus set before us a clear picture of the ethical import of God's act, and that here is portrayed precisely the kind of conduct required in our relations with our fellows."[4] A christocentrism, understood as God's self-disclosure as self-giving love, is central to Kaufman at this point, as it is consistently for Yoder.

But for Kaufman this love penetrates human history and human society in general through the community of reconciliation. He continues to talk about a separation of church and world in this early work and characterizes the empirical church as a "believers' church" along sectarian lines, yet he already clearly feels uncomfortable with the strict response-dualism of Yoder's Schleitheim. The community cannot afford to separate itself from the world if it takes its missionary task seriously. The church, seen both eschatologically and empirically, "is taking up the world into herself and transforming it into the community of the love of God ."[5]

This rich image of the church taking the world into herself in the process of transforming the world has important ethical implications. The world is no longer seen simply in terms of apostasy (although Kaufman too occasionally uses the term "rebelliousness" for the world) but as the place of human need, and the church no longer is a place devoid of sin but is made up of those living by the gracious forgiveness of God. A 1958 *Concern* essay, published the same year Burkholder completed his doctoral thesis, shows what Kaufman's theological position means for ethics. "Love," he says, "goes to the very heart of the most sinful situations that it can find."[6] Love does not retreat from the realm of power struggles, self-centredness, selfish individualism, domination, and exploitation, as Mennonites have historically tended to do, but enters into the heart of darkness in an attempt to transform it and bring it to light. Ethically this means that we also enter the political realm in the attempt "to help the society come to a deeper understanding of *its own* deepest convictions before God."[7] This may mean on occasion supporting a military bill which corresponds to the best insights of American society, and participation in the making of political policies with which we as individuals or a Mennonite community may disagree but which accords with the best insights of our nation. In a quotation that sounds remarkably like what Burkholder might say, Kaufman says:

> Yoder has argued for the recognition of a dualistic principle in Christian ethics which takes seriously the dichotomy between church and world, Christian and non-Christian action. The present essay has tried to take seriously the existence of this dichotomy, but without drawing the conclusion that this implies that the church need not "assume responsibility for the moral structure of non-Christian society." Rather, as God's agent here on earth—the very body of Christ—the church has absolute responsibility for the moral structure and activity of all of the world.[8]

This theme of the Christian's "responsibility for the moral structure and activity of the world" preoccupies Burkholder's thought. It could be argued that Burkholder's paradigm stands midway between the position of Yoder and early Kaufman. He agrees with both that the starting point for Christian theological and ethical reflection and for moral action are the tough sayings and nonviolent love of Jesus. But Burkholder differs in how this is made concrete. He is as strong as Kaufman in his call for Christians to enter responsibly into the ambiguities of social and political existence. But he has a keener sense of the inescapable contradictions, paradoxes, guilt, sin as wrongdoing, and tragedy of such social involvement. He is much more pessimistic and has a more tragic sense of life, a sensibility shaped by personal experience of suffering and death on the front lines of social action. There is less of the liberal and more of the neo-orthodox in Burkholder. This is perhaps expressed in the conclusion of his doctoral dissertation:

> It is the writer's conviction that the present crisis in Mennonite life will require a revision of the present Mennonite approach to society. This is not to suggest that Mennonites should consider "selling out" to world culture because of the intrinsic difficulties of embodying the ethic of Christ in the power arena. Rather it is to suggest that Mennonites must seek their traditional goals of brotherhood, peace and mutuality under the conditions of compromise. Mennonites must realize that they are a part of the world system, and that they share the guilt and responsibility for corporate evil, and that their attempts to be obedient to Christ and "be" the true church must take into consideration the "ambiguities" of their actual situation. This realistic approach will prevent perfectionist illusions and despair.[9]

Mennonites, according to Burkholder, will need to make a place in their theology for the ambiguities of the exercise of power, which in reality they already do in business life, educational institutions, mutual aid societies, etc. They will need to give up the idea of nonresistance, which if followed literally would take them out of this world, and replace it with "non-violent resistance." As well, they will need to find a place in their theological and ethical vocabulary for justice and the ambiguous struggle for justice. All this they must do, without giving up the unique nonconformist witness of Mennonites to the world.

Burkholder's theological and ethical paradigm ought to be compared with the other theological paradigms of his contemporaries, like Yoder and Kaufman, to help us understand his distinctive sociological analysis of Mennonite life and modern culture. I have just begun to think in these comparative terms, suggesting above a few lines of thought. In what follows I concentrate on Burkholder's autobiographical reflections, bringing in additional observations emerging from wider reading of his works, and I conclude with theological proposals concerning the direction I think Mennonites should be heading.

J. Lawrence Burkholder: Taking Responsibility for the World

The Role of Experience in Theology

Where does Burkholder begin methodologically? Christology obviously plays a central role in his theological ethic but experience, for him, is methodologically almost as important. One of the striking features of Burkholder's moving self-portrait as he gives it to us in his autobiographical essay[10] is how concrete personal experiences shaped or modified his theology. His Mennonite upbringing and the influence of educators Daniel Kaufman, Harold Bender, and Guy F. Hershberger firmly implanted in him the idealism of Jesus' love ethic as central to the gospel and a nonconformist/ separatist stance toward the world. The memory of his mother's kindness to battered women in the 1930s reinforced his idealistic conviction that unselfish acts of Christ-like love were in fact possible. His studies at the Lutheran Seminary in Gettysburg introduced him to grace and to liberal pacifism as a politically prudential possibility—an optimistic attitude shattered by Hitler and World War II. His witnessing before the draft board on behalf of conscientious objectors brought him face to face with a Christian board chairman who asked some tough but intelligent questions which his background had not adequately prepared him for. His MCC relief work in India, his work as National Director of Church World Service in China, and as Director of the National Clearing Committee of the United Nations in China, all led him in a new theological direction, quite distinct from that of Bender, Hershberger, and the Concern group.

What does it mean to take background, experience, and context seriously as theologically significant? It means that the human condition, the existential situation, the fact of sin, and life's ambiguities are taken into consideration in formulating one's theology and ethics. Here I stand with Tillich, when he argues for a method of correlation between the existential question and the theological answer. These experiential and social factors are not irrelevant to how one understands the very essence of the Gospel. Further, it means recognizing as legitimate a diversity of views even on the most serious of topics, because people come from different backgrounds, and have different experiences of life. I teach a course at the Toronto School of Theology entitled "War and Peace in Christian Theology." I have Catholics, Anglicans, Evangelicals, Methodists, Presbyterians, Pentecostals, and occasionally Mennonites in this course. These different groups think differently about war and peace, depending on how they have been raised and what they have experienced. Many of them come up with different answers than I am used to as a Mennonite. To call them apostate because they reach different conclusions does not take seriously their experience, Christian faith and commitment, and struggle for moral integrity.

Burkholder's Christology: A Jesus of the Sermon on the Mount

It is fair to say that Burkholder's Christology, except for a few wrinkles, stands firmly in the Mennonite tradition of the Bender, Hershberger, and Concern group. That is, the life and teachings of Jesus, as most clearly articulated in the Sermon on the Mount, are the basic point of reference for ethics. The Jesus ideal for discipleship is pure love, disinterested love, unreciprocating love, sacrificial love, nonviolent love, nonresistant love, *agape*—all terms Burkholder uses frequently and interchangeably. "I cannot escape the 'extraordinary'. . . character of Jesus' demands," he says. "Perfectionism is patterned in the Gospels; it is not occasional or accidental."[11] He is not about to weaken or soften the hard sayings and tough demands of Jesus to make life in this world easier. "We cannot avoid the 'offense' of Jesus' radicality . . . . Hence we must decide what to do with an 'impossible' ethic or, as Reinhold Niebuhr put it more positively, an 'impossible possibility'."[12]

This is why Burkholder is so critical of much of the contemporary middle-class Mennonite talk of discipleship, what he calls a domestication of Jesus according to the demands of assimilation. Mennonites are now doing pretty well what everyone else is doing, without clearly admitting that a fundamental paradigm shift has occurred. "I am becoming slightly uncomfortable with the frequency and the unguarded use of terms like 'discipleship' and 'Anabaptism' when used to describe Mennonite middle class life in a democratic context of religious freedom such as ours."[13] He calls this "loose talk," which no longer means "the gold standard of Jesus' sayings as rigorous, sacrificial, 'upside down,' extraordinary, impractical Sermon on the Mount presuppositions."[14] Burkholder continues to hold that "all human relationships must be judged by their approximation to *agape*."[15]

Where, then, is the rub? What in his theology would make his doctoral thesis "inadmissible" to old and young Mennonites of the 1950s, and prevent it from being published? One word: "compromise."

Burkholder's Ethic: Love, Justice, and Power

What made Burkholder's thesis inadmissible was not his christology *per se* but his claim that it was impossible historically to actualize and be obedient to the Sermon on the Mount ethic of Jesus, because every historical situation is morally ambiguous. As such it necessitates making compromises. One can realize the absolute ideal of pure love only proximately. Here Burkholder in fact has taken the Niebuhrian turn. It is in the world of ambiguity, complexity, and social responsibility that love meets justice (he defines justice as "love divided, distributed") and power (power is what is required to bring about justice). Mennonites, according to Burkholder, have never adequately come to terms with these two elements of all human life: justice and power.

Burkholder's autobiographical sketch is a moving account of how his personal experiences in India and China put on him the awful burden and guilt that come with positions of power and social responsibility: when corporate responsibilities sometimes take priority over personal relations; when the language of rights, due process, and legalities takes precedence over consideration of particular human needs; when the need to fire a dishonest employee no longer justifies infinite forgiveness; when coercive measures need to be taken to evict refugees from an overcrowded evacuation plane; when military escort is required to ensure safety.

Burkholder is the most persuasive in his analysis, in my opinion, when he moves away from the dramatic. His own personal experiences in foreign service are certainly interesting and explain his own tragic dilemmas and problems with the historical impossibility of a pure love ethic. But for most of us they are not in the realm of our personal lives, and for that very reason they do not become a convincing critique of the historical Mennonite position. Also, his tendency to concentrate on the ambiguities of high-level government and politics tends to polarize positions before the issues are sufficiently clarified. Much more persuasive are his close-to-home examples, where we all live and have our being: marriage, family, institutional life of various kinds, life insurance, medicare, security benefits, business, wealth, education, art, music, and so on. It is on this level that we have *de facto* always made choices that compromise the radical Jesus ethic. Burkholder not only calls us to a new ethic of responsibility but to honesty in admitting what in effect always has been the case. We have always exercised power, for instance, in the church and in our educational institutions, and we ought to do so openly and responsibly.

A Theological Proposal: A Theocentric Christology

Burkholder straddles two worlds: that of a traditional Mennonite sectarian ethic based on an Anabaptist Vision reading of the New Testament, and that of modern culture and its social demands. He finds himself firmly rooted in both and faced with the impossibility of living in both comfortably. He does not resolve this dilemma. While he is obviously attracted to the Niebuhrian option, he is less ready than Niebuhr to relegate one to the realm of the ideal and the other to the real: the two stand in more immediate tension with each other for Burkholder than they do for Niebuhr.

The question is, how do we as Mennonites now move forward into the future theologically and ethically? Where do we go from here? This is where Burkholder does not give us a great deal of help, although he offers some hints. I suggest that in our attempt to find a viable moral and ethical stance toward culture we need theologically as Mennonites to go back to the drawing board in four areas: 1) our reading of the Bible; 2) our reading of church history, particularly early church history; 3) our reading of the sixteenth- century Anabaptist movement(s); and 4) our reading of modern and postmodern culture.

Our Reading of the Bible

The church I belong to has a "Statement of Faith" that begins as follows: "To follow Christ daily in life, I will try to think, talk and act in the spirit that moved his acts and teachings. I must aim to do this day in and day out, in family, vocational, and social life. I recognize the Sermon on the Mount as Christ's guide for the Christian life." Here we have a pristine Bender version of what we as Mennonites are called to do. But is it adequate? A person from a Christian Reformed background who recently joined our church commented to me privately how inadequate she found this statement. And as I reflected on it I realized how narrowly we tend to define the basis for our ethic. The Sermon on the Mount in itself can simply not bear the freight that it is asked to bear. It does not give sufficient advice for family, vocational, and social life. We need the whole Bible as a guide for Christian life—a theology of the whole Bible, grounded in what I would like to call a theocentric christology.

A theocentric christology is one which (a) places the Jesus of the Sermon on the Mount within the context of the whole incarnation of the eternal Christ—the birth, life, teaching, ministry, death, resurrection, ascension of Jesus—and understands this Christ event in relation to (b) the God (Yahweh) of the Jews, as that God acted in Jewish history, and to (c) the Holy Spirit that gives birth to the Christian church and is present to the ongoing Christian community and to the world as God's continuing self-revelation. There is both a plenitudinous diversity within the biblical narrative and a comprehensiveness about the creation-fall/redemption-consummation drama that cannot be summed up exhaustively by the Sermon on the Mount ethic. To take the whole Bible as a guide for Christian faith would not mean that we treat all parts of it the same way but that we struggle with the Torah, Historical Books, the Prophets, the Wisdom Literature, the Gospels, the Acts of the Apostles, the Letters, the Pastoral Epistles, and the Apocalypse with equal seriousness.

I believe that the Sermon on the Mount ethic can and ought to continue to be the central ethical marker for Mennonites, but it ought not to function as a canon within a canon. The Sermon on the Mount should itself be understood in the light of the whole Bible and not the other way around. To make it into a hermeneutical key with which to understand everything—the whole Bible, the whole of God's relation to the world—is to make ethics the starting point for theology. It is not clear to me where Burkholder stands on this issue, although I heard him say that, while discipleship is certainly important, Christian faith should begin and end with grace rather than with discipleship. I agree.

The one wrinkle in Burkholder's christology that I mentioned above, which gives it a different tone from the Bender-Hershberger-Concern Sermon on the Mount christology, is his attraction to the universal *logos* christology of Colossians and Ephesians. This brings a universal cosmic element into christology itself which transcends the more narrowly defined, literal Sermon on the Mount ethic, at least as normally understood by Mennonites. Also at various other points Burkholder strains at the Mennonite bit. He observes, for example, that Jesus' life was not representative of ordinary life: he never married, did not need to worry about looking after a family, did not run anything, did not pay taxes, had miracles at his disposal, was a free-lance, lived to be only thirty-three, and so on.[16] At another place Burkholder says he is drawn both to the radical discipleship rigour of sectarianism and the "'fullness' of Catholicity in which, quite apart from Constantinianism, an attempt is made to bring Christ to bear upon 'all things' essential to human existence."[17] But in the end he remains suspended between these two extremes, and thus ironically remains a dualist, a position which he criticizes in others. We need, as Mennonites, to move forward theologically to a new synthesis, not as a way of escaping the tensions but as a way of offering viable witness to the modern world. To do this, we could benefit by re-examining the early period of the Church and its attempt to come to terms with a fast-changing world to find some guidance for our own project.

Our Reading of Early Church History

I have argued strenuously that Mennonites need a trinitarian theology as a framework (better, ground) for their ethics, and have recently tried to show how the classical trinitarian orthodoxy of the early church both grows naturally out of the biblical materials and should be distinguished from the Constantinianism that Mennonites, together with other so-called

"Believers' Churches," rightly reject.[18] Rather than concentrating here on trinitarianism, I would like to reflect briefly on what has come to be known as Constantinianism, because our view of this phenomenon has coloured our whole attitude toward culture and politics.

It is for Mennonites almost a truism to say that Constantine and what he represents in the fourth century constitutes the fall of the church. I have shown in some detail, in the work noted above, how two interpreters of Mennonite theology, John Howard Yoder and J. Denny Weaver, are fairly representative of the Mennonite position on this question. Constantinianism embodies everything that is bad and apostate about the church. I would like to re-open the case, not necessarily to reverse the judgment.

I want to propose that we have considered the third, fourth, and subsequent centuries too monolithically as the fall of the church, and written them off simply as the church accommodating itself to the state. This is a highly complex period, but here I will make just two observations about these early centuries.

The development within early Christianity that led to the so-called Constantinian synthesis was a direct consequence of the obedience to and success of the great commission of Matt. 28: 18-20: "All authority in heaven and on earth has been given to me. Go therefore and make disciples of all nations, baptizing them in the name of the Father and the Son and of the Holy Spirit, teaching them to observe all that I have commanded you; and lo, I am with you always, to the close of the age." This was a universal message, not a sectarian one. It was not a mandate to call the nations out of the world but to make disciples of them. We define discipleship too narrowly if we see it only in terms of nonconformist morality and ethics. Discipleship included spiritual regeneration and salvation. It was the seriousness with which the early church took these words of commission and its success that got it into trouble. The world, including high culture and politics, was drawn into the church.

In *Christianizing the Roman Empire A. D. 100-400*, Ramsay MacMullen explores why the non-Christian world was attracted to and came over to the church, and how authentic that coming over was.[19] He estimates that from the end of the first century there were in the order of half a million converts in each generation, that by 312 AD there were some 5,000,000 converts and by the end of the fourth century there were up to 30,000,000. With the massive influx of new members, particularly in the fourth century, the level of commitment to "discipleship" decreased, as people joined for mixed or nonreligious reasons. This is the dilemma for all missionary-minded movements like the early church, sixteenth-century Anabaptists, and modern evangelicalism.

There was considerable diversity in the type of solutions offered to the Christianity-culture dilemma in the period leading up to and during the fourth and fifth centuries. Tertullian (160-220 AD), living in passionate eschatological expectation, rejected outrightly Roman politics and society, and for the most part called for Christians to live in rigid, ascetic isolation from Roman culture, including not only the holding of office and military service, but also from some forms of commerce, attending circuses, certain types of greetings, and so on. And yet, even he, anticipating the Mennonite *Dordrecht Confession*, believes the emperor serves a limited function in keeping the peace, restraining the evildoers, and protecting innocent people in the secular realm. To the extent that the emperor does this he should be obeyed.[20]

Eusebius of Caesarea (c. 260-340 AD) represents the other extreme solution. He was a close friend and confidant to Constantine, a respected and influential churchman. He reluctantly supported the Nicene formulation of 325, was at the council (Tyre) that condemned the staunch defender of orthodoxy, Athanasius, and played a leading role in the council that readmitted Arius. Eusebius espoused a conservative political theology of culture, in which piety and temporal success are correlated. Constantine's reign was seen as the realization of the messianic age. Eusebius regarded Constantine himself as a saint, even the incarnation or vice-regent of the divine *logos*. The Christian Empire is the earthly image of the eternal archetype or exemplar in heaven. On the whole, western Christianity rejected this kind of fusion of theology and politics in favour of Augustine's solution.[21]

A contemporary of Eusebius was Lactantius. Somewhat paradoxical and inconsistent in his thinking, he was much more critical than Eusebius of the Roman empire, which Lactantius saw as the product of corrupted power and selfishness. Like Tertullian, in some of his earlier works at least, he was suspicious of wealth; condemned military service, war, plays and circuses; and warned against music and poetry. Only within the Christian community, within a dissident minority group, can God's golden age be restored. He called for social justice and economic levelling. Yet he rejected a Tertullian-like withdrawal, and tried to reconcile Christian theology with Greek philosophy and literature. As the attitudes of the Empire changed toward Christianity he too became more conciliatory, and ended his life as a high-ranking employee of Constantine.[22]

It is Augustine (354-430 AD), however, who provides western Christianity with its classic solution to the dilemma concerning Christ and culture. He is no longer able to see Rome as the eternal city and the crumbling empire as the actualization of the kingdom of God. Like Tertullian, Augustine sharply distinguishes between Jerusalem (the city of God) and Babylon (the temporal city, the Roman empire or any empire), the first defined by love of God and the second by love of self and coercive power. But, unlike Tertullian, he does not counsel rejection and separation from the earthly city, which he considers a transient good. All states and empires, including the Roman, are for him fleeting realities. That which lasts is personal and spiritual attachment to Christ and God.

Augustine therefore both counsels inward detachment from the temporal city and supports the dutiful carrying out of societal tasks, including military service and government office. Because one's personal destiny far outweighs any other considerations, however, he subordinates the state to the church, and is willing with some misgivings to recommend the use of force not only against those who invade the empire but against Donatist Christians themselves. This theocratic assumption, in which the church tells the state what to do, becomes the predominant theme of the Middle Ages.[23]

Our final example is Salvian, writing in the mid-fifth century, after Carthage had been sacked in 439 and after the decline of the empire was virtually complete. He no longer defends the virtues of the empire but, like the Hebrew prophets, denounces its sins, attributing its fall to the just punishment by a wrathful God for class division, official corruption, exploitation of the poor, imposition of heavy taxation on the peasantry, and social injustice generally. He holds before society the absolute ideal of Christian monasticism, and somewhat naively reverses earlier contempt for the barbarians by idealizing them despite their theological Arianism. He is deeply pessimistic about strong political leadership, and calls for moral and spiritual regeneration.[24]

The point of these examples is that we ought not to demonize a whole era with one grand generalization. There was a rich diversity of attempts to come to terms with the changing fortunes of Christianity and its role within larger culture, some less acceptable than others. To call the whole period apostate is not to take seriously the struggle of the church, both its leaders and its members generally. Some of our theologians have tended to identify the theological development of trinitarian and christological orthodoxy with the so-called Constantinianization of the church. This is too simple an analysis of what happened, and does not take into account the diversity of the period. That something went seriously wrong at the point where the church made the choice to theocratically identify itself with, and engage the state in, coercive suppression of dissent, heterodoxy, and diversity generally must not be covered up. To re-examine this period is not to soften our critique of what happened but to look empathetically at an age to see what we can learn from it in our own attempts to address similar dilemmas. Simply to close the chapter on the fourth century, labelling it apostate, and thereby also to close the chapter on all other traditions—Catholic, Anglican, mainline Protestant—identifying them as heirs of that tradition, while identifying ourselves with the true church, is a form of self-righteous hypocrisy. We too are heirs of that tradition, we too face similar challenges in our relation to larger culture, we too make compromises. There never has been a pure church within history, a pristine Christian community.

Our Reading of Anabaptist History

Historian Werner Packull has recently put in serious doubt whether sixteenth-century Anabaptists actually lived up to the Anabaptist vision.[25] The twentieth-century Anabaptist ideal does not fit the sixteenth-century reality: "Revelations of bickering, of nasty interpersonal and group relationships—not to mention sexual failings and financial embezzlement among first-generation leaders—seem hardly the right stuff to inspire contemporary church renewal or stave off the inroads of secularization."[26]

Early Hutterite leaders and their wives enjoyed special privileges at the table (good wines and better foods) in separate dining rooms not enjoyed by ordinary believers. They were authoritarian in their approach to leadership. Caspar Schwenkfeld, with some justification, accused Anabaptists of splintering into numerous sects for ridiculous reasons— "The Swiss, Hutterites, Gabrielites, Pilgramites, Netherlanders, Friesians, Mennonites, Hoffmanites, etc., ..."[27] Each tended to have self-appointed leaders accusing the other of holding to private property, of despising proper leadership, of disregarding family and economic obligations, of sexual misconduct, and so on. In the end, Packull asks: "Could Mennonites, after all, learn something from the Augustinian tradition and Lutheran theology in regards to imperfection within the church, just as Lutherans should learn something from the Anabaptists concerning discipleship and separation from the powers that be?"[28]

Ordinary Christians in our congregations have always recognized the reality of sin more clearly than the theological idealists, who develop ideologies of perfection. There is a dark underside to the Mennonite psyche which the official keepers of the tradition (preachers, deacons, patriarchs, theologians, teachers, bishops, ministers, leaders) have frequently managed to disguise through ingeniously contrived public personas, rules, regulations, myths, dogmas, and so on. The recent spate of abuse stories in our Mennonite media is making us all too aware of our imperfections right within the church. Myths about ourselves are being shaken regularly. Our artists and our journalists have frequently done a better job of communicating to us our true reality than have our theologians.

Burkholder has in his own powerful way struggled precisely with this contradiction between the Anabaptist ideal and the real world of sin, ambiguity, and moral dilemmas in which we find ourselves. He too, like Packull, in the end turns to the doctrine of justification and grace as a way of coping with this incongruity between the ideal and the real. The theological way forward for us as Mennonites in modern culture, I would argue, lies in two directions: a re-reading of Anabaptist history, which recognizes the diversity of possible connecting points beside Schleitheim; and a re-examining of other than Anabaptist theological traditions which can supplement and complement our own theological strengths.

Our Reading of Modern and Postmodern Culture

Classical Christianity is under massive attack these days. This attack is coming from three major directions: (a) from those concerned with saving our planet who want a more environmentally friendly God; (b) from those concerned with social and economic justice who want a more historically active God; (c) from those concerned with dialogue between Christians and between religions who want a more ecumenical God. It is interesting to consider how each of these either complements or contradicts the other. All, however, have negative things to say about classical Christianity, whose God they see as too masculine and environmentally unfriendly, as too authoritarian and oppressive, as too exclusive and judgmental. It is an attack that is not new; it began with the Enlightenment and continues unabated. It is justified on some levels. In the end, however, it will reach a dead end, and as always we will reach into our distant past for wisdom for our future.

In my undergraduate and graduate teaching, as well as in my work with pastors and in congregations, I find that the dualism between church and world which preoccupied Mennonites even thirty or forty years ago is largely unknown or irrelevant. We are surrounded by and have been shaped by contemporary culture on all levels. In this situation we can no longer assume a monolithic reading of the Bible, of our history, of present culture. We live in a world that lacks theological and cultural cohesion. We live in a Mennonite church that lacks cohesion. It is the loss of cohesion that characterizes modern and, even more so, postmodern culture. We can no longer delude ourselves into believing that we can isolate ourselves from other traditions, ignore the diverse readings of our own origins and traditions, escape the influence of major theological trends around us and so on.

I have come to believe, however, that in this period of fragmentation a reinterpretation of the biblical and early Christian doctrine of God is not only possible but urgent for all Christians, including Mennonites, as a way not of avoiding but of handling diversities and distinctives. It is my conviction that we need spiritual and moral renewal not by deconstructing and replacing the classical doctrine of God with a novel one, but by rereading the Bible, classical history, and Anabaptist history to find things there that we have overlooked. For instance, our Mennonite view of discipleship, peace, and social justice might possibly be more fruitfully grounded in the mystical, sacramental, and *Gelassenheit* thought of certain Anabaptists than in the harsher obedience-oriented thought of others.

I believe that the best in Anabaptist-Mennonite theology can and ought to be framed by a classical trinitarian theology in which: 1) God as transcendent creator and mystery of the world is wholly free of our own moral systems, including our own Mennonite view of nonviolence (God is not a pacifist); 2) Christ as eternal *logos* and *sophia* takes on flesh in Jesus of Nazareth who, through his birth, life, teachings, ministry, death, resurrection, and ascension redeems us (through him we have been and are being saved from our sins) and shows us an alternate way of peace and reconciliation; and 3) the Holy Spirit as the very spirit of God and the very spirit of Christ is present to the whole world and to us as Christians, empowering us and leading us into ever greater freedom—freedom to think new thoughts and find new answers to our existential concerns and moral dilemmas.

SEVENTEEN

Mennonites, Christ, and Culture: The Yoder Legacy*

John Howard Yoder died on December 30, 1997. I attended his funeral at the Goshen College Chapel on January 3, 1998.[1] A special issue of The Conrad Grebel Review (Spring 1998),[2] containing the funeral orations and critical essays devoted to the thought of Yoder signals the beginning of what will surely be a raft of articles, dissertations, and books reappraising Yoder's contribution to Mennonite self-understanding and to ecumenical discussions worldwide.

Yoder represented what I would call the second wave of self-conscious North American Anabaptist-Mennonite thought in the twentieth century. The first wave was that of Harold S. Bender and his generation of scholars, including thinkers like John C. Wenger, Guy F. Hershberger, John Horsch, C. Henry Smith, Cornelius Krahn and Eduard G. Kaufman (Gordon D. Kaufman's father). These were all men of similar age who were part of the renaissance of sixteenth-century Anabaptist and historical Mennonite studies—a movement driven by a fresh look at original sources and contemporary identity questions.[3] The nucleus of the second wave was a group of seven young American Mennonites in post-

---

*Originally published in *Essays & Tributes: John Howard Yoder 1927-1997* in *The Conrad Grebel Review* 16.2 (Spring 1998). Reprinted in *What Mennonites Are Thinking—1999—*. Edited by Merle Good and Phyllis Pellman Good (Intercourse, PA: Good Books, 1999), 151-65. For all notes on the text see the Notes section below.

World War II Europe who first met at a two- week retreat in Amsterdam in April 1952 to reflect upon their experience as graduate students, missionaries, and MCC workers. The group consisted of John Howard Yoder, John W. Miller, Paul Peachey, A. Orley Swartzentruber, David Shank, Calvin Redekop, and Irwin Horst[4] and came to be known as the "Concern Group," a name associated with a series of pamphlets, known as Concern, in which they published their views from 1954 to 1971.

There were numerous other scholars on the periphery of this group whose intellectual careers were similar, among them Gordon D. Kaufman, J. Lawrence Burkholder, Norman Kraus, William Klassen and Walter Klaassen, J. B. Toews (to name just a few)—all university, college and seminary teachers who had either directly studied with the first wave or been significantly shaped by them, many of them publishing articles in these pamphlets.

This larger circle represented a growing diversity of viewpoints on issues having to do with the relation between Christianity, Mennonites, and culture. Yoder, perhaps more sharply than the others, was critical of the older Bender generation for a compromised denominationalism and for not applying its historical and theological findings more consistently to the congregational life of present-day Mennonites. Yoder articulated this critique in the legendary unpublished letter written to Bender from Europe, entitled "The Cooking of the Anabaptist Goose."[5]

The third wave in twentieth-century Anabaptist-Mennonite historiography was the "social historical" school of thought, associated with scholars like James Stayer, Werner Packull, and Hans-Jürgen Goertz. This group, which included scholars from outside the Mennonite community, criticized both the first and second wave for a too theological, selective, and homogeneous reading of Radical Reformation history. However, in its legitimate concern for disclosing the diverse economic, social, and political factors at work in sixteenth-century revolutionary thought, these social historians tended to underestimate the common theological factors that motivated the martyrs and gave them their ideological staying power.

An exception is C. Arnold Snyder's work in Anabaptist history and theology. Snyder has one foot in the social-historical school of thought and one in theology. He seeks to take seriously the truths of polygenesis (an emphasis on the heterogeneous beginnings of sixteenth-century Anabaptism) while moving beyond it by exploring the core theological elements in all early Anabaptist groups.[6]

Now, a fourth wave of young academics is seeking to interpret the Anabaptist-Mennonite experience from a wide range of inter-disciplinary perspectives including the natural and social sciences, history, philosophy, literature, and theology. The flurry of current interest in Mennonites and postmodernity is just one example of this.[7] Increasingly clear is that no longer can the Mennonite tradition be adequately understood or passed on to the next generation by a small elite group of scholars, teachers, or leaders, let alone by one or two disciplines like history or theology.

This application of a multi-disciplined approach to Mennonite identity questions, combined with the plethora of new issues facing an increasingly urbanized, acculturated, and professionalized middle-class Mennonite community, compels the reassessment of Yoder's thought, one that is already well under way. It is not entirely clear whether Yoder's particular reading of the Christian tradition is the flagship for this new postmodernism (with its antifoundationalist assumptions) or whether it is but the most elegant and consistent synthesis of a previous paradigm.

My own reading of the situation is that the nonfoundationalism of postmodernity is not sturdy enough for carrying the ethical and theological load of historic Christianity. The centrifugal force of postmodernity threatens the magnetic centre of Christianity—a trinitarian theology, christology and pneumatology. It is from the perspective of this 'trinitarian foundationalism'— defined biblically, historically, ontologically, and metaphysically—that I have in my writings over the past twenty years sought to engage Mennonite and ecumenical Christian thought. It is also the standpoint from which I have evaluated Yoder's legacy in a number of recent articles, two of them reprinted below.[8] Although I have consumed Yoder's thought for some twenty-five or more years, it is only in his last few years that I came to know him on a more personal basis, the consequence of some casual encounters, a Believers Church conference at McMaster Divinity College in October 1996, and a series of lectures at Conrad Grebel College and Toronto Mennonite Theological Centre in the Winter of 1997.

In the following essay I acknowledge the crucial importance of Yoder's political-ethical challenge to contemporary Mennonites and Christians of all stripes. What I plead for, however, is the rejection of all ethical reductionism, and the grounding of that ethical message in a Christian doctrine of God as Trinity; not to weaken the peace witness but to strengthen it. It is this Christian doctrine of God which I argue is not fully developed in Yoder's thought.

◆ ◆ ◆

Recollections

John Howard Yoder was not the easiest man in the world to relate to casually and informally. I would run into him regularly at the American Academy of Religion meetings, an annual gathering of academics teaching at universities and colleges, but our greetings to each other until recently were no more than perfunctory. I was always surprised at how well he was known outside Mennonite circles, even though he was always an enigmatic and silent presence at such international academic conferences. He would virtually never say anything but would take notes prolifically.

What did he do with all those ideas? Write books, I guess! I do remember him once accusing me in front of others of trying to Catholicize the Mennonites at Conrad Grebel College. I punched him good-humoredly. He seemed to be taken aback.

Then in the 1990s, up to his untimely death, we managed to establish what I would consider to be a kind of relationship. In fall 1994 I had breakfast with him in Chicago, at a conference on theology for which I had flown in from Amsterdam, where I was spending my sabbatical. He was sitting alone and I joined him. We talked about Dutch Mennonites and how they differed from North American Mennonites. I told him about my wife's (Margaret Loewen Reimer) article on Mennonite hymnody. He was particularly interested in the high regard Harold S. Bender had had for the Russian Mennonite choral tradition. An issue that was of special interest to me, but one that Yoder never fully answered, was the role that dogmatics (as in Barth's *Church Dogmatics*) played in his ethics.

In October 1996 I drove him back and forth to the Believers Church conference sessions at McMaster Divinity College, which we were both attending. We rode the hour distance between Waterloo and Hamilton a number of times. The discomfort of my 1982 AMC Concord, an awkwardness compounded by trying to find a place for his ever present crutches, did not hinder us from engaging in lengthy conversations on a range of topics, including his reflections on Karl Barth, with whom he had studied in Basel. The influence of Barth on Yoder's thought always fascinated me, but my probings into the matter never received satisfactory answers.

Then in March 1997, I helped to arrange a series of lectures by Yoder at Conrad Grebel College and the Toronto Mennonite Theological Centre (at the Toronto School of Theology). Again we spent a lot of time in conversation at lectures, in my car, and at my house. I was struck by the "patriarchal" style of his presentations and interaction with audiences. Discussions were question-and-answer periods more than conversations. He lectured on Tolstoy, "The Politics of Jesus Revisited," "Judaism as a Non-non Christian Religion," and "The Jewishness of the Free Church Tradition."

These lectures confirmed what had been my impression over the years: here was a man who seemed never to have changed his mind. His 1972 *The Politics of Jesus* was simply a working out of his Concern Group theology of the 1950s and 1960s. And in his last book, *For the Nations*, he sets the record straight about what he has always thought, said, and meant, to those who misunderstand him. In this book he is especially concerned to defend himself against the charge of a sectarianism that is apolitical and withdraws from engagement with contemporary culture. My last memory of Yoder is a vigorous handshake at the American Academy of Religion meetings in San Francisco in November 1997.

Yoder's influence on the Mennonite church in the twentieth century and now into the twenty-first is irrefutable. Through his writings, his lectures at Associated Mennonite Biblical Seminary, his administrative responsibilities for a variety of Mennonite institutions, and his ecumenical presence he has profoundly shaped the Mennonite self-understanding of generations of pastors, lay persons, and academics. While his importance should not be underestimated, his passing does free the next generation of Mennonite theologians and ethicists to reconfigure the question that preoccupied him above all others: What does it mean to be "in the world but not of it?" What does it mean to follow Christ in contemporary society and culture? The impact of Yoder's reading of the sources and the logic of his argument does not preclude the possibilities of other interpretations of what it means to be faithful in the world at the turn of the millennium.

Yoder's Claims Reconsidered

Yoder's intellectual pursuits were eclectic: biblical studies (*The Politics of Jesus, The Fullness of Christ, Body Politics*), historical and systematic theology (*Preface to Theology: Christology and Theological Method*), Reformation Studies (his German doctoral dissertation on the Swiss Anabaptist disputations, *The Legacy of Michael Sattler*, [ed.]*Balthasar Hubmaier*), ecclesiology (*The Royal Priesthood*), ecumenicity (*The Ecumenical Movement and the Faithful Church*) and innumerable other articles and pamphlets on topics from capital punishment to sexuality. Underlying all of these impressive contributions, however, lies one over-riding concern: the nonviolent peace witness that all who confess "Jesus as Lord" are called upon to give without compromise. It was the topic that compelled him and is the explicit focus of many of his books (*The Christian Witness to the State; He Came Preaching Peace; The Original Revolution; Christian Attitudes to War, Peace, and Revolution; Nevertheless; The Priestly Kingdom; For the Nations; Karl Barth and Pacifism; Reinhold Niebuhr and Christian Pacifism; What Would You Do If?; When War is Unjust*). His views on this subject, part of the much larger issue of the relation of church to world, Christ to culture, might be summarized with the following six propositions.

1. To say that Jesus is the the Messiah is to say that the "way of the cross" is the way to particular and universal reconciliation (at-one-ment). The "suffering servant" vision of the the Messiah, already present in the messianic passages of the Hebrew Scriptures (e.g., Isaiah 53), is the one appropriated by Jesus from a number of options, a fateful choice forged through struggle with intense temptation in the desert in preparation

for his mission. Retrospectively, it is most profoundly expressed in the Pauline *kenosis* (Jesus emptying himself of his divinity) passage of Philippians 2, one of the oldest hymns of the early church. This "way of the cross" (the resurrection somehow does not get equal treatment), the way of self-sacrificial love, is not a *means* to salvation but is itself the gospel, the good news, the *kerygma*. It is not primarily an existential, inner reality but a social-political alternative for how people ought relate to each other in community. The existential dimension (one's individual stance before God) is subordinated to the "political" message—"political" interpreted not in any narrow sense but as a whole new way of living with others in the world. To confess Jesus as Lord is to commit oneself to the way of the cross in human relations.

This is the gist of Yoder's best known work, *The Politics of Jesus*. The question for us is whether this is an adequate christology. In his effective corrective to the evangelical tendency to interiorize the gospel, and that of the mainline churches to sacramentalize it, Yoder offers a powerful political reading of the New Testament which unfortunately devalues the existential-sacramental power of Jesus's message—that part having to do with divine grace, the personal forgiveness of sin, the inner renewal of the spirit, and the individual's stance before God.

2. The earliest Christian community consisted of messianic Jews who accepted Jesus' messianic vision. The Jesus movement in its earliest phase was quite compatible with the range of Jewish possibilities at the time. It was in the synagogue tradition of exilic Judaism. Only gradually, with its transformation into a Gentile religion, did Christianity and Judaism separate into two discrete, even hostile religious entities. Until the end of the third century, there were still Christians who went to the synagogue on Saturday and heard Origen preach on Sunday. This tragic split emerged gradually with the Hellenization of the Christian movement. The apologists of the second century (like Justin Martyr) are at least partly to blame for this. They use non-Hebraic philosophical categories to make universal, rational claims for Christianity (what in modern academic jargon might be referred to as "foundationalism"). The struggle against so-called "heresies" (Jewish, on the one side, and Hellenistic, on the other), together with the conversion of the Emperor Constantine in the fourth century, signal the completion of the rift. In the process Christianity isolates Judaism into a defensive, non-missionary religious culture quite different from its earlier Babylonian version.

In Yoder's reading of the Hebrew Scriptures, the dispersion of the peoples in the Babel story (Gen. 11) was not a punishment but a blessing. It represented God's "nonfoundationalist" intention in creation—

diversity (plenitude) rather than conformity. Again and again God's people were tempted by a "foundationalist" tendency to conform and unify. Centralized military and religious bureaucracies were the result of falling away from God's intent. Through the Babylonian captivity and the consequent scattering of the Jews from their homeland, God (as God had done in the Tower of Babel event) once again was trying to teach his people the missionary task of contributing to the welfare of alien cultures in foreign cities. The formation of the Hebrew canon was not orchestrated by a central hierarchy in Jerusalem but emerged in the diasporic community as a way of achieving Jewish identity—an identity based not on central authority but on text(s). This is the line of argument in Yoder's last book, *For the Nations*.

Yoder's compelling interpretation of the exilic Jewish and early Christian story fails to do justice to the importance of organized, institutional religious and political life both in Judaism and in historic Christianity. Jerusalem and Constantinople/Rome, symbolically speaking, played a more important role (both historically and theologically) in the development of Judaism and Christianity, respectively, than Yoder allows for. His selective reading of the history of each appears to be driven by his "free church" agenda. Furthermore, there is diversity in the prelapsarian biblical vision of creation, to be sure. But underlying this plenitude is a foundational unity and divine harmony that Yoder underestimates. It is the Fall that brings disunity, fragmentation, and estrangement.

3. The great Christian reversal took place with the so-called "Constantinian shift." The conversion of Constantine in the fourth century is for Yoder the dominant symbol for the reversal of the messianic vision of early Jewish-Christianity. Whereas the early Christian community was a suffering and persecuted minority within a larger, hostile culture, Christianity gradually becomes first the privileged minority and eventually, in the medieval period, virtually coincident with society. It now supported the state in persecuting non-Christian minority groups like the Jews. *Constantinianism* becomes a shibboleth in Yoder's theology for all that is wrong, especially centralized and military top-down authority which presumes to be in charge of running the world. It is a code word for everything that faithful Christianity should not be and characterizes the basic stance of all mainline denominations in Eastern and Western Christianity up to the present.

Within this Constantinian world view, Christian ethics is always premised on what is universalizable and pragmatic. Only if it is possible to think that something works for everybody can it be considered realistic. In this way of thinking Jesus' "way of the cross," and nonviolent love (*agape*) no longer is the one criterion—you obviously can't run a society that way. Other criteria, taken from the larger culture (norms based on what is considered rational or common sense) are now more important than the christological one.

Now the theory of the Just War, originating with Ambrose and Augustine, replaces the official "pacifism" of the early church during the time of Constantine. The medieval church (in exempting the clerical estate from bloodshed) still bore witness to the higher nonviolent ideal—war was an evil only to be tolerated ("justified") in extreme circumstances and required penitence. But with the Reformation the duty to defend one's country militarily becomes imbedded in the very articles of faith (it in effect is dogmatically justified). Meanwhile the "crusade" (or "holy war"), in contrast to the "just war" which plays by certain restraining rules, is divinely ordained violence. This was a position adopted by the Church during part of the Middle Ages and by certain groups in the modern period (some Puritans and Liberation movements).

Only the Jews of the Middle Ages, some medieval Christian "sectaries," the Anabaptists, parts of the modern believers church (Mennonites, Quakers, Church of the Brethren, etc.), and some humanists and Christian dissenters in mainline traditions have kept the pacifist vision alive. The Constantinian reversal is to blame for this loss of Jesus-based pacifism. Christians began thinking they were responsible for running the world, that Jesus' love ethic was irrelevant, unrealistic, and irresponsible. This is the basic argument of Yoder's twenty years of lectures on the subject published as *Christian Attitudes toward War and Peace: Companion to Roland Bainton*, and *When War is Unjust: Honesty in Just War Thinking*.

There is no denying the power of Yoder's critique of Constantinianism and the "fall of the church." It is a message that is not original with Yoder, and one that the church caught in "civil religion" needs to hear over and over again. But there is an injustice to history, including the Constantinian era, that is committed by Yoder and others for whom "Constantinianism" is a shibboleth for all that is bad. The third and fourth centuries were a time of great upheaval and diversity. There were many serious Christians, including theologians, clerics, and statesmen, who were attempting to address the profound issues raised by their cultures in the light of the gospel. One cannot dismiss the working of the divine in the movements of history even in its most unlikely places and persons (like Constantine). What Yoder, in my view, does not adequately account for are the tragic ambiguities of human existence and the ethical dilemmas of concrete social-political (including ecclesiastical) life in the fallen world in which all of us still find ourselves. Theologians like J. Lawrence Burkholder have seen these matters more clearly.

4. The history of Christian theology and ethics from the time of the second century to the present is predominantly the story of Constantinian apostasy. Although the theologians of the second to fifth centuries asked some significant questions, and the ecumenical councils and creeds (Nicea, Constantinople, Chalcedon) dealt with important issues, they transposed the narrative approach of the apostolic message into a Greek metaphysical and ontological way of thinking. In the process, obedience to the moral-ethical challenge of Jesus' life, teaching, and ministry was no longer central.

This Platonizing of Christian theology suited imperial politics. Constantine called the council of Nicea to unite the Empire. He chaired the Council and played a key role in its theological formulation, using Greek philosophical terminology. Dissenting voices were pronounced anathema (heretical) for the sake of unity. This becomes the story of institutional Christianity from then on. It is not altogether clear whether Yoder believes that the trinitarian and christological developments of the classical period were necessarily linked to the Constantinianization of the church. He equivocates on this issue. It is also not entirely evident whether or not he thinks the truth lies with those minority views (the heretics) who were excluded. What Yoder certainly objects to is the exclusion of the dissenters for the sake of unity.

Yoder's over-riding concern in his historical-theological approach to the treatment of Christian thought through the millennia is with the unfaithfulness of the church to the original messianic vision of Jesus. Yoder does not claim that we can in any simplistic sense turn the clock back, return to the origin, but again and again the Christian community needs to loop back (as a vine) to the initial Christ-event for renewal and reform in the present. This is the substance of Yoder's *Preface to Theology: Christology and Theological Method*.

Yoder's encyclopedic grasp of the variety of theological controversies and systems throughout the ages never ceases to amaze. Yet the sharply focused ethical glasses through which he views every event, text, and theory too cleanly filter out the rich plenitude of historical possibilities and contingencies. The theological seriousness of historical moments and individual Christians caught in the messiness of life never quite get their due. The development of a Christian doctrine of God in the first few centuries, with its distinctive metaphysical and ontological character, is not sufficiently appreciated as the grounding for the ethic that Yoder proclaims. Both *theology* and *pneumatology* are eclipsed by a low *christology* interpreted primarily in ethical-political terms. In the process the mystical, spiritual, and sacramental get lost.

5. The Believers Church tradition, prototypically present in the Anabaptists of the sixteenth century, is a reform movement in which the concerns of the early, pre-Constantinian Jewish-Christian community are recovered. Anabaptism, and the Free Church tradition it exemplifies, represents the retrieval of the Jewishness of Christianity. Although Yoder had been interested in the early Jewish period of Christianity for a long while, the similarity of the Free Church tradition to exilic Judaism seemed to engage him more intentionally toward the end of his life. He saw not only sociological parallels between Mennonites and Jews, but also sociological-theological ones between the synagogue culture of Babylonian Judaism and the ecclesiology of the believers church more generally. Both were suspicious of centralized authority structures, particularly those enforced by the state. Both were small messianic-type communities intent on living faithfully in alien cultures, their identities similarly shaped by the reading and discussion of texts and the pre-eminence of ethical obedience. Both espoused nonviolence.

These insights are spelled out in Yoder's essay "The Jewishness of the Free Church Tradition" (a lecture he gave at the Toronto Mennonite Theological Centre in March 1997). In drawing out the historical and ethical similarity between the synagogue culture of diaspora Judaism and free church Christianity—a valuable analogy which is illuminating and helps to mitigate anti-semitic elements present in the Christian tradition—Yoder does not do justice to the genuine theological differences that developed early on between the two religions (seen from both perspectives). He also, thereby, distances Mennonites and the believers church movement even further from the historic development of catholic Christianity, particularly from its ecumenical, "dogmatic" foundations.

6. The task of the Christian in contemporary culture is not to run the world, not to make history turn out right, but to live faithfully within a believing community as a witness in and to the world of the coming of the kingdom of God. Christians have only one norm—Jesus Christ who incarnates the way of self-sacrificial, nonviolent love in the world. Christians cannot expect the world (dominant culture and society in general) to live by this christological nonviolent standard. This can be presumed only for those who have voluntarily joined the believing community, for whom faith is a presupposition, and who have committed themselves to a life of Christ-like love. Yoder identifies many different forms of pacifism, but the one he espouses is "the pacifism of the messianic community." It is a pacifism that does not depend on effectiveness in any usual pragmatic sense, but on the *corporate* confession of "Jesus as Lord." Such a community is not sectarian, it is not quietistic, it does not withdraw from the world but seeks

to live out the way of Jesus in human relations. It does not take direct responsibility for the political life of the state but does so indirectly by "witnessing" to the state. It does so with the use of "middle axioms," by which Yoder means norms that society in general can understand (justice, freedom, equality, etc.).

For Christians these norms receive their content from the one christological norm of redemptive love; but in communicating with society this ultimate criterion remains indirect. At no point in the church's engagement with society is the Christian justified in compromising this christological basis for ethical thinking or behavior. The "church" is to be distinguished from the "world," not sociologically and institutionally, but in terms of response. It is a community of faith response to the way of Jesus Christ. This is the heart of Yoder's theological ethics and is found throughout his work, but is concentrated in books like *The Christian Witness to the State, Nevertheless*, and *The Priestly Kingdom*.

The logical tightness of Yoder's system makes it difficult to refute. But its inner consistency fails to square with the inconsistencies, ambiguities, fallenness, and messiness of real life either in the church or in the world. There is little room for personal or group failure within the messianic community. Nevertheless, his is a powerful critique of much mainstream ethics which is too prone theologically to justify failure, sin and violence.

After Yoder What?

Yoder was known in recent years to say with just a tad too much modesty that others had passed him by. It is tempting to think that after a great era that produced thinkers like Bender and Yoder, we the epigones enter a period of mediocrity. It is certain that Yoder himself would rightly refute any such conclusion. He would encourage those who come after him to find new ways of being more faithful to Christ within contemporary culture. Yoder's death has ushered in a time of intense scrutiny and reappraisal of his way of reading the gospel. In his lifetime there were other contemporaries of his, like Gordon D. Kaufman and J. Lawrence Burkholder, who saw things quite differently. Even fellow members of the original European-based Concern Group, like John W. Miller, have come to interpret the Bible and the responsibility of the Christian within society differently than Yoder.

I myself believe that the trinitarian foundations for Christian ethics are not sufficiently worked out in Yoder's thought. The Christian doctrine of God that emerged in the biblical and post-biblical period is the foundation for all Christian ethics, and is not exhausted by an ethic of *agape*. God cannot be said to be a pacifist in any strict sense (he gives and takes life;

"'Vengeance is mine,' says the Lord")—this, of course, does not justify our human use of violence. But there is a sense in which a theology that begins and ends with a Jesus-ethic of nonviolent love cannot fully account for the irrational depths of evil and suffering in the world, which also are mysteriously in the hands of God and can be used for divine purposes. God is an unfathomable and inexhaustible abyss, and the disclosure in Christ does not fully (without residue) annul the hiddenness. Wasn't it William Blake who asked, "Did he who made the Lamb make thee [the Tiger])?" Where is the tiger in Yoder's God? In Yoder's Christ?

EIGHTEEN

Theological Orthodoxy and Jewish Christianity: A Personal Tribute to John Howard Yoder*

In his 1999 doctoral thesis on John Howard Yoder, Craig Carter takes issue with my interpretation of Yoder as I express it in this and other essays—namely, that I question Yoder's commitment to theological orthodoxy.[1] Carter claims that Yoder's social ethics presupposes and is in fact based on christological (Chalcedon) and trinitarian (Nicene) orthodoxy. I fully agree that the ethical project Yoder propounds can succeed only if based on such presuppositions—this is the thread that runs through all of my theological essays in this volume. Furthermore, I acknowledge that there are times in Yoder's theology when he speaks positively about theological orthodoxy.

Nevertheless, as I try to show here, ultimately Yoder is highly ambivalent about the dogmatic theological developments that occurred in the Classical period of Christianity. This is particularly evident in his writings on the early Jewish-Christian community, to which he returned in a more concentrated form toward the end of his life. In my essay below, published in a Festschrift *for Yoder,[2] I acknowledge my great indebtedness to Yoder's thought, but then proceed to*

---

* Originally published in *The Wisdom of the Cross: Essays in Honor of John Howard Yoder*. Edited by Stanley Hauerwas, Chris K. Huebner, Harry J. Huebner, and Mark Thiessen Nation (Grand Rapids: Eerdmans Publishing Co., 1999), 430-48
For all notes on the text see the Notes section below.

examine his thinking on the first Jewish Christians, his provocative claim that the Free Church tradition of Radical Protestantism is a recovery of the Jewishness of Christianity which was lost during the Constantinian period, to take issue with his reading of the Jewish story, and to suggest that he shortchanges the distinctively Christian doctrinal developments of the classical period that distinguish early Christianity from the Jewish tradition, on the one side, and the Greco-Roman worldview, on the other.

◆ ◆ ◆

A Tribute

I've lived intellectually with John Howard Yoder for at least thirty years. I've gone to bed with him, woken up with him in the morning, dragged him to class with me regularly, argued with him over dinner, travelled with him on trips, and accompanied him to concerts. I've taken him as arsenal into 'enemy' territory (Foundationalists and Constantinians in 'Yugoslavia,' Germany, and Toronto). It's been a virtual cohabitation, with all the resulting domestic squabbles and quarrels that come with the territory. In this posthumous *Festschrift* for Yoder, I pay a personal tribute to this man by sharing with readers the ups and downs of my life with an intellectual sphinx, whom I will always remember as that bearded figure on crutches.

Sometime in the late 1950s, I first heard Yoder speak in my home congregation—the Bergthaler Mennonite Church in Altona, Manitoba. I don't remember what he said but I was impressed. Since then I have heard him on numerous occasions, read virtually all of his books, and within the past two years spent hours in conversation with him. While I never had him as a classroom teacher (I didn't follow the usual Mennonite seminary route in my educational career), he has been my teacher in every other sense and has permanently shaped my Mennonite self-understanding. I developed a love-hate relationship to his thinking, and found that within Mennonite circles I tended to be critical of him, seeking emancipation from his claustrophobic grip on me. In non-Mennonite circles I discovered him to be most useful for debate and Mennonite apologetics. It's too early to tell what the nature of his legacy for the Mennonite church and the larger Christian community will be. He leaves a weighty one—of that there is no doubt.

I recall studying at Union Theological Seminary, New York, in 1971-72, trying to come to terms with Yoder's reading of our Mennonite heritage in that bastion of Niebuhrianism. That year I wrote a paper on "Mennonite Nonresistance in the Light of Reinhold Niebuhr's Critique of Pacifism" for American church historian Robert Handy, who in a written evaluation of the paper responded: "I happen to know John Yoder and respect him very much; I was somewhat surprised to find him using the 'middle axiom' concept, usually related to the realist, responsible society, ecumenical ethics of Oldham and Bennett." Niebuhr had died a year earlier but his presence was palpable in teachers like Roger Shinn, with whom I took a course on "Conflict and Reconciliation," and to whom I gave a copy of Yoder's just-published *Nevertheless: The Varieties of Religious Pacifism*.[3] Shinn had been a Major and Company Commander in Europe in World War II, been captured by the Germans, and held the Reinhold Niebuhr Professorship in Social Ethics at the Seminary.

One of the texts he assigned was Frantz Fanon's *The Wretched of the Earth*, which introduced me to the powerful psychological nature and "need" for violent revolt by oppressed peoples.[4] During that year I wrote to Yoder, at the time president of Goshen Biblical Seminary, telling him I was working on a paper on Niebuhr vs. Anabaptists/Mennonites and asked him to send me "any relevant material especially . . . [his] thought and work on the subject."[5] He replied promptly, sending me some texts and advising me how to get other material, with the words: "If you come up with any conclusions which you think are convincing, I would be grateful for the privilege of seeing a carbon of your paper."[6] I never sent him my paper. With Yoder one had the sense that he had already thought of all the arguments—to disagree with him was either not to have understood him or to have gone over to the other ("apostate") side.

A normal objection to Yoder's nonviolent alternatives to solving conflict was: "They don't work!" His characteristic reply: "They haven't really been tried." This begged the question, of course, of how hard one would have to try before establishing that nonviolent options did in fact work or not. In the final analysis, the power of Yoder's prophetic word lay not in the effectiveness of various strategies but in their fidelity to what he took the Jesus message to be. He had an admirable assurance of the rightness of his reading of the biblical materials and history. He gave the impression of one who had never substantially changed his mind on anything. I have often wondered whether Yoder could have written once what his teacher Karl Barth wrote three times for *The Christian Century* on "How I have changed my mind."[7]

Despite his rejection of universal, rational truth claims as in classical foundationalism, his razor-sharp logic always seemed to me to presuppose some foundational rationality implicitly, if not explicitly. He had a way of logically disarming the opponent that seemed irrefutable. It was a style of argumentation that placed a premium on consistency, and he was usually able to show how the opponent was being inconsistent in one way or another. His book *When War is Unjust: Honesty in Just War Thinking*[8] is one of the most impressive examples of this way of arguing. It was an approach that left many a reader and listener on the defensive, at times highly effective, at other times greatly alienating. Whether alienating or convincing, it was a witness to the truth of Jesus Christ that could not be ignored in ecumenical circles. He left no doubt that a commitment to "Jesus as Lord" was the heart of his intellectual and ethical project.

My occasional uneasiness with Yoder's uncompromising theological-social ethic may have been at least partly due to my being a Canadian Mennonite and the progeny of Dutch-Prussian-Russian-Mennonites rather than American-Swiss Mennonites. My great, great, great grandfather was the founder of the *Kleine Gemeinde* church in Russia in 1812, and my ancestry moved to Manitoba in 1874.

There are important historical differences between the two streams of Mennonites that have significant theological-ethical ramifications. Despite the many migrations within the Dutch/North German Mennonite stream through the centuries, there was a greater tendency among the "northerners"(in Europe and in Canada) toward "assimilationism" of various kinds, particularly among those who stayed behind during periods of mass migrations.

This is most dramatically evident, of course, in the Dutch Mennonite story, but is present in subsequent periods of acculturation in Russia and in Canada. Many Swiss Mennonites assimilated into American culture, but more often than not it appears they left the church in the process. It is not surprising, therefore, that a theological, ethical, and ecclesiological recovery of Anabaptist-Mennonite distinctives in this century, which would highlight the differences between the descendants of sixteenth-century Anabaptists and other mainline Christian groups, would emerge from within the American, Swiss Mennonite tradition rather than my Canadian stream. This renewal movement emphasized the distinction between Christian community and civil society as it was experienced within the largest imperial power in the world.

Most Canadian Mennonites, although they benefited greatly from the Swiss Mennonite renewal movement, never had the same passion about noncomformity, partly for historical reasons, partly for contextual reasons. Canada was not a superpower and the special multicultural fabric of Canadian society gave a different colour to the relationship of Mennonites to wider culture in Canada.

As I look back on my religious, ethnic upbringing in the village of Altona, Manitoba, I note that, true, we were an ethnic enclave, surrounded by the English, German Lutherans, French Catholics, native Canadians who lived in nearby reserves, and a few Jewish families. The primary distinguishing factor, however, was our language (a Low German, High

German, Dutch, Russian amalgam) and distinctive eating habits. Our worship services and theology were not that different from German Lutheranism, both in form and content.

I knew Mennonites were pacifists but the rest of my theology was a mix of conservative and evangelical Protestantism, shaped just as much by my experience with Interschool Christian Fellowship and American-style revivalism as Anabaptist theology. As a challenge to this frame of mind I encountered Bender and Yoder in my years at Canadian Mennonite Bible College. They had a strong impact but never totally convinced me. There were other theological and philosophical streams to my education that modified my reading of Bender and Yoder. It always seemed to me that Yoder was "right" in a limited sphere of life and knowledge, but that his thought could not provide a comprehensive foundation for many other areas of reality and human existence—music and the arts, to give just one example. There were also theological and philosophical issues to be dealt with that were not exclusively or even primarily ethical in nature—e.g., existential meaning in the face of personal suffering and death, or the numerous issues raised by science and cosmology.

Questions of the where from and where to of cosmic reality and human existence, I continue to believe, are not to be defined as exhaustively in moral-ethical categories as Yoder's work suggests. And even within ethics, the parameters of Yoder's ethics are not large enough to include many of the frontiers of modern ethical dilemmas in the area of risk analysis, biomedical research, and cloning that my colleague Conrad Brunk is working on for Canadian government agencies.

My first serious intellectual engagement with Yoder's theological-ethical thought was in the early 1970s, with issues arising out of his 1964 book, *The Christian Witness to the State*.[9] I still think this is one of Yoder's best books, in that it lays out in simple and graphic terms his neo-Schleitheimian view of the church and state in contrast to the views held by other traditions. Reading Chapter 7, "The Classic Options Graphically Portrayed"—in which he contrasts his own proposal with the medieval Roman Catholic, Lutheran, Calvinist, Liberal, Niebuhrian, Jehovah's Witness, and Amish-Mennonite views—was an eye-opener for me.[10] There were two main 'revelations' I received from this book: 1) the "middle axioms"—that rights, freedom, justice, equality language can be used by the church in its communication to larger society in a way that does not compromise its christological norm of unconditional love (*agape*); and that 2) while Christians always fall short of the christological standard, "sin" can never be systematically factored in as a relevant variable for Christian ethics the way Reinhold Niebuhr did it.[11]

The first insight I found theologically helpful; the second continues to give me difficulty. It has always seemed that Yoder did not allow adequately for the human fallibility of individual Christians as well as the Christian community. I grant that the fact of 'sin' (the 'is' of sin) ought not to be built into one's ethic in such a way that it anticipates and excuses sinful behavior (that is, virtually functions as an 'ought'). But I do believe that sin is a theologically relevant category for doing Christian ethics; particularly in how we understand the God-given role of religious, social, and political institutions in a post-lapsarian world.

When his new, expanded edition of *Nevertheless: Varieties of Religious Pacifisim* appeared in 1992, I was curious whether in his chapter on "The Pacifism of the Messianic Community" (which represents his own view) he might have modified his thinking on sin in the church from the time of the first edition in 1972.[12] I discovered a slight modification. What he adds is a brief allusion to individuals even within the Messianic community being "moral cripples:" "Being crippled," he says, "I am unashamed of needing a crutch; and most of us are moral cripples."[13] This is an admission of a sort, but it is biological metaphor which in my view does not adequately address the continuing moral-volitional nature of fallenness even amongst the "saints."

What Yoder resisted, and here he remains our prophetic guide, is compromising the public witness of the church by too easily slipping into existential excuses. The above "moral cripple" reference is immediately followed by this assertion: "Yet the social meaning of a peace witness is far more fundamental than that. The existence of a human community dedicated in common to a new and publicly scandalous enemy-loving way of life is itself a new social datum. A heroic individual can crystallize a widespread awareness of need or widespread admiration. However, only a continuing community dedicated to a deviant value system can change the world."[14]

One of my first public critiques of Yoder's thought came in a 1983 article, "The Nature and Possibility of a Mennonite Theology."[15] There I place Harold S. Bender, Robert Friedmann, Yoder and Gordon Kaufman on a theological continuum in which they share some common assumptions about the world, the church and theology; assumptions which stand in tension with classical Christian thought. What they have in common, I suggested, is a suspicion of metaphysical-ontological thought in favour of historical-ethical categories. This puts them, I proposed, within the modern Enlightenment project. If I had to rewrite that essay, I might well highlight the differences among these four thinkers more than I did at the time. I would also want to acknowledge to a greater degree the theological orthodox or neo-orthodox aspects particularly of Bender's and Yoder's thought. However, my basic thesis still holds.

I argue that Yoder, like Bender and Friedman before him and the more radical historicist Kaufman, prefers a "prophetic-eschatological" reading of the Judeo-Christian tradition to a "priestly sacramental" one.[16] In his polemic against liberal and political realists (Niebuhrians) on the one side and pietistic existentialists on the other, he interprets the Gospel essentially in social-political terms—i.e., as a nonviolent way of living in this world which presupposes the lordship of Christ. Jesus' message is a political one, albeit a politics of a different kind (one premised on nonviolent relationships). This is the basic thesis of his best known book, *The Politics of Jesus*.[17]

My quarrel with Yoder in that article is not so much his strong emphasis on the Gospel as a historical-political-ethical message, but the virtual eclipse of what I call the sacramental, mystical, cultic, metaphysical, and ontological dimension(s). This historicist, anti-metaphysical orientation makes Yoder's thought less critical of our age than he intends it to be—it in fact buys into modern historicism. In that article I also cite passages from his *Preface to Theology*[18] in which he, like Kaufman, identifies with the Hebraic view of things over against the Hellenistic and later Greco-Roman views in a way which positively links that Hebraic view with modern historicist thought. In his separating of "Athens" and "Jerusalem" he has much in common with Tertullian of the second century, but in his linking "Jerusalem" with modern historical thinking he parts company with classical thought. The ancient ecumenical creeds, particularly in their trinitarian affirmation, represented a coming together of "Athens" and "Jerusalem" that I believe important for Christian theology and ethics. I find this perspective lacking in Yoder's thought as well as in others of the so-called "non-foundationalist" school of theology.

My own theological project has been largely shaped by my growing interest in the classical imagination, especially as it developed in the encounter between Jewish-Christianity and Greco-Roman culture, and the trinitarian and christological debates of the Patristic period. It has come to be my firm conviction that in the context of this encounter and these debates, a distinctive Christian doctrine of God emerged that is *foundational* for later Christian thought and ethics.

The critical issue for Christians, and in particular for Mennonites in the "Free Church" tradition, is the "Constantinian" problem. The question quite simply put is: Can the development of classical Christian orthodoxy be distinguished from the Constantinianization of the church (usually assumed to be the fall of the church by those in the Believers Church stream)? It is at this point that I have done some of my most serious engagement with three of Yoder's texts: *The Priestly Kingdom, Christian Attitudes to War, Peace, and Revolution,* and *Preface to Theology.*[19] For many years I have taught a course on "War and Peace in Christian Thought," both at Conrad Grebel College and at the Toronto School of Theology. A staple of my textbook diet in this course has been *The Priestly Kingdom* and *Christian Attitudes.*

Where I have found Yoder one of the most stimulating debating partners in this course is around the question of Constantinianism. Since most of my students come from what Yoder would call "Constantinian" traditions—Catholics, Orthodox, Lutherans, Anglicans, so-called mainline Protestants of various stripes—Yoder's Constantinian thesis usually gets me a lot of intellectual mileage. I have found, however, that the "Constantinian shift" axiom in Yoder's thought ("axiom" in the sense that the spectre of Constantinianism is an evil ghost that hovers behind virtually every sentence Yoder writes, a bit like Schleiermacher was the unseen enemy behind everything Karl Barth wrote) to be both right and troubling.

In two of my published writings I spar with Yoder on this issue. One is "Trinitarian Orthodoxy, Constantinianism, and Theology from a Radical Protestant Perspective."[20] There I try to show how, despite Yoder's respect for what the early church theologians did with the Trinity at Nicea and with christology at Chalcedon, he has a fundamental suspicion of this so-called post-biblical *Hellenistic* development and its link to imperial power. It is for Yoder a departure from biblical narrative into metaphysical-ontological thinking: "If we call into question the acceptance of *Hellenistic* thought forms which are foreign to the way the Bible thinks, which don't fit with the *Hebrew* mind, or with the *modern* mind either for that matter, then again we have to challenge whether it does us much good."[21]

I try to establish that theological orthodoxy as it developed in the first five centuries stands in fundamental continuity with the Scriptures, that it went beyond the Scriptures in formulating a uniquely Christian doctrine of God. Furthermore, classical trinitarian orthodoxy need not be identified with sociopolitical Constantinianism but can function as a critique on all forms of Constantinianism and is in fact a necessary framework and grounding for Christian ethics.[22]

In a subsequent essay, "Towards a Theocentric Christology: Christ for the World," I go further in defending a more pluralistic reading of the Constantinian period.[23] The Constantinian problem challenges all of us, emerging as the consequence of successful missionary activity as it tries to deal with the problems of relating Christian faith to culture. It was not a monolithic "apostate" phenomenon. There was a multiplicity of responses to this challenge in the third, fourth, and fifth centuries (Tertullian, Eusebius of Caesaria, Lactantius, Salvian, and Augustine, to name only a few). It is not helpful to demonize this whole era. Doing so not only does an injustice to the diversity of the period (is bad history) but robs us of creative possibilities for engaging culture and politics in our own era. That something went seriously wrong with the Eusebian type of political theology in the Constantinian court is undeniable. But to label the whole of the fourth century era as apostate, thereby closing the chapter on all other "mainline" traditions—Orthodox, Catholic, Anglican, Protestant—simply won't do.[24] And this leads me to the central topic of this essay: What about "theological orthodoxy" as it developed in the first five centuries in its relation to early Jewish-Christianity as Yoder understands it?

Messianic (Diaspora) Judaism

In March 1997, Conrad Grebel College and the Toronto Mennonite Theological Centre invited Yoder to give a series of lectures in Waterloo and Toronto. Two of the lectures dealt with a theme that seemed to be of increasing interest to Yoder toward the end of his life: diaspora Judaism and its relevance to Christianity, particularly the Believers Church tradition.[25]

Yoder's reading of the biblical and early church's theological development is a serious challenge to my own defence of theological orthodoxy. I devote the following pages to an exposition of Yoder's view as expressed in these lectures, and in his book *For the Nations*, with my response.

Jews as non-non-Christians

In the lecture, "Judaism as a Non-non-Christian Religion" (a typical Yoder turn of phrase), Yoder makes the case that early Christianity was a voluntary form of Judaism, a messianism within Judaism that led to the Christian movement.[26] From the second century onward, mainstream Christianity has been anti-Jewish, at first in the form of the theory of supercession, and by the fourth century outright antagonism and political ostracism, frequently manifesting itself in expelling Jews and forcing them into ghetto culture. The Jew came to be viewed not as honest "non-Christian," but as "infidel," responsible for "deicide." Responses by Christians in turn have varied from missionizing Jews, ignoring them, giving them a permanent priority in the plan of God, to a post-holocaust biblical perspective in which any explicit Christian proclamation to the Jews is rejected. For Yoder, the gospel is a message of reconciliation between Jew and Gentile, two peoples becoming one, the rejection of all coercion in matters relating to faith and civil governance of churches, as the Radical Reformation understood it.

Jesus, himself a Jew, was not anti-Jewish; and in those areas where he differed from other Jews, he was "well within the parameters of tolerable diversity which the Judaism of the time could support, and which Judaism today can support. The same is true of the nonviolence or the nonresistance of Jesus."[27] Similarly, Paul was fully Jewish even in his mission to the Gentiles, a mission which he saw as related to the coming of the Messianic age. Only a Jew could have believed that the Messiah had come. Paul's mission in a Gentile city always began from the synagogue.

Only in the second century did Gentile minority groups begin separating church from synagogue. For some eighty years after Pentecost, synagogues were open to Messianic believers. The churches were in effect "messianic synagogues" that did not split off communion with Jewry. Ethically (as in the rejection of violence) non-messianic Jews acted the way Christians did at the time. Only later did non-messianic Jews come to be known as Jews and messianic Jews as Christians. Jews became through this process an ethnic enclave which ultimately led to Zionism: The "abandonment of missionary perspective on the part of Judaism is an adjustment not to the Gentile world but to Christianity," says Yoder.[28]

For this reason, the fall of the church which has frequently been associated with Constantine in the fourth century really begins in the second century: "The 'apologists' like Justin Martyr, who reconceived the Christian message so as to make it credible to nonJewish culture, whether to philosophers or religious people or practical or powerful people, detached the message of Jesus from its Jewish matrix and thereby transposed it into an ahistorical moral monotheism with no particular peoplehood and no defences against acculturation."[29] In this process the church lost the globalness of its message, the Torah (law) as grace, and diaspora life as suffering servant. It was these elements that the Radical Reformers set out to retrieve.

Christianity as a Jewish "free church" movement

In the second of the lectures mentioned above, "The Jewishness of the Free Church Vision," Yoder makes the connection between messianic Judaism, or the early Jewish-Christian community, and the Believers Church tradition more specifically.[30] He calls the "Free Church" a "renewal movement within Jewry." For two centuries, Christianity and Judaism were overlapping circles, with a small segment of non-messianic Jews and some Gentiles outside. Origen and later Chrysostom, notes Yoder, still preached on Sunday to those who on Saturday had worshipped in the synagogue.[31]

He repeats the claim that the "christianizing of Judaism" resulted in the abandonment by Jews of their missionary vision and the division of Jews into an ethnic Jewish minority and a Christian establishment. Modern Zionism is the culmination of this process, with the synagogue becoming in effect one more "church" in North America, and the State of Israel modelling itself on Western thinking—the state no longer a believing community, but as individualized as in the West.

The magisterial Reformers were critical of medieval unfaithfulness—wrong turns in the development of the papacy and in the doctrines of salvation and the sacraments:

> The deviation they deplored had not taken place before the sixth century, since these "Reformers"did not intend to abandon the great creeds of the fourth and fifth centuries, or the achievements of Constantine, Theodosius, and Justinian in creating the Christian Empire. The "radicals" of the Reformation on the other hand dated the "fall" earlier, beginning at the latest with the persecution of dissenters at the order of Constantine, and perhaps much earlier at the death of the last apostle. *For our purposes the exact date does not matter, but we are learning something about how to define the substance of the loss. The first dimensions of the loss to become visible are precisely those traits of early Christianity tied to the Jewishness of the gospel.* (Emphasis mine)[32]

Yoder blames the "apologetes" (at least partly) for this loss of Jewishness, in their changing the faith into an "ahistorical moral monotheism" to make it more palatable to Gentile culture.

Exilic Jewish identity defined by the synagogue made it flexible and able "to live without central administration." When this diaspora notion was lost with the separation of the "church culture" from the "synagogue culture," Western Christianity looked to Rome for centralized identity. The Radical Reformation was a return to a "synagogue-free-church" model.

> Thus in principle, the issues raised by the radical reformers (Hus and Cheltschitksy, Sattler and Marpeck) were transpositions of the old Jewish identity agenda, now restated as an intra-Christian critique. *The anticlericalism, the anticentralism, the warning against antinomianism, the rejection of national-governmental control of the churches, which had marked earlier Christianity, were rooted jewishly just as truly as was the nonviolence of the free churches.* (Emphasis mine)[33]

What Judaism and Radical Reformation have in common include seeing God as continuing agent of critique and historical change more than sanctification of a static present, unembarrassment about their particularity and minority status, derivation of group identity from a book more than from clergy and ritual, and a distinctive and serious moral commitment (although sixteenth-century free churches did not transcend the antisemitism of their age, and contrasted too easily between the Old and New Testaments).[34] The Jewish-Christian schism was not part of Jesus' or Paul's vision for the coming Rule of God, and Yoder implies in the latter part of his lecture that reconciliation between Judaism and Christianity is the way to religious renewal: "The recovery of our sense of the Jewishness of original Christianity and especially of free church renewal should give a second wind to the forces of renewal. Whether the impact be commonality or dialogue, confession or guilt or joy in reconciliation and common witness, to restore the recognition of the sister communion might just call Christians back to their roots as the free church minorities in the West have been failing to do."[35]

Yoder is unapologetic in his particular reading of the Jewish story— making "Heschel [more representative] than Ben Gurion, Arnold Wolf than Meir Kahane, Anne Frank than Golda Meir."[36] It is appropriate particularly within the Jewish story to identify this particular stream of inner-Jewish thought, he says, because "there is not, as for most other ethnic communities and most nations, any one central authority within the community to define from what perspective it must be read."[37] It is this latter point, namely Yoder's reading of the Jewish story, that we want to consider, and for that we look at one essay in Yoder's most recent book, *For the Nations*, "See How They Go with Their Face to the Sun."[38]

Diaspora: Jewish and Christian paradigm

Yoder consciously entitles his most recent book *For the Nations* to correct what some have incorrectly labelled his "sectarian" or "against the nations" stance.[39] This, Yoder claims, is not a change of conviction but was always his view— namely "that the very shape of the people of God in the world is a public witness, or is 'good news,' for the world, rather than first of all rejection or withdrawal."[40] This witness to the nations is best understood, according to Yoder, in the words of JHWH through Jeremiah: "Seek the peace of the city where I have sent you"—that is, witnessing as a diaspora living amid foreign peoples.[41] For Yoder, the time of Jeremiah and Constantine represent two ancient turning points more significant than the Reformation or the Enlightenment for clarifying the Christian faith. The one (Jeremiah) symbolizes the birth of a new concept of "believing community" and the other (Constantine) the apostasy of that diaspora vision.

In Chapter 3, "See How They Go with Their Face to the Sun," Yoder develops most fully this Jeremian turning point. Citing God's command to the Jewish people in Babylon, "Seek the welfare of the city where I have sent you into exile, and pray to the Lord on its behalf, for in its welfare you will find your welfare" (Jer. 29:7 RSV), Yoder defends the view of Jewish writer Stephan Zweig that the scattering of the Jews was the beginning of a new divine mission. It represented God's negative judgment on monarchy and the start of a "fresh prophetic mandate, of a new phase of the Mosaic Project."[42] Diaspora (the "Joseph paradigm") was not a brief detour after 586, but a model for normal Jewish existence for the next millennium and a half.

Babylon, not Jerusalem, becomes the cultural centre of world Jewry until the Middle Ages. What has come to be known as "canonization," the process of selecting a manageable body of defining literature, is what helps to give the scattered community its identity ("Face to the Sun," 55ff).

Other markers of identity are the Torah, rabbinate, circumcision, and the synagogue. The transition from a temple culture to a synagogue culture was, for Yoder, "the most fundamental sociological innovation in the history of religions ... " ("Face to the Sun," 71)—a shift from centralized authority to dispersed communities of believers. It is this synagogue culture which continues in earliest Christianity:

> Messianic Judaism in the first century, which we now call "Christianity," went from here with no basic change as far as social structure and worldview are concerned. "Christians" (most accurately described for the first generations as "messianic Jews") modified the synagogue pattern only slightly by their openness to non-Jews, and by their love feasts; the lay, book-centered, locally managed format of the synagogue remained. When the synagogue polity came later to be overshadowed among Christians by sacerdotalism and episcopacy, that represented a fall back into the pre-Jeremian patterns of Hellenistic paganism ("Face to the Sun," 71, n48).

God's judgment on Constantinian and neo-Constantinian Christianity is thus the same as it was on the pre-Jeremian imperialistic-monarchical Jewish culture. The intent of God in the pre-lapsarian world was heterogeneous "nonfoundational" diversity. The sin of Babel is the attempt by the human community to absolutize and homogenize itself, and the punishment of dispersion of tongues is really a blessing—the demonstration of God's initial primeval ordination of multiplicity and diversity. The people of Babel, says Yoder, were the first foundationalists ("Face to the Sun," 62-63). The later scattering of the Jews into dispersion was therefore a continuation of God's initial nonfoundationalist purpose. What would never have occurred to the "polyglot Jews" at home in Babylon:

> ... was to try to bridge the distance between their language world and that of their hosts by a foundationalist mental or linguistic move, trying to rise to a higher level or dig to a deeper one, so that the difference could be engulfed in some *tertium quid*, which would convince the Babylonians of moral monotheism without making them Jews, and to which the Jews would yield without sacrificing their local color. They did not look for or seek common ground ("Face to the Sun," 73).

Another Reading of the Jewish Story

Yoder admits that his is not the only reading of the Jewish story, even within Judaism. In response, I draw here on an alternate reading by my colleague John W. Miller, a specialist in Hebraic literature who has published extensively in the area.[43] Miller is a contemporary of Yoder's, and with Yoder and five other American Mennonites spent time studying and doing voluntary service in postwar Europe in the 1950s. They published a small periodical called *Concern*, and were known as the "Concern Group."[44] Miller's theological stance on the role of the state in society, and the relation of the church to the state, is markedly different from that of Yoder, as is his reading of Israel's story.

Canonization and the transition to synagogue culture

Miller agrees with Yoder that it was probably during the exilic period that Jews began the canonization process—the collection of a body of authoritative literature from their history for purposes of identity. Where he disagrees with Yoder is on the role of the Jewish establishment in Jersualem in compilation and dissemination of the Jewish Scriptures. Miller finds Yoder's "pejorative brushing aside of the whole second temple period as portrayed in Ezra and Nehemiah" as "mind-boggling."[45] While, according to Miller, we know little about exactly how and when synagogue culture began, "John's notion that the canon and synagogue arose without there being any centralist organization is ahistorical and fantastical."[46] Miller believes that some kind of centre at Jerusalem did continue to play an important role in the religious life of the Jewish community after the Exilic period, thereby in effect relativizing the normative nature of the diaspora as Yoder sees it.

Jews and the Nations

Miller's much more fundamental disagreement relates to his view of the role of the Jews in witnessing to the nations. Miller takes particular issue with Yoder's claim that it would never have occurred to Jews in Babylon to attempt to mediate in a foundationalist way between their world and that of their hosts, to seek common ground, that "Jews knew that there was no wider world than the one their Lord had made and their prophets knew the most about" ("Faces to the Sun," 73).

According to Miller, Yoder is simply wrong on this point: "The Jews (through their Scriptures) did seek to locate their story within the wider world story, and in Genesis 1-11 ascribe a very clear place to the nations (and to the role of the nations) in God's post-diluvian will for the world. It is of this that Paul speaks in Romans 13, a text which John [Yoder] dislikes and marginalizes (as he dislikes and marginalizes Genesis 9)."[47]

Miller agrees with Yoder that God calls Israel and the church to be a blessing to the nations of the world as a covenanted, believing people rather than a state. Where Yoder falls short is in not seeing this blessing in the context of the whole of creation and history. For Miller, the God of Creation, the God who "sovereignly guides all nations, charging them with responsibility for protecting human life," is the same God as revealed in Christ. Yoder "advocates a universal pacificism that does not feel responsible for making history come out right. These ideas and ideals have become normative for many modern Mennonites. This is not, however, what the Bible teaches, nor what Mennonites have believed historically."[48]

According to Miller, the diaspora and Jerusalem scholarly community told the Jewish story (law and prophets) in the setting of the Creation story at one end and the Wisdom writings at the other. The Genesis story (creation [Genesis 1 and 2], fall [Genesis 3], building of cities and involvement in skills and trades [Genesis 4ff], increasing fragmentation, chaos and account of various nations [Genesis 9-11]) is an attempt to understand the Jewish experience theologically in the largest context of the nations. God is seen as a God of all nations, not just of the Jewish nation; Adam and Eve were not only the ancestral parents of the Jews but of all humans; and the promise to Abraham that his descendants would become a great nation with a special covenant is for the blessing of all nations. Messianic expectations have to do with how this will happen.

It is true, as Yoder says, that an important paradigm shift took place in the second temple period, when the synagogue throughout the diaspora becomes important (a type of "believers church" is born). However, the synagogue does not displace the temple, and there is always a hope for restoration of the temple—Babylon is never considered to be the exclusively normative symbol.

What about Classical Theological Orthodoxy?

What are the implications of these two different readings of the Jewish and early Jewish-Christian tradition for theological orthodoxy as defined by the classical period of Christianity? Yoder is rather selective in his choice of a slice of Jewish experience (diaspora synagogue culture, the "Joseph" paradigm), and making it normative not only for the whole of Judaism but also for the whole of Christianity. Is this a comprehensive enough picture of the Jewish story, and the Christian narrative as it has developed over the millennia?

Miller recognizes the importance of the "scattered-exilic" model but places it within a broader, global, national, and inter-national vision. Yoder, it is true, sees the role of exilic Jewish culture as seeking the blessing of the host nations, although he never, in my view, satisfactorily shows how that blessing is actualized in concrete situations. Yoder is (and was) a non-foundationalist if not anti-foundationalist, long before the present postmodern disenchantment with foundationalism. He idealizes decentralized diversity and is suspicious (he would call this being realistic) of all institutional centres of power and authority. Yoder reads this antifoundationalism back into the prelapsarian intent of God in Creation. One wonders where the ontological and theological grounds for ultimate unity and reconciliation lie in Yoder's theological ethic. Miller, on the other hand, gives more weight to a type of what I would call theological foundationalism (although he doesn't use the term) existing at the very heart of Creation. God's intent for the human race, from the beginning, is not fragmentation, diversity, diaspora, and exile, but unity. The theological foundation for this in both Jewish and Christian thought is the one God of the Jews, Christians, and all nations. Ultimately, the difference between Yoder's and Miller's vision is the relation between "exilic" culture (both for Jews and Christians) and larger global, world culture. For Miller, the same God is at work in both, using different means to achieve God's divine purpose with the nations. For Yoder, because exilic culture is ethically and politically normative, it is not clear whether and how God is at work outside that alien community. If exile and diaspora are the norm, how is a unified vision ever possible?

More specifically, does the logic of Yoder's position not finally end up being incompatible with the trinitarian councils of Nicea and Constantinople, and the christological definition of Chalcedon? He does say in *The Politics of Jesus*:

> To deal with the many ways, ebionitic and docetic, of avoiding the normativeness of Jesus, would call for a different kind of study from the present one. Such questions are of a dogmatic, not exegetical character, and would need to be encountered on that level.... If we were to carry on that other, traditionally doctrinal kind of debate, we would seek simply to demonstrate that the view of Jesus being proposed here is more radically Nicene and Chalcedonian than other views. We do not here advocate an unheard-of modern understanding of Jesus; we ask rather that the implications of what the church has always said about Jesus as Word of the Father, as true God and true Man, be taken more seriously, as relevant to our social problems, than ever before.[49]

In this passage Yoder implies that the early church was right in rejecting the "heretical" reductions of Jesus either on the human side (ebionitic) or the divine side (docetic), and that his own challenge to take Jesus' normativity for ethics seriously presupposes classical orthodoxy, and is in fact strengthened thereby. After carefully examining his writings on Jewish Christianity, however, I am not so sure. They seem to confirm my earlier suspicions. In these lectures he seems more radically restitutionist than ever. He suggests that the fall occurred not in the fourth century but in the second century with the apologists and the consequent loss of the early Jewish-Christian paradigm. The fall now occurs at the point where the Hebraic-Christian and Greco-Roman world views encounter each other in a creative synthesis.

What does one do with the success of the missionary movement to the Gentiles (the Greeks and the Romans)? Is this shift from synagogue to church, from Hebraic monotheism to Christian trinitarianism (the rejection of Greco-Roman dualism or polytheism), truly to be seen as the fall of the Christian vision? Yoder rightly identifies and denounces the tragic nature of the historic split between Judaism and Christianity, and the consequent anti-semitism. But in emphasizing the continuity between the early Christian community and the messianic diaspora community of the Jews, does he not underestimate the discontinuity that sets in immediately with the emerging success of the missionary movement as we find illustrated already in Acts 15 (the giving up of the critical ceremonial marks of Judaism even in the diaspora)? Is one not finally faced with some radically new developments in the Christian understanding of God that include the move toward Nicea and Chalcedon, incorporating both Judaism and Hellenism in a new third way?[50]

There are theologically complex issues present already in the New Testament writings that Yoder's thesis does not adequately address. To claim that in the first 500 years following the death of Christ a new "religion" with a distinctive "doctrine of God" evolved surely does not necessarily entail supercessionism and antisemitism.

The theological inadequacy of Yoder's thesis also applies to his rather univocal identification of the Reformation Radicals with the free church movement of messianic Judaism and the early Jewish-Christian community. This strikes me as an ahistorical approach to the rather heterogeneous social and intellectual origins of the Anabaptists in late medieval society (not to mention historic Judaism and early Christianity). He is right in noting some sociological and ethical parallels between the Radicals of the Reformation and early Jewish Christians (really messianic Jews, according to Yoder), and between later Mennonites and Jews. But are there not some profound theological differences that Yoder avoids? Aside from the *heterogeneity* of the Anabaptist movement, are there not significant theological-anthropological differences that stem from the rise of the modern world, which provide the context of the rise of the modern Free Church tradition? Voluntaristic-nominalistic assumptions shape the Radicals' view of individual freedom and responsibility in a way quite foreign to the classical period.[51] Noble and prophetically important as Yoder's political-ethical agenda is, in the end it short-changes critical theological insights central to the Christian tradition. More than that, the central theological affirmations found in classical orthodoxy are needed to undergird the very moral and ethical claims that Yoder witnesses to so singularly.

PART THREE

THE CLASSICAL IMAGINATION

NINETEEN

Lost Horizon: Whatever Happened to Classical Theology?*

In Part III of this volume, I begin applying the insights of the more formal, methodological essays of Part I and Part II to the material substance of Christian theology. I use the word "begin" deliberately because my methodological concerns are never far beneath the surface even in this third part (evident especially in the first few essays), and in none of the essays do I presume to be offering comprehensive, systematic treatments of any given doctrine.

It might also be noted that despite my defence of an Alexandrian orientation throughout this volume—one which seeks to combine Athens (philosophy) with Jerusalem (historical theology)—in my actual method of dealing with systematic themes I shy away from prolonged speculative treatises. Instead, I tend inevitably to arrive at my philosophical-theological conclusions via a good deal of historical narrative. Essays in the first Part dealt primarily with the crisis of the modern world illuminated for me in a special way by diverse thinkers such as Gordon Kaufman and George Grant, the former accommodating modernity unapologetically and the latter being its severest critic.

---

* Originally published as "Lost Horizons: Whatever Happened to Classical Theology?" in *CMBC Alumni Bulletin* (Fall 1983): 3-12. For notes on the text see the Notes section below.

My turn to classical theology was occasioned by my dissatisfaction with the modern answers to the modern crisis. The essays in the second Part focus more specifically on the uneasy alliance of Mennonites with modernity, and how they have responded theologically or in other ways to the dominant assumptions of the modern period. I examined the thinking of numerous Mennonites but engaged myself most critically with the work of the late John Howard Yoder, who more than any other has left a mark on my generation of Mennonite intellectuals. In the following essays, making up the third Part, I begin offering constructive proposals for how one might go about thinking classically in the modern period on the main themes of systematic theology.

There is no clean division between the three Parts—similar themes, both formal and material, recur in all three—partly due to the chronological order in which each of the Parts is organized, each division beginning with my earliest thinking on the subject. Nevertheless, these last essays deal with the material substance of theology: Revelation, Trinity, Christology, Pneumatology, Creation, Ethics, Anthropology, and Ecclesiology.

At points my decision to deal with the material autobiographically—i.e., to structure the section sequentially according to the year in which the essays were written rather than thematically—means that I don't follow strictly the classical sequence of systematic theology. When this happens, as for instance, when the doctrine of creation is considered after the doctrine of the Holy Spirit, this is for pragmatic rather than theological reasons, although it is interesting to consider creation from a pneumatological perspective. If there is one consistent thread that runs through virtually all the essays, it is the conviction that the Christian doctrine of God as Triune is foundational to all theological thinking.

The first essay in Part III sets the stage, functioning as a bridge between the earlier two sets and the subsequent one. It was presented in 1983, as the first annual Distinguished Alumnus Lecture at Canadian Mennonite Bible College in Winnipeg, Manitoba.[1] *At the time my apology for a recovery of classical trinitarian thought especially within Mennonite circles appeared to go against the grain of dominant North American theology, not to mention Mennonite thought.*

Since then, there has been a virtual explosion of interest in trinitarian thought, including among Mennonites. I have since then realized that I was myself riding on a wave that had begun in Germany with Jürgen Moltmann and Wolfhart Pannenberg, who were themselves cashing in on what Karl Barth had already put in motion much earlier. However, my way of reappropriating classical theology is more "Alexandrian" in its orientation than much of this recent trinitarian thinking. By this I mean that I am much more positively inclined toward the bringing together of "Athens" and "Jerusalem" (Hellenistic and Hebraic thought). In the concluding essay of this volume, in which I engage the projects of Thomas Oden, Wolfhart Pannenberg, and Miroslav Volf, I spell out in greater detail how I understand the recovery of the classical imagination for our time.

The essay below, together with an article of the same year, "The Nature and Possibility of a Mennonite Theology" (reprinted as Chapter 10 above), represented the first public expression of my growing conviction that not only Mennonites but Christians of all traditions needed to retrieve the classical imagination. It brings together my thinking at the time concerning the nature of theology, the crisis of modernity, and some rather loose suggestions about the imaginative potential of classical trinitarian thought for the religious and ethical issues facing us today.

The autobiographical nature of much of the address has to do with the context and audience—many of the listeners knew me and my past well, although they were less aware of my intellectual life. In particular, I identify the three theological facts that have shaped my Christian faith: 1) the Evangelical fact: the need for an immediate experience of forgiveness (justitication by grace) and a personal encounter with a personal God; 2) the Anabaptist-Mennonite fact: the emphasis on moral and ethical obedience to Scripture, especially Jesus' teachings; 3) the Catholic fact: a respect for tradition, historical development, liturgy, sacrament, and the mystical dimension of religious life.

◆ ◆ ◆

The title I have chosen for this occasion, "Lost Horizon: Whatever Happened to Classical Theology?" is deliberately put in the form of a question. It expresses the present state of my theological questioning. Actually this question holds within it three implicit questions: What is theology? What is classical theology? What is modern theology and what, if anything, may have been lost in modern theology? In fact, I do think something of great significance, a pearl of great value, an intellectual and spiritual horizon, has been lost not only to much modern theology but to many of us. It has to do with the way we think about the world, about ourselves and about God. But I'm getting ahead of myself.

What Is Theology?

Historically, we as Mennonites have rightly been suspicious of systematic theologians, the "learned ones" who build intellectual edifices of Christian thought removed from real life. We have been able to see the importance of studying the Bible, the very foundation of Christian life. We have even been able to understand why we should study church history and ethics. But academic theology has always been suspect. Theology is the systematic reflection on God, ourselves, and the world in which we live. It is once removed from experience and practice. And Mennonites, particularly sixteenth-century Anabaptists, have always put experience and practice ahead of theological reflection.

What attracted the great Anabaptist historian Robert Friedmann as a Jew to the Mennonites in this century was precisely their emphasis on concrete practical Christianity. He felt they truly embodied the essence of the gospel through an "existential [concrete, lived] Christianity."[2] In fact, Friedmann makes the case that the Anabaptists were *in principle* opposed to theological systems of thought because this would separate faith from action, belief from obedience. The Anabaptists believed that we are called first and foremost to be obedient to the ethical teachings of Jesus.

What am I then doing in systematic theology at a university? Two very simple reasons have driven me to theology: first, understanding and accepting the basic doctrines or tenets of the Christian faith as we find them in the Bible and in the teaching of the Church has never come easy to me; second, my own experiences, anxieties, and doubts have more often than not clashed with traditional Christian beliefs. I have become a theologian more by fate than by choice, always driven to try to bring together these two poles: traditional Christian beliefs and the modern world of human experience. I have found it difficult simply "to accept" or simply "to believe." Belief has been a struggle for me. This is why I have in my academic work had an interest in history, philosophy, and theology but in the end come back to theology. It is in my blood, or, as the Germans put it, *Es ist mein Schicksal!*

The term *horizon* has become increasingly important in contemporary theological discussion. It is often associated with the name of Bernard Lonergan, an internationally recognized Canadian Catholic theologian. It has to do with one's conceptual field of vision from a particular viewpoint. This conceptual horizon is made up of two poles. The *subjective* pole is the person at a particular stage of development with all of the factors that have shaped his/her thinking. The *objective* pole is the whole set of questions and possibilities open to the person at a given stage in his/her development. The important point about horizon-language is that thought, meaning, and consciousness are dynamic, not static. We all have and think within certain conceptual horizons from particular vantage points. We change, and as we change, our horizons change. Not only do we as individuals have horizons which change, but historically there have been what Lonergan calls numerous "horizon-shifts." One such major horizon-shift in western history was the shift from a classical way of thinking about God, human beings, and the world to a modern way of thinking about these things.

My own theological horizon has been shaped by what I would call three facts: the "Evangelical fact," the "Mennonite fact," and the "Catholic fact." I suggested earlier that theology is my obsession and passion more by fate than by choice. I believe this may have to do with the question that haunted me as a little boy and that probably still hovers in some way over all my theological work, although I no longer put the question quite the same way I used to. The question quite simply is: "What must I do to be saved?" or to put it the way Luther did: "What must I do to be justified, made righteous before God?" Incidentally, Luther's answer to this question was "Nothing!" We don't do anything for our salvation. It is accomplished for us by God's grace in Christ. Our reception of that gift through faith is itself a gift.

I have always had a deep sense of my own inadequacy, unworthiness, and sinfulness, and the question of salvation continues to be relevant for me. This probably explains why I think Evangelical concerns ought to be taken seriously in all good theological thinking, even though the above question seems anachronistic to many modern theologians. This is why I find it difficult to accept Robert Friedmann's assessment of early sixteenth-century Mennonites or Anabaptists. He says that these early Anabaptists did not experience ongoing inner doubt, "no feeling of despair," but rather the opposite, "*the certainty* of resting in God's gracious hands."[3] Friedmann claims that these early Mennonites rejected Luther's view that a believer is justified and sinner at the same time, Luther's deep sense that after the experience of forgiveness and justification one continues to be plagued and tempted by sin and inner doubt. If this is the case, I find myself closer to Luther than to my own early Anabaptist ancestors on this point. For me the reality of personal sin, anxiety, doubt, and inner struggle has always been an intrinsic part of my faith.

Whether there is something important lacking here in our theology or emphasis as Mennonites, which drives many out of the Mennonite church into the more "evangelical" camp, I don't know. But increasingly I feel that Evangelicals point to something extremely significant in human religious experience. It is a kind of intuitive recognition on their part that is often poorly expressed either because of a wooden literalism or a poor conceptual vocabulary. Nevertheless, the Evangelical rightly points to and yearns for a direct and immediate experience of forgiveness and an encounter with a personal and transcendent God. This is not to say that the God the Evangelical ends up with is not much too often a projection of his/her own needs and desires and not truly transcendent. In an age of technology, when the experience of genuine otherness and transcendence is increasingly in jeopardy, this evangelical yearning is refreshing. It is the weight of this Evangelical-Lutheran question in all my theological thinking, what I call here the *Evangelical fact*, that keeps me from fully accepting the "de-privatization" of religious experience in some forms of modern political theology. In an age when everything tends more and more to be deprivatized through technology and mechanization, we need to retain or recover some sense of genuine inwardness.

What is the *Mennonite fact* that shapes my theological horizon? If the Evangelical-Lutheran question is "What must I do to be justified (saved)?" the Anabaptist-Mennonite question might be stated as being "What must I do to *be* Christian?" or "What must I do to be an obedient Christian?" J. C. Wenger, one of the few Mennonite systematic theologians we have had in our history, says that what made the sixteenth-century Anabaptists unique was not a matter of doctrine but a matter of ethical obedience. "It was not an unbalanced movement," he writes of early Anabaptism, "it was rather *a more earnest effort than the other Protestant groups made to break with religious and ecclesiastical tradition to render absolute obedience to the text of Scripture.*"[4]

This strong moral and ethical sense is the Mennonite fact which shapes my personal consciousness and theological thinking. One of my graduate professors once commented snarkily on my typical Mennonite moralism by saying that what I ought to do is think of the worst sin I could possibly imagine and then go and do it. After this, I would no longer be able to rely on my own moral righteousness for salvation but on God's gift of grace alone.

It is this ethical and social-political sensitivity which attracts me to certain modern theological movements such as Latin American "Liberation Theology" and German "Political Theology" and "Hope Theology." In all of these there is this same Anabaptist-type of stress on the unity of theory and practice, belief and action. This has recently been referred to as "orthopraxis," denoting the importance of both "right belief" and "right action," rather than the more traditional term "orthodoxy," which connotes primarily "right belief." As a Mennonite systematic theologian I do not have the option of building a beautiful neutral edifice of thought. All my thinking needs to be done in the context of a commitment of obedience to Jesus as Lord, which means also a commitment to social justice and human liberation, whether it is the emancipation of the poor, the oppressed minorities, or any other victimized and marginalized people in society. This is what I call the Mennonite fact in my theological thinking.

But consciously or unconsciously I have always felt a kind of tug of war between my Evangelical fact and my Mennonite fact. The Evangelical fact tends to make me pessimistic about the possibility of my sinful human nature actually to change for the better. It tends to become inward and somewhat passive in its reliance upon the grace and forgiveness of God. The Mennonite fact is more optimistic about human nature and expects a kind of legalistic perfectionism both on the level of individual morality and on the level of a social commitment to justice and equality. It is often difficult for me to reconcile these two facts which tend to push in opposite directions, to contradict each other and cause a type of theological schizophrenia.

Third, there is the *Catholic fact*. I have studied for a number of years in a Catholic university, have developed some close Catholic friendships, and have learned to greatly appreciate certain aspects of the Catholic tradition. One could go on at length to talk about the important Catholic view of comprehensiveness or universality and the Catholic view of the sacramental nature of reality. But it is particularly the Catholic notion of tradition and the development or evolution of Christian belief that has added something new to both my Evangelical and Mennonite facts. I have often felt that we as Mennonites (not to mention Evangelicals) hop, skip, and jump a bit too quickly from the present straight to the Bible, maybe with a brief touch-down in the sixteenth century. We do not have a strong enough sense of the historical development of ideas and beliefs.

The Reformation gave us the profound and to a great extent right conviction that each one of us can enter directly the biblical world and find there immediate nourishment for our souls and principles for action. Increasingly, however, I sense that what has gone on between the first and sixteenth centuries, and the sixteenth and the twentieth centuries, has shaped us much more profoundly than we have admitted; that we have access to the scriptural text largely through the eyes of the tradition that has passed on the written and unwritten Word of God to us. Increasingly, it seems to me also that particularly the classical doctrines, especially the Trinitarian formulations of Nicea-Constantinople, the Christological formula of Chalcedon, and the writings of the Church Fathers need to be taken more seriously, not only by Mennonites but by modern Christians and modern theologians.

The Catholic fact has also given me a much greater appreciation for the liturgical, sacramental, and mystical dimensions of life and religious experience. One of the great battles between the Anabaptists, Catholics, and Magisterial Reformers in the sixteenth century concerned the nature, number, and role of the sacraments in the church. The Anabaptists basically rejected the sacramental-sacerdotal system in favour of a "low" or "non-mystical" view of the sacraments and church polity. Instead of the seven Catholic sacraments (baptism, eucharist, penance, ordination, last rites, confirmation, marriage) the Anabaptists had two ordinances (baptism and the Lord's supper) and these were seen as signs of remembrance rather than supernatural or mystical events. In the sixteenth century there may have been too much mysticism, too much of the superstitious and the magical in the church.

In contemporary times, however, there is too little of the sacramental, the mystical, and the supernatural. In an age of technology, where technology itself has become "sacralized," where the sense of the mystical experience of the truly transcendent is missing almost totally from our everyday experience, it may be time that we re-examine our own traditional anti-sacramentalism.

These three facts—the Evangelical fact, the Mennonite fact, and the Catholic fact—live in an uneasy alliance in my soul. The fact that I as a Mennonite wrote my doctoral dissertation on two Evangelical-Lutheran theologians, Paul Tillich and Emanuel Hirsch, for a Catholic university under a Catholic advisor, illustrates this rather odd constitution of my theological horizon. This uneasy alliance of various traditions and religious impulses in my theological thinking has driven me to systematic theology. Systematic theology has a passion for comprehensiveness, for illuminating *all* dimensions of human experience—politics, economics, psychology, sociology, philosophy, art, business, agriculture—in light of the gospel. Someone from the Mennonite tradition, however, finds himself in a dilemma. A "sectarian" tradition like ours is not so much concerned with comprehensiveness—in fact it is more often opposed to universality—as in calling a small visible group of believers to obedience in certain areas of acceptable social life. It is extremely difficult to do systematic theology as a Mennonite for this very reason.

Yet this is precisely what I am interested in and what I think needs to be done. I am interested in whether it might be possible to develop a comprehensive systematic theology from the vantage point of the Anabaptist-Mennonite understanding of the Believers' Church and obedience to Christ. To do this, however, Mennonites need once more, as they did in the sixteenth century, to sit down with Catholics, Anglicans, Lutherans, Calvinists, and others to debate the theological issues confronting all of us in the modern world. In this process we ourselves will undoubtedly be changed. But the issues facing us in the contemporary situation are also vastly different than they were in the sixteenth century, and may demand new positions cutting across traditional denominational lines.

What Is Modern Theology?

As hinted at above, there was a major horizon-shift in western history during the time of the Enlightenment (in German: *Aufklärung*) in the eighteenth century, with intellectual roots in the sixteenth-century Reformation and the fourteenth-century Renaissance, usually thought of by historians as the birth of modernity. People gradually began thinking differently about God, themselves, and the world. This change or shift is usually referred to as the shift from classical consciousness to historical consciousness. People began to take history, development and change more seriously than before.

I do not want to dwell on a technical discussion of this shift except to say that in the classical world view it was generally assumed that there existed an eternal order or divine purpose in which human beliefs, lives, and actions took place. There were eternal and objective norms of right and wrong by which human morality and ethics were judged. These eternal norms were accessible to human beings. To use Roman Catholic language, there were unchanging eternal laws and natural laws according to which human laws had to be judged. The shift to historical consciousness meant that the human subject became profoundly aware of the historical and dynamic nature of all knowledge and all reality. Catholic theologian Karl Rahner describes this shift as "that turn to the subjective at the beginning of modern thought."[5] This turn meant that human beings either rejected the existence of a transcendent and objective realm of absolute norms or thought of themselves as not having access to such norms.

This shift had serious consequences for ethics. Human beings began to view themselves as the prime movers of history, as being alone in the world, free to shape and master human and non-human nature in total freedom, without a sense of accountability to a divine source outside of themselves. They began to consider themselves as being essentially the products of and the managers of history.

This change in thinking has had far-reaching consequences for each one of us in this room, particularly in the way we look at ethical issues. One Canadian philosopher who has influenced my own thinking on this subject a great deal maintains that the most persuasive modern assumption lying at the basis of modern technology is the view that "man's essence is his freedom." He argues that we have a whole new notion of justice in the modern world based no longer on non-negotiable norms of right but on convenience and social contract. This means that those who are too weak to enforce social contracts will be left without justice—"the imprisoned, the mentally unstable, the unborn, the aged, the defeated and sometimes even the morally unconforming."[6] In short, when we ourselves start making the rules and changing them on the basis of self-interest, not one of us is secure any longer.

One of the most important issues facing us today is the possibility of a nuclear holocaust. The real possibility that human history as we know it may come to an end forces us to think seriously about what we believe as Christians and Christian theologians. Let me tell you how one modern theologian, who has been called a "postmodern," "post-liberal," or "revisionist" theologian deals with this most important question. His name is Gordon D. Kaufman.

Kaufman, an ordained Mennonite minister in Boston, argues in a paper entitled "Nuclear Eschatology and the Study of Religion," that humankind finds itself in an entirely novel situation today. We have the possibility of totally obliterating the present and future human species. This possibility has never existed before. This means that some of the most basic traditional religious concepts are no longer adequate or applicable. In the past the end of history was seen by the Christian to be the consummation of God's divine purpose. The nuclear extinction of humanity would, however, be brought about by human beings themselves and could not be conceived in any way as being within the scheme of "an active creator and governor of history."[7]

The symbol of the "ultimate sovereignty of God over the events of history," a symbol indispensable for biblical faith, no longer holds in the face of the present situation. To argue, as some American fundamentalist Christians do, that a nuclear holocaust, if it occurred, would be an expression of God's divine plan, is totally unacceptable to Kaufman. Or, to affirm that God will not allow the nuclear holocaust to occur, or, if He does allow it to come to pass, that He will rescue a few human beings in a kind of Noah's ark rescue operation, is also unacceptable to Kaufman. Neither of these, he says, fully recognizes the radical nature of the human predicament and its implications for Christian theology. Neither is an ethically responsible stance in the face of this massive potential evil.

The possibility of total self-annihilation is a "hard empirical fact," says Kaufman. It is a "fact-which-is-not-yet-a-reality."[8] Confronted with this actual possibility none of us can remain neutral or aloof, he concludes. We must join forces to prevent this fact from becoming a reality. But to do so we will have to give up, or at least radically alter, some of our most precious theological beliefs. Here is how he puts it:

> Instead of assuming that we already know from revelation or authoritative tradition the correct values and standards—the faith-orientation—in terms of which life is to be understood, and decisions and actions formulated, we must recognize and acknowledge that humankind has moved into a historical situation unanticipated by biblical writers and subsequent theological commentators alike, a situation of much greater human knowledge, power and responsibility than our religious traditions had ever imagined possible.[9]

The only reasonable alternative for theologians, according to Kaufman, is to give up a traditional or classical understanding of Christianity:

In consequence, instead of understanding ourselves largely as handers-on of these traditions, as having a task simply of interpretation, we must be prepared to enter into the most radical kind of deconstruction and reconstruction of the traditions we have inherited, including especially their most central and precious symbols, God and *Jesus Christ* and *Torah*.[10]

Kaufman does not explain here what he means by this radical deconstruction and reconstruction of our views of God and Jesus. It is obvious, however, that he thinks the traditional-classical view is no longer adequate for the present crisis. We must come up with a more adequate concept of God. Here we see in a most remarkably clear way the basic assumptions behind much modern theology. Kaufman's view of the deconstructive and constructive task of theology, his belief that theologians must free themselves from the authority of revelation and tradition to fashion new concepts of God more adequate for the present human task, is based on the modern historical consciousness mentioned earlier, a view which emphasizes the primacy of the human subject in shaping humanity, history, and the world.

I agree with Kaufman at a number of important points. I should say right at the start that in many ways he is my alter ego and his agenda is also mine. I agree that the possibility of an imminent nuclear holocaust is one of the most important issues facing the Christian theologian today. I agree that this is a novel situation in human history which puts traditional Christian beliefs about God, ourselves, and the world under severe strain. I agree that it is not good enough for us simply to take the passive route of saying either that such an event, if it occurs, would be in the plan of God; or that, if it occurs, God will save at least a handful of human beings. We need to take responsibility for history in the sense that we actively struggle against evil of whatever kind, including imminent nuclear disaster. I also believe that traditional theological categories may need to be reinterpreted in the face of these novel events.

Where I do not agree with Kaufman is in his basic assumption and conclusion. Implicit in his whole argument is his belief that human beings are the primary if not the only movers of history, and that meaning and value are somehow dependent on the continuance of history as we know it. He assumes that the truth of God's sovereignty over history and creation is somehow dependent on whether time and history as we know it continue. His conclusion, therefore, follows logically. We must radically change our view of God and Jesus Christ to fit this new historical situation. I find myself rejecting both Kaufman's assumption and his conclusion.

I cannot see why the truth and meaning of traditional Christianity is contingent upon whether time as history continues the way we know it today. I do not believe that the objective reality and sovereignty of God depend upon what we do to the world. There are levels of meaning, value and truth which are not intrinsically historical but transcend time—that dissect the temporal sequence. This is why I increasingly find the classical world of meaning more attractive than the modern view as expressed so dramatically by Kaufman. I believe the classical world view was more multidimensional in its perception of reality than the modern view, and had the capacity to deal with dimensions of human experience and truth that the modern historicist view as represented by Kaufman cannot do.

It is for this reason that I have much greater regard for the authority of tradition and revelation than does Kaufman, and that I cannot accept Kaufman's challenge to radically deconstruct or dismantle older concepts of God and replace them with modern, more historicist notions. In fact, I suspect that Kaufman has mis-diagnosed the modern problem. What has brought us to the modern abyss of nuclear self-annihilation is not that we have not taken active responsibility for shaping the world in which we live. No! Precisely the opposite. We have come to this point because we have taken things into our own hands, because we have perceived ourselves arrogantly as free, as the shapers and managers of the world, without a sense of accountability to the Lord of history who transcends His own creation. It is this sense of a transcendent God to whom we are accountable individually and corporately that has been lost in modern theology.

We define and treat life increasingly within the framework of the historical movement from past to present to future. The modern horizon seems to me to be a narrower and more restrictive horizon than the classical one.

What Is Classical Theology?

By the classical period of Christian theology I mean the theological thought that arose in the formative period of Christianity, including the historical events of Jesus of Nazareth, the historical response to those events, and the theological interpretation of those events by the biblical writers and the early church, including the early Church Fathers. I include here very specifically the Trinitarian and Christological creeds of the early church at Nicea-Constantinople (A.D. 325-381) and at Chalcedon (A.D. 451), which were formulated with the use of both Jewish religious thought on the one hand and Greco-Roman thought on the other, but which nevertheless maintained their own distinctive revelatory character. It was in this Jewish-Hellenistic-Roman matrix that Christianity as we have come to know it first took shape. Here in the encounter of Christianity with classical culture a distinctively trinitarian and christological way of thinking about God, human beings, history, and reality as a whole was born that continues to be normative for us today. Here we have expressed a comprehensive Christian world view which is particularly significant in the modern context. It provides us with a model critical of all theological and anthropological reductionism, truncation, one-sidedness, and heresy, dangers so apparent in modern historicism.

Why and how is trinitarian thinking about God, as found implicitly in the biblical text and systematized explicitly in the Apostles' and Nicene Creeds, significant for us today? Trinitarian thinking about God guards against an unbalanced and one-sided emphasis in our theology and in our personal religious life. To emphasize the first article of the Nicene Creed, "We believe in one God, Father all-sovereign, maker of all things seen and unseen," is to affirm the God who is beyond all human imagination and construction, the God who is a judge and preserver of all of creation, including human history. This God is the one who created everything good but who nevertheless transcends creation and limits human action. It is an affirmation that God (not the human species) is the Lord of creation and of history. Everything that has existence, in so far as it exists, has its existence from and in God.

To confess the second article of the creed, "We believe in one Lord Jesus Christ, the Son of God, begotten from the Father as only begotten...," is to assert that this transcendent God is not an abstract God about whom we know nothing but one who has been concretely revealed to us in human history, in the birth, life, teachings, death, resurrection, and ascension of Jesus of Nazareth as the Christ. To affirm faith in the second article is to take history seriously. I am not denying that there are some serious epistemological and historical problems in any wooden or literalist understandings of this historical revelation in Christ. These epistemological (how does one know?) and historical (what really happened?) questions need to be honestly faced and may lead to significant reinterpretation of what the claims of this second article mean in the modern context. Central to all such interpretation and reinterpretation, however, is to understand the nature and function of theological language. My point here has to do with the importance of retaining the specifically *theological claims* expressed in the three articles of the creed.

Our affirmation of the third article, "We believe in one Holy Spirit...," is to assert the reality of God's dynamic presence in our lives in an ongoing way. Not only is God wholly transcendent! Not only is God historically concrete in Christ! God is existentially present to us as individuals, in the church and outside the church, within creation and human history, as a whole. These three articles and the three distinct *theological* claims they express are always dynamically related to each other and need to be affirmed simultaneously if theological truncation is to be avoided. The Mennonite who puts special weight on absolute obedience to the teachings of Jesus needs to confess faith in the three articles of the Creed to guard against a Christo—or Jesu—monism. The Charismatic who quite rightly puts special weight on the gift(s) of the Holy Spirit needs to see the leading of the Holy Spirit in the context of the entire Creed to avoid unchecked spiritual enthusiasm and fanaticism. The main point I want to make here is simply that there is a kind of one-dimensional view of reality and of what it means to be human in the modern horizon which is reflected in the modern caricature of the classical world.

Gordon Kaufman expresses such a caricature in his essay, "Biblical Authority in a World of Power," where he contrasts the modern scientific world view with the ancient mythological perception of reality:

> In its statements about the world we live in, the Bible reflects the primitive three-story cosmology characteristic of ancient humankind—the heavens above being the abode of God and the heavenly host; the underworld below, the place of the dead and of the legions of Satan; the earth in between, a flat disk floating on the waters, the place where humankind dwells and the battleground between the forces of light and the forces of darkness. All of this, of course, has become completely incredible to the modern scientific mind with its belief that the earth is really but a second-rate planet revolving around a third-rate sun somewhere in one of the millions of galaxies which make up the universe—a far cry indeed from the very center of the cosmos where the Bible places humankind.[11]

Kaufman illustrates the kind of one-dimensional modern scientific historical consciousness *vis-à vis* the classical world and ancient mythology that appears to me increasingly to be inadequate. In the modern world in which autonomous scientific and technical reason have become our new mythology, we have lost the multi-dimensionality of the classical horizon. I am not at all convinced that the new horizon is a more adequate one by which to understand ourselves, the world, and God than the traditional classical one. At least the classical horizon had a "three-tiered cosmology"—a description which is itself a modern caricature, the kind of language that only a modern literalist could use about the ancient world view. The modern horizon has reduced reality to "one tier"—the material, physical, empirically verifiable, and historically horizontal tier. We need more dimensions, more tiers to our thinking, rather than fewer. I want my children, for instance, to believe that Jesus was born of a virgin

Mary, conceived by the Holy Spirit, could calm the seas, and could walk on the water.

I would describe my own theological movement over the past decade or so as a kind of conversion. This conversion can best be illustrated by looking at three periods of my thinking during the past twelve years. Some of you may remember my participation in a music group called "The Faith and Life Singers." In 1971 we cut a record. I recently listened to that record and heard with some chagrin the words of one of the songs which we all sang with such conviction. It's a song by Sydney Carter which goes as follows:

> Your holy hearsay is not evidence;
> Give me the good news in the present tense.
> What happened nineteen hundred years ago
> May not have happened—how am I to know?
> The living truth is what I long to see;
> I cannot lean upon what used to be.
> So shut the Bible up and show me how
> The Christ you talk about is living now.

There is to be sure a certain truth to these words, particularly when viewed in the context of the times and the spirit in which they were sung. They express the yearning for a Christianity that is real, lived, practical, concrete, and dynamic rather than merely a static and formal repetition of a creedal past. But they also contain an implicit scepticism about the objective truth of classical Christianity.

In 1978, seven years later, I expressed a scepticism that was even stronger but one which held within it a new yearning for a more classical orientation:

> The dilemma of modern man, however, is precisely the following: while a more transcendent God who stands above history and judges, restricts, and limits man's *hubris*, such a worldview is impossible in the modern age after the philosophical (Kant), psychological (Freud), social (Marx), and scientific (Einstein) enlightenments. In short, we desperately need a more traditional concept of God, but we cannot believe in such a God. And, to deliberately and self-consciously fashion such a concept for pragmatic and humanistic reasons begs the question. This is the dilemma confronting the modern theologian.[12]

This statement, made at a Mennonite graduate seminar, reflects a major shift in my theological horizon. My disillusionment with the modern human project and the modern horizon is clearly evident, but I find myself in a stalemate. The Enlightenment assumptions about the world and human beings do not allow me to see the possibility of accepting the classical view of a transcendent God.

Since 1978 I have found myself thinking, speaking and writing more and more in defence of the classical trinitarian and christological understanding of God, humankind, and the world as a way of overcoming the above dilemma and stalemate. I am not suggesting that we can or even ought to recover the classical way of thinking in its pristine purity. We cannot turn the historical clock backwards. To try to do so would be to become theologically obscurantist and reactionary. We cannot go back to first century Christianity as if nothing has transpired in between, ignoring the radical changes in human self-understanding that have occurred during the Renaissance, the Reformation, and the Enlightenment. What I am suggesting is that we recognize the poverty of the modern horizon and re-examine, seriously listen to and engage ourselves with the classical Christian doctrines from within the modern horizon. What I am calling for, in short, is a renewed interest in orthodoxy, in right belief, in the doctrinal basis for Christian praxis.

My theological shift has come about not as an escape from the Anabaptist-Mennonite concern with ethics. On the contrary, it has come by way of my ethical concerns. Increasingly it seems to me that individual and social-political ethics must ultimately be rooted in the *Credo* (the I believe) of the Christian Church if it is not to deteriorate into human beings freely managing history and ultimately destroying themselves and the earth which they inhabit. True conversion, genuine faith, however, is never an autonomous human choice but always a gift. To the degree that one receives such a gift, one ought to be truly grateful.

TWENTY

A Confessional Reading of the Scriptures*

Protestants, and especially radical Protestants with their cry of sola scriptura *against the Catholic emphases on* scriptura et traditio, *have frequently forgotten that the believing and confessional tradition came before the Christian writings, both temporally and theologically. If one takes Anselm's definition of Christian theology as "faith seeking understanding" (as I do), then rational reflection on the Christian faith theologically presupposes an existential faith encounter (either individually or corporately) with God. Faith itself is not rationally produced but is a divine gift, a response to a divine address, a response which is itself made possible by the Holy Spirit. The biblical account of Peter's initial response to Christ, his pathetic attempt to walk on the water, his confession, his denial, his first sermon, and his epistle, is a helpful way of understanding the sequence: faith to rational reflection.*

One can identify at least seven moments in Peter's path from faith to understanding.[1] First on this path (or continuum), one can assume, was Peter's being nurtured in a believing Jewish community, as we find it described for us in

---

* Originally published in *The Conrad Grebel Review* 4.2 (Spring 1986): 125-40; see also: "Further Reflections on 'The Theological Framework for the Authority of the Scriptures.' A. James Reimer responds to Glenn Brubacher," *CGR* 5.1 (Winter 1987): 71-75. For notes on the text see the Notes section below.

Deuteronomy, where the community is instructed on how to pass on their beliefs to succeeding generations. We are told that when the Jewish children ask their parents "What is the meaning of the decrees that God has commanded?" parents shall tell the story of God's action in their history and in their lives (Deut. 6).

Second, Peter's immediate response to Jesus' call at the seaside was to leave his fishing nets and follow (Matt. 4:20). There may have been events leading up to this moment, but in the biblical account it represents the initial, personal encounter between Peter and Jesus, the second moment on the way from faith to systematic reflection. It is pre-reflective (to the extent that anything can be pre-reflective). He is confronted by a call from the outside and responds.

The third moment in the continuum of "faith seeking understanding" is Peter's confession. Having spent some time following, observing, and reflecting as a disciple on the meaning of Jesus' life, teaching, and way he responds to Jesus' question "But who do you say that I am?" with the cryptic statement: "You are the Messiah, the Son of the living God" (Matt. 16:15-16). This is the foundational claim of the early church ("You are the Christ"), the second and core article of faith in the creed. It signifies a considerable degree of rational reflection by Peter on the meaning of that initial, existential encounter of faith. But it was not purely intellectual, for Jesus answers him, "Blessed are you, Simon son of Jonah! For flesh and blood has not revealed this to you, but my Father in heaven." Appropriating the faith through a public confession involves our emotions, our intellect, our will, but only as response to the movement of God in our lives.

The fourth step from faith to understanding is Peter's denial. He had been raised in a nurturing, believing community, and had left his nets to follow Jesus. He had personally confessed Jesus as the Christ. But his battle was not nearly over. Even as earlier, overly self-confident in his faith, he had tried unsuccessfully to walk on the water like Jesus, he continued to be a weak person, a sinner like all of us, who could fall into serious temptation. He sank in doubt when going to meet Jesus on the water, and at the end publicly denied that he had ever known Jesus (Matt. 14 and 26).

Peter's sermon as recorded in Acts 2 represents a fifth moment in Peter's understanding of faith. Recounting the Christ-events in the light of the Old Testament prophetic tradition, including the basic elements of the **kerygma** (the "rule of faith") as it is formulated in the creeds—foreknowledge of God, crucifixion, abandonment to Hades, resurrection, ascension to the right hand of God, call to repentance, forgiveness of sins, gift of the Holy Spirit (Acts 2:14-36)—Peter gives us a highly systematic interpretation of all the events leading up to Christ's death and resurrection, and the coming of the Holy Spirit.

Sixth, in 1 and 2 Peter we have a full-blown systematic-theological interpretation of the Christian faith for a new situation. Taken together with some of the great Pauline texts (such as Col. 1:15-23) we have a level of "metaphysical" philosophical-theological reflection on the Father, Christ, and the Spirit that rivals *any of the later ecumenical creeds. The basic elements of the later creedal confessions are present within the earliest apostolic hymns and writings of the New Testament. More particularly, Peter gives us the following advice: "Do not be intimidated.... Always be ready to make your defence to anyone who demands from you an accounting for the hope that is in you; yet do it with gentleness and reverence" (1 Pet. 3:15).*

This "accounting," however, is never an esoteric intellectualism separated from morality and ethics. It is an accounting that receives its verification in Christian conduct: "Keep your conscience clear, so that, when you are abused, those who revile your good behavior in Christ may be put to shame." (1 Pet. 3:16). Dogmatic confession is, for Peter, the foundation for Christian ethics, and ethics is the litmus test for the authenticity of confession.

Finally, seventh, we can talk about a posthumous moment in Peter's life—the legacy he leaves behind is as important as the Jewish legacy he inherited. When Peter confessed Jesus to be the Christ, Jesus replied: "You are Peter, and on this rock I will build my church" (Matt. 16:18).

This critical verse has been interpreted in two different ways. Roman Catholics have understood the church to be founded on Peter as the first bishop in the long continuous apostolic tradition. Protestants have interpreted the rock to be the content of Peter's confession: "You are the Christ." These two views can be combined to say that the Christian community is founded on the apostle Peter and his confession. Peter represents the disciples and the historical church community, and his confession represents the apostolic message. When people are called to faith, confession, witness and defence, it is important that they see themselves as part of a historical institution that is much larger than their local congregation or denomination. They are part of the church universal which extends through time and throughout the whole world.

The interpretation here given of the historical and theological movement from faith to dogma in the early church contrasts sharply from that of the liberal theology of the eighteenth and nineteenth centuries which claimed confession, credo, and dogma were a form of later Hellenistic corruption of the synoptic gospel narrative. The post-Easter believing community, having experienced a Petrine-like encounter with the risen Christ, heard the kerygma proclaimed, confessed Jesus to be the Christ, and engaged in various degrees of reflection on the meaning of the events for their lives, wrote texts, used these in worship, and gradually collected and canonized them. Based on this sequence of events, we now too read and interpret the biblical text most adequately from the perspective of personal and corporate confession. The Christian writings were collected and given authoritative status on the basis of the apostolic witness, the core of which was the confession that Jesus was the Christ.

The following essay reflects an early state of my thinking on the relation of faith to understanding, and of confession to hermeneutics.[2] It was first presented at a "Dialogue on Faith and Biblical Interpretation and Practice" at Camp Wonderland, Camp Lake, Wisconsin in November 1985 as part of an ongoing discussion between conservative, evangelical, fundamentalist, and liberal voices within the Mennonite community. It was later published in slightly revised form as "The Theological Framework for the Authority of Scriptures," and defends the authority of Scripture on confessional rather than rigid-literalistic grounds. It thereby takes seriously the "conservative" concern for theological orthodoxy but rejects the reductionist anti-tradition view that frequently accompanies modern "fundamentalist-orthodoxy."

◆ ◆ ◆

An Autobiographical Perspective

The topic under consideration in this essay is a sensitive and serious one, not only for the Mennonite community but for the Christian church as a whole in the contemporary era, an age which cries out for an authoritative voice in the face of religious and moral-ethical crises of a magnitude which boggles the mind. To begin to address these issues from a personal, autobiographical perspective is to run the risk of psychologizing and subjectifying what is in fact an urgent, objective, and universal crisis: the problem of truth in the historicist and relativistic age of which we all are a part. The issue is: By what authority is the church to know, to preach, to teach, to counsel, and to practise the truth of the gospel as it applies to the whole world? How is the world to be saved? We are dealing here not with small sectarian visions of the truth but with the possibility or impossibility of a universal message of salvation.

Having stated my reservations about beginning such a discussion as this autobiographically—an approach which is intrinsically self-indulgent and tends to make individual experience the starting point— I will nevertheless go against my better judgment and start with a few personal reflections. I come to this topic not as a professional biblical scholar—not as one who practises the intricacies of the historical-critical method as it has dominated most biblical scholarship for the last 200 years in the form of historical criticism, literary criticism, form criticism, redaction criticism, and so on. I come rather as a systematic theologian. I come also as a Christian believer who has a deep reverence for the world of the Bible, convinced that the Bible is God's word for us in the modern and postmodern era even as it was for the ancients, persuaded also that this Bible has an integrity of its own and stands over against us as an authoritative text by which our individual and corporate faith, experience, and moral-social life needs to be measured over and over again.

I have a firm conviction that our attempts to control the Bible either from the left or the right, from the conservative or liberal side, rather than allowing the Bible to control us, is an example of modern *hubris*. When I use terms like conservative, liberal, fundamentalist, evangelical, and so on, I have no desire to label anyone unfairly. I use the terms simply as ideal types by which to get at some of the basic issues behind different approaches to the Bible.

I have never paid all that much attention to the passionate debates between the various factions on questions of biblical inspiration, inerrancy, and infallibility. I have often felt that there was, on the surface at least, something misplaced about the debate itself, a missing of the mark. I have come to suspect, for instance, that the strident defence of inerrancy and infallibility by the more conservative-evangelical wing of the church is a code for something else, something deeper. The question for me is: What is the deeper meaning? What is at stake?

I was raised in a staunchly Mennonite environment in southern Manitoba before the age of general Anabaptist-Mennonite self-consciousness; the "recovery of the Anabaptist vision," which was already exciting Mennonite scholars to the south, had not yet filtered down into my own immediate family and church milieu. Much more important for me during my growing-up years was the evangelical and pietistic emphasis on personal salvation and a personal relationship with Jesus. It is clear to me now in retrospect that my early theological thinking was a strange mixture of Mennonite moralism and evangelical-pietistic experientialism. It was always assumed in my home and church that the Bible was the one totally inspired word of God, from beginning to end, which ought to be read fervently and never tampered with. Nevertheless, from early days my primary concern was not with textual accuracy but with "sin" and "salvation." Actually, I had three related concerns: a *moral* one (how can I be good?), an *experiential* one (how can I be saved?), and an *epistemological* one (how can I know with certainty?). Pat answers to these questions did not satisfy me. The repeated response to my youthful queries with the plain "the Bible says" never appeased my struggle or curiosity, not because of rebellious inclinations but because I was unable to translate what the Bible says into my own experience.

It was not until my years at Canadian Mennonite Bible College in Winnipeg, where I was introduced to a moderate form of historical biblical criticism and what was known as biblical theology, that I experienced a kind of liberation which I had not known before. The historical, contextual, and critical-exegetical approach to the Bible combined with thematic biblical theology opened up a whole new world for me which did not provide cut-and-dried answers to my earlier concerns but led me to ask different sorts of questions of the biblical material. As I continued my studies in history and philosophy at the University of Manitoba and theology at the bastion of modern liberalism, Union Theological Seminary in New York, I moved further and further away from what I might loosely call my early evangelical-Mennonite background.

Then a certain disillusionment with some aspects of the "liberal project" set in. A number of factors in the past decade or so have gradually contributed to my seriously questioning the adequacy of the modern Enlightenment and post-Enlightenment scientific understanding of the biblical materials, including not only the exclusiveness of the historical-critical method itself but also the one-dimensionality of the modern fundamentalist preoccupation with literal inerrancy and infallibility. Both underestimate the richness and power inherent in ancient readings of the text.

First, and probably most important, was my encounter with ancient classical and medieval texts to which I was introduced at a Catholic university. Here I found myself in a world that I had never known before— the world of an older and much longer Christian tradition of texts, doctrines, creeds, and piety which appeared to me to be based on some valid presuppositions quite foreign to my own Mennonite, evangelical, and liberal past—a creedal hermeneutical tradition.

Second, my encounter with the method of studying and teaching religion within the context of the modern secular university, together with the reading of modern theology, philosophy, history, and the social sciences, led me to the forceful conclusion that the real issue for us in the modern scientific and technological age is not "errancy" versus "inerrancy" but the very possibility of belief in a transcendent reality itself, the possibility of making any universal truth-claims whatever, be they of a Christian, non-Christian religious, or secular-humanist vantage point. The burden of proof used to lie with those who professed unbelief in eternal truths; now the burden of proof appears to have shifted to the other side: to those who profess belief. In this context I found myself becoming strangely sympathetic with those in my classes, including the fundamentalists, who dared to take an unequivocal stand on the question of truth, whether from a "naive" or a more "sophisticated" standpoint.

The crucial issue for the universal Christian church and for the particular Mennonite church is not primarily whether we recognize the historical conditionedness of the Bible—this we already know and accept and dare not downplay—but whether anything at all of God's universal and objective word to us can be allowed to shine through and in the text. It is this affirmation—that in the biblical text as a whole we have an authoritative word addressing us which cannot be controlled and manufactured by us—that I want to make as strongly as possible in this presentation.

The Nature of the Crisis and the Present Debate

What is the nature of the urgent issues facing us and how can we move to address them? That is the question. I was not part of the October 1984 "Dialogue on Faith" and have not followed the debate closely since. But it appears from what I have read and heard about that conference that there was at least at the time, and probably still today, some consensus within both the Mennonite Church and the General Conference Mennonite Church (the two are now merging) that we are facing serious crises within the church on a number of pressing issues, including leadership and authority, male and female ordination, abortion, homosexuality, divorce and remarriage, social and political involvement in the light of our own traditional stance on peace, "nonresistance" and political power, among others, and that our way of reading the Bible has something to do with the answers we give to these concrete issues.

What strikes me as I read various publications and the reports on the "Dialogue on Faith" is the genuine diversity within the Mennonite community on how to read and interpret the Bible in the face of these questions. Part of the problem for us as a biblically oriented people is that we cannot find a clear unmediated biblical answer to some of these difficult and complex issues. For this we need mediating theological principles which help us relate biblical themes and imperatives to our present situation. This is the task of systematic theology. Unfortunately, we have historically been weak in the area of systematic theology, opting rather for biblical theology, historical theology, and practical theology.[3] My proposal at the end of this paper has to do with a systematic or "doctrinal" reading of the Bible which is not "biblicist" in the bad sense of that term but tries to remain faithful to the Bible while at the same time creatively addressing twentieth-century issues.[4]

It is in this light that I examine the concerns of George R. Brunk II and Ted VanderEnde. In *A Crisis Among Mennonites* Brunk speaks out of a specific theological tradition, harking back to the fundamentalist stance in its controversy with the modernists in the 1920s. Brunk's position is not a pure fundamentalist one, for he brings to his theological themes certain Mennonite concerns. While his book represents an oversimplification of the issues and an unfair caricature of certain individuals, books, and institutions in the Mennonite Church, still it reflects a consistent line of argument which is widely espoused and needs to be taken seriously. For integrity."[5] By sound doctrine he means the basic doctrines of the Christian church as traditionally espoused: the virgin birth, the resurrection of Jesus, the inspiration and infallibility of Scriptures, a doctrine of peace based on the discontinuity between the Old and New Covenants while at the same time considering both to be fully inspired, the centrality of the cross and the substitutionary death of Jesus, sin and the need for personal salvation.[6]

What has caused this crisis and uncertainty within the Mennonite Church, this erosion of the fundamental doctrines? For Brunk, the causes are the following: the historical-critical method and a scientific approach to the Bible,[7] the allegorizing of biblical books and passages, and the search for deeper spiritual truths instead of adhering to the literal meaning,[8] liberation from orthodoxy in the name of academic freedom,[9] an emphasis on ethics, discipleship, and following Jesus outside of personal salvation and the experience of the new birth,[10] and a preoccupation with social justice apart from a recognition of personal sin, guilt, and the need for accepting Christ.[11]

What bothers Brunk especially is the fundamentalist-bashing that goes on in our academic institutions and books, the general "anti-fundamentalist tide that has been moving across the church," and a simultaneous lack of criticism of liberalism, modernism, and the "threat of humanistic Bible-denying, Christ-rejecting modernistic heresy."[12] He feels that the leaders of the past and the doctrines of the past are being contemptuously treated and rejected in the name of freedom from bondage, when in fact this very rejection constitutes a new form of bondage.[13] While Brunk appears at points to feel uncomfortable identifying himself with fundamentalism (he calls for a "balanced view of salvation which does not ignore social-ethical issues such as peace and justice but sees personal conversion as the starting-point for discipleship,"[14] a position which he refers to as "the orthodox, evangelical view"[15]), his list of concerns and the militancy with which he conducts himself on this issue is reminiscent of the classical fundamentalism of the 1920s.[16]

I must say right from the start that my own theological orientation and temperament is quite different from that of Brunk. I cannot accept his easy classification of the opponents and the culprits, his liberal- and modernist-bashing. In fact, I dare to suggest that he, like all of us, has drunk more deeply at the well of the Enlightenment and modern scientific assumptions about the Bible than he would care to admit. We cannot as easily as he suggests extricate ourselves from a particular time period and the modern presuppositions which have shaped us all.

Yet I find myself in strange agreement with many of the things Brunk says. His call for *sound doctrinal and theological thinking* as a basis upon which to address the fundamental issues of our age, and for an *experiential*

Yet I find myself in strange agreement with many of the things Brunk says. His call for *sound doctrinal and theological thinking* as a basis upon which to address the fundamental issues of our age, and for an *experiential spiritual foundation for Christian moral and social ethics* is quite timely. There appears to be an anti-creedal, anti-doctrinal, anti-confessional, and anti-theological bias in our recent history and possibly also within our Mennonite heritage in general which threatens to make our admirable emphasis on ethics, discipleship, and right-living one-sided and rudderless.[17] I want to make this point cautiously, fully recognizing that we have in our tradition quite an impressive series of confessional and catechetical formularies which have had a marked influence in shaping the life and thought of our community, as is illustrated in Howard John Loewen's recent book, *One Lord, One Church, One Hope, and One God: Mennonite Confessions of Faith*.[18]

Nevertheless, I do believe there is that in our heritage which is suspicious of doctrinally systematizing the contents of the Bible for fear that it will diminish our obedience to the actual literal sense of Jesus' words, for instance.[19] I believe that our road into the future as Mennonites should be based on a doctrinal and theological reading of the Bible which seeks to reappropriate and interpret the classical doctrines of the Christian church without disparaging the ancient creeds.

I move now from Brunk and the Mennonite Church context to Ted VanderEnde and the General Conference Mennonite Church. In the first issue of *Consultation: A Hermeneutical Newsletter for Concerned Mennonites*, published before but in anticipation of the October 1984 "Dialogue on Faith," VanderEnde manifests concerns which have some continuity with those of George Brunk, but he expresses them much less militantly and with a sensitivity and openness to other views which are absent from Brunk's pamphlet.

Although fully aware of the dangers inherent in easy classifications, VanderEnde draws a line between two theological-hermeneutical camps: the evangelical-orthodox-conservative-traditional versus the liberal-modernistic-critical. For him "evangelical" refers to the acceptance of the "centrality of Scripture as the unique and sole source of divine revelation": "To be evangelical (supported by terms such as `conservative, orthodox, traditional') is to be rooted in the apostolic witness to Jesus Christ."[20] VanderEnde recognizes the "common concern for obedience to God's leading" but thinks that the widely held "traditional, or conservative viewpoint," that is, an "intelligent and authentic evangelical voice, speaking from an Anabaptist perspective," is generally absent on conference floors and leaves many feeling lonely, isolated, and having little to identify with.

sees theology in terms of process and movement, a hermeneutical community of faith which reinterprets Scripture and then applies it to modern culture, or (2) a scriptural approach, which views the biblical canon as the "once for all product of God's work in and through selected prophets, after which the church seeks to apply its content to various historical situations."[21]

VanderEnde's position becomes clearer in the second *Consultation* article, "Apostolic Versus Process Hermeneutics: A Mennonite Dilemma," presented at the 1984 Dialogue on Faith, in which he more directly deals with the concepts of divine inspiration and infallibility. He reduces the divisions within the Mennonite community to two diverse approaches to the Bible: 1) the "apostolic-Mennonite view" which, in line with Thieleman van Braght's notion of doctrinal succession in the *Martyr's Mirror*, perceives "Scripture as absolute and constant," and 2) the "process-existential Mennonite view" espoused, according to VanderEnde, by certain writers in *Explorations of Systematic Theology* and *Essays on Biblical Interpretation: Anabaptist-Mennonite Perspectives.*[22]

In these latter writings VanderEnde detects a shift from a more traditional evangelical-Mennonite view which places the locus of authority squarely in the Scriptures to the hermeneutical community which, itself in process, interprets Scripture progressively. According to VanderEnde, "The task of the community of faith is not to make a restatement of faith in Christ and His gospel to a new complex historical situation, but to re-live and re-apply dynamically and obediently this divine guide for faith and practice. Thus in each age since the apostolic age, in different cultural and historical settings, believers have sought to live out the propositional principles of God's Word."[23]

VanderEnde does not want to be accused of holding to a "flat" view of the Bible if that means allowing "no place for the historical and cultural context." However, he is willing to accept a "flat" view if that means that "God inspired each word and sentence and chapter and book," that Scripture is "fully inspired in each detail, including seemingly that what does not fit in man's eye."[24]

I have sympathy for two of VanderEnde's key points: (1) the importance of maintaining doctrinal continuity with the past; and (2) the importance of making the Scriptures *as a whole* the starting point for theological authority, rather than placing final authority within the present believing community, personal experience, or the latest critical thinking — and in the process disregarding huge chunks of the Bible simply because they don't seem to suit us.

Nevertheless, I have some basic quarrels with VanderEnde's stance: I find his rejection of the "higher critical methodology of the early part of the process disregarding huge chunks of the Bible simply because they don't seem to suit us.

Nevertheless, I have some basic quarrels with VanderEnde's stance: I find his rejection of the "higher critical methodology of the early part of this century or modern relativistic and existential thinking" too unnuanced and immediate; his unqualified reference to a normative "apostolic Mennonite" and "evangelical Mennonite" approach highly problematic in the light of the historical heterogeneity of the Anabaptist and Mennonite tradition; and his consequent polarization between an absolute scriptural approach and a process-historical hermeneutic much too sharp. Most of all, I consider his particular "flat" version of verbal inspiration an abstraction which does not take seriously the selection process that takes place in every church community as it seeks to appropriate the Scriptures to contemporary issues.

What is at Stake?

What is at stake in this debate, not only for the Mennonite church but also for the Christian church in general? What is at stake is the locus of authority. Where are our norms to be taken from by which we can address the issues that face us? What is the measure by which the church can determine its message? Do our standards come from the natural sciences, from the social sciences, from the world of politics and economics, from the human sciences, from individual experience or conscience?

Ultimately, I would argue, the source and content of the church's message is a theological one, the word of God as most definitively revealed to us from Genesis to Revelation. Other sources of authority (biology, psychology, sociology, anthropology, politics, economics, experience, conscience) are important secondary sources for understanding, reinterpreting, and applying the theological authority. They remain, however, servants of a theological reading of the Scriptures which sees the word of God in terms of creation, redemption, and consummation.

For this reason I am not as willing as is VanderEnde to separate an absolute scriptural approach from a hermeneutical-community approach. If we take seriously the doctrine of the Holy Spirit implicit in the Bible and explicit in the early creedal formulations, we need to take seriously the ongoing hermeneutics of the church using whatever means available, including the historical-critical method, to ferret out the original intent and context of the biblical writings and to translate these original writings into the language of each new generation. How is this translation to retain its fidelity to the original revelation? It is the second article of the *Credo*, the

It is, however, the first article, the doctrine of a totally free and transcendent God, Yahweh, the one God of the Old and New Testaments, of whom no human images can be constructed, who created the world *ex nihilo* and cannot be controlled by any human system or language, that appears to me to be most often missing in the present discussion and in the modern situation. All of us, including the inerrantists, the progressivists, and the traditionalists tend to control God's self-revelation by imposing upon God our own hermeneutical schemes, which more often than not are premised on extra-biblical presuppositions.

In the present debate, both the so-called "Conservative-Evangelical-Mennonite" approach and the "Process-Existential-Mennonite" perspective, to use VanderEnde's terminology, presuppose certain assumptions. These have their source in modern understandings of science and reason largely foreign to the ancient understanding of the world and God's interaction with that world, and prevent their proponents from gaining the wanted distance from their own stance to allow the totally other to break through. The issue for me is, therefore, not so much whether we use or do not use the language of inerrancy and infallibility, but whether we allow God the freedom from our own systems to come to us from the outside, so to speak, both creatively and judgmentally. Both sides tend to want to control the text in the light of their own self-interests, and thereby also control God's self-revelation through and in the text, and in so doing prevent the genuinely new possibilities that the age requires.

I am persuaded, for instance in studying the fundamentalist-modernist debates of the early part of this century, that the particular line of argument between the inerrantists and the evolutionists is foreign not only to the New Testament church, the Patristic church, the Medieval church, and the Reformers, but also to the more recent German Pietists, British Methodists, and American revivalists as well as many nineteenth-century conservative evangelical American Protestants. It is interesting to note here that the historical-contextual-critical method itself was to a large extent born in the context of eighteenth-century Pietism with its concern to go back to a study of the original sources.[25]

George M. Marsden, in his definitive study, *Fundamentalism and American Culture: The Shaping of Twentieth-Century Evangelicalism 1870-1925*, convincingly demonstrates that the fundamentalists of the 1920s were not as anti-scientific and anti-intellectual as they are often assumed to have been, but that in fact:

> They stood in an intellectual tradition that had the highest regard for one understanding of true scientific method and proper rationality. In science they were steadfastly committed

were not as anti-scientific and anti-intellectual as they are often assumed to have been, but that in fact:

> They stood in an intellectual tradition that had the highest regard for one understanding of true scientific method and proper rationality. In science they were steadfastly committed to the principles of the seventeenth-century philosopher Francis Bacon: careful observation and classification of facts. These principles were wedded to a "common sense" philosophy that affirmed the ability to apprehend the facts clearly, whether the facts of nature or the even more certain facts of Scripture. This philosophy, essentially the "Scottish Common Sense Realism" . . . that had dominated mid-nineteenth century America, was the basis of much of the unity of fundamentalist thought.[26]

When the second scientific revolution came along—that of Darwin and an evolutionary explanation of reality which conflicted with their own previous reconciliation of science and Christianity—they had to give up their own earlier openness to scientific investigation.[27]

Before the 1920s there was no unanimity amongst American conservative-evangelical Protestants on the question of infallibility, inerrancy, and evolutionary theories. A considerable diversity is still evident in the famous *Fundamentals*, a series of pamphlets written by different authors, published and distributed between 1910 and 1915. Marsden makes the following interesting statement about the conservative Baptist theologian August H. Strong, whom George R. Brunk happens to cite in defence of his own position: "While holding a high view of biblical authority, Strong's starting point was that truth was not doctrinal or propositional, but rather `the truth is a personal Being, and that Christ himself is the Truth.'"

Marsden goes on to tell us that Strong "rejected very explicitly the idea of Scripture as inerrant and in his influential *Systematic Theology* eventually dropped language that might suggest such a conclusion."[28] It was only in the 1920s in a very specific crisis that "inerrancy" became a united rallying cry. Basic to this new position was the weight that it placed on the *written word* and *objective facts* as distinct from religious experience, rituals, traditions, and unrecorded words.[29]

I see the present crisis as being remarkably different from that faced by fundamentalists and modernists in the early part of this century. The call for an authoritative voice in addressing the issues of abortion, divorce and remarriage, homosexuality, ordination of women, world hunger and injustice, and the nuclear threat cannot be answered in terms laid out by the classical fundamentalists and modernists. But then and almost inevitably moves beyond the purely historical method, particularly in the field of biblical scholarship. The great temptation of the biblical critic is that he is not critical enough — of his own presuppositions.

One does not need to belabour the point that the various historical-critical methods of biblical scholarship have been under siege of late.[30] Before joining in the fray too hastily it is good to remind ourselves of the invaluable contribution to our understanding of the biblical materials and times made by the various types of historical-critical-contextual approaches to the Bible. It also bears repeating that the method in its earlier phase originated in the framework of German Pietism with its rejection of Protestant scholasticism and orthodoxy and its passionate concern to go back to the original sources themselves. One of the most valuable contributions of the historical-critical method is that it helps us—at least that is its intent—to distance ourselves from ourselves.

Nevertheless, the method is itself rooted in specific modern rationalist and historicist assumptions, and is inclined to become more than merely a method. Peter Stuhlmacher, in his *Historical Criticism and Theological Interpretation of Scripture*, while staunchly defending the value of the method, admits to its inherent functionalism and autonomy and the need for additional types of exposition.[31] I would suggest that the classical fourfold sense of Scripture (literal, allegorical, tropological, and analogical) might bear re-examination as a model for a multidimensional approach to the Bible which could incorporate the historical-critical method as one crucial but not exhaustive approach. Stuhlmacher challenges us to "take fully into account the fact that in the vacuum and exegetical uncertainty in which we find ourselves we are actually summoned to recall the original, emancipating, and enlightening power of historical-critical method...."[32] He calls for a "willingness to open ourselves anew to the claim of tradition, of the present, and of transcendence."[33]

More specifically he suggests that a way out of the present dilemma in Protestant exegesis would be "to strive for contact and connection with a dogmatics able to correct and guide it, above all a dogmatics which not merely exhausts its strength in theological-historical analysis, but moves toward its own affirmations and judgments."[34] It is this coming together of biblical scholarship and systematic theology that I think is imperative for us in the present situation in the Mennonite church.

A Theological Reading of the Bible as a Whole

I come now to my own proposal on how I think this coming together of historical-critical biblical scholarship and systematic or "doctrinal" theology might occur and help us address the problems that face us. I

A Theological Reading of the Bible as a Whole

I come now to my own proposal on how I think this coming together of historical-critical biblical scholarship and systematic or "doctrinal" theology might occur and help us address the problems that face us. I call this a direct theological reading of the Bible as a whole in the context of the Christian community of faith. I reject the sharp division between an "absolute scriptural approach" and a "hermeneutical community approach," or, to put it in more ordinary language, between "Scripture" and "tradition." The two are so intrinsically linked as the medium of God's self-revelation that we dare not separate them, even while affirming that the "scriptural tradition" has precedence over succeeding tradition. For my views in this last section I am deeply indebted to Henry Vander Goot's book *Interpreting the Bible in Theology and the Church*.

Let me outline Vander Goot's line of argument, a position which is close to my own. His main contention is "that before and outside of the scientific study of the Bible in the Christian community of faith, interpretation is already there and that this existing phenomenon of interpretation and immediate confessional response to the Bible is what should fund the theoretical enterprise of theology and biblical studies."[35] In modern thought this order tends to be reversed—that is, scientists and experts deconstruct, dissect, and dismantle the biblical materials first and then offer interpretive models for the believing community.

Vander Goot's argument goes like this: First, a distinction must be made between first order knowing (pre-scientific) and second order knowing (scientific), with the pre-critical reading of the Bible taking precedence over the critical reading.

Second, the Bible as a whole or in its "overall narrative sweep" should be accepted as God's word to us. This word has to do minimally with the "creation-fall-redemption-consummation structure of the biblical narrative;"[36] this is not to deny the importance of specific verses, chapters, or books but to emphasize the intended unity of the material.

Third, and in my mind one of the most important contributions of Vander Goot's book, is the point that "this overall sense of the biblical story is directly comprehensible to the naive Christian reader."[37] This is so because "The Christian understanding of the biblical story takes place in the context and tradition of the Christian community of faith and is at once directly and naively grasped."[38]

Fourth, this overall meaning can legitimately be called "the real *literal sense* of the *canon*."[39] Vander Goot distinguishes between a "literal" sense and a "literalistic" reading, the latter being an unacceptable positivistic grammatical approach. A literal reading, as

Christian understanding of the Bible's overall message as a creation-fall-restoration-consummation story, which should be the controlling ingredient in the interpretation of the Bible's parts."[42]

For Vander Goot the biblical canon as a whole is the locus of authority for the Christian, but this by no means devalues the importance of the believing community as hermeneutical community. According to him, no one exposure of the individual believer to the Scriptures can give a sense of the whole; "Rather a sense of the whole emerges in the course of ordinary experience in the church, which involves recurrent exposure to the stories of the Bible that as taken together comprise the Bible's single storyline.... Direct reading is a concept intended to refer to a fundamental level of apprehension that exists within the Christian community in which the reader-believer participates."[43] In this pre-scientific, pre-critical, or naive reading of the Bible, the Scriptures are seen not primarily as "God's word to the Hebrews or as God's Word to the early church, but as God's revelation to us, the present readers."[44]

Seeing the Bible as having an integral unity is a "function of faith," and "the function of faith is the primary context within which the truth of the Bible is able to come to expression, setting the framework within which second order study (that is the critical or scientific examination) of the text should take place."[45] Crucial for Vander Goot's whole position is that a critical, scientific, and contextual study of the various parts of the Bible is not to be rejected or minimized but is to be considered secondary to the direct reading of the Bible as a whole in the framework of a believing community. Thus the context of proper understanding is the "community of those who appropriate Scripture in obedient and believing affirmation of it, and, hence, by the tradition of Christian orthodoxy, which has come to its most normative expression in the ecumenical confessions of the early church."[46] In this approach, therefore, summaries, confessional statements, and creeds are all taken with great seriousness because they "serve to remind us that the Bible is a single, ongoing, cumulative narrative and thus can be viewed as a canonical unity."[47]

It may be that Vander Goot, in his concern for rescuing the overarching unity of the biblical story, does not adequately take into consideration the genuine diversity of the Scriptures or, for that matter, the various interpretations of the content of the creation-fall-redemption-consummation scheme by divergent Christian communities. Nevertheless, there is something persuasive about the priority he puts on the direct reading of the Bible as a whole by the believing community, especially in the face of the fragmentation of the Scriptures that the scientific method leaves us with in the present situation.

something persuasive about the priority he puts on the direct reading of the Bible as a whole by the believing community, especially in the face of the fragmentation of the Scriptures that the scientific method leaves us with in the present situation.

Further, this priority of a direct reading is consistent with our own Mennonite heritage. While there was no absolute unanimity within early Anabaptism(s) on biblical interpretation, there was by and large a consensus that the Bible as a whole was authored by the Holy Spirit, that it contained the "good news of salvation through Christ" and also "specific directions for the individual and the corporate life of those who respond to the good news."[48] While the Bible itself was for most sixteenth-century Anabaptists clearly the locus of authority, the authority of interpretation rested not with the individual in isolation but with the congregation. In the words of Walter Klaassen, "It is therefore not the hierarchy as in Roman Catholicism, nor the scholar-teacher as in Protestantism who decides what the Word means in any given instance, but the gathered community under the guidance of the Spirit."[49]

Both Klaassen and John Howard Yoder emphasize this congregational framework in which biblical interpretation, translation, and application to specific situations and problems takes place.[50] What appears to me particularly important in the present discussion is that while the primary source of authority is recognized to be the word of God as expressed in and through the biblical text, no sharp distinction can in fact be drawn between this primary source of authority and the interpretive authority of the congregation. Without the interpretive process the Bible as a source of authority remains an abstraction.

Where Vander Goot's proposal is somewhat different than what I often hear emphasized in Mennonite scholarly circles is that for him this congregational hermeneutic ought to be seen in continuity with a much larger and longer interpretive tradition in which the Christian church's doctrinal, confessional, and credal expressions are taken seriously. I am thinking here not only of the Apostles' Creed but also of the creeds of the early ecumenical councils (Nicea, Constantinople, and Chalcedon). One dare not take these specific creeds with their particular formulations as normative in any absolute sense, or as superseding the authority of the "Scripture principle;" nevertheless, there is a genre of theological thinking inherent in this credal tradition which takes sound doctrine and right thinking (orthodoxy) with utmost seriousness. Intrinsic to this dogmatic tradition is a trinitarian hermeneutical scheme which places emphasis on God's threefold being and work — God as transcendent creator, God as and obedience to the teachings of Jesus. There is an enigmatic silence in the great creeds concerning the ethical dimensions of the creation-redemption-consummation story, which we as Mennonites are apt to notice. It is probably in this particular area—that is, our concern for taking quite literally Jesus' teachings on love and nonviolence in every area of life—that we as Mennonite readers would want to ask some probing questions of Vander Goot's sweeping analysis and proposal.

Nevertheless, I find his overall prescription convincing and would urge that we reappropriate this ancient model of interpretation in our congregational preaching, teaching, worshiping, and counselling ministries. When we address particular issues such as abortion, divorce and remarriage, homosexuality, and ordination we take seriously God's intent in creation, the reality of sin and the fall, the possibility of redemption, and, finally, consummation and perfection at the end of time and history. These doctrines ought not to remain on the level of formal generalities and abstractions but need to be given substantive content.

In conclusion, I would suggest that in this present discussion the more conservative, evangelical, and so-called "orthodox" wing of the Mennonite church has a special contribution to make. Why? Because I sense in this circle a special sensitivity to "sound theology" and "right thinking." It may be that we will never reach total agreement on the important matters facing us, but there is something to be said for placing our emphasis once again on right thinking and believing as the basis for right action. I am not calling for a kind of wooden, oppressive, and tyrannical orthodoxy but for the recovery of a systematic, doctrinal, theological reading of the biblical texts as the theological framework for scriptural authority in moral, social, and political ethics.

TWENTY-ONE

Confessions, Doctrines, and Creeds: Symbols and Metaphors of Ultimacy*

A growing conviction in my reading, writing, teaching, and preaching in the 1980s was that contemporary Christian theology in general, and Mennonite theological reflection in particular, needed disciplined theological thinking, which would bear some resemblance to what Elizabeth Johnson more recently has called a "disciplined theological imagination"[1] —that is, a theological imagination that is disciplined by the doctrinal categories, not interpreted literalistically but as the ancients did: symbolically and analogically. This theme began appearing repeatedly, as a leitmotif *in my "Mennonite" essays of that decade.*

In this essay, which was initially entitled "Doctrines as Metaphors of Ultimacy" and delivered at a conference on Christian doctrine at Laurelville Mennonite Church Center, February 15-17, 1991, I elaborate on how I understand doctrines and their function, and why I think we need them.[2] Since that time there has been a growing interest in confessions, doctrines, and creeds even in the Mennonite community, reflected most dramatically in the ten years of consultation on a new joint confession of faith between the Mennonite Church and the General Conference

---

* The present form of the essay is a revised version of what appeared in *The Conrad Grebel Review* as "Doctrines: What are They, How do They Function, and Why do We Need Them?," 11.1 (Winter 1993): 21-36. For notes on the text see the Notes section below.

Mennonite Church, culminating in the official acceptance in 1995 of Confession of Faith in a Mennonite Perspective.[3]

In retrospect, I find that my use of the term "metaphor" in this essay is much too ill-defined, as it is in much contemporary talk and writing. Much work has been done recently in defining carefully and distinguishing between terms like sign, image, symbol, allegory, analogy, parable, and metaphor, which I did not take into account at the time. The ancient understanding of "symbol" and "analogy" more closely conveys the meaning I was trying to communicate about doctrine.

A metaphor, as a figure of speech, is the juxtaposition of two unlikely images, emphasizing their discontinuity and dissimilarity for the purpose not of describing external reality but of opening up new imaginative possibilities. This is not what the ancients had in mind when talking about creedal confessions and doctrines. For them there was a sense in which this type of language, in all its fallibility and human inadequacy, conveyed something about the ultimate mysteries, and even helped mediate the reality to which it pointed. The core doctrines of the Christian faith are more than arbitrary constructions or the rules of a language game that regulate Christian God-talk; they have become powerful symbols that help mediate the ultimate reality in which Christians believe.

Symbols can of course become adulterous when they are absolutized and no longer mediate divine reality, and they can lose their power (as Tillich tells us). It is for this reason that the Christian community needs again and again to revisit the age old symbols, interpreting them in new and imaginative ways.

I end this essay by exploring how the doctrine of the Trinity might be imagined in ways that have relevance for our age. Appropriating Don S. Browning's notion that "the way we metaphorically represent the world in its most durable and ultimate respects influences . . . what we think we are obligated to do," I explore how the doctrine of the Trinity helps us address in creative ways our obligations in relation to the environment, a world of violence, and new ethical issues facing the church that are not directly addressed by the Scriptures.

◆ ◆ ◆

Introduction: Definitions

For many people of my generation or older, "doctrine" is an anachronistic concept. The word brings up images of authoritarian male bishops or ministers who laid down the law. It frequently connotes rigidity as in derivative terms like "doctrinaire" or "dogmatism."

There is some historical justification for the fear that people have of doctrine-talk. The eighteenth-century Enlightenment, sometimes referred to as the age of reason, referred to the previous age as the "age of dogmatism"—referring to the sixteenth and seventeenth centuries when the major denominations developed confessional statements and then proceeded to fight each other. The Thirty Years War (1618-48) that laid waste many cities of Europe is an extreme example of this confessional intolerance. The "enlighteners" identified doctrinal self-definition with intolerance and the inhumanity of human beings toward each other.

Mennonite churches have also had their "ages of dogmatism." In such eras harsh lines have been drawn between the right and the wrong, between those who are in and those who are out, leading to excommunications, shunnings, and numerous church splits.

So why would anyone in their right mind suggest that we bring back doctrine? Why do Mennonites need doctrine? Because it is scriptural! Because the church has considered it important! Because we need it in the context of contemporary culture!

Before proceeding to elaborate on each of these three, we need some working definitions. Jaroslav Pelikan defines the term "doctrine" as follows: "What the church of Jesus Christ believes, teaches, and confesses on the basis of the word of God: this is Christian doctrine."[4] Beliefs have to do with the contents of Christian faith, teaching has to do with passing it on, and confessing has to do with committing oneself to it. Pelikan correctly states, I believe, that doctrine is not the primary activity of the church—worship, service, the transformation of the world are perhaps more important—nevertheless, doctrine had better not be ignored.

Mennonites have been more ready to talk about doctrine—especially Bible doctrines—than "dogmas," let alone "creeds," the latter suggesting a system imposed on the Bible from the outside. However, doctrine, dogma, creed, and confession are all part of a family of words referring to something similar: what the church of Jesus Christ believes and teaches to be true.

Doctrine is the most general term for the church's teachings. The word *dogma* refers more specifically to a particular doctrine or set of doctrines as officially adopted and pronounced by the church as authoritative or normative. *Confession* is the act of personally and corporately appropriating and witnessing to what one believes to be true, frequently in the face of attacks, false accusations, and a falsification of doctrine, even to the point of martyrdom. The *Credo* (literally "I believe") is confessing to a summary of the essential doctrines of the church, usually in the context of worship or liturgy.

There is historically a close connection between the experiential (or subjective) and the content (or objective) aspects of doctrine which should not be lost. Doctrines are not literal pictures of divine realities, nor are they simply models or archetypes; they are symbols (they were in the classical period called symbols) in the Tillichian sense—they participate in the reality to which they point; that is, through them deeper levels of reality are opened up to us in a way that ordinary literal language is incapable of doing.

Don S. Browning talks about "metaphors of ultimacy."[5] He says that "it is not only in theology but, to a surprising extent, in the modern psychologies as well that the way we metaphorically represent the world in its most durable and ultimate respects influences (although not necessarily determines in all respects) what we think we are obligated to do."[6] Doctrines are more than literal signs, more than rules by which religious communities order their beliefs and communal life; they are "metaphors of ultimacy"—the way we as Christians represent and confess what is most important to us and in a way that has profound implications for how we live and act.

Scriptural Basis

Why do we need doctrines? Because it is biblical! If one looks at the early confessions of Mennonites (of which there are many), what immediately stands out is how Scripture is treated. First, these confessions (like the Dordrecht Confession of 1632) are an orderly listing of our basic doctrines, or "metaphors of ultimacy;" our representations of what we hold to be the most important things that can be said about God, creation, Christ, salvation, the world, the church, the end of history.

Second, it is noteworthy how seriously Scripture is taken. Each of the many articles makes only doctrinal claims that can be backed up by scriptural references, which are listed either in the body of the text or beneath.

But third, what understandably confounds the modern biblical exegete is that the Bible is scanned backwards and forwards with little regard for context or original intent. This is another reason why dogmatic or systematic theologies defined along dogmatic lines are suspect among many biblical scholars. They are critical of what they see as an extrinsic deductive schema used to interpret Scripture. The Bible, they say, is more messy than this.

So what kind of case can be made for biblically based doctrinal thinking? One can go to a concordance and find a list of passages that specifically refer to "doctrine" or "sound teaching" (Matt. 16:12; Mark 1:27; Acts 17:19; John 7:16-17; Acts 5:28; Rom. 6:17; 16:17; Eph. 4:14; 1 Tim. 1:10; 4:1; 6:3; 2 Tim. 3:10, 16, 4:3; Titus 2:1, 7; Col. 2:22; Heb. 13:9). These passages include references to false doctrines, new doctrines, sound doctrines, human doctrines, the doctrines of demons, and so on. In all of these, doctrine refers to sound or unsound teachings of some kind, and it is assumed that what one believes is important, ought to be true, and related to virtue or upright moral character. In other words, the content of one's beliefs is related to ethics.

A good example is the "warning against false teachers" found in 1 Timothy 6:3-5:

> If anyone teaches otherwise and does not agree with the sound words of our Lord Jesus Christ and the teaching which accords with godliness, he is puffed up with conceit, he knows nothing; he has a morbid craving for controversy and for disputes about words, which produce envy, dissension, slander, base suspicions, and wrangling among men who are depraved in mind and bereft of the truth, imagining that godliness is a means of gain.

Sound doctrine, and a concern for truth, is directly linked to godliness. There is no place for controversy and verbal disputation for their own sake, an occupation that academics are particularly fond of.

Specific references to doctrine in the Bible are not sufficient, however, to develop a basis for doctrinal thinking. For an adequate doctrinal theology one needs to look at the Bible as a whole: beginning at the beginning (Genesis) and moving toward the end (Apocalypse), taking seriously not only historical and narrative books, or the prophetic books (all of which are in vogue, especially among Mennonites), but also the more explicitly theological books, which take seriously systematic and rational reflection on the profoundest of questions, including the nature of God, the meaning of history and especially suffering, and the universal significance of the Christ-event.

The book that most immediately comes to mind is, of course, Paul's epistle to the Romans. We tend to overlook the Wisdom literature of the Old Testament (Job, Psalms, Proverbs, Ecclesiastes, the Song of Songs) and the wisdom writings of the New Testament, especially the gospel of John, as "systematic" reflection on human experience. Here wisdom and reason are extolled as the great gift of God. Take especially the book of Proverbs, which begins by exalting wisdom, discipline, an enlightened attitude of mind:

> For learning about wisdom and instruction, for understanding words of insight, for gaining instruction in wise dealing, righteousness, justice, and equity; to teach shrewdness to the simple, knowledge and prudence to the young—Let the wise also hear and gain in learning, and the discerning acquire skill, to understand a proverb and a figure, the words of the wise and their riddles. The fear of the Lord is the beginning of knowledge; fools despise wisdom and instruction (Prov. 1:2-7, NRSV).

Here we have the biblical starting point for a systematic and doctrinal reflection on what we believe as related to human experience. Here there is no sharp dichotomy between faith and reason, between a Christ-centred and a God-centred theology. Ancient doctrinal thinking is not a rigid dogmatism but a proverbial wisdom of the ages, a wisdom born of experience and faith in a Providential God, faith seeking understanding. While Hebraic and Christian wisdom literature provides us with a kind of formal rationale for systematic thinking, for the content of one's beliefs one turns to a more comprehensive look at the general sweep of the biblical story, at the early *kerygma*, and at the way this story and *kerygma* are formalized in the context of classical culture and passed on in the tradition of the church.

In making his case for systematic theology Thomas Finger alludes to the "recitals" of significant events in Jewish history that occur in the Hebrew Scriptures (Deut. 6:20-24; 26:5-9; Josh. 24:2-13; Neh. 9:6-37). In the New Testament the early Christian community continues such recital of events, now expanding them to include the *kerygma* (Acts 2:14-36; 3:12-26; 10:18-43).[7] Such recitals are narrative in their structure but, in their very repetitive nature, they take on a form that is more than merely historical retelling; they become a teaching device to pass on faith content. Truth claims are being made about the nature of God and the meaning of God's actions within and through history.

More specifically, however, the *kerygma* itself has an implicit theological and confessional or doctrinal component to it. The *kerygma* is the central message, core, or content of Christian preaching. Although there are many places in the New Testament where the content of the early *kerygma* is evident, the first sermon of Peter in Acts 2 probably gives clearest expression to it:

> You that are Israelites, listen to what I have to say: Jesus of Nazareth, a man attested to you by God with deeds of power, wonders, and signs that God did through him among you, as you yourselves know—this man, handed over to you according to the definite plan and foreknowledge of God, you crucified and killed by the hands of those outside the law. But God raised him up, having freed him from death, because it was impossible for him to be held in its power....
>
> Since he [David] was a prophet, he knew that God had sworn with an oath to him that he would put one of his descendents on his throne. Foreseeing this, David spoke of the resurrection of the Messiah, saying, 'He was not abandoned to Hades, nor did his flesh experience corruption.'

This Jesus God raised up, and of that all of us are witnesses. Being therefore exalted at the right hand of God, and having received from the Father the promise of the Holy Spirit, he has poured out this that you both see and hear....

Peter said to them, "Repent, and be baptized every one of you in the name of Jesus Christ so that your sins may be forgiven; and you will receive the gift of the Holy Spirit. For the promise is for you, for your children, and for all who are far away, everyone whom the Lord our God calls to him." And he testified with many other arguments and exhorted them, saying, "Save yourselves from this corrupt generation." (Acts 2:22-24, 30-33, 38-40, NRSV)

Here you have the essential building blocks of what later gets developed further into the Apostles' and Nicene Creeds: God the Father, the human Jesus of Nazareth (as the Christ), delivered up and crucified according to the eternal foreknowledge of God, abandonment to Hades, resurrection and exaltation, the promise and coming of the Holy Spirit, the call to repentance and promise of forgiveness.

Historical Precedence

Why do we need doctrines? Because historically the church has considered them important! History does not bear the burden of proof against contemporary experience. It is the other way around. If a contemporary fad suggests that a major departure from historical precedent is necessary that new direction bears the burden of proof. That we are smarter today than they were 100, 500, or 2000 years ago is generally assumed but unfounded. Our scientific and empirical method has made us more linear and one-dimensional in our thinking than the ancients. The Einsteinian and post-Einsteinian revolution may be bringing us back again to a more multidimensional universe—something the ancients already understood better than we.

There are three paradigmatic periods of doctrinal thinking in the history of Christianity which can provide models for us: the Classical period (100-500), the period of Protestant Orthodoxy (1550-1700), and the period of Neo-Orthodoxy (1920-1960). Classical orthodoxy begins with the biblical period and ends roughly with the definition of Chalcedon in 451, with the major lines of orthodoxy drawn on the questions of the Christian doctrine of God (the Trinity) and the Christian doctrine of Christ (the two natures). Many individual and corporate creedal confessions were written during this period but the dominant ones are the Apostolic, the Nicene-Constantinopolitan, the Athanasian, and the Chalcedonian Christological confessions.

Most interesting about this period is the development of the very notion of the development of doctrine.[8] The early church theologians and bishops began to take historical development and novelty seriously, and accepted the idea that the church had the authority, under the guidance of the Holy Spirit, to further clarify and elaborate upon what was already essentially given in Scriptures. Scriptural confirmation of the development of doctrine can be found in texts like John 16:12-15:

> I have yet many things to say to you, but you cannot bear them now. When the Spirit of truth comes, he will guide you into all the truth; for he will not speak on his own authority, but will speak whatever he hears, and he will declare to you the things that are to come. He will glorify me, for he will take what is mine and declare it to you.

It was not a free-for-all development but a development within certain parameters:

1) The primary concern was *theological and soteriological*: the nature of the Christ-event in relation first of all to the one God, Yahweh, of the Hebrew Scriptures, and second, to the outpouring of the Holy Spirit after his departure; especially as it affected salvation. Heresy endangered soteriology.

2) A related concern was *scriptural*: although Hellenistic language was employed it was clear that the primary texts were the Scriptures—both the Jewish Scriptures and the Christian writings; it was to preserve both, in the face of anti-Jewish Marcionism, that largely focused the discussion around the formation of the biblical canon.

3) Another concern was *ecclesiastical*: the preservation of the catholicity (universality/ecumenicity) of the church under the guidance of duly appointed leaders. Heresy (too narrow, rigid and fragmentary an understanding of the faith) was a threat to that catholicity.

4) The last concern was *apologetical*: defending the truth of the Christian faith in the face of Greco-Roman philosophical critics. All four of these criteria are still valid for evaluating doctrine and doctrinal development. The questionable role of Constantine and his political agenda in the development of the early creed, the first "political theology" in his court, and the general *Gleichschaltung* (coordination) of the church and its doctrines with the state that occurred during the so-called Constantinian shift, I have dealt with in another context.[9]

The Eastern Orthodox churches split with Rome in part over the dispute as to whether the development of doctrine legitimately continued past the early ecumenical councils. We do not need to pursue that issue further here. We conclude this historical section with a few brief comments about seventeenth-century Protestant Orthodoxy and twentieth-century Neo-Orthodoxy.

Beginning shortly after the initial wave of the Reformation, a process of consolidation occurred in Roman Catholicism at the Council of Trent and in all of the Protestant denominations: Lutheran, Reformed, Anglican, and Mennonite. For Protestants this denominational consolidation took the form of confessionalism—the development of confessions and accompanying theological manuals of orthodoxy for each group. It was a kind of scholasticism, ironically, not that different from the medieval Thomistic scholasticism that the Reformers had so strongly protested against. These confessions, while they have some similarities with the classical period, are not to be simply equated with them. The most important difference, is that they take shape in the context of the birth of the modern world, i.e., in the context of the first scientific revolution—that of Nicolaus Copernicus (1473-1543), Francis Bacon (1561-1626), Galileo (1564-1642) and Isaac Newton (1642-1727).[10]

This means they reflect a kind of static propositional universe, rationalist systems of thought, literal ways of talking about God and the world in a way foreign to the ancients. There is little of the dynamism and developmentalism, and the metaphorical, symbolic use of language that characterizes the ancient creeds.

In these later confessions and scholastic manuals we have the beginning of a preoccupation with a biblical literalism that was quite foreign to the Reformers and the early church theologians. This Protestant Orthodoxy lives on in some later Lutheran and Calvinist confessionalism as well as in twentieth-century Fundamentalism. The Oxford Movement (Tractarianism) in England around men like John Henry Newman was a return to the classical period quite different from late Protestant Orthodoxy. While there are some valuable things about this period of Protestant doctrinal consciousness, including the detailed manuals that came out of it, there are some serious shortcomings. Mennonite confessions which take shape during this same period up to the present, beginning with the Dordrecht Confession of 1632, share in some of these same weaknesses, a kind of doctrinal rigidity and literalism. Most valuable about this era, however, is the seriousness with which theological questions are discussed, the clarity with which doctrines are defined and articulated, and the comprehensiveness with which the doctrines are related to each other.

The third of the periods mentioned above is Neo-Orthodoxy. With Karl Barth's interest in dogmatics, beginning in the late 1920s and early 1930s, especially as it finds expression in the Barmen Declaration during the time of crisis within the German Evangelical Church, there emerges amongst Protestants a new interest in classical doctrine as dogma. Barth sees dogma as the church's judgment concerning the truth of the matter in the face of grave danger to the gospel.

Earlier, Barth had been very much committed to the political task of Christianity (he was a member of the Religious Socialist movement in Switzerland). Now, in the face of the growing fascist threat, and in the face of the politicization of both left-wing and right-wing theological fronts, he turned to dogmatics not as an escape from social and political responsibility but as a way of formulating a sound dogmatic framework for responsible personal, social, and political ethics. Doctrine and dogmatic theology became for him the primary task of the church; the foundation and grounds for sound moral and political choices. In this he stands in continuity with the classical tradition.

In Barth one has the beginnings of what I would call a postmodern dogmatics; that is, a dogmatics which is fully aware of the serious epistemological, historical, and religious questions that the Enlightenment paradigm raises for theology, but which also recognizes that the uncritical belief in scientific progress and historicism of the seventeenth, eighteenth, and nineteenth centuries is itself coming to an end.

The Present Situation

Why do we need doctrine? Because our present situation in the Mennonite church urgently calls for it in three areas: church unity, catechesis, and ethics.

1. ***Church Unity*** The diversity and pluralism that exists within the Mennonite tradition— the heterogeneity of sixteenth-century Anabaptist groups; the differences historically between Dutch, German, Swiss, Russian traditions; not to mention more recent divisions and multi-ethnic additions— calls for an overarching theologically defined identity rather than (or in addition to) an ethnic one. My wife has written a small book in which she identifies more than twenty groups within the Mennonite family in Canada alone, many of them the result of divisions amongst the two traditional Dutch-German and Swiss streams.[11] Some of the divisions are doctrinal ones, some of the diversity is due to ethnic and geographic factors.

How can we as a Mennonite communion maintain unity while respecting this diversity? We cannot impose, as traditional ethnic Mennonites have tended to do, a Swiss or German-Dutch-Russian ethnocultural identity on all members of the Mennonite family. We have to come together theologically or confessionally. Although I disagree in significant ways with John Redekop's proposal in his book *People Apart*, I do accept his basic point that if the Mennonite church is going truly to be the church, incorporating a variety of ethnicities within itself, it will need to have a theological foundation rather than an ethnic one.[12] This theological/confessional basis I think will need to be a doctrinal one.

But our diversity does not consist only of ethnic, geographic, and cultural pluralism. We have fundamental differences ideologically. In one article I listed some fourteen different theologies that seem to be vying with each other for dominance, including liberation theologies of various kinds, therapeutic theologies, conservative-evangelical-fundamentalist theologies, process theologies, narrative theologies, and so on.[13] We will need to develop some confessional-doctrinal-dogmatic framework within which to hold together our diversity. It will need to be some kind of postmodern dogmatics which stands in continuity with the classical creedal tradition and historic Mennonite confessions but takes more seriously than these the profound pluralism of the contemporary situation. An attempt was made by the Faith and Life Committee of the Mennonite World Conference Assembly 12 in Winnipeg in July 1990, with a confessional statement "Our Witness to Christ in Today's World," but the statement was so broad and so situational that it bore little resemblance to the historic creeds. A much more substantive undertaking is the Mennonite Church and General Conference Mennonite Church Confessions of Faith Committee's effort at developing *Confession of Faith in a Mennonite Perspective*.[14]

2. *Catechesis* Doctrines answer the questions children ask. Who made the mountains? Where did we come from? Where do people go when they die? Is there a God? Where is he? Why did people kill Jesus? At seven years of age my son asked questions like this. When my daughter was fifteen she came home depressed after a fight with her best friend over freedom and predestination. It is adults more often than children who seem to give up on such questions.

Catechesis is the passing on of Christian beliefs concerning the most fundamental questions of meaning to children, to converts, to baptismal candidates, to adults. Beliefs or doctrines are not themselves the reality which they represent nor are they the same as the experience of faith, but they are closely related. Chronologically the teaching of the doctrines usually comes first and the experience of the reality which the doctrines symbolically point to comes later, but the experience of an encounter with God stands ontologically before the doctrinal articulation of that experience. Because doctrinal teaching is usually prior historically or chronologically, it is important that the church ritualistically pass on through catechesis what it believes.

I am taking our youth class (ages 14 to 17) through Helmut Harder's *Guide to Faith*,[15] systematically dealing with the major doctrines of Christian faith from a Mennonite perspective. Catechesis should be done regularly, repetitively, and in an orderly fashion, along the lines of the ancient creeds and Dordrecht-type confessions. In Dordrecht for instance we have all the basic categories outlined[16]: God and creation; the Fall; Christ; repentance; baptism; the church; offices of the church; the Lord's supper; washing of feet; marriage; civil government; use of force; oaths; church discipline (excommunication and shunning); resurrection and the last judgment.

A postmodern dogmatics will take the historical questions much more seriously than did the framers of the seventeenth-century confessions, will accept some notion of the development of doctrine, and will grapple with the post-Kantian theory of knowledge, reflecting a turn to the human subject and the experiential ground of talk about God. It will also be more critical of any political theology (whether of the left or the right) that uses doctrine as political ideology. These factors will influence our translation of traditional doctrinal categories as found in Dordrecht, for example, into contemporary terms. The basic categorical framework will remain the same: this framework will include God as triune; Creation as finite (i.e., dependent on God); creation as fallen and human beings as sinful; salvation through the being and work of Christ; the church as the body of Christ incarnated in the world as empowered by the Holy Spirit; the end of time and history; and judgment and the resurrection.

Old Order Mennonite Isaac R. Horst writes interesting columns regularly in the *Mennonite Reporter*, under the title "Old Order Voice." In the January 21, 1991 issue he writes about how the Old Order keep their youth, and how "on six consecutive Sunday afternoons, from about mid-June through mid-July, instruction meetings are held for the candidates at various locations, to catechize them in the 18 Articles of Faith (Dordrecht), before being baptized."

In a sequel he explains in much greater detail how this is done. How on each of the six Sundays three articles are considered. How on the Saturday before baptism the candidates gather at the meetinghouse for one final review of the 18 articles with the "applicants counselled and exhorted to Christian faith, charity, and forbearance." On baptism Sunday, before a full house, the bishop, with the candidates in a semi-circle before him, asks them the following questions: "first, whether they believe in God, who created heaven and earth, in Jesus Christ, the son of God, as their Saviour, and in the Holy Spirit, flowing from the Father and Son; second, whether they have repented from sin, and are willing to forsake their own will and the works of Satan; third, whether they promise, through God's grace and guidance, to follow the teachings of Christ until death." Here we have what I consider the true genius of Mennonite catechetical instruction: the melding of doctrine and discipleship, orthodoxy, and orthopraxis. And this leads me to my final reason why we need doctrine.

3. **Ethics** We need doctrine because of ethics! Doctrine can never be a substitute for ethics or an escape from an upright moral life. Nor can ethical theology [*Nachfolge*] be an alternative to a doctrinal theology. Further, doctrine and discipleship should not be seen as existing side by side, in tension with each other. Nor should ethics be attached to the end of a list of doctrines as their conclusion. Doctrine is, you might say, the ontological or theological framework, ground, or basis for ethics. It is in this sense before ethics, functioning as its foundation. As Browning states so well: " the way we metaphorically represent the world in its most durable and ultimate respects influences . . . what we think we are obligated to do."[17] Doctrines are our "metaphors of ultimacy," the way we metaphorically represent the world to ourselves. To illustrate in greater detail how a doctrine becomes the ground for ethics (and not the other way around), we now take a look at the doctrine of God.

Ethics and the Doctrine of God

How might one go about thinking about the doctrine of God for today? Ideally one would begin by looking at the *Bible*, both in its specific references to God and in its general sweep, recognizing that reading the biblical text is a hermeneutical task with text as object and interpreter as subject having a symbiotic relation to each other.

One would look at *history*, beginning with the classical period of orthodoxy as having a certain pre-eminence over later movements, and tracing the development of doctrine in the thought of individual theologians, conciliar statements, catechetical documents, and artistic expressions of various kinds. Starting with the Reformation, one might pay greater attention to "confessional" differences. One would look carefully at the Enlightenment and the shift that took place in human consciousness and generally take seriously the numerous so-called "paradigm shifts" that have occurred throughout history. Finally, one would look at the *present situation*, what Tom Finger calls the "apologetic context,"[18] and attempt to interpret the biblical and classical views concerning God in light of the most pressing academic, religious, churchly, and moral-ethical issues facing us.

The importance of a christological starting point for all theology has, ever since the 1920s with the emergence of Neo-Orthodoxy, been widely recognized. While there is much to be said for this, there is always the danger of becoming too narrowly Christocentric or Christomonistic. I therefore prefer to begin with a theocentric or trinitarian perspective, with Christ, the second article of the creed, taking the place of pre-eminence.

A trinitarian approach ought not to be a post-biblical systematic imposition upon the biblical text but one that emerges out of the three-fold encounter early Jewish-Christians had with divine reality: 1) the historic experience of Yahweh's acts in their history as a people; 2) their experience of Jesus as the Christ, as the Messiah both in his being and works, including the forgiveness of sins; and 3) their experience of the outpouring of the Holy Spirit in the early believing community, especially at and beyond Pentecost. The question was not whether there were here three gods of equal status but whether the early Christians had in fact encountered the one divine, living reality in all three experiences. Their answer was "Yes!" This is what the church tried to articulate with fallible human words at Nicea and Constantinople.

The Christian doctrine of God as it found expression in the earliest confessions and creeds was the affirmation by the early Christian community that the one divine reality was all three: transcendent creator, provider and preserver; historically incarnated and revealed in Jesus as the Christ; and immanent energy and power within us, the church and creation. Sixteenth-century Anabaptists not only perceived themselves within the Apostolic-Creedal tradition but saw repentance and upright moral life, including communal life in the case of Hutterites, already intrinsically part of this trinitarian view of God. Later Mennonite confessions and catechisms (like the one I grew up with) deal with the doctrine of God in continuity with the ancient tradition, highlighting more specifically the ethical and ecclesiological implications. This three-fold ancient affirmation of the divine reality continues to be indispensable for defining the Christian Mennonite identity and for grounding Mennonite worship and discipleship.

1. *"I [We] believe in God the Father Almighty, Creator of Heaven and Earth."*
One of the most pressing issues facing contemporary civilization is modern technology and its devastation of the natural world. It is frequently claimed by critics that a good part of the blame for the environmental crisis is the Judeo-Christian view of a sovereign, willing and controlling God who is separate from nature and acts upon it, expecting human beings to be His

deputies on earth by also willing God's will over nature. One could contest the accuracy of this charge by an exegesis of the two creation stories of Genesis, one calling upon humans to "Be fruitful and multiply, and fill the earth and subdue it; and have dominion over the fish of the sea and over the birds of the air and over every living thing that moves upon the earth" (Gen. 1:28); the other asking humans "to till it [the garden] and keep it" (Gen. 2:15). But this would not absolve Christian history for its inexcusable rape of the earth.

Of particular interest for the environmental issue are the two subdoctrines usually associated with the first article of the Apostles' Creed: Providence and Preservation. First, the doctrine of God's *providence*. In this doctrine God is viewed as above and outside of nature, the transcendent and sovereign ruler who has a plan for creation and acts upon it to achieve his purpose. Here the masculine image of God as "Father," so prevalent in biblical literature, may have been appropriate (although one can no longer distinguish masculine and feminine in this way). This view of God as distant is not only biblical but a necessary one for environmental concerns, for it means that we are not on our own in human history, to do with the world as we please. We are accountable to an external reality for what we do with nature. The wonderful concept of "nature revolting" (George Grant) is in some sense an analogy for viewing transcendence as outside us, for it suggests that there is that which is outside our own nature, standing over against us, limiting us in our willing. Further, it grounds our hope that despite all our exploitation of nature, there is a mysterious transcendent purpose toward which the cosmos is directed.

The second subdoctrine is God as *preserver*. In this doctrine God is perceived as bearer and immanent ground of the world, keeping it safe from harm. God in this image is not distant and far away but near to nature, within nature. We feel ourselves not as cut off from nature but as part of it, and our harming of any segment of nature as a wounding of ourselves. The whole natural world is in some sense unified through God's Spirit in this way. The Thomistic notion of God as *ipsum esse* (being itself) suggests this closeness of God to all manifestations of being, wherever they are found. Here the image of God as feminine, "mother earth," may be appropriate; while frequently identified with non-Jewish, polytheistic religions, it nevertheless can be found in biblical literature as well. Both of these doctrines—God as sovereign providence and God as creative ground—need to be held together. Unfortunately, they frequently get separated, with Protestants tending to stress the one and Catholics the other. I wonder whether the Eastern Orthodox tradition does not hold them together more successfully than western Christianity.

2. "*[I believe] in Jesus Christ His only Son our Lord.*" The early Christians' high claims for Christ are premised on his unity with Yahweh and the Holy Spirit (a trinitarian claim). It is imperative that Mennonites not forget this in their concern for discipleship and the peace witness. Here the doctrines of the full deity and humanity of Christ are crucial. I will concentrate on the deity of Christ, for it is this doctrine which seems to give moderns the most difficulty. As Mennonites understand it, Christ's life and teaching of non-violent love culminating on the cross is at the heart of the gospel. The question is whether this is one more school of thought, or whether this is a "metaphor of ultimacy," that is, whether it is believed to lie at the heart of reality itself. Is this *God* being revealed to us here in the non-violent love of Christ? Is *God* dying non-violently on the cross? It is precisely because we want to say "Yes" to this question that we want to defend the doctrine of the deity of Christ.

What a trinitarian theology does not allow us to conclude, however, is that *this* exhausts the reality of God, or is all that can be said about God—that God is a pacifist in the Mennonite sense. There is a plurality within God's own unity. It is true that the Christian tradition affirms Christ as being fully God, yet the first mode of God's being (God as creator, provider, preserver) cannot be collapsed into God's second mode of being (the Christ).

In other words, Jesus of Nazareth is not equated with God as "Father." The unexplained existence of evil and violence in our world—especially in those realms of human and non-human nature which are beyond human ethics—pushes us to use images of ultimate reality which allow for a dark, wrathful, even judgmental side of God. This dark side cannot be fully grasped by the non-violent love ethic (*agape*) of God or Christ. This is why the historic church has held that, while "Father," Son and Holy Spirit are of the same substance, they can never be simply equated. The "Father" is unbegotten and therefore absolutely free of human moral/ethical systems; Christ is begotten and becomes the norm for all our behavior both in his humanity and divinity; and the Holy Spirit proceeds from the "Father" (in the Eastern Church) or proceeds from the "'Father' and the Son" (in the West). In effect we have one God who has unbegotten, begotten and proceeding modes of being. This plurality within God allows us to claim meaning within suffering and violence, while at the same time rejecting all violence as a norm for human behavior, from a christological perspective.

3. "*[I believe] in the Holy Spirit.*" Simply in terms of immediacy, God's third mode of being, the Holy Spirit, is the most important for us in our present encounter with God. God's Spirit identifies with our spirit and thus mediates Christ and "Father" to us. Without the Spirit we would not have existential and personal access to God's two other modes of being. Christ

and the transcendent creator are mediated to us by the Spirit. The question here is: Does the Spirit have moral and ethical relevance? Traditionally, of course, it was through the Spirit that regeneration and sanctification properly occurred. But is there not a fresh interpretation that can be made here that is particularly relevant for our age?

Take a third example of an issue facing us in the church: the gender issue (homosexuality could be another example). By now this may be a mundane question for some—many of us have made our theological and biblical moves to justify gender equality in all levels of church life and polity (and some have done so in the area of homosexuality), even though the actual situation in many cases remains appallingly far from the ideal. Nevertheless, I would like to use this case to illustrate how a doctrine of the Holy Spirit as the third mode of God's very being can help us address new situations as they arise historically in the church.

A sound doctrine of the Holy Spirit allows and calls upon the church to make genuinely new decisions which go beyond the biblical text and beyond classical texts and dogmas while remaining fundamentally true to them. John Henry Newman already dealt most comprehensively with the question of novelty and continuity in doctrine in his nineteenth-century classic, *An Essay in the Development of Christian Doctrine*. To say that the Holy Spirit is very God is to open history to God's continuing dynamic and new action in the name of Christ. To paraphrase Gayle Gerber Koontz's formulation, there is a trajectory in Scripture that moves out beyond the text, breaking through rigid patriarchal structures in liberating ways.[19]

If one wants to take the whole Bible seriously with its many seemingly conflicting images on such matters, then how can one move forward in a united way to meet new challenges for which the Bible as a whole does not give adequate direction in the specifics? One takes Christ's own words at face value: "I still have many things to say to you, but you cannot bear them now. When the Spirit of truth comes, he will guide you into all the truth; for he will not speak on his own, but will speak whatever he hears, and he will declare to you the things that are to come. He will glorify me, because he will take what is mine and declare it to you" (John 16:12-15, NRSV). It is because of this doctrine of the deity of the Holy Spirit, God as immanent power of self disclosure to us in the church, the body of Christ, that we can and are called upon to make *genuinely new judgments* on the nature of truth.

The question of how we determine when we are truly being guided in our decision-making by the Holy Spirit or when we may be misled by a false god (or wish fulfilment) is, of course, a serious matter. For this very reason the three modes of God's being need to be seen in relation to each other.

TWENTY-TWO

Biblical and Systematic Theology: Two Parallel but Related Activities*

The legendary suspicion with which biblical scholars and systematic theologians regard each other is premised on a fallacy—the assumption that 1) the Bible comes first and that 'systematic' reflection on the faith comes second, is derivative, and almost necessarily distorting of biblical truth, that 2) the biblical scholar is dealing with primary data ideally devoid of systematic-theological presuppositions, and that 3) the systematician by definition is engaged in an extra-biblical enterprise.

Systematic confession, both historically and theologically, preceded the written New Testament text(s) and their canonization. The primitive church's "Rule of Faith," by which fidelity to the truth of the Christian kerygma was determined, predated canonization by some two centuries, and played a role in distinguishing authoritative texts from others. The "Rule of Faith" was the Creed in nutio.

---

* Originally published as "Biblical and Systematic Theology as Functional Specialties: Their Distinction and Relation," in *So Wide a Sea: Essays on Biblical and Systematic Theology*, ed. Ben C. Ollenburger (Elkhart, IN: Institute of Mennonite Studies, 1991), 37-58. The same volume published a response to my essay by Gordon D. Kaufman, "Critical Theology and the Bible: A Response to A. James Reimer," 59-64, in which he criticizes me for ignoring the critical function of theology. For notes on the text see the Notes section below.

> The Rule of Faith ... is of course that by which we believe that there is but one God, who is none other than the Creator of the world, who produced everything through his Word, sent forth before all things; that this Word is called his Son, and in the Name of God was seen in divers ways by the patriarchs, was ever heard in the prophets and finally was brought down by the Spirit and Power of God the Father into the Virgin Mary, was made flesh in her womb, was born of her and lived as Jesus Christ; who thereafter proclaimed a new law and a new promise of the kingdom of heaven, worked miracles, was crucified, on the third day rose again, was caught up into heaven and sat down at the right hand of the Father; that he sent in his place the power of the Holy Spirit to guide believers; that he will come with glory to take the saints up into the fruition of the life eternal and the heavenly promises and to judge the wicked to everlasting fire, after the resurrection of both good and evil with the restoration of their flesh.[1]

Systematic theology, as I understand it, is not undisciplined imagination, but has its prototype in the confessional tradition as illustrated in the above "Rule of Faith" as articulated by Tertullian.

It is my contention in this essay—first presented at the Mennonite Scholars session at meetings of the American Academy of Religion and the Society of Biblical Literature in Boston, December 4, 1987,[2] responded to by Gordon D. Kaufman—that biblical theology and systematic theology are specialities within the larger generic discipline of theology, broadly understood as "the reflection on the grounds, contents and experience of the Christian faith."

It's not that biblical theology is the foundation and systematic theology the elaboration, but that they are parallel activities sharing a symbiotic relationship with each other. The biblical theologian focuses on the world of the biblical text and translating that world, whereas the systematic theologian focuses on the content and meaning of the confession (kerygma) in ever new situations and cultures. Insofar as the biblical theologian engages in reflecting on the content and meaning of the early Christian confession, she is engaging in systematic theology. Insofar as the systematic theologian tries to understand the biblical world within which the kerygma was first proclaimed and textually preserved, she becomes a biblical theologian. The time has come for mutual respect between these two essential specialities within Christian theology.

◆ ◆ ◆

Abstract: The Basic Argument

Christian theology in general is the reflection on the grounds, contents, and experience of the Christian faith. It is an activity which assumes the transcendent reality of God, God's self-revelation in Jesus Christ, and God's ongoing presence in the life of the church and the world as Holy Spirit, the unifying theme(s) running through the diversity of the church's foundational texts and historical events and manifold interpretations of those texts and events. To the extent that a scholar (whether biblical, historical, systematic-dogmatic, or practical-pastoral) is engaged in this activity with these assumptions, to that degree she can be considered to be engaged in Christian theology. Technically speaking, therefore, the prevalent distinction between biblical theology, historical theology, systematic theology, and practical theology, as though these were four different theologies, is a false one.

All Christian theologians are engaged in one set of interdependent tasks or functions, based on a common collection of foundational texts and their historical interpretation, directed toward a common goal. They specialize in different areas for mainly practical reasons of skill, temperament, convenience, and so on. Biblical theology, for instance, is not a separate genre of theology (although it is often seen to be just that) set over against systematic theology, as though it alone were truly biblical and were unconcerned about coherence, unity, synthesis, systematization, mediation, or even dogma. If it is a form of Christian theology it is interested in these things. All theology is to a greater or lesser degree systematic, and all theology if it is Christian ought to be biblical.

With these provisos, however, there is some value in differentiating between the different areas of specialization (sometimes referred to as "functional specialties")—biblical, historical, systematic, and practical—as long as it is remembered that if their respective practitioners want to attach the common noun "theology" to their speciality, then they are admitting to being engaged in a common enterprise with the others: Christian theology.

The primary focus of *systematic theology*, as a functional specialty, is the church within the world of contemporary culture (its language, values, assumptions, and demands) and its task the summarizing and schematizing of the essential tenets of the Christian faith (as revealed in the Scriptures and interpreted historically) for the purpose of helping the church to shape the beliefs and values of her adherents, to mediate between the world of the Bible and her life within contemporary culture, and to address critically the assumptions and demands of the present age. The primary focus of *biblical theology*, as a functional specialty, is the world of the Scriptures — that is, it seeks to research, analyze, synthesize, elucidate, interpret, and translate the biblical texts and identify the assumptions of the biblical age using all the tools of modern culture and insights from tradition to do so.

Both are essential to the life of the church. Biblical theology, with its greater concentration on the inner diversities and infrastructure of the biblical materials, including the milieu of those writings, has the responsibility toward systematic (or dogmatic) theology of keeping it from ideologically falsifying the biblical texts (and world) in its necessary task of summarizing. Systematic theology, with its greater concentration on the assumptions of the contemporary world and the *summarized unities* of the tradition, has the responsibility toward biblical theology of identifying and unmasking contemporary presuppositions that are inescapably present in and may threaten to distort biblical studies, such as the positivistic fragmentation and quantification of the Scriptures.

While any given individual or group of individuals may specialize in one or the other, they may in fact do both. The two, while distinct, in actual practice overlap considerably. Both, for instance, attempt to be faithful to the Christian revelation and to mediate the world of the Scriptures to members of the Christian community, but they do this in different ways. The primary rationale for distinguishing between the two functional specialties is to preserve, paradoxically, both the distance and the closeness between the world of the Bible and our own world. For this reason it is imperative for the scholar to be clear about what she is doing and when she is doing it.

Introduction: The Importance of Catechesis

The divisions and specializations in the general field of Christian theology are fluid and vary significantly from historical period to historical period, from tradition to tradition, from institution to institution, and from scholar to scholar.[3] What this fluidity suggests is that these various schemas are relative and developed to meet the exigencies of particular situations. One may lament this increasing differentiation as a deplorable fragmentation of what once was and ought still to be one basic unified set of activities: the reading, interpretation, appropriation, and application of the Scriptures. Nevertheless, the specializations seem to be here to stay and have to do with the accumulation of data which needs to be absorbed but can't possibly be mastered by any one group of scholars, let alone individuals. A division of labour not only between individuals but between groups of specialists, therefore, appears to be an unhappy necessity.

The most common and perhaps most useful contemporary curricular categorization is the one that divides Christian theology into biblical, historical, systematic, and pastoral (or practical) specialities. I intend in this paper to concentrate on two of these commonly accepted separate disciplines—biblical theology and systematic theology—and attempt to delineate what I consider to be, at least functionally, the distinctive operations and methodologies of each, giving special attention to systematic theology and its relation to biblical theology.

Leaving aside the thorny issue of whether or not the practitioners of biblical and systematic theology can properly fulfill their functions outside the community of faith, I will assume in this essay that in both cases the said theologians belong existentially to a believing community of Christians (that is, they have experienced conversion in some sense of that term[4]) and are seeking to be faithful in proclaiming the Christian understanding of God in and to the present age. They are, in short, engaged in a common enterprise: *theology*. Neither biblical nor systematic theology is antiquarian, interested in the past for its own sake. Each views its respective task as a form of piety and fidelity to God in the contemporary context.

The German-English *Catechism* which first initiated me into the life of the Altona Bergthaler Mennonite Church,[5] and which first introduced me to the "systematic" categories of creation, fall and redemption, began with the following question: "Was ist das Notwendigste, wonach ein Mensch in diesem Leben trachten soll?" The answer: "In Gottes Gemeinschaft und Gnade zu leben und nachmals die ewige Seligkeit zu erlangen." There followed what was a rather questionable translation. Question: "What should be our chief aim in this life?" Answer: "To live in God's fellowship, enjoy his favour, and obtain eternal happiness hereafter."

Despite the weak translation, and despite all of the modern Enlightenment and postmodern problems associated with this answer, I hold this affirmation to be fundamentally true and applicable to all Christians, including professional theologians. The *alpha* and *omega* of our theological work and reflection is to live in God's fellowship and grace, and to proclaim the same to others in the context of contemporary pluralism.

What this catechism did, and what I consider to be one of the essential tasks of systematic theology, was to summarize what its writers considered to be the essentials of the Christian faith for the purpose of educating baptismal candidates. The opening statement of the "Foreword" reads as follows: "This catechism was first published in the year 1783 at Elbing, Prussia, with the purpose of presenting to the Mennonite young people the cardinal truths of Christianity in a brief and simple form."[6] This catechetical manual, which characterizes itself as giving "Brief lessons from the Holy Scriptures," consists of 202 questions and answers, each supported by one or more Bible verses, divided into the following major sections: Introduction; Part One: The Creation [ranging from God as Creator of all things, the Trinity, to God as preserver and ruler of the world]; Part Two: the Fall of Man [dealing with the condition of humanity before, during, and after the Fall]; and Part Three: The Redemption of Man [covering the promise of redemption, the role of law, Christ and his death, resurrection, ascension, the Holy Spirit, faith, regeneration, justification, sanctification, the church, baptism, the Lord's supper, non-resistance, government and the oath, the future destiny of humanity, judgment, and so on].

What is going on here? For one thing, from the perspective of modern contextual-critical biblical scholarship this catechism commits the unpardonable sin: it assumes without question an underlying canonical unity, ranges freely backwards and forwards across the Old and New Testaments, moves with ease from one book to another, and uncritically selects isolated Bible verses in support of its particular doctrinal framework without ever asking any social-historical and contextual questions, admitting of any genuine heterogeneity in the biblical materials, or allowing for any hermeneutical difficulties. And yet, it seems to me that this catechism is engaged in a very legitimate task and in its own distinctive way does what the Christian Church has always done from ancient times until recently — namely, simplifying, summarizing, and schematizing what it believes to be true for the purpose of shaping and nurturing the beliefs and values of her existing or potential adherents.

Whatever the strengths and weaknesses of George A. Lindbeck's "cultural-linguistic view of religion and . . . rule theory of doctrine," a subject I want to return to later in this essay, I do think he helps us understand sympathetically what is going on in a catechism like this.[7] For one thing, Lindbeck's analysis lends support to my own long-standing contention that doctrinal language (I might add here that I consider confession, doctrine, creed, and dogma to be family members of the same literary and theological genre, even though important differences exist between them) is indispensable for the Christian church, including the Mennonite church. Doctrinal formulations, while not the whole, are an intrinsic part of the work of systematic theology. They represent the attempt by the Christian community to develop some kind of coherent picture out of the multiplicity of diverse concepts, images, and symbols particularly in reference to God, Jesus Christ, and the Holy Spirit as found in early Christian writings,[8] for the purpose of catechesis.

Lindbeck is right in arguing that historically catechesis rather than translation "has been the primary way of transmitting the faith and winning converts for most religions down through the centuries."[9] This has also been an important aspect of the Mennonite way. Whether Lindbeck's postliberal cultural-linguistic model is the best way in which to conceive of doctrine or catechesis is another question. The point is that Lindbeck is justified in stressing the importance of doctrine and catechesis in the life of religious communities and in the work of systematic theology, which he problematically refers to as a "descriptive" discipline. "The task of descriptive (dogmatic or systematic) theology," he says, "is to give a normative explication of the meaning a religion has for its adherents."[10] For Lindbeck there is no such thing as "creedless Christianity." Doctrines, at least operationally if not officially, are a requisite for communal identity: "a religious body cannot exist as a recognizable distinctive collectivity unless it has some beliefs and/or practices by which it can be identified."[11]

Lindbeck is also clearly right in asserting repeatedly that the modern age and its theology has an antipathy to catechetical-doctrinal thinking and an accompanying dogmatic-systematic theology. This is so for a number of reasons. First, doctrines in the narrow sense (meaning those central beliefs considered essential and normative for the existence of a particular religious community) and dogmatic-systematic theology in the broader sense (the explanation, interpretation, and justification of those doctrines) presuppose the existence of an organic religious community. The modern age, however, is characterized precisely by the breakdown of community and community norms, as sociologists have been at such pains to point out. This disintegration of a cohesive communal society, or communal enclaves, is the consequence of modern notions of individual freedom and autonomous authenticity. What we have, in fact, is an increasingly global-homogeneous society in which only a privatized and interiorized religiosity appears to be able to survive. The experiential-expressive approach to religion (the liberal alternative to what Lindbeck somewhat questionably refers to as the traditional, classical "propositional" approach, his own third option being a postliberal cultural-linguistic model[12]) is more attractive to a culture defined by "religious privatism" and "subjectivism."[13] The prevalent aversion to dogmatic standards reflects a theology inclined to accommodate and legitimate rather than stand over against a pluralistic-atomistic age.

This contemporary resistance to doctrinal norms cannot, however, simply be attributed to the perversity of modern culture. There are, according to Lindbeck, some correctly perceived conceptual difficulties with doctrinal propositionalism. It cannot account for the development of doctrine over time, it is unable adequately to distinguish between what is essential and what is non-essential when interpreting doctrines in new situations, and it is incapable of dealing satisfactorily with ecumenical issues.[14] In another context I have pointed to the fact that in Mennonite churches, and I believe this could be said about other traditions as well, various other ways of speaking about the Christian faith in the present situation have replaced the doctrinal-dogmatic approach; the therapeutic and socio-political models being two of the most obvious.[15] Whether these alternatives improve substantially upon the doctrinal-confessional genre is doubtful. What is required is an understanding of the nature of doctrine and dogmatic theology that can meet some of these objections. To what an extent Lindbeck's own cultural-linguistic approach meets these requirements remains to be discussed. Here I want to introduce catechesis or doctrinal thinking as an essential aspect of systematic theology, and of theology in general, and as a way of distinguishing it from biblical theology as it is often perceived.

I make no claims for originality here but am simply defending what I consider to have been an ancient understanding of the task of Christian theology. My own view is very close to that of Karl Barth's, for whom "Christian doctrine is the attempt, undertaken as a responsibility of the church, to summarize the gospel of Jesus Christ, as the content of the church's preaching. Its source and its goal is the authentic witness to the gospel in Holy Scripture."[16]

For Barth, dogmatics is a critical, human science, located halfway between exegesis and practical theology, a means for testing the church's teaching and preaching, "not an arbitrary testing from a freely chosen standpoint" but a measuring of "the Church's proclamation by the standard of the Holy Scriptures, of the Old and New Testaments. Holy Scripture is the document of the basis, of the innermost life of the Church, the document of the manifestation of the Word of God in the person of Jesus Christ."[17] Dogmatics has not fallen from heaven. It is a "human and earthly" science by which the "Church draws up its reckoning in accordance with the state of its knowledge at different times." Thus, "Christian dogmatics will always be a thinking, an investigation and an exposition which are relative and liable to error."[18]

What is noteworthy is the high regard Barth has for the dogmatic formulations of the early patristic period of the church, particularly the development of the classical trinitarian and christological dogmas, and the relative authority he is willing to assign to them.[19] "Holy Scripture and the Confessions do not stand on the same level," he says. "We do not have to respect the Bible and tradition with the like reverence and love, not even tradition in its most dignified manifestations." Nevertheless, confessions do have a certain kind of normativity: "If Holy Scripture has binding authority, we cannot say the same of the confessions. Yet there is still a non-binding authority, which must be taken seriously."[20]

For Barth, then, "dogma" is simply the term we give to that which we in the church, and based on the Holy Scripture, consider to be normative or valid in the church's proclamation and life. While this is the proper sphere of systematic or dogmatic theology, to the extent that biblical theology (or a biblical theologian) does this, to that extent it is engaged in what I consider systematic-dogmatic theology.

Biblical Theology: Ollenburger versus Stendahl

In his provocative 1986 essay, "What Krister Stendahl 'Meant'—A Normative Critique of 'Descriptive Biblical Theology,'" Ben C. Ollenburger persuasively points out the logical and semantic confusions inherent in Stendahl's classic program for "biblical theology."[21] In his famous 1962 essay, "Biblical theology, Contemporary," an article which significantly shaped the way biblical theologians understood their task thereafter, Stendahl proposed that biblical theology be limited to *describing* what the biblical texts *meant*, whereas systematic theology be left with the *normative* task of *interpreting* what the texts *mean*.[22] Unfortunately, although Ollenburger hints at how biblical and systematic theology might differ from each other, he deliberately restricts himself to dismantling Stendahl's proposal and does not give any constructive proposal of his own. He succeeds in undermining the usefulness of Stendahl's distinctions concerning the differences between biblical theology and systematic theology.

First, Ollenburger maintains that Stendahl's division between "'the descriptive study of the actual theology and theologies to be found in the Bible [biblical theology]'" and "'any attempt at a normative and systematic theology which could be called 'biblical,'" in the end leaves biblical theologians with little more than historical studies, that is— studying the "*meanings* ascribed to the text by interpreters over history" without any means of adjudicating between alternate meaning statements.[23] For Stendahl, hermeneutics (that is, the attempt to find the normative meaning of a given text) consequently would appear to belong solely to the domain of systematic theologians. Hermeneutical decisions, according to him, do not naturally grow out of the text itself but are made from a "specific theological stance," a stance which presupposes a community of faith and canonicity.

In Ollenburger's eyes Stendahl reduces all biblical studies to two types: historical (the realm of non-normative description) and normative systematic theology. Stendahl, so argues Ollenburger, gives us no clear method of relating the one to the other, of methodologically moving from descriptive to normative work. By inference one can assume here that

Ollenburger thinks of biblical theology itself as being a transitional method or discipline standing halfway between history and systematic theology.

My reading of Stendahl on this point differs from Ollenburger's. I think Stendahl does provide us with what he considers to be a connecting link between descriptive and normative statements, a bridge which grows out of historical description itself. It is this which colours Stendahl's whole view of what systematic theology should be. But I'm getting ahead of myself.

Second, Ollenburger claims that the distinction between "descriptive" and "normative," which lies at the basis of Stendahl's whole argument, entails a logical and semantic confusion. For one thing, there is no reason why something cannot be both descriptive and normative at the same time. It is possible to have "normative description." Dogmatics, in the Barthian sense, for instance, claims to be both descriptive and normative. Further, normativity can mean different things: a) it can mean "to be constrained by a given set of rules or standards," or b) it can refer to "a set of rules by which something else is to be constrained."[24]

Thus biblical theologians, for the most part, consider descriptions governed by the rules of the historical-critical method as normative in trying to understand texts. Stendahl assumes a much too narrow definition of normativity, taking it to refer to those accounts that are considered binding or authoritative by rules other than the historical-critical ones. Stendahl thinks that "[n]ormative interpretations (accounts) of Scripture are to be understood as those interpretations by which we are constrained to order our beliefs and actions as Jews and Christians."[25] Ollenburger allows that "There is nothing at all wrong with this tendency ... it merely shows that descriptions can be offered of different things."

The point Ollenburger wants to make is that "'normative' accounts are no less descriptive than, say strictly historical ones, and, on the other hand, strictly historical accounts are no less normative than these."[26] His agenda appears to be quite a modest one; namely, to demonstrate that even in its use of what is ordinarily considered to be a purely descriptive method—historical-criticism—biblical theology is making normative judgments. This is an extremely significant point, for it means that all biblical-theological work, including even its most descriptive tasks, is coloured by *philosophical* presuppositions.

What is important is not that historical description can also, and often does, make normative judgments (that to make normative descriptions is logically possible); but that historical descriptions necessarily entail normative presuppositions and in doing so have a philosophical (or systematic) side to them. The strength of Stendahl's argument is that he correctly identifies the "normativity" issue with systematics. The problem is that he separates description and normativity into two distinct disciplines. What Ollenburger's essay demonstrates is that biblical theology is much more systematic (or philosophical) than it sometimes likes to think of itself. What Ollenburger unfortunately does not address is in what sense the descriptive-normative components of biblical theology might differ from the descriptive-normative components of systematic theology, or, for that matter, whether there is a rationale for their separate existence as disciplines within Christian theology at all.

Finally, in Ollenburger's opinion Stendahl's problems are simply compounded when he goes on to differentiate biblical and systematic theology further on the basis of the "meant/means" distinction. The problem with this dichotomy becomes evident as soon as one seeks a criterion by which to determine the property of a text (meant) apart from its interpretation (means). As Ollenburger once again convincingly shows, first by way of an inserted discussion of Samuel Terrien's problematic understanding of biblical theology, then by a feat of complicated "symbolic logic," any attempt to describe what a biblical text meant apart from what it means involves one in the logical oddity of asserting that a simple entity T (Text) possesses two exclusive properties, M (Meant) and M' (Means), one capable of being described without reference to the other. The upshot of all of this, for Ollenburger, is that to say something about what a text meant is invariably also to say something about what it means, and that biblical theologians are always engaged in both.

The fundamental problem with Ollenburger's essay, despite its obvious strengths as outlined above, is that it does not tell us when biblical theology (which evidently Ollenburger assumes to be a legitimate discipline in its own right) is doing historical work and when it is engaged in theology. He appears to be drawing an invisible line between "biblical theology as history" and "biblical theology as theology," without ever identifying how they are different. In fact, at some points he seems to imply that Stendahl's distinctions do after all apply to one but not to the other. Here is what Ollenburger says:

> That biblical theologians describe texts (or their theologies) and determine what they meant is of little use in differentiating biblical scholarship from other historical disciplines, or in distinguishing biblical theology from other kinds of biblical scholarship. But this characterization has proven extremely useful in differentiating biblical scholarship from theological inquiry generally, and for preventing biblical scholarship, as a historical discipline, from being given theological responsibilities that historical disciplines cannot legitimately exercise. While it has not always been recognized, it seems to me that this is where Stendahl's real contribution lies.[27]

What is Ollenburger saying here? Is Stendahl's proposal helpful in distinguishing between historical work and theological work or not? What is "theological inquiry generally" as something incompatible with "biblical scholarship, as a historical discipline?" Is biblical theology, then, not engaged in theological inquiry in general? Is this to be left to the systematic theologians? The only sense I can make out of these statements is that Ollenburger is drawing a distinction between "history" and "theology" within the discipline of biblical theology itself.

This becomes a little clearer later in the essay when Ollenburger states that "Stendahl is right to distinguish between history and theology, and to urge us to practice the kind of civility that does not try to mount historical arguments that depend on theological warrants. But to contrast descriptive and normative as he does is to confuse the issue by asking us to contrast the descriptive component of one discipline with the normative component of another."[28]

What appears to be going on here is an attempt by Ollenburger to make of biblical theology a self-sufficient discipline, with both a historical and a theological component, but quite different from and independent of "systematic (or dogmatic) theology." My contention is that theology, when conceived of in this way—that is, as one part of a separate discipline known as biblical theology, the other part being history—tends to be defined primarily in terms of the historical-critical (if not historicist) paradigm. This I think is implicit in Ollenburger's observation that "Stendahl seems to think theology tells us how we *ought* to believe or *what* we ought to believe. In a sense, this is the case—in the same sense that it is true that history tells us how and what we ought to believe, only about different things. In fact, theology describes Christian belief, or Christian faith. It is, we might say, an account of the grounds and content of Christian faith, and there are properly descriptive and properly revisionary such accounts."[29]

Ollenburger may not have intended as much, but he does appear here to be suggesting that history and theology use the same methodology; it is just in their subject matter that they differ. That is, biblical theologians ought to see their normative task as similar to the way history makes normative judgments. The strength of Ollenburger's essay—his main intent—is in showing how the biblical theologian (as also the historian) is never doing purely descriptive work but always also normative work.

I read Stendahl's 1962 essay, as well as his 1984 introduction to a reprint of it ("Meanings") before reading Ollenburger's article. What struck me positively about Stendahl's differentiation between biblical theology and systematic theology, despite its weaknesses, was how seriously he tried to limit the scope of biblical theology in order 1) to preserve the integrity of the biblical texts and that world as distinct (or distant) from our world, and 2) to make room for the legitimate and ongoing task of systematic theology. He was very deliberately counteracting an anti-systematic prejudice and methodological imperialism among biblical theologians. He says so quite explicitly in his 1984 introduction: "In restricting the primary role of the biblical scholar to the descriptive task, it was my intention to liberate the theological enterprise from what I perceived as `the imperialism of biblical scholars' in the field of theology. The more clearly one sees `what is meant,' the more obvious it becomes how impossible it is to live without the ever-ongoing work of systematic theology. Biblical categories stimulate and guide, but do not confine the task of contemporary theology be it in the academy or the churches, in seminars or in sermons."[30] To adapt Kant's famous dictum, Stendahl was limiting biblical theology to make room for systematic theology.[31]

Whether or not he pulled it off is another question. Now, especially after reading Ollenburger's critique, it seems to me that Stendahl's strict distinction between description and prescription (or interpretation), especially when divided according to disciplines, will not work. How ought one, then, to differentiate between biblical theology and systematic theology? I propose that before one can answer this question one must first be clear about the difference between history and theology, both in terms of method and of content.

Contrary to Ollenburger's charge that Stendahl does not provide us with a means of moving from the one discipline (the descriptive) to the other (the interpretive and normative), Stendahl does in fact give us what he considers to be the bridge between the two — namely, *history itself*. Even the biblical theologian can find an organic unity running through the diversity of the biblical texts, that is the unity of "sacred history": that is, the unity "which actually holds the material together in the Bible itself."[32]

Thus "the thrust of an OT theology," in the words of Stendahl, "is ultimately to establish how history is not only a stage upon which God displays his nature through his acts, but that the drama itself is one of history."[33] Thus there is to be found within the historical world of the biblical materials themselves, open to the non-normative methodology of description, that which leads naturally into the world of systematic theology if understood historically. Here is what he says:

> The descriptive approach has led us far beyond a conglomeration of diverse ideas, the development of which we may be able to trace. We are now ushered right into a world of biblical thought that deserves the name 'theology' just as much as do the thoughts of Augustine, Thomas, Calvin,

and Schleiermacher. . . . The relation to the historical record is not any more one where systematic theology takes the raw material of nonsystematic data of revelation and gives to it systematic structure and theological stature. . . . It is a relation between two highly developed types of theology: on the one hand, theologies of history, from which all statements about God, Christ, man, righteousness, and salvation derive their meaning and connotations, in terms of their function within the plan and on the plane of history; and on the other hand, theologies of an ontological sort, where Christianity is understood in terms of the nature of God, Christ, man, and so forth.[34]

It is not entirely clear from this passage whether Stendahl allows for the legitimate role of both types of theology, one historical and the other dogmatic. This is also not quite clear from some of his other statements in the essay. It does seem, however, that Stendahl, while not wanting to reject outrightly the "ontological" approach to theology (or what he calls the "once for all" or "perfect tense" of biblical thought, as the Greeks viewed it), the over-riding paradigm by which he wants to understand theological categories is the "radically historical" one. This historical model, for him, stands in direct contrast to the "radical, ahistorical" model of a Bultmann.

I want to argue that, while theology should take history with great seriousness, as a discipline it needs to retain its own distinct methodology which is quite different than the historical one in the assumptions it makes and the way it deals with its subject matter. While both biblical and systematic theologians are accountable to the historian, in some sense, both, to the degree that they are Christian theologians, make what I call "ontological" assumptions that the historian *as historian* cannot make. There is no doubt that the historian is both descriptive and normative and may even make ontological assumptions. In fact, the historicist gives history itself ontological status. The Christian theologian, however, cannot make history the primary ontological category. For her the underlying unifying assumption, I would argue, is a trinitarian one: the suprahistorical reality of God, God's self-disclosure *in history* (not *as history*), and God's ongoing presence historically in the life of the church and the world.

These are not solely historical assertions. They are also ontological affirmations; that is, they purport to say something *theologically* (a nonliteralistic way of speaking and thinking about things) about the structure(s) of reality. The historian as historian cannot make these assumptions *methodologically* determinative. The oft-perceived conflict between biblical theology and systematic theology is really a conflict within biblical theology itself. It cannot make up its methodological mind between history and theology. In naming itself "theology" it is clearly committed to making assumptions and speaking a language that the historian *qua* historian (including the biblical historian) cannot make or speak. The temptation for the biblical theologian, therefore, is either to disguise her extra-historical theological presuppositions and commitments as descriptive history, or not to be theological at all but positivist in her treatment of the Bible.

There is an important place for the biblical scholar as historian (with all the historical presuppositions peculiar to the historian) in biblical studies. If there is such a discipline as biblical theology, however, in adopting this terminology it *ipso facto* joins the methodological family of theology (of which systematic theology is also a member), and in doing so it acknowledges making theological assumptions about God, Jesus Christ, and history that the biblical scholar as pure historian cannot make. That the biblical theologian's specialized sphere of study is the biblical world itself does not change her underlying theological assumptions, which she has in common with the systematic theologian and with which she approaches the biblical materials.

Systematic Theology: What is its Task?

Biblical theology ought, strictly speaking, not to be conceived of as a separate discipline but rather as a functional specialty within theology in general, of which systematic theology is another specialty.[35] To help us differentiate between these two specialties it may be useful to look at the first few centuries of the Christian church. During the Patristic period two parallel movements were going on side by side, more or less during the same period and basically for the same reasons: one was canonization and the other creedalization.[36] While it is true that socio-political forces were at work in both movements, nevertheless, both were attempts by the early Christian community to establish norms by which to preserve the truth of the apostolic witness; or to put it negatively, to guard against the heretical distortion of that truth. Further, both were theological developments beyond the earliest form and content of the witness. The selection process of canonization, whatever the primary criteria may have been, was in fact a narrowing for normative purposes. The process of creedal formulation was a more intensified narrowing for normative purposes. Creedalization, in short, was doing the same thing canonization was doing, except in summary form.

The importance and strength of the canonical writings over the confessional-creedal statements of the early church was that they preserved within themselves a much greater (although still selective) diversity of historical and theological materials and positions. The importance and strength of the confessional-creedal formulations was that they systematized the multiplicity of images, symbols, experiences and accounts within the canonical writings 1) for catechetical purposes, and 2) for apologetic purposes, both necessary in the missionary task.

Biblical theology and systematic theology are parallel theological activities and are related to each other somewhat like the parallel early church movements of canonization and creedalization were related to each other. Biblical theology takes its cue from the one, systematic theology from the other. Both are essential to the life of the church in the world and both have their particular strengths and dangers for which they need the compensating strengths of the other. Biblical theology has as its specialty the analysis, interpretation, and translation of the multiplicity of the biblical texts,[37] using all the various critical tools and methodologies available to it (historical, literary, archeological, sociological, and philosophical[38]). In its being theological, however, it is more than a scientific methodology and acknowledges a hermeneutical bias: it takes its subject matter to be the Word of God,[39] and, consequently, as having a normative (or canonical) claim over us. Systematic theology has as its speciality the summarizing and schematizing of the essential tenets of the Christian faith for the purpose of helping the church in shaping the beliefs and values of her adherents, mediating between the world of the Bible and her life within contemporary culture, and critically addressing the assumptions and demands of the present age. In this task the concern for doctrinal formulations plays a vital role.

A recent example of the confessional-doctrinal imperative of Christian theology is the Barmen Confession. The point of division amongst Christians in the Third Reich was not solely between those who claimed fidelity to the Scriptures and those who did not. Both the German Christians (at least a significant number of them) and Confessing Christians based their positions on the Scriptures. In fact, some of the best biblical scholars sided with the German Christians. Good biblical scholarship in itself did not guarantee sound theology, let alone right politics.

In this situation members of the Confessing Church found it necessary to summarize the essentials of the Christian truth, as they perceived it, into propositional form, clearly dividing between right belief and wrong belief. A confession or doctrinal statement does in itself also not guarantee good theology or good politics, but it does recognize the need for articulating as clearly as possible what one believes to be true and how this applies in a given situation. The danger in such confessional-dogmatic narrowing, especially when it becomes a tool in the hands of political power, is that inevitably other legitimate points of view are excluded. This danger does not cancel out, however, the need for or legitimacy of such doctrinal summarizing; it simply means that all such systematization and narrowing must be recognized for what it is: a finite human activity and language subject to error.

Confessional-doctrinal thinking is important to systematic theology not exclusively for its own sake but for three reasons: 1) to inculcate certain beliefs and values in the actual and potential adherents of the Christian church (catechesis); 2) to mediate between the world of the Bible and the world of the church within contemporary culture; and 3) to address critically the assumptions and demands of contemporary culture. I have spoken to the first earlier in this paper. Let me conclude with a few observations concerning the second and third. I have in another context argued that doctrines are really mediating principles or "middle axioms" which bridge the world of the Scriptures and the contemporary situation, and are useful in dealing with new situations and new issues as they arise for the church.[40]

In a recent *Mennonite Reporter* article I have indicated how this might work when dealing from theological perspective with a specific issue like homosexuality.[41] Although I take biblical theology to be interested in mediation as well (mediation as translation),[42] the kind of mediation that systematic theology is compelled and ready to undertake is more radical than that of biblical theology. Systematic theology is prepared to move beyond the biblical texts quite deliberately and consciously in attempting to address contemporary issues which the biblical text itself does not address adequately. But it does this in a way continuous with or growing out naturally from the biblical materials. Its paradigm is the way the early ecumenical creeds, in their addressing of the trinitarian and christological issues, moved from within and yet beyond the biblical writings. In other words, systematic theology does not simply translate, it mediates; but it does this not through free association or unrestrained individual imagination. It follows certain formal guidelines, known as doctrines, which have their foundation in the Scriptures and have received their most universal articulation in the early ecumenical creeds. *There is, thus, a kind of classical balance between formal restraint and creative imagination in the work of systematic theology.*

The danger of such mediation is that one capitulates to the dominant assumptions of an age. It is incumbent upon biblical theology to provide a bulwark against a simple accommodation of the church's foundational writings to contemporary culture. Biblical theology's primary focus as a specialty is the world of Scripture and its interest in the language, assumptions, methodologies, and insights of contemporary culture is primarily directed toward the illumination of the world of the Bible and the translation of that world into contemporary language. Thus biblical theology guards jealously the distance between the biblical world and the contemporary world. The main focus of systematic theology is the contemporary situation; that is, the illumination of the church's life within contemporary culture from a Christian perspective. In this it is uniquely torn between what might be called a "prophetic-critical no" and a "priestly sacramental yes" to the assumptions of the modern age.[43]

The triumph of technical-analytical reason in modern technology, with its accompanying view of reality, nature, and history has its own metaphysic and ontology, which in my view is difficult to reconcile with classical Christianity and God as transcendent creator to whom human beings are accountable.[44] The privatization of religion that comes with the victory of a therapeutic understanding of human nature in modern post-communal culture, as manifested in the "cult of self-worship," may be seen as a direct counterpart to the dominance of modern technique, and equally as irreconcilable with biblical Christianity.[45] These are just two examples of the assumptions of the modern age which suggest that we are becoming a much more globally homogeneous culture than a superficial analysis of modern diversity and pluralism would lead us to believe. It is these assumptions which need critical analysis and addressing by systematic theologians in the light of the Christian *kerygma*.

One of the strengths of George Lindbeck's "cultural-linguistic" approach to religion and "rule theory" view of doctrine is the importance it places on foundational texts and "intratextual theology." In this model believers conform their experience to the Bible rather than the other way around. "Intratextual theology," he says, "redescribes reality within the scriptural framework rather than translating Scripture into extrascriptural categories. It is the text, so to speak, which absorbs the world, rather than the world the text."[46] Or to put it in other words, "To become a Christian involves [not so much making a decision as] learning the story of Israel and of Jesus well enough to interpret and experience oneself and one's world in its terms."[47] The danger, according to Lindbeck, has always been that extrabiblical materials have become the framework for biblical interpretation. This was the case in rationalism, pietism, and historical criticism in which the biblical text became not a lens through which one viewed the world but an object of study through the lens of the external world.

The irony is that Lindbeck's whole model grows out of a contemporary agenda: ecumenism. Here is what he says: "Although the focus of this book is on intra-Christian theological and ecumenical issues, the theory of religion and religious doctrine that it proposes is not specifically ecumenical, nor Christian, nor theological. It rather derives from philosophical and social-scientific approaches; and yet, so I shall argue, it has advantages, not only for the non-theological study of religion but also for Christian—and perhaps also non-Christian—ecumenical and theological purposes."[48] His "cultural-linguistic" model is in some ways, I would suggest, more faithful to recent linguistic theories à la Noam Chomsky and Ludwig Wittgenstein than it is to traditional understandings of Christian theology or doctrine. This is most clearly evident in his attempt to address the thorny issue of truth claims. According to Lindbeck, "a religious utterance, one might say, acquires the propositional truth of ontological correspondence only insofar as it is a performance, an act or deed, which helps create that correspondence."[49] Further, "just as grammar by itself affirms nothing either true or false regarding the world in which language is used, but only about language, so theology and doctrine, to the extent that they are second-order activities, assert nothing true or false about God and his relation to creatures, but only speak about such assertions."[50]

This touches upon the fundamental problem with Lindbeck's model. How does one ultimately arbitrate between competing cultural-linguistic systems? It is well and good that as Christians we ought to shape our experience in accordance with the biblical stories and not in terms of propositional truth claims. I think Lindbeck is right to criticize wooden propositionalism with its particular correspondence theory of truth, although he fails adequately to differentiate between modern propositionalism and classical creedal thinking. The question remains: why one story over another, why one semiotic system over another?

For Lindbeck, despite his admirable efforts to do so, there is ultimately no way of answering this question because all criteria are internal to a particular cultural-linguistic framework. In the end, he is caught in hopeless cultural-linguistic relativism, a fate that haunts all of us. Where in Lindbeck's system is there the possibility of a radical breaking in from the outside. Where is the basis for missions and conversion? It seems to me that in an age no longer defined by a variety of traditional cultural-linguistic systems but by one dominant technological cultural-linguistic system, Lindbeck's proposal does not offer the radical critique of contemporary culture that is demanded from the systematic theologian.

The primary focus of systematic theology is the church within contemporary culture, and its task the summarizing of the tradition (particularly its biblical moment) for the purpose a) of catechesis, and b) of mediation. In order for it to be able to do this comprehensively, however, it must understand and address the particular contemporary culture within which it finds itself: its language, art, philosophy, religions, politics, economics, and so on. Only as it listens to and understands these bearers of culture can it determine what is authentic and positive (supportive of the created order) and what is negative (destructive of that order) within contemporary culture in the light of the Christian revelation.

Where Lindbeck's proposal is useful is in emphasizing the particular cultural-linguistic conditionedness of all our religious and theological feeling, thinking, and acting. It is not clear to me, however, whether his model allows for the radical breaking in, shattering, and judging of a particular cultural-linguistic context, or contemporary technological culture as a whole, from the outside.

Seen purely from a "profane" perspective the crises of modern and postmodern culture—the injustices perpetrated by both western capitalist and eastern communist-socialist countries on minority groups; the grave moral perils arising out of medical advances and biogenetic experimentation; the objectification and destruction of nature brought about by the *hubris* of modern technology; the growing gap between rich and poor both within our own societies and between first, second, and third worlds; the nuclear threat; not to mention the unimaginable atrocities of the past century—would appear to call for more universal, transcultural, and translinguistic answers than Lindbeck's model offers.

Seen from the Christian perspective, the underlying affirmations imbedded in the church's confessions, doctrines, creeds, and dogmas are more than rules intrinsic to a language game. They assert something fundamental (call it ontological, metaphysical, whatever you like) about God as transcendent reality, and God as freely entering into and acting within history (paradigmatically in Jesus Christ). They point toward God as ultimate author of human dignity and the dignity of the created order as a whole.

These fundamental affirmations by the Christian church are conditioned but not exhausted by a cultural-linguistic-semiotic view of religion and theology. It is at the point of this claim— that Jesus Christ and the biblical witness to Jesus Christ is not simply one among a number of stories, not simply our story, but *the story*, the Word of God to us— that biblical theology and systematic theology become Christian theology.

TWENTY-THREE

God as Triune*

God as Triune is not one doctrine among many, it is the foundational doctrine of all other teachings of the Christian church. It is the doctrine which distinguished the Christian doctrine of God from the polytheism of the Greco-Roman pantheon and qualified (in a nuanced way) the Hebraic view of God. Although monotheistic, it is not Jewish monotheism pure and simple—it developed further the plurality within the one divinity hinted at but not defined in the Hebrew Scriptures, without fragmenting into polytheistic religion. It is a doctrine which gradually evolved as a distinctive Christian understanding of God in the encounter between Hebraic and Greco-Roman cultures in the classical period.

In the essay below, written for The Mennonite Encyclopedia, vol. 5, in 1990,[1] I trace the historical emergence of the Christian doctrine of God, with a special interest in the Anabaptist and Mennonite understanding of God. I show how, with a few exceptions, the sixteenth-century Anabaptists accepted the classical trinitarian and christological formulations. There were minority Socinian (unitarian) deviations from Nicea and Melchiorite (docetic) departures from Chalcedon, but the mainline position was true to historic Christianity. What

---

*Originally published as "God (Trinity), Doctrine of," *The Mennonite Encyclopedia*, vol. 5 (Scottdale, PA: Herald Press, 1990), 342-48. For notes on the text see the Notes section below.

Anabaptists did bring to classical orthodox Christianity was a heightened ethical consciousness that appeared to be missing in the ancient creeds.

My challenge to Mennonites therefore is not, as some contemporary theologians are suggesting, to do an end run around the ancient ecumenical Credo and plead a special non-trinitarian reading of the biblical text alleging greater fidelity to the gospel. Rather, my concern is to situate the Mennonite ethical agenda squarely within the trinitarian and christological claims of historic Christianity. I would now make my case even more strongly than when I first wrote the article below. The Trinity is not only the framework for ethics but is the essential foundation or ground of all our ethical concerns. Further, I would concur with Wolfhart Pannenberg, when he argues that not the economic Trinity (trinitarian actions outward in relation to creation) alone but the immanent Trinity (intratrinitarian relations between Father, Son, and Spirit) is the essential theological prerequisite for our understanding of God's way with the world and our responsibility within that world.[2] It is the self-sufficient immanent Trinity which guards the transcendence of God in relation to the created order. My problem with Pannenberg is that he appears at times to collapse the immanent Trinity into the economic Trinity by historicizing the former.

If John R. Loeschen's interpretation of Menno's trinitarian theology is right—that Menno stresses not the "transcendent Trinity" but the Trinity of Christ's nature, Word and Spirit—I would take issue with Menno's theology at this point. The economic Trinity alone is not an adequate grounding for ethics. However, I would first have to be persuaded by Loeschen's thesis. I remind the reader that the essay below was written for a specific venue and is not meant to be a balanced, systematic treatment of the Christian doctrine of God.

◆ ◆ ◆

Introduction

The doctrine of God is central to Christian theology. The term *theology* in the broad sense means the study of God and is not restricted to Christianity. Usually Christian theology is understood more specifically, however, to include reflection on the nature of God, God's self-disclosure in creation and especially in Christ as witnessed to by the Scriptures, God's ongoing interaction with the world through the Holy Spirit, and the final consummation of God's purpose beyond time. It is quite appropriate therefore to say that Christian theology begins and ends with the doctrine of God.

A distinction needs to be drawn between a "doctrine" of God and a "concept" of God. The term *doctrine* denotes a "teaching" (Latin: *doctrina*) that is handed down by the church in accordance with the Scriptures. The term *concept* is more individualistic and has a more cognitive, philosophical connotation. It is noteworthy that as one moves into the modern period one tends also to talk about God more in terms of concepts than doctrines. This shift is reflected in this article's concluding discussion of three theologians' notions of God.

For much of modern theology, characterized by the anthropocentric turn that came with the eighteenth-century Enlightenment, the notion of God has become the primary issue or problem. In contemporary life and thought, be it psychological, sociological, political, philosophical, literary, or theological, a recognition of the transcendent reality of God can no longer be taken for granted. This has led many Christian theologians, including Mennonite thinkers, to find ways of reconceiving the concept of God to make it more comprehensible for moderns. We will come back to the modern view of God as a problem and various attempts at reinterpreting this doctrine for today.

Here we want merely to say that until the modern age there was no general agnosticism or rejection of the "existence" of God. The Bible itself simply assumed the reality of God (Exod. 3:14: God says to Moses, "I am who I am") and the biblical authors were not *explicitly* preoccupied with metaphysical or philosophical speculation about the nature of God. Their primary concern was with God's self-revelation and historical action in the lives of people and the appropriate human response.

Implicitly, however, the Bible already raises theological and philosophical issues about who God is and how God can be known that set the agenda for a development of a doctrine of God in the post-biblical period. In the Old Testament, for example, there is the problem of evil which confronts Job and the fact that God allows the righteous to suffer. How can God be good if God brings about or tolerates such seeming injustice? Further, a variety of anthropomorphic images and metaphors, both masculine and feminine, used in Old Testament references to the divine stimulate the theological imagination to contemplate more fully the nature and attributes of God.

While both the Old and New Testaments are thoroughly monotheistic, new experiences of the acts of God in the New Testament era raise for early Jewish-Christians and Gentile-Christians much more sharply the issue of the nature of God. The early church's experience of salvation in Christ and divine power through the Holy Spirit poses the problem of how to reconcile these two phenomena with an unequivocal belief in the one God of the Old Testament.

Patristic and Medieval Period

During the first five centuries after Christ these issues were hotly debated by the Christian church around the question of the Trinity (Nicea, 325; and Constantinople, 380) and Christology (Chalcedon, 451); the former dealing primarily with the relation of Christ to the Father, and the latter with the relation of the divine and the human in the person of Christ himself.

The trinitarian controversy is particularly important for us here and has ongoing relevance for any contemporary understanding of God. It revolved around two intrinsically related and archetypal concerns: the nature of God within Himself and the nature of God for us. The first has been referred to as the *immanent trinity* (the threefold inner nature and relations of God as Father, Son, and Spirit), the second as the *economic trinity* (God's threefold mode of being for us— as transcendent mystery above us, as historically disclosed to us in Jesus Christ, and immanently present in us and the world through the Holy Spirit).

Unfortunately, we cannot here take the time to discuss at greater length the biblical concept of God nor these highly significant debates of the Patristic period. It is important, however, to recognize that what occurred already within the Scriptures and continued during the post-biblical period was a *development of the doctrine of God* that has shaped all later Christian thinking in this regard, including our own.

Medieval theology contributed to this development in a number of important ways. Based particularly on passages like Romans 1:18-21 and 2:14ff, which suggest that God in some sense reveals God's self to believers and non-believers alike, a distinction was drawn between what is naturally knowable about God by everyone (sometimes referred to as natural revelation), and what can be known only by special revelation, like the mystery of the Trinity and the incarnation.

Thus, in the Platonic-Augustinian tradition a pre-rational awareness of the reality of God is the condition for the very possibility of the moral and spiritual life. In the Aristotelian-Thomistic tradition the natural knowledge of God takes a more rational form, reflected in the five arguments for the existence of God, although for Aquinas this rational knowledge was also closely linked to morality and spirituality.[3]

There was another stream of medieval theology concerning God which was especially important for certain segments of sixteenth-century Anabaptism: the *unio mystica* traditions of Meister Eckhardt, John Tauler and the *Theologia Deutsch*. While there were differences between the various mystical traditions on how the union between the divine and the human takes place, there was a common emphasis on the immanence of God, and the capacity of human beings for sharing a common nature with God.[4]

Reformation and Anabaptists

The indebtedness of the Reformers to these various Medieval streams concerning the doctrine of God is a highly complex and even controversial topic and cannot be summarized here without doing injustice to the thinkers involved. In general, however, it can be fairly said that the major Reformers, with their emphasis on human sinfulness and the need for a personal experience of justification through faith, tended to be suspicious of the more rationalistic, scholastic natural law tradition as well as the *unio mystica*. Both Luther and Calvin stressed the transcendent sovereignty of God and the accompanying doctrines of grace and predestination, and tended to accentuate the gulf between the human and the divine. The Anabaptists, on the other hand, rejected predestination (although they did espouse a notion of election) in favour of free will and consequently were less inclined in their theology to emphasize the unbridgeable separation between God and humanity.

In our attempt to understand sixteenth-century Anabaptist notions of God it is critical, first of all, to note that what distinguished Anabaptism from its Reformation counterparts—the Catholic, Lutheran, Reformed, and Anglican traditions—was the extent of its theological and sociological diversity. It was not one homogeneous mass but a collection of diverse movements spread throughout Europe, defined by local differences which affected their theology. Consequently, one cannot assume that there was one Anabaptist doctrine of God. Here as in other theological doctrines there was a dynamic plurality of views, cross-fertilizing each other and in the process of evolution, especially during the early period.

Despite this heterogeneity, it is remarkable how similar most of the early Anabaptists were in their concern for practical Christian living as an outgrowth of theological orthodoxy (orthodoxy defined as fidelity to the traditional teachings of the church concerning christology and the Trinity). It was not their formal acceptance of the church's historic creed in itself that is interesting but the way the formal confession of a triune God received content and functioned in their theology.

Both Robert Friedmann and John C. Wenger have argued strongly that, while the weight of their concerns was not with doctrine but with discipleship, on the whole sixteenth-century Anabaptists were orthodox in their fundamental beliefs, accepting the Apostolic creed, Nicene trinitarianism, and Chalcedon christology with few exceptions. Friedmann especially has taken care to defend the Anabaptists against the thesis that their theology tended toward Socinian rationalism and anti-trinitarianism and thus could be seen as a source for modern Unitarianism.[5]

Wenger's and Friedmann's claim that the Anabaptists were orthodox in their doctrine of God, but more faithful than other Protestant groups in their obedience to the ethical imperatives of Scripture, contains elements of truth. One needs, however, to guard against defining Anabaptism too narrowly and thus passing over the rich theological diversity that is part of the tradition. While it is true that on the whole the majority of early documents manifest a fidelity to the articles of the Apostles' Creed, for example, there is in much early Anabaptism a rather sophisticated reappropriation and reinterpretation of the theological tradition.

Although there was a formal acceptance of the creedal affirmations, Anabaptists' preoccupation with the morally regenerated life was not simply an addition to the other doctrines but gave these doctrines, particularly the doctrine of God, a new flavour. The trinitarian nature of God, while fully accepted by most of the Anabaptists, received a new and distinctive interpretation. It was for them no abstract speculative doctrine of God but the necessary theological framework for ethics, as we shall see below. This is much more than simply accepting traditional orthodoxy as espoused by the mainline traditions and adding ethical elements. We need only turn to individual and corporate writings and confessions of the sixteenth century to discover this close link between the primary Anabaptist concern for a regenerated life and the doctrine of God.

We will look at three varieties: 1) the South German-Austrian Anabaptism of Hans Denck and Hans Hut; 2) the Hutterian Anabaptism of Peter Riedemann; and 3) the North German-Dutch Anabaptism of Menno Simons. (The Swiss Schleitheim Confession of 1527, with its seven articles—all concerned with practical matters of Christian life and distinctiveness—is perhaps the least doctrinally oriented. Even here, however, the cover letter begins with a three-fold invocation of Father, Christ Jesus, and Spirit).

1. While there were strong mystical elements in many early Anabaptists, it was the South German-Austrian stream, directly influenced by the cross-mysticism of the revolutionary Thomas Müntzer, that most clearly reflected the themes of the *unio mystica* tradition alluded to above: no radical distinction between the natural and the supernatural, the immanence of God within the human soul, the potential capacity of human beings to participate in divine nature, the close identification of justification and sanctification as a single process of gradual deification.[6]

There was in this branch of Anabaptism a strong link between the immanence of God (rebirth interpreted as the birth of the son within the human soul), deification (participation of human nature in divine nature), and moral-ethical perfection (a gradual process of sanctification). This mystically oriented doctrine of God was in its early phase not sectarian or quietistic but, as illustrated by Müntzer himself, could be interestingly combined within an apocalyptic ideology directed at social-political transformation and even revolution.[7]

2. The Hutterian Anabaptism of Austria and Moravia was a later phase of South German-Austrian Anabaptism and reflects a more separatist and internally disciplined spirit, achieved primarily through an imposed communitarian uniformity. As in its earlier phase the doctrine of God was explicated primarily in terms of its moral and ethical implications for human behavior but was now more directly framed in terms of the concern for moral perfection within a separate community where all things were to be held in common.

The clearest example of this is Peter Riedeman's *Account of Our Religion, Doctrine and Faith* (1545).[8] The first part of the book is devoted to a theological commentary on the twelve essentials of the Apostolic Creed with the Anabaptist-Hutterite ethical concerns introduced right into the context of the various classical doctrines. What is remarkable is how each of these doctrines immediately receives practical application.

To confess the first article of the creed—that God is almighty Father, creator of heaven and earth—is itself a moral act for "every sinner who remaineth and continueth in sin, and yet nameth God father, speaketh what is not true. . . ." Further, the whole purpose of confessing the second and third article of the creed—belief in Jesus Christ as the only begotten son of God, and the Holy Spirit as proceeding from the Father and the Son (the phrase "and the son" [*Filioque*] was inserted into the creed at the Council of Toledo in 589 and is accepted here without question)—is to acknowledge that through them we are "grafted . . . into the divine character and nature." This phrase or various versions of it, like the "participation in the nature of Christ (or God)," appears repeatedly in many of the Anabaptist writers and suggests, as we have already seen, the deification of human nature in a way quite foreign to Luther and Calvin.

Concern for genuine moral regeneration is present in the *Account* from the start, and the Hutterite commitment to Christian communalism is linked to the very immanent plurality within God Himself: "Community, however, is naught else than that those who have fellowship have all things in common together, none having aught for himself, but each having all things with the others, even as the Father hath nothing for himself, but all that he hath, he hath with the Son, and again, the Son hath nothing for himself, but all that he hath, he hath with the Father and all who have fellowship with him."[9]

3. In our third representative Anabaptist group—North German-Dutch Anabaptism—we find one of the most explicit and straightforward treatments of the doctrine of God in Menno's "A Solemn Confession of the Triune, Eternal, and True God, Father, Son, and Holy Spirit" (1550), written in defence of the orthodoxy of his movement. It is a work intended to counteract the views of Adam Pastor, an Anabaptist bishop who had come to deny the full deity of Christ and was consequently excommunicated by Menno Simons and Dirk Philips, the very ones who had earlier ordained him.

While Menno remains simple, biblical, and non-philosophical in his language, his expression of trinitarian orthodoxy is remarkably classical in outline. God (the Father) is Spirit, the "one and only eternal, omnipotent, incomprehensible, invisible, ineffable, and indescribable God . . . not physical and comprehensible but spiritual and incomprehensible." Jesus Christ is not a literal Word but "the eternal, wise, Almighty, holy, true, living, and incomprehensible Word, which in the beginning was with God, and was God, by whom all things were made . . . ."

This Christ "did in the fullness of time become, according to the unchangeable purpose and faithful promise of the Father, a true, visible, suffering, hungry, thirsty, and mortal man in Mary, the pure virgin, through the operation and overshadowing of the Holy Spirit, and so was born of her." In like fashion, Menno confesses the Holy Ghost to be "divine with His divine attributes, proceeding from the Father through the Son, although He ever remains with God and in God, and is never separated from the being of the Father and the Son."[10]

In the words of Menno, "these three names, activities, and powers, namely, the Father, the Son, and the Holy Ghost (which the fathers called three persons, by which they meant the three, true, divine beings) are one incomprehensible, indescribable, Almighty, holy, only, eternal, and sovereign God. . . . And although they are three, yet in deity, will, power, and works they are one, and can no more be separated from each other than the sun, brightness, and warmth. For the one cannot exist without the other."[11]

What gives Menno's orthodox-sounding language its distinctive quality, as it does with the other Anabaptists, is his concern not so much for doctrinal orthodoxy in its own right as for the ethical function of the doctrine of God. John R. Loeschen gives a persuasive analysis of precisely this characteristic in his fine treatment of various Reformation views of the Trinity, church and ethics, in his *The Divine Community*.

Loeschen's thesis is "that the Christian understanding of the church, as hence of ethics, depends upon prior assumptions about God in his trinitarian functions."[12] While all the Reformers were sensitive to the charge of doctrinal novelty, and argued that theirs was a genuine restoration of ancient views, what emerged were in fact new interpretations of Christ and the Trinity. The Holy Spirit received greater emphasis and the Trinity was valued more for its practical implications (the economic Trinity) than for its own sake (the transcendent or immanent Trinity).

This is particularly the case with Menno, who more than Luther or Calvin understood the classical doctrine of the Trinity christologically. His numerous references to the Holy Spirit, for instance, are directly associated with the "Spirit of Christ."[13] His trinitarian theology is derived not from a "transcendental Trinity" but from the immanent trinity of Christ's nature, Word, and Spirit."[14]

While Menno's writings are full of biblical imagery pointing to the transcendence of God, his thought patterns are not explicitly ontological, metaphysical, or philosophical but historical and narrative. In the words of Loeschen, "Simons' effective trinity is an actual historical trinity of Christ's Word, Spirit and life, and not the transcendental, philosophical Trinity of Father, Logos, and Holy Spirit."[15]

Once again with Menno as with the other Anabaptists we see how doctrinal theological language, including trinitarian language, is linked to moral-ethical concerns. Trinitarian theology is important not for its own sake but as a necessary framework for the regenerated life. Christ and more particularly, the Spirit of Christ, is that which unites the Christian with the nature and character of God. This participation in the character of Christ and through him in the very nature of God is one of Menno's most repeated themes; a form of sanctification (or even deification) which can occur only in the context of the visible believing community: the church. Menno's paradigm for this community is not a static one but the dynamic and evolving apostolic church which began at Pentecost and continued through the Patristic period, receiving important theological definition in the early creeds, including that of Nicea.[16]

Mennonites, Sixteenth to Twentieth Centuries

Hans-Jürgen Goertz has recently emphasized the discontinuity between sixteenth-century Anabaptist confessions, which were primarily individual confessions of faith arising out of widely different situations, and later seventeenth-century Mennonite confessions which had an ecclesiastical doctrinal character functioning more like mainline Reformation confessional statements. According to Goertz,[17] the Anabaptists saw the whole of life as a confession, and rejected what they perceived as the intellectualization and codification of faith by the other Reformers; for them verbal and lived confession was more important than fixed statements of belief. When they did come up with statements of orthodoxy it was usually in response to charges of heresy made against them.

This, Goertz maintains, changed during the seventeenth century with the conservative reaction to the onset of modernity, and reflects a narrowing of the gap between Mennonites and the Reformed state church. In effect, what developed during this Protestant scholastic period was an authoritarian Mennonite orthodoxy, expressed in doctrinal statements like the 1632 Dordrecht confession and the many subsequent confessions, for the purpose of uniting various factions around normative ecclesiastical formulations of belief and thereby guarding against free-thinking subjectivism and nonconformity.

We cannot here trace the rather complex development of doctrine from early Anabaptist origins to later Mennonite church confessions, nor give a thorough analysis of the many individual church confessions up to the present. What we want to do is make a few observations about the doctrine of God as articulated in these Mennonite confessional statements between the sixteenth and twentieth centuries.

First, what is remarkable is the multiplicity of confessions in a tradition that is supposedly non-creedal in orientation.[18] Ironically, Mennonites have throughout their history probably produced more confessions and catechetical statements than any other group. Noteworthy in this regard is the fact both of diversity of confession (arising out of particular social, historical, and religious contexts) and unity, reflecting the heterogeneity and homogeneity of their origins. While there are significant differences between the General Conference, Mennonite Church, Mennonite Brethren, and other independent confessions, there are some remarkable common elements, in particular the fourfold axis around which most of the confessions are structured: creator, Christ, church, and consummation, with a particularly weighty emphasis on the life of the church and mission. Further, virtually every confession begins with an article on God, often an extended article or series of articles on the Trinity and revelation.

Second, Mennonite confessions of the seventeenth century reflect a church that is beginning to consolidate its theology, Christology, ecclesiology, and eschatology as a way of establishing a separate "sectarian" identity. With this comes a greater concern for spelling out in a *systematic* and *orderly* fashion the doctrine of a triune God and placing it in the proper sequence in a litany of doctrines. In most cases the chronology of these doctrines parallels the classical confessional and creedal tradition. While some of the confessions are more metaphysically oriented than others, there is a common concern to remain faithful to biblical language as much as possible.

Third, what becomes evident when one studies these confessions is the centrality of ethics and the Christian life (reflected in the weight given to ecclesiology and mission). The doctrine of God is carefully articulated at the beginning not for its own sake but as the starting point for the more practically oriented articles that follow, including "free will, conversion, footwashing, church discipline, Christian life and non-conformity, integrity and oaths, non-resistance and revenge, the Christian and the state."[19] In this ethical orientation the later Mennonites manifest a continuity with their early Anabaptist ancestry despite the discontinuities that historians like Goertz legitimately point out. With the systematization of their various beliefs, including the doctrine of God, there is the increasing danger of intellectualizing faith, and of separating ethics into sectarian dogmas held on to rigidly as a means of preserving static denominational purity.

One final observation may be in order before we leave this cursory summary of Mennonite theology before the twentieth century. It would be erroneous to leave the impression that there was a uniform adherence to theological orthodoxy amongst Mennonites in the post-Reformation period. Friedmann, who takes great pains to point out the orthodox trinitarianism of early Anabaptists and later Swiss and Hutterian Mennonites, does allow that early on there was a softening of confessional orthodoxy among some European Mennonites, particularly in the Netherlands where certain "Dutch Mennonites became rather imbued with the spirit of Socinian (unitarian) rationalism" beginning in the second half of the seventeenth century.[20]

Contemporary Mennonite Theology

Ever since the eighteenth-century Enlightenment the concept of God has become a dominant preoccupation for much of Christian theology. As the relation of grace to nature (or revelation to reason) was a primary theological issue for Medieval theology, justification and salvation for Reformation theology, and confessional orthodoxy for seventeenth-century Scholastic theology, so the very possibility of belief in a benevolent transcendent reality (God) has become *the* problem for nineteenth- and twentieth-century theology.

Within modern theology itself there has been a shift. The earlier period, beginning with the Copernican revolution in philosophy associated with Immanuel Kant, saw the problem of God mostly in terms of epistemology: how can finite sentient beings have any knowledge of supra-empirical reality? Kant has been immensely influential for modern theology, and his conclusion that we cannot have rational knowledge of God but that God remains a necessary postulate for ethics continues to surface in various ways in contemporary theology, including certain forms of political and liberation theology.

In the twentieth and twenty-first centuries, marked by the novel experience of total wars, unimaginable atrocities, global environmental crises, growing disparity between the rich and the poor, the spectre of a totally administered society, and the threat of the nuclear self-destruction of the human species, attention has shifted away from epistemological concerns to the question of transcendence and theodicy (the problem of good and evil).

Is it possible to experience a transcendent reality in our technological age and, if so, how might that be expressed theologically and liturgically? Is it possible to believe in an all-loving and all-powerful God in the face of unmitigated evil and the suffering and annihilation of innocent victims throughout history? How might such a God be understood, so as to preserve a belief both in God's providential sovereignty and control over the course of creation *and* the historical freedom of human beings to participate actively in the shaping of their own destiny?

One of the characteristics of contemporary theology is the diversity of answers given to these pressing questions concerning God. Whereas until recently, Mennonites did little explicit systematic theological thinking in general, let alone systematic reflection about the nature of God (other than that of a few isolated individuals here and there, and the confessional and catechetical statements as we have seen above), they now contribute significantly to and reflect the diversity of views in contemporary theological discourse. We can here offer only a brief sampling of this growing literature. We choose three systematic theologies to illustrate three different twentieth-century concepts of God.

Early in the twentieth century there was the influential (for Mennonites) systematic work of Daniel Kauffman, who devoted much of his time to articulating the fundamentals of the Christian faith, which he preferred to call *Bible doctrines*. Deeply concerned about the direction of the modern Mennonite church, his theology reflects both the influence of Fundamentalism in its fight against modernism (particularly the theory of evolution) and historic Mennonite concerns such as non-conformity to the world and non-resistance. In his major work, *Doctrines of the Bible*,[21] his lengthy treatment of the doctrine of God resembles both in order and in content the scholastic method of seventeenth-century Protestantism, so evident in the leading Fundamentalist theologians of his time. He even devotes considerable space to enumerating the various proofs for the existence of God.

Kauffman sought to present biblical doctrines as a bulwark against what he called the "critical age of liberalistic and modernistic tendencies" that he felt distorted modern theology. His theological orientation, while largely eclipsed by the so-called "Recovery of the Anabaptist vision" school of thought, still attracts significant elements of the Mennonite population.

The more recent work of another systematic theologian, Gordon D. Kaufman, represents the other end of the twentieth-century theological spectrum, someone for whom the issues raised by modern thought and life become the determinative factors in the theological enterprise. Gordon

Kaufman has without a doubt given more attention to the "problem of God" (in both its epistemological and in moral-ethical dimensions) than any other Mennonite thinker.[22] Demonstrating a broad understanding of contemporary philosophical and social thought, he has sought in his many writings to reinterpret traditional doctrines, especially the doctrine of God, from a post-Kantian historicist (non-transcendent) perspective.

His earlier writings, particularly his *Systematic Theology: A Historicist Perspective*,[23] attempts to bridge traditional trinitarian language about God and biblical revelation with modern philosophical theories of knowledge, and historical and social-scientific views of human development. Becoming increasingly more radical in his dissatisfaction with the theological formulations of the past in his later writings, however, he argues that traditional concepts of God as unchanging and sovereign are no longer adequate to our nuclear age.[24] It is imperative that we reconstruct imaginatively our doctrine of God to reflect our novel freedom as human beings to change fundamentally and even destroy totally our global environment, and to assume fully our responsibility not to do so.[25]

The most recent attempt to write a full-length systematic theology from a "Believers Church" perspective but with a strong ecumenical orientation is Thomas Finger's two volume *Christian Theology: An Eschatological Perspective.*[26] Finger's theology can be seen as a middle position between Kauffman and Kaufman; it takes contemporary experience seriously while at the same time emphasizing the importance of God's sovereign initiative and the once-and-for-all nature of divine revelation. What is unique about Finger's approach is that he reverses the usual ordering of Christian doctrines. He begins not with the doctrine of God but concentrates in his first volume on the eschatological themes of the New Testament *kerygma*, including the resurrection, judgment, heaven and hell, the nature and work of Christ, and ends his system with a consideration of the nature of God.

This method is consciously intended by Finger to highlight first God's activity in the world, then from the historical data of the church's experiences rather than through metaphysical speculation to infer certain attributes about divine reality itself. Particularly significant is the weight Finger places on a doctrine that has, he admits, received little systematic treatment within the Believers Church tradition: the trinitarian nature of God. Here also, as with the other doctrines, Finger starts "from below"; that is, he develops a case for both the dynamic diversity and unity within the Godhead from a consideration of the data of the human experience of divine reality and need for community. In this way he manages creatively to accentuate both the transcendence and immanence of God.

These are only three examples of contemporary Mennonites systematically thinking about the doctrine of God. One need only turn to the pages of *The Conrad Grebel Review* in its first six years of publication (1983-1988) to discover the plethora of views concerning God within the Mennonite community. These positions range all the way from a defence of classical creedal trinitarianism[27] to a God perceived in terms of modern process theology,[28] and even a strident Arian anti-trinitarianism.[29] A major new and creative impetus for reconceptualizing the doctrine of God has come from feminist theologians like Gayle Gerber Koontz who challenge the almost exclusively male-dominated thinking of God as Father.[30]

Whether a synthesis of these various theological positions that are now vying with each other for prominence within the Mennonite communion is possible or even desirable remains to be seen.[31] The theological diversity that is reflected in the historical Mennonite confessions and that is evident in the present is in line not only with the pluralism in contemporary Christian theology in general but with the heterogeneity of the early Anabaptist movement itself. It seems clear, however, that historically Mennonites on the whole espoused a high, trinitarian view of God, a doctrine that is in perpetual need of translation and interpretation but, nevertheless, one that continues to have relevance for every age.

More important, however, is the urgency with which the modern challenges in the field of technology, environmental concerns, medical ethics, the nuclear threat, and the growing concern for political and economic justice call for a renewed sense of God as transcendent mystery and human beings as accountable stewards of the world. The common Anabaptist concern for a doctrine of God that is intrinsically related to a morally and ethically regenerated life in the world would appear to be a good theological starting point for facing the challenges of the postmodern age.

This heightened moral-ethical consciousness is the particular contribution that the Anabaptist and Mennonite traditions can make to the ecumenical discussion of the doctrine of God. Implicit in this our historic strength is, however, a danger: that of reducing the teaching concerning God to a notion of linear, ethical obedience to the historical Jesus alone. The challenge for Mennonites as a Mennonite communion will be to maintain a trinitarian framework for Mennonite ethical, historical, and communal concerns, a trinitarian framework which will guard both the transcendence and the immanence of God.

TWENTY-FOUR

The Two Natures of Christ: Reconsidering Chalcedon[*]

Paul Tillich's mediating theology has fascinated me and influenced my thinking for at least thirty-five years. His singular way of imaginatively reinterpreting the classical tradition, without deconstructing it, I believe has foundational possibilities for us in the antifoundationalist ethos of postmodernism. His method of correlating the existential questions arising from contemporary culture with the revelatory answers provided by traditional theology continues to have validity amid the myriad options available. Perhaps most compelling for me is Tillich's ability to hold philosophy (Athens) and theology (Jerusalem) together in a creative, dynamic tension, which does not reduce Christian reflection to either pure rationalism or fideistic revelationism.

This paper was first presented at the Fifth International Tillich Symposium in Frankfurt, Germany, under the title "Tillich's Christology in Light of Chalcedon."[1] Read to a group of German academics, the language becomes rather technical at points, especially in the second part, but it does show the general direction of my

---

* Originally published as "Tillich's Christology in Light of Chalcedon," in *The Theological Paradox/Das Theologische Paradox* (Berlin: Walter de Gruyter, 1995), 122-40. For notes on the text see the Notes section below.

christological thinking. *This is not a comprehensive christology; these are some narrowly focused reflections on the being of Christ and make no reference whatever to the atoning work of Christ, for instance. In this paper I combine my specialized studies in Tillich scholarship and my ongoing interests in the classical trinitarian and christological synthesis.*

Relying heavily on the works of Patristic scholars R.P.C. Hanson and Aloys Grillmeier, I make the following observations about the two-natures formulation of Chalcedon (451 C. E.): 1) existential Christian faith and piety are not conditional upon accepting the technically correct doctrinal formulation; 2) the formulations of Nicea and Chalcedon are forms of 'mediating' theology—they mediate between what had been passed on in the kerygma *and the exigencies of the time; 3) in the post-Easter and continuing in the post-biblical periods there evolved a) a new doctrine of God and Christ intrinsically linked to cosmology and soteriology, and b) a new language and understanding of human personality that was to shape western anthropology (freedom and historical consciousness). In his early essays, particularly as they relate to classical christology, Tillich wants to replace the "nature-language" of Chalcedon with the "historical language" of modernity in a way that I find problematic. Nevertheless, I argue that there is within Tillich's sacramental theology and ontology the potential for reaching a proper balance between nature (space) and history (time) that is required for an adequate ethic in the contemporary world.*

◆ ◆ ◆

I. Introduction: The Issue Identified

My choice of this topic is part of a larger renewed interest of mine in the classical imagination as holding fascinating possibilities for us as we move into a postmodern period. A revisiting of the classical Greek or Christian vision—and it is a vision—becomes ever more urgent for us as we bear the fruits of our own Promethean exercise of historic freedom on our natural and social environment in the past two hundred years. Paul Tillich was a mediating theologian who was intent not on simply denying the classical tradition but on reinterpreting and reimagining it in the light of the contemporary world and its challenges. How he does this with the two-natures christology of Chalcedon is interesting in its own right but also for how it sheds light on other aspects of his theology.

In 1935 Tillich draws on the fifth-century christological formulation of Chalcedon to illumine the differences between his own understanding of the political situation in Germany and that of Karl Barth, on the one hand, and Emanuel Hirsch, on the other. He argues that Barth's critique of political and social life too radically *separates* the human-cultural sphere from the divine realm of the kingdom of God. Barth's heresy is that he separates the divine and the human. Hirsch (a German Christian who was a strong supporter of Hitler) commits the opposite heresy: he *mixes* the divine and the human by hallowing in an unbroken and unmediated way human-historical existence. Tillich remains faithful to the intent of the fathers of Chalcedon: holding the human and divine in their proper relation to each other.[2]

Tillich's characterization of Barth and Hirsch could be challenged. My object here, however, is not to examine the accuracy of Tillich's portrayal of these two theologians. Of greater interest to me is Tillich's self-perception: that he—in contrast to Barth and Hirsch—is in fact the preserver of theological fidelity to Chalcedon.

This is noteworthy for at least three reasons. First, Tillich's faithfulness to the tradition (particularly in his christology) has sometimes been questioned. Second, Tillich is himself highly critical of theological orthodoxy at times, especially the Protestant orthodoxy of his day. There is, however, third, a further point of interest. It is how Tillich applies the fifth-century christological formulation to his own political situation that I find intriguing, especially in the light of his own strong statement in *Systematic Theology* vol. II where he says that "if the use of the dogma for political purposes is acknowledged to be a demonic distortion of its original meaning, one can, without being afraid of authoritarian consequences, attribute a positive meaning to dogma generally and to the christological dogma in particular."[3] Is Tillich himself not using the traditional christological dogma for political purposes in this case, one might ask. And how faithful is Tillich's political reading of the christological formulation to the intent of the fifth-century council?

We begin by taking a look at the Council of Chalcedon and its christological definition, with a particular interest in the social-political context and theological implications of the formulation arrived at in 451 C.E. Second, we will examine more closely Tillich's christology in light of the above.

Chalcedon: A Theological and Political Reading

Background: The Christian Doctrine of God

The Councils of Nicea (325) and Constantinople (381) were concerned with the dogma of the Trinity—primarily the relation of Christ to God and derivatively the Holy Spirit to God. They concluded after much controversy that the proper theological way to speak of Christ was that the Son was of the same substance (*homoousion*), not of like substance (*homoiusion*) as the Father. What occurred in the first four hundred years of trinitarian debate was the development of a Christian doctrine of God, a Christian language about God. According to R.P.C. Hanson, the Fathers of trinitarian orthodoxy rejected the literalistic language and theology of the Arians. Instead they employed analogical imagery to talk about God "as one substance or *ousia* who existed as three *hypostaseis*, three distinct realities or entities ... three ways of being or modes of existing as God."[4] The term *ousia* represented universality and *hypostasis* particularity (at least for Basil of Caesarea).[5]

That the classical trinitarian imagination was an analogical one and not literalistic is an important observation, because it reverses the frequent reading of the past as being more literalistic in its thinking patterns than ours. It is the modern understanding of reality which is more inclined toward linear and literalistic thinking. The doctrine of the Trinity was an attempt to express in imaginative terms an answer to the question raised but left unanswered by the experiences of the first Christians—how their experience of Pentecost was related to their experience of Jesus as the Christ, and both of these to their profound commitment to the one transcendent God of the Jews as the one who acted in Jewish history.

Theological orthodoxy as defined by Nicea/Constantinople has historically come under attack from at least two directions. One, that of nineteenth century liberal theology, is the charge that the development of dogma in the first few centuries after the New Testament represents a Hellenization and, consequently, a corruption of the meaning of the historical Jesus and of the *kerygma* of the earliest Christian community.

The other not unrelated charge, held in one form or another by so-called "Free Church" or "Believers Church" traditions, as well as contemporary political and liberation theologies, among others, is that Classical orthodoxy was little more than political ideology: a political theology of Constantinian politics. These traditions have interpreted the Constantinian period of the fourth century as the fall of the Church. Since Constantine called and resided over the Council of Nicea, and is said to have offered the crucial terminology, theological orthodoxy is itself suspect.

For Constantine, so the argument goes, the unity of the church was indispensable for the unity of the empire. As someone who comes from the Radical Protestant tradition (Anabaptist-Mennonite), I have some sympathy for this reading but have in another context pointed out some of the problems with such an over-simplification of the period.[6] I have argued, for instance, that the *homoiousian* language of the Arians was more prone to a political ideology of the right (as in Eusebius of Caesarea, Constantine's court theologian) than the orthodoxy of Athanasius, political *persona non grata*, exiled five times for his views. This does, however, raise the important question: What are the political-ethical implications not only of imperial power in the shaping of theological orthodoxy but also of the doctrine of the Trinity itself? It also speaks to Tillich's concern that dogma not be demonically distorted for political purposes.

Chalcedon: The Christian Doctrine of Christ

Like the Council of Nicea, the Council of Chalcedon was called by the Emperor (Marcian) in October 451 for the sake of seeking unity both within the Church and the Empire. Ever since the Councils of Ephesus (431, 449) the church had been torn apart by internal disputes between two christological extremes: the Eutychians and the Nestorians. It was to a large extent a conflict between the East and the West, the Eutychians concerned with maintaining the unity of Christ (one nature: monophysitism) and the Nestorians with the duality of Christ (two natures: diophysitism). Nestorius was seen to be adoptionist, too radically separating the humanity of Christ from the eternal Logos; Eutyches a docetic with Manichaean tendencies—not giving the humanity of Christ its due. The bishops who gathered in Chalcedon were under pressure by Emperor Marcian, against their wishes, to come up with a formula that went beyond the Councils of Nicea and Constantinople in defining both the unity and distinctions of the divine and human in Christ.

In the end several hundred bishops from representative parts of the church reached a verdict which was intended not to supersede previous Councils but to clarify a very particular question: *"how the confession of the 'one Christ' may be reconciled with belief in the 'true God and true man', 'perfect in Godhead, perfect in manhood'."*[7] The crucial sentence was: "One and the same Christ, Son, Lord, Only begotten, made known in two natures (which exist) without confusion, without change, without division, without separation...." Representing all the major centres (Rome, Alexandria, Constantinople and Antioch) and trends, the bishops formulated a language for christology which tried to mediate the concerns both of the East and the West, and attempted to remain faithful both to the Scriptures and to the tradition.

Implications for Theology and Politics

1. *Theological* There are theological aspects and implications of Chalcedon which have relevance for us, especially as we look at Tillich's theology in the next part of this essay. First, the general life of faith in Christ in the early Christian community continued independently of correct philosophical formulations, and allowed for diverse expressions of faith. "Such faith," says Aloys Grillmeier, "drew its vitality from a picture of Christ which could not be fully comprehended in the formula of 451 about the person of Christ."[8]

This faith was equally accessible to the pro- and the anti-Chalcedonians. Nevertheless, second, the framers of the christological doctrine were developing a language for speaking about Christ which had profound repercussions for the church's understanding of soteriology. Despite the static-ontic sounding language of "two natures" and the "one person," the concern was a dynamic one: the basis and the means of salvation. This is evident in Pope Leo's writings both before and after Chalcedon.[9]

In fact, what happened in the dogmatic formulations of the first centuries was the emergence of the very notion of the development of doctrine.[10] Dogma in the classical period was the dynamic attempt to interpret and reinterpret the traditional *kerygma* in light of contemporary exigencies, quite the opposite to what theological orthodoxy came to mean in fundamentalist groups of the modern era. One might even say these bishops were "mediating" theologians, mediating between the apostolic tradition and the era in which they were living, not unlike Tillich's own mediating methodology.

The soteriological concerns behind the christological formula were both personal and general. In the words of Grillmeier: "All the same the relation between God(head) and man(hood) in Christ as understood by Chalcedon is the model and supreme case of the relationship between 'God' and 'world' in general—a matter which had already come under debate at Nicea in the face of Arianism . . . . Christianity itself intends to be and to offer a *Weltanschauung*."[11] A similar thesis is also defended persuasively by the Canadian classicist Charles Cochrane, in his *Christianity and Classical Culture*.[12]

This point is perhaps most dramatically reflected in the Church's fight against Manichaeism. Manichaeism offered Christians an alternative doctrine of salvation, a way of dealing with the problem of evil in the world.

> The message of Manes took those who were converted to it into a movement which above all had a more comprehensive effect than the Church's message of salvation in Christ and its mediation in faith and sacrament. For on the one hand there are the human primordial experiences which one has in dealing with nature, in witnessing the cosmic event, and of one's own instincts and yearnings; on the other there are the hopes which the message of Christ—however much it may be distorted—was able to arouse and, in Manes' preaching, produce. In the Manichaean myth of creation and redemption, in which gnostic ideas have been incorporated, an enticing vision manifests itself.[13]

Manes's vision had three stages: original separation of light and darkness, their subsequent mingling, and their present dissociation in the movement toward ultimate division. Manes's ethical agenda for the present therefore was a call for the radical renunciation of evil (the material realm) in favour of the good (the spiritual).[14] The Chalcedonian bishops' formulation, supported by the writings of Pope Leo, saw this alternative Manichaean soteriology, which they associated with Eutyches, as fundamentally endangering the Christian vision. It did not take the material, natural world seriously enough. The "two natures" language is in fact "nature friendly" (to use contemporary jargon), without absolutizing nature. In the seeming speculative interest in the relation of the two natures in Christ, the theologians of Chalcedon were genuinely concerned with a concrete issue: the relation of the material to the spiritual within the incarnation, and therefore within the world in general. Whereas the Greek conceptuality tended to deprecate the material, the early Church's nature language was a dynamic, analogical attempt to emphasize the importance of the material realm.

Chalcedon, however, was not only important in developing a theologically balanced view of the relation of the spiritual to the material in general. In the debates leading up to Chalcedon and following, the Christian understanding of the human personality evolved, including the notion of human autonomy. Here is what Grillmeier says:

> Perhaps the most important result of the trinitarian, christological "scholasticism" of the fifth and sixth centuries was the discovery of the concept of "person", which was highly fruitful not only for theology but also for philosophy and the history of thought. In the discussion about the fullness of Jesus' humanity, or about the "one" or "two" wills in Christ, or about one or two modes of operation in him, important anthropological problems came to be spoken about. Then for the first time the theme of the "autonomy" of created being in concurrence and cohesion with divine being made itself heard. Thus the development of the fifth and sixth centuries should not be assessed simply as a "scholastic" aberration of patristic theology.[15]

If Grillmeier's reading is correct, and I find it persuasive, then modern historical consciousness is indebted to the notion of human autonomy and agency that took shape in the christological debates. This would put in question Tillich's strong polarization of the nature-language of Chalcedon and modern historical language and consciousness, as we shall see below. This way of interpreting the debate about the two natures in

Christ—which are properly juxtaposed "without confusion, without change, without division, without separation" and yet within one unified personality—has profound personal, ecclesiological, and political implications. If salvation creates the possibility for individuals to participate in the new being in Christ (to use Tillich's expression), then the way the divine and the human are related in Christ is a prototype for the relation of the two dimensions within us as human beings (anthropology).

Furthermore, if the church is the body of Christ, to use Pauline imagery, then our understanding of the relation of the divine and the human in Christ determines our ecclesiology. This is quite compatible with Tillich's own view of the church as the "social existence of the new being." It is, according to Tillich, the community of those who have experienced the new being in Christ and are called to bring salvation and healing. Although later the church came to be identified with an institution, in fact it ought to mean not a group beside other groups, but the realization of the powers of salvation belonging to the new being, within the social sphere.[16]

2. *Political* In light of Tillich's political interpretation of Chalcedon, as we noted at the beginning of this essay, it is appropriate that we examine briefly the political context and implications of the fifth-century christological formulation. The imperial political pressure under which both the Nicene trinitarian creed and the Chalcedonian christological definition were formulated should make us wary of accepting without critical reflection the boundaries for orthodoxy set by these and other early Councils.

The Emperor played a decisive role, particularly in the important sixth session of the Council of Chalcedon on October 25, 451. On February 7, 452 he proclaimed the Council's conclusions as imperial law, leaving no room for dissenting views, doubt, or criticism. "It is evident," says Grillmeier, "that the Christology of Chalcedon was tailor-made for the Emperor. The Chalcedonian concepts and distinctions ... the doctrine of the two natures, the whole picture of Christ, seem to correspond to his clear, orderly mentality and uncomplicated character. His simple clarity of mind cannot understand the restless urges of the Monophysites. Above all they do not fit into the picture of religious order which he would like to have for the empire and which it is his commission to protect. That the goal which Marcian set for the Council of Chalcedon was to favour the imperial Church is no secret."[17]

Did Emperor Marcian totally manipulate the delegates and the theological conclusions for his own political purposes? Does the validity of the Council not hinge on whether finally the decisions were reached on theological rather than political grounds? Grillmeier believes that, despite the flawed imperial church-state involvement, the bishops and Pope Leo, where it concerned the actual theological content and basis of faith, appealed to Scripture and apostolic tradition rather than imperial authority: "But while the Emperors in the long run were all too clearly ready to buy 'unity' in faith through compromises, the Pope remained consistent and placed purity of faith above a false unity. In this sense, therefore, Leo I abandons the principle of the imperial Church at a decisive point."[18] In the end Leo's primary concern was soteriology and not politics. One also needs here to guard against the genetic fallacy—determining the validity of something primarily on the basis of its origin or social context. Perhaps the more important question is whether there is something about the "two natures" definition which tends toward political or ethical conservatism. Tillich seems to suggest, as we will see below, that the Greek nature ontology behind fifth-century christological language gives priority to space over time and therefore is intrinsically conservative.

Preliminary Conclusion

In conclusion, one can say that the church fathers who framed the dogmatic formulations of the fourth and fifth centuries were first and foremost concerned about preserving the biblical picture of Christ, and thereby the means of salvation.[19] For this they used the philosophical language at their disposal. To discredit their efforts as a form of Hellenization of the gospel, as does Harnack, is to misunderstand the task of Christian theological reflection in every age. For they knew, as R.P.C. Hanson observes in his *Studies in Christian Antiquity*, "that you cannot interpret the Bible simply in biblical terms. If your intention is to explain the Bible's meaning, then on crucial points you must draw your explanation from some other vocabulary apart from that of the Bible. Otherwise you will be left with the old question in another form still unanswered."[20] The charge of Hellenism can in fact be levelled more accurately against those like the Arians and the Manichaeans who were offering pseudo-solutions for salvation.[21]

Second, one of the most significant aspects of the Chalcedon and post-Chalcedon debates was the evolution of new language not only about Christ, and by implication about the Christian view of God, but about the very notion of human personality. New understandings of the terms *hypostasis* and *prosopon*, and their relation to each other, had profound significance for future theological, philosophical, and ethical reflection. As Grillmeier so incisively puts it:

> If the person of Christ is the highest mode of conjunction between God and man, God and the world, the Chalcedonian "without

confusion" and "without separation" show the right mean between monism and dualism, the two extremes between which the history of Christology swings. The Chalcedonian unity of person in the distinction of the natures provides the dogmatic basis for the preservation of the divine transcendence, which must always be a feature of the Christian concept of God. But it also shows the possibility of a complete immanence of God in our history, an immanence on which the biblical doctrine of the economy of salvation rests.[22]

This balance between divine transcendence and immanence, between monism and dualism within the context of a trinitarian doctrine of God, I maintain, is crucial for contemporary theology. It is a way of guarding against the modern temptation toward monistic nature idolatry, on the one hand, and gnostic/docetic depreciation of nature on the other. Tillich, therefore, quite rightly identifies the historical and political implications of Chalcedon. Such an interpretation stands in continuity with the intent of the Chalcedonian theologians. They wanted a balance which Tillich also attempts to maintain. To the extent that he succeeds in doing so he remains within the general framework of Chalcedonian orthodoxy. Tillich's legitimate critique of his contemporaries' absolutization of nature over history is, in my view, not sufficient reason to reject the nature-language of classical christology but rather the ideological misuse of the nature language.

II. Tillich's Christology: Christ, Nature and History

We come now to our examination of Tillich's christology in the light of Chalcedon. Throughout his work Tillich makes many fleeting references to the ancient trinitarian and christological formulations, generally looking more kindly on classical orthodoxy than on post-Reformation Protestant orthodoxy. He sees his own reinterpretation of classical trinitarian and christological thought as being distinct from that of Protestant orthodoxy on the one side and nineteenth-century liberal theology on the other. We will look at some of his specific references to Chalcedonian christology to shed light on his quarrel with traditional formulations.

Theological Paradox

The terms "paradox(ical)" and "dialectic(al)," when considered in the context of Tillich's thinking, can be quite problematic and confusing. Tillich uses these terms in different ways at different times. For example, in an early article on Barth's so-called "Dialectical Theology" he argues that

Barth is not really a dialectical thinker but a paradoxical thinker (that is, the "yes" and "no" are juxtaposed in a non-dynamic, non-dialectical manner). It is he, Tillich, who is the dialectical thinker. His own theology is not paradoxical but dialectical, in that the "yes" and "no" do not stand over against each other in a static sense but are related to each other dynamically.[23] In some contexts, however, Tillich uses the term "dialectic(al)" in a more "paradoxical" sense. In his 1936 book *On the Boundary*, for instance, he refers self-critically to his own thinking as always being on the boundary, between two poles of every issue—caught between a yes and no to every question. This is fruitful for thought, he admits, but not adequate to historical decision-making.[24]

It is interesting that in his *Systematic Theology* II, he uses the term "paradox" positively, but only in a highly restrictive sense. He argues that there is only one true paradox: that is the paradox of the New Being in Christ: "The appearance of the New Being under the conditions of existence, yet judging and conquering them . . . ." "This," he says, "is the only paradox and the source of all paradoxical statements in Christianity" (*ST* II, 92).

Paradox, as used in this sense, is not to be confused with rational thinking, dialectical thinking, irrationality, the absurd, the nonsensical. It means quite literally that which contradicts the *doxa*—the opinions of human beings based on ordinary experience; it is an offense against "man's unshaken reliance upon himself, his self-saving attempts, and his resignation to despair" (*ST* II, 92). In this same context, Tillich limits the use of the term "dialectical" to describe life-processes: "In a dialectical description one element of a concept drives to another" (*ST* II, 90). There is a rational dimension to dialectical thought that is not present in paradoxical thinking, which is defined more by contradiction and the appearance of a new reality into life-processes (as in the New Being in Christ).

The Problem with Chalcedon: Time (History) over Space (Nature)

Tillich's covert and overt references to classical trinitarian and christological dogma are ubiquitous. It is not my task here to do a comprehensive quantification of these references, but to examine the fundamental problem Tillich has with the way the "two nature" concept was formulated in the ancient church.

Tillich's Specific Comments on Chalcedon Tillich thinks Harnack's liberal critique of early trinitarian and christological dogma as being the intellectualization and Hellenization of the Christian faith is misplaced. Classical Greek philosophy was not intellectualistic by nature, and

Hellenization was inevitable for a church concerned with missionary activity (*ST* II, 140-41). Furthermore, the fifth-century church quite rightly recognized that "any diminution of human nature would deprive the Christ of his total participation in the conditions of existence. And any diminution of the divine nature would deprive the Christ of his total victory over existential estrangement. In both cases he could not have created the New Being. His being would have been less than the New Being. Therefore, the problem was how to think the unity of a completely divine nature" (*ST* II, 142). "In the two great decisions of the early church," Tillich says, "both the Christ-character and the Jesus-character of the event of Jesus as the Christ were preserved. And this happened despite the very inadequate conceptual tools" (*ST* II, 145). The questions of the early church fathers were right, but their conceptual tools were wrong. What were these conceptual inadequacies of Nicea and Chalcedon?

It was their concept of nature. Not only is the static-essentialist language inadequate to a discussion of human beings and divine reality (*ST* II, 147-48), it is the language of an age which lacks historical consciousness. Reality was still understood spatially (in terms of nature) rather than temporally (time as history). This is at the basis of Tillich's problem with classical christology. And this is the place where we need most carefully to examine his critique, for in some sense he continues the modern (not necessarily the postmodern) historicist critique of classical dogma. What distinguishes Tillich from some of the more radical historicists of the modern period is the importance he places on nature and spatial thinking in his theology.[25] In the end, however, historical thinking takes precedence over nature and space thinking.

Historical Consciousness: Loss of the Imagination In his 1939 essay "History as *the* Problem of our Period," Tillich claims that every period has its ultimate concern, and the ultimate concern in our period is history—that is, existence viewed historically. The Middle Ages were preoccupied with "a theonomous culture supported by a hierarchical church."[26] From the fifteenth-century Renaissance to the early part of the twentieth century, the primary concern was "the control of nature and society by human reason" ("History," 226). Anthropocentrism replaced theocentrism, and religion became a rational instrument for morality. In the modern period a sense of our historicity has replaced the previous era's confidence in natural rationality. Marx and Nietzsche each in their own distinctive way represent this modern forceful recognition that "[h]istorical consciousness is the consciousness of history as one's fate" (228).

Tillich too thinks this historical consciousness is our fate as human beings, even though there continues to be a struggle between nature-consciousness and history-consciousness. Writing this at the high point of Nazi power in Germany, Tillich admits that in many ways nature-consciousness continues to have the greater alluring power:

> It is much more natural to the human mind to interpret existence from the point of view of nature. Nature, the all supporting and creative reality, her eternal laws of birth and growth and decay and death, her abundant gifts and her violent acts of destruction, seem to give the universal pattern of being and existence. According to this pattern, history is the process by which human groups, tribes, nations, empires, cultures, rise and grow, decay and disappear ("History," 229).

It is the view held by the most powerful political groups in the contemporary world: "Nature and history, space and time, again contend with each other, as they did in the first Christian centuries" ("History," 230). The difference between the ancient world and ours is that for the ancients the eternal, timeless realm bestowed meaning on existence. But this non-dialectical notion of an eternal supra-natural realm is no longer conceptually adequate for our age.

A few observations might be made concerning Tillich's juxtaposing of modern historical-consciousness over against classical nature-consciousness. First, is it still true to say that our primary concern at the turn of the century and millennium is to recognize and promote historical consciousness? Some, like American theologian Gordon Kaufman, in his most recent book *In Face of Mystery*, would say yes and draw stronger historicist conclusions than does Tillich.[27] Others, like Canadian philosopher George Grant and the Jewish philosopher Hans Jonas, say no. For them, historicist thinking is part of the problem. It has brought us to our present environmental and technological impasse. A new, more classical view of reality and nature, as a grounding for human values and ethics, is urgently called for.[28]

Second, why does the modern inability to think the Eternal, and history as the fleeting shadow of the Eternal (Plato), need to have the last word? What is it that will not allow us to imagine the existence of the radically other which gives meaning to the historical? Tillich himself suggests that history derives its meaning from that which breaks into history from beyond. Third, can one so readily identify a) the early Church's notion of the two natures in Christ, with b) the more general Greek nature-consciousness? Although the ancient Church adopted nature language it drew quite different conclusions about the material world than did the Greeks. Finally, how legitimate is it for Tillich to connect the triumph of nature (space) over history (time) in certain neo-pagan groups in the 1930s with the nature language and consciousness of classical Christian thought? These observations and questions lead us into the final section of our paper.

Conclusion: Christ as the Middle of History

Tillich's most extensive discussion of christology in relation to history is found in his 1930 essay, "Christologie und Geschichtsdeutung."[29] Christology, he maintains, leads necessarily to the interpretation of history; and, conversely, the interpretation of history leads necessarily to the christological question. The old discussion about the two natures of Christ and their unity, or the two wills in Christ, are no longer relevant unless we transform them into the problem of the interpretation of history in our present situation. In a footnote in the 1936 English translation of this essay, "The Interpretation of History and the Idea of Christ," Tillich elaborates on what he means:

> The German situation of today shows with surprising clarity the truth of this statement. The old Christological struggle has been transformed into a struggle about a Christian or a half pagan interpretation of history: whether the kingdom of God or a national kingdom is the center of history and principle of meaning for every historical activity, and what the relationship should be between divine and human activity with respect to the kingdom of God. These questions replace the old question as to the relationship of these two natures in Christ.[30]

In other words, Classical theology focused exclusively on the problem of the two natures—divine and human—in Christ. But to consider being fundamentally in terms of nature is to think cyclically and spatially. To view being historically is to break through cyclical-nature thinking about being. It is to give priority to time over space. It is to decide for the meaning of being; for historical freedom and meaning are intrinsically related. To think christologically is "to describe the concrete place where 'that which is unconditioned-meaning-giving' enters history and provides it with meaning and transcendence. . ." ("Christologie," 190).

This is what Tillich calls the "middle of history." Both the beginning and end of history are defined and given meaning by the middle. Wherever historical consciousness arises there is a middle of history, a "concrete-meaning-giving" principle by which history is constituted. Jews, Mohammedans, Enlighteners, Marxists, and Imperialists all have their middle of histories by which their historical consciousness is constituted. There is no such a possibility as universal history, only particular history and particular middles of history. The christological claim is that Christ is the middle of history.

Christian theology identifies "as meaning-giving middle of history a personal life, that is fully defined through the relation to the transcendent" ("Christologie," 201). This is a matter of faith, what Tillich calls a "transcendental decision." It is a matter of destiny; being grasped by the transcendent. "Only a breaking in from the beyond of history can overcome the threat to history" (202). Being can become the bearer of history only to the extent that something new can shine through it. "Freedom is the possibility of being, to establish something new," and "the freedom of being from its necessity is the lifting up of being to meaning" (197-98).

Salvation is the overcoming of that which is against being, and the content of the christological problem is nothing other than the determination and description of the place of salvation. Christ is a sacramental reality in the sense of the "anticipated fulfillment" of history. In the pagan sacramental view of the middle of history ethical demand is excluded. It is in the final sense ahistorical and absolutizes space over time. Christ as the middle of history gives priority to time over space. Christology is, therefore, no longer concerned with the applicability of questionable mythical categories (like the two natures dogma) of an historical personality but with identifying the place, meaning and content of the middle of history as it applies to us ("Christologie," 204-205).

These early essays, perhaps more than later ones, reveal the extent to which Tillich replaces "nature-language" with "historical-language." His very strong sense of the "sacramental" dimension of reality guards him against a radical historicism. Nevertheless, his intent as expressed in these essays is to replace the nature-thinking of the classical vision with the historical-consciousness of the modern period. We have in this essay suggested that in doing so he too radically polarizes the two ways of speaking and thinking.

We have, following Grillmeier's interpretation of the classical christological dogma of Chalcedon, also suggested that: a) the early Christian view of nature was quite different from the general Greek view, and b) in the process of defining the two natures and two wills in Christ, the modern understanding of individual personality, freedom, and historical consciousness began to take shape. It is precisely the retrieval of the proper balance between nature (space) and history (time) that is required for an adequate ethic in the contemporary world. By and large Tillich's own theology is premised on the need for such a balance.

TWENTY-FIVE

Angels, Demons, and the Holy Spirit*

The following four essays have much in common. Although they differ in style—the first two were originally presented as sermons, the third was written for a popular church periodical, the fourth was an academic paper—there are material similarities. They all are related to and use the language of pneumatology, although none is a systematic treatment of the subject.

Of the spate of recent books on pneumatology, Michael Welker's God the Spirit *and Harvey Cox's* Fire from Heaven: The Rise of Pentecostal Spirituality and the Reshaping of Religion in the Twenty-first Century *are among the best, although for very different reasons.[1] Welker's study is a systematic, biblical-theological treatment of the subject; Cox's is a socio-historical look at twentieth-century pentecostalism and an indirect apologetic for pneumatological renewal in contemporary theology. These two complementary works figure prominently as background to my treatment of the subject in the essay below, originally published in the* Mennonite Reporter *under the title "Angels and Demons and the Holy Spirit."[2]*

---

* Originally published as "Angels and Demons and the Holy Spirit," *Mennonite Reporter*, 27.10 (May 12, 1997): 8. For notes on the text see the Notes section below.

Welker's study deserves more careful treatment than circumstances allowed for in writing this essay, which was intended for a popular audience. Mine is not a systematic treatment of the doctrine of the Holy Spirit but *a reflection on the renewal of interest in the supernatural and spiritual in our time that bears on pneumatology*. Since the doctrine of the Trinity is the theme that more than any other ties together the very different essays in this volume, the doctrine of the Spirit is alluded to and expanded upon at various points throughout; but nowhere is there a comprehensive treatment of pneumatology, due to the occasional nature of these articles.

My interest here was in the way our understanding of the Holy Spirit should help orient us as we engage the so-called "new age spiritualities." I have at a number of points made a few additions to the original article, identifying them as such with square brackets. In the end I suggest a way in which our pneumatology might be applied to ecclesiology, in particular how the different gifts of the Spirit might be understood as the gifts of individual church traditions in relation to the universal church. I deal with this latter subject at greater length in an essay at the end of this volume, "Mennonites and the Church Universal: Ecumenical Gifts of the Spirit."

Michael Welker, Professor of Systematic Theology at the University of Heidelberg, has emerged as one of Germany's most respected theologians. He held teaching positions in Tübingen and Münster and has been a guest professor at McMaster University in Hamilton, Ontario, and at Princeton. I first made his acquaintance at a Tillich conference in Germany in 1978, at which time he was assistant to Jürgen Moltmann at Tübingen, and we've visited each other and corresponded over the years. He knows Mennonites well, having lived with his family in the parsonage of the Hamilton Mennonite Church while guest professor at McMaster and attending the congregation during that year. There are affinities between his theology and that of Mennonites, evident in his *God the Spirit*, a work preparing the ground for a sequel on Law.

Welker's underlying interest in the compatibility of "Spirit" and "Law"—a fascination that might be traced to his Reformed background and one not uncommon to Mennonites—is both the strength and the weakness of his approach. It corrects a frequent misperception that the two are opposed, one having to do with irrational enthusiasm and the other with ethics. For Welker, the Spirit of God has to do with "universal righteousness, mercy and knowledge of God." A theology of the Holy Spirit ought to concern itself not with the sensational and the unusual but with an understanding and experience of the actions of the Spirit "open to sober and realistic perception."

To experience the Spirit of God is not some vague, abstract form of ecstasy but has concrete ethical criteria: "The messianic promises assign the name 'Spirit of God' to the power that both promises and realizes new community for poor and rich, strong and weak, people separated and alienated by economics, politics, racism, and sexism." Welker calls this a "realistic" theology of the Spirit; one which stands in contrast to the old form of European metaphysics on the one hand and to overly enthusiastic charismatic movements on the other.

What Welker—in his otherwise legitimate concern for rationality, law, and ethics—does not quite manage to attend to sufficiently is the unexplainable, irrational, and personal nature of the world of the Spirit and the spirits.

In a 1999 letter to Welker, I wrote:

> I do want to raise one critical point about your book, however. Despite your eloquent attempt to do justice to the variety of spiritual fruits and gifts of the Spirit, both her diversifying and unifying power, and your wonderful journey through the Bible, I do not think you adequately catch the ecstatic, irrational, even dark dimensions of the Spirit. I don't know if it's your subliminal Reformed background that is at work, but in your concern for 'law' and fear of antinomianism you do not in my opinion quite get at what in fact, historically and phenomenologically, has been at the heart of twentieth-century Pentecostalism.[3]

He responded:

> I am particularly thankful for your remarks concerning my Spirit-book. You are right, that I don't adequately work out the ecstatic, irrational and dark dimensions of the Spirit. Really, I am preoccupied too much with the outpouring of the Spirit and not enough with the working of the Spirit "from below." [Geisteswirken "von unten her"]. That has occurred certainly under the influence of Barth's Reformation theology, with his strong recommendation that one hold oneself to the clarity of Revelation and to consider the dark side, as Barth says so beautifully, only with a 'brief sharp glance.'[4]

Here Harvey Cox's book supplements Welker's treatment. It is precisely the irrational dimension of the Spirit's manifestations that Cox probes in his history of the Pentecostal movement. Even Cox, however, virtually dismisses the importance of what he calls the third wave of Pentecostalism—the recent "Spiritual Warfare" literature. It is this issue which I take up in the subsequent essay, "The Grammar of Spiritual Warfare and Apocalypse," which follows the one below.

◆ ◆ ◆

We are living through a "spiritual" renaissance in Western societies! It is a remarkable age of "re-enchantment." We produce new computer technology at such a feverish pace that we are forced to get rid of obsolete equipment every few years to remain competitive. At the same time, we breed fantasy worlds like Star Trek and bizarre cults like the Gates of Heaven whose members recently left this earth for a distant star where they imagine life is perfect.

The very society that since the eighteenth century has become secular (disenchanted) is now devouring books such as *The Celestine Prophecy*. New Age spiritualities in the form of environmentalism, "love-your-body" mysticism, and self-awareness therapies are the rage. How can one and the same culture worship both the god of modern technology and the mysteries of the spirit? Might it be that after the human atrocities of this century, after the nuclear night of the past fifty years, after our dangerous gambles with the ecosystem—that after all this we are being given a new "spiritual" chance?

The evidence of spiritual yearning is everywhere. The word "spirituality" has become commonplace. The question is: What does this have to do with Christian spirituality? Christian spirituality is not to be equated with spirituality in general. Christian spirituality is rooted in our experience of the Holy Spirit, and the Holy Spirit has characteristics by which we can discern her working.

My interest in the doctrine of the Holy Spirit goes back to my childhood, when three of my father's sisters left the *Kleinegemeinde* church (Evangelical Mennonite Conference) for the Pentecostal church. They found Mennonite church life too constricting. I remember the arguments at family gatherings over the Christian status of those who had not been "baptized with the Spirit" (speaking in tongues). So I did not find it surprising to learn from J. Howard Kauffman ("Mennonite Charismatics: Are they any different?" *Mennonite Quarterly Review*, Oct. 1996) that between 5 and 10 per cent of Mennonites are "seriously involved in charismatic experiences and forms of worship" (from a 1989 survey). He concludes that the Mennonite charismatic movement is a form of spiritual renewal.

Three Waves of Pentecostalism

Thirty years ago a Harvard University professor named Harvey Cox wrote a book called *The Secular City* in which he, like many, predicted the end of institutional religion and the advent of a "post-religious" age.[5] In 1995, Cox published *Fire from Heaven: The Rise of Pentecostal Spirituality and the Reshaping of Religion in the Twenty-first Century*. It is a remarkable reversal.

Cox now believes that it is secularism, not religion, which may be heading for extinction. Over 400 million Christians (one out of every four) are connected in some way with the pentecostal experience. Pentecostalism, which emphasizes the experience of the Holy Spirit at Pentecost, is the fastest growing religious movement in the world. One can talk, according to Cox, about three waves of pentecostalism in the twentieth century.

Classical Pentecostalism

On April 9, 1906, the Holy Spirit descended upon a small group of domestic workers of mixed background in Los Angeles. Five days later this motley crew had grown to the point where it had to move to a warehouse. The leader was a self-taught black preacher named William Joseph Seymour. The most remarkable thing about this outpouring of the Spirit was its racially mixed character: blacks, whites, Asians, Mexicans, male and female, saw visions, prophesied in tongues, and went into ecstatic trances. From the start, the movement splintered into factions, primarily a split between Seymour's followers and an exclusively white group known as Assemblies of God.

Initially, Seymour thought speaking in tongues was the primary sign of the new age. He changed his mind after the split: "If you get angry, or speak evil, or backbite, I care not how many tongues you may have, you have not the baptism with the Holy Spirit"(Cox, 63). The white faction became more fixed on tongues, while for Seymour the true mark of the new age was overcoming racial barriers. [Cox emphasizes the radical, social and apocalyptic nature of the movement's original vision. Only in time did the white wing of the movement lose this critical social message and become identified with more conservative, rightwing political and theological thinking. American black pentecostalism managed to maintain the prophetic element much more clearly than did white pentecostalism.]

Charismatic Movement

Since World War II, a second wave, the neo-pentecostal or charismatic movement, has seen phenomenal growth within virtually all mainline Christian traditions. The desire to go beyond the rational in speech, in worship, and in hope makes the charismatic experience so appealing to the postmodern world. The traits—speaking in tongues, spiritual ecstasy, raising of hands, physical healing, being "slain in the spirit"—remained similar to classical pentecostalism but its incorporation into mainline Christianity contributed to its becoming less "sectarian" in its stance toward modern culture.

Spiritual Warfare

The most recent wave is a preoccupation with the battle against demonic forces. C. Peter Wagner articulated this kind of pentecostalism in his book *Wrestling with Dark Angels*.[6] He depicts the world as populated with demonic principalities and powers seeking to control human behavior. It is against these powers we must fight, says Wagner.

An Ontario Mennonite pastor, Laurence Burkholder, has recently written a Masters thesis on "A Mennonite Theology of Exorcism." He is convinced that pastors, doctors, and therapists need to recognize forces of evil that are beyond normal powers of healing and require the gift of exorcism. [According to Burkholder, "He [Jesus] treated them [demons] as real creatures complete with names, emotion, social organization and the evil capacity to afflict people. And then he cast them out of people."[7]]

Wagner and others like Burkholder rightly draw our attention to the reality of the demonic, too often ignored by liberally inclined theology and culture. Where in my view they go wrong is in a) giving too much credibility to the demonic, bordering on a Manichean view of creation, and b) reifying (objectifying) the spirits without sufficient attention to the nature of biblical and theological language when speaking about the paranormal. (It is to this linguistic issue that I turn in the next essay.)

I agree with C. S. Lewis when he says, in his *Screwtape Letters*: "There are two equal and opposite errors . . . about devils. One is to disbelieve their existence. The other is to believe and to feel an excessive and unhealthy interest in them. They themselves are equally pleased by both errors, and hail a materialist and a magician with the same delight."[8] This third wave is part of a much broader phenomenon— the "new spirituality" of our time, which is preoccupied with demons and angels and the world of spirits.

Relation to Christian Spirituality

How is all of this, (particularly the contemporary interest in spirituality and demonology) related to the Christian doctrine of the Holy Spirit? When the biblical understanding of creation was taking shape, there were a number of ways of understanding the spirit world. The Greeks and neighboring religions saw the world as intrinsically spiritual. Every sphere of nature and life was the domain of some god or spirit. From Gaea (mother earth) and Uranus (father sky) descended Poseidon (god of the sea), Hephaestus (fire), and Demeter (harvest). Aphrodite personified love and Athena, wisdom. Nature was filled with spirits which manipulated life in unpredictable ways. [Barth, in his *Church Dogmatics,III/I*, has made the point that the polytheistic myths of the cultures surrounding the Hebrews were in fact monistic in their thinking—gods, humans, creatures, all of creation came from the same primal reality.[9]]

The ancient Hebrews developed a rather different view of the world. The two Genesis stories of creation portray one God (Jahweh) creating the heavens and the earth from nothing.

Each part of creation is good and has its purpose. Human beings are the only parts of the universe created in the "image of God." They are part of nature but also have a special relation to the divine. Their most important spiritual trait is freedom—unlike stones, plants and animals, they can make moral choices. We know the rest of the story—the order, beauty, and harmony of the world is destroyed by the arrogance of human freedom.

Here we have two different spiritualities. The ancient Greeks experience spirituality everywhere, but it is a polytheistic, capricious spirituality personifying the forces of nature. The ancient Hebrews believe the world is created good, but not divine. The world receives its value extrinsically, from its maker, the God of whom no images can be made. The world is not God's body, it is God's creation.

Christian spirituality continues in the Hebrew tradition with some added Greek elements. Christians confess that the one God created the world separate from its creator, but that in Christ the divine assumes flesh and dwells with creation. Furthermore, the divine Spirit "indwells" human beings who thereby bear God's image. This is the same Spirit that hovered over the waters at the beginning of creation, that is "breathed" into the clump of earth that becomes a human being, that brings the dry bones back to life in Ezekiel's vision, that Joel prophesies will come to everyone in the messianic age.

The Old Testament has numerous references to the Spirit coming upon individuals and taking possession of them. It is a Spirit of freedom that makes moral demands. In the New Testament, the Spirit takes on more focused characteristics. Jesus is conceived by the Spirit; the Spirit leads him into the wilderness and descends on him at baptism. Jesus promises the Holy Spirit to his disciples and is raised from the dead by the Spirit as a forerunner of our own resurrection (both now and in the future).

The most dramatic event is the outpouring of the Holy Spirit at Pentecost (Acts 2). The Apostles' witness throughout Acts is made possible through the power of the Holy Spirit. Paul is the "Apostle of the Spirit" whose writings emphasize that the Spirit is the power which transforms people into children of God, into a new creation. In fact, Paul sees the whole of creation longing for the children of God who have the first fruits of the Spirit (Rom. 8). The fruits of the Spirit are symbolized by the tree of life in John's great vision of the New Jerusalem (Rev. 22).

Meanwhile, we live in the old Jerusalem, with many spirits calling for allegiance. These spirits, says John, need to be tested to see whether they bear the fruits referred to by Paul and incarnated by Christ. In my Pastors' Theology Seminar our text one year was *God the Spirit*, by Michael Welker. He argues that the "Spirit of God" is the biblical name of the power which creates unity between widely diverse people: "old and young, rich and poor, socially privileged and subordinated men and women of various religious, national, and cultural backgrounds"(23). The Spirit does not erase differences but cultivates them as long as they do not contradict "justice, mercy, and knowledge of God"(40). The Spirit is the power that seeks to "protect, liberate, renew, and enliven other creatures" rather than itself (297). It is a self-giving, not a possessing Spirit.

This is surely what Paul means when he talks about the different gifts of the Spirit in 1 Cor. 12: wisdom, faith, healing, prophecy, discernment, tongues, interpretation. These are given to individuals not for selfish fulfillment but for the benefit of the whole body of Christ. This body is much larger than our church, our denomination, or even the Christian religion. It is ultimately the whole world, including all of creation. Each Christian denomination has a special gift of the Spirit to bring to the ecumenical body. Eastern Orthodoxy brings the wonderful sense that the whole universe is the mystical body of Christ (Eph. 1). The Roman Catholic Church brings the mystery of the sacraments as visible means of invisible grace. Lutherans remind us that we are justified only by grace through faith in Christ (Gal. 3). Methodists strive for holiness (1 Pet. 1). These can all be seen as gifts of the Spirit.

What about Mennonites? We bring to the ecumenical table our peace witness and discipleship—a theology of the Sermon on the Mount. What is often forgotten, however, is that the Anabaptists were the charismatics of the sixteenth century. The doctrine of the Holy Spirit was the key to Anabaptist faith. The main debate in early Anabaptism was between those who emphasized the "inner word" (spirit) and those who focused on the "outer word" (letter).

With time, the "outer word" people won the day, but all early Anabaptists were convinced that the inner regeneration (baptism of the Holy Spirit, if you like) was essential for discipleship. A witness to this conviction may be our Mennonite gift of the Spirit. It is the conviction that our spirituality is grounded in the Holy Spirit who indwells us, makes a moral demand on us, and empowers us to live by the spirit of Christ.

TWENTY-SIX

The Grammar of Spiritual Warfare and Apocalypse*

In the essay below I elaborate on themes introduced in the previous chapter. In this sermon, preached at Rockway Mennonite Church on April 18, 1999,[1] I examine the language of "spiritual warfare" and "apocalypse," and suggest that the two genres of speaking about the invisible realm of spiritual forces have much in common. The Bible, including Jesus, tends to anthropomorphize and personify spiritual powers in both cases, but it is theologically unsound to understand these anthropomorphisms literalistically. To do so—to "thingify" spiritual powers—is to slip into paganism, where gods are little more than personifications of material forces. Spiritual powers (both divine and human) are by definition not objects defined in usual temporal and spatial terms.

That is why we use figures of speech to talk of these powers, even when talking about God. Technically, only Jesus Christ, who is God incarnated in a particular human being, can be defined in spatial and temporal terms, and even in his case, it is important to make a distinction between the human being Jesus of Nazareth (a Jewish male) and Jesus as the Christ (who is not to be reduced to humanness or

---

* The original title of the Sermon was "Apocalypse: the curtain tore, the earth shook, rocks split, tombs opened, saints rose and went into the holy city (Matt. 27: 51-53)." For notes on the text see the Notes section below.

maleness). *The scandal of particularity is, of course, that these two are so inextricably connected (as was expressed by the "two natures" formula of Chalcedon in 451). Jesus himself, we are told, spoke only in parables when speaking about eschatology (Matt. 13:34). What is important in all of biblical eschatological literature, including Jesus' Kingdom parables, are always the ethical implications for human behavior here and now, in this world.*

One of the most unsettling experiences I have had recently is my supervision of a Masters thesis on "A Mennonite Theology of Exorcism." It's a lengthy scholarly treatment of the subject by a bright, mature student who sincerely believes in the subject matter and speaks from personal experience. He came into theology with an M.A. in history from the University of Toronto. He is not alone. There are a lot of Christians who see the world as the field of battle between invisible demonic and divine powers.

These people believe we are personally and corporately engaged in spiritual warfare and need to be constantly alert to Satan and a hierarchy of demonic beings who seek entrance through cracks in our psyches. There are voluntary and involuntary entry points in us through which these evil powers seek to control us. These demons are beings that can be exorcized only through constant vigilance, prayer, communal liturgies, and the actual utterance of the name of Christ and the use of the phrase "the blood of Christ." There are curses that plague individuals and families generation after generation until they are released through exorcism. Certain practices amongst Mennonites in the past (like charming and various other forms of "magic") are the cracks through which these demonic forces enter the Mennonite community. Personal sins, vices, and secrets are the garbage which the so-called demonic rats feed upon.

My Masters student shows how the ancient world firmly believed in such a battle against the evil powers, and how throughout history there have been individuals and groups who have recognized the importance of the fight against these principalities and the powers. These are not just abstracts forces, they are real personal beings that try to invade and control us. We disregard these beings at our own great peril.

I found supervising this thesis unsettling for the following reasons. First, the student is right: there is a lot of scriptural support for his views. Second, throughout most of history such views have been held by many Christians. Third, he cites as evidence many accounts of dramatic encounters with demons and their exorcism, personal testimonies which cannot easily be explained away. Fourth, he is not denying the reality of mental illness, the importance of psychotherapy, and the use of medication. He is just saying that frequently psychology cannot answer all the questions, and that there are situations in which there are objective causes of illness that go beyond the ability of the medical doctor or psychologist to treat. In such cases exorcism may be necessary. Fifth, I myself have often argued over the years against reducing everything to materialistic and psychological explanations. I also strongly believe in the reality of an invisible and spiritual world behind the physical world we see.

What then is it that bothers me about all of this? C. S. Lewis in his Screwtape Letters *once said there are two dangers when speaking about the Devil and his Angels: Either one does not take them seriously enough or one is too preoccupied with them. I think Lewis is exactly right. But what bothers me most is what I would call the "reification" of the spiritual world. To reify means to "thingify," to think of the spiritual world as made up of things or objects flying around within time and space.*

This, I believe, is to misunderstand the spiritual realm. The whole point of the spiritual dimension of reality is that it cannot be defined in strictly spatial and temporal terms. Take God and the good angels, for example. I think it's quite appropriate to talk about God and angels in personal terms, as long as one remembers that one is using anthropomorphic imagery to describe a reality that is not human. One is personifying spiritual forces in a way that does not do justice to their reality.

It is really a question of language. How does one speak in temporal ways about realities that are not essentially spatial and temporal, and yet enter space and time? All our thinking, experiencing, and speaking is within time and space, and yet as Christians we claim to be experiencing that which comes from beyond space and time. At the bottom of all of this is the question: Do we truly believe in a spiritual world, and if so, how does it interact with the physical world in which we live? To answer this we need to go back to core Christian beliefs about God, the world, and history. In the following pages I concentrate on apocalyptic imagery as a case in point, for the grammar of apocalypse is closely related to the language of spiritual warfare.

◆ ◆ ◆

The Christian View of God, the World, and History

The foundation of Christian faith is not history, not human beings, not nature or matter, not even faith or personal experience. It is God. And the two most direct biblical statements about the essence of God are: "God is Spirit" (John 4:24) and "God is Love" (1 John 4:8,16)—both non-spatial, non-temporal images for God, who is not an object beside other objects but the ground, source, basis, and creator of all objects. Our faith begins and ends with this God (who is Spirit and Love) and what this God is doing in and through the World. There are many different religions with different views of the divine. As Christians, however, we believe that God is the one who is creating the world, who is saving the world through Christ, and who is completing the world through the Holy Spirit. For God (who in His immanent trinitarian relations is beyond time and history) these activities are all in the present tense. Only for us humans are these three—creation, redemption, consummation—seen as past, present and future. We humans are bound by space and time, and anything we say about God therefore is expressed in spatial and temporal terms. We as human beings either participate in these divine activities or shut ourselves off from them. And even if we shut ourselves off from them, God uses us in achieving divine ends, for in some mysterious sense we have no choice in the matter. This is the unresolved mystery: we have a choice to be on God's side and we don't have a choice. God is ultimately not dependent on us.

Of the three divine activities—creation, redemption, consummation—it is the third that I want to think about here. The word frequently used for this third doctrine is "eschatology" or the teaching about the end times. It is a subject that seems to get a lot of attention at certain periods of history—particularly at the turn of centuries and millenniums. Especially in anticipation of 2000 there have been a host of movies and books written about the subject. In 1970 Hal Lindsey wrote the *Late Great Planet Earth*, which made many predictions about the end-time (most of which have proved false) and sold over 25 million copies, more than any other book in history except for the Bible.[2] The year 2000 has taken on special meaning for many religious forecasters. Drawing on speculations by Jewish rabbis about the world running its course in a six-day world week, depending on Psalm 90:4 and 2 Peter 3:8 which identify one day with a thousand years, and using sixteenth-century Archbishop Ussher's calculation of Old Testament numbers that the world was created around 4004 B.C., these people predict that in the year two thousand our world will come to an end.

The word "apocalypse" comes from the Greek term meaning the revealing of that which is hidden. The Bible is full of apocalyptic imagery prophetically speaking about a future time when the hidden meaning of the universe will be revealed. The books of Daniel and Revelation are the two biblical sources full of such imagery, but there are many other places (like Matt. 24) which talk about the end of the world, tribulation, punishment and reward, and so on. There are many related biblical themes that come under the general doctrine of eschatology: the return (or second coming) of Christ, the rapture of the saints, the general resurrection, eternal life (a quality of existence), heaven (a place of eternal bliss), hell (a place of eternal damnation), judgment (God's reward of the good and punishment of the evil), and the kingdom of God (*Basileia*: the final reign of God).

There is no doubt that for early Christians all of these various end-time notions had great meaning and immediacy. It is also the case that there was no one unified view of what the end-time would look like. Some seemed to think the eschaton (end-time) was already present as a new quality of

SPIRITUAL WARFARE AND APOCALYPSE / 433

existence in Christ. Others like Matthew seemed to think of it as a dramatic future event. Without question, Jesus saw his primary message as being the proclamation and inaugurator of the kingdom of God, the rule of God, beginning in the present and fulfilled in the future.

Very quickly in church history the preoccupation with eschatology or end-time thinking became secondary, if not forgotten altogether.. Fringe groups like the second-century Montanists who did stress eschatology were anathematized. Periodically other peripheral groups would again emphasize Old Testament and New Testament end-time imagery, only to be sidelined by a more mainline institutional approach to faith. In the Reformation, it was the Radical Anabaptist groups which most dramatically interpreted the social, political, and religious upheavals in Europe as signs of the end (the end of the world as they knew it). But predictions of when, where, and how the world would end have always proven false.

One of the best books on the subject is Walter Klaassen's *Armageddon and the Peaceable Kingdom*. Klaassen's interest in the subject is driven by the bizarre events of the 1880s in which his great -grandfather Martin Klaassen was involved—a disastrous trek by a group of Mennonites who considered themselves the church of Philadelphia (Rev. 3:7-13) from the Volga River in southern Russia to Kazakhstan in Central Asia, where they vainly awaited the return of Christ. Klaassen's book is a careful study of all the relevant texts in the Bible having to do with eschatology. First, he examines the texts to see if they really say what all the end-time predictors say they say; second, he explains what he thinks they really say.

Klaassen accuses the forecasters of a cut-and-paste job, a kind of science-fiction approach to eschatology which falls far short of Christ's true teaching of the peaceable kingdom. The God we get in much of this literature is a vengeful, wrathful God who at the great final battle of Armageddon is depicted as littering the earth with corpses lying in rivers of blood, having little to do with the suffering servant God of Isaiah 53, the God of Christ who dies for the sins of the world at Easter, and the victory of the God of the Lamb in the book of Revelation.

As I see it, there are two great dangers when dealing with end-time thinking. Either 1) we are complete cynics, sceptics, agnostics, and materialists who write off totally the reality of the supernatural, spiritual world, the invisible realities behind the visible, physical world we perceive with our five senses. Or, 2) we become gnostics (spiritualizers), those who become so obsessed with the invisible world of spiritual beings, forces, powers, realities that we lose touch with this world of matter, nature, body, senses, economics, politics, institutions, structures, etc. Most moderns in the past 200 years have in effect become materialists. In reaction to this modern secularism, materialism, and consumerism, there are however a growing number who escape into the world of gnosticism.

Conclusions

So, what conclusions can be drawn? It's not good enough to say we need a balanced view between these two extremes: the overemphasis on the material on the one hand, and the overemphasis on the spiritual on the other. We need a clearer understanding of how the spiritual realm relates to the material world, and the material to the spiritual. We can understand this properly only in the context of our faith that a loving God has created the world, that this loving God is redeeming the world, and that this loving God will bring this world to completion, despite all the evidence to the contrary.

But what do we do with strange texts like the one in Matthew 27 that first struck me recently while listening to Bach's St. Matthew's Passion. We read in the account of Jesus' death the following:

> And behold, the curtain of the temple was torn in two, from top to bottom; and the earth shook, and the rocks were split; the tombs also were opened, and many bodies of the saints who had fallen asleep were raised, and coming out of the tombs after his resurrection they went into the holy city and appeared to many. (Matt. 27:51-54)

What is one to make of this? The secular materialist will of course write the whole thing off as nonsense. The extreme gnostic will take this as evidence of the reality of spiritual bodies making their appearance. There is also a kind of Fundamentalist materialism which would see these bodies as actual, physical, material, biological bodies resuming ordinary life. Another fashionable approach nowadays is to say: it's a mystery and we should just leave it at that.

All four are unsatisfying interpretations of what's going on in these kinds of passages. Some kind of serious claim is being made here about the theological significance of historical events—in this case, of Jesus' death and resurrection. What is this theological significance? It has to do with interpreting specific historical events as part of an overall view of what God is doing with the world. Only this way can one understand the obvious connection between this Matthew passage and the Ezekiel text, where we read:

> 'Our bones are dried up, and our hope is lost; we are clean cut off.' Therefore prophesy, and say to them, Thus says the Lord God: Behold, I will open your graves, and raise you from your

> graves, O my people; and I will bring you home into the land of Israel. And you shall know that I am the Lord, when I open your graves, and raise you from your graves, O my people. And I will put my Spirit within you, and you shall live, and I will place you in your own land; then you shall know that I, the Lord, have spoken, and I have done it, says the Lord. (37:11-14)

What we have here is a way of speaking about the world which makes sense of historical events from a theological perspective. The Ezekiel text is interpreting the meaning of the exile of the Jews in Babylon and the meaning of hope in that context. The Matthew text is interpreting the events of Jesus' death and resurrection and what hope means for the early Christians. The writer of Matthew connects the Christ events with the fulfilling of the prophesy of Ezekiel. Paul in 1 Corinthians 15 connects our own resurrection with Christ's resurrection. In Romans 8 Paul connects the resurrection of the whole world with our resurrection. It is a non-scientific, non-literalistic, non-historicist way of speaking about the meaning of historical events and connecting them as a basis for hope and action in the concrete present. More to the point, it is a figurative way of interpreting our own moral responsibility within the world of history in the light of what we think God is doing with the world.

It is interesting that Jesus himself uses figurative language when speaking about the kingdom of God and the end-times. In Matthew 13:34-35 we read:

> Jesus told the crowds all these things in parables, without a parable he told them nothing. This was to fulfill what had been spoken through the prophet: 'I will open my mouth to speak in parables; I will proclaim what had been hidden from the foundation of the world.'

Remember the meaning of the term *Apocalypse:* a revealing of that which is hidden. When Jesus talked about the future, about things to come, he was talking about those things that were hidden, and to do this he chose to speak in parables, or figuratively. In John 16, he says, "I have said these things to you in figures of speech. The hour is coming when I will no longer speak to you in figures, but will tell you plainly of the Father" (16:25).

We are dealing here with the world of images, the imagination. But always—in all the parables of the kingdom and the parables of Hell and Judgment—the point is not speculation about future events but moral responsibility in the present. Belief in the Spiritual realities (whether divine or demonic) is not to preoccupy us for its own sake, or for means of escape from this world and its moral, social, and political responsibilities, but precisely as a motivation for engagement with life. This is what I take to be the meaning of Acts 1: 6-11, the account of Jesus' ascension. We read: "While he was going and they were gazing up toward heaven, suddenly two men in white robes stood by them. They said, 'Men of Galilee, why do you stand looking up toward heaven? This Jesus, who has been taken up from you into heaven, will come in the same way as you saw him go into heaven'" (verses 10-11). *In short: Get to work here on earth.*

TWENTY-SEVEN

Apparitions: The Virgin Mary Appears in Yugoslavia[*]

The language of dream, vision, apparition, and epiphany have always intrigued me because the normal rules of space (up and down, in and out, substance, extension and causation) and time (historical sequence from past to present to future, backwards and forwards, duration) don't apply. The language of night dream and day dream are not that different and bear similarities to the grammar of spiritual warfare and apocalypse as discussed in the previous essay. To reduce this way of speaking to psychological or materialist explanation (some form of epiphenomenon) does not do justice to the archetypal patterns that have consistently characterized such religious phenomena through the centuries. On the contrary, to objectify the spiritual subjects of such apparitions, to literalistically objectify the spiritual beings inherent in such visions—to debate or justify their concrete reality or even corporeality—is itself a form of materialist reduction. The important issue is the recognition that truths can be mediated through these epiphanies.

The challenge is to differentiate between authentic and inauthentic mediation of the divine Word. Inauthentic mediation occurs frequently and is vulnerable to the critiques of the nineteenth-century German philosopher Ludwig Feuerbach and to that of psychoanalyst Sigmund Freud, who said that religion was little

---

[*] Originally published as "Medugorje: The Virgin Mary Appears in Yugoslavia," in *IRF: A Newsletter of the International Religious Foundation, Inc.* 2.6 (Nov. - Dec. 1987): 1-2, 11. For notes on the text see the Notes section below.

more than psychological projection and human wish-fulfilment. There is, however, authentic mediation through such means—apparitions which convey the truth of God in given historical situations leading to healing, salvation, and social justice. Throughout biblical literature and church history there are those who have been especially attuned to divine communication of this sort. One has only to read about how God revealed the divine will to the early church mother Perpetua (c. 181-203), as recorded in her personal diaries,[1] to realize that alongside the rational and institutional ways of perceiving the Word of God there is another more intuitive lineage of receiving God's message. The glamorous, psychic powers of the fictional characters Jonathan and Nicholas Darrow in Susan Howatch's novels are a contemporary version of such classical epiphanies and apparitions.[2] The following essay, written before the collapse of communism in Eastern Europe, speaks to these issues in connection with apparitions of the Virgin Mary to a group of young people in former Yugoslavia, on the hillside of the small rural village of Medugorje, which I visited in April, 1987.[3]

◆ ◆ ◆

The recent appearances of the Virgin Mary and dramatic revival of the Mary cult in Yugoslavia raise profound questions for a socialist society, for the post-Vatican II Roman Catholic Church, and for all believers in the modern technological age. In April this year a friend and I were guided by Fr. Marko Orsolic, a Franciscan professor of theology in Sarajevo, and Fr. Peter Krasic, vice-president of the Franciscans in Herzegovina, to the small rural village of Medugorje, rapidly taking its place alongside other modern holy cities famous for Marian apparitions, such as Paris, LaSalett, Lourdes, and Fatima.

Whatever one thinks of the authenticity of such supernatural visions, the fact remains that a significant religious event is taking place here which has caught the imagination of millions of pilgrims, rich and poor, who have painstakingly made their way up the holy hill of Medugorje in the past six years. It is an ecumenical event which cannot easily be dismissed by secular society, established church officials and institutions, and observers of religious phenomena in the modern age.

In 1981 a group of five (some report six) children were innocently playing on a lonely hill just outside the small impoverished village of Medugorje, located in a predominantly Roman Catholic area in the Yugoslavian Republic of Bosnia-Herzegovina. They were interrupted in their play by a vision of a beautiful woman claiming to be the Blessed Virgin. Since that initial apparition she has appeared regularly to these same children in the parish church down in the village below and, after the vigils there were prohibited by the local bishop, in the nearby church rectory basement. The actual contents of the messages from Mary are hard to determine with any amount of accuracy, although reportedly they have become less political over the years, evolving from earlier promises to save the world from socialism to later more spiritualized and apocalyptic allusions to the end of the world.

Since 1981 some seven to eight million visitors from a variety of different countries, cultures, and Christian traditions have climbed up the holy hill of Medugorje. These pilgrims, some out of curiosity, most of them sincere seekers with various forms of physical and spiritual ailments coming to be miraculously helped by the "Mother of Sorrows," daily wend their way up the stony path, strewn with crosses and offerings of all kinds. The church below is filled to overflowing during daily mass, and long lines of fervent penitents, young and old, wait to make their personal confessions and pray for healing. At 7:30 every evening pilgrims and tourists anxiously crowd around the dark rectory, staring at the small basement window, hoping to catch a glimpse of the stream of light which will signify that once more the children, who still gather there daily, are having their private audience with the Blessed Mother.

The immediate consequence of all of this for the surrounding area and for the Republic as a whole is an obvious economic renaissance. Travel agencies, touring companies, builders, and private entrepeneurs seem to be the ultimate material beneficiaries of this spiritual revival. The most glaring example of this are the scores of little souvenir vendors who have been allowed to set up shop on state property right next to the parish church, to the chagrin and embarrassment of the local pastor, Fr. Tomislav Pervan. The public officials evidently find themselves in an awkward situation, sceptical of the religious phenomenon as such but willing to put up with it for its economic benefits. Foreign agencies are benefitting as well.

We met one travel agent from Chicago whose business had picked up dramatically since a nationally televised ABC News special on the apparitions. Her agency alone had brought 8,000 people to Medugorje. She attributed all of this to divine intervention. Another Italian travel company, reputedly on the brink of bankruptcy when the story broke, had experienced a remarkable economic recovery.

Yugoslavia is one of the most open and liberal of socialist countries. It prides itself in having developed an independent, decentralized form of socialism distinct from the centralized socialism of the USSR. Nevertheless, religion continues to be a troubling issue. First of all, the vitality and growth of religious faith and practice, particularly among young people, confounds Marxist theory, which predicts that with the revolution the need for a religious superstructure will gradually wither away. This is driving many of the younger sociologists of religion in Yugoslavia to drastic revisions of the doctrine of Marxist critique of religion to the point of seeing religion playing an ongoing positive role even in a socialist state. Religion, they say, will not die out but will continue to answer the existential needs of people.

Further, the fundamental problem for national unity in this country has been the age-old rivalries between national-ethnic peoples divided historically along three major religious lines.

Catholic, Orthodox, and Islamic religion has in the past often helped to intensify ethnic conflict. This combined with the fact that the established church reputedly cooperated, if not outrightly collaborated, with the Fascists during the revolutionary and Second World War years, continues to make religious belief suspect for being a reactionary force in society. Nevertheless, the hard line taken against religion immediately following the revolution of 1941-45 has softened over the years. Now, theoretically at least, religious affiliation is no longer seen as necessarily incompatible with the "progressive" aims of the socialist state.

The *sine qua non* for religious toleration in Yugoslavia, however, is that it be relegated to the private sphere and not become a political force. The church and individuals can believe what they want, as long as they do not become a political lobby criticizing or interfering with the Party's vision of what constitutes a just society. The Medugorje event is evaluated by public officials in terms not of its authenticity but of its political implications. Filip Simic, Deputy Minister for Religious Affairs in Bosnia-Herzegovina, whom we had the privilege of interviewing, saw no political threat from the growing Mary cult and confirmed the official line concerning religion in Yugoslavia namely that it be seen as a private affair."As long as religion preaches the general well-being and worth of individuals in Yugoslavia we have nothing against it," he added. He acknowledged that initially some people had apparently tried to take political advantage of the apparitions. This the state would not tolerate. The state did, however, have a responsibility along with the church to meet the needs of these suffering people on Yugoslavian soil.

If state officials find themselves in an awkward position, so do the church representatives. Vatican II saw a dramatic change in the church's official attitude toward Mary. The nineteenth and twentieth centuries experienced a noteworthy intensification of officially approved Marian devotion. With the Council, however, the role of Mary was explicitly subordinated to the worship of God mediated through Jesus Christ. Arguments for the adoration of Mary were no longer based on extra-biblical sources but firmly tied to the New Testament. As a result, Marian devotion as a separate cult subsided considerably. Despite the obvious affinity of Pope John Paul II for the adoration of Mary, the church hierarchy is highly sceptical of the Medugorje apparitions. This scepticism is evident right from the Vatican down to the Yugoslavian bishops and the local Franciscans in whose jurisdiction the appearances are taking place. The stringent form of investigation by the hierarchy of the children's stories is illustrative of the extent to which the Church has appropriated modern means of critical verification in the testing of such supernatural religious experiences.

A fifteen-member commission, including representatives from ten major theological faculties in Yugoslavia and two neuro-psychologists, was set up to investigate the authenticity of the children's claims. We talked to some of the members of this commission and found that the report concluded, by a wide margin (12 to 3), that their claims were false, full of contradictions and outright lies, and that the reported messages of the Virgin did not coincide with the teachings of the New Testament and the church. To our astonishment, however, the details of the report were not released because of pressure from the business community. Instead, another commission was set in motion to further investigate the evidence. In one thing the Franciscans and the public officials seemed to agree—that they had an obligation to meet the physical and spiritual needs of the pilgrims. Fr. Orsolic, himself a sceptic, had spent five hours hearing confession at Medugorje the previous Sunday.

What is one finally to make of this renewed interest in Marian appearances and devotion in the latter part of the twentieth century? Marian devotion has of course been around for a long time, at least since the fifth century. The intensification of the Mary cult in the nineteenth and twentieth centuries does suggest, however, that something deeper is going on here than an anachronistic spiritual aberration in certain impoverished parts of the modern world. Simple social-scientific and political explanations are inadequate. It is not enough to argue with Michael P. Carroll, as he does in his recent book *The Cult of the Virgin Mary*, that Mary "gratifies Oedipal desires of both sexes" or that Marian piety flourishes mainly in "areas where the father-ineffective family prevails."[4] Nor is it sufficient to explain all such eruptions of Mary worship as politically reactionary. Marian devotion, like most forms of spirituality, can become a powerful force for progressive social reform.

What we see in Medugorje is a genuine cry of suffering people for physical well-being and spiritual healing, a massive human yearning for the supernatural and the metaphysical which crosses ideological boundaries. Implicit in this is a profound critique of the technological exploitation of people in both capitalist and socialist countries. We are living at the end of the modern age. Our confidence in scientific panaceas is being shattered daily. There is manifest in Medugorje a longing for reconciliation with the mystical ground of human existence, an experience of that which transcends the mundane and the ordinary. Mary becomes for the pilgrims in Yugoslavia and for all of us an archetypal human being who bears within her womb not only the sorrows of humankind but also fresh hope for the birth of a new humanity.

The challenge for the church is to teach the theological significance of Marian devotion for authentic spirituality without allowing the magical and superstitious to distort that spirituality for reactionary purposes. Marian piety can lead to a genuine spirituality in the modern age only if Mary is seen as a bearer of the transcendent and eternal *logos* in whom the mighty are put down from their thrones and those of low degree are exalted. It is in this spirit that we too can exclaim with Elizabeth: "Blessed are you among women, and blessed is the fruit of your womb!"

TWENTY-EIGHT

Chiliastic Imagination and Social Change: Bloch's Interpretation of Müntzer*

I began working on Ernst Bloch's interpretation of Thomas Müntzer in a graduate course taught by Gregory Baum in the late 1970s, part of my interest in the neo-Marxist critique of religion as it found expression in the Frankfurt School of Critical theory.[1] Bloch, peripheral to this circle of philosophers, taught at the University of Tübingen and was influential in the work of Jürgen Moltmann.

I include this historical essay in the classical, dogmatically oriented section of this volume for a number of reasons. First, my own systematic theological reflections generally emerge out of the history of ideas. Second, this article illustrates, together with the immediately preceding essays, the nature of apocalyptic and chiliastic language. Third, it provides a bridge between earlier, more strictly theological essays to those focusing on political-ethical issues, of historical interest particularly to Mennonites. Bloch's revisionist interpretation of Müntzer, taking more seriously than dogmatic Marxists the mystical, religious, and theological impetus for social-political transformation, is especially pertinent to my overarching theme in this volume: that ethics needs to be metaphysically and theologically (dogmatically)

---

* What started as a paper in a graduate course was later published as "Chiliastic Imagination and Social Change: Bloch's Interpretation of Müntzer," in CLIO: A Journal of Literature, History and the Philosophy of History 9.2 (Winter 1980): 253-67. For notes on the text see the Notes section below.

grounded if it is not to be reduced to human action pure and simple. In Bloch's understanding of Müntzer, the mystical-theological and the political are inseparable. For Müntzer to talk apocalyptically, drawing on the eschatological imagery of Daniel and Revelation, is not an escape into another spiritualistic world but to talk about the transformation of this world into a new world.

Since 1980, when this essay was first published, I have become somewhat more cautious about thinking of theology and politics as two sides of the same coin. Through my study of how political theologies of the left (Paul Tillich) and right (Emanuel Hirsch) functioned in the 1920s and 1930s in Germany—where the criterion of "good" theology tended to be what side you were on politically—I have moved in the Barthian direction of saying that good theology has its own dogmatic ground distinct from and before all political ethics.

This transition in my thinking is reflected in some of my critiques against an Anabaptist-Mennonite theology that too quickly identifies itself as an alternative social-political option—one that is different from others not in that it is less political but that it has a different politics, a non-violent one. Nevertheless, one of the criteria for discerning between inauthentic and authentic dream, vision, spiritual warfare and apocalyptic language is their moral and ethical effects.

Cardinal John Henry Newman, in one of his sermons, makes a relevant point in this regard: "To know God is life eternal, and to believe in the gospel manifestation of Him is to know Him; but how are we to 'know that we know Him'? How are we to be sure that we are not mistaking some dream of our own for the true and clear vision? . . . St. John says, 'Hereby do we know that we know Him, if we keep His commandments,' Obedience is the test of faith."[2] One of the tests for the authenticity of the language of the imagination is its transformative moral and political power.

◆ ◆ ◆

Ernst Bloch's somewhat romantic treatment of the radical reformer Thomas Müntzer, in his *Thomas Müntzer als Theologe der Revolution* (1921), is a remarkable defence by a neo-Marxist of the religious-mystical dimensions of social change.[3] In this masterfully written book, which has never been translated into English, Bloch combines historical narrative, theological insight, and a powerful literary style to support a new interpretation of Müntzer. Not only does Bloch correct traditional Lutheran and Catholic diatribes against Müntzer; he goes beyond some of the orthodox Marxist reductionist theories of the Reformation. For Bloch, religious imagination is the central factor in Müntzer's revolutionary vision, and must be taken seriously for understanding the Reformation and in formulating modern theories of social change. Bloch appropriates historical-sociological analysis and theological-philosophical synthesis brilliantly for the purpose of understanding as well as furthering the ongoing human search for the kingdom of God on earth.

Unfortunately, however, Bloch's work on Müntzer has not been given the attention it deserves. While modern theologians have recognized the importance of Bloch for theology, both Marxist and non-Marxist historians of the Reformation have paid little or no attention to Bloch's book.[4] Marxist historians question Bloch's fidelity to their interpretation of history, and non-Marxists dislike his revolutionary romanticism and legitimately point to some grave historical inaccuracies in Bloch's analysis of Müntzer.[5] It is easy to see why historical "purists," concerned with historical objectivity and an analytic-quantitative approach to historical research, would find distasteful Bloch's more synthetic approach to historical objectivity and an analytic-quantitative approach to historical research, his overt revolutionary bias, and his deliberate *appropriation* of history. Bloch makes no pretension of being interested in historical facts *for their own sake*. He uses his study of Müntzer as a paradigm with which to challenge his readers to carry on the revolutionary tradition and work for a more just and free social order.

Bloch's passionate, though not doctrinaire, portrayal of Müntzer as a class-conscious revolutionary may tell us more about Bloch himself and the neo-Marxism of postwar Germany than it does about the historical Müntzer. Nevertheless, his picture of this heroic revolutionary figure is a powerful one, and it is so because he catches something of the sixteenth-century *Zeitgeist*, a feat which positivistically oriented historians cannot hope to rival. The importance of Bloch's book rests not primarily on a meticulous presentation of historical minutiae, but on its capturing the mood and spirit of a man and his times. Müntzer becomes for Bloch an ideal type in the Weberian and Troeltschian sense, one representative product of a time when economic forces and religious imagination, political realities, and apocalyptic dreams flowed into each other.

Not only, however, does Bloch grasp the mood and spirit of the "mystic with the hammer." His historical treatment of Müntzer and his theological insight into the Reformation, while obviously dated on many points, have an integrity of their own and anticipate some of the most recent scholarship in the field. Bloch, for instance, places Müntzer in the tradition of medieval mysticism, a line of thinking which is increasingly being accepted by leading Müntzer scholars.[6] All this is to say that, while Bloch's book admittedly raises some serious methodological questions concerning the utilization of history and theology for political purposes, it is the conviction of this writer that Bloch makes a plausible case, and that his historical-literary portrayal of Müntzer deserves closer attention than it has so far achieved, particularly by historians in North America. This essay will attempt to examine Bloch's historical and theological picture of Müntzer, giving particular heed to the role of religion in movements for social change as Bloch envisions it.

Bloch's *Thomas Müntzer* cannot be studied in isolation, as a work of pure history. It was written just after World War I, after Bloch had joined the communist-oriented KPD.[7] It follows upon the heels of *Geist der Utopie* (1918) and a small article, "Blick in den Chiliasmus des Bauernkriegs und Wiedertäufertum," published in 1920 and incorporated almost verbatim into his *Thomas Müntzer*.[8] His study of the Reformation is obviously an attempt to find historical roots for his socialist and utopian ideas. Bloch's view of history is as much determined by the future as it is by the past, if not more so. This is most vividly stated in the last few lines of his magnum opus, *Das Prinzip Hoffnung*: "The true origin is not at the beginning, but at the end, and it truly begins when society (*Gesellschaft*) and existence (*Dasein*) become radical, that is, when they grasp themselves at the root (*Wurzel*)." The real root of society, for Bloch, is the working, creating, and rebuilding activity of man. Once society has truly grasped its root within a real democracy without alienation, humanity will have reached its real home.[9]

These few lines from Bloch's greatest work express the underlying revolutionary presupposition and bias of all his writing, including his historical and theological treatment of Müntzer. Müntzer is not merely a heroic figure of the past, to be studied as objective history. He graphically represents the ongoing struggle of oppressed humanity for its own liberation and the creation of a new heaven and a new earth. This future, however, remains *an open one,* forever unfinished. This point cannot be stressed too strongly in defending Bloch against those non-Marxist historians who accuse Marxists of imposing an ideological theoretical framework on historical facts.[10] While Bloch is clearly committed to the struggle for a just social order and reads history from this perspective, he refuses to construct ideological images of the future.[11] Here he, like the neo-Marxists of the Frankfurt school, remains true to the Jewish tradition with its rejection of idolatrous images of God and the future.[12]

As *Das Prinzip Hoffnung* retroactively sheds light on Bloch's book on Müntzer, in the same way Bloch's earlier *Geist der Utopie* anticipates and prepares for *Thomas Müntzer*. In this book, which has been referred to as a "'system of theoretical messianism,'" one of "Judeo-Christian and philosophical-theological beginnings," Bloch already shows his ambiguous relationship both to Marxism and religion.[13] While he wants to expose the "humbug of the bourgeois-feudal ideology of the state," he is just as deeply critical of the Marxist tendency to empty people of all subjectivity and reduce reality to economic explanations, banishing all dreams and concrete utopias.[14]

In a most effective passage, Bloch says of Marxism: "Dialectics has voided the economy, but the soul and the faith it was to make room for are missing.... [It] helps us neither to comprehend the inherent utopian tendency, nor to grasp and judge the substance of its miraculous images— even less to dismiss primal religious desire. Throughout all the movements and goals of worldly transformation, this has been a desire to make room for life, for the attainment of a divine essence, for men to integrate themselves at last, in a millennium, with human kindness, freedom, and the light of the *telos*."[15] It is to answer this question—of the historical significance and meaning of utopian movements, miraculous images, primal religious desire—that Bloch writes his *Thomas Müntzer*. The book is a sociology of a historical religious movement, in which Bloch in a Weberian and Troeltschian fashion examines the sociological meaning and historical effect of religious phenomena.

Hans-Jürgen Goertz has rightly argued that "Müntzer must be released from the narrow confines of Marxist, non-Marxist, and confessional interpretations, from the premises of an Anabaptist scholarship which has been shy of revolution, as well as from the acclamations of a political theology which has made a fad of revolution."[16] It is true that Müntzer has been held captive by these various competing points of view. Until recently, the Lutheran interpretation has been the predominant one, by and large seeing Müntzer as a spiritualist fanatic, a revolutionary primarily responsible for the peasant revolt of 1525, an extreme visionary guided by the inner word, in contrast to Luther's much more reasonable reliance on the outer word.[17] From this perspective, Müntzer is defined by his relation to the extreme Zwickau spiritualist Nicholas Storch, rather than by the medieval mystical tradition as represented by Tauler and Suso.[18] Catholics, on the other hand, have tended to see Müntzer as the logical outcome of the rebellious Lutheran spirit and its rejection of ecclesiastical and papal authority.[19] Finally, scholars of the Anabaptist tradition, concerned with correcting a distorted historiography concerning their peace-loving tradition, have been preoccupied with dissociating themselves as far as possible from the revolutionary Müntzer phenomenon.[20]

All of these various groups—Lutherans, Catholics, and Anabaptists/ Mennonites—have been concerned with separating themselves from this revolutionary sixteenth-century figure on the basis of a one-sided, largely negative interpretation. Not until recently has Müntzer received a less hostile hearing by non-Marxist scholars such as Willis Stoesz, Abraham Friesen, James Stayer, Werner Packull, and Hans-Jürgen Goertz, to name just a few.[21] Ironically, it was Marxist historiography that was largely responsible for a more sympathetic Müntzer scholarship. Unfortunately, the Marxist historians have tended to swing the pendulum to the other extreme and have used Müntzer for narrow revolutionary purposes, reducing and distorting the image of this complex reformer once again.

Nineteenth-century socialists and revolutionaries saw Müntzer as a heroic forerunner of modern revolutionary causes. This was especially true of Friedrich Engels who argued that Müntzer was a class-conscious revolutionary and communist. According to Engels, the battle lines of the Reformation were quite simply drawn between 1) the Catholic reactionaries, 2) the bourgeois reformers (primarily Lutheran), and 3) the left-wing revolutionaries.[22] With great oversimplification, Engels put the peasants, the labourers, the Anabaptists, and the Müntzerites rather generally into this third category.[23]

Engels is of course right in stressing the economic and class character of the peasant upheavals, but he does grave injustice to the religious character of the revolution by calling it a screen and a disguise for the political struggle.[24] It is at this point, as we shall see, where Bloch goes beyond the traditional Marxist interpretation. He takes the religious element much more seriously, viewing it as essential rather than merely a peripheral ingredient of this and other revolutionary movements.

Unlike many non-Marxist historians who profess to strive after an objective understanding of the past, often not recognizing their very pronounced denominational, political, or other presuppositions, Bloch makes his intent clear from the start. *Thomas Müntzer* begins with a forthright statement of intentions. "We want always to remain only with ourselves," he says. "In no way do we want to look back. But we become existentially involved . . . the dead return, their works will rise again in our midst." "Müntzer," he adds, "is above all else history in the fruitful sense; he and his, and everything that is worth writing about, exist for the purpose of challenging and enthusing us. . . ."[25] This in a nutshell is Bloch's historical method.

How and in what direction is history to be used? Here again Bloch makes himself perfectly clear. His purpose is to further the cause of human liberation and freedom, whatever that may consist of. In the concluding section of the book, he draws an implicit comparison between the utopian dreams of Müntzer and those of Marx: "Marxism and the dream of the Unconditional unite in a similar process and campaign plan. . . ." They are both committed to the total end of the present order, in which the human essence is oppressed, contemptible, and forgotten. Both are devoted to the rebuilding, in some way, of this earth and the creation of the kingdom. "Müntzer together with all the chiliasts remains the prophetic voice on this stormy pilgrimage" (229). Not only Müntzer, but Bloch himself becomes the prophet. Remaining true to his statement of intent, Bloch becomes existentially involved at almost every point. Freely using biblical and Judaic language, he calls for a messianic vision: "We have here no abiding city, other than the future one we are seeking; a messianic disposition is preparing its approach . . . (228).

One cannot help but notice the contrast between Bloch's approach to writing history and that of a non-Marxist Müntzer historian such as Werner O. Packull. For Packull the goal of history is not to change society but to understand the past. "History," he says, "is not primarily a search for truth *in* the past, but a quest for a true, accurate perception and understanding of the past."[26] Packull goes on to charge Marxist historians with having more "monistic, politicized pedagogical criteria of truth," in contrast to non-Marxist historians, who tend to view truth more relativistically and pluralistically.

It is of course true that a neo-Marxian reading of history, as Bloch's obviously is, raises some serious methodological questions. There is a danger of imposing nineteenth and twentieth-century political, economic, and Enlightenment categories onto the sixteenth century. But then no historian is exempt from these dangers. It is also highly questionable whether western non-Marxist historians do in fact operate on the basis of a less monolithic perception of truth. Packull's desire for a "true, accurate perception and understanding of the past"[27] is beyond reproach. But he also argues that the historian needs to admit openly his methodological presuppositions and biases. The problem in writing history is precisely the attempt to remain true to the historical past and to acknowledge one's own methodological biases. In my opinion, Bloch makes an admirable effort to do just that.

Bloch divides his book into two main sections: one dealing generally with the life of Müntzer, and the other discussing directions in his theology and preaching. Since we are interested here more in Bloch's own presentation of the material than in the actual historical facts concerning Müntzer and the sixteenth century, we will review thematically the story as Bloch tells it without examining the historical accuracy of his portrayal except in a few instances.

The most striking aspect of Bloch's portrayal is the respect he shows for the fusion of the *political* and the *religious* in Müntzer's life and thought. While Müntzer's interest, especially in the earlier part of his career in Zwickau and Allstedt, was primarily religious and liturgical, increasingly the religious and the political nature of his reform concerns became inseparable. In a most remarkable description of this fusion of the theological and the political, Bloch remarks that "with the active theologian of revolution the one is interchangeably intertwined with the other, the deed with the distant goal, the ideological with the pure religious idea . . . ." (21). In such a revolutionary situation hostility toward the lord, anticlericalism, desire for church reform, and the ecstatic anticipation of the advent overflow into one another. Bloch rightly rejects a strict separation between a "spiritual realm" and a "political realm," prevalent among some theologians and historians.[28]

In Bloch's opinion Müntzer's final break with Luther came in a July 1523 letter to Luther, even though "the break had long since taken place inwardly." After this open break, Müntzer became essentially a class-conscious revolutionary and chiliastic communist (25). His revolutionary class consciousness was couched in biblical imagery. His famous message to the princes *(Fürstenpredigt),* which he preached in an Allstedt chapel on July 13, 1524, illustrates Müntzer's use of Old Testament apocalyptic imagery to wage his own cause. Just as in the dreams of Nebuchadnezzar in the book of Daniel, where the pillar of the builders is smashed by the rolling stone and a new kingdom is set up, so Müntzer predicts the smashing of the princely kingdoms and the coming of a new order. The essence of this new order is recognized by the lower classes and not by Luther and the princes (33ff). The rejection of his call for this new order by Luther and the princes drives Müntzer more and more into an identification with the poor farmer *(armen Ackersmann)* and artisan *(Handwerksmann)* (45-46).

At no point, however, despite his growing political involvement with the poor and the oppressed, does Müntzer leave his theology behind or consciously use it simply as a screen. His religious apocalypticism and his revolutionary politics grow and intensify together and reinforce each other. The growing resentment, anger, and revolutionary fervour of both the leaders and the masses go hand in hand with an increasing chiliasm, apocalyptic visions and imagery, and cosmic signs of coming events. The rainbow in the sky is taken by the masses of peasant and poor labourers, gathered on the Frankenhausen battlefield, as the sure sign and covenant of God's protection and their victory over the enemy (76).

The battle of Frankenhausen, which has been called the turning point of the Peasant War, ended in a tragic defeat of the peasant cause, the horrendous massacre of thousands by the princes, and the execution of Müntzer himself. Müntzer's chiliastic and apocalyptic spirit, however, according to Bloch, lived on and surfaced even more remarkably in the Anabaptist uprising in the city of Münster in 1535, where leaders, influenced by Müntzer's earlier teaching and preaching, took over the city and established a type of theocratic-communistic city state. Münster was conceived of as the New Jerusalem where Christ would set up his earthly kingdom.

Here, in Bloch's opinion, Müntzer's life and preaching reached its highest fulfilment (83ff). Proletariat and petty-bourgeois alike, driven by a mixture of revolutionary motives and an anticipation of the millennium, attempted to realize their earthly yearning for salvation, the resurrection of the world (87-88). But the Münster experiment in communism also came to a tragic end. Men and women were slaughtered without discretion. The polemical nature of Bloch's writing is evident in his rather one-sided portrayal of the terrors and violence perpetrated by the princes in Münster and at Frankenhausen. He tends, further, to romanticize the leaders of both episodes. Particularly romantic is his treatment of the last days of Thomas Müntzer. The historical connection between the preaching of Müntzer and the theocracy of Münster can also be seriously questioned.

All of these criticisms, however, do not substantially undermine the success with which Bloch demonstrates the interdependence between social, political, historical, and religious phenomena. The *religious* consciousness of these sixteenth-century revolutionary movements grew out of concrete historical circumstances, then in turn helped to create a new *historical* consciousness in these people, helping thus to shape the very course of history itself. While Bloch tends to overrate Müntzer's organizing role in the Peasants War of 1525, he legitimately illustrates that the apocalyptic and chiliastic imagination that Müntzer espoused was a broad and significant phenomenon, not concocted by Müntzer but grasped by him. Müntzer was a "type" or representative of a prevalent mood. His chiliastic rhetoric effectively caught the imagination of a large number of people.

With Müntzer's death, a highly worthwhile, adequate, and embodied world view was laid to rest (99). Müntzer demanded the extraordinary but not the illusionary (101). The real and the surreal were united in his preaching. He embodied the brief dream of a democracy, a mystical world republic, a theocracy under Christ. He postulated communal property in the nature of primitive Christianity, preached the removal of all oppressive governmental authority, and urged that law be based on morality and the anticipation of Christ (98). History, since it was written by the victors, has underestimated the significance of this revolutionary hero.

After Müntzer, and after Münster, the fighting spirit of Anabaptism capitulated before the pressures of the surrounding world and princely powers. With the coming of Menno Simons, according to Bloch, Anabaptism made a shallow peace with the world, just like the early Christian church had done (92). Bloch tends, like Engels, to throw Müntzer, the Münsterites, the Anabaptists, the peasants, and the poor working class all into one homogeneous revolutionary group. He tends to oversimplify the commonality of these rather divergent groups under the general rubric of Anabaptist (*Wiedertäufer*) or Baptist (*Täufer*). Anabaptist scholarship has convincingly demonstrated the heterogeneous and pluralistic nature of early Anabaptism, both in beliefs and in origins. Consequently, it is a grave distortion and oversimplification to accuse Anabaptism, as Bloch does, of generally making a shallow peace with the world.

Nevertheless, Bloch is right in stressing the political significance of early Anabaptism. He rightly argues that the deeper the Protestant Church sank into a state-church mentality, the more politically significant was the Anabaptist espousal of adult baptism, for instance. Late baptism was essentially a rejection of state-church alliance. The Anabaptists, in Bloch's narrative, proclaimed in Bakunin-like fashion voluntary association, an internationalism of the poor and elect. Bloch argues convincingly that Müntzer and the Anabaptists (*Täufertum*) represented the *political* left, a new and radical principle of the Reformation, in their search for external freedom, in their emphasis on absolute ethical and religious independence (102). What gives Bloch the crucial edge over traditional Marxist interpretations, however, is not so much his analysis of the political implications of early Anabaptism but his examination of the *religious basis* for their political radicalism.

As the title of Bloch's book clearly states, Müntzer must be seen as both theologian and revolutionary. Even Marxist scholars like Steinmetz have noted the significance of Bloch's contribution in this area.[29] And Hans-Jürgen Goertz confirms what Bloch had said more than fifty years earlier: "The decisive problem of interpreting Müntzer today," says Goertz, "consists in discovering how he provides a *theological* basis for revolution."[30] While Bloch's analysis of precisely *how* Müntzer's theology provides a framework for revolution differs from Goertz's own view, the important observation here is that Bloch does in fact stress the theological dimensions of social change.

The second part of Bloch's book is devoted largely to the sociological analysis of Zwinglian, Calvinistic, Lutheran, Catholic, and sectarian theology. Bloch is especially interested in showing how these various theologies related to the social, economic, and political world in which they found themselves. None of them, he argues, has an adequate theology for instigating social change, except for the sect type. Depending heavily on Weberian and Troeltschian social analysis, Bloch becomes much more polemical than in his harsh critique of the church types, particularly that of Lutheranism.

Only with the sect-type do we arrive at an adequate theological basis for social change. The early Anabaptists, of which Müntzer is a representative type, fall into this sect-type category, in contrast to the Zwinglians, Lutherans, Calvinists, and Catholics who make up the church-type. Obviously depending heavily on Troeltsch's *Social Teachings*, Bloch enumerates the theological and social strengths of the sect-type *contra* the church-type: voluntary membership, strong sense of community, belief in the fundamental goodness of humanity, hope in the immanent transformation of the world, identification with the poor and the oppressed, a yearning for the *parousia*, and inclination toward an allegorical-spiritualistic understanding of the world and the Bible, and a propensity for single-mindedness, homogeneity, and monotheism. While the church-type is syncretistic, eclectic, and polytheistic, intent on coming to terms with the present order, sects are future-oriented, eagerly anticipating the advent of a new order, a heavenly Jerusalem on earth (169-75).

The dated nature of Bloch's treatment is most evident in this rather simple and neat classification of church and sect types. His long list of all the positive political attributes of the sect type, fitting into his own revolutionary bias, is grossly overstated and tends to mitigate somewhat the strength of his analysis. Nevertheless, his fundamental point—the positive connection between theology and social transformation—remains intact. While Bloch laments the fact that Müntzer and the other Anabaptist radicals did not more fully think through the revolutionary theology which was latent in their preaching, he maintains that it was their *theology* which gave them the power, energy, and endurance necessary for social transformation (200). Although Müntzer had strong spiritual and intellectual ties with mystics such as Joachim of Fiore, he himself was not primarily a contemplative soul and did not escape into a mystical land of the soul (208). He was concerned with the transformation of the real world; he strove for a new heaven and a new earth.

It is at this point where Bloch's interpretation of Müntzer differs most substantially from that of Goertz, who also stresses the mystical roots of Müntzer's theology of revolution. Goertz explains Müntzer's theology from the standpoint of an inner mystical process of salvation. The inner transformation comes first and is then directed outward to the social realities around him. But inherent in this mystical concern for the transformation of the soul is an element of world-negation which proves to be the downfall of Müntzer's social effectiveness.[31]

For Bloch, however, it is the *dialectic* between a chiliastic imagination and the real historical world that distinguishes Müntzer from his teachers, Eckhart and Tauler. The content of his apocalyptic vision was the kingdom of God on earth—the descent of the heavenly Jerusalem to earth. Translated into more earthly language, this is the *metapolitical* and *metareligious* principle of all revolution—the advent and the breaking in of the freedom of the children of God (210).

In his article, "Blick in den Chiliasmus des Bauernkriegs und Wiedertäufertums," Bloch summarizes the main thrust of his later book on Müntzer. Contesting the orthodox Marxist explication of history, Bloch argues that, while economic and political forces helped to hasten the changes brought about by the Reformation, they are not an adequate explanation for the power behind the explosive emotions of the masses and the powerful enthusiasm of the chiliasts. Something more than mere economic theory is needed to explain the revolutionary fervour and strength of these movements for social transformation. What is required is an analysis and understanding of religious imagination. Dreams, emotions, enthusiasm, and inspiration are clothed by more than pure necessity and suffering, and are never only hollow ideologies. These daydreams arise from a definite point in the soul and burn longer than any empirical disaster, graphically illustrated by the chiliasm of the Peasants War of the sixteenth century.[32] All the prescriptions of the radical preachers during that time would have remained meaningless and incomprehensible to the masses had they not been accompanied by a religious imagination and fantasy.

An essential ingredient of this chiliastic movement was its egalitarian and communistic tendency. The masses banded together on a totally new basis and for a new cause—a communistic-spiritualistic state, a mystical, democratic republic. They did not fight for *better* days, or *gradual* reform of society, but for the end of all days. Their hope was for a radical breakthrough of a new society. Bloch concludes this brief but brilliant article with the statement that gives the kernel of his thought about theology and revolution: "However, what was dreamed and intended yesterday," he says, "must come to pass tomorrow, neither power nor darkness has conquered the longing; behind the desert awaits Canaan, and God always remains the cloud during the day, and a pillar of fire during the night of affliction."[33] The mystical and the religious are not negated but are fleshed out in the concrete and the real. The *mystical* democracy must precede the *actual* democracy.

While Bloch's historical accuracy may be questioned at a number of points, and his specific research on Müntzer may have been surpassed, he has something to teach us in terms of historical method, theological insight, and sheer brilliance of literary style. In Müntzer, Bloch has found a man with a kindred spirit. It has been said of Müntzer that he "conceived a theology of revolution which contains on the one hand embryonic elements of the Marxist theology of society and revolution, and, on the other hand, the elements of a theology of revolution as it is developed today in the ecumenical movement."[34] Bloch too, in his life and thought, combines a radical Marxist view of history and societal change with a theoretical messianism rooted in the Judeo-Christian tradition.

Although it is true, as Packull argues, that the Marxist-Christian dialogue may not be an adequate *a priori* starting point for Müntzer research in a strictly historical sense,[35] one can surely assume that both Marxists and Christians are committed to a theory of social change and in this have something in common. As such it is at least conceivable that their respective readings of history may have points of coincidence, neither of them starting from a methodologically neutral point.

Here Bloch's existential involvement in his historical narrative is instructive. Placing Müntzer in the company of a long subterranean list of non-conformist heretics and movements—Marcionites, Montanists, Cathari, Waldensians, Albigensians, Joachamites, Brethren of the Good Will, of the Common Life, of the Free Spirit, Eckhart, Hussites, Anabaptists, Sebastian Frank, Illuminati, Weitling, Tolstoy, and Religious Socialists—Bloch makes no attempt at hiding his historical sympathies and methodological biases.[36] He is reading history from the perspective of the underdog, and is committed to a theory of social change. Writing in the tradition of Karl Mannheim, he assumes that economic conditions and means of production depend upon higher simultaneous mental constructs for reinforcements, and that these mental constructs are never socially and politically neutral—they either reinforce given social reality, as in ideology, or they critique socio-economic conditions, as in utopian thinking.[37]

TWENTY-NINE

Theology and the So-called "Orders of Creation": Nationality as an Instance*

It has been my conviction for some time now that when social ethics (in the form of discipleship) gets placed after a discussion of the doctrine of the Church, as you find it in most historic Mennonite confessions of faith and in virtually all Mennonite systematic theological reflection, the true theological significance of "God-ordained" institutions (Rom. 13) throughout human history, by which God preserves the world from total chaos and disintegration, is not adequately understood or acknowledged.

This problem becomes even more pronounced when, as is the case in the Believers Church tradition, the Church is understood not in a universal comprehensive sense, but in the sense of a small group of believers gathered together from out of larger culture and society. In this scenario, how God governs the world "outside the perfection" of Christ remains largely unaddressed; the focus is primarily, if not exclusively, on what it means to be faithful "inside the perfection of Christ" with little analysis of what positive role human institutions of family, tribe, ethnicity,

---

* Originally published as "Theology and Nationalism," in *Canadian Mennonites and the Challenge of Nationalism*, ed. Abe J. Dueck (Winnipeg: Manitoba Mennonite Historical Society, 1994), 1-20; and "Mennonites, Theology and Nationalism," in *Journal of Mennonite Studies* 12 (1994): 89-103. For notes on the text see the Notes section below.

nationality, government play in the divine economy of the world at large and the cosmos as a whole. The church is of course, for Christians the primary community of allegiance—the community within which our ultimate values and commitments are shaped, a theme I turn to in a later essay of this volume, "Virtue, Justice and the Moral Community: A Critical-Appreciative Appraisal of Alisdair MacIntyre and the Narrative School of Theology."

This present essay, which does not deal with the church itself but with the larger context within which the church seeks to live out its commitments, was first presented at a symposium on "Canadian Mennonites and the Challenge of Nationalism," held in Winnipeg in May 1993, and later published twice.[1] In it I begin to reflect on the nature and theological significance of what Paul Tillich has named the "myths of origin" (like nature, soil, blood, family, tribe, nation). This and the following three essays, "War as a Theological Litmus Test: Hirsch, Tillich, Barth, and the Confessing Church," "God is Love but not a Pacifist," and "Christians, Policing, and the Civil Order," all explore related issues having to do with church and world, and the place and role of Christians in national and international life, the latter two more specifically with the Mennonite peace witness. What ties them together is their attempt to think dogmatically about Christian social ethics.

A systematic treatment of a Christian social ethic from the perspective of the historic peace church and classical Christian theology ought to include a careful analysis of the historical, sociological, economic, and political factors determining modern societies. This does mean, methodologically, that one is founding Christian ethics on universal, natural reason (although one ought not to disregard classical understandings of natural revelation, including reason, too quickly). Christian ethics is grounded in the Christian revelation, most specifically the Christian doctrine of God.

It is interesting here to observe how Karl Barth, thought of by some as the "father" of contemporary Christian nonfoundationalism, engages secular philosophy (natural reason) in his own dogmatic work. The amount of time and effort Barth, in his Doctrine of Creation, for instance, devotes to reading carefully the primary sources and explicating the thought of philosophers such as Schopenhauer, Descartes, and Leibnitz, on the way toward articulating his own biblically based view of Creation is really quite remarkable.[2] While he is unequivocal in his rejection of making philosophy the starting point for the Christian doctrine of creation (only Revelation can be that), he consistently engages the modern Western philosophical tradition as a negative conversation partner in formulating his own alternative biblical reading. My approach is more Alexandrian than is Barth's. This means that some form of natural theology and reason play a more foundational role in my thinking about ethics than they do for Barth.

In this essay I look at the lessons one can learn from twentieth-century nationalist movements (German National Socialism in the 1920s and 1930s, and more recent ethnic conflicts in former Yugoslavia), and the role the Christian religion has played *in these movements, in my effort to gain greater clarity on how Christian theology might more adequately deal with the myths of origin, or the so-called "Orders of Creation." Some of my proposals anticipate what Miroslav Volf has more recently so powerfully argued in his book* Exclusion and Embrace.[3] *I conclude with a look at the Bible and nationality and some of the theological ramifications for the contemporary world. At the 1993 symposium I was justifiably criticized for not dealing with the church as the new* polis. *My views on ecclesiology are partially spelled out in subsequent essays of this volume.*

◆ ◆ ◆

Definitions

Modern nationalism is a response to modernity, a response to the loss of cohesion in contemporary culture. A theology that intends to deal adequately with the issue of nationalism, therefore, will need to address this crisis—the fragmentation and disintegration of communal life in the modern and postmodern world.

The first challenge is a definitional one. What is "nationalism" and what is "theology?" Let us consider nationalism first. How does the term *nationalism* connect to other terms such as *nationality, nation, ethnicity (ethnos), Volk* (a people)? These are all related although not synonymous concepts, and deserve to be carefully defined if one wants to do justice to the moral, ethical, and theological issues involved.

I find helpful Paul Tillich's way of speaking about this group of terms. He goes behind them to a common root: the notion of the "powers of origin"—nature, soil, blood, family, tribe, nation.[4] These are the biological powers that give us individual and group identity and tie us to nature and being (space), in contrast to those which tie us to history, history-making, and becoming (time). All these concepts are related to each other; yet it is important that we not equate all respect for powers of origin (like ethnicity and nationality) with nationalism, or with their demonization in certain forms of nationalism.

The second concept needing definition is *theology*. Among the variety of historical attempts to define theology I continue to find Anselm's notion the most adequate: Theology is "faith seeking understanding" *(fides quaerens intellectum)*, or put in another way, "I believe to understand" *(credo ut intelligam)*. This means that theology takes its starting point to be faith (or revelation, in Barth's terms) not reason. And yet reason continues to play a highly significant role in the task of theology (Barth may not have given reason a sufficient place in the essential task of theology, although even he had a place for it[5]).

Appropriating Anselm's definition for myself, I would say: Christian theology is "faith seeking understanding" concerning God and all things in relation to God; premised on faith in God as transcendent mystery of the world, made known historically in the Christ-event, and immanently present as dynamic power in the Holy Spirit; in the light of the Scriptures (first), the church's historical confessions (second), and (finally) insight from all areas of human knowledge and experience, past and present. I take the "powers of origin" (to use the language of Tillich) to be some of those realities of human existence and experience that have theological significance—especially in their relation to the Christian doctrines of God, God's creation of the world, and God's providence and preservation of the world.

The Problem Identified

Contemporary theology is faced with a conundrum. Ever since the triumph and demise of National Socialism in the 1930s and 1940s, with its accompanying atrocities, many have equated nationalism (and related concepts) with un-Christian bigotry and injustice. Can one so easily, however, identify a concern for elements of origin, like ethnicity and nationality, with reactionary politics and oppression in the present situation? Is there not a sense in which the dynamic "myths of origin"— such as nature, soil, blood, family, tribe, and nation—are positive and defining characteristics of what it means to be human and, therefore, are to be affirmed? The dilemma faced by contemporary theology is the following: Is nationalism (or nationality) to be rejected theologically as a *negative power* driving peoples to ethnocentricism, intolerance, racism, and barbarism? Or can it be a *positive force* for understanding oneself, for the liberation of oppressed peoples, and to be theologically supported on the grounds of justice, autonomy, the right to dignity ,and self-determination? Are nationality, ethnicity, and family not intrinsic goods of creation?

Structure and Methodology

I will first look at historical lessons to be learned from the experiences and debates on these very questions in Germany in the 1920s and 1930s; then examine the contemporary revival of nationalism both on the right and the left, illustrated most dramatically in the nationalistic wars in Eastern Europe, particularly in the former Yugoslavia. Finally, I will look at Mennonites, theology, and nationality.

Historical Lessons: German Theology and Nationalism in the 1920s and 1930s

My doctoral work was in the area of German nationalism in the 1920s and 1930s. I concentrated in particular on two "political theologians" of the period: Emanuel Hirsch on the right and Paul Tillich on the left. My research was published in a book entitled *The Emanuel Hirsch and Paul Tillich Debate: A Study in the Political Ramifications of Theology.*[6] Hirsch and Tillich came from similar Lutheran pastors' homes, both studied theology under liberal professors in Berlin, where they first met in 1907. Both were ordained as pastors. They early developed a close friendship, wrote a play together, Hirsch fell in love with Tillich's sister, and they shared many similar theological ideas, with a life-long interest in each other's books and careers. However, World War I changed them significantly. Hirsch became a passionate *national* Lutheran and Tillich became an ardent defender of *socialist* Christianity and a founding member of the German "Religious Socialist" movement.

Throughout the 1920s they had extensive personal contact with each other and exchanged substantive correspondence. The final rupture between them occurred in 1933. Hirsch became a strong believer in Hitler and National Socialism as the God-ordained destiny for Germany and Protestant Christianity. Tillich may have been attracted to some aspects of National Socialism but in the end rejected it, and together with Jewish friends was on the first list of those who lost their jobs at the University of Frankfurt. He moved to New York, where he began a brilliant theological career in North America. Hirsch became a leading protagonist in the German church struggle on the side of the pro-Hitler "German Christians" and as dean of the theological faculty at the University of Göttingen. He wrote many books during this period and after 1945, when he resigned from the University and lived virtually in exile in his own country until his death in 1972. Tillich died in 1965. The controversy between Hirsch and Tillich raises many of the central theological issues concerning nationalism.

Hirsch: A Theological Defence of Nationality

The case of Hirsch illustrates my thesis—that modern nationalism is a way of coming to terms with the legacy of the Enlightenment. Hirsch was deeply disillusioned with the Enlightenment while accepting much of what it stood for. Theologically, on the one hand, he rejected conservative traditional Lutheran orthodoxy and confessionalism in the face of modern critical thought. On the other hand, he also rejected just as strongly the individualism and loss of authority and moral discipline that he felt characterized nineteenth-century liberal cultural Protestantism. He regarded National Socialism and a theology in tune with National Socialism as a third way—a way into the future. He was one of several prominent theologians in Germany who in the War and in the post-world War I period had re-discovered the concept of *Volk* as central for their theological work. It was a concept which for them served to counter the individualism of nineteenth-century liberal theology in favour of the virtues of community, solidarity, commitment, and self-sacrifice for the sake of the common good. *It was a contextual theology, in which theology was seen always to be in the service of a community—the national, ethnic community within which one finds oneself.*

In order to understand Hirsch's perspective properly, one has to understand what he means by nationality. Hirsch distinguishes between *Volk* (folk) and *Nation* (nation). *Volk* is a concept before nation, and refers to a group of people with a common biological-racial, cultural, ethnic, linguistic, and religious heritage. It is more than a biological-racial entity, but blood-relatedness is an important aspect of its group identity. It is family or tribe writ large. The word *nation* refers to this people (*Volk*) having become conscious of its group identity in social, political, and historical terms. Human beings, he says, do not grow like wild flowers—isolated and mixed up. According to Hirsch, humans are not like such wild flowers but are born into and grow up within a national community, or more accurately, self-conscious "peoplehood" (*Volksgemeinschaft*). This is a historical fact which powerfully shapes individuals and which they experience as law-defining and binding them. The individual receives his/her external fate and inner being from this inescapable fact. This is why any conversion from one nationality to another is a slow and painful process that can be completed only in succeeding generations, for the character of one's nationality shapes one's soul or personality.[7]

Hirsch calls this the God-given boundary which we dare not cross, the "hidden sovereign" which is the ground for every healthy nation-state. Such national-consciousness (*Nationalgefühl*) is a pre-Christian good, an order of creation.[8] It is a good which must be respected within the temporal order. As long as the sun shines there will be such distinctions between different national and ethnic groups. Only in the eternal spiritual realm are these distinctions transcended and the christological norm of unity between all becomes applicable. Only spiritually can one speak of a universal human community. Anyone who, like Tillich, avoids commitment to particular historical communities in favour of a universal human community is confusing the temporal/external and the eternal/spiritual and has a faulty understanding of what it means to be human, what it means to be morally and ethically responsible within a given historical context.

Hirsch maintains that the holy boundary of nationality cannot be crossed. One's nationality—not synonymous with but certainly including biological, material, racial as well as spiritual qualities—is the highest earthly communal bond, created by God, to which one must submit oneself and be obligated if one is to find meaning within human existence. Hirsch is tragically aware of the origin, givenness, and inescapability of one's own historical situation.

I find much that is persuasive in Hirsch's treatment. In the end I must however reject it, for by giving such a high status to nationality and, further, by linking it so closely to the legal, political, and coercive arm of the state, he makes nationality into an untouchable entity. Because it is part of the created order, nationality remains beyond and outside of the realm of rational and theological critique, public discussion and, open questioning. Nationality, for Hirsch, is a historical given which cannot be challenged.

It is true, Hirsch believes that nationality ought not to be absolutized (that is why he does not like to be called a nationalist). Nationality, he maintains, is a temporal reality and therefore subject to change and evolution and stands under the judgment of God—a fact born out in the birth, growth, power, decline, and defeat of nations, most dramatically manifest during times of war and crisis. This, however, is God's doing. Even though Hirsch was less strident than many in his comments about Jews, and even spoke warmly of individual Jews he nevertheless did not shrink from drawing objectionable but logical conclusions from his assumptions. He declared that Jews and Germans were racially distinct and therefore ought to be kept separate from each other. Jews ought to be given "guest status" in Germany;[9] they were not inferior, just different.

Tillich: In Defence of Internationalism

Tillich saw more clearly than most how the preoccupation with national identity in National Socialism and among "German Christians" such as Hirsch was a contradictory attempt to meet the challenges of a modernity in crisis. It was an attempt by people who had been shaped by modern consciousness to create an artificial pre-Enlightenment-type of national cohesion. Tillich too found a place in his theology for nationality but in a way that he felt remained more faithful to modern experience and the Judeo-Christian prophetic tradition.

Like Hirsch, Tillich began as a strong German patriot and nationalist, volunteering enthusiastically in 1914 to fight for the fatherland. He was appointed army chaplain on the Western Front. The war experience, however, soon radicalized him. It was not long before he became disillusioned with the usual conservative interpretation of the war as nations fighting each other for survival. He became a convinced Religious Socialist and internationalist, rejecting the Lutheran two-kingdom doctrine, espoused by nationally oriented Christians like Hirsch. He was also, however, critical of both liberalism (the spirit of capitalism) and doctrinaire Marxism for destroying all communal relationships in family and nation through the pure rationalization of existence.[10]

He conceded a certain legitimacy to groups committed to national renewal but ardently protested against any unmediated identification of Christianity and the nation, the cross, and the swastika. Christianity must always exercise a critical function over against nationality. He called for a genuine socialist decision in which National Socialists take seriously the second part of their name. Tillich's argument rests on his analysis of the two roots of political thought. The first, consciousness directed to the myth and powers of origin (nature, blood, family, tribe, race, nation) is the root of all romantic and conservative thought. It is the *priestly sacramental* view of reality which says yes to being, to the wherefrom of existence, to the ground of reality rooted in nature. It stresses the past and the present. The second root is the consciousness of the whereto of existence, the future, the ought, not being but becoming. It is the *prophetic-eschatological* emphasis of the Hebrew prophets working toward a just social order—a universal, international human community.[11]

The crucial point, for Tillich, is that the priestly sacramental and the prophetic-eschatological must be emphasized. Liberals and Marxists have tended to empty history of all religious, sacramental substance and emphasized pure prophetic form. Conservatives (both romantic and revolutionary) have stressed the sacramental to the exclusion of the prophetic. Religious Socialists, he says, recognize the importance of the powers of the origin but only as ultimately subordinated to the prophetic. Another way of putting it: while nationality is an important ingredient in what makes us human, it must ultimately be seen as the means toward the universal human community which in the final theological sense is the kingdom of God. Tillich uses a wonderful analogy of emigration (physical and spiritual) to describe the Christian's relation to nation.

Shortly after his emigration to the United States he addressed the American Committee for German Christian Refugees and made the following appeal:

> I would like to close with an appeal to support emigration, be it for the sake of Christian love, moral indignation, or political conviction. But behind all these reasons there should be the

recognition that *emigration is a religious category*, which applies to every Christian; for it points to the majesty of God and the exclusiveness of his demand that people at certain times ought to tear themselves away from home and family, homeland and nation, and all other things on this earth.[12]

In a series of broadcasts to the German people during the war years he encouraged them to emigrate spiritually while remaining physically within Germany. This metaphor of emigration to describe the whole of life, the existence between what is one's own and what is foreign to one, what Tillich frequently calls standing "on the boundary," "on the frontier" between two equally alluring alternatives, is what perhaps most clearly separated him from Hirsch's unqualified allegiance to one's own family, nationality, and country.[13]

In a remarkable 1933 article (Hitler came to power in January, 1933), entitled "Das Wohnen, der Raum und die Zeit [Habitation, Space and Time]," Tillich gives positive value to all three concepts.[14] To live in a house, to have a home, to create space for oneself is the way everything that lives comes into existence. Space for Tillich takes on a primal and holy quality, especially that space which has the character of preservation and grounding of life. One's own house, the neighbor's house, village, city, country, and *Volk* all participate in the sanctity of space which makes possible human existence. In the end, however, time (or history) takes precedence over space—we have again and again to forsake present space for the sake of the future. Abraham, of the Old Testament, in leaving his living space (*Lebensraum*) for an unknown future becomes the archetype for all of humankind. Physical and spiritual emigration (time) have greater theological significance for Tillich than allegiance to one's own (space).

Lessons to be Learned

There are a number of lessons that can be learned from the German experience of the 1930s. First, the powers or myths of origin (including ethnicity and nationality) have a primal power that can hardly be overestimated. They shape peoples' identity and are a fact of human existence which cannot be denied without grave consequences, for they erupt again and again in the course of history.

Second, in the modern and postmodern period a static or pristine national-ethnic homogeneity is no longer possible; we live in a fragmented world—a world in which the powers of origin have been broken. To presuppose a communal society composed of a cohesive ethnicity is an illusion; and to enforce coercively such uniformity as Fascism and Nazism endeavoured to do is to sink into barbarism.

Third, the only possible alternative is to view ethnicities as dynamic kaleidoscopic configurations which are in constant flux. I do believe that the powers of the origin—that is, those dimensions of human existence which root us in nature—are defining characteristics of what it means to exist as human creatures, both as individuals and as groups. It is that which ties us to nature and to fellow human beings and, therefore, is to be taken with utmost seriousness in an age of technical reason which uproots us from our origins. The root cause of injustice, I propose, is not the affirmation of nationality/nationalities as such but rather the domination by one configuration of the powers of origin over another. In short, the political and moral "ought" has to do not with overcoming or denying nationality or ethnicity but with the breaking of the domination of one nationality by another. Nationality has to be relativized and put in its rightful place.

Contemporary Experience: Religion and the Renewal of Nationalism

The media has brought home to all of us the fact that the widely accepted thesis that we live in a disenchanted secular global society does not stand up to careful scrutiny. We live in an age of "religious" renewal throughout the world. Ironically, this renewal is taking place most blatantly in former socialist countries—societies that until recently prided themselves in gradually overcoming religion. Along with the renewal of religion, frequently fundamentalist religion, has come a renewal of nationalism. Here too, ironically, the forces of nationalism seem to be the most powerful in societies that have for decades de-emphasized the importance of national in favour of class analysis. The two—religious renewal and national renewal—are frequently intrinsically linked. This is all-too-evident in what used to be Yugoslavia.

In the past sixteen years I have visited the former Yugoslavia six times and have come to understand at least partly the political, national, and religious landscape of this beautiful and diverse country. My association with Yugoslavia began in 1977 in connection with an annual course on the "Future of Religion," at the Inter-University Centre for Postgraduate Studies in Dubrovnik. Out of this involvement has come a recent volume of essays edited by me.[15] All of the essays address the question of the nature and role of religion in the modern world, and a number deal specifically with the relation of religion to nationalism.

In the fall of 1992 our family had the opportunity of assisting a Yugoslav family—Marinko and Djurdja Cvjeticanin, and their two children Dina and Srdjan—to emigrate to Canada. Marinko is Serbian, from the Serbian minority community within Croatia, and Djurdja is Croatian. They have deliberately avoided communicating to their children their own national backgrounds and organized religion. Marinko is a sociologist of religion, who taught for the University of Zagreb in Osijek, and was a therapist with a private practice. He has a thorough grasp of the political, national and religious contours of the former Yugoslavia; and a deep insight into the human psyche in search of national and religious identity. My reflections in the following pages are based mainly on my own experience in Yugoslavia, and what I've learned from my many personal "Yugoslav" friends.

Nationalities in the Former Yugoslavia

The modern Yugoslavia, largely the legacy of World War I, consisted of six Republics: Slovenia, Croatia, Bosnia/Herzegovina, Montenegro, Serbia, and Macedonia; and two independent provinces: Vojvodina and Kosovo. According to a 1981 census, the former Yugoslavia was made up of seven major nationalities: Serbian (36.6%), Croatian (19.7%), Moslem (8.9%; most of them converted Serbs and Croats), Slovenian (7.7%), Albanian (7.7%), Macedonian (5.9%), Montenegran (2.9%), not including 5.4% identifying themselves simply as Yugoslavian, 1.9% as Hungarian, and 1.0% as Other.[16] The same census identifies the distribution of nationalities as follows: Slovenia the most homogeneous with 90.0% Slovenes; Serbia, the second most homogeneous with 85.4% Serbs; and Croatia the third most homogeneous with 75.0% Croatians and 11.5% Serbians; Montenegro the fourth with 68.5% Montenegrans, 13.3% Moslems and 3.3% Serbians; and Macedonia the fifth, with 67.0% Macedonians, 19.7% Albanians, and 4.5% Moslem Turks. The most complex and therefore also the most war-torn is Bosnia-Herzegovina, with 39.5% Moslems, 32.0% Serbians, and 18.3% Croatians.

The point is that the nineteenth-century concern for nation states, in which political-geographical boundaries would be ideally drawn according to homogeneous ethnic-nationalistic lines has been far from successful and is virtually impossible, as the Balkans demonstrate. According to Marinko, one-third of all children in the former Yugoslavia come from mixed marriages. There is virtually no extended family which does not have mixed ethnic blood in it. This means that frequently two brothers will choose to fight on opposite sides, depending on whether they identify with their father or mother. For most it is not clear where their national-ethnic identities and loyalties lie. Nationality has become an ambiguous notion within modernity, even while it is being defended and fought over more aggressively than ever. This confirms my thesis that any claim made on behalf of a large-scale cohesive ethnicity is illusory;

and that the desire and need for community in the contemporary world (*Gemeinschaft* rather than just *Gesellschaft*) will need to be satisfied in some other way.

Religion in the Former Yugoslavia

The most important fact to consider in this context is that historically religious identity and national identity has been fatefully linked in the Balkans. The three major religions in former Yugoslavia are Roman Catholicism, Orthodoxy (Serbian and Macedonian), and Islam, coinciding remarkably closely with the ethnic-national make-up of the various republics and provinces: Slovenians and Croatians are predominantly Catholic; Serbians, Montenegrans, and Macedonians primarily Orthodox; and Muslims, Islamic. This historical identification of religious identity with national identity has in effect made Balkan wars into "holy" or religious wars. It is for this reason that the initial post-revolutionary socialist government of Josip Broz Tito was characterized by all-out hostility toward religion.[17] Religion had historically played a reactionary and oppressive role in Yugoslav society. This fact largely motivated the socialist disenfranchisement of public religion.

Since the demise of the socialists, the renewal of national independence movements has brought with it once more also a renewal of public religion. In the words of Paul Mojzes, a former Yugoslav, "The role of religion has changed drastically. No longer treated under a Marxist formula the churches and religious people are no longer discriminated against due to ideological considerations. Rather the large Orthodox, Catholic, and Muslim religious establishments have gained in importance and have become among the most important players as the ethno-religious mix typical of Eastern Europe propels them into defenders of nationhood."[18]

Besides the three major religions, there were by the late 1970s more than thirty different smaller religious groups in Yugoslavia, including Lutheran, Baptist, Pentecostal, Methodist, Nazarene, and so on. In fact, it seemed that these small Protestant groups, who were not nationally identified, earned special respect within the socialist period. Peter Kuzmic, president of a Pentecostal Bible Institute in Osijek, whom I visited in 1990, was highly respected by politicians and had high-level political contacts.

A Mennonite, Gerald Shenk, has been involved with that Institute of Osijek and Zagreb for some fifteen years. In an article, "The Protestant Experience in Yugoslavia: Response to Modernity," Shenk persuasively argues for the social and political significance of the dissenting traditions in modern societies such as Yugoslavia. Their significance lies in their emancipatory potential—liberating persons from old cultural, religious, and ethnic obligations in favour of a free gospel, offering in place of older national and religious identities "a smaller-scale intimacy of family, and immediate community on a face-to-face basis."[19]

In a prophetic statement, Shenk said in 1988:

> Across the country we see some evidence that the society itself is showing a new openness to the contribution of small Protestant communities. There is a potential for social reintegration on the local community level that will be more and more needed as this country attempts to recover from deep and debilitating social crisis. In particular, as nationalism becomes more and more divisive, these groups are a model of integration across lines matched only by the Army and (originally) the Party, but on a completely voluntary basis.[20]

Lessons to be Learned

The fact is that around the globe today there are major political liberation movements that perceive themselves as struggling for the rightful place of soil, blood, family, tribe and nation. The black majority in South Africa, the minority native population of Canada, French Quebecers, Arabs and Israelis in the Middle East, a variety of national groups in the former Soviet Union, not to mention the Republics in former Yugoslavia. All of these point to the significant role which the powers of origin play in the contemporary struggle for historical freedom and justice. It is frequently not clear whether these are reactionary or progressive movements. Often religion functions as a powerful factor in these struggles.

This brings me back to my original question: Is nationalism to be rejected theologically as a negative power driving peoples to ethnocentricism, intolerance, racism, and barbarism? Or is nationalism a positive force for the liberation of oppressed peoples, to be theologically supported on the grounds of justice; autonomy; the right to dignity and self-determination; and the notion that nationality, ethnicity, and family are intrinsic goods of creation? I will come back to this question.

Mennonites and Nationality

I recently heard someone call a convert to the Mennonite church a non-ethnic Mennonite. What was meant was that she was a non-German, non-Dutch, or non-Swiss ethnic Mennonite. In fact there is no such thing as a non-ethnic. We are all defined ethnically to a lesser or greater degree. We are defined by the language we speak, by the food we eat, by the rituals we perform, by our cultic behavior and by other customs we inherit and live by. To use Tillichian language, to be human is to be defined by both space and time. Mennonites as an ethno-religious people are also defined by both space and time; as a group we have perhaps more than many other groups lived with a tension between space and time: sometimes defining ourselves primarily spatially (that is, by ethnic, national, characteristics), at other times in terms primarily of time (as a pilgrim, emigrating, non-territorial people, identifying ourselves historically and religiously).

Werner Packull, my colleague at Conrad Grebel College, tells me that in the diversities of the sixteenth-century Anabaptist movement ethnic differences played a significant role. The three major linguistic groups were the Swiss, German, and Dutch, but within these there were local variations having to do with differences in dialect, eating habits, dress and so on. These differences led to conflict and splinter groups. It is of interest that Anabaptist groups in what are now the Czech and Slovak Republics maintained their German or Swiss dialects and did not adopt the Slavic languages.

How important this is theologically is not clear, but that religious beliefs and ethnic-cultural factors cannot be easily separated is indisputable. What is important about the early Anabaptists is that because their ethnic differences did not take on self-conscious political-institutional form (they were a non-territorial church), there was a universalistic possibility within the movement. This universalistic potential, grounded in their reading of the biblical text, finds strongest expression in "Free Church" ecclesiology—the conviction that church membership is not to be determined by territory, political allegiance, or family ties, but by personal confession of faith and a moral, regenerated life.

This universalistic impulse has, however, again and again been frustrated by historical Mennonite religious and ethnic sectarianism. In the Russian Mennonite stream, this happened in Holland in the sixteenth century, in Prussia in the seventeenth and eighteenth centuries, in Russia in the nineteenth century, and in North America and Latin America in the twentieth century. That we have moved from one country to another shows that we are a people of time and the diaspora; but again and again we have become a people of space, types of nation-states within states (e.g. former Mennonite colonies in Russia).[21]

The reason for this is that all of us consciously or unconsciously recognize that to be human is to be bound in some sense to space—in this sense Emanuel Hirsch is right. We are defined by how we come into this world: gender, colour, race, language, customs. The liberation movements throughout the world—Black, Hispanic, African, Quebecois, Arab, Jew, Feminist, Lesbian, Gay, and so on—are all ample proof of this. The passion with which French Mennonite Sonia Blanchette, in her recent visit to four

Mennonite schools in Ontario, defended the notion of French separatism, and her own identity as Quebecois rather than English Canadian illustrates this fact. She refused to "equate God's unity with Canadian unity" and stressed that God's grace operates not independent of but *through* culture and nationality.[22]

The Bible and Nationality

My theological proposal at the end of this presentation emerges out of a survey reading of the biblical understanding of the nations, to which I now turn.[23] At the end of the Bronze Age (thirteenth century B.C.E), at about the beginning of the biblical period (the Iron Age), the tribal element took on new significance, with states beginning to define themselves along lines of tribal kinship (people linking themselves together in terms of blood-ties, common traditions and languages). The movement from the Patriarchal period to the Judges is the movement from tribe to state, from "pastoral groups" to a larger unity which might be called a "nation," with common leaders, a political structure based on kinship relationships, and the worship of a national god, Yahweh.

By about 1000 B.C. this development culminated in a larger kingdom or centralized monarchical state inhabited largely by Israelites but not exclusively. With the Babylonian exile, ironically, national consciousness takes on a new intensity. With the return to Palestine there is a strong push for national political recovery with racial overtones (the forbidding of mixed marriages), and the desire to re-establish, largely unsuccessful, "the myth of a lost national identity and history." But also, to quote Mario Liverani,

> From the model of the national state emerged that of a religious community . . . devoid of any political power and competence, and re-using the previous projects of national recovery as a metaphor for the eschatological salvation. The 'national' origin of the Jewish religious community kept important features, however, in the ethnic and racial limitations of its membership— to be eventually overcome by the 'universalistic' character of Christianity (under the impact of the Hellenistic-Roman cosmopolitanism).[24]

This dialectic between a narrow nationalistic self-interest and a universalistic salvation runs as a theme throughout the Hebrew Scriptures.[25] After the Flood, humanity is divided into "families, languages, lands and nations."[26] In Genesis 10 we have some seventy different racial-type groups listed, a listing without parallel in the ancient world, indicating the importance the Bible places on history and nations as a vehicle for God's revelation. Genesis 11 and the tower of Babel story identifies this division into many nations and languages as a punishment for human pride: "then the Lord confused the language of all the earth; and from there the Lord scattered them abroad over the face of the earth" (Gen. 11:9). John H. Yoder sees the dispersion of the peoples at Babel not as a punishment but as a blessing. According to Yoder, it is centralization ("totalization," to use the language of postmodern deconstructionists) that represents the departure from God's intent in creation, that intent being diversity and decentralization.[27]

The Hebrew Scriptures are to a large extent a record of the Jewish people defining themselves over against other peoples and nations. A large portion of the prophetic literature is devoted to oracles against other nations. Yahweh is frequently depicted as a divine warrior miraculously delivering the Hebrews from their enemies. But with the destruction of Jerusalem in the fifth century B.C. there is a turn to a more universal eschatological and messianic hope. Yahweh is seen as the God of all nations and pagan empires are envisioned as gathering in Jerusalem to worship the one God. Anticipating the Pentecost coming of the Spirit of God on all people alike (Acts 2), Zechariah prophesies: "In those days ten men from the nations of every tongue shall take hold of the robe of Jews, saying, 'Let us go with you, for we have heard that God is with you'"(8:23); and Zephaniah says: "Yea, at that time I will change the speech of the peoples to a pure speech, that all of them may call on the name of the Lord and serve him with one accord" (3:9).

This tension within the canon between a narrow nationalistic view and a universalistic perspective is represented dramatically in the contrast between Jonah-Micah, on the one side, and Nahum-Habakkuk, on the other. In Jonah, God shows compassion on the wicked city of Nineveh, capital of Assyria. In Nahum, God destroys Nineveh. The Jewish covenant community was open to the foreigner and the stranger from the start, narrated so powerfully in the book of Job and the book of Ruth. The universalistic principle is a logical conclusion of monotheism, which affirms the unity of the cosmos and the sovereignty of the one God over all nations.

This universalism becomes the fundamental theme in the *kerygma* of the New Testament. The earliest Jewish-Christian community saw the messianic age as having come upon them in Christ; and the most definitive aspect of that age was its inclusiveness. The message of John the Baptist, of Jesus, Paul, Peter, and all the Apostles is that the old walls of partition have been broken down. At Pentecost in Jerusalem, "devout people from every nation under heaven" began speaking in tongues other than their own. "There is neither Jew nor Greek, there is neither slave nor free, there is neither male nor female; for. . . [all are] one in Christ Jesus" (Gal. 3:28).

John Miller, in a soon to be published study of how the Hebrew Scriptures came to be collected, ordered, and canonized devotes considerable space to the concept of the nations in Hebrew literature. From the early chapters of Genesis the disparate linguistic, ethnographic groups and nationalities remain a central theme. The covenant God makes with the Hebrews is that they will become a great nation through which "all clans on earth" will be blessed and come to know Yahweh as the true God. Miller claims that the "architecture" of the Law and the Prophets has, in its final redaction, been deliberately shaped to proclaim the message of the overarching plan of God for all the nations of the world. It is the world vision and mission to all nations foreshadowed in the Law, the Prophets, and the writings that is taken up by the Spirit-inspired Church of Jesus Christ.[28]

A Theological Summing Up

Theologically, I take the powers of origin (sexuality, family, tribe, clan, peoples, nationality, race) to be part of what defines us as human beings. I understand these as falling under the Christian doctrine of creation, including God's providence and preservation of the world. That is, they are givens, facts of existence that we do not freely determine. Using Heideggerian language, we are thrown into existence this way. Having said this, however, I would draw the following distinctions and conclusions.

First, these powers of creation are not fixed orders of creation the way theologians like Hirsch tended to view them in the 1930s. Although the powers of origin have a certain enduring quality and intransigence to them, they are not totally in the realm of inevitability and necessity. They are dynamic powers, and there is an element of human freedom and accompanying moral responsibility in how the contours of these powers of origin take shape and then function in societies. Dietrich Bonhoeffer also rejects the notion of orders of creation and uses the term "mandates" for them. This in my opinion puts them too easily into the realm of moral freedom. There is a created givenness to them which is not quite so easily at our moral disposal.

If one were to use a metaphor it would be, I suggest, that of the scrabble game in contrast to the jigsaw puzzle. The dynamics of the scrabble game I think best describe God's providence in this regard (the limits of the board, the luck of the continued picking up of letters, one's own vocabulary and skill in playing, one's dependence on other players, and the ultimate design which emerges [always unique] through the interaction of all these factors). Ethnicities in fact change and develop in this way rather than being totally predetermined as in the jigsaw puzzle. This is another way of saying that creation needs to be understood not only as original creation but also as ongoing creation.

Second, I believe distinctions need to be made between 1) ethnicity (small group identity through local kinship ties, ritual behavior, eating habits, dress and, most important, dialect); 2) nationality (larger group identity in which ethnic ties are expanded, a common language increases in importance, and above all the group becomes self-conscious); and 3) nation state (the politicization of the ethnic-national concept so that political boundaries are made to coincide with ethnic-national borders). Historically the nation state, and also to a lesser degree nationality, is a modern eighteenth- and nineteenth-century Romantic notion, which is politically and theologically highly problematic. Politically it is problematic because it flies in the face of the absence of such homogeneity and coherence in the modern and, even more so, the postmodern world.

This means that any attempt to create such a state is based on an illusion and must be done by force; exactly what happened in Germany in the 1930s and 1940s and what is happening now in the former Yugoslavia. Ethnic and national differentiation I believe to be assumed in the Bible and theologically defensible as human givens—factors which give us a natural sense of communal belonging and rootedness, to be encouraged in the contemporary deracinated world. But the nation-state defined along ethnographic lines, especially when shored up by civil religion and a political theology, in my view leads to the intolerance and "ethnic cleansing" that continues into the present.

Finally, I would like to defend theologically the ethnic- and nationally polymorphic state in which ethnically defined groups are treated equally and fairly on the basis of a shared humanity. In other words, the powers of origin are taken seriously and treated with respect as created goods that define us as humans, but they are not given absolute political or theological status. Politically, they are relativized by a higher good: the shared humanity between all humans represented by transnational institutions and constitutions. Theologically, they are relativized by the affirmation of the unity of all as created in the image of God, redeemed in Christ, and unified in Holy Spirit within a voluntary church community. This is what I take to be the biblical vision of the kingdom of God, which all human societies, including the church, can always only imitate by analogy.

THIRTY

War as a Theological Litmus Test: Hirsch, Tillich, Barth, and the Confessing Church*

My interest in Paul Tillich goes back to my undergraduate years in the 1960s. He had that unique ability to rephrase traditional answers to universal questions in both philosophical and theological ways. There was something about his philosophical ontology and his existentialist Lutheran theology that filled a void in my Mennonite soul. My brief period of study in New York, at Union Theological Seminary (1971-72), where Tillich had taught from the time of his emigration in 1933 to 1955, furthered my interest especially in his early German years and his encounter with National Socialism. Dietrich Bonhoeffer, in whom I had also had a long, keen interest, had studied at Union in 1930 and come back briefly in 1939, wrestling with himself and others whether to stay or return, but in the end deciding, fatefully as it turned out, to go back to Germany.[1]

So when I was faced with choosing a topic for my doctoral dissertation in the 1970s I quite naturally turned to Tillich and the years leading up to his dismissal by the Nazis. What I had not anticipated was my growing fascination with another theological figure: Emanuel Hirsch, a long-time personal friend of Tillich's, someone

---

* This essay was first presented at the American Academy of Religion meetings in San Francisco in November 1997, and not previously published. For notes on the text see the Notes section below.

who went in the opposite direction politically. Hirsch turned into a strong nationalist and supporter of the pro-Hitler "German-Christians." In the 1989 Preface to my Tillich-Hirsch study I allude to this fascination with Hirsch:

> I had never heard of Emanuel Hirsch, let alone read any of his works, and began what I expected to be a rather straightforward exposé of what I presumed must be Hirsch's flawed theology, and a simple apology for what I uncritically assumed to be Tillich's more intelligent and coherent position. It did not take long, however, before I realized that the issues were considerably more complex than I had imagined. In the process of studying the writings of Emanuel Hirsch, meeting friends and colleagues of his, and talking to some of his post-war students, I found myself increasingly fascinated by this intellectual giant . . . and his particular way of grappling with the 'crisis of modernity.'[2]

What was it in Hirsch that bore this unlikely fascination for me as a Mennonite? It had something to do with his stress on "peoplehood" (Volk: folk or nation) and his view that theology could only be done properly in the context of an ethnic/cultural community, not by deracinated, free-floating, autonomous individuals. Like Jews, Mennonites have historically sought to integrate faith and life, religious belief and life in community ("historically" for the most part defined ethnically). Hutterites are the most dramatic example of this fusion of religion and ethnic culture within the Anabaptist heritage. It is perhaps, ironically, this very wholistic notion of the integration of belief and life, faith and things of the earth (as expressed in the Wiebe poem at the beginning of this volume) that led to the confusion (even identification) of religion and ethnicity among some European, North and South American Mennonites, even to the point of supporting Hitler and National Socialism.[3]

But there was something also in Tillich that struck a familiar chord in me as a Mennonite—a critical, prophetic, and eschatological principle which protested against the hallowing of the so-called "powers of origin" (one's own blood, land, ethnicity, nationality). Tillich names this the "Protestant Principle" but the more radical form of this might well be called the "Anabaptist Principle"—the protest against all forms of idolatry and uncritical religious sanctification of culture (the anti-Constantinian principle).

In the previous essay I identified some of the lessons that can be learned from Hirsch and Tillich concerning the theological significance of ethnicity and nationality. In this essay, first presented at the American Academy of Religion meetings in November 1997, I venture further in examining the theology of Tillich and Hirsch, especially as it relates to another topic of interest to Mennonites: the issue of war. I point out that on this issue the conservative nationalist Hirsch and the liberal internationalist Tillich are really not all that different. Neither is biblical pacifists. *Neither's theology is rigorous enough to be able to judge violent contemporary culture. Both in the end justify war theologically.*

For a more stringent and critical social ethics one must turn to the theology of Karl Barth. In contrast to Hirsch, for whom theological work is identified with German national consciousness (what he calls the "hidden sovereign"), and contrary to Tillich, for whom the theological task is an international humanistic one, Barth centres theology and dogmatic work firmly in the confessional life of the church. It is Barth, in his understanding of theology, ecclesiology and social ethics, who of the three has most in common with the Anabaptist-Mennonite view.

This is borne out, for instance, in the thought of John H. Yoder, who despite his critique of Barth's notion of Grenzfal *(the exceptional case in ethics),[4] bears the marks of Barth's influence—he studied with Barth in Basel—and the non-foundationalism of Stanley Hauerwas, who attributes so much of his thinking to Yoder. It is in no small part because of these theologians and the so-called Yale school of contemporary theology (associated with names such as Hans Frei and George Lindbeck[5]) that the thought of Barth is experiencing a renaissance in North American circles.[6] In my own theological work I find myself both drawn to Barth and departing from his theology and that of the circle influenced by him.*

This is perhaps where Tillich's influence is present but, more so, my growing appreciation for the classical creedal and apologetic tradition. I do not follow what to me is Barth's too stark Tertullianism: the strict separation of Athens and Jerusalem.[7] I am drawn more to the Alexandrian model of ancient apologetics, which finds commonalities between Athens and Jerusalem, between philosophy and the Jewish-Christian revelation. Christian social ethics—even of the Anabaptist-Mennonite kind—is better served and more biblical when God's revelation in nature, human consciousness, and reason is seen not as alien to but consistent with God's revelation in Christ, although it is only through the latter that the former is most clearly and fully understood.

Nevertheless, the article below ends rather abruptly, suggesting that Barth's confessional-dogmatic theology is a more adequate foundation for developing a Christian perspective on war and violence in particular than is Tillich's more philosophical-dogmatic approach. In the subsequent two articles I explore in greater detail how such a confessional-dogmatic approach might be applied to the question of war and peace. How I reconcile this move with my Alexandrian leanings awaits further clarification in future writings.

◆ ◆ ◆

I. Introduction

My specialized area of research is German theology in the 1920s and 1930s, focusing especially on the early Tillich, and his close friendship and later public debate with Emanuel Hirsch over theology and National Socialism. My findings were published in 1989 in *The Emanuel Hirsch and Paul Tillich Debate: A Study in the Political Ramifications of Theology*, published in German by Walter de Gruyter in 1995 under the title *Emanuel Hirsch und Paul Tillich: Theologie in einer Zeit der Krisis*. I conclude that study with the following statement:

> For Tillich the *kairos* doctrine (and later the category of revelation which he correlated with the notion of *kairos*) remained largely a formal category without sufficient Christological and ecclesiological content. For Hirsch, revealed theology (in particular his Christology) pertained to the spiritual realm and had little to do with social and political choices. Our study suggests but does not demonstrate (this must remain the goal of another study) that Barth's more classical dogmatic theology was not an escape into supernaturalism, as charged by Tillich and Hirsch, but was precisely an attempt to develop normative theological-dogmatic criteria relevant for historical and political action.[8]

In this paper I pick up where I left off in my earlier study by contrasting further the political and ethical ramifications of the three theologies: Hirsch's religious nationalist theology, Tillich's religious socialist theology, and Barth's "confessional" theology. *The issue of war is not overtly the single unifying theme of this paper, but it does serve as a kind of litmus test for evaluating the ethical ramifications of each of the three theologies.*

As someone active in the Mennonite community, I come to the subject matter with a particular historical predisposition in favour of Barth's "virtual pacifism," even though in the end Barth also finds a place for the exception (*Grenzfall*). When I published my work on Hirsch and Tillich I was not acquainted with Karen Schäfer's untranslated work on the early political theology of Tillich, entitled *Die Theologie des Politischen bei Paul Tillich unter besonderer Berücksichtigung der Zeit von 1933 bis 1945*.[9]

So I want to take this opportunity to rectify this omission by engaging her and her thesis at a number of key points. Schäfer rightly observes that Tillich's debate with the political theology of Hirsch on the one side, and the orthodox ("non-political") theology of Barth and the Confessing Church on the other, had a profound impact on Tillich's first years in the United States and were determinative in his subsequent theology (Schäfer, 85-123).

In the following pages I examine Hirsch's theological apology for Germany's engagement in war in the years 1914-18 to elucidate his theological presuppositions for doing ethics; Tillich's debate with Hirsch's political theology especially as the latter uses it ideologically to support National Socialism in the 1930s; and, finally, Tillich's quarrel with Barth and the Confessing Church.

II. Hirsch on War

Barth's disillusionment with nineteenth-century liberal theology was a response to liberalism's impotence at a time of political crisis—most especially its uncritical support of World War I. In stark contrast to Barth, both Hirsch and Tillich were enthusiastic supporters of Germany's entrance into the war in 1914. In a 1914 article "Unsere Frage an Gott," Hirsch interprets war as the nation's encounter with God. Although war as such is not to be glorified, and although God is a God of the whole world (French, Slavs, and Germans), nevertheless war becomes the final court of appeal to God for his judgment on the destiny of a nation—that is, whether a national-people (*Volk*) has a right to exist and what role it has among the nations in history.[10] It might very well be that the historical role of a country (like Germany) has come to an end, but this can only be discovered through a serious encounter with God's holy will and a struggle to the end. In this sense war can be called a "holy war" or "holy venture."

Hirsch's keen sense of duty during time of war suffered a serious blow when his application for military service was turned down for health reasons, a fact which bothered Hirsch greatly and contributed to his growing intellectual support for the war and increasing nationalism. In a series of three articles in 1916 to 1918 he spells out his theological presuppositions for Christians and war: "Luthers Gedanken über Staat und Krieg" (1917), "Ein christliches Volk" (1918), and "Der Pazifismus" (1918).[11]

In the first of these, Hirsch outlines Luther's understanding of the two kingdoms and deliberately constructs an apology for German Christians' unqualified support of the war effort.[12] The kingdom of God is an *invisible* eternal realm having to do with the individual conscience and the internal disposition to love. In this inward and personal realm (the gospel) Christians are justified by grace alone and reject all forms of coercion, bearing injustice patiently. The temporal kingdom is the *visible* external realm of law and political realities. In this sphere Christians are called to serve their fellows in the spirit of love; however, some are called to the task of governing, and in this role have the divinely authorized task of using the sword to carry out justice. The legitimacy of war rests in the legitimacy of the state. There are two conditions for a just war: a) it cannot be directed against governmental authority itself; and b) it must arise out of the basic duty of the state to protect its subjects. In other words it must be a defensive war.

The modern case for a just war, according to Hirsch, has altered little from the time of Luther with one exception. Our understanding of the state has expanded to include the concept of nationality (*Volksgedanken*). It is the task of the state in the modern context to preserve the state as grounded in the sovereign will of a people with a national consciousness (*Volk*).

In "Ein christliches Volk" Hirsch elaborates on this theme. He admits that "nationality" as such is a pre-Christian reality. Consciousness of it is granted to us through nature and history, but this in itself does not make a "national-community" (*Volksgemeinschaft*) Christian. To be considered Christian a nation must have a "Christian-cultivated conscience [*christliche gebildetes Gewissen*]." The character of a nation is defined by what it considers to be right, and the moral conscience of the German nation in this regard, as that of other European nations, has been shaped largely by Christian values, in particular the value of the individual human being before God. The political task of theology in the temporal sphere is to keep the nation Christian in this limited sense: to foster an ethos in which the individual conscience can remain free and inviolable, and one in which the first kingdom (the stance of the individual before God) can flourish. This is not, however, to equate the political task of theology with the gospel—it is in effect a pre-Christian task.

In "Der Pazifismus" Hirsch more systematically develops his views of the political task of theology as it relates to war. There are two options for humanity; either: a) to value the genuine diversity of nations and the different forms of life they represent, or b) to idealize an international communal culture (*Lebensgemeinschaft, Staatsgemeinschaft*) through a world peace alliance (*Weltfriedensbund*). Pacifists are deluded if they think that nations can become equal, independent partners in such a world alliance. Smaller nations will always become colonized nations subordinate to the powerful nations and the dominant vision of life they represent. While primitive nations with a relatively underdeveloped history and culture of their own might allow themselves to be thus dominated, more developed nations with a unique spiritual and political identity will refuse to allow themselves to be absorbed into an internationally homogeneous culture.

This is where the limitations of the pacifist ideal truly become evident. It might of course be the case, as mentioned above, that not every nation is destined to live out its own unique character, but the final test of that is war, not peace at all costs. Furthermore, pacifists confuse the kingdom of justice (a realm of conflicting egos and nations) with the kingdom of God (the realm of love and the renunciation of rights as defined by the Sermon on the Mount). The principles of the Sermon on the Mount are guidelines on how to become members of the invisible kingdom of God, *not* how to order the nation state. The state would relinquish its God-given task if it tried to apply Jesus' teachings on nonresistant love to the running of the government.

This does not mean, however, that the nation state is free from every ethical law. It stands under the ethical norm of justice (*Gerechtigkeit*): "Thus a nation can indeed begin a war when an aim, which appears to it as indispensable for the unfolding of its nature and life, cannot be attained in other ways. But woe to the nation that takes such a step lightly, that in boundless darkness or base rapacity transgresses against the rigorous spirit of historical righteousness. Nations must answer for their deeds, and the grandchildren atone for the crimes of the fathers."[13]

Here we see Hirsch moving beyond the traditional defensive just war to the offensive just war, carried out, however, under certain historical norms of justice, presumably the criteria as formulated in the classical just war tradition. The Christian statesman who unleashes a war does so because of the welfare of the nation, out of love for the neighbor, just as the Christian soldier fights and destroys the life of other people out of love and service for the national community. As a member of the invisible kingdom of God, the Christian is a member of an international community without distinctions and with a universal loyalty; but as a member of the visible earthly kingdom, where peoples are by destiny divided into diverse nation states out of which they receive their life and character, the first loyalty is to their own peoples.

III. Tillich on Hirsch and War

World War I had opposite effects on the two old friends. Hirsch became increasingly more nationalistic, with war as the highest court of appeal before God on the historical destiny of a nation. For Tillich's, the romanticism of war in 1914 came to an abrupt end within the first year. "The first weeks had not passed before one's original enthusiasm disappeared," he said in retrospect. "Above all, I saw that the unity of the first weeks was an illusion, that the nation was split into classes, and that the industrial masses considered the Church as an unquestioned ally of the ruling groups."[14]

The war radicalized Tillich. He no longer saw war as a struggle between nations but as a symptom of the crisis of imperialism within late capitalist culture, and the birth pangs of a new humanity mediated through the international proletariat. His role in the founding of the Religious Socialist movement in Germany after the war and his numerous writings on behalf of the movement are common knowledge. What is possibly not as well known are some aspects of his debate with Hirsch and the different readings of this debate both in Germany and in North America.

It is a debate that bears close scrutiny because of the light it sheds on the strengths and vulnerabilities of Tillich's early political theology, not to mention Hirsch's nationalist theology. In North America the debate is usually read only through the eyes of Tillich, a one-sidedness which I try to correct in my study. One assumption that most North Americans bring to the debate is quite simply that Tillich was right and Hirsch was wrong, and that's that. In actual fact, Hirsch made some remarkably astute criticisms of Tillich's political theology which are virtually never read (because Hirsch's writings have not been translated into English) or, if read, simply dismissed as false because of his pro- "German Christian" sympathies. I have examined and evaluated the charges on both sides carefully in my longer study, so I won't repeat them here.

There is, however, one puzzling, little known postcard that Hirsch sends to Tillich on April 4, 1933, just before Tillich's suspension and departure for North America, a postcard also highlighted by Karin Schäfer. In it Hirsch suggests that Tillich's just published book *The Socialist Decision* has elements that reveal Tillich's sympathies with the nationalist cause, and urges Tillich to consider staying in Germany to lend his weight and influence to the cause. In my thesis I suggest that in his German writings, despite Tillich's very clear rejection of National Socialism, there was a romantic element in his thought from the beginning which makes some of his statements about the movements devoted to the "myth of origin" seem ambiguous.

Schäfer unequivocally rejects any suggestion that there is ambiguity in Tillich's thought on this issue. She considers it to be a completely unjustified claim by some Tillich interpreters in Germany (like E. Schwerdtfeger) that Tillich had an ambivalent attitude toward National Socialism at first and that only gradually in the United States he exorcized his fascination with that movement. Her strongest critique is reserved for Wilhelm Pauck's complicity in this interpretation, with his suggestion that Tillich avoided practical political involvement. Schäfer cites Tillich's work with the "Neuen Blätter für den Sozialismus" as a conscious political activity, as well as his letter to his friend Hermann Schafft, in which he expresses his thorough disgust at Hirsch's political orientation (Schäfer, 88ff).

What is clear in the debate (and Schäfer acknowledges this) is that Tillich now sees the need to strengthen the revelation pole of *revelation-kairos*. This has the effect of drawing Tillich closer to Barth's confessional theology. In fact, says Schäfer, after the debate with Hirsch the *Kairos*[15] concept never plays an important role in Tillich's theology (Schäfer, 92).

In my own analysis of the debate between Hirsch and Tillich, I suggested, with the late historian Klaus Scholder, that there were actually important formal, categorical similarities between the two political theologians even though the political contents they put into these formal categories were on opposite sides. In contrast to Barth who turned increasingly to confessional dogmatics, both Hirsch and Tillich politicized theology: one on the right and the other on the left. This is why there was a certain kind of interchangeability between their theologies, not because of "plagiarism" on Hirsch's part, as Tillich suggests at one point in the debate.

Since I published my research I have done more work on Tillich's ontology and think Scholder's conclusions may have been one-sided and mine somewhat premature. Tillich's early work on dogmatics (in 1913 and again in 1925 in Marburg) clearly show that he was concerned to ground his social and political ethics in ontological theology and not the other way around, as Scholder's thesis would suggest.

Nevertheless, I maintain that there continued to be "romantic" elements in Tillich's thought which weakened the critical-prophetic element in his political thinking, a tendency that increased rather than decreased in his later years. Interestingly, despite his disillusionment with the war, Tillich remains ambiguous in his statement on war. Many years after his debate with Hirsch, in his book *Love, Power and Justice*, he describes the historic encounter and struggle between social groups and nations in a way remarkably similar to what we read in Hirsch:

> For every power group experiences growth and disintegration. It tries to transcend itself and to preserve itself at the same time. Nothing is determined *a priori*. It is a matter of trial, risk, and decision. And this trial has elements of intrinsic power united with compulsion whether the group or their representatives want it or not. These encounters are the basic material of history. In them man's political destiny is decided. What is their character? The basis of all power of a social group is the space it must provide for itself. Being means having space or, more exactly, providing space for oneself. This is the reason for the tremendous importance of geographic space and the fight for its possession by all power groups.[16]

In the same book Tillich rejects the notion that permanent peace and the union of humankind (the kingdom of God) is achievable on earth. It would mean that creativity would have come to an end, history would have transmuted into post-history. Only fragmentary anticipations of such a peaceable kingdom are possible. The church is one such fragmentary anticipation, but there are also groups and movements outside of the "manifest" church, which as the "latent" church can represent such fragmentary anticipations. But within history, power, and tragedy (and presumably war) will always be part of the human condition.[17] So Tillich too, no matter how critical he is of Hirsch's stance toward nation, politics and war, in the end himself also justifies the 'war-like' struggle between nations for their space under the sun.

IV. Tillich on Barth and the Confessing Church

Of the three theologians, Barth comes the closest to rejecting war in principle.[18] This is possible for Barth because his is not a political theology in the sense of Hirsch or Tillich, but a dogmatical-confessional theology. Tillich, like Barth, rehabilitated the term *dogmatics* for theological thinking in the 1920s. The same year that Barth was lecturing on dogmatics in Göttingen, as a colleague of Hirsch, Tillich was giving his first full series of lectures on dogmatics in Marburg. I have done an analytical comparison of their [Barth and Tillich's] different approaches to dogmatics elsewhere.[19] The difference between them is that Tillich develops a universal dogmatic philosophical theology not imbedded in any exclusive sense in the Christian church as an institution, while Barth's dogmatics is done by, for, and in the Christian church.

Here I want to consider Tillich's view of Barth and the Confessing Church.[20] Tillich left Germany at the point where things were beginning to heat up for the Protestant church. It is interesting to speculate to what extent if at all he would have been personally involved in key events of the church struggle—the Emergency League of Pastors, the Barmen Synod of 1934, the subsequent confessing synods, alternate seminary training institutions, and public statements on the part of pastors and theologians (like Barth and Bonhoeffer)—had he stayed.

As it is, we get astonishingly little specific insight into what Tillich's views on these attempts at witnessing and resistance were. I would be interested, for instance, whether Tillich had any extensive conversations with Dietrich Bonhoeffer in 1939, when Bonhoeffer briefly visited Union Theological Seminary where Tillich was teaching, before returning to Germany and his undercover activities on behalf of the conspiracy. What we are left with are bits and pieces, and some comments on the church situation in Germany in general and his criticisms of the Confessing Church.

In 1934-35, the years of the Barmen Synod and his debate with Hirsch, Tillich wrote three articles which have a bearing on his attitude toward the Confessing Church and its theology: "Die religiöse Lage im heutigen Deutschland " (1934), "The totalitarian state and the claims of the church" (1934), and "What is wrong with 'Dialectical' Theology" (1935).[21] In these texts the main themes of Tillich's disagreement(s) with those involved in the church struggle are identified. First, the church struggle is not a political struggle against National Socialism at all. Only a few liberals and radicals are in the church opposition; most belong to the old conservative parties. This manifests itself in the silence of the Confessing Church on the persecution of Jews, communists, and trade unions. It is interested mostly in dogmatic issues and its own survival. Second, a church struggle devoted to internal, dogmatic-confessional issues and avoiding the larger political issues does not address the fundamental problem of our time: secularism and the loss of meaning (whether in the form of empty liberalism or the atheism of the upper classes and the proletariat).

The consequence of this secularization is the leaving of a religious vacuum which, if not filled in some other way, will be filled by totalitarian world views like National Socialism. Religious Socialism was an attempt to fill the vacuum with an alternative meaning—an alternative between the secular orthodoxy of Marxism on the one hand, and traditional Lutheran orthodoxy on the other. Tillich is aware that the Religious Socialist movement unfortunately miscarried, and was supplanted by the new heathenism of National Socialism (cf. Schäfer, 97.).

Third, Barth and his confessional theology contributed significantly to the fact that the Religious Socialists were ineffective in carrying through their program. Confessing Church theology tries to separate the theological from the political. Such a non-political theology is ineffective and illusory in a situation where the political sphere makes totalitarian worldview claims (cf. Schäfer, 100ff.). A church premised on such a division of reality can ultimately not address the human, political situation adequately. Tillich presents his own political-theological alternative as the *genuine* Chalcedonian solution: keeping the two spheres (spiritual and material, theological and political) in their proper dialectical relationship with each other, in contrast to what he characterizes as Hirsch's collapsing of, and Barth's separation of, the two. Tillich's 'quarrel' with Barth and the Confessing Church, therefore, is a fundamental disagreement over how the principalities and powers of this world can be effectively wrestled with. Because the Barthian solution separates itself from the political, it ultimately abets rather than challenges the evil powers of this world (cf. Schäfer, 105).

Despite this argument, Tillich is in support of the resistance of the Confessing Church as far as it goes in the present context. In attempting to save the German Evangelical Church from paganism premised on the doctrine of Revelation, it is to be applauded. In a 1935 letter to his friend Hermann Schafft, Tillich confirms his belief that, according to news he is receiving from Germany, the Confessing Church represents an "orthodox narrowing in priestly garments" (Schäfer, 108). All the same, in the present crisis there seems to be no other option, and one must clearly side with the Confessing Church. For in a situation where the final theological criterion, the Christian substance itself, is being threatened by pagan nationalism, it is imperative that we come to its defence, in the way Athanasius needs to be defended against Arius, despite all the problems of Athanasian orthodoxy. No one in the present has the right to come between Bishop Ludwig Müller and Martin Niemöller.[22] But this is to be seen only as a temporary measure in a time of extreme crisis, when the very essence of Christianity is at stake. In the future, theology, if it is interested in the salvation of the world, not just of the church, must once more develop a theology of the political (cf. Schäfer, 109).

V. Conclusion

We have looked at Hirsch's theology particularly as it becomes an apology for war in the years 1914-18; we have examined Tillich's rejection of Hirsch's nationalist theology but his own similar sounding rhetoric when it comes to the issue of war; and, finally, we have identified certain themes in Tillich's critique of Barth's dogmatic theology while giving conditional support to the struggle of the Confessing Church against Hitler and the German Christians. What we have not done is shown how Barth, even though he allows for the exception in the extreme case, has a much more rigorous position on war and Christian social ethics in general.

Karin Schäfer rightly notes that uppermost in Tillich's analysis of the situation in the 1920s and 1930s is the issue of secularization, the loss of meaning, uncertainty and disintegration of autonomous modern culture (cf. Schäfer, 110). The political and cultural task of theology, as Tillich envisioned it within the Religious Socialist movement, was to contribute to the discovery of new forms of theonomous meaning and cultural integration without falling into either political heteronomy on the one side, or orthodox heteronomy on the other.

Is this truly the challenge that faces modern culture? Is it the case that such grand theonomous-cultural synthesis is either possible or desirable? There is an irony in the fact that in the present, fragmentary, postmodern culture, it is Barth's brand of theology that appears to have more appeal to many than Tillich's. This in itself, to be sure, does not make it better or truer. It does, however, raise this question: Might it not be that in the long run it is Barth's dogmatic-confessional theology that has more ethical-political power than Tillich's ontological-political theology? On the issue of war this would seem to be the case. For Barth, Bonhoeffer, and the Confessing Church neither nationality (Hirsch) nor international humanistic reason (Tillich) can be determinative for Christian ethics. Only the church, based on the Revelation of the one Word of God in Jesus Christ, can be foundational for theological ethics.

THIRTY-ONE

God Is Love but Not a Pacifist*

This and the following essay should be read as two parts of a whole. The first, preached as a sermon at Rockway Mennonite Church on June 7, 1998, and later published in a slightly modified form in the Canadian Mennonite,[1] *is my initial attempt to lay the trinitarian groundwork for my personal coming to terms with the Mennonite peace witness. I have taught a course, "War and Peace in Christian Thought," for many years at Conrad Grebel College, Toronto School of Theology, and McMaster Divinity College. Gradually, what I would call my own "Mennonite theological peace position" has been evolving in dialogue and debate with students, colleagues, and other Christian traditions. I hold both viscerally and intellectually to the historic Anabaptist-Mennonite peace stance, and try to pass this conviction on to my own children and my students. I have come also, however, to recognize some of the problems (even contradictions) inherent in our own view—not the least of which is our hermeneutical avoidance of some biblical texts—and the compelling aspects of other traditions and other views.*

What follows is my preliminary effort at addressing some of these issues through a reconsideration of what I consider a classical trinitarian doctrine of

---

* Originally published as "God is not a Pacifist," *Canadian Mennonite* 3.15 (July 26, 1999): 8-9. The biblical texts for the sermon were Deut. 32:18-34 and Rom. 12:9-21. For notes on the text see the Notes section below.

God. What needs to be more fully explored is how the distinction between the "immanent Trinity" (the unity and distinctions within the divine being itself) and the "economic Trinity" (the unity and distinctions of the divine as they relate to God's creation) bear on social ethics. To say that "God is Love" is to say the most profound thing one can say about God, but it begs the question of the nature of divine love and how that love expresses itself in relation to the world.

What it must surely mean is that God has the good of the created order at heart and everything that God does and allows to happen is for the ultimate good of that creation. One might theologically spell this out further as follows: God is love in God's inner trinitarian relations—that is, following Augustine, God is the source of all love, God is the object of love, God is love itself; and the inner trinitarian life of love (immanent Trinity) is the foundation of the economic Trinity.

I do not agree that the two can be collapsed into one, as some contemporary theologians seem to be advocating, for the economic Trinity is the life of God as expressed outwardly and as experienced by us within the 'history of salvation.' There is a historicity to the economic Trinity that is not there in the immanent Trinity. Even in the context of the economic Trinity—God as the mysterious origin of the world, God as revealed to us in Christ the redeemer, and God as present to us in the Holy Spirit as the fulfiller—God works in ways that are frequently not entirely clear to us, even though the Christian church confesses that in Christ the very hidden nature and providence of God has in some mysterious way been revealed to us.

What I try to say below is that the nature and workings of God (in God's economic relations), despite this revelation in Christ, continue to have a hidden, mysterious quality to them. God cannot be said to be nonresistant and pacifist in any strict, univocal sense. I wrote the essay before I had read Miroslav Volf's Exclusion and Embrace, in which he says some of the very things I am getting at here—namely, that God's wrath and judgment does not translate into a justification of our own use of violence. In fact, Volf rightly says, it is precisely because vengeance is transferred to the divine that we humans are free not to exercise it.[2] The reader should be reminded that this and the subsequent essays were occasional pieces and, as such, are loosely-stated, preliminary reflections. They are not tightly-argued, systematic treatises. As I re-read these articles in preparation for this volume, what struck me were two problem areas: one, the concept of God, in which God's "absolute freedom" is so strongly emphasized, seems now to be too voluntaristic a notion; and, two, my view of civil institutions (e.g., the state) is too one-sidedly negative. I think the second essay, "Christians, Policing, and the Civil Order," begins to espouse a more positive role for such institutions.

◆ ◆ ◆

The Reality of Violence

I have for a long time thought that as Mennonites we don't quite get to the reality, root, and tenacity of violence and our complex involvement with it. Not a day goes by but that we encounter the reality of violence in ourselves, in our society, in nature.

Recently, I woke up to the shocking news of a local murder and suicide: a bright, ambitious young artist took the life of her child and then hanged herself. Which is the greater tragedy, the mother's violence toward herself or toward her "innocent" daughter? Tragic as it is for the mother, we could argue that *she* exercised her right of free choice; *the child* had all choices taken from her. But let's consider more closely the roots of violence in human actions like this mother's.

We know from history and the insights of modern psychology that our freedom is not nearly as unfettered as we like to think. There are hidden forces and motivations, genetically inherited personality traits, traumatic childhood experiences, moments of uncontrolled rage and fears that drive us to act in ways that free, rational beings normally don't act. The Old Testament, particularly the Psalms, gives powerful expression to the violent, irrational depths of the human and social psyche, as well as the dark forces of nature and the cosmos that determine us. Again and again, the Psalmist despairs in the face of these forces: "Save me, O God, for the waters have come up to my neck. I sink in deep mire, where there is no foothold; I have come into deep waters, and the flood sweeps over me. I am weary with my crying; my throat is parched. My eyes grow dim with waiting for my God" (Psalm 69:1-3).

The truth of the Calvinist teaching of predestination lies precisely in the recognition of this unexplainable, mysterious force behind all our actions. This is the insight that most forcefully came to me in reading John Irving's *A Prayer for Owen Meany*. The "problem" in Irving's Calvinistic novel is that human freedom and choice are lost. Destiny! (The German word is *Schicksal*). We all have a "destiny." The word expresses the inter-relatedness of all things past and present. There is no such thing as an isolated moment or action. Innumerable variables led up to the mother's murder of her child. Her violent act in turn permanently affects (destines) her child, her family and friends, and all of us. Now comes the difficult question. If all things are interconnected, if we are destined, can we still meaningfully speak of free choice?

Freedom! What do freedom and responsibility for our actions mean amid our destiny? I have used the metaphor of the Scrabble game to describe how we might understand the paradox of destiny and freedom. Unlike the jigsaw puzzle (where everything is predetermined), the scrabble game functions as a complex combination of predetermined factors: luck, skill, intelligence, memory, and interaction. While there are predetermined components, they do not absolutely predetermine the outcome of the game. The design and outcome emerge with the inter-relating of all the variables, not least of which is the freedom of choice of each player. We could say the destiny of the game emerges gradually and is fully clear only in retrospect. The non-believer might call this emergence of the destined end of the game of life as impersonal fate. The religious person believes that behind, beyond, or before this emerging end is a divine power which weaves all the variables together, a power in which we human beings participate.

To give this divine power a personal name is to declare that behind the game of life is not pure necessity but freedom. To say that we as human beings participate in this divine power is to say that we too have freedom. To say that we have freedom is to say that we are responsible for our actions amid our destiny. No matter how bad things are, no matter how deep the abyss, no matter what the genetic variables we have been given, we have freedom (limited though it is) to act responsibly. Therefore, we need to take responsibility for our actions and their consequences for others.

In the historical debate between the traditional Calvinists and their rather harsh view of predestination and Arminians (followers of Jacobus Arminius, a sixteenth-century Dutch theologian) and free will, Mennonites have been decisively on the side of the latter. We have stressed the free possibility of human beings to act lovingly and non-violently in this fallen world of evil. In doing so, however, we have never quite gotten at the root, irrationality, and tenacity of evil and violence. Our Mennonite peace theology, if it is not to deteriorate into a false romanticism, a kind of modern-day legacy of nineteenth-century liberalism, will need to deal seriously with these dark forces in the cosmos, in nature, and in our own psyches and communities.

Violence and the Christian Tradition

The Christian tradition has not been united in its understanding of violence within ourselves, within society and within the natural world. It is not simply a matter of disobedience or faithfulness to the teachings of Jesus—it has to do with serious differences about how to think of God, Jesus, human beings, and the world.

Christians have taken three different approaches: holy violence, justifiable violence, and non-violence—all supportable by the Bible. Central to the Mennonite understanding of the gospel of Jesus Christ is the message of peace and non-violence. Also central to Mennonite belief is the primary authority of the Bible for all faith and action. What happens when these two conflict? We have had tremendous difficulty reconciling the many stories of violence (even God-ordained violence) in the Old and New Testaments with our conviction about the basic non-violent character of Jesus and the kingdom of God. We have also had trouble dealing with the reality of violence in our fellowships and within ourselves.

We have in our history held to a minority position on the issue of violence and peace. First, we have for the most part rejected the view of *justifiable violence*. This position, held by the majority of Christians throughout history, is frequently referred to as the "just war" approach. But this is really a misnomer. Augustine, with whom this view originated, did not think violence was just, but he did believe that in our fallen and sinful world violence was sometimes justified as the tragic but lesser evil. Augustine had a keen sense of destiny and our involuntary connectedness with historical events. Most Anabaptists partly accepted the Augustinian view—the world was fallen and the sword was a tragic necessity for worldly people. Where they differed was in their view of the church. The Anabaptists believed that in the church—defined as Christians regenerated by the power of the Holy Spirit—violence was no longer to be practised. Augustine had less faith in the possibility of Christians to extricate themselves from violence within a fallen and violent world.

Second, Mennonites have for the most part rejected the Puritan notion of *holy violence*. This view has its roots in the Old Testament passages that depict God as holy warrior, a God of wrath, vengeance, and righteousness who uses nations to punish the wicked and set up a kingdom of justice. The Hebrew Scriptures are full of stories where God ordains holy slaughter against the wicked, and the Psalmist frequently calls upon God to vindicate his people by punishing and even killing the enemy. The New Testament apocalyptic literature (especially Revelation), which speaks prophetically about the end time, judgment, hell, and eternal damnation, falls into this same genre of thinking about God. It was because of the seemingly vengeful nature of the Hebraic God that some early Christians (for example, Marcion and his followers in the second century) wanted to separate themselves completely from the God of the Old Testament. They claimed that the God of Jesus was a God of love and nonviolence, totally different than Yahweh, the violent God of the Old Testament. Fortunately, Marcion's view was rejected by the majority in the early church. The development of the biblical canon (holding together both the Jewish and the Christian Scriptures), as well as the development of the doctrine of the Trinity, was an unqualified confession by the Christian church that the God of the Jews and the God of the Christians was one and the same God.

The third characteristic of our minority position is that Mennonites, in our strong commitment to *non-resistance*, are always tempted by Marcionism, by separating the God of Jesus and the God of the Old Testament. One way

Mennonite scholars have gotten around this is to identify another stream of thought in the Old Testament, the "suffering servant" motif of Isaiah 53, but this does not solve the problem of the many references to the God who judges, punishes, kills, and orders his people to do so on God's behalf.

There was a tremendous diversity among sixteenth-century Anabaptists on the use of violence. There were those like Balthasar Hubmaier who leaned toward the justifiable use of violence under certain conditions. Thomas Müntzer and Jan van Leyden were in the holy violence tradition. But the view that became dominant was the rejection of all overt violence. What Mennonites could never escape, however, was the reality of violence in their own midst. The ban brought a new form of psychological and social "violence" into the community of believers. I'm not criticizing the ban; I'm making the point that the reality of violence and force is a fact, both outside and inside the Christian community and Mennonites have participated in their share of it.

The God of Abraham, Isaac, Jacob, and Jesus

So what are we to do? How can we take seriously both 1) the reality of violence in our lives and in our world, and 2) the Christian witness to peace and non-violence? How can we reconcile the apparent violence of the God of Abraham, Isaac, and Jacob, and the non-violence of Jesus as found in his teachings in the Sermon on the Mount and his death on the cross?

This is where the Christian doctrine of the Trinity is so important. The trinitarian teaching of the early church can be applied to the issue of violence, especially as a challenge to Mennonite pacifists. Some Mennonite theologians have implied that if we take Jesus to be the full revelation of God, and if we understand the gospel of Jesus essentially as the rejection of all violence, then it follows that God is a pacifist. This, in my view, has dire consequences. It implies that all violence (such as the death of children or even the suicide of a distraught mother) is ultimately meaningless and outside the providence of God. It also suggests that evil will not be punished and judged.

The basic claim behind the trinitarian confession is that God the Creator, God the Son, and God the Spirit are one, yet distinct. God the Creator is the invisible, absolutely transcendent, unknowable, mysterious source of all that is, both being and non-being. This is the unknown God who destroyed all life in a flood, with the exception of Noah and those in the ark, spoke to Moses in the burning bush, drowned the Egyptians in the Red Sea, commanded Abraham to sacrifice his son Isaac, tested Job by destroying his family and property, the God to whom Jesus cried on the cross: "Why hast thou forsaken me?" This is the God of whom the author of Deuteronomy says: "See now that I, even I, am he; there is no god beside me. I kill and I make alive; I wound and

I heal; and no one can deliver from my hand" (32:39). This is the unknown God to whom the Athenians built an altar in Acts 17.

This God is no Mennonite pacifist. This God is beyond all human ethical systems, beyond our rules of good and bad. This is the God one meets not in the living room but on the boundary, at the abyss, at the point where one is faced with the threat of non-being. Does this mean God the Creator is arbitrary, like the Greek and Roman gods? No, the pagan divine arbitrariness is precisely what the Jews and the Christians rejected. God is not arbitrary—God is just, righteous, good, and loving, but in ways that are not fully transparent.

God's revelation through the Son in Jesus Christ is a revelation of this mystery—the mystery that despite the reality of violence and evil in the world there is a movement of divine redemption and reconciliation in the cosmos. God's justice and love will ultimately triumph even for the murderous mother and her child. The loving God is amid death and violence in ways that are not clear to us. The non-violent way of the cross, mediated to us in Jesus the Christ, reveals the hidden purposes of God. What this means for Christians, as followers of Jesus Christ, is that we give ourselves over to the non-violent undercurrent of God's purposes, empowered by the dynamic power of God as Holy Spirit—the Spirit of reconciliation. Though God in his mysterious ways with the world may not be self-evidently "pacifist," we are called to be so.

God's means of achieving the ultimate reconciliation of all things are not immediately evident to us. God cannot be subjected to our interpretation of the non-violent way of Jesus. Our commitment to the way of the cross (reconciliation) is not premised on God's pacifism or non-pacifism. It is precisely because God has the prerogative to give and take life that we do not have that right. Vengeance we leave up to God. Anabaptists called this *Gelassenheit*—surrender to and trust in God. We do not avoid the reality of violence in ourselves and in our world, but we side with the dynamic power of peace and reconciliation which is mysteriously at work in the scrabble game of life, knowing that ultimately all things rest in God's providential and loving hands.

THIRTY-TWO

Christians, Policing, and the Civil Order

The theological reflections below are an elaboration of my remarks made at a day-long symposium, "In Search of a Mennonite Response to Kosovo," held at Conrad Grebel College on June 22, 1999.[1] At the symposium I made the claim that whereas Anabaptists in the sixteenth century for the most part accepted some form of two-kingdom thinking, twentieth-century Mennonite thinking about church and society has tended to collapse the two kingdoms into one—the historical kingdom of peace and justice of which the church is a witness and the vanguard. I argued that we need to retrieve a form of two-kingdom thinking in which there is a distinction between church and world, the spiritual and temporal realms, the kingdom of God and the kingdom of Christ premised on a trinitarian doctrine of God.

The previous essay, "God is Love but not a Pacifist," makes the claim that God is absolutely free, beyond all human ethical systems, and is not a pacifist strictly speaking. In the following analysis I take this one step further, spelling out the consequences for the Christian's role in civil society. I make a distinction between "policing" and "warring." Although on occasions it may not be easy to identity

---

* Originally published as "Christians and the Civil Order" in *The Grebel Scholar* 2.1 (August 1999): 5-7 and in a shortened and modified form in *Canadian Mennonite* 3.17 (August 30, 1999): 6-7. For notes on the text see the Notes section below.

with precision when police-keeping shades into war-making, nevertheless these are two quite different ways of engaging force, premised on different assumptions, one to be theologically defended and the other rejected.

Policing, consistent with the biblical mandate for institutions of authority, ought to be devoted to the legitimate task of protecting good and restraining evil, always guided by the principle of "loving the enemy"—that is, respecting the dignity of the other as created in the image of God.

War, by its own inner logic, despite the rhetoric of nation states engaging in it, disregards the mandate to protect good and restrain evil, by in fact violating the good and itself using unrestrained evil (violence) to counter what it considers evil. The most recent, blatant example of this, is the unjustifed bombing of Belgrade.

Policing, on the other hand, as I am using the term in this article, is a metaphor for all forms of institutional life in civil society in which the exercise of power is necessary for maintaining disipline and order on domestic, municipal, provincial, and international levels. For pacifist-Mennonite intellectuals to argue against "policing" is a form of dishonesty.

John H. Yoder wrote a book called When War is Unjust: Being Honest in Just-War Thinking, in which he rightly presses those in the Just War tradition (most mainline Christians) to apply the criteria of Just War thinking consistently. Were they to do so, he argues, they would in virtually all cases join with pacifists in condemning war. I would propose another title: "When Policing is Just: Honesty in Pacifist Thinking," in which all Mennonites and others in the Historic Peace Church traditions are urged to overcome the dishonest disjunction between abstract theories of pacifism, on the one hand and their actual human life within civil society (i.e., calling 911 in an emergency) on the other.

I am not recommending deriving an "ought" from an "is." I am, however, urging us not to use high-sounding theological rhetoric ideologically to distort the situation in which we actually find ourselves in our family, professional, business, political, civil, and church lives or to read the Bible selectively, thereby misreading the positive biblical mandate for institutional life. In short, we need a more honest theology of institutions and their function to help shape and keep life human.

A brief excursus following the essay is an elaboration of my thinking on how Mennonites might through research contribute to the police function of the state in a way that is consistent with our historic peace witness. It was a presentation given to the Conrad Grebel College Council on whether or not the College should accept funding from the Department of National Defence for human security research. I argued in favour of such funding under some very strict conditions, taking as my point of departure sixteenth-century Anabaptist Pilgram Marpeck's view of Christian involvement in civil institutions.

◆ ◆ ◆

Foundational to any Christian thinking about the role of the church in society is our doctrine of God as One and Three. The first article of the creed, "I believe in God almighty, creator of heaven and earth," has implicit within it three sub-doctrines: a) the doctrine of creation (God has created the world and everything in it, visible and invisible)—the created order is good and God loves it in its entirety despite its fallenness; b) the doctrine of preservation (God bears, carries, preserves, and sustains this world as a mother cares for her child) despite the world's fallenness; c) the doctrine of providence (God has a purpose [*telos*] for this world and turns evil [the result of the world's fallenness] into good in achieving the divine goal.

It is not immediately clear how God is moving the world toward the final end—this is what it means to speak about the *hiddenness* of God. God in this first sense (God as creator, provider, providence) is no pacifist in any obvious sense. God is absolutely free, beyond good and evil, not captive to human moral and ethical systems. God's ultimate purpose is reconciliation as revealed in Christ (as we shall see below) but because of the fallenness of the world God has instituted so-called social "orders" or, better, "mandates" of creation.[2] These are institutions of society like family, nation, state, worldly authority to preserve the good and restrain the evil (Rom. 13). My own view is more Augustinian than Thomistic in this regard. Augustine, influence by both Jewish-Christian and Platonic thought, had a less benign view of these institutions than did Thomas. Augustine thought that force, including the use of the sword, was tragically necessary in a fallen post-lapsarian world but they were not intrinsic to creation. Thomas, influenced by Aristotle at this point, had a more optimistic view of the role of these institutions of power and was inclined to identify them as created goods.

The second article of the creed, "I believe in 'His' only begotten son. . . ," is God as the Christ, the saviour and reconciler of the world through sacrificial love. Here God's will for the world is revealed in an immediate, direct way.[3] In Christ God is reconciling the world through self-sacrificial love, peace, and non-violence (the way of the cross). Here what is hidden in the first sense is made manifest. The problem is that what is made manifest in Christ as God's ultimate goal for the world continues to have a hidden quality within historical time in the larger world, as God deals with the fallen world in God's own way and time.

The framers of the Schleitheim Articles of 1527 (Swiss Anabaptists) understood this, and distinguished between the ways of God with the church "inside the perfection of Christ" and world "outside the perfection of Christ." The challenge for us is to unravel what it means to be "in the world" but not "of it." The question that interests me here is: What role does the Christian play in the realm designated as "outside the perfection of Christ," where God works through the orders, mandates, institutions of power, and force to preserve [and further] the good and restrain/punish the wicked? The one task of the church is clear: to incarnate God's reconciling work in Christ (Rom. 12). What is not so clear is the role Christians have in being instruments of God's work to protect the good and restrain/punish the evil (Rom. 13) on the way toward the reconciliation of the world.

There are four basic possibilities:[4] Medieval Catholic, Augustinian-Lutheran, Anabaptist-Mennonite, Contemporary.

1. In the Medieval-Catholic view, the religious orders are called to a higher vocation—a few follow the call to live radical Christian lives of sacrificial love inside the perfection of Christ, while the majority follow a lesser standard, but also in obedience to God.

2. In the Augustinian-Lutheran view, the loving perfection of Christ tends to be spiritualized and internalized (it's a disposition premised on faith and the love of God), while the external world is characterized by force and power—that which is necessary for earthly justice, law, and order. Christians live in both worlds and have to decide situation by situation which norms apply: the rule of Christ's perfect love or the norm of law, force, and justice.

3. Generally speaking (although there were significant differences between them, as I indicate in my essay below) Anabaptists, like Luther, distinguished between two kingdoms—the spiritual and the temporal. But for them, unlike for Luther, both were external-social realms demanding allegiance: the spiritual was identified with the church and the temporal with the world, and one had to choose between them. The dualism is most graphically presented in the Schleitheim Articles but is present to a greater or lesser degree in most Anabaptist tracts.

4. There has been a dramatic shift in twentieth-century Mennonite thought toward what I will call here "one kingdom" thinking. In this Mennonites are not alone, but reflect a change in mainline Christian theology in this century from various forms of dualisms to what is called "wholistic" thinking, but which upon closer examination is really a type of monism. It is a monism in which the kingdom of God is understood as a "historical" or temporal future which is "not yet" fully here but is "already" being realized in the historical-temporal present within the church as a society of Christians. Christians involved in relief work, non-violent protests, reconciliation between warring factions, mediation between conflictual parties, and so on, are helping to build and bring about within society in a preparatory way the kingdom of God.

Within this latter understanding there is little or no recognition of divine activity in those areas of social life which have no concrete, visible, or direct connection with the positive work of reconciliation but are related to the restraining of evil and protection of the good in a fallen world. There is also scant appreciation for the invisible, spiritual realm that unites all Christians, despite their differences on social issues. The Anabaptists of the sixteenth century had a much livelier sense of the strange, or "left-handed" work of God in the world through the institutions of authority.

In my view, some form of dualism, or better, trinitarianism, is a more adequate foundation for Christian social-political ethics, also for Mennonites, than an "already-not-yet" historical-temporal monism. The "already-not yet" schema readily dissolves into a one directional, linear, past-present-future historicism and progressivism that does not take seriously enough the distinctions, paradoxes, even antagonisms between dimensions of reality that the Bible and Classical-Patristic thought take for granted. Trinitarian thought, when understood properly, is able to combine both distinctions and unity in a way that neither monism nor dualism can do. This is why I argue throughout this volume for trinitarian foundations for Christian ethics. A few of the implications of a trinitarian theology for Christian social-ethics are as follows:

1. It is important to distinguish between the kingdom of God and the kingdom of Christ. Ultimately, of course, these two are essentially one and will become actually one, but in the present the preservation and providence of the world is in the hands of God in ways that are hidden and that may appear to be in conflict with God's work in Christ. This has to do with the fallenness of the world. The sixteenth-century Anabaptists were right in talking about God being at work in the world outside the perfection of Christ before the *Basileia* when God's rule will be fully realized and there will no longer be any distinction between the two kingdoms—there will be only one kingdom.

2. The church as church has one primary task: to proclaim and incarnate the perfection of Christ within the fallen context of the world. The perfection of Christ is the work of restoration and reconciliation of that which is fallen and estranged as a result of the Fall. It does so through the transforming and empowering work of the Holy Spirit. It is this to which the third article of the creed speaks: "I believe in the Holy Spirit. . . ." Theologically and ethically for the church, the most important doctrine associated with the Holy Spirit is the Resurrection. The Spirit gives new life and the possibility of living the new life under the fallen and estranged conditions of time and history. Jesus's own resurrection is directly attributed to the Holy Spirit as is ours, beginning in the present and completed in the eschaton. To live "inside the perfection of Christ," to use Anabaptist terminology, can be misinterpreted as living perfectly according to some divinely revealed ethical system taught by Christ

which includes pacifism and non-violence. It might be better understood as "living in" or participating in the Spirit-empowered resurrection of Christ which entails the resurrecting of the world as a whole.

3. This, however, begs the question, given the church's primary role to proclaim and incarnate the so-called "perfection of Christ," of how it is involved, if at all, in the providential and preservative activity of God in a fallen world through the institutions of authority, power, and force identified above. I offer the following suggestions:

a) The church ought not to look upon such institutions of authority (the Principalities and the Powers) as by definition demonic, enemy territory but as having legitimate, divinely ordained tasks within a fallen world. The church ought to pray for and support the limited but nevertheless legitimate functions of these "orders" of authority, in which the restricted use of power and force are necessary. For want of a better metaphor, I call this the "policing" function of civil institutions. This policing, whether on the domestic (family), local, provincial, national, or international level, is most properly understood as protecting good and restraining evil with a minimum amount of force. It ought to be guided by one over-riding criterion: to respect the dignity of offended and offender alike as human beings created in the image of God whom it is our obligation to love. At the point where this criterion is transgressed, the Christian says, No.

b) The church acts as a prophetic watch-dog or gad-fly, critically watching and reminding institutions of authority not to overstep their limited mandate of restraining evil and protecting the good through power and force. War, for instance, is an over-stepping of the boundary, a moving beyond the peace-keeping activity of policing. It is to be unequivocally rejected.

c) This means that the church, although not directly involved itself, will support in prayer, wisdom, and guidance not only *direct* work of peace and reconciliation in the world but also *indirect* peacemaking activities by government-sponsored and non-governmentally sponsored work in areas of policing, prison work, social services, civil rights, peace-keeping, and so on. Support takes the form of helping groups and individuals within its ranks to discern whether they are called to be instruments of God's preserving and providential functions, and what it means to be faithful within limited parameters.

d) There are times of crisis when the church, to be faithful to its primary task, is called upon to "put a spoke in the wheel" (Bonhoeffer). On rare occasions, the church finds itself in a *status confessionis* (state of confession) when it separates itself dramatically from the given institutions of power and authority and goes underground, as did the Anabaptists in the sixteenth century and the Confessing Church in the Hitler period. But this is not the normal state of affairs—it is an extreme situation where the divinely ordained powers have clearly become illegitimate, transgressing their limited mandates. It is through much careful deliberation, prayer, and discernment that such drastic steps are taken.

e) Within the church, there are a variety of callings, from vocations of direct peacemaking (Christian Peacemaker Teams) to less direct peacemaking through involvement in all levels of cultural and civil life. The church cannot compromise its unequivocal commitment to loving the enemy, but it can expect disagreement on how that principle is interpreted and applied in civil society—i.e., what form loving the enemy might take in diverse situations of everyday life as well as times of crises.

Excursus: Should Conrad Grebel College Accept Department of National Defence (DND) Funding for Human Security Research

I would like my following remarks to be seen as standing firmly within the historical Mennonite commitment to peace. However, I have thought for some time that the radical Anabaptist vision which emerged amongst 1950 and 1960 Anabaptist-Mennonite theologians and ethicists, who rehabilitated the vision of the Schleitheim articles (which in effect became their confession) of the Swiss radicals does not fully reflect the broad stream of early, particularly second and third generation Anabaptist-Mennonites, nor does it adequately represent where and how we as Mennonites have managed to live historically and at the present.

From very early on for Mennonites (even for Swiss Mennonites, as Arnold Snyder and Werner Packull are showing in their research) it was Pilgram Marpeck's approach to living within culture that actually won the day. Conrad Grebel College situates itself most authentically within Marpeck's vision, where political institutions (like the "magistracy") are not seen as evil in themselves but as potentially positive venues for human and also Christian activity. It is only at the point where they transgress their legitimate roles that one says No, as did Marpeck. This is the background for my subsequent comments on the issue before us. It is not simply a question of whether we are departing from our historical peace position and compromising ourselves on the slippery slope to the mainstream. It is, rather, our candid recognition of who we are, how we live, with which of our historical positions we identify ourselves, and what it means to be faithful Christians in the world.

1. The request for me to respond to the issue before us is forcing me to ask myself some hard preliminary questions. Do I think the Department of National Defence should be disbanded? If not, what role should it play? And what

attitude should I as a citizen of Canada, as a Canadian Christian, and as a Mennonite Christian have toward it? Until I can be persuaded otherwise, I do not think DND should be disbanded. It's like asking myself: should Kitchener-Waterloo get rid of its police-force? No, I do not think so. There is much about DND and the local police force, and their actions, that I don't agree with; that's why it is my responsibility as a citizen, Christian, and Mennonite to keep on reminding them of what their true role ought to be. Their role should be peace-keeping, peacemaking, and "policing," not killing.

2. To accept money from DND for a well-defined project which is in keeping with our historical-Mennonite peacemaking position is not to agree with or condone everything the Canadian military establishment does, just like paying taxes to or taking money from the government does not mean one agrees with everything the government does.

3. As Ernie Regehr's article shows, Canadian foreign policy, and by implication the Canadian military establishment as one of its instruments, has been historically (and is increasingly) interested in peace-keeping, peacemaking, peace-building and "policing," which Christians, and especially those in the historic peace church, ought to welcome and support conditionally and with reservation.[5] I see this as a form of witness. It is important to remember in all of this that one ought not to compromise the clarity of one's witness, and that this is but one of many forms of witness.

4. As I have argued elsewhere, a distinction needs to be drawn between "policing" and "war-making." Policing can and ought to respect the biblical mandate of governments to "preserve the good and restrain the evil" while respecting (loving, if you like) the enemy or perpetrator of evil. As Christians we ought to reject all war-making but support well-controlled, limited "policing." This reasoning is I believe biblically and theologically supportable. I have been impressed recently, for instance, with the comparatively benign view the Lukean materials, especially Acts, have of the Roman establishment (in contrast to the book of Revelation). It is really quite remarkable how frequently in Paul's travels he takes advantage of his Roman citizenship for a kind of police protection against the threat of mob violence.

5. So as far as I now see it, I would support applying for research funding from DND on the strict condition that a) such research proposal be focused strictly on issues of human security and peace-building, as Regehr defines it in his article, and b) we in our proposal clearly identity ourselves as standing within a tradition which has a long history of rejecting war and all participation in war as a way of solving conflict—and that it is precisely for this reason that we are engaged in such research.[6]

THIRTY-THREE

Virtue, Justice, and the Moral Community: A Critical-Appreciative Appraisal of Alasdair MacIntyre and the Narrative School of Theology*

In this and the subsequent three articles I begin reflecting on the nature of the church as a worshiping and moral community—I say "begin" deliberately for, I do not present a comprehensive doctrine of the church. The essays are no more than occasional reflections on some aspects of ecclesiology.

The following previously unpublished piece was presented upon invitation at Brock University, St. Catharines, for a conference on "Love and Justice in the Writings of Alasdair MacIntyre," sponsored by the Brock Philosophical Society on February 13, 1993.[1] Since then, other Mennonite theologians than those cited here have critically explored the theology of narrative thinkers like MacIntyre and Stanley Hauerwas in relation to Mennonite theology.[2] My own fuller acquaintance with the person and thought of Hauerwas came later that same year, through the organizing and moderating of a special session of Mennonite scholars at the American Academy of Religion and Society of Biblical Literature meetings in Washington, D. C. This event, sponsored by the Toronto Mennonite Theological Centre, was called "Mennonites on Hauerwas: Hauerwas on Mennonites," and consisted of five presentations by Mennonites (Lydia Harder, Scott Holland, Harry Huebner, P. Travis Kroeker, and Ben C. Ollenburger) and a final response by Hauerwas.

Each of the presentations together with an introduction by me were later published.[3] In my introduction, written on the island of Korcula off the coast of Croatia while the ethnic war in Bosnia was still going on, I noted that while Hauerwas

---

* The original title was "Virtue, Justice and the Moral Community: A Mennonite Theological Appraisal of Alasdair MacIntyre." For notes on the text see the Notes section below.

challenges Mennonites to be faithful to their historic vision of the church as an alternate model to mainline ecclesiology, all the Mennonite respondents raise critical questions of their own tradition. I suggest that "maybe this generation of Mennonite theologians needs to take Hauerwas's challenge to us [more] seriously. In our eagerness to identity the weaknesses in our tradition and to be open to the world around us, are we not in danger of losing our own souls?"[4] I do, however, make reference to the anomaly, even irony, that the historic Mennonite view of the church as made up of "resident aliens" (Hauerwas's term), is now come of age, discussed and debated as the postmodern option in the religious pantheon of American academia (AAR/SBL) in Washington.

In the Brock University presentation as it appears below, I give an appreciative reading of the narrative school of theology of which both MacIntyre and Hauerwas are representatives. I am especially sympathetic with their turn to the classical period of Christian thought. What I am most critical of, however, is MacIntyre's open embrace of modern historicism—that is, the acceptance of classical thought apparently eviscerated of its metaphysical foundations. This appears to me to be the danger of much contemporary narrative thinking: in its postmodern critique of all forms of metaphysical foundationalism it collapses metaphysical and ontological thinking into "story," or better, "stories." In an April 20, 1998 letter to me by Stanley Hauerwas, in which he responds to my contribution to the Yoder Festschrift (reprinted above), Hauerwas says the following:

> Just a note to say I got the essay and thanks so much. It is very good and presents a challenge that is crucial. Of course, like you I want to separate Catholicity from Constantinianism. Where I would differ from you, however, is contrasting the prophetic/eschatological with priestly/sacramental. I think that is not a good contrast and that Yoder belies it in many ways. It is a kind of history versus metaphysics contrast that does not do justice to the fact that the gospel is about historic events which require witness. Of course, metaphysical claims are intrinsic to that, but they're not in contrast to it.[5]

My point is not so much to contrast metaphysical claims to historical claims, although I may have said things that suggest that, but to see metaphysical-ontological-theological claims (understood in the classical, apologetic sense not in the Enlightenment rationalist sense) as foundational for historical-ethical claims. As I state repeatedly in a variety of ways in this volume, it is only thus that our common humanity (transcending all particular narratives) can truly be taken seriously and the universal, global ethical challenges arising out of modern technology adequately addressed.

◆ ◆ ◆

The Mennonite Connection

I have been asked to address the philosophy of Alasdair MacIntyre from a Mennonite perspective. This is a most unusual challenge, for historically Mennonites have not been known for their philosophizing—nor their theologizing, for that matter. And yet, as will become clear in this paper, there is an appropriateness to asking how a Mennonite might respond to MacIntyre's thought. For Mennonites have historically found themselves as tightly knit traditional communities on the margin of dominant culture (with the possible exception of Dutch Mennonites). Rooted in the radical left wing of the sixteenth-century Reformation, they have found themselves throughout the centuries in the minority for moral and religious reasons— one group emigrating from Switzerland to Pennsylvania to Canada, another from Holland to Prussia to the Ukraine to Canada to South America, and so on. My own ancestors, for example, emigrated from the Ukraine to southern Manitoba in 1874. My first language as a child was low German, a hybrid reaching back to sixteenth-century Holland.

For some 400 years this small emigrating community had lived with a common language. My children are the first generation not to speak low German. I grew up in a Manitoba Mennonite village, similar to the villages in southern Russia, which themselves bore resemblances to villages from an earlier period. These villages in southern Manitoba—as those in Russia had been—were built as communal villages (one main street, with house-barn farmyards on each side, a common pasture at one end).

The church in these villages was the focal point. The theology was a simple one—to follow Jesus in daily life. Only with modern urbanization and industrialization did this village life begin to come apart, as individuals with entrepreneurial spirit left communal-village life and moved onto individual estates—a phenomenon that had begun already in Russia. This also brought a change in theology: a less communal-oriented theology was found that could accommodate assimilation into a more individualistic culture. By the time I was growing up, these villages were well on the way to disintegration.

Like the medieval monasteries, Mennonites for centuries had preserved in their communities values and virtues from a previous age, a notion of the good quite in opposition to the dominant cultures surrounding them. According to MacIntyre, in an individualistic culture like today's, "conceptions of the virtues become marginal and the tradition of the virtues remains central only in the lives of social groups whose existence is on the margins of the central culture."[6] In the fragmentation of modern and postmodern culture, traditional virtues survive in some such fringe cultures (MacIntyre mentions Catholic Irish, Orthodox Greeks, Orthodox Jews, but

one might add Mennonites) who continue to have strong ties to the past—
"communities that inherit their moral tradition not only through their
religion, but also from the structure of the peasant villages and households
which their immediate ancestors inhabited on the margins of modern
Europe."[7] Mennonites in the not-too-distant past were carriers of such
traditional virtues. And some contemporary groups which trace their
lineage back to the sixteenth-century Anabaptists (like the Hutterian
Brethren, and the Old Order Amish and the Old Order Mennonites of
Waterloo County) continue to be strong traditional communal cultures;
but on the whole Mennonites too have lost the cohesion and shared values
of their past.

Some of our contemporary Mennonite theologians have seen in the
communal-narrative theology of Hans Frei, George Lindbeck, Stanley
Hauerwas (and indirectly, I would argue, also in the narrative-philosophy
of Alasdair MacIntyre), a theology most congenial to recovering or
preserving a distinctive, Mennonite way of living and thinking in the
present situation. In the following pages I will approach the topic of
MacIntyre somewhat through the back door—that is, through establishing
a Mennonite connection with the narrative school of thought, which
ultimately leads back to the philosophy of MacIntyre. It has been through
the thought of Hauerwas, I want to show, that MacIntyre's narrative
philosophy has found a home within some forms of Mennonite theology
recently, although in my own theology I rest uneasily here in this
appreciation of MacIntyre, for reasons which will become evident later.

Ted Koontz

One example of such a theology appears in a recent article by Ted Koontz,
professor of ethics at the Associated Mennonite Biblical Seminary in
Elkhart, Indiana. In a 1989 essay, "Mennonites and 'Postmodernity,'"
Koontz laments the Mennonite loss of a sense of "over-againstness"
toward modern culture amongst the present generation of Mennonites.
He urges Mennonites to resist "modern liberalism" and witness to the
Mennonite distinctives of "community, discipleship, active service and
peace"[8] Although Koontz does not explicitly refer to MacIntyre, he draws
heavily on Stanley Hauerwas, whose early work on the ethics of character
bears the unmistakable stamp of MacIntyre's philosophy.

Let me paraphrase Koontz's Hauerwas-MacIntyre-sounding argument.
Liberalism defines modernity. It is a belief in the supremacy of the
individual, the priority of individual rights and freedoms over everything
else. John Rawls's *A Theory of Justice*, with its vision of "hypothetical rational
individuals, behind a 'veil of ignorance'. . . who seek to construct social

arrangements which will best allow them . . . to maximize their freedom to pursue their own visions of the good"[9] is the greatest representative of contemporary liberalism. Here there is no search for a common good by which to frame individual goods. What defines postmodernity is the overcoming of this liberal individualism in favour of communitarianism.[10] Communitarians stress the larger communal endeavours within which individuals can lose themselves and find meaning. They emphasize the priority of the common good over the individual good; and consequently they also subordinate the language of rights and justice to the language of virtue (benevolence, love, compassion). While for liberal educators moral education is not necessary, communitarians think of the formation of moral character as a central task.

Central to the communitarian position, as Koontz sees it, is its historicism (although he never uses the term). Narrative-communal thinking is linked to a pure historicism. I take the following historicist claim to be the most important and also the most problematic made by Koontz and the whole narrative school, including MacIntyre:

> Implicit in the communitarian view of reality is the notion that there can be no position outside history, behind particular commitments, from which to make universally binding moral judgments. Every moral perspective is a particular one. The task of the philosopher or theologian is not to try to escape from this inevitable particularity, but to demonstrate the interpretive power of a given framework, to explore its coherence and its ability to provide meaning. There can be no "neutral" ground upon which to stand and pass judgment on competing religious and philosophical traditions. Pluralism, not unity, prevails at a foundational level. The liberal enlightenment dream of finding a way to adjudicate truth claims—as symbolized in liberal political thought by the prevalence of hypothetical "state of nature" theories—is a pipe dream.[11]

In other words, meaning, coherence, and truth are self-referential, intratextual,[12] intra-communal, intra-narrative. It is true that a narrative is always larger than any particular story, for particular narratives take on significance and meaning only within larger frameworks, larger histories and stories. Nevertheless, one cannot make universal truth claims. I will comment on the problems with such historicism, including MacIntyre's self-proclaimed historicism, at the end of this essay.

Koontz places himself within this communitarian camp, and appears to lament the Mennonite yearning to become modern in its movement toward individualism, softening of family bonds, increasing emphasis on self-fulfilment, loss of traditional forms of church discipline or mutual discernment, preoccupation with social justice without a clear notion of the good that is sought. In the end, however, Koontz remains ambivalent about postmodernity, wanting to balance individual rights and communal goods, freedom and virtue, justice and love—recognizing both the emancipatory gains of modernity as well as the need for renewed community. Koontz suggests one way out of the dilemma for Mennonites with their historic suspicion of the state and larger culture. The state ought to exercise the legitimate task of guarding individual and group rights and freedoms; and the church ought to be the place where a communal vision of the good is fostered. The logic behind this is that membership in the church is voluntary whereas citizenship in the nation-state is not. Ultimately, the good cannot be enforced.

Scott Holland

A much more critical look at the narrative school of thought by a Mennonite is found in a recent article by Scott Holland, a Mennonite minister and Ph.D. candidate working on narrative theology at Duquesne University in Pittsburgh, PA. Holland critically evaluates the narrative theology of Hauerwas. He identifies the major influence on Hauerwas's thought as being that of the Yale School of narrative hermeneutics associated with Hans Frei, George Lindbeck, and Paul Holmer. Central to their project is an "antifoundationalism," in which "there can be no ontological grounding or extrabiblical foundations that can be used to prove the truth or falsity of the Christian story."[13] Right or wrong belief is not as important, if at all, as living by the rules and principles intrinsic to the narrative, similarly, I take it, to MacIntyre's claim that goods and virtues are only intrinsic to practices. Intratextual and intrasystematic coherence replaces concern for universal truth claims and inter-communal (not intra-communal) expressions of common experience.

Holland shows how, more recently, Hauerwas has moved from his earlier Aristotelian-Thomistic emphasis on the ethics of character and virtue, in which "being good" takes precedence over "good actions," to discipleship and anti-Constantinian Free Church theology profoundly shaped by John Howard Yoder, our most influential Mennonite ethicist. Holland cites Yoder as arguing that "'the church precedes the world epistemologically' and . . . 'the church precedes the world axiomatically.'"[14] What is more, according to Holland, is that "Stanley Hauerwas has such high regard for the Yoder reading of the Jesus story that the Texas-born Methodist theologian at Duke calls himself 'a high-church Mennonite'!"[15] I take it that, according to Holland, Hauerwas has moved from a loosely defined MacIntyre-like notion of community to a more narrow, well-defined notion of moral community as church under the Mennonite influence of John Howard Yoder.

Although Holland manages to say some good things about Hauerwas's hermeneutics of suspicion directed to liberalism with its view of general rationality, the conscious self, and the idea of progress on the one hand, and the problems of traditional foundationalism and orthodoxies on the other, he identifies some key difficulties in Hauerwas's methodology. These, I believe, can be applied also to other representatives of the narrative school of thought, including MacIntyre. Holland thinks that in a world of competing narratives and increasing pluralism, Hauerwas's (and also Yoder's) "ecclesiastical positivism"—where God appears to be working only through a particular church community—leaves us with an unacceptable religious tribalism.

My response to Hauerwas would be somewhat different from Holland's. My diagnosis of the contemporary situation is different. I do not believe that what defines the modern and postmodern period is a new communitarianism but a fundamental paradox: the increasing fragmentation and disjunction of human experience in the face of a growing homogenization—brought about by the all-pervasive fact of modern technology (in the form of computers, television, and so on). It is not pluralism and competing stories which ultimately define the postmodern age but one monolithic story—the technological story. In the face of this a narrative philosophy and theology is powerless. In fact, I see the historicism of the narrative school as itself the most radical manifestation or product of modernity.

Holland argues for "a method of mutually critical correlation between one's religious community and culture" along the lines suggested by David Tracy, without appealing to metaphysics or a meta-narrativist approach. Only this way, Holland thinks, can one hear the "voice of the Other, who often comes to us as the stranger."[16] For Hauerwas, according to Holland, "God appears to be absent in the world of general cultural experience.... God appears to be so confined to linguistic-narrative activity that any pre-conceptual, pre-verbal mystical experience of the divine is not possible."[17]

Here, in my view, Holland has put his finger on the fundamental problem of historicist-narrative schools of philosophical and theological thought. I do not see how within such historicism there is room for the experience of that which is given to us from the outside (the wholly other) either in the Heideggerian sense of the "givenness of being" or the traditional theological sense of God's coming to us and breaking into our world of narrative chronology. This brings me to a more direct confrontation with the philosophy of Alasdair MacIntyre.

MacIntyre: A Mennonite Theological Appraisal

The Mennonite Peace Debate: A Test Case

Mennonites pride themselves in belonging to a small cluster of so-called "Historic Peace Churches"—churches which believe not only that war is wrong (a view held also by most churches in the just war tradition), but that it is not permissible for Christians, who claim to be followers of Christ, to engage in any kind of violence, let alone military violence. For Mennonites, this is an ideal (sometimes referred to as the Anabaptist vision) which has been the most distinctive and universally shared moral tenet of all of the numerous Mennonite splinter groups (more than twenty-five groups of Mennonites in Canada alone).[18] It is what holds Mennonites together today, despite the fact that in the sixteenth century not all Anabaptist groups were united on this question; and despite the fact that in their nearly five-century history Mennonites have repeatedly compromised this ideal. (In Germany during the 1930s many Mennonites found themselves supporting Hitler, and in World War II many Canadian Mennonites left the church to join the armed forces and were in effect excommunicated from the church.)

The recent events in Iraq and in Somalia have once again raised the issue for Mennonites of what we believe in this regard. The Mennonite church press has been printing articles with contradictory opinions. Some hold to an absolute, non-compromising, non-resistant biblical pacifism. Others are waffling, especially in the face of ambiguous situations like Somalia, where food convoys need military protection to feed starving people. This debate in the Mennonite media simply reflects a more general diversity on theological issues, particularly those related to our historic peace position. A publication entitled *Mennonite Peace Theology: A Panorama of Types*,[19] illustrates this diversity and fragmentation of positions on what once seemed to be a unified position. Thus, within the Mennonite community itself there exist what MacIntyre refers to as the diverse moral claims which compete for allegiance in the present situation.

I teach at a Mennonite college, Conrad Grebel College, affiliated with the University of Waterloo. At an event sponsored by our graduate programme in theological studies, seven faculty members became involved in a heated exchange over "the moral ambiguity of military intervention in Somalia." We ended up spelling out sharply contrasting positions on the issues—all the way from a pragmatic Niebuhrian political realism, to a strict non-compromising pacifist absolutism, to a so-called "vocational pacifism" (where some Christian communities like the Mennonites might perceive themselves as having a special calling to be pacifist while recognizing that society as a whole could not operate on such a principle).

I articulated my own position as follows. I am confronted with a number of equally intellectually and theologically coherent positions on the issue, based on equally compelling readings of the biblical text. At the same time, I find myself existentially committed to one of these— namely, an uncompromising pacifism, which I also convey to my children. My position is therefore not based on superior rational grounds or on a superior reading of the Bible, but on pre-rational and pre-cognitive (not irrational or noncognitive) factors which have to do with my upbringing, my personal experiences, my reading of the sacred texts, and so on. My own conscience acts therefore as a sieve garnering all the data from my personality, my upbringing, my reading of the Scriptures, my experiences, my reasoning powers, etc. And out of these various factors emerges a coherent position.

MacIntyre: *After Virtue*

We come back now to see how MacIntyre's proposals fare in light of the above. I take his argument in his *After Virtue* to go roughly as follows.

1. *Moral Pluralism* In our contemporary world we are faced with competing moral claims but we have no general, rational way of evaluating or adjudicating the validity of these claims and reaching a reasonable solution.

2. *Emotivism* Most, if not all, moral discourse in the modern world is based on judgments of personal preference, for "emotivism asserts . . . that there are and can be no valid rational justification for any claims that objective and impersonal standards exist and hence that there are no such standards."[20]

3. *Enlightenment* The loss of rational criteria by which to make moral judgments can be understood historically as a consequence of the failure of the Enlightenment project—namely , the unsuccessful attempt to replace the Aristotelian/Thomistic notion of the human being as having an essential nature and telos with an abstract, secular, rational justification of moral allegiances (using the language of effectiveness, utility, and rights), freed from any external, religious restraint. Nietzsche successfully unmasked the complete failure of this Enlightenment rationality.

4. *Aristotle* One is left with one of two options: either to follow the Enlightenment through to its ultimate demise in Nietzsche, a direct consequence of the rejection of the Aristotelian tradition; or to vindicate an Aristotelian-like version of the virtues, and with it a "classical" understanding of the human being. MacIntyre opts for this latter alternative.

5. *Teleology* As I see it, MacIntyre divests the Aristotelian tradition, as filtered through Thomistic Christianity, of its metaphysical grounding and translates the left-over teleology into a historicist, narrative account of moral behavior. "A central thesis," he says, "then begins to emerge: man is in his actions and practice, as well as in his fictions, essentially a story-telling animal. He is not essentially, but becomes through his history, a teller of stories that aspire to truth. . . . I can only answer the question 'What am I to do?' if I can answer the prior question 'Of what story or stories do I find myself a part?'"[21] We find our moral identity through our membership in communities: families, neighborhoods, cities, tribes, nations, and so on.[22] This runs directly counter to abstract rational Kantian-like moral oughts, which ultimately lead to the irrational and motivist aporias (dead ends) of the contemporary moral scene. MacIntyre remains vague about the specific nature of these communities—something theologians like Hauerwas try to correct by defining more specifically the moral community as the Christian community.

6. *Justice and Rationality* In his book *Whose Justice? Which Rationality?* MacIntyre tries to show how competing views of justice and rationality emerge in different historical-social contexts and different traditions.[23] There are different traditions of rationality, each with internal criteria for the rationality of a position. Through imaginative reasoning one can understand someone from another tradition not one's own; but to persuade someone from another tradition to appropriate for himself/herself the rationality of another tradition would require a conversion of sorts.

7. *The Postliberal University* In his Gifford lectures, published as *Three Rival Versions of Moral Enquiry*, MacIntyre argues that the modern liberal university is premised on "unconstrained [pragmatic] agreement" based on "neutral objectivity," thus excluding "substantive moral and theological inquiry from its domain."[24] He proposes that the postliberal university become "a place of constrained disagreement, of imposed participation in conflict, in which a central responsibility of higher education would be to initiate students into conflict."[25] There can be no way of adjudicating between stories with criteria abstracted from one's own story.

A Critical Concluding Appraisal

I find much of MacIntyre's argument compelling. I think, for example, to answer my earlier question, that MacIntyre's narrative understanding of how individuals make moral decisions—like Mennonites holding a strong peace position—is quite persuasive, for it allows for pre-cognitive formation of moral opinion in the face of other coherent views. There are, however, a few problem areas.

1. I find most persuasive his critique of the Enlightenment project of abstract so-called uncommitted rationality, and his attempt to reappropriate aspects of the Classical tradition for a postmodern age. Enlightenment rationality seems to have run its course. What I find most problematic, however, concerns those aspects he reappropriates and those he leaves out. He builds a case for a narrative-communal historicism on the basis of classical teleology divested of the latter's metaphysical framework.[26] This leaves him with a radical historicism (and he frankly admits he is a historicist[27]) which is the product of modernity *par excellence*; for it was precisely classical metaphysics and ontology which the moderns and postmoderns (deconstructionists, for example) have rejected. While I would not suggest that we rehabilitate classical metaphysics as is, it has been shown by Hans Jonas among others, for example, that some form of postmodern metaphysics is not only necessary but possible for contemporary ethics.[28]

2. My second area of disagreement has to do with MacIntyre's understanding of the nature of modernity and postmodernity. He believes that what defined the modern period was a notion of liberal consensus and that what characterizes the postmodern period is the unravelling of this agreement into competing moral and rational claims, ultimately not based on reasoning at all but on emotivism. It is true that loss of cohesion, disjunction, and conflict defines our present situation on a superficial level; but, I would argue, that to linger on this so-called pluralism is to miss the fundamental character of contemporary life. We live in a world that is in fact coalescing around a shared vision of a perceived "good"— the good as defined by modern technology. There is *de facto* a shared rationality—the instrumental rationality of *techne*. Heidegger, Jonas, Ellul, and Grant have illuminated this situation. A narrative-communal historicism cannot, in my opinion, address the monolithic nature of the modern technological phenomenon.[29] It can not adequately meet the universal, global nature of the moral challenges coming to us from technology, nuclear power, the environment, the Third World, and so on. A more universalist ethic is required.

3. Finally, my membership in the Mennonite tradition has given me a great appreciation for community defined both ethnically and religiously. Mennonites have historically seen the church (not the society at large, nor the nation-state) as a moral community. The church is a voluntary community of shared values, shared beliefs, and shared assumptions about morality based on the biblical text and passed on from generation

to generation. Ideally, this is a praiseworthy model, especially when the basic assumption behind it is that the church is a dynamic reality, open to the experience of divine reality and the spirit of truth equally available to all members. Practically, however, there are dangers inherent in this model of church when such communitarianism becomes rigid and closes itself to that which is outside; drawing sharp boundaries and defining itself as standing over against the rest of the "evil" world, devoid of individual freedoms and rights within its own ranks, and characterized by the loss of love for art and beauty.

God as cosmic mystery addressing us within and through our particular histories and narratives is that universal which transcends the narrative—the Absolute before which all of us stand and before which/whom we also are held morally accountable for what we do with the created order and with each other. A pure narrative-communal-historicist ethics of tradition, without some such type of metaphysical, ontological underpinnings leads, in my opinion, to an anthropocentric *cul-de-sac*.

THIRTY-FOUR

Homosexuality: A Call for Compassion and Moral Rigour*

The ethical issue of homosexuality, apart from its intrinsic importance, is also a useful test case for looking at how one interprets biblical texts and doctrinal development. While the discussion of gay and lesbian sexuality is an important window into one's biblical hermeneutics, this is not the primary interest in the following essay. Rather, the focus is on how one's understanding of doctrine, particularly the development of dogma, can help deal in creative ways with tough moral and ethical issues like homosexuality. Homosexuality, then, is a case example of ways of proceeding that should be applicable as well to other ethical problems like women's ordination, war, policing, social justice, euthanasia, biomedical advances—issues which are not directly addressed here but could be, using the same general doctrinal approach. In fact, as argued elsewhere in this volume, to address the complex issues of contemporary society demands moving beyond the biblical text in dynamic ways. This is made possible through some notion of "doctrinal" development in the context of a discerning believing community (the church) led by the Holy Spirit.

---

* Originally published as "A forum on homosexuality," in *Mennonite Reporter*, 17.3 (June 22, 1987), 7-9. This essay was later that year discussed at a Conrad Grebel College Faculty Forum. For notes on the text see the Notes section below.

It is this developmental principle which is assumed in the discussion of homosexuality below, an essay which first appeared as an article in the Mennonite Reporter[1] and reflects my treatment of the subject in various venues in the 1980s and 1990s, including a lecture to Conrad Grebel College students,[2] an adult Sunday school class at Rockway Mennonite Church, a presentation to Brethren/Mennonite Council for Lesbian and Gay Concerns,[3] and my work as chair of the Theological Concerns Council of Mennonite Conference of Eastern Canada (MCEC) in 1993-94.

In the Council we spent a good deal of time discussing the issue and planning a workshop on the subject for MCEC Executive Board, pastors, and other groups with an interest in the topic. Most recently, I was invited to respond to a United Methodist study of homosexuality.[4] This study used the traditional fourfold set of authorities—Bible, tradition, reason, experience—to examine the issue, which although not without its own problems is surely an advance over a purely biblicist method of determining divine will in given situations.

The Catholic "development of doctrine" way also has its set of dangers—it still begs the question of how authentic development is to be distinguished from inauthentic development—but presupposes a high view of tradition and the church (church history becomes the history of biblical interpretation) that bears some resemblance to the high ecclesiology of Anabaptist-Mennonite theology. Catholics and Mennonites both have a high view of the church—moral and ethical issues need to be addressed not on the basis of individual hermeneutics, reason,or experience but corporately in the context of the church. Where they differ is in the nature of their church polity—the way they go about determining what is divine will in given situations.

I continue to find helpful John H. Yoder's characterization of Believers Church decision-making. For Yoder, ethical discourse in the church, as understood by the Anabaptists, is characterized by four indispensable elements: the Spirit, the gathering of believers, the Scriptures, and the moral challenge of the situation. Taking seriously these four elements in determing God's will is what constitutes the "hermeneutic community."[5] My emphasis on the "dogmatic foundations for Christian ethics" in this volume is not meant to replace Yoder's method. Rather, I mean to add a higher regard (than Yoder has) for the importance of doctrinal tradition and development; to spell out how confession, doctrine, catechesis, dogma, and creed function within this 'Yoderian' process of reading the Bible and interpreting the moving of the Spirit within the believing community. It allows for diversity within unity on divisive issues such as homosexuality. What the confessional/dogmatic/creedal approach does is distinguish between the universal language of faith which ties all Christians together everywhere and ethical particulars on which sincere Christians disagree within the believing community.

This is why the ancient creeds do not become as ethically specific as one might wish. What they do is give expression to the most fundamental affirmations of faith—faith in God the Creator, Christ the redeemer, and Spirit the consummator—the theological/ontological foundation for all human ethics. The 1983 "Pastoral Letter on War and Peace" by the National Conference of Catholic Bishops makes the further distinction between universal moral principles and specific applications of them as follows:

> In doing this we realize, and we want readers of this letter to recognize, that not all statements in this letter have the same moral authority. At times we state universally binding moral principles found in the teaching of the Church; at other times the pastoral letter makes specific applications, observations and recommendations which allow for diversity of opinion on the part of those who assess the factual data of a situation [sic] differently.[6]

In applying to homosexuality the distinction between universal affirmations of faith and ever more specific applications of this faith to moral and ethical issues on which believers genuinely disagree, I draw the following conclusions for the Mennonite church. The ultimate criterion for belonging to the church within the believers church tradition is to be baptized on the basis of a personal confession of faith in Jesus Christ, and a commitment to living a regenerated life as far as is possible in the context of a fallen world in which all forms of sexuality are imperfect.

Our congregational church polity—and in this we differ from the Catholic traditions—allows for local congregations to deal with ever more concrete applications of this confession, especially in areas of morality and ethics, in freedom within certain agreed upon limits. This is where I end up in the following essay: namely, that it is on the local level, where believers of different sexual orientation confront each other face to face, that divine leading on such divisive issues will need to be discerned. It is dangerous for some centralized body to make authoritative pronouncements on matters of concrete application, and as a rule such denominational-wide 'decrees' should be limited to affirming more general, universal, confessional principles and leaving detailed application to the local congregation.

◆ ◆ ◆

The extensive public airing of the controversial topic of homosexuality in the Mennonite press, at conferences, and in a variety of study documents indicates the extent to which the Mennonite community is willing to face openly one of the tough issues of our time.

When I read the poignant pleas for acceptance and understanding by gay persons and those close to them on the one side, and the sincere and passionate arguments against homosexual activity on the other—both using biblical texts and persuasive reasoning—I recognize the difficulty the church faces.

What is required, in my judgment, is compassionate listening to all members of our community, an openness to all the empirical, social-scientific data available, a serious reading of the biblical materials, sound theological thinking, open public debate, and prayerful receptiveness to the leading of the Holy Spirit. We're into the long haul here. The church is called to make moral judgments but we ought not to make them prematurely.

The first distinction we have to make is between compassionate solidarity with suffering persons (with those who represent "the other") and the developing of moral positions. I call these the "priestly pastoral" and the "prophetic-ethical" tasks of the church, respectively. Both are necessary but they are not the same. Charity for those who suffer, particularly the stranger, takes precedence over "correct moral positions." In fact, a commitment to charity is itself a moral imperative.

This does not, however, absolve the church from the difficult task of developing biblically-based moral positions on an urgent issue like homosexuality. The public debate about homosexuality points out the need to re-examine in a fundamental way our method of biblical interpretation and some of the basic tenets of what we believe.

I want here not so much to offer a definitive position of my own as to ask some basic questions of belief and to offer some suggestions on how we might approach the issue. My observations grow partly out of a Pastor's Theology Seminar on homosexuality which I conducted at Conrad Grebel College from September to May 1987.

The biblical texts that refer directly to homosexuality are quite meagre and are open to a variety of interpretations. What this demonstrates is the need to move beyond quoting and exegeting isolated verses and passages. We need to read the Bible as a whole and find a thematic way of weaving together the variety of biblical materials and of relating them to the present situation in a dynamic way.

The most fruitful way of doing this is by seeing the Scriptures as a drama of salvation with a threefold structure: creation (created nature), sin and the Fall (fallen nature), and redemption (redeemed nature). What does God intend in creation? What is the nature and extent of the Fall? How and when does redemption take place? These questions are difficult to answer and in fact drive us to the very foundation of what we believe and hold dear.

Simply collating all the texts that have to do with homosexuality is not adequate. For one thing, the texts are diverse and subject to different interpretations. For another, we do not consider all parts of Scripture of equal value. New Testament texts, particularly for Mennonites, supersede in importance Old Testament texts. For Christans Old Testament texts are read through the lenses of New Testament texts, which means that Jews will read the Hebrew Scriptures somewhat differently than Christians do (which is not to assume that their reading is inferior).

Further, even within the New Testament certain theological or interpretive decisions have to be made. Christ's own life and teachings are generally considered to be for us the definitive Word of God, the norm by which we evaluate the rest of the Bible. For our position on war and peace, for instance, we begin not with Old Testament "divine warrior" texts, even though these need to be taken seriously, but with Christ's ethic of non-violent love. In the end, we need a kind of hierarchy of normative values by which we interpret the Bible and make moral judgments, including judgments on the issue of homosexuality. [I should add here that my thinking has evolved further than when I first wrote this piece, as my article "God is Love but Not a Pacifist" (Chapter 31 above) shows.]

Created Nature

We believe that God created the world and that what God created was good. Part of this good creation and what it means to be human is human sexuality. But what kind of sexuality did God intend in creation? The answer to this question is not as clear as it might first appear. First of all, where do we go to find an answer?

Traditionally, Roman Catholics, for example, have maintained that we can discover God's intent in creation by looking both at revelation (Scriptures) and nature (natural law). Sex, they said, is for procreation, and by looking at nature we can conclude that homosexuality is unnatural since procreation is impossible. A certain reading of the Genesis account supports this understanding of natural law.

The problem is that nature is ambiguous. The argument from nature can be used to support both heterosexual and homosexual ethics. One of the central claims made by the gay community is that homosexual orientation is such by nature. This is not to deny the importance of considering nature for Christian ethics. In addressing the issue of homosexuality, as well as other urgent moral issues, we need to take into account all the available empirical (including biological) data.

Protestants, and particularly Mennonites, have at least in theory given less credence to natural law and restricted themselves more to the Scriptures themselves as the source for norms on ethical questions. Unfortunately, this has its own set of problems. For one thing, the biblical text itself is ambiguous.

The Genesis account of creation presents at least two models for the purpose of human sexuality: procreation and companionship. A biblical case for homosexuality from Genesis, if one wanted to make one, would have to be made on the basis of the second model—unless, of course, advances in medical technology would make possible male conception.

A straightforward reading of Genesis, not to mention other parts of Scripture, in my opinion clearly places sexual activity (both for procreation and for companionship) within a male-female context. The problem, however, is that male/female language itself has become ambiguous for us today. Medical possibilities make male/female differentiation increasingly fluid. Potentially, at least, males can be made into females and females into males.

There is also a further consideration. When one speaks of God's intent in creation, is one speaking about God's original creation, as represented in the Genesis stories, or does one include God's ongoing acts of creation (the creation of each unique individual, for instance)? Surely, Christians want to say—and there is good biblical support for this—that God continues to create and what God creates is good.

Individuals with a self-perceived homosexual orientation from as early as they can remember could, then, persuasively argue that they have been created with a particular orientation, and that this is a created good; and to deny this would be to deny the goodness of God's ongoing creation. Here the crucial question, of course, is whether the gay person has perceived himself or herself correctly. Surely we are all masters at self-deception. Has the homosexual in fact been born (or created) with a particular orientation, or is it in the end all a matter of psychological or social conditioning, some of it perhaps prenatal? Here, in my opinion, the empirical data is consequential but not conclusive at the present.

For Mennonites, who place such a high premium on the life and teachings of Jesus, there is however something strange about beginning chronologically with Genesis to discover God's intent for sexual ethics. Ought we not to begin with Jesus and read backwards and forwards through his eyes?

What a christological approach to ethics does, I believe, is to put the emphasis not on what is the case but on what ought to be the case. In other words, the central question becomes not what we are, or how we were born, but what we can and ought by God's grace to become. This applies to heterosexuals and homosexuals alike. What would our redeemed natures look like? Before we address that question, we need first to examine the reality of the Fall.

Fallen Nature

Even if we were to know clearly what God's intent in creation was, we believe that creation is fallen in an impersonal sense (evil and "original sin") and in a personal moral sense ("personal sin"). The implication here is that all human sexuality, whether in orientation or in activity, whether heterosexual or homosexual, has been distorted. None of us can live up to God's intent completely until the whole order is redeemed. To say this is not to excuse all sexual behavior. It is, nevertheless, to recognize that none of us is unblemished sexually, and that to identify homosexual activity as the one supreme example of the Fall, sexually speaking, is hypocritical.

How we understand the Fall—whether total or partial—will determine to some extent how we look at homosexuality. If we believe in the total depravity of the created order (as Lutherans and Calvinists traditionally do), then the orientation we are born with must be seen as much more fateful in determining our sexual behavior. Whether homosexuals can be held accountable for their orientation in a situation where their own freedom to choose an orientation does not exist then becomes highly questionable.

If, on the other hand, we believe with traditional Catholics and most Anabaptists that the Fall is only partial—that substantial amounts of human freedom have remained intact despite the Fall—then individuals shoulder a much greater degree of responsibility in choosing sexual behavior, for instance, regardless of how they were born. In short, initial orientation, whether viewed as a "created good" or the consequence of "original sin," is then less of a determining factor in sexual activity.

The really important issue, however, is how we view the church. For Mennonites, with their historic belief in a pure redeemed church, the pervasiveness of sin in all human life and activity, even after regeneration, is a central problem. If homosexual orientation is seen as a departure from God's intent, and homosexual practice as freely chosen sinful behavior, then it follows that a pure church cannot allow practising homosexuals within its ranks.

How the Mennonite church is to deal with members of its communion who either 1) do not share some of the dominant values or beliefs of the communion, or 2) have "fallen" from the normative position, is proving to be increasingly problematic on a wide range of issues (divorce and remarriage is another example). Our tendency in the past has been to exclude them. We are finding more and more, however, that the concept of the pure church is no longer adequate for our growing conviction that the church is not only a redeemed but also a redeeming community, in which individuals are not expected to be immediately perfect but are gradually nurtured to a fuller realization of God's intent.

Redeemed Nature

We come now to what is perhaps the most difficult question. What does regeneration and ultimate redemption mean for human sexuality? We believe that Christ is the *alpha* and *omega* of creation, that in the life, work, and teachings of Jesus Christ creation in general and individuals in particular have begun to be restored to God's initial intent. What this suggests is that the redemption of human sexuality is on the way but not yet perfected, both for the heterosexual and the homosexual.

There are a number of possibilities. For instance, we could hold the position that in Christ our fallenness is forgiven but our natures will not be restored until the end of time. Behavior that falls short of the ideal, then, could be seen as tolerable within the church although not normative, waiting for final redemption. Or, we could maintain (a view closer to the Anabaptist position) that in Christ we are not only forgiven but our natures can be transformed (either suddenly or gradually through the Holy Spirit) already in the present, although not perfected until the end of time.

If we accept the normativity of heterosexuality within the second of these two options, then we might argue that the homosexually oriented person can not only be forgiven for his or her orientation and practice, but can gradually be changed in the context of the church toward heterosexuality through God's grace, pastoral care, a loving community, therapy, and so on.

If, on the other hand, we believe that heterosexuality is not the standard for all persons, but that some are in fact created by God with a homosexual orientation, and that redemption has to do not with giving up a particular sexual orientation but with mutuality and self-giving love in human relationships, then the task of the church is to foster fidelity within a monogamous relationship of whatever kind.

What is of paramount importance is to recognize that when we talk of the redeeming process of God's grace we are talking not only about the transformation of individuals but also of the entire created order. It is my firm conviction that the final transformation of individuals cannot take place separately from the redemption of the whole of creation. In short, we cannot expect individuals to be perfect until the total context has been perfectly restored.

What final perfection, when applied to human sexuality, will look like is, of course, a mystery, especially when we consider enigmatic biblical passages such as the one in Luke 20: 34-36:

> The sons of this age marry and are given in marriage; but those who are accounted worthy to attain to that age and to the resurrection from the dead neither marry nor are given in

marriage, for they cannot die any more because they are equal to angels and are sons of God, being sons of the resurrection.

Practical Implications: Three Options

In the light of all of these questions, what are we to do as a church? We have a number of options.[7] We can continue to maintain what the church has traditionally held: namely, that homosexual activity is *intrinsically evil* and must therefore be rejected. According to this view, biblical revelation teaches that God created human beings male and female, and that sexual activity, whether for procreation or for companionship, is legitimate only within a monogamous heterosexual marriage. A homosexual orientation must in this view be seen as part of imperfect nature and homosexual activity as sinful.

For theologian Karl Barth, homosexual activity represents "the physical, psychological and social sickness, the phenomenon of perversion, decadence and decay, which can emerge when man refuses to admit the validity of the divine command. . . . "[8] While our heterosexuality or homosexuality does not determine our ultimate destiny—God's objective grace in Christ justifies regardless of orientation, inclination, or activity—homosexual practice cannot be condoned by the church.

Implicit in this position is the assumption that change can occur through repentance, forgiveness, and God's transforming power, including therapy. Whether or not change in orientation does occur, however, celibacy for the homosexual is imperative. I think the church should take this first point of view with utmost seriousness. It does reflect the historic position of the church; it is one legitimate historic reading of the biblical text; and it does represent the need for the church to take strong moral positions against trends in society which it considers wrong. Further, it does emphasize the legitimate place of celibacy in the Christian life—something which we as Protestants and Mennonites have tended to undervalue in our traditions.

The weakness of this position, however, is that it does not adequately reflect the diverse interpretations of biblical texts on this and related issues, nor does it sufficiently take into account the empirical and historical data on the subject.

There is a second option which considers homosexual acts as *intrinsically imperfect*, as a departure from the biblical view, but is willing to consider making exceptions under certain extreme conditions.

Helmut Thielicke holds this view. According to him,

> [t]he fundamental order of creation and the created determination of the two sexes make it appear justifiable to

speak of homosexuality as a perversion—in any case, if we begin with the understanding that this term implies no moral depreciation whatsoever and that it is used purely theologically in the sense that homosexuality is in every case not in accord with the order of creation.[9]

Thielicke's conclusion is that when change is possible (according to empirical evidence, in most cases it is not) it should be actively sought. If change is not possible, homosexuals ought to sublimate their desires and not act on them. In certain exceptional cases, he asks, where sublimation seems not to be possible, ought homosexuals not at least to be expected to structure their sexual relationships "in an ethically responsible way" without idealizing them as the standard?

The third option is to view homosexual activity as *morally neutral*, to be evaluated only in terms of its relational integrity. This position holds that God's intent is determined not primarily in terms of 1) divine command in Genesis, or 2) some static notion of natural law, but on the basis of a relational christology.

Sin is seen primarily as the exercise of power and domination over others and applies equally to heterosexual and homosexual activity. Homosexuality is inherently no more prone to such domination than is heterosexuality. The church, in this view, needs to recognize homosexuals as an oppressed group in our society who need to be accepted for who they are. Both heterosexuals and homosexuals need to find an equal place within the church where they ought to be encouraged to grow in their mutual, loving, permanent monogamous relationships. This is what I take Gregory Baum's position to be when he says:

> The important question . . . is whether homosexuality is open to mutuality. Is the homosexual orientation capable of grounding friendship that enables the partners to grow and become more truly human? This is the crucial question. For the structure of redeemed human life is mutuality. There are gravely damaged sexual inclinations, e.g., sadism, masochism, and paedophilia, which may not be acknowledged without a struggle: for they exclude mutuality. They bind the participants in a cruel game of possessor and possessed. The important question, therefore, is whether homosexuality is open to mutuality. Can it be integrated into the kind of human life to which God summons us?[10]

What I find appealing in the third alternative is the weight it places on the sin of domination and the importance of mutuality. What I find less convincing is the too easy disregard of what I consider the biblical emphasis on the "normativity" of heterosexual monogamous relationships.

This is why I find myself, at this point at least, leaning toward the second option, although I have some difficulty with the use of the term "perversion." This view recognizes the diversity of homosexuality itself. It assumes that some homosexuals can change in their orientation while others cannot. For those who cannot change, for whatever reason, and find themselves unable to practise celibacy, it asks of them as of heterosexuals that they structure their sexual behavior responsibly.

What impresses me as I read the literature on the subject is the diversity of views and approaches that are present in the current debate. I support this diversity, at least at this stage of the discussion, and would caution the church against closing off the conversation prematurely through some kind of rigid, unilateral declaration. The subject is too complex.

At some point the church will need to make judgments about what it believes, but hopefully these declarations will have a tentative tone to them, reflecting an openness to new insights from all quarters. Most important of all, heterosexuals and homosexuals need to discover each other as human beings on the local level where they must learn to live and worship together.

THIRTY-FIVE

Christian Anthropology: The Perils of the Believers Church View of the *Humanum**

The Protestant and Radical Reformation were strongly influenced by the late Medieval shift from a realist to a nominalist world view. This shift had serious consequences for all of theology. Particularly significant was its influence on the Christian view of what it means to be human.

In this essay, which was first presented as "The Adequacy of Voluntarism in a Voluntaristic Age" at a Believers Church conference at McMaster Divinity College in 1996,[1] I critically examine an anthropology shaped by nominalistic voluntarism. I look at Balthasar Hubmaier's tripartite view of human beings in the light of Joan Lockwood O'Donovan's critique of contemporary voluntaristic traditions. I ultimately come to a qualified defense of this older premodern form of voluntarism, like Hubmaier's, which takes individual freedom to choose between good and evil seriously but assumes that all human willing is grounded in divine willing (a modified form of realism). What I am critical of, and here I agree with Lockwood O'Donovan, is the modern propensity to reject all realist assumptions in favour of

---

* Later published as "The Adequacy of a Voluntaristic Theology for a Voluntaristic Age," in *The Believers Church: A Voluntary Church*, ed. William H. Brackney (Kitchener, ON and Scottdale, PA: Pandora Press, co-published with Herald Press, 1998), 135-48. For notes on the text see the Notes section below.

pure, unadorned voluntaristic individualism—where human freedom and willing is grounded in the individual subject herself.

Where this becomes crucial is in our Believers Church ecclesiology. By grounding church membership in the individual's choice to be baptized upon the confession of faith—presupposing a level of rational capacity to understand—are we not implicitly defining what it means to be fully human too narrowly? In doing so, are we not (without wanting to) relegating those who do not fully meet the criteria of "full rational capacity" to lesser status in the human and Christian family? These are the questions I begin to explore in this essay.

◆ ◆ ◆

I. Introduction: Definitions and Presuppositions

Voluntarism is one of those ill-defined terms which can readily be used to obfuscate rather than illumine theological discussion. In the most technical sense it refers to the theology of Duns Scotus (c.1265-1308) and William of Ockham (c.1285-1347) who, against Thomas Aquinas (c.1225-74), argued that the divine will precedes in importance the divine intellect. This emphasis on divine willing had significant implications for ethics, and was part of a larger ideological shift occurring in the late Middle Ages—the transition from a realist worldview to a nominalist one. Christian realists heavily indebted to the Greek, particularly Platonic tradition, assumed an eternal cosmic order. Moral universals such as ideal justice were part of this unchanging order, and were considered more real than any earthly particulars, which were but imperfect imitations (or analogies) of eternal perfections.

From the second-century Apologists to the high middle ages of Thomas Aquinas, this intellectual realism had dominated western Christianity. With Aquinas and the rediscovery of Aristotle, a theological shift began, which took the empirical and observable world of the senses more seriously. It was a shift that would lead, after Thomas, to nominalism and voluntarism. Nominalists, like William of Ockham, turned their attention from the ideal world of universal forms to particulars (particular beings rather than being in general, specific justice rather than abstract justice). Particular existents were real, universals were but "names" or "abstractions," useful in language but having no independent existence. For the nominalists, even God was understood not as universal, metaphysical essence, supreme intellect in whose mind existed all ideal forms, but as absolutely free, singular and willing subject (or agent). Things or actions were good or evil because God willed them to be so, not because they corresponded to some eternal ideal form or essence.[2]

This shift from seeing the world as a rationally structured and ordered universe to one in which personal subjectivity and willing was at the heart of things helped to give shape to the Renaissance, the Reformation, the Enlightenment, and all of modern western thought. A voluntaristic understanding of God had deep roots in the Hebraic monotheistic tradition, which thought of God freely creating the world (visible and invisible) out of nothing through Word, creating "Adam" with free will and responsibility, freely making a covenant with his chosen people and dynamically intervening in their history.

What distinguished this long premodern Hebraic voluntaristic tradition from the voluntarism that was now emerging with the rise of the modern world was that "human willing" was earlier thought to be derived from and subject to, "divine willing." With modern nominalistic voluntarism there began a process not only of seeing the world in terms of "volition" but human willing as independent of divine willing, a process leading ultimately to human willing without any divine horizon whatever (Nietzsche and the "will to power"). Classical Christian orthodoxy creatively combined Hebraic personalism and voluntarism with Hellenistic metaphysics.

This is evident in the trinitarian and christological formulations of Nicea and Chalcedon, and is still the case with Thomas for whom human law is derived from natural law, in turn reflecting eternal law, superseded ultimately by divine law. While Christian realism dominated western thought up to the modern period, nominalistic voluntarism has dominated the modern period to the present, existentialism perhaps being the most dramatic example. It remains to be seen in what direction the postmodern age will take us. If pluralism, fragmentation, and discontinuity are seen to be the defining characteristic of the postmodern age (a thesis which can be debated) then nominalistic voluntarism would appear to have won the day. This technical discussion of late medieval voluntarism, with its nominalistic presuppositions about God and the world, provides an essential background for the rest of this presentation.

Often, however, voluntarism is understood in a broader sense, as referring to those Christian traditions which have historically espoused the "freedom of the will" (Radical Protestantism or the so-called "Believers Church") rather than the "bondage of the will" or predestination (Calvinism and, in a modified form, Lutheranism). Some version of "free-will" unites the rather disparate group making up the Believers Church tradition, is at the heart of its distinctive theology and ecclesiology, and is considered to be essential for ethics and moral responsibility. Free will within Radical Protestantism has generally been connected with Christian ethics and moral accountability. The proposition *implicit* in most Believers Church theology goes something like this: to be virtuous is to choose the morally good over the morally evil, but to choose good over evil one must have the freedom to do so, otherwise one could not be considered either virtuous or culpable for one's actions. If one were not free, if one's actions were pre-determined (as in Greek notions of fate or some Christian views of predestination), one could not be held accountable for one's behavior, neither would there be any motivation toward the good. The Fall (original sin) has distorted the human will but not to such an extent that the knowledge of good and evil, and the ability to respond positively or negatively to God (divine grace), has been altogether removed. Although qualified and interpreted in a variety of ways, this proposition or set of propositions I take to be implied in all Believers Church theology, ecclesiology, and ethics. In sum, intrinsic to Believers Church theology, ecclesiology, and ethics is voluntarism of one type or another.

It is this claim—that voluntarism is indispensable for all responsible Christian ethics—that I want to test. I want to examine it in light of the strong challenge by Oxford theologian Joan Lockwood O'Donovan, who argues that a sound Christian ethic is not well served by the voluntarism of the modern age. We in the voluntaristic tradition need to take seriously Lockwood O'Donovan's critique. I will argue, however, that classical voluntarism, as reflected in the theology of Balthasar Hubmaier, for instance, does not presuppose the radical nominalism present in the voluntarism of the modern period. It is grounded in a trinitarian realism that has both Hebraic and Hellenistic elements, but offers a securer foundation for social and personal Christian ethics than do the less voluntaristic traditions.

II. The Challenge to Modern Voluntarism: An Inadequate Anthropology

Joan Lockwood O'Donovan, a theologian in the Church of England, has been strongly influenced by the late Canadian philosopher George Grant's critique of modern liberal understandings of freedom[3] (as I have been). In a number of recent articles she has challenged the adequacy of an ethic premised on modern notions of voluntarism and freedom, especially with regard to the most vulnerable in the human community. Her treatment of this subject deserves careful attention, for, in my estimation, she has identified a sensitive spot in Believers Church theology and ethics, especially in the modern period.

Lockwood O'Donovan situates herself within the realist camp, espousing what she refers to as non-voluntaristic "theological realism." By voluntarism she has in mind the modern turn to the individual person understood as "self-determining subjectivity." In an article on the debate over Britain's participation in the evolving European community, "Subsidiarity and Political Authority in Theological Perspective," she examines the evolution of Catholic social theory in the last century from traditional political Thomism to modernized political Thomism.

Her thesis is that the Aristotelian aspects of Thomas's political synthesis have abetted the modernization (liberal democratization) of Catholic thought at the expense of classical Christian features. In Christian thought, as systematized by Augustine, political authority was understood primarily in *juridical* terms—as restraining evil and protecting the good. Aristotle gave a more positive and creative (*directive/legislative/ integrative*) role to political authority:

> [H]ere, the essential purpose of government is less the adjudication of right and wrong on the basis of received communal understandings of divine and natural law, than the active orienting of the political whole to the order of right defined by positive law.[4]

With Thomas these two traditions—the juridical (Christian) and the directive (Aristotle)—were held in tension with each other. The modernization of Catholic social theory, however, has seen the liberalization of the Aristotelian concept of law and political authority at the expense of the Augustinian Christian understanding. Modernization, for Lockwood O'Donovan, is the acceptance of historical progressivism, in which the inalienable natural rights of individuals is seen to take precedence over all other rights. She traces this gradual modernization process through various papal encyclicals/letters in this century, concluding with the liberal-democratic, post-war Thomism of Jacques Maritain and Pope John XXIII. Both subscribe to a concept of political society in which government is authorized to make provision for the common good seen as "a body of universal natural political and social rights and obligations (principally of individuals)."[5] Modern liberal democratic society, she claims, suffers not from moral pluralism but from "moral monism, being enslaved to one universally acclaimed good, that of individual self-determination. The public hegemony of this good is both disclosed and maintained in the public hegemony of the language of individual rights."[6]

Common to biblical, patristic, medieval, and Reformation Christian thought was the "concept of natural law as the permanent moral order within which God intends human life in its individual and social aspects to be lived."[7] It distinguished between prelapsarian (the structures of created nature) and postlapsarian (fallen nature) orders. Political rule was placed within the realm of fallen nature. With Thomas and the subsequent evolution of politico-ethical thought, the distinction between created and fallen nature has gradually diminished to the point where we have a moral monism: the "hegemony of a single language ... the language of individual rights."[8] This is the modern civil religion:

> In this civil cult, the final public good, which is the measure of all others, is the self-determination of the individual subject, who stands as God, outside nature, and makes him/herself and the world around out of the resources of his/her own unlimited willing.[9]

Lockwood O'Donovan is not rejecting the value of individual subjectivity and personal right. Quite the opposite! Her concern is how these are conceptualized and safeguarded. In classical Christianity (biblical, patristic, medieval, reformation) human subjectivity and right is derived from divine subjectivity in relation to the structure of created nature and fallen nature. In modern liberal thought (Renaissance-Enlightenment) natural and civil law is no longer understood in relation to the divine and eternal. Human subjectivity and right is no longer seen as derived but as inalienable—that is, as innate and intrinsic to itself (or self-determined). The ethical consequences of this shift are profound.

In a second article, "Man in the Image of God: The Disagreement Between Barth and Brunner Reconsidered," the Anglican theologian spells out her alternative to this modern voluntarism. She calls it "Theological realism" and "Christological realism." She offers her own realist alternative by revisiting the well-known 1934 debate between Barth and Brunner over Christian anthropology, focusing especially on the concept of *imago dei*. In his book *Natur und Gnade* Brunner had distinguished between a formal and a material aspect of the created image of God in human beings. The formal image is that which separates human beings from other parts of creation: rationality, responsibility (subjectivity), and the capacity for language. Brunner claims that this formal image is neutral and not destroyed by the Fall and human sin—it is that which makes human beings human. The material image, in contrast, is that which makes a person truly personal, existence in love. This has been lost: "Sinful man remains 'a person'—that is, a responsible subject—but is 'an anti-personal person.'"[10]

Lockwood O' Donovan takes Barth's side in this debate, arguing with Barth that Brunner is not able to maintain the neutrality of this "formal image" but is forced to define it qualitatively and materially—"the capacity for recognizing God in external nature and in the events of history; the capacity for moral judgment and conduct, and for knowing one's guilt."[11] It is not the distinction between formal and material image as such that

Barth rejects, but giving the formal a qualitative character. For Barth, as for Lockwood O'Donovan, there can be no such dialectical precondition for the work of grace. Divine grace, in which the essential being of human persons is understood christologically and relationally, has absolute, undialectical priority. This is not to deny all structure to human being, but to insist that both the form and content of human being is determined by "God's being-as-love."[12]

Why is this issue so important for both Barth and Lockwood O'Donovan, and why is it imperative that we in the Believers Church address it? It has to do with how we understand the uniqueness of being human in an age where the assault on human dignity by scientific and technological advances is pervasive. More specifically, it has to do with how universally inclusive our understanding of the *humanum* is. Brunner's "transcendental structural concept of person" forces him to make freedom, responsibility, and capacity for decision-making the criteria for defining human persons. But this excludes some children of Adam. Only a transcendent-relational, or christological-trinitarian conceptualization is adequate to safeguard the unique humanity of human beings, says Lockwood O'Donovan.[13] This is what she calls Theological or Christological realism. It focuses on God's transcendent act rather than on human decision-making responsibility. Let me quote her at length:

> Barth's Christological realism is a significant theological gain in the ethical realm, particularly in the realm of judgments concerning those individual beings at the borders of human life: the unborn child, the severely defective infant, the very old and senile, the comatose patient. For it forces upon us the consideration that these individuals are human beings created in the image of God, that they have a share in human uniqueness because elected in Jesus Christ, the objects of God's judgment and mercy. It forces this consideration upon us by disallowing all immanent conceptions of human being, either structural or qualitative, which would place such creatures beyond the pale of humanness. It stands as a refutation of the favourite argument of the technicians and humanists of our age: that only those beings are "persons," are uniquely human, that manifest the qualities of subjectivity, of personality. Against this argument it pits an uncompromising theological understanding of the particularity and uniqueness of human being in terms of its transcendent determination by God's covenant of grace in Jesus Christ. It sets forth human uniqueness as the incomprehensible particularity of God's

elective Will, the transcendent mystery of "the person" as the mystery of God's gracious action.[14]

This is the challenge that Karl Barth, as interpreted by Lockwood O'Donovan, places before us in the voluntarist tradition, one that I want to take up and answer in the final section of this presentation. At issue is the following: Is there a way of safeguarding the humaness of all "children of Adam" within the voluntaristic heritage, one which places such a high price on personal decision making, illustrated most dramatically in the insistence on adult baptism at the age of accountability upon the personal confession of faith?

III. The Christian Anthropology of Classical Voluntarism

Here I want to explore the Christian understanding of human being within what I am calling the classical voluntarist heritage, by which I mean that understanding which precedes the Enlightenment and post-Enlightenment, predominantly nominalistic world view. I take the Believers Church tradition, at least in its origins, to stand within this earlier stream, and will analyze in some detail the anthropology of Anabaptist theologian Balthasar Hubmaier, as representative of this classic voluntarism. In his theology of human freedom and responsibility he stands in the tradition of a long line of Christian thinkers (medieval, patristic, and biblical). Common to all of them are "realist" assumptions about the world, and at the same time a strong emphasis on human freedom, subjectivity and responsibility to make decisions, capacities which are not immanent-structural but derived from divine subjectivity.

Hubmaier, born around 1480 in Friedberg, near Augsburg, studied at the University of Freiburg (1503-1506), where he learned to know as his teacher the Catholic scholar John Eck, whom in 1512 he followed to the University of Ingolstadt, where he received his doctorate in theology. He had been ordained to the priesthood earlier and now in Ingolstadt served both as theology professor and priest of the largest parish church in the city, and in 1515-16 became prorector of the University. At some point, after a stint as cathedral preacher at Regensburg and activities in Waldshut, he came in contact with Christian humanists and the Zwinglian reformation, and eventually converted to Anabaptism. He was burned at the stake in Vienna on March 10, 1528. Hubmaier was a distinguished theologian, who of all the Anabaptists gave the most systematic attention to Christian anthropology in his Catechism of 1526-27, and in his two treatises on the Freedom of the Will: the first dated April 1, 1527, dedicated to Count George of Brandenburg-Ansbach, a follower of Luther;[15] the second dated May 20, 1527, dedicated to Duke Friedrich II of Liegnitz, Brieg, and Wohlau, in Silesia, who through Caspar Schwenkfeld had been converted to the evangelical faith.[16]

What interests us here, in light of Lockwood O'Donovan's powerful critique, is how Hubmaier defines the *humanum*, in a realist or nominalist fashion, in transcendent derivative terms or in an immanent-structural sense (i.e., along the lines of Emil Brunner). With Hubmaier's publication of the two treatises on the freedom of the will, he joined one of the hottest debates of the Reformation: the debate between Erasmus and Luther on whether the will is free or bound. He clearly sides with Erasmus, using many of the same scriptural texts and arguments. It is also obvious that he has strong nominalist leanings:

> The schools call the revealed power and will of God an ordered power and will. Not that the first will is unordered for everything that God wills and does is orderly and good. He is not subject to any rule. His will is itself a rule of all things. Therefore they call the will 'ordered' since it occurs according to the preached Word of the Holy Scriptures in which he revealed to us his will.[17]

How does this divine voluntarism translate into his anthropology? That's our question.

Hubmaier understands the human person as the dynamic interaction of soul, body, and spirit. In conceiving human being in this tripartite fashion, he is not original; but in the way he tries to hold together in tension both the "bondage of the will" and the "freedom of the will" he puts his own stamp on the debate. He begins with the assumption that only God is good, and any good works we do is the work of God and God's grace within us.[18] How is it then that we have the responsibility to choose good over evil, as the Scripture teaches? He gives us a traditional answer: we were created free, lost our freedom after sinning, and had our freedom restored with the death and resurrection of Christ. But what precisely is lost with the Fall, and what exactly is freed through Christ? And, further, is what is freed in Christ seen in a realist fashion; that is, as something happening objectively to all humans whatever; or in a nominalist way (contingent upon individual, subjective volition and response)? What, in short, is the *imago dei* for Hubmaier, and what is lost, retained, and restored in this image?

With these questions we come to the heart of his discussion of the tripartite nature of human being. "The human being," he says, "is a corporal and rational creature, created by God as body, spirit, and soul, Gen. 2:7. These three elements are found essentially and in varying ways in every human being, as the Scripture thoroughly proves."[19] These three things, substances, or essences, he says, "are made and unified in every human being according to the image of the Holy Trinity."[20]

Here we have a trinitarian "realism," if you like, in which humans are images of the divine in the state of innocence (before the Fall). Let us look at each of these three elements more closely. The flesh (*soma* in Greek, *corpus* in Latin, *Leib* in German) is the material physical body which derives from the earth. It is that which we share with the rest of creation. The soul (*psyche*, *anima*, *Seele*) is the life principle in us, that which made the dust of the ground alive when God breathed upon it. The spirit (*pneuma*, *spiritus*, *Geist*) is the image of God, the divine, in us. Hubmaier distinguishes between the divine Spirit as such, and the divine spirit as a component of human being. It is the human spirit which is the point of contact for the divine Spirit. The soul (the life principle) finds itself hovering, as it were, between the flesh and the spirit: "the soul, which has become flesh through the disobedience of Adam, must through the Spirit of God and his living Word be reborn to a new spirit and become spirit, for what is born of the Spirit is spirit, John 3: 6."[21]

In the prelapsarian state all three (soul, body and spirit) were good, and wholly free in the recognition, capability, and performance of good or evil. This power to will the good is not self-originating but is derived from God. It is, however, part of our created structure: "Whether now such a power for willing what is right and good is in us, it is not in us as if it were from us, for it is originally from God and his image, in which he created us originally...."[22] After the Fall, because of disobedience (the wrong use of this freedom), this structure has been distorted. Free will has been lost. Each of the three elements, however, has lost it in a different sense. The flesh has been completely ruined (total depravity, one might call it). The soul has been seriously wounded, half-dead, not even knowing good or evil. Only the spirit retains its original righteousness in which it was created. However, it is captive and can only "bear internal witness to righteousness against evil."[23] It would appear, therefore, that for Hubmaier, there is at least one element in the *humanum* which can never be destroyed and which remains the point of contact for God's Word in Christ (the spirit).

With the restoration in Christ, appropriated by the human being through the spirit which has remained whole although captive all along, the soul regains its capacity to know good and evil, and the freedom to choose. The flesh remains ruined, although harmless, until the resurrection of the body. The soul remains between flesh and spirit, and can choose to follow either. If it chooses the way of the flesh, it sins willingly and is held accountable; if it did not sin willingly, it would not be sin. So the human destiny now lies with the human choice: "If I now will, then I will be saved by the grace of God; if I do not will, then I will be damned, and that on the basis of my own obstinacy and willfulness."[24]

Free will, in Hubmaier's view, is "nothing other than a power, force, energy, or adroitness of the soul to will or not will something, to choose or flee, to accept or to reject good or evil, according to the will of God, or according to the will of the flesh...."[25] He has nothing but scorn for those who deny such freedom, and through this denial excuse themselves and blame God for their sins, leading people to laziness and despair.

Having said this, however, Hubmaier insists that the good we do is not due to our merit but is God's grace working within us. First, we were originally created free by God in body, soul, and spirit. Second, having lost our freedom and capacity to know good and evil, our freedom was restored by "a special and new grace of God through Jesus Christ."[26] Through the sent Word of God we are now able to choose and do the good, with the exception of the flesh, which before the resurrection cannot do anything but sin and struggle against the spirit.[27] Like Adam, we can choose to reject the Word of the Spirit; to do so is not God's doing but our own. Our ability to choose comes from God, but not our choice itself. Hubmaier does allow a place for "God's omnipotence, omniscience, and eternal foreknowledge, predestination, providence, or reprobation,"[28] but these lie beyond human investigation and have to do with the hidden, absolute will of God, who owes no one anything.[29]

Hubmaier is without a doubt a voluntarist with nominalist leanings; but he is a voluntarist in the premodern sense—that is, there is a strong component of what might be called trinitarian, theological or christological realism. The ontological structure of being human (body, soul, spirit) remains the same for all humans. This structure is not self-determined or innate in the modern sense, but derived from God originally and restored by a new act of God's grace in Christ. Furthermore, the good human beings do after the restoration of their freedom is not of their own merit but is a response to the sent Word of God within them. The "spirit" (the divine image in human beings) remains unspoiled by sin throughout and is the point of contact for God's Word.

IV. Conclusion: What about the Idiot?

This brings us to the conclusion of our exploration, with the most difficult question still unanswered: Where do those on the boundary of the human, those exemplars of humanness who are without free will in the ordinary sense of the term (the unborn fetus, the baby, the mentally handicapped, the insane, the comatose) belong, when the very essence of the human (the image of God) is defined as the capacity to make responsible decisions?

Anabaptists such as Pilgram Marpeck had a simple answer to this: Such people are covered by the objective work of God's grace in Christ. In the words of Marpeck:

> [T]he law is given for those who can know and not for those who cannot (such as children or idiots, for whom there is no law either with man or God). . . . All who know and recognize their sin can only then receive comfort and security. To this part of man's recognition and faith belongs the baptism of the apostolic church, and not to young children or the ignorant, who have no law or knowledge of sin even though they are under law and sin. That is why the young children had to be circumcised under the law, for whoever received circumcision is responsible for the whole law, but only after he knows it. Where in the old law was any child punished for his own transgression? Much less so in the new, where the children never bear the penalty of the parents nor the parents of the children.[30]

According to Marpeck, children and the ignorant (it is not clear what he does with those who have never heard the proclamation) "are without justification pronounced blessed by Christ, and regarded as belonging to the sanctified of the kingdom of God."[31]

At the point where persons reach the age of accountability—are able to know good and evil, and choose the good over the evil—human beings become responsible for their actions; before that or outside of that they are "simply received by Christ." Although Paul says, "without faith no man can please God," children and the ignorant "are not required to believe or disbelieve these words, but those who are born from the knowledge of good and evil into the innocence and simplicity of faith are required to believe."[32] Only when children receive the knowledge of good and evil, only at that point "sin, death, and damnation begin."[33] Only where there is knowledge there is sin.

Although Marpeck is theologically not as sophisticated as Hubmaier, especially in spelling out the nuances of God's prevenient grace operative in choosing good over evil, the general sentiment and logic is the same. Believers Church ecclesiology is premised on the assumption that at some point in the development of personhood one gains the knowledge of good and evil, and the capacity and responsibility to respond to God's grace voluntarily. Before this a kind of christological realism is assumed (the ignorant are saved by God's objective act of grace);

after this there is a shift to a kind of nominalistic voluntarism, in which a particular person truly becomes a subject (a free moral agent) in the fullest sense.

Is this not an incoherent conceptualization of the *humanum*? In the premodern voluntarist tradition, free will was ultimately derivative, and subordinate to the mystery of divine will, election, and providence (as we have seen in Hubmaier). Free will and human accountability (even in Augustine) was never completely annulled by divine election. However, with the radical nominalism of the modern period, and the loss of all sense of transcendent realism, voluntarism as understood by the Believers Church is in danger of undermining the very ethic it once sought to undergird.

THIRTY-SIX

Mennonites and the Church Universal: Ecumenical Gifts of the Spirit*

Of all my theological conversation partners I am in my general approach (method and substance) perhaps closest to that of Miroslav Volf, even though I have some points of disagreement with him and find myself more drawn to the classical philosophical and theological synthesis than Volf appears to be. Volf is more nominalistic and voluntaristic than I am.

In my next and concluding article of this volume I spell out my own theology in relation to Volf, Wolfhart Pannenberg, and Thomas Oden in some detail. In this essay, originally presented at a conference on ecclesiology in Elkhart, Indiana, in February 2000,[1] I focus on Volf's ecclesiology as he develops it in critical conversation with the Roman Catholic Cardinal Joseph Ratzinger and Eastern Orthodox theologian and Metropolitan John D. Zizioulas.

I applaud Volf for taking seriously the work of Ratzinger and Zizioulas as well as for some aspects of his Free Church view of the church. I criticize him,

---

*The venue was a conference on ecclesiology for scholars, church leaders, and students of theology hosted by the Institute of Mennonite Studies, at Associated Mennonite Biblical Seminary, Elkhart, Indiana on February 5, 2000. The theme of the conference was "Without Spot or Wrinkle: Reflecting Theologically on the Nature of the Church." For notes on the text see the Notes section below.

however, for not taking more cognizance of the sixteenth-century Anabaptists as progenitors of the Free Church movement and of the thought of John Howard Yoder.² To have done so would have had significant consequences for his analysis. I sent Volf a copy of the paper and he responded to me at some length during a recent visit for lectures and conversations at Conrad Grebel College and the Toronto School of Theology.³

◆ ◆ ◆

Theological Foundations

The Christian doctrine of God is the starting point for all theological and ethical reflection. It is also the foundation for any thinking about the church, as we shall see below.

1. The first article of confession asserts the absolute *transcendence* of God, the unbegotten and uncreated origin of all things visible and invisible (God the Creator).⁴ It is the notion of the divine as the unbegotten origin of, and distinct from, the created order that is the essential theological claim here.

2. Implicit in the second article, confessing belief in God's only "Son," is the claim that the eternal Word (*logos*) present in the first verses of Genesis as the principle of differentiating order in creation, and in the Wisdom literature as "lady wisdom" (*sophia*), incarnates itself historically in the phenomenon of Jesus as the Christ. While the first article stresses the transcendence (beyondness) of the divine reality, the second highlights the *historicity* and incarnational *specificity* within time and space of that divine reality. The danger of idolatry is always near in the second article: that is, to equate "God" with the *man* "Jesus of Nazareth." The ancient trinitarian and christological debates revolved around how best to avoid such idolatrous claims. Asserting the deity of Christ is to claim that in the being and work of Jesus the Christ—conception, birth, life, teachings, ministry, death, resurrection, and ascension—the God of the Jews was truly manifest in the Christ-event, and was experienced by those who responded in faith and life.⁵

3. The third article—"I believe in the Holy Spirit" and the various "sub-doctrines" that follow (the holy catholic church, the communion of the saints, the forgiveness of sins, the resurrection of the body, and the life everlasting)—are most appropriately understood as the dynamic life-giving (quickening) *immanence* of the divine reality present within all of creation but in a particular leavening (or "sacramental") way in the *community of believers* (the church), the "firstfruits" of the resurrection of the world.

These three Christian affirmations about the divine reality are confessions concerning the one true God who has a plurality within unity in such a way that the one God can be said to be all three simultaneously: transcendent, historical, and immanent.

In recent discussions of the Trinity by Karl Barth, Jürgen Moltmann, Wolfhart Pannenberg, Miroslav Volf, and others, much has been made of the distinction and close connection between the immanent Trinity (the relations between the three persons eternally within God) and the economic Trinity (the relation of God in God's threefoldness to that which is external to God—i.e., the world). What is astonishing is how much these theologians seem to know about the immanent Trinity. While they make their claims on alleged biblical-theological grounds, it appears to me that most of this talk of the immanent Trinity is highly speculative. There are important theological reasons for maintaining a belief in the immanent Trinity as distinct from and as the ground for the economic Trinity, and there are also biblical texts which can be drawn upon to make certain inferences about immanent Trinitarian relations. However, my own statements about the Trinity above and their application to a doctrine of the church below apply to what I have identified as the economic Trinity: our understanding of God's ways with the world, and in particular, a Christian doctrine of the church from a pneumatological perspective.

I have a limited purpose in what follows: to offer some tentative suggestions about what an ecumenically open ecclesiology might look like for Mennonites: one which respects both the plurality and unity within the global Christian community, both the distinctives each tradition brings to the ecumenical table and that which all have in common. I will begin by critically engaging the thought of Miroslav Volf on the subject of a Free Church ecclesiology, then briefly examine the views of Balthasar Hubmaier as representing an Anabaptist view, and conclude with a proposal of my own using Paul's "one body, many gifts" model as offering some creative possibility for an ecumenical Mennonite ecclesiology.

Miroslav Volf: Congregational Catholicity

In his tour de force, *After Our Likeness: The Church as the Image of the Trinity*, Miroslav Volf develops his own Free Church version of the church as a viable alternative to Roman Catholic and Eastern Orthodox ecclesiologies.[6] He takes Joseph (Cardinal) Ratzinger, Prefect of the Vatican Congregation for the Doctrine of the Faith as representative of Catholic ecclesiology, and Metropolitan John D. Zizioulas as spokesperson for Orthodox ecclesiology. His theological sparring partner for Free Church theology is John Smyth (1554-1612), an early

English separatist, for him the originator of the Free Church. His choice of Smyth as Free Church representative, with no reference to Continental Anabaptism and its quite different view of the church, is highly dubious but serves him well as he seeks critically to build his own theology of the church without some of the weaknesses he sees in Smyth. The great contribution of Volf's work is his serious treatment of Ratzinger and Zizioulas, and his apology for a congregational theology and polity taking especially Ratzinger's criticisms into account. Some of the shortcomings of Volf's analysis will be identified below.

Ratzinger

In preparation for this paper, and well before I had come upon Volf's book, I had begun reading Ratzinger on the church. I was astonished at the vehemence with which Ratzinger referred to Free Church ecclesiology, fueled by an obvious fear that contemporary post-Vatican II Catholicism was moving in the Free Church direction. I found myself agreeing at least with some of Ratzinger's criticisms of Free Church ecclesiology, but not persuaded by his alternative, especially the hierarchical conclusions he draws for church polity. There is a crisis in Catholic ecclesiology, he says; many, even bishops, are attracted to a North American type of Free Church ecclesiology in which the church tends to be a human project, the "Gospel becomes the *Jesus project*, the social-liberation project or other merely historical, immanent projects...."[7]

Although the Free Church properly understood does not necessarily lead in the direction of church understood primarily in socio-anthropolitical terms (Volf has made this clear, as we shall see), there is something within the voluntarist tradition that can easily lead in that direction. In contrast, according to Ratzinger, the Catholic church views itself as "a *more than human* reality, in which reformers, sociologists, organizers have no authority whatsoever" (Ratzinger, 46). According to Ratzinger, there is a *human* exterior which constantly needs reform but behind this exterior is the divine reality; it is in its essence the "Body of Christ"—this is its New Testament character which is more distinctive for her than the image of the "People of God," which gives it its continuity with the Old Testament. "One is Church and one is a member thereof, not through a sociological adherence, but precisely through incorporation in this Body of the Lord through baptism and the Eucharist" (Ratzinger, 47).

For Ratzinger, this translates into a hierarchical polity: "But the Church of Christ is not a party, not an association, not a club. Her deep and permanent structure is not *democratic* but *sacramental*, consequently *hierarchical*. For the hierarchy based on the apostolic succession is the indispensable condition to arrive at the strength, the reality of the sacrament. Here authority is not based on the majority of votes; it is based on the authority of Christ himself, which he willed to pass on to men who were to be his representatives until his definitive return. Only if this perspective is acquired anew will it be possible to rediscover the necessity and fruitfulness of obedience to the legitimate ecclesiastical hierarchies" (Ratzinger, 49).

Volf accepts Ratzinger's criticism of the individualism of Free Church ecclesiology but rejects his hierarchical alternative, and develops a version of Free Church ecclesiology based on an egalitarian, nonhierarchical, communal trinitarianism. He wants, he says, to redeem the voluntarism and the egalitarianism of the Free Church from its tendency toward "self-enclosed individualism" (Volf, 3). Seemingly unaware of sixteenth-century continental Anabaptist ecclesiology,[8] which had a non-individualistic, communal understanding of the church, in some cases quite explicitly grounded in an egalitarian, communal doctrine of the Trinity, Volf develops what he considers to be a novel view of Believers Church ecclesiology.[9] Not altogether convincing, he says he intends to offer a Free Church model of the church *not* as the best or only possible understanding but as at least one legitimate option; not altogether convincing because in the end he does appear to propose his congregational alternative as the theologically most justified approach (253). Let me summarize Volf's underlying argument, beginning with his helpful portrayal of Ratzinger's and Zizioulas' theology of the church.

For Ratzinger, Christ (the new Adam) is a corporate reality, not an individual.[10] The church as the body of Christ is a single whole, a subject with Christ (Volf, 33). The corporate reality of the church always takes precedence over the individual subject. The consequence, according to Volf, is that in Ratzinger's thought, the subjectivity and the rights of the individual remain obscure if not nonexistent (38, 72). The fundamental structure of the ecclesial community is the "being from" and the "being toward" the universal church (39). As far as church polity is concerned, the local congregation receives its being from the universal church. The universal church is always before the local church. The local assembly has the Lord totally through the celebration of the Eucharist, but always has so in a *receptive* mode. Every local church derives its catholicity from the universal church, which antecedes and sustains it. How is this divine reality mediated from the universal church to the local church? Through the office of the bishop. In the person of the properly consecrated bishop, the faith of Christ is transmitted to the local congregation and to the individuals in that congregation (56-59). The "primacy of reception" operates on every level of Ratzinger's ecclesiology: the local church, liturgy, the individual Christian, the bishop (64).

Volf rightly questions Ratzinger's assumption that anything not based on such a sacramentalism (as, for example, Free Church ecclesiology) must be seen as "self-constructed" (Volf, 65). What protects the Free Church from this kind of reductionism is its understanding of the Holy Spirit at work in the church. Is not Ratzinger's own hierarchical sacramentalism just as vulnerable to the charge of self-construction, rightly asks Volf. Ratzinger's ecclesiological "wholism" is based on a view of divine trinitarian personhood as "pure relationality." Standing firmly in the Western tradition, Ratzinger stresses the unity (the dominance of the one divine substance) of the Trinity over the plurality. The differentiation between the persons is nothing more than relational. Since Christ is the prototype of all human personhood, and since the goal of Christ is to integrate all individual persons into the divine trinitarian life of God, in the end the subjectivity and rights of the individual and the local congregation are overwhelmed by a concern with totality, the whole.

Zizioulas

Like Ratzinger, Zizioulas models the church after the Trinity. Nevertheless, his different ecclesiology is grounded in a different understanding of that Trinity. In traditional Eastern fashion, the "person" is emphasized more strongly than in Ratzinger's thought. Instead of differentiation within the Trinity consisting of "pure relationality" (as in Ratzinger), divinity is understood in terms of "personhood"—the person represents the ultimate ontological reality" (Volf, 77). Personhood means communion. The very concept of personhood rests on the divine communion of Father, Son, and Spirit. This does not, however, translate into egalitarianism either on the divine or the human level. Divine and, consequently, human communion "is always constituted and internally structured by an asymmetrical-reciprocal relationship between the one and the many" (78). Sin and the Fall consist of separation, isolation, and individualization. The fallen world is defined not by freedom and personhood but by substance, biology, and the realm of necessity. Salvation is the process of deindividualization and personalization, which occur concretely in the church. Christ, understood as a corporate reality (in this Ratzinger and Zizoulas agree), is person *par excellence*, "a corporate personality who incorporates the many into himself" (84).

It is in the church, which in a very real sense is Christ on earth,[11] that this incorporation of the many into the one occurs. This transformation from an isolated individual into a divine person in the church is not merely a moral transformation but an ontological one, mediated through baptism, effecting a union of created nature with the uncreated God in Christ. In this transformation the filial relationship between the Son and the Father becomes ours also (Volf, 88). What are the implications for ecclesiology? While for Ratzinger the universal church antecedes the local church and gives it its being, for Zizioulas it is the local church that takes precedence over the universal church. In this regard, there is an interesting congruence between Eastern and Free Church ecclesiology.

Even more central than the Mass for the Western church is the Eucharist in Eastern thought.[12] It is as expected the critical point of Zizioulas' whole ecclesiology. He understands each celebration of the Eucharist, as does the East generally, as the point where the eschatological gathering is realized in the present. Since the Eucharist is a local event, it is the local congregation that truly represents the universal, catholic church. The local church is the whole, catholic church every time the Eucharist is celebrated.[13] It stands in collegial communion with other local churches who also are catholic in this sense, but there is no sense as in Ratzinger that the universal church has precedence over the local congregation. The decisive components in the celebration of the Eucharist are the bishop and the people. The bishop is the icon of Christ, the corporate reality standing in for Christ in front of the congregation, he is the *alter Christ* who mediates between God and human beings. The people are important but not on equal terms; they are those who say "Amen."

The Eucharist is a strictly bipolar event. As there is a hierarchical, asymmetrical-mutuality between the divine persons (with the Father as the monarch), so there is a hierarchical, asymmetrical relationship between the bishop and the laity, and within all human relationships. In Christ, mediated to the local congregation through the bishop in the context of the Eucharist, laity are lifted up into the divine life itself, thereby becoming persons. While there are important differences between the Catholic and Orthodox doctrines of the church, between Ratzinger and Zizioulas, in both cases according to Volf the subjectivity and rights of the individual and the local church get lost in a hiearchically structured church polity, where individuals are absorbed into the whole.

Volf's Congregationalism

In his carefully developed doctrine of the church, Volf tries to rescue the Free Church from the two charges levelled against it by Ratzinger: its individualism ("liberal, personalistic, or existentialist") and its reduction to sociology ("group-dynamic interaction") (Volf, 30). I restrict myself here to examining three aspects of Volf's theological defence of Free Church ecclesiology: his view of the Trinity, his view of the church and its polity, and his view of Catholicity, before turning to my own sympathetic critique of Volf and proposal.

1. *Trinity* Like Ratzinger and Zizioulas, Volf, to avoid the individualism that he too thinks Free Churches are inclined toward, models his view of the church on the Trinity itself, all the while aware of the limits of the analogy. The Trinity ultimately remains a mystery that we as human cannot imitate but only worship (Volf, 192). Despite the differences between Eastern and Western theology, the inner trinitarian life of God for both Ratzinger and Zizioulas remains asymmetrical, monocentric and monarchical with unity preceding and overcoming plurality (236). In contrast, Volf, following his mentor Jürgen Moltmann, argues that unity and multiplicity are equiprimal in God (193). Even the unity within God must be understood *perichoretically*—that is as the three persons coinhering in each other: "each divine person[sic] stands in relation not only to the other persons, but is also as a personal center of action internal to the other persons" (Volf, 203).

There can be no analogy between the one divine identity and the church, only between the egalitarian communion of the three persons within the divinity and a corresponding communion of persons within the church. The trinitarian persons must be understood not as one single subject (God) but as three personal subjects (Father, Son, and Spirit), just as individual members of the church need to be understood as equal subjects (Volf, 205-206). Where the analogy breaks down is with the concept of *perichoresis*. Human beings do not coinhere in each the way the divine persons do (211). Nevertheless, despite his earlier cautionary note about the mystery of the divine Trinity, and not trying to draw too straightforward an analogy between the church and the Trinity, it is surprising how much Volf seems to know about the communal nature of inner Trinitarian life and how closely Volf draws the analogy between the divine and the human. One is left wondering, in the end, whether Volf himself does not fall prey to the same criticism he makes of Ratzinger and Zizioulas: namely, that he projects his own understanding of what the Free Church should look like onto the inner nature of God.

2. *The Church and its Polity* Volf takes as his starting point for discussing Free Church ecclesiology and polity the *Works* of the English dissenter and "first Baptist" John Smyth, someone from within "The Reformed tradition, from which," he says, "the Free Churches derive" (Volf, 270). This is, of course, a highly questionable thesis, as anyone having read the literature ought to have known.[14] Volf at no place acknowledges the sixteenth-century Anabaptists as the possible source for Free Church ecclesiology, nor does he seem to know of John Smyth's and Thomas

Helwys's connection with the Waterlander Mennonites in Amsterdam, before the beginning of the first Baptist church by Helwys at Spitalfields in England in 1611-12.

The reason these details are important is that Volf is critical of the early Free Church ecclesiology and soteriology of Smyth for being too individualistic and generally not being trinitarian enough (Volf, 172-77). Volf does, however, accept the basic principle of Smyth's Free Church ecclesiology: "the fundamental *theological* conviction that *Christ's dominion is realized through the entire congregation* (132). Christ is present in an unmediated way to the entire local church and to every individual believer in that congregation, a presence that does not have to be mediated through the narrow gates of office as in the theology of Ratzinger and Zizioulas (152).

Like the Anabaptists did many years before, Volf takes as his foundational text Matthew 18:20 for defining what the church is and where it is manifested: "*Where two or three are gathered in Christ's name, not only is Christ present among them, but a Christian church is there as well...*" (Volf, 136). Two of the essential conditions for ecclesiality are a common confession of faith, and a common commitment to live in the power of the Spirit. Although the church ought to strive to live "without spot and wrinkle," its ecclesiality does not depend on its holiness but "on the presence of Christ promised to be there wherever people gather together in his name, believe in him as Saviour and acknowledge him as Lord to live in the power of the Spirit" (148). Where Volf believes he is making a contribution to the Free Church ecclesiology of Smyth is in applying Ratzinger's and Zizioulas's notion of the sociality or ecclesiality of salvation to Free Church ecclesiology. No one is saved alone. It is only in the context of the church that salvation occurs. But in contrast to the soteriology of Ratzinger and Zizioulas, salvation does not occur by the church but through the church. This is the crucial distinction. Christ is the only subject of salvific activity, and a direct personal acceptance is required (164), but the mediation of this salvation is intrinsically communal (162). What Volf does not seem to realize, is that early Anabaptists for the most part saw soteriology ecclesiologically the same way he does, as Robert Friedmann argued (not unproblematically, I might say) in the early 1970s in his book *The Theology of Anabaptism*.[15]

3. **Catholicity** Both Ratzinger's and Zizioulas' church is episcopocentric. Volf is congregational-centred. Furthermore, the congregation modelled after the Trinity is itself polycentric in contrast to the monocentric church of Ratzinger and the bipolar church of Zizioulas. Although it is the confession of and commitment to Christ that is the defining characteristic of the church, it is the Spirit through

its charismata that gives the congregation its inner dynamic. Every person (not different persons through their offices) acts in the power of Christ through the Spirit, who in her sovereignty chooses to allot different gifts and ministries to each member (230-31). In both the Roman Catholic Church and the Eastern Orthodox Church there is an "asymmetrical-monocentric distribution of power." The Free Church, on the contrary, presupposes "institutions with symmetrical-decentralized distribution of power and freely affirmed integration" (236).

This is quite directly linked to Volf's understanding of the Trinity. In a most remarkable, in my view questionable, comparison, Volf says: "the more a church is characterized by symmetrical and decentralized distribution of power and freely affirmed interaction [integration], the more will it correspond to the Trinitarian communion" (Volf, 236). There are two reasons why I find this statement remarkable and questionable: 1) it presumes to know too much about the inner workings of God; 2) it, despite his earlier caveats in this regard, draws much too tight an analogy between the divine life and human relationships.[16] That is why, in my own work—including my proposal below—I prefer to remain within the realm of the economic Trinity, although not denying the reality of the immanent Trinity and its ultimate antecedence and grounding of any assertions in the realm of "salvation history."

Although Volf wants to distinguish himself from both Ratzinger and Zizioulas, by not excluding the ecclesiality of either the episcopally or congregationally understood church, thereby in effect being more catholic than they, he in my view cannot hold his position consistently. He draws the distinction between office holding and its theological justification in the following way.

1. On the level of institutional office holding, Volf assumes "that Christ can rule in the church both through bishops and through the whole people" and proposes that the thesis "that a participative church structure is the only correct one for all times and places is just as false as the thesis that the hierarchical church structure is God's unalterable decree" (Volf, 253).

2. On the level of theological justification, Volf makes what would appear to be a contrary claim: "This applies even if the strictly *theological* arguments with which the hierarchical understanding of church organization is justified are in *every* context false (which, with regard to a participative understanding of church organization, is not the case)" (*Ibid.*).

It would appear that Volf wants it both ways: to be fully tolerant of all church polities and at the same time to be theologically convinced of the correctness of the congregational participative model. One reason that this dilemma becomes such a problem for Volf is that he wants in fact to theologically justify church polity ontologically—i.e., to ground polity in the very inner being of God. In the end, this asks the very human, external structures and organization of the church to carry far too much theological freight.

That, in the end, Volf identifies himself fully with a theologically justified Free Church congregational model becomes ever more clear toward the conclusion of his study when he talks about the meaning of "catholicity" for a church and for individuals. For him, the episcopal and congregational churches have diametrically opposed views of catholicity: the episcopalists dissolve catholicity into a false totality (Volf, 261-62), while the congregationalists respect multiplicity, diversity, and personal subjectivity. What must be guarded against within congregationalism is falling prey to a false particularism (270). Full catholicity will be achieved only in the future eschatological gathering of all the people of God. The catholicity of the local church is always broken and partial, and exists not in an already concretely existing universal church of some kind but rather in anticipation of that future eschatological gathering (272).

In this expectation or anticipation, according to Volf, rests the full catholicity of the local church. There is no need for any reference to a concrete universal church. The marks of catholicity do not include the local congregation receiving its being from the universal church (Ratzinger) nor standing in communion with other local churches through bishops (Zizioulas), but simply an openness to other churches which also anticipate the eschatological gathering, and fidelity to the apostolic tradition that comes by way of the presence of the Spirit to each and every one (Volf, 274-275). It is at the point of Volf's understanding of the *charismata* that I now proceed to my specific proposal of how Christians in general and Mennonites in particular might understand their own catholicity.

Proposal: Mennonites and the Ecumenical Gifts of the Spirit

I accept Volf's point that the Holy Spirit is present to the church as first fruits of the eschatological gathering of the whole people of God, and that in this sense each congregation can only be partly catholic (Volf, 268).

Although I disagree with his too nominalistic and voluntaristic view of the church,[17] find his teleological-directional eschatology a problem, I do also—albeit differently—base my subsequent proposal on the notion that every local congregation can be only partly catholic. Volf does not, however, consistently follow through on this basic insight. He proceeds in effect to argue that full catholicity can reside only in local congregations and in individuals in their communion with others in the local church. This has to do with his understanding of the *charismata*. He maintains that "the catholicity of charismata thus means that each congregation contains *all* ministries within itself necessary to mediate salvation, and that the totality of its members is the bearer of these ministries. Here catholicity means *the fullness of spiritual gifts allotted to the local church*" (Volf, 273). Further on, he says this even more strongly: "The local church is catholic in the full sense," and this without any necessary reference to the universal church (274).

It is here that my own proposal begins to differ from that of Volf. He is in the end too congregationalist for me. I want to argue that just as no individual can have all the gifts of the Spirit (with which Volf would agree), similarly no local congregation can have all the gifts of the Spirit. It might be argued that a congregation is a congregation only to the extent that it has sufficient number of gifts, and related ministries, for its existence as church to be theologically justified.

I am more of a realist when it comes to an understanding of the universal church than Volf appears to be. By this I mean that the concept of a universal church consisting concretely, presently, of all those believers throughout the world who confess Christ in whatever tradition does really exist, and can be referred to as the "Body of Christ." All Christian traditions—Catholic, Orthodox, Protestant, Free Church—where the apostolic confession of faith in Christ is present, belong to this real, universal church. No one local church, no one denomination, no one tradition (whatever its church polity) can claim to be the exclusive guardian of the "Body of Christ." Each is given a set of spiritual gifts which contribute to the body as a whole. I believe Hubmaier had this in mind when in his 1528 *Apologia* he refers to the Universal Church as "mother" and the local congregation as "daughter":

> The church is an outward assembly and community of Christ-believers in one Lord, one faith and one baptism, Eph. 4:4f. It should be noted here that the word *church* is used in the Scriptures for two kinds of church: First, for the universal holy, Christian communion and assembly of all who believe in Christ, wherever on earth they be, in the whole circle of the world. And so we believe in a holy Christian church, which is a community of the saints. Christ also speaks of the church in this sense, Matt. 16:18. This church is the body of Christ. Christ is the head and we are the members of the body of Christ, 1 Cor. 12; Eph. 2; 4; Col. 1; 3. Second, the church is understood in

the Scriptures as a particular community of some believers in Christ, such as the church of the Galatians, Gal. 1, the church of the Corinthians, 1 Cor. 1. It is this specific congregation that is commonly called the daughter and the general church the mother. Now the daughter has equal authority with the mother, which is the general church, to bind and to loose sin according to Christ's command, as the Scripture testifies concerning the Corinthian church, 1 Cor. 5; 2 Cor. 2. This authority the particular church now commends and gives over to its chosen, established, and ordained minister and priest, so that all things may be done in an orderly manner. *Both of these churches are outward communities and not imaginary, conceivable, or logical essences,* as I explained in my booklets on the catechism, on brotherly discipline, and on the ban. (The emphasis is mine.)[18]

My proposal builds on this, Hubmaier's, organic understanding of the universal church as mother and the local church as daughter, both concretely existing communities, but one a part of the whole. I go beyond Hubmaier in at least one sense, however: I apply Paul's explication of the gifts of the Spirit in 1 Cor. 12 to the way the relationship of a local church/denomination to the universal church might be understood. A second point at which I might go beyond Hubmaier, although I will not do so in this context, is where he gives full powers of church discipline to a local congregation. There is a third point at which I part company with him: I do not believe his view of the universal church as purely a concrete, visible community of presently existing believers throughout the world is an adequate one. There is a sense—and here my realism is evident over against Hubmaier's nominalism—in which the universal church is an invisible reality behind the concretely, existing universal church; it is the invisible community of all those who have come before and will come hereafter who confess the Christ.

There are three New Testament texts which list the gifts of the Spirit: Rom. 12: 4-8 (prophecy, service, teaching, exhortation, contribution, giving aid, acts of mercy); Eph. 4:11-16 (apostles, prophets, evangelists, pastors, teachers); 1 Cor. 12:1-26 (wisdom, knowledge, faith, healing, miracles, prophecy, discernment, tongues, interpretation). The fact that each of these lists is different, although there are similarities, would suggest that none of the congregations Paul is talking to has a comprehensive set of gifts that makes it totally self-sufficient.[19] From the start, congregations in the different centres of the Greco-Roman world (Jerusalem, Alexandria, Antioch, Constantinople, Rome, Ephesus, Corinth, etc.) had their own individual character, and developed different theological orientations out of which emerged different historical traditions. This is already evident in these Pauline letters and the gifts that he cites for each.

What these lists have in common is the call for humility, love, and unity in the light of this diversity. The most comprehensive set of gifts is the one found in the Corinthian text. Paul describes the spiritual *charisms* given to individual Christians in Corinth as not their own possession but as belonging to the community. He envisions the church as an organic body with each of the organs (those which appear weaker as well as those which seem stronger) being indispensible parts of the whole. In fact, "God has so adjusted the body, giving the greater honor to the inferior part, that there may be no discord in the body, but that the members may have the same care for one another." (12: 24-25) The whole point is that while there is a diversity of gifts, there is one Lord, one Spirit, one God (12: 4-6).

Customarily we think of these various gifts as the *charisms* given to a particular congregation as the spiritual basis for the different ministries on the local level. This is also how Volf interprets the gifts of the Spirit. I want to suggest here, however, that without doing an injustice to these New Testament texts we can apply these gifts to the larger theological traditions within the universal church as Hubmaier thinks of it. I am not seeking to draw a strict parallel between each of the separate gifts itemized by Paul with specific Christian traditions, but rather to say that each of the major Christian groups contributes a valuable emphasis to the Christian body as whole, an emphasis which has a biblical basis and is pneumatically given: 1) *Eastern Orthodoxy*: the church as the mystical body of Christ, Pentocrator, the Lord of the Universe (Eph. 1 : 15-23); 2) *Roman Catholicism*: the historic, institutional church as the official guardian of the tradition through the apostolic succession and the sacraments (Matt. 16:13-20); 3) *Anglicanism*: worship and liturgy (the Psalms, Isa. 6, *The Book of Common Prayer*); 4) *Lutheranism*: justification by grace through faith (Gal. 3: 6-14); 5) *Calvinism*: the sovereignty of God, covenant, election and the cultural mandate (2 Pet. 1:10; Rom. 9:6-18; Gen. 1: 27-28, 2:15-17); 6) *Methodism*: holiness and sanctification (1 Pet. 1:13-21); 7) *Anabaptists/Baptists*: Church as voluntary, gathered community (Matt. 18:15-20); 8) *Quakers*: quiet meditation and spontaneous worship based on light within (1 Cor. 14:26-33); 9) *Pentecostalism*: gifts of the spirit, especially glossolalia (Acts 2:1-4); 10) *Mennonites*: discipleship and the historic peace witness (Matt. 5; Rom. 12: 9-21).

This is not meant to be an exhaustive list but it does illustrate my point. I do not suggest that these emphases are exclusive to one tradition, let alone exhaust the gifts of that tradition, but rather that they are highlighted by that tradition. Furthermore, the whole body of Christ, the universal Christian community (in Hubmaier's understanding of the term) needs all of these gifts for its well-being. None can do without the other. This way of looking at the relationship of the local church to the universal church allows for diversity without relativism, and unity without dogmatism. The question might be asked, Is any one of these emphases (gifts) incompatible with any other? As I have identified them above, I do not think so, but that would have to be explored in greater theological depth, something I cannot do here. The *sine qua non* would be the confession of one God, one Lord, one Spirit.

Conclusion: Implications for Mennonites

Certain implications for confession, church polity, and ethics follow from the above proposal. I would argue that there is a reverse "hierarchy" of sorts, or graduation of levels, from the more general (the universal church level) to the more particular (congregational level); the lowest level being the foundational level at which universal consensus is critical, and the highest level being farthest away from the theological core of the confession, where agreement is not as critical. An alternate way of visualizing this would be from a central core to ever larger concentric circles:

1. A first circle would have to do with core theological/confessional issues that all Christians have in common (affirmation of the Christian doctrine of God as Creator, Christ, Spirit) and properly belong on the universal level.

2. Structural questions of polity and certain historical, theological distinctives would be located on the denominational level. The recent integration of Mennonite Church and General Conference on the denominational level can, in my view, be justified theologically *in a way* that the division of the denomination into two nations (Canada and United States) cannot be justified theologically, although there may be good pragmatic and sociological reasons for doing so. This raises the question, for instance, what theological significance "nationality" has for Christians.

3. Particular matters in which sincere Christians who confess the faith in the one God, the one Christ, and the one Spirit find themselves in honest disagreement even within a denomination would be dealt with on the local, congregational level (e.g., homosexuality). Disagreements between denominations (second level) or congregations (third level), do not however justify excommunication or schism, where schism is defined as separation from the universal body of Christ as understood above. This does not mean that the second and third levels do not have theological

relevance, just that the further you move away from the core, the less foundational are the matters dealt with on that level.

What are the specific implications of this proposal for Mennonites and their historic peace witness? One's gift is an essential aspect of the whole, but it is not the whole. One definition of "heresy," using this model would be the reduction of all gifts to one's own gift, and the absolutization of that gift as though it were the total truth. No one tradition can fulfill all the gifts; to attempt to do so would be the dilution of each gift and a sure way to lose the singular power of the individual gifts.

The Mennonite emphasis on discipleship and peace (variously named nonresistance, pacifism, nonviolence) is one gift among many, but it is an essential one for the whole church. For Mennonites to understand their peace emphasis as a "gifted" ministry to the whole body of Christ is more than a vocation (as, for example, "vocational pacifism"). It is a truth that applies to the whole body, and is the Spirit working through their particular tradition in the transformation of the entire body, and through it the resurrection of the entire world.

However, it ought always to be remembered that there are other gifts that other traditions have which are just as important, and maybe more important in the fulfilling of God's divine purpose for creation. For example, I have frequently in my writing argued that the Mennonite peace witness cannot be the foundation of our theology although it is intrinsically part of Christian theology. The ultimate foundation is God in God's threefoldness.

THIRTY-SEVEN

Conclusion: The Dynamic of the Classical Imagination

It's really all about the imagination and how one understands the imagination. Does it emerge from the collective unconscious, is it miraculously given to us from the outside, is it passed on as tradition, or is it constructed bottom-up either by individuals or cultures? What imagination is it that inspires one's view of reality– one's vision of the divine, the cosmos, the world of visible and invisible nature, what it means to be human, one's relation to the divine and role within the world? The concern of this volume of essays has been the *theological* imagination and how this theological imagination informs human action. Imagination as understood here is more literary than scientific, although scientific curiosity may itself be inspired by the imagination. Theological imagination as understood here is less a constructive activity, although it possesses constructive moments, than a kind of spiritual day-dreaming where the usual categories of fixed space and sequential time are transcended, thereby opening up new worlds of possibility. We are told by the Gospel writer that "all these things Jesus spoke to the crowds in parables, and he did not speak to them at all without using parables— to fulfil the prophecy: I will open my mouth in parables; I will utter things hidden from the foundation of the world" (Matt. 13: 34-35).

Theological language is univocal (literal) only in a very limited sense. Of far more critical importance are allegorical (mystical), tropological (moral), anagogical (futuristic), symbolic, metaphorical, analogical, parabolic, and dialectical forms of speech. Dogmatic thinking in contemporary theology is frequently identified with rigid, univocal speech. This is a misunderstanding of classical dogmatic language, which was thought of as symbolic and analogical, and was an imaginative way of preserving the faith and dealing with new issues as they arose. To enter the classical imagination is to enter this dynamic, creative process of thinking "dogmatically" in ever new and changing circumstances within the basic framework of a Christian doctrine of the triune God.

What holds together the diverse essays of this volume, articles written over a period of more than two decades, is the conviction that: a) the classical imagination— the biblical and post-biblical vision that saw the world theocentrically and that held sway up to the modern period— is far richer and more fruitful for Christian systematic theology than acknowledged in much modern and postmodern thinking; b) dogmatic thinking as it developed in antiquity was imaginative thinking about ultimate reality, intended not to ossify but to express things dynamically that are too deep for ordinary human speech and thought; and c) Mennonites, in their concern with moral rectitude and a social-political ethic dedicated to radical non-violent love ("pacifism"), dare not attempt an end-run around creedal antiquity on the way to the biblical text itself, or an unqualified identification with heterodox traditions (the peripheral voices). Critical issues related to the Christian doctrine of God, christology, and pneumatology were imaginatively addressed in the first few centuries to preserve the integrity of the faith in the face of various reductionist views. In these essays I have called for a retrieval of the classical imagination, and argued strongly that Mennonites ought to situate themselves and their ethical concerns firmly within this classical Christian tradition. In this concluding chapter I explore further how one might fruitfully *enter* the classical imagination, by engaging a number of writers from outside the Mennonite tradition whom I consider especially pertinent for my own theological project: Thomas C. Oden, Wolfhart Pannenberg, and Miroslav Volf.

Of these three, Thomas Oden, Professor of Systematic Theology at Drew University Divinity School, perhaps more than any other has argued persuasively for a return to classical origins. Oden, an ordained Methodist minister and author of many books, has since the 1970s espoused what he calls a "post-critical, postmodern orthodoxy," most succinctly and popularly articulated in his 1990 book *Agenda For Theology: After Modernity . . . What?*[1], systematically worked out in his three-volume *Systematic Theology* (Volume One: *The Living God*, Volume Two: *The Word of Life*,

Volume Three: *Life in the Spirit*[2]), and technically applied in his editing of an ambitious biblical commentary project, a compilation in twenty-five volumes of what the ancients have said about the entire Bible.[3]

I am drawn to Oden's turn to the classics, which is so similar to mine. I have, however, serious reservations on three counts: first, his critique of the Enlightenment, modernity, and all things new is too one-sided and undialectical, and does not take seriously enough God's doing novel things with the world through the Spirit; second, he does not enter the classical imagination in its comprehensiveness—i.e., in his avowal of the Vincentian method (according to Vincent of Lerins of the fifth century that which has always, everywhere, and by all Christians been believed to be true) he excludes important voices; and, consequently, third, the moral-ethical conclusions Oden draws from the classics do not adequately reflect the full range of the biblical message (e.g., the prophetic-eschatological is short-changed) or the ever-new challenges facing Christians in new historical situations.

Oden's one-sided critique of the Enlightenment In his impressive three volumes of systematic theology, Oden's way of retrieving classical theology and what such a retrieval means for treating systematically all the themes of Christian theology becomes transparent. He never tires of telling us that he is committed to unoriginality and to making "no new contribution to theology . . . pledged to irrelevance if relevance means indebtedness to corrupt modernity" (Oden, *ST* 3, vii). The decisive question for Oden is whether the Christian testimony is true, not whether it is palatable to the modern mind. Although he seeks "language that makes plausible today the intent of classical Christianity" (*ST* 2, x), he intends to restrain his own idiosyncrasies and as much as possible let classic Christianity speak for itself and in its own language. After many years of worshiping at the altar of the modern agenda, he now disavows the contemporary obsession with all that is new and gives his unqualified allegiance to classical Christian thinking:

> The only promise I try to make to my readers, however inadequately carried out, is that of unoriginality. I hope to present nothing whatever original in these pages. . . . Nothing of my own, that would have my initials stamped upon it, is important in this discussion, as I see it. Admittedly the classic language must be reappropriated and articulated in sentences written and organized by some particular person. Yet I hope my own voice does not intrude inordinately upon the likes of Polycarp, Anthony, or Athanasius. I wish to provide neither a new interpretation of old ideas, nor a new language that is

more acceptable for modern sensibilities.... I do not pretend to have found a comfortable way of making Christianity acceptable to a deteriorating modernity (*ST* 2, xvi).

Is his approach reactionary or antiquarian, he asks. "I can think of nothing more forward-looking than taking the risk of allowing ourselves to be addressed by the texts of Scripture and tradition" (*ST* 3, ix). Although we learn from other sources that Oden does not reject modernity and the historical-critical method entirely, but calls for post-critical thinking,[4] the vehemence with which he polemicizes against the modern project as a whole betrays his true colors. A return to the classical church fathers (or "influential mothers," some of whom he is willing to include [*ST* 2, xvii]), would entail, in my view, a more radical openness to historically new divine workings in history than Oden's theology allows for. For the ancient development of trinitarian and christological dogma was precisely such a dynamic openness. Many of the early maternal church mystics (e.g., Perpetua) were visionaries to whom God revealed new things. This is not to rehabilitate modernity in all its forms— I am as critical as Oden of modern reductionism and historicism, but can we so easily say that the divine is not in some strange way present, working mysteriously in the very things we deplore? Oden describes the ancient tradition as living, not dead and archaistic, the ancients as having an "originally fresh sense of imagination..."(*ST* 3, ix), but does this very same lively imagination not free us similarly to exercise our *own* imagination?

Oden's exclusion of peripheral voices This brings me to my second reservation. Oden's purpose in his systematic theology is not to offer novelty or originality, but to set forth faithfully, in a simple and ordered way, the Christian faith following the ancient ecumenical consensus. This consensus is, according to Oden, the core of faith agreed upon by the majority of Christians throughout two millennia of Christian history, a core described by Vincent of Lerins as "that which has always, everywhere, and by all Christians been believed about God's self-disclosure" (*ST* 1, xiv). Oden's pyramid of sources makes clear where his loyalties lie: Scripture at the foundation, then the Ante-Nicene and Post-Nicene Writers, followed by the Medieval Sources, then the Reformation Writers, and finally the Modern Interpreters (*ST* 2, xv).

Because the concepts of "consent" and "consensus" are so problematic for some of us standing in a nonconformist tradition, we need greater clarity as to exactly how Oden understands these notions. Consensus for him means the dominant interpretation of the Bible throughout history; for him, the history of Christian thought is really the history of biblical exegesis. In determining the dominant ecumenical interpretation of the

Bible, priority is given to the seven ecumenical councils: Nicea, A.D. 325 (the triune God); Constantinople, A.D. 381 (Jesus' full humanity and the Spirit's full divinity); Ephesus, A.D. 431 (the unity of Christ's Person, and Mary as *theotokos*); Chalcedon, A.D. 451 (two natures of Christ); Second Council of Constantinople, A.D. 553 (against Nestorianism); Third Council of Constantinople (against Monothelitism); and the Second Council of Nicea, A.D. 787 (against Iconoclasm) (*ST* 1, 349-350). Further, priority is given to the "four great ecumenical 'Doctors of the Church' of the Eastern tradition (Athanasius, Basil, Gregory Nazianzen, and John Chrysostom), [and] the four 'Doctors of the Church' of the West (Ambrose, Augustine, Jerome, and Gregory the Great)" followed by others such as Gregory of Nyssa, Hilary, Leo, John of Damascus, Thomas Aquinas, Luther, and Calvin (*ST* 2, xvii). His aim, Oden claims, is not to focus on the many varieties of dissent, nor on "centrifugal variations" of apostolic teaching, but on the "cohesive central tradition of general lay consent to apostolic teaching" (*ST* 3, vii). This means nonconsensual authors like Origen, Novatian, and Menno Simons are quoted sparely and only on such points in which they agree with the consensus (*ST* 2, xx).

This raises a fundamental problem for a Mennonite, for it might be precisely at the point where a peripheral voice has historically been nonconsensual and noncentrist that it needs to be listened to by the majority. Is it not possible that at certain critical points the dominant position (the so-called ecumenical consensual position) was wrong and the nonconsensual voice right? Here Oden's method falls short. In deferring so completely to the actual words of ancient texts, councils, and authors, without wanting to interfere via his own voice and critical analysis he, first of all, presupposes an ecumenical consensus where there may not be one. Second, in effect he assumes that the dominant position is the right one— the one inspired by the Holy Spirit— without making a case for it.[5] My objection is not to the priority he gives to the ecumenical councils, and to those Christian thinkers who by virtue of their writings stand head and shoulders above many other minor figures, but rather to his deliberate attempt to limit our own era's critical engagement with *all* the classical sources. He has excluded some so-called marginal voices, and is left with a kind of mechanistic, collating-of-sayings approach to what the ancients have said about Christianity. This is surely a failure to truly enter the dynamic of the classical imagination.

Oden tells us that his systematic theology is really little more than a reproduction of classical Christian sources and the "*text is an introduction to its annotations*" (*ST* 2, xiv). "Theological argument does well to view itself modestly as merely an introduction to its annotations" (*ST* 3, viii). The problem really is that Oden cannot apply his own method consistently;

he makes choices of interpretation that bear the marks of a contemporary agenda. This is perhaps most evident in his attempt to include the concerns of liberation theology, feminist theology, black theology, and even process theology. He defends this by arguing that "traditional study is not a flight from relevance" and that the ancient "texts relentlessly address modern and postmodern problems" (*ST* 2, xviii). But there is no way in which the agenda, concerns, and methodologies of these contemporary theological movements can be said to emerge naturally from within the classical texts without reinterpretation. When Oden includes "influential mothers and not fathers alone" (Macrina, Perpetua, Caecilia of Rome, Agatha of Sicily, Margaret of Antioch, Paula, Eustochium, and Amma Theodora) in his list of classical thinkers, he is making a methodological move that would not have been obvious to the ancient ecumenical bishops meeting at Nicea. *He is, in other words, bringing to bear his own critical judgment in novel ways. This is as it should be, but is not fully consistent with his own declared intent of denouncing all originality and novelty.*

This is where I find Wolfhart Pannenberg's approach more helpful. His *Systematic Theology*, also in three volumes,[6] outlines a careful reading of ancient, medieval, Reformation, and modern texts which, like Oden's, attempts to remain faithful to the tradition but, unlike Oden's, understands the need to ask much more deeply the historical questions raised by the Enlightenment. The truth of Christian doctrine, says Pannenberg, cannot simply be methodologically presupposed; it needs to be debated. This is precisely the task of systematic theology: to debate the truth of the revelation. There is no *a priori* guarantee of truth. Systematic theology presents, tests, and confirms the truth claims it makes. What is needed is open, rational discussion and debate concerning the universal truth of doctrines of faith without steering the line of argument. Doctrinal statements have the status of hypotheses that need historical confirmation and correction (Pannenberg, *ST* 1, 47-56). What is true, reliable, and lasting will come to light only eschatologically, in the progression of time: "as time advances it brings to light what is constant and true in the world of our beginnings" (Pannenberg, *ST* 1, 55). In stark contrast to Oden, Pannenberg maintains that in the process the tradition will not remain unchanged: "theological thinking now faces the task of revising traditional ideas of God. It cannot escape this challenge if it is to remain in intellectual dialogue with modern criticism of the traditional doctrine of God and with atheism, and if it is not to fall back upon loose symbolic language in its statements about God" (Pannenberg, *ST* 1, 367). Our understandings of the world and of God are mutually conditioning and, consequently, need redefining and reformulation (Pannenberg, *ST* 2, xiv).

CONCLUSION / 559

Pannenberg also has a much more nuanced view of historical, ecumenical consensus than Oden does. The issue for Pannenberg is: How is consensus to be determined? For the Eastern church, consensus has always to be tested by the whole body of believers. The Western church makes no mention of such reception of the consensus by the whole body; instead it stresses the ecclesiastical teaching authority guaranteed by bishops and the pope. According to Pannenberg, the weakness of the consensus approach is that it can express convention as well as universal truth. Therefore, consensus alone is not a sufficient criterion. Lutherans and Reformed regard evangelical teaching — the Word of God witnessed to by Scripture — as the definitive criterion. The problem with the Protestant view, as rightly recognized by Roman Catholics, is that the diversity of the Scripture requires more than private judgment. It therefore adds the teaching authority of the Church. Pannenberg's own solution is that all interpretation must be measured against the truth of the subject matter, which is itself determined in the process of expository debate. The subject matter common to the New Testament is "the act of God in Jesus of Nazareth." This is the core of the New Testament confession. The final truth and content of God's act in Jesus of Nazareth will be verified only eschatologically, at the end of time and history. In the meantime consensus stands in constant need of renewal and testing. The testing and exposition of dogma in the light of history is the task of dogmatics (Pannenberg, *ST* 1, 8-26).

Although I find Pannenberg's more critical engagement with the classical texts, and his wariness of the consensual argument, more congenial than Oden's, there are a number of areas where I disagree.

1. In the end, Pannenberg is too much of a rationalist and historicist. He is so fearful of a pietistic subjectivism that he has too high a confidence in rational debate and the progressive, historical confirmation of the objective truth of the Christian faith, ultimately to be verified eschatologically (at the end of time and history). This is not the place to engage in a thoroughgoing critique of Pannenberg's view of time and history, except to say that he, like many contemporary theologians who make eschatology the hermeneutical key to their theological understanding, tends to collapse the immanent Trinity into the economic Trinity, thereby historicizing all of reality. One of the main themes of all my essays has been an on-going argument against this kind of reduction of reality to linear, directional, historical thinking.

2. As in Oden's system, one searches Pannenberg's opus in vain for any discussion of the Radical Reformers and their understanding of the church. Had he engaged the Radicals more seriously, he might have considered

another approach to consensus different from the Magisterial Reformers (Lutherans and Reformed) on the one hand, and the Roman Catholics on the other, and in some ways closer to the Eastern position. Consensus needs to be tested by the whole body of believers. Mennonite ethicist John Howard Yoder has suggested that for the Anabaptists and later Puritans there were three indispensable elements needed for consensus: the Spirit, the Scripture, and the gathered community of believers.[7] The problem, as I have articulated it in "Mennonites and the Church Universal," (Chapter 36 above) is that for Anabaptist-Mennonites the church is frequently understood in too sectarian a way. Ecumenical consensus is important. In this Oden is right. But consensus needs testing by the whole Christian community, which I have argued includes the universal church both in its visible and invisible aspects. My reservation with Oden's understanding of the concepts of "consent" and "consensus" is that he understands them too restrictively. He does not listen adequately to the peripheral voices. Here again Pannenberg is more nuanced. He distinguishes between heresy and apostasy, and recognizes the positive function that so-called "heresies" have played throughout Christian history, without rehabilitating the heresy itself (Pannenberg, *ST* 3, 412-13).

Oden's conservative social-ethical conclusions My third reservation about Oden has to do with the ethical conclusions he draws from his ecumenical-consensual approach. My encounter with Oden's theological turn to the classics came some years after I had myself been thinking along similar lines. I was introduced to Oden first through reading his *After Modernity... What?*[8] which I subsequently reviewed. I found myself agreeing with much of what he was saying theologically but disagreeing with his unqualified return to antiquity, and what seemed to me to be the conservative social-political ethics that went along with it. I reviewed Oden's book alongside a publication of the same year by Daniel Liechty, *Theology in Postliberal Perspective*,[9] which proposed the exact opposite agenda for theology: one which deconstructs the past in favor of new notions of God, Christ, and church to suit more adequately the age within which we live. Liechty offers us a left-wing critical social ethic, supposedly rooted in the Anabaptist tradition as interpreted by Mennonite thinkers like John Yoder, combined with a postcritical, deconstructionist theology learned from theologians like Gordon Kaufman. In my reviews of these two books I sought to combine the "conservative" theological orthodoxy of Oden with the "radical" ethics of Liechty:

> In conclusion, I can support Liechty's ethics but not his theology. I do not believe that his historically and psychologically immanentist theology can bear the weight and

high demands of his moral and ethical passion. The mystical motor is missing. I am attracted to Oden's theology and the need to recover classical thought as a framework for ethics. What I object to is his ethics— his social and political conservatism couched in language of "tradition-maintenance"— and his virtual disregard for the contribution of long-standing nonconformist traditions. In the end, I would like, with some modifications of each, to combine Liechty's ethical concerns with Oden's theological orthodoxy. Without a grounding in theological orthodoxy Liechty's ethics is in danger of ending up as little more than a human-centered project. Without the prophetic-eschatological themes found in the dangerous Jesus narratives, Oden's pastoral and communal "tradition-maintenance" is in danger of ending up as a religious ideology of the right.[10]

In Oden's entire *Systematic Theology* there is no serious analysis of the Constantinian shift that is such a watershed in the history of the church; no critique of the alliance between political, imperial power and the institutional church against voices of dissent, protest, and reform. Here again Pannenberg, while not giving an extended treatment of the Constantinian period, manifests a much greater sensitivity to the theological and political ambiguities of the classical synthesis. According to him, Eusebius still saw the church as the bearer of, and witness to (not the guarantor of), the truth claim of revelation. Beginning in the fourth century and culminating with Justinian in the sixth century, codification of dogmas becomes legally binding, taking on a status of virtual equality with Holy Scripture and enforced by the state. From then on doctrinal truth and legal codification, undergirded by state coercion, become fatefully intertwined and confused (Pannenberg, *ST* 1, 10-11). Further, there is in Oden's christology and ecclesiology no discussion of the "politics of Jesus," his message of non-violent love, and the important contribution of Radical Protestantism to a Christian understanding of a Free Church.

In this regard Miroslav Volf has made a more significant contribution, particularly in his two volumes *After Our Likeness* and *Exclusion and Embrace*.[11] *After Our Likeness* is the most thorough analysis of the differences between Eastern Orthodox, western Roman Catholic, and Free Church ecclesiologies that I am aware of. I will not repeat my critical assessment of Volf's understanding of and apology for a congregational doctrine of the church, as presented in "Mennonites and the Church Universal" (Chapter 36). What I conclude with instead is a glance at Volf's most prominent book, *Exclusion and Embrace*. In it, he develops the kind of theological ethic—grounding a commitment to Jesus' way of nonviolent love and reconciliation upon a classical trinitarian theology—that is of all three views, the closest to my own theological project, with a few qualifications, one of which I will identify below.

In *After Our Likeness* Volf proposes a Free Church ecclesiology which, distinct from Eastern Orthodox and Roman Catholic ecclesiologies, emphasizes not hierarchy but an egalitarian community theologically reflecting the mutually self-giving divine community of Father, Son, and Holy Spirit. In *Exclusion and Embrace*, he draws out the ramifications of "the self-giving love of the divine Trinity as manifested on the cross of Christ" for social-political ethics (*Exclusion and Embrace*, 25). In highly imaginative ways, Volf reappropriates the classical trinitarian tradition, interpreting and reinterpreting it creatively to address the contemporary world of ethnic conflict: "This book seeks to explicate what divine self-donation may mean for the construction of identity and for the relationship with the other under the condition of enmity" (*Ibid.*, 25). He does not shy away from engaging in a critical conversation with any modern and postmodern voices that have something to say on the subject.

The issue Volf seeks to address in the last chapter of *Exclusion and Embrace* is "how to live under the rule of Caesar in the absence of the reign of truth and justice." He considers three modern proposals for countering violence: the Enlightenment proposal of a universal reason, modern interreligious dialogue, and the deconstructionist denunciation of both religion and reason as promoters of terror in favor of a nonjudgmental and de-centered self. Volf rejects all three proposals as inadequate. 1) The Enlightenment notion that the rational, civilizing process leads to peace and nonviolence is a naive myth; savage cruelty and rational, civilized culture have been shown not to be antithetical, as the holocaust illustrates (*Exclusion and Embrace*, 278-82). 2) Religious tolerance, or reducing all religions to one, also does not necessarily lead to peace between peoples, for gods fight because people fight, not vice versa; what is needed is a critique of religion itself when used to legitimate violence (*Ibid.*, 282-86). 3) The postmodern deconstructionist belief (à la Gilles Deleuze) that terror can be eliminated by getting rid of the subject (the "I") and all boundaries (no judgments) is also an illusion: "The attempt to transcend judgment—whether it be judgment of reason or of religion—does not eliminate but enthrones violence" (*Ibid.*, 290).

The only way the cycle of violence can be broken, says Volf, is the way of the cross. The cross is not the consequence of a form of self-denial that leads to violence, as Deleuze thinks, but rather breaks the cycle of violence, unmasks the mechanism of scapegoating, and represents the struggle of

Jesus for God's truth and justice. The cross is the divine embrace of the unjust. The only alternative to violence is self-donating love, imitating the self-giving love between members of the Trinity. The cross is not a form of divine weakness that condones or overlooks violence, but is a means of transforming violence. On the other hand, God is not the nice, weak-kneed deity of the liberal imagination. The image of the victorious rider of Revelation (Rev. 19: 11-17) represents divine anger against those who have immunized themselves against redemption (whose hearts have been hardened), an image that needs to supplement the divine self-giving image of the cross of Jesus. There are those who will experience God's terror, not because they have done evil but because they refuse to accept the offer of divine embrace. This by no means translates into a justification for human terror. It is precisely because God has a monopoly on vengeance ("the transcendence of violence") that humans are freed from the cycle of violence (*Ibid.*, 295-304).

In the end, however, after so powerfully making the case for the way of the cross as a way of overcoming violence and embracing the other, Volf loses nerve. In a Niebuhrian-like move, he undermines his whole previous argument:

> It may be that consistent non-retaliation and nonviolence will be impossible in the world of violence. Tyrants may need to be taken down from their thrones and the madmen stopped from sowing desolation . . . . It may also be that measures which involve preparation for the use of violent means will have to be taken to prevent tyrants and madmen from ascending to power in the first place or to keep the plethora of ordinary kinds of perpetrators that walk our streets from doing their violent work. (*Exclusion and Embrace*, 306)

But, says Volf, when one puts on one's soldier gear rather than wearing the cross, one should not use religion to legitimate this move. Either Volf's whole book has been a romantic, unrealistic proposal for how Christians should live in a world of violence, and Niebuhrian realism is after all the way of achieving relative justice, or Volf has in the end not followed through consistently on what he has so masterfully proposed throughout the volume. I suggest the latter is the case rather than the former.

We *do* live in a world with tyrants, madmen, and violent criminals where a sentimentalization of the way of the cross is not adequate. We do need as Christians to be involved in civil institutions that protect the good and restrain the evil. It is the legitimate role of such institutions that Volf has not adequately addressed in his volume.

In "God is Love but not a Pacifist" (Chapter 31), I attempt to come to terms with a world of violence (in nature, history, ourselves, and our communities) and to lay the trinitarian groundwork for Christian non-violence. I argue that while "God is Love" is the most profound thing one can say about God, God is not a pacifist in the strict sense of the term. In fact, as Volf also argues, it is precisely because we leave vengeance to God that we are free to live non-violently. In "Christians, Policing, and the Civil Order" (Chapter 32), I draw out some of the implications of a trinitarian theology for Christian social ethics. In particular, I distinguish between "policing" (a metaphor for the legitimate use of power in the domestic, municipal, provincial, national, and international arenas) and "warring" (the illegitimate use of force) and biblically, historically, and theologically justify the former but not the latter.

Nowhere in this volume, however, have I engaged in a sustained, systematic treatment of Christian social ethics. This remains the challenge for a future work. In these essays I have argued not that we repristinate, word-for-word, ancient terminology (as Oden is prone to do) but that we enter the classical imagination in creative ways. At the heart of the classical imagination is a different view of time than our modern view of time as historical becoming. Ancient Christians did not absolutize historical time (the movement from past to present to future) as moderns do, as even someone like Pannenberg is inclined to do, but saw history as the temporary stage upon which divine and human action takes place. Ultimately the created order, including time and space, was seen as contingent upon that which was eternal and uncontingent. The Christian doctrine of God as Triune (both immanent and economic) is the core of the classical dogmatic imagination, the basis of all other doctrines, and the ground for all thinking about the cosmos, nature, history, and human action.

NOTES

Introduction

[1] Frederick Copleston, S.J., *A History of Philosophy*, vol. 1, *Greece & Rome: Part I* (Garden City, NY: Image Books, A Division of Doubleday & Company, Inc., 1962), p. 132. I am not one of those who believes the case against classical and medieval metaphysics is closed and that the postmodern anti-foundationalists have said the last word on the subject.

Chapter 1

[1] Originally published in *Prophetic Vision Applied to One's Academic Discipline: 1978 Mennonite Graduate Seminar* (Elkhart, IN: Mennonite Board of Missions, 1978), 109-21.

[2] Larry Schmidt ed., *George Grant in Process: Essays and Conversations* (Toronto: House of Anansi, 1978).

[3] See George Grant, *Time as History* (Toronto: Canadian Broadcasting Corporation, 1969), 10-11; see also Grant, *Technology and Empire* (Toronto: House of Anansi, 1969), 138-39. For my whole analysis of modernity I am deeply indebted to George Grant, as will be evident throughout this essay.

[4] Much of my conceptual framework for theological method comes from Gordon D. Kaufman's *An Essay on Theological Method* (Missoula: Scholars Press, 1975). The last three sections of the paper are loosely fashioned after Kaufman's three moments of theological construction as he outlines them on pp. 41ff.

[5] "Whatever Happened to Theology?"*Christianity and Crisis* 38.8 (May 12, 1975), 106-120 The quotations that appear in the text are all taken from this article..

[6] Kaufman, *An Essay on Theological Method*, 60, 57ff.

[7] *Ibid.*, 19ff.

[8] *Ibid.*, 54

[9] While Kaufman does not deny the relevance of particularist approaches to theology, it is clear that he is trying to develop a theology that transcends particular and "parochial" traditions. See *ibid.*, 61ff.

[10] *Ibid.*, 35

[11] *Ibid.*, 44

[12] *Ibid.*

[13] Grant, "Conversation," *George Grant in Process*, 144.

[14] Grant, "'The Computer Does not Impose on us the Ways it Should be Used,'" *Beyond Industrial Growth*, ed. Abraham Rotstein (Toronto: University of Toronto Press, 1976), 124.

[15] Grant, "Conversation," *George Grant in Process*, 143.

[16] *Ibid.*, 145.

[17] *Ibid.*, 144.

[18] *Ibid.*, 14.

[19] Grant, *Technology and Empire*, 45-59.

[20] Grant, "'The Computer Does not Impose on us the Ways it Should be Used,'" 122.

[21] Grant, "Conversation," *George Grant in Process*, 15.

[22] *Ibid.*, 14ff.

[23] *Ibid.*, 21
[24] *Ibid.*, 62
[25] Grant, *Technology and Empire*, 43.
[26] Grant, "Conversation," *George Grant in Process*, 21.
[27] *Ibid.*, 20
[28] For an insightful discussion of the relation between Christianity and modernity in Grant's thought, see Bernard Zylstra, "Philosophy, Revelation and Modernity: Crossroads in the Thought of George Grant," *George Grant in Process*, 148-56.
[29] "Conversation," *George Grant in Process*, 20.
[30] Kaufman, *An Essay on Theological Method*, x.
[31] *Ibid.*, 7.
[32] *Ibid.*, 3.
[33] *Ibid.*, 8.
[34] *Ibid.*
[35] *Ibid.*, 41.
[36] *Ibid.*, 54-55.
[37] See Rudolf Siebert, "Max Horkheimer: Theology and Positivism I," *The Ecumenist* (January-February, 1976): 22. See also A. James Reimer, "Theological Debate in Yugoslavia," *The Ecumenist* (September-October, 1977): 90.
[38] Seibert, 22
[39] Kaufman, *An Essay on Theological Method*, 49.
[40] Grant, *Philosophy in the Mass Age* (Toronto: Copp Clark, 1959), 81.
[41] Kaufman, *An Essay on Theological Method*, 48.
[42] *Ibid.*, 55
[43] *Ibid.*, 50
[44] *Ibid.*, 51-52
[45] *Ibid.*, 71-72
[46] *Ibid.*, 21
[47] *Ibid.*, 23
[48] *Ibid.*, 56
[49] *Ibid.*, 59-60
[50] *Ibid.*, 71
[51] For a survey of Grant's political development from an early liberalism to a profound conservatism, see my "George Grant: Liberal, Socialist, or Conservative?" in *George Grant in Process*, 49-57.
[52] Abraham Rotstein, *The Precarious Homestead* (Toronto: New Press, 1973), 242.
[53] Cf. Friedrich-Wilhelm Marquardt, "Socialism in the Theology of Karl Barth," *Karl Barth and Radical Politics*, ed. and trans. George Hunsinger (Philadelphia: Westminster Press, 1976), 47-76.
[54] Cf. Stephen Sykes, *Friedrich Schleiermacher* (London: Lutterworth Press, 1971), 45.
[55] Grant, "Conversation," *George Grant in Process*, 62-63.

Chapter 2

[1] According to Canadian philosopher George Grant, greatly influenced in his critique of modern thought by Heidegger and Nietzsche, "liberalism" and "technology" presuppose the essence of humanity as being the freedom to shape human and non-human nature in an unlimited way. Justice in the modern world has come to mean something that it did not mean in the Greek and the Biblical tradition. The affirmation of reality that accompanies technology signifies a new view of justice as human creativity, in which "some human beings have no due." See George Grant, "Conversations: Philosophy," in *George Grant in Process: Essays and Conversations*, ed. Larry Schmidt (Toronto: House of Anansi Press, 1978), 144-45.

There is a certain "oblivion of eternity" that characterizes modern technology, says Grant. "In the pre-technological era the central western account of justice clarified the claim that justice is what we are fitted for. It clarified why justice is to render each human being their due, and why what was due to all human beings was 'beyond all bargains and without an alternative.'" Cf. George Grant, *English-Speaking Justice* (Sackville: Mount Allison University, 1974), 93.

[2] Members of the neo-Marxist Frankfurt School of Social Research, particularly Theodor W. Adorno and Max Horkheimer, were especially interested in the question of "Negative Dialectics" and the "Dialectic of Enlightenment." Cf. Theodor W. Adorno, *Negative Dialectics* (New York: Seabury, 1974); idem and Max Horkheimer, *Dialectic of Enlightenment* (New York: Seabury, 1972). Cf. also Martin Jay, *The Dialectical Imagination: A History of the Frankfurt School and The Institute of Social Research 1923-1950* (Toronto: Little, Brown & Co., 1973), 156-57.

[3] Grant, "A Platitude," *Technology and Empire* (Toronto: House of Anansi, 1969), 137.

[4] David Tracy, *Blessed Rage For Order: The New Pluralism in Theology* (New York: Seabury, 1975), 32.

[5] *Ibid.*, 22

[6] *Ibid.*

[7] *Ibid.*, 24-25

[8] *Ibid.*, 25-27

[9] *Ibid.*, 27-31

[10] *Ibid.*, 31-32

[11] *Ibid.*, 32-34

[12] Gordon D. Kaufman, *An Essay on Theological Method* (Missoula: Scholars Press, 1975), 44.

[13] A. James Reimer, "Theological Method, Modernity, and the Role of Tradition" [1979] (Chapter 1 above).

[14] Grant, "Conversation: Theology and History," *George Grant in Process*, 105.

[15] Reimer, "Theological Method, Modernity, and the Role of Tradition" (Chapter 1 above), 24.

[16] Kaufman, *Relativism, Knowledge, and Faith* (Chicago: University of Chicago Press, 1960), ix.

[17] *Ibid.*

[18] *Ibid.*
[19] Cf. G. W. F. Hegel, *The Phenomenology of Mind*, trans. J .B. Baillie (New York: Harper & Row, 1962). According to Hegel, "[t]he truth is the whole. The whole, however, is merely the essential nature reaching its completeness through the process of its own development. Of the Absolute it must be said that it is essentially a result, that only at the end is it what it is in very truth, and just in that consists its nature, which is to be actual, subject, or self-becoming, self-development" (82).
[20] Kaufman, *Relativism, Knowledge, and Faith*, 44.
[21] *Ibid.*, 81-82
[22] *Ibid.*, 82
[23] *Ibid.*, 51
[24] *Ibid.*
[25] *Ibid.*, 65-66
[26] *Ibid.*, 66-67
[27] *Ibid.*, 71
[28] *Ibid.*, 73-74
[29] *Ibid.*, 77
[30] *Ibid.*, 82
[31] *Ibid.*, 86
[32] *Ibid.*, 96
[33] *Ibid.*, 114, 102
[34] *Ibid.*, 114
[35] *Ibid.*, 117
[36] *Ibid.*, 116
[37] *Ibid.*, 124
[38] *Ibid.*, 119
[39] *Ibid.*, 122
[40] *Ibid.*, 108, n 3
[41] See A. James Reimer, "Theological Method and Political Ethics: The Paul Tillich—Emanuel Hirsch Debate," *Journal of the American Academy of Religion* 47.1 Supplement (March 1979): 173.
[42] Gordon D. Kaufman, *Nonresistance and Responsibility and Other Mennonite Essays* (Newton, KS: Faith and Life Press, 1979), 7.
[43] *Ibid.*
[44] Kaufman, "Biblical Authority in a World of Power," *Nonresistance and Responsibility*, 31.
[45] Kaufman, "The Christian in Church and World," *Nonresistance and Responsibility*, 115, n 8
[46] Kaufman, "Preface," *Nonresistance and Responsibility*, 9.
[47] Kaufman, "What is our Unique Mission?" *Nonresistance and Responsibility*, 15-17.
[48] *Ibid.*, 18
[49] Kaufman, "Biblical Authority in a World of Power," *Nonresistance and Responsibility*, 22-23.
[50] *Ibid.*, 27

[51] *Ibid.*, 32
[52] *Ibid.*
[53] *Ibid.*, 29
[54] Kaufman, "Nonresistance and Responsibility," *Nonresistance and Responsibility*, 63.
[55] *Ibid.*, 64
[56] *Ibid.*, 65
[57] *Ibid.*, 66
[58] *Ibid.*, 68
[59] *Ibid.*
[60] *Ibid.*, 71
[61] *Ibid.*, 71-72
[62] *Ibid.*, 74
[63] *Ibid.*, 75
[64] *Ibid.*
[65] *Ibid.*, 78
[66] *Ibid.*
[67] *Ibid.*, 79
[68] *Ibid.*
[69] *Ibid.*, 78
[70] Kaufman, "Preface," *Nonresistance and Responsibility*, 9.

Chapter 3

[1] Originally published as: "Doctrinal Renewal: An Adequate Alternative to Theological Liberalism?" in *The Future of Anglican Theology*, ed. M. Darrol Bryant (Lewiston, NY / Toronto, ON: The Edwin Mellen Press, 1984), 73-86.

[2] Max Horkheimer and Theodor W. Adorno, *Dialectic of Enlightenment* (New York: Seabury, 1972), xiii; first published as *Dialektik der Aufklärung* in 1944.

[3] The Institute for Social Research was founded in 1927 by Max Horkheimer in Frankfurt am Main, Germany. It was closed in 1933 when the Nazis came to power, and moved to New York City where it continued its critical analysis of modern society as the New School for Social Research. Names associated with this school, sometimes referred to as Critical Theory, included Theodor Adorno, Walter Benjamin, Herbert Marcuse, and more recently, Jürgen Habermas.

[4] Horkheimer and Adorno, *Dialectic of Enlightenment*, 3.

[5] *Ibid.*, 9

[6] *Ibid.*, xv

[7] Stephen W. Sykes, *The Integrity of Anglicanism* (Oxford: A.R. Mowbray, 1978).

[8] George Grant, "Conversation," *George Grant in Process: Essays and Conversations*, ed. Larry Schmidt (Toronto: House of Anansi, 1978), 144; cf. also my own essay in *George Grant in Process*: "George Grant: Liberal, Socialist, or Conservative?," 49-57.

[9] David Tracy, *Blessed Rage For Order: The New Pluralism in Theology* (New York: Seabury, 1975), 25-26.

[10] *Ibid.*, 32-34
[11] Sykes, *Integrity*, 32
[12] *Ibid.*
[13] *Ibid.*, 51
[14] *Ibid.*, 29
[15] *Ibid.*, 29-30
[16] *Ibid.*, 34
[17] *Ibid.*, 35
[18] *Ibid.*, 8
[19] Tracy, *Blessed Rage for Order*, 92ff. See also Gordon Kaufman, *An Essay on Theological Method* (Missoula: Scholars Press, 1975), 47ff.
[20] Sykes, *Integrity*, 95
[21] *Ibid.*, 38
[22] *Ibid.*, 89-90
[23] *Ibid.*, 42-43
[24] *Ibid.*, 19
[25] *Ibid.*, 61
[26] *Ibid.*, 35
[27] *Ibid.*, 6
[28] *Ibid.*, 49
[29] *Ibid.*
[30] *Ibid.*, 50
[31] *Ibid.*, 59
[32] *Ibid.*, 68
[33] *Ibid.*, 72
[34] Paul Tillich, *Systematic Theology*, vol. 1 (Chicago: University of Chicago Press, 1951), 86.
[35] Sykes, *Integrity*, 88-89
[36] *Ibid.*, 99
[37] *Ibid.*
[38] *Ibid.*, 98
[39] *Ibid.*, 98
[40] Tillich, *Systematic Theology* 1, 86

Chapter 4

[1] Originally published as "How Modern Should Theology Be? The Nature and Agenda of Contemporary Theology" in *The Church as Theological Community: Essays in Honour of David Schroeder*, ed. Harry Huebner (Winnipeg: CMBC Publications, 1990), 171-98.

[2] Stephen Spender, *The Struggle of the Modern* (Berkeley: University of California Press, 1965), 78.

[3] For an examination of Grant's understanding of the modern, especially in relation to Nietzsche and Heidegger, see Chapter 5 below.

⁴ George Grant, *Technology and Empire* (Toronto: House of Anansi, 1969), 114, n 3.
⁵ Cf. Grant, *Time as History* (Toronto: Canadian Broadcasting Corporation, 1974).
⁶ We should also note other important thinkers in this development, such as a view of modern science as represented by the inductive-empirical method of observing nature put forward by Francis Bacon (1561-1626), the turn to the rational human subject as the only ground for certainty as espoused by the philosopher René Descartes (1596-1650), the protest against all heteronomy (external authority) in favour of autonomous reason most forcefully present in the thought of Immanuel Kant (1724-1804), and modern views of historical and evolutionary time beginning with G.W.F. Hegel (1770-1831). Together these figures, among others, and the influential intellectual currents they represent, including their social, economic, political and religious consequences, mark off the seventeenth and eighteenth centuries (often referred to as the Enlightenment) as a crucial turning point in western history and as the birth of the modern world.
⁷ Cf. Claude Welch, *Protestant Thought in the Nineteenth Century*, vol. 2: 1870-1914 (New Haven: Yale University Press, 1985), 277.
⁸ For an overview of the nature of scientific paradigms as applied to theology, and the various paradigm shifts in theology throughout history, including the most recent one, see Hans Küng, "Paradigm Change in the History of Theology and the Church: An Attempt at Periodization," *The Conrad Grebel Review* 3 (Winter 1985): 19-20. Küng, basically following Thomas S. Kuhn's view of paradigm and paradigm shifts in the natural sciences, defines paradigm and paradigm shifts as the "values, techniques, and so on shared by the members of a given community" (*ibid.*, 20). He identifies six basic paradigms in the history of Christian theology: primitive Christian apocalyptic, early Christian Hellenistic, medieval Roman Catholic, Protestant Reformation, modern enlightenment, and contemporary. What characterizes the contemporary post-enlightenment paradigm is its diversity (its profusion of theologies and paradigms).
⁹ Hans Jonas, "Wissenschaft als persönliches Erlebnis," *Wissenschaft als persönliches Erlebnis* (Göttingen: Vandenhoeck & Ruprecht, 1987).
¹⁰ *Ibid.*, 19ff.
¹¹ *Ibid.*, 28. See also Jonas, *The Imperative of Responsibility: In Search of an Ethics for the Technological Age* (Chicago: University of Chicago Press, 1984), where he says:

> My main fear rather relates to the apocalypse threatening from the nature of the unintended dynamics of technical civilization as such, inherent in its structure, whereto it drifts willy-nilly and with exponential acceleration: the apocalypse of the 'too much,' with exhaustion, pollution, desolation of the planet. Here the credible extrapolations are frightening and the calculable time spans shrink at a frenzied pace. Here averting the disaster asks for a revocation of the whole lifestyle, even of the very principle of the advanced industrial societies, and will hurt an endless number of interests (the habit interests of all!). It thus will be much more difficult than the prevention of nuclear destruction, which after all is possible

without decisive interference with the general conditions of our technological existence (202).

[12] Jonas, "Technik, Freiheit und Pflicht," *Wissenschaft als persönliches Erlebnis*, 32-46.

[13] *Ibid.*, 40

[14] *Ibid.*

[15] Jonas, "Im Kampf um die Möglichkeit des Glaubens," *Wissenschaft als persönliches Erlebnis*, 47-75.

[16] *Ibid.*, 54

[17] *Ibid.*, 60-61

[18] *Ibid.*, 64

[19] *Ibid.*, 63-64

[20] Subsequent page references to this book appear in the text.

[21] Carl Mitcham and Jim Grote, eds., *Theology and Technology: Essays in Christian Analysis and Exegesis* (New York: University Press of America, 1984).

[22] Joan E. O'Donovan, *George Grant and the Twilight of Justice* (Toronto: University of Toronto Press, 1984), 159.

[23] *Ibid.*, 169-70

[24] See Walter Klaassen, ed., *Anabaptism in Outline* (Scottdale: Herald Press, 1981), 41-70, especially 50. There is in some early Anabaptists the basis for developing a natural theology; related to the concept of the "gospel of Christ" and "the whole of the Scriptures" being already manifest in creation and in the work and suffering of creatures. According to Klaassen,

> the idea is basically that knowledge of God comes to man first through the created world which prepares the way for the gospel of Christ. But it is also more than that; the suffering of Christ was seen to be already inherent in the processes of nature which require suffering and death that there may be life. Again, it is the idea of 'the Lamb slain from the foundation of the world' (42).

[25] Gregory Baum, *Theology and Society* (Mahwah, NJ: Paulist Press, 1987). The page numbers that appear within the body of the text in the following section of the paper refer to this book. See also Baum's CBC Massey Lectures published as *Compassion and Solidarity: The Church for Others* (Montreal: Canadian Broadcasting Corporation Enterprises, 1987).

[26] Rudolf J. Siebert, *The Critical Theory of Religion: The Frankfurt School* (New York: Mouton Publishers, 1985). For a review of this book see my "Hegel's Contemporary Relevance," *The Ecumenist* 26 (July-August 1988): 75-78.

[27] A Mennonite example of this preoccupation with diversity and identity is the recent book edited by Calvin Wall Redekop and Samuel J. Steiner, *Mennonite Identity: Historical and Contemporary Perspectives* (Lanham, MD: University Press of America, 1988).

[28] George Lindbeck, *The Nature of Doctrine: Religion and Theology in a Postliberal Age* (Philadelphia: Westminster Press, 1984), 74.

[29] William A. Christian, Sr., *Doctrines of Religious Communities: A Philosophical Study* (New Haven: Yale University Press, 1987), 1-2.

³⁰ Lindbeck, *The Nature of Doctrine*, 47-48.

³¹ See, for example, my "Mennonite Theological Self-Understanding and the Challenge of the Third Millennium" and "Toward Christian Theology from a Diversity of Mennonite Perspectives" (Chapter 14 below).

³² Don S. Browning, in his brilliant book, *Religious Thought and the Modern Psychologies: A Critical Conversation in the Theology of Culture* (Philadelphia, PA: Fortress Press, 1987), convincingly shows how all the modern psychologies, whether they like to admit this or not, have theories of moral obligation that grow out of certain "deep metaphors" or "metaphors of ultimacy," behind which lie distinctive ontological, metaphysical, or cosmological worldviews. I view Christian doctrines similarly as deep metaphors of ultimacy; they are more than rules in a particular language game. Cf. my essay, "Confessions, Doctrines, and Creeds: Symbols and Metaphors of Ultimacy" (Chapter 21 below).

³³ "Mennonites: Theology, Peace, and Identity: J. Denny Weaver responds to A. James Reimer and Thomas Finger," *The Conrad Grebel Review* 7.1 (Winter 1989): 73.

³⁴Cf. A. James Reimer, "God as Triune" (Chapter 23 below).

Chapter 5

¹ See *The Chesterton Review: George Grant Special Issue* XI, 2 (May 1985):183-98; republished in Wayne Whillier, ed., *Two Theological Languages by George Grant and other Essays in Honor of his Work* (Lewiston, NY: The Edwin Mellen Press, 1990), 105-20.

² My letter of June 21, 1991 reads as follows:

> To the New Democratic Party of Ontario: I am a long-time supporter of the New Democratic Party, and have been a contributing member for many years. I was delighted when Bob Rae and his NDP colleagues were elected to head the government of Ontario. There are many NDP policies with which I heartily agree, and some I have felt uncomfortable with [I was thinking here of the NDP alliance with big unions to the neglect of small farmers and small business]. But there is one policy I simply cannot support. The NDP stance on abortion has disturbed me for a long time. I believe that public money should not be used to fund abortions, either in hospitals or clinics. Your recent decision to fund abortions forces me to withdraw my membership from your party. I cannot in good conscience belong to a party that believes abortion is a "right" and that abortions should be supported with public money. It is my profound conviction that abortion, although understandable in some situations, is always a tragic option and has serious consequences for the woman who chooses it. I believe that a society that promotes abortion as an acceptable option — as a "right" — is in danger of eroding the value of each human life and is not fulfilling its responsibility to care for its weakest members. In my opinion, the NDP policy on abortion is contrary to its policy of caring equally

for all members of society. Because of my convictions, I am withdrawing my membership in the New Democratic Party and immediately terminating my monthly contribution. I hope you will reconsider your policy on abortion. I wish you well as [you] seek to bring responsible government to this province.

[3] George Grant, "Conversation: Philosophy" in *George Grant in Process: Essays and Conversations*, ed. Larry Schmidt (Toronto: House of Anansi, 1978), 143. Cf. also Grant, *Time As History* (Toronto: Canadian Broadcasting Corporation, 1969), 48, 51-52.

[4] Grant, "A Platitude" in *Technology and Empire* (Toronto: House of Anansi, 1969), 137. Cf. also Grant, *Time as History*, 45.

[5] In some literary circles, for instance, the word "modern" denotes the very opposite to what Grant means when he uses the term. For the literary critic Stephen Spender, the "modern" figure (writers such as Joyce, Lawrence, Eliot, and Woolf) is someone who "is acutely conscious of the contemporary scene, but . . . does not accept its values." According to Spender, it is the modern to whom "it seems that the world of unprecedented phenomena has today cut us off from the life of the past, and in doing so from traditional consciousness." Stephen Spender, *The Struggle of the Modern* (Berkeley: University of California Press, 1965), 78.

[6] Grant, *Technology and Empire*, 114, n 3. The best account that Grant gives of the relationship between modern technology and liberalism is found in the first chapter of his *English-Speaking Justice* (Sackville: Mount Allison University Press, 1974), 1-13.

[7] Grant, "Conversation: Intellectual Background" in *George Grant in Process*, 67.

[8] Cf. Laurence Lampert, "The Uses of Philosophy in George Grant" in *George Grant in Process*, 186, 218, n 22.

[9] Grant, "Conversation: Intellectual Background," 66.

[10] *Ibid.*

[11] Grant, "Conversation: Philosophy," 142.

[12] *Ibid.*

[13] *Ibid.*

[14] *Ibid.*, 144. See also *English-Speaking Justice*, 24-34.

[15] Grant's best treatment of the concept of justice, both old and new, is found in his *English-Speaking Justice*. Note particularly p. 47. See also Grant, "Conversation: Philosophy" in *George Grant in Process*, 144-45.

[16] Grant, "Conversation: Philosophy," 145.

[17] *Ibid.*

[18] A. James Reimer, "George Grant: Liberal, Socialist or Conservative?" in *George Grant in Process*, 51. Grant's respect for the English legal system and its concern for individual rights is evident throughout his lectures published in *English-Speaking Justice*. The problem is that these rights are wrongly based on contract and fairness rather than on eternal dues and the nature of things. Cf. especially p. 47.

[19] Grant, "Conversation: Intellectual Background," 67.

20 *Ibid.*

21 Grant, *Technology and Empire*, 129-30, n 6. Grant's main criticism of Ellul, from whom he has learned a great deal, concerns his "positivist Christianity"—namely, his failure to address the question "to what extent is modern technological society connected to, and a product of, the western interpretation of Christianity?" For Grant, modernity and western Christianity are somehow intimately linked. Both have an inadequate view of reason and the philosophical tradition of the Greeks. Cf. also Grant, "Conversation: Philosophy," 146-47.

22 While it is true that Heidegger considers the preoccupation of the western philosophical tradition since Plato and Aristotle with Being separate from beings as a kind of decline, still, his great respect for the early Greek tradition is evident throughout. This is particularly obvious in his characteristic return to the original Greek language for the meaning of terms and for its sensitivity to the immediate experience of beingness. For an excellent treatment of this move, see George Steiner, *Heidegger* (New York: Viking, 1978), especially 15, 32-33. Also, Heidegger's continuing indebtedness to the medieval scholastic tradition is often overlooked. Cf. John D. Caputo, *Heidegger and Aquinas: An Essay on Overcoming Metaphysics* (New York: Fordham University Press, 1982).

23 Lampert, "The Uses of Philosophy in George Grant" in *George Grant in Process*, 186.

24 *Ibid.*

25 *Ibid.*, 187

26 Grant, "'The Computer Does not Impose on us the Ways it Should be Used'" in *Beyond Industrial Growth*, ed. Abraham Rotstein (Toronto: University of Toronto Press, 1976), 130.

27 Grant, *Time As History*, 22.

28 *Ibid.*, 26-27

29 *Ibid.*, 29

30 *Ibid.*, 30

31 *Ibid.*

32 *Ibid.*, 35-37

33 *Ibid.*, 45

34 *Ibid.*, 46

35 *Ibid.*, 47

36 *Ibid.*

37 *Ibid.*, 48

38 Grant, *Lament for a Nation: The Defeat of Canadian Nationalism* (Toronto: McClelland and Stewart, 1970), 2-3.

39 Grant, *Technology and Empire*, 139.

40 Grant, "Introduction," *Lament for a Nation*, x; "'The Computer Does not Impose on us the Ways it Should be Used,'" *Beyond Industrial Growth*, 30.

41 Grant, *Time as History*, 49-52.

42 See particularly Martin Heidegger, "The Question Concerning Technology" in *The Question Concerning Technology and Other Essays*, trans. William Lovitt (New York: Harper & Row, 1977), 34-35.

⁴³ Heidegger, "The Word of Nietzsche: 'God Is Dead'" in *The Question Concerning Technology and Other Essays*, 53-54.
⁴⁴ *Ibid.*, 111
⁴⁵ *Ibid.*, 108
⁴⁶ *Ibid.*, 55
⁴⁷ Heidegger, "The Turning" in *The Question Concerning Technology and Other Essays*, 41. Cf. also "Science and Reflection" in the same volume.
⁴⁸ Heidegger, "The Word of Nietzsche: 'God Is Dead'," 102-5.
⁴⁹ *Ibid.*, 108
⁵⁰ *Ibid.*, 100
⁵¹ Heidegger, "The Question Concerning Technology," 27.
⁵² *Ibid.*, 33
⁵³ Heidegger, "The Turning," 38-9, 42.
⁵⁴ Heidegger, *The End of Philosophy*, trans. Joan Stambaugh (New York: Harper & Row, 1973), 82.
⁵⁵ *Ibid.*, 83
⁵⁶ *Ibid.*
⁵⁷ Heidegger, "Nur noch ein Gott kann uns retten," *Der Spiegel* 23.30 (May 31, 1976): 193-219, 204. The interview took place in 1966 and was published posthumously. Cf. also *George Grant in Process*, 141-42.
⁵⁸ Grant, "Conversation: Intellectual Background," 66.
⁵⁹ Heidegger, "Nur noch ein Gott kann uns retten," 214.
⁶⁰ *Ibid.*, 209
⁶¹ *Ibid.*
⁶² Cf., e.g., Grant, "Conversation: Theology and History," 21, 103-7.
⁶³ Heidegger, "The Question Concerning Technology," 31.
⁶⁴ Grant, "Conversation: Theology and History," 21, 103-4.

Chapter 6

¹ First published as "Christian Theology and the University: Methodological Issues Reconsidered," *The Conrad Grebel Review* 9.3 (Fall 1991): 223-41.
² Ron Neufeldt, "Religious Pluralism and Christian Understanding: Toward a Theological Understanding of Other Religions" (unpublished paper presented at the American Academy of Religion meeting in New Orleans, November, 1990).
³ For the following pages dealing with the medieval origin of universities, I am dependent on Charles Homer Haskins, *The Rise of Universities* (Ithaca/London: Cornell University Press, 1957), first published in 1923.
⁴ *Ibid.*, 8-9
⁵ *Ibid.*, 30
⁶ *Ibid.*, 51
⁷ *Ibid.*, 55-56
⁸ Immanuel Kant, "An Answer to the Question: What is Enlightenment?" (1784), *Perpetual Peace and other Essays on Politics, History, and Morals*, trans. Ted Humphrey (Indianapolis: Hackett Publishing Company), 41-48.

⁹ *Ibid.*, 41
¹⁰ Immanuel Kant, *Critique of Pure Reason*, trans. Norman Kemp Smith (Toronto: MacMillan Publishers, 1985), Bxxx, 29.
¹¹ Allan Bloom, *The Closing of the American Mind* (New York: Simon & Schuster, 1987), 337.
¹² *Ibid.*, 339
¹³ *Ibid.*, 372
¹⁴ *Ibid.*, 374-75
¹⁵ *Ibid.*, 381
¹⁶ George Grant, "Faith and the Multiversity," *Technology & Justice* (Toronto: House of Anansi, 1986), 35-70.
¹⁷ *Ibid.*, 36
¹⁸ *Ibid.*
¹⁹ *Ibid.*, 42
²⁰ The American Academy of Religion Task Force for the American Association of Colleges, *The Religion Major: A Report*, ed. Stephen D. Crites (American Academy of Religion, 1990).
²¹ *Ibid.*, 3
²² *Ibid.*, 4-5
²³ *Ibid.*, 10
²⁴ Hans-Georg Gadamer, *Truth and Method* (New York: Seabury, 1975), 246.
²⁵ "Liberal Learning and the Religion Major," *The Religion Major: A Report*, 12.
²⁶ *Ibid.*, 15
²⁷ *Ibid.*, 15-6
²⁸ *Ibid.*, 17
²⁹ *Ibid.*
³⁰ M. Darrol Bryant, "Religion in a New Key: Notes Towards the Symphony of Living Faith" (unpublished paper used with permission).
³¹ *Ibid.*, 2
³² Alasdair MacIntyre, *Three Rival Versions of Moral Enquiry: Encyclopedia, Genealogy, and Tradition* (Notre Dame: University of Notre Dame Press, 1990), 221.
³³ Rodney Sawatsky, "In Defence of Proselytizing: A Contribution Towards Interfaith Dialogue," *Interfaith Dialogue: Four Approaches*, ed. John W. Miller (Waterloo: University of Waterloo Press, 1986).
³⁴ Charles Davis, "The Reconvergence of Theology and Religious Studies," *Studies in Religion*, 4.3 (1974/5): 205-21.
³⁵ *Ibid.*, 207
³⁶ *Ibid.*, 211
³⁷ *Ibid.*, 219
³⁸ Gregory Baum, "Response," *Studies in Religion* 4.3 (1974/5): 222, 224.
³⁹ William O. Fennell, "Response," *Studies in Religion* 4.3 (1974/5): 231.
⁴⁰ Donald Wiebe, "The Failure of Nerve in the Academic Study of Religion," *Studies in Religion* 13.4 (Fall 1984): 401-22.
⁴¹ *Ibid.*, 407
⁴² *Ibid.*, 409

43 *Ibid.*, 412
44 *Ibid.*, 420
45 *Ibid.*
46 Charles Davis, "'Wherein There is no Ecstasy,'" *Studies in Religion* 13.4 (Fall 1984): 395.
47 *Studies in Religion* 15.2 (Spring 1986).
48 John W. Dixon, Jr., "What Should Religion Departments Teach?," *Theology Today* 46 (1990): 364.
49 Bernard Lonergan, *Method in Theology* (New York: Herder and Herder, 1972), 5.
50 *Ibid.*, 136-37. A converted person, according to Lonergan, in effect becomes a better scholar for she transcends her own ideological self-interest and truly becomes open to the available data.
51 Justin J. Meggitt, "Fragmentalism as Authentic Theological Method" (unpublished paper, University of Waterloo, 1990), 17.
52 For a detailed discussion of this period of Christian thought see Jaroslav Pelikan, *The Christian Tradition*, vol. 1, *The Emergence of the Catholic Tradition (100-600)* (Chicago: University of Chicago Press, 1970). In the following paragraphs I am indebted to Pelikan's account of the apologists.
53 John C. Meagher, *The Truing of Christianity: Visions of Life and Thought for the Future* (New York: Doubleday, 1990), 221.
54 *Ibid.*
55 A. James Reimer, "Trinitarian Orthodoxy, Constantinianism, and Theology from a Radical Protestant Perspective" (Chapter 15 below).
56 See especially John Howard Yoder, "The Constantinian Sources of Western Social Ethics," *The Priestly Kingdom: Social Ethics as Gospel* (Notre Dame: University of Notre Dame Press, 1984), 135-47.

Chapter 7

1 "On Bringing Forth 'the New Individual' at the University: A Call to the Church Colleges," *University of Waterloo Gazette* (June 3, 1998): 2.
2 For helpful background to these two different approaches to learning see Hugh T. Kerr, ed., *Readings in Christian Thought* (Nashville: Abingdon Press, 1990, second edition), 80ff; and William C. Placher, *A History of Christian Theology: An Introduction* (Philadelphia: The Westminster Press, 1983), 140-61. The classic multi-volume history of the medieval universities is Hastings Rashdall, *The Universities of Europe in the Middle Ages*, 3 vols., rev. and ed. F. M. Powicke and A. B. Emden (Oxford: Oxford University Press, 1997).
3 For an informative discussion of the beginnings of the University of Berlin and its concept of the academy, see Hans Frei, *Five Types of Christian Theology* (New Haven: Yale University Press, 1992): 95-132.
4 For two helpful articles dealing with teaching of religion in the universities and the need to bridge the distance between the disciplines and foster a sense of a community of scholarship in the academy, see Paula P. Brownlee, "'I was a Stranger and You Welcomed Me': Bridging between Language," *Christianity and Culture in*

the Crossfire, ed. David A. Hoekema and Bobby Fong (Grand Rapids: Eerdmans, 1997): 171-79; and Andrew A. Sorensen, "The Role of Religion in a Public University," a paper presented to David Epstein's class in October 20, 1999.

Chapter 8

[1] Nancey Murphy, *Reconciling Theology and Science: A Radical Reformation Perspective* (Kitchener: Pandora Press; Scottdale: Herald Press, 1997).

Chapter 9

[1] Originally published in Alain Epp Weaver, ed., *Mennonite Theology in Face of Modernity: Essays in Honor of Gordon Kaufman* (North Newton, KS: Bethel College, 1996), 227-43.

[2] See my "Towards a Theocentric Christology: Christ for the World" Chapter 16 below. In this essay I discuss Burkholder's theology in relation to John H. Yoder on the one side and to Gordon Kaufman on the other.

[3] See Kaufman, "Preface," *Systematic Theology: A Historicist Perspective* (New York: Charles Scribner's Sons, 1978), xivff. Kaufman considers his *An Essay on Theological Method* (Missoula: Scholars Press, 1975) to be a transition to his new understanding of theology as construction.

[4] Kaufman's rejection of the classical Platonic notion of an eternal, unchanging order, within which time and history is to be understood, is at the basis of his doctoral dissertation published as *Relativism, Knowledge, and Faith* (Chicago: University of Chicago Press, 1960).

[5] Some of George Grant's most important works are: *Philosophy in the Mass Age* (Toronto: Copp Clark, 1959); *Lament for a Nation: The Defeat of Canadian Nationalism* (Toronto: McClelland and Stewart, 1965); *Time as History* (Toronto: Canadian Broadcasting Corporation, 1969); *Technology and Empire* (Toronto: House of Anansi, 1969); *English-Speaking Justice* (Sackville: Mount Allison University Press, 1977).

[6] These include: "Theological Method, Modernity and the Role of Tradition" (1978), "The Ethical Implications of Gordon Kaufman's Theology" (1980), and "The Nature and Possibility of a Mennonite Theology" (1983), all reprinted in this volume. In the latter essay I place Kaufman at the end of a Mennonite theological continuum beginning with Harold S. Bender and continuing through Robert Friedman and John H. Yoder. I argue that Kaufman is the logical conclusion of a theological tradition in which ethics tends to take precedence over everything else.

[7] Grant's critique of modern science and technology appear to me to be too strong. There is a "mystical" dimension to much modern scientific work which is not adequately accounted for by Grant's criticism of modern science as pure *techne*. Also, the Christian tradition calls us to look more hopefully at the world (even the modern world) as God's creation—and, therefore, open in every historical era to God's redemptive purposes—than is present in Grant's Christian philosophy.

⁸ Gordon D. Kaufman, *In Face of Mystery: A Constructive Theology* (Cambridge, MA: Harvard University Press, 1993). Hereafter, references to this work will be indicated in the body of the text as *Mystery*.

⁹ See Hans Frei, *Five Types of Christian Theology* (New Haven: Yale University Press, 1992). There are times when Kaufman does idealize the academy in a way that might justify Frei's interpretation. For example, Kaufman says: "It may be that the only institutional context available in modern society for such open and unfettered theological conversation is to be found in our great liberal university" (*Mystery*, 67).

¹⁰ Stephen Hawking, *A Brief History of Time: From the Big Bang to Black Holes* (London: Bantam Books, 1990), 143-53.

¹¹ Hans Jonas, *The Imperative of Responsibility: In Search of an Ethics for the Technological Age* (Chicago: University of Chicago Press, 1984), 125. Hereafter, references to this work are given as "Jonas" in the body of the text.

¹² Hawking, *A Brief History of Time*, 122-23.

Chapter 10

¹ Originally published in *The Conrad Grebel Review* 1.1 (Winter 1983): 33-55; Howard John Loewen responded to this article in the subsequent issue (*CGR* 1.2 (Spring 1983): 56-58, and my rebuttal appeared in *CGR* 1.3 (Fall 1983): 51-4.

² Cf. C. Arnold Snyder, "The (Not-So) 'Simple Confession' of the Later Swiss Brethren. Part I: Manuscripts and Marpeckites in an Age of Print," *The Mennonite Quarterly Review* 73. 4 (October 1999): 677-722; "The (Not-So) 'Simple Confession' of the Late Sixteenth-Century Anabaptists. Part II: The Evolution of Separatist Anabaptism," *The Mennonite Quarterly Review* 74.1 (January 2000): 87-122. In this paper Snyder discusses the Swiss Brethren response to the Frankenthal Disputation in 1571, and shows how, under the influence of the Marpeck Circle, second generation Anabaptist-Mennonites related their ethical concerns to the doctrine of the Trinity in rather sophisticated ways.

³ Historicism is the modern view that humans are captive to and essentially defined by their history. It rejects the belief that humans have access to some form of eternal unchanging truth, either in more traditional orthodox perceptions of God's authoritative revelation of himself or in Greek-Platonic notions of eternal forms, or in later concepts of the eternal laws of nature. In the words of George Grant, "Historicism was the belief that the values of any culture were relative to the absolute presuppositions of that culture which were themselves historically determined, and that therefore men could not in their reasoning transcend their own epoch" ("The University Curriculum," *Technology and Empire* [Toronto: House of Anansi, 1969], 123). The problem thus becomes in the post-Enlightenment west the problem of epistemology. How is it possible to know? If human knowledge is radically historical, how can one speak of truth and knowledge at all, how can one speak of universal norms by which the relativities of human history can be judged? In his important book *Relativism, Knowledge,*

and Faith (Chicago: University of Chicago Press, 1960), Gordon Kaufman attempts to show how it is possible to speak about faith, truth, knowledge, and normativity while espousing the thoroughgoing historicity of human beings. In *Time as History* (Toronto: Canadian Broadcasting Corporation, 1969), Grant also examines "what it means to conceive the world as an historical process, to conceive time as history and man as an historical being" (7). Unlike Kaufman, Grant sees modern historicism as an inadequate understanding of truth and goodness.

4 The modern person assumes that he or she is essentially and radically free. George Grant claims that (1) the reality of technology more than anything else defines the modern age and that (2) this technological spirit is fundamentally rooted in the almost unanimously accepted liberal assumption that "man's essence is his freedom." At the heart of the modern western view of self and the world is a historicism which assumes that humans are on their own and have an unlimited capacity, potential, and freedom to shape and control nature, history, and themselves. See Grant, "The University Curriculum" in *Technology and Empire*, esp. 114, n 3. My own views owe a great deal to the thought of Grant. The problem with this second assumption—humanity's radical freedom—is that of "limit." Is there not in fact some external sphere beyond or external to nature (human and non-human) which puts absolute limits on human activity and experimentation, and holds humans accountable for their actions? Interestingly, recent "revolts of nature" against human arrogance in dominating the environment suggest by way of analogy that humankind is not as free as the Enlightenment envisioned—that the human person is seriously limited in what he or she may or may not do.

5 Max Horkheimer and Theodor W. Adorno, founding members of the Frankfurt School of Critical Theory, have precisely this kind of ambiguous relation to the Enlightenment and modern liberalism. On the one hand, they are deeply committed to the fundamental assumptions and aims of the Enlightenment tradition, particularly in their use of critical reason to examine and unmask contradictions in Western society and to work toward a more just and humane social order. On the other hand, they are profoundly aware of the most inevitable tendency of the Enlightenment to destroy itself by converting into "positivism"— the reduction of all metaphysics into objectivity, transcendence into immanence, spirit into matter and subjectivity into objectivity. See *Dialectic of Enlightenment* (New York: Seabury, 1972), xiii. In his recent book *Theology and Political Society* (New York: Cambridge University Press, 1980), Canadian theologian Charles Davis, while keenly aware of the ambiguities of the Enlightenment tradition, and particularly critical of its modern children, positivism and scientism, believes that Christian theology must carry on the Enlightenment program of human emancipation, preserving all the while a strong sense of religious tradition, mystery, and transcendence. It is the religious dimension in politics, he believes, which prevents it from deteriorating into positivism and administration. Although I agree with much of what Davis says, in the end he is too ready to evaluate spirituality primarily in terms of its political and social efficacy.

6 While I am quite willing to admit to the "constructive" role of the theologian in formulating and interpreting theological concepts—there has always been

this constructive element in theology—I am unwilling to make as radical a break with traditional forms of theologizing on the basis of a thoroughgoing historicism as is Gordon Kaufman in his *An Essay on Theological Method* (Missoula: Scholars Press, 1975). In a sense my own theological movement is precisely the reverse of Kaufman's. Kaufman continues to become increasingly more disillusioned with traditional concepts of God and his authoritative revelation and seems to be moving in the direction of an increasingly more radical historicism, arising largely out of his epistemological concerns. See especially Kaufman's "Preface" to *Systematic Theology: A Historicist Perspective* (New York: Charles Scribner's Sons, 1978), xivff. I find myself becoming increasingly more disillusioned with the modern Enlightenment agenda, historicism, and the post-Enlightenment obsession with epistemology, and moving in the direction of a re-examination of the power of traditional theological models. It appears to me that they have a more profound understanding of reality, human nature, and moral accountability than do modern historicist options.

[7] Harold S. Bender, *The Anabaptist Vision* (Scottdale: Herald Press, 1944): 4. "The Anabaptist Vision" was first given as an address before the American Society of Church History in 1943, a society of which Bender was the president at the time.

[8] It has sometimes been argued, correctly, I think, that the Believers' Church tradition of the eighteenth and nineteenth centuries (German Pietism, British Methodism, and American Revivalism), in its suspicion of Protestant scholastic and creedal orthodoxy, was in fact part of the spirit of the Enlightenment and, as such, had much in common with rationalism and its protest against traditional authoritarian institutions and theological ideas in favour of individual autonomy. It is interesting, in the light of this, that Donald F. Durnbaugh places the origin of the Believers Church tradition with the early Swiss Anabaptist movement. See *The Believers' Church: The History and Character of Radical Protestantism* (London: Collier-Macmillan, 1968), 18ff.

[9] Bender, *The Anabaptist Vision*, 20.

[10] *Ibid.*, 35

[11] *Ibid.*, 35-6

[12] Robert Friedmann, *The Theology of Anabaptism* (Scottdale: Herald Press, 1973).

[13] The use of the term "existential" is problematic, because it has come to mean in modern thought precisely that which Friedmann wants to exclude in his interpretation of Anabaptism: namely, a non-historical, highly personal, individual, lonely, subjective, and inward experience of reality and the courageous affirmation of faith in the context of and despite inner doubt, meaninglessness, fear, anxiety, and despair.

[14] Friedmann, *The Theology of Anabaptism*, 21.

[15] *Ibid.*, 22

[16] *Ibid.*, 25

[17] *Ibid.*, 27

[18] *Ibid.*, 29

[19] *Ibid.*, 31

[20] *Ibid.*, 45

[21] *Ibid.*, 117

[22] David Tracy discusses this distinction between a "mystical-priestly-metaphysical-aesthetic" emphasis and the "prophetic-ethical-historical" emphasis and says: "That any religion is really *only* mystical-metaphysical or *only* ethical-political seems an illusion produced by some partial vision of the complexity of the whole." See *The Analogical Imagination* (New York: Crossroad, 1981), 204. My own contention is that Yoder does not adequately allow for the "mystical-priestly-metaphysical-aesthetic" dimension essential to the Christian religious experience. This is not to say that he dismisses it completely.

[23] John H. Yoder, *The Politics of Jesus: Vicit Agnus Noster*, revised ed. (Grand Rapids: Eerdmans, 1993).

[24] *Ibid.*, 5

[25] I see the recent move from orthodoxy to orthopraxis in political and liberation theologies—a move which incidentally has much in common with the Anabaptist refusal to separate theory and practice—as theologically sound only if it does not represent a collapsing of metaphysics into historicism. It is true that theory and doctrine must not be separated from ethics as it so often has been in the past. Nevertheless, I maintain that theory always in some sense is prior to and even separate from practice. Theology must remain prior to politics even though all theology is political in a certain "relative" sense. The new doctrine of orthopraxis can be sound only if it is based on affirmation not only of the second person of the Trinity (God as historical Christ), nor only of the third person of the Trinity (God as immanent Holy Spirit), but also on an affirmation of the first person (God as absolutely transcendent creator, beyond time and space); otherwise, God once more becomes a puppet of social-political-ethical programs either inside or outside the church.

[26] Yoder, *The Politics of Jesus*, 11.

[27] *Ibid.*, 39

[28] *Ibid.*, 43

[29] *Ibid.*, 46

[30] *Ibid.*, 47

[31] *Ibid.*, 130-1

[32] *Ibid.*, 132

[33] *Ibid.*, 250

[34] John Howard Yoder, *Preface to Theology: Christology and Theological Method* (Elkhart, IN: Goshen Biblical Seminary, 1981).

[35] *Ibid.*, 286

[36] *Ibid.*, 32

[37] *Ibid.*, 42

[38] *Ibid.*, 226

[39] This is not to disparage Yoder's thought; it is simply to point out that Yoder too has been profoundly influenced by modern conceptions of history in his biblical interpretation, as we all have been. Further, the linking of the "Hebraic view of history" with modern historicist views—an association which seems to be almost unanimously accepted in theological circles—has some serious

problems. While it may be true that the Hebraic view of history was more eschatological and teleological than that of the Greek ontological and cyclical view, and in this sense has greatly influenced western conceptions of history up to the present, both classical views had this in common: they presupposed an absolutely transcendent spiritual reality (God), a presupposition which is lacking in the modern historicist view. In this sense, I would argue, Jerusalem and Athens had more in common with each other than either has with the modern world.

[40] Tracy describes five theological models: orthodox theology, liberal theology, neo-orthodox theology, radical theology and revisionist theology. Tracy places himself, Kaufman, Gregory Baum, Michael Novak, Langdon Gilkey, and Van Harvey into this fifth category, a theological approach which is aware of the disillusionment with some of the oppressive consequences of the Enlightenment but refuses to return to a form of mystification. Instead, the revisionist theologian "believes that only a radical continuation of critical theory, symbolic reinterpretation, and responsible social and personal *praxis*, can provide the hope for a fundamental revision of both the modern and the traditional Christian self-understanding." According to Tracy, "For the post-liberal theologian both secularity and traditional Christianity should be challenged in accordance with publicly available criteria for meaning, meaningfulness, and truth." See *Blessed Rage For Order: The New Pluralism in Theology* (New York: Seabury, 1975), 33-4. In my view, Kaufman is much less willing than Tracy to incorporate into his theology a radical critique of modern assumptions on the basis of more traditional theological categories. Tracy's rootedness in the Catholic tradition guards him against the severe doctrinal and theological iconoclasm that marks Kaufman's work.

[41] A reading of Kaufman's collection of essays written over a period of almost twenty years, published under the title *Nonresistance and Responsibility and Other Essays* (Newton, KS: Faith and Life Press, 1979) gives one important insight into Kaufman's theological engagement with his own Mennonite tradition. Particularly revealing is how Kaufman applies his theological method to social and political ethics.

[42] Kaufman, *Relativism, Knowledge, and Faith*, 65-66.

[43] There are certain fundamental human experiences—looked at purely phenomenologically—that cannot be defined in essentially historical terms. I would cite the birth of a child, the death of a loved one, the facing of one's own death, just to name a few, as examples of experiences which, while clearly taking place within history cannot in themselves be defined in terms of the movement of past to present to future, let alone in terms of ethics, but break into our temporality in a radically vertical, a-temporal or even non-temporal sense.

[44] Kaufman cannot be accused of an absolute relativism in metaphysics or ethics. His whole book *Relativism, Knowledge, and Faith* is an attempt to take seriously both the historical relativity of all human knowledge and the belief "that our knowledge somehow participates in that which transcends the relativities of our situation," a grounding of our norms of right and wrong, truth and falsity ("functional absolutes") in that which "is ultimately real, beyond all illusion" (Kaufman, *Relativism, Knowledge and Faith*, 86). Nevertheless, Kaufman's

historicism drives him to a relativization of ethical norms in concrete situations. The ultimate metaphysical reality which stands beyond or above history remains without concreteness and particularity. Thus the application of the Christian norm of "redemptive love" and "nonresistant love" in actual situations becomes highly relative and situational. Redemptive love which must by definition go into the heart of the sinful situation may demand that we *"support"* the military bill most in accord with the highest ideals and best moral insights of the total American society (Kaufman, "Nonresistance and Responsibility," *Nonresistance and Responsibility*, 71). Love must adapt itself to the needs of very new situation: "Love thus never becomes a rigid absolute, the ethical implications of which are clearly and absolutely defined for every situation" (75).

[45] This Kaufman tries to do in his carefully argued book, *An Essay On Theological Method*, in which he maintains that there are three essential moments in all theological construction. In my article "Theological Method, Modernity and the Role of Tradition," Chapter 1 above, I try to point out the strengths and weaknesses of Kaufman's theological method.

[46] Kaufman, *Systematic Theology: A Historicist Perspective* (New York: Charles Scribner's Sons, 1968).

[47] Ibid., 329, 332

[48] Ibid., 332

[49] Ibid., 346

[50] Ibid., 94ff.

[51] Ibid., 10-11

[52] For instance, in a "Theological Brief," included in *Christian Theology: A Case Study Approach*, R. A. Evans and T. D. Parker, eds. (New York: Harper & Row, 1976), Kaufman is highly critical of what he calls "the ideational development of Christianity" with its "tendency to regard the approved ideas and formulas as definitive and unchangeable dogmas. Faith becomes understood as a matter of assenting to or 'believing' certain verbal formulation or ideas about God and Christ, sin and redemption" (119). He suggests that Christ must be seen less ideationally and more existentially: "Ideas, concepts, verbal formulations—especially those about 'God' and 'Christ'—will be used by thoughtful Christians only insofar as they help to promote the upbuilding of human community and the realization of free personhood, for these are the actual incarnation of Christ in contemporary life" (120). Aside from the difficulty inherent in trying to separate ideas, concepts, and verbal formulations from the substance and content of the faith, the problem with substituting new "myths" for "old myths," existential Christianity or ideational Christianity is that we create the kind of Christianity for ourselves that accommodates our modern culture rather than perceiving the revelatory content *and* expression of classical Christianity as standing in judgment of all human ideology throughout the ages.

[53] Chapter 1above.

[54] Kaufman, *An Essay on Theological Method*, 54-5.

[55] Kaufman, "The Christian in Church and World," *Nonresistance and Responsibility*, 115, n 8.

[56] Ibid., 9

[57] Kaufman, *Systematic Theology: A Historicist Perspective* xvii.
[58] Kaufman, "God and Humanity," *Nonresistance and Responsibility*, 35.
[59] Kaufman, *Systematic Theology: A Historicist Perspective*, 333.

Chapter 11

[1] "Anabaptist-Mennonite Systematic Theology," *The Ecumenist* 21.4 (May-June 1983), 21.5 (July-August 1983): 68-72.
[2] Thomas Finger, *Christian Theology: An Eschatological Perspective*, vols. 1 and 2 (Scottdale: Herald Press, 1989).
[3] John C. Wenger, *The Doctrines of the Mennonites* (Scottdale: Mennonite Publishing House, 1952), 1. In Wenger's view, "This lack of theological treatises is not without its significance; it indicates the fundamental fact that Anabaptism and Mennonitism are more biblical that theological" (1). In my view, this unqualified distinction between biblical fidelity and theological interest does not adequately account for the hermeneutical-theological nature of all biblical understanding.
[4] Harold S. Bender, *The Anabaptist Vision* (Scottdale: Herald Press, 1944), 12-13. Quite a different understanding of early Anabaptism is espoused by Mennonite church historian Walter Klaassen, who argues that Anabaptism is a third Reformation alternative: "Anabaptism was neither Protestant nor Catholic but in fact a movement of different dimensions. It is the conviction of this author that it represents some of the best of both traditions. This judgment is made in retrospect and in the light of current developments in church renewal. Anabaptists in the sixteenth century did not consciously choose the best of both; in fact they would have vigorously rejected any suggestion that they did so. They merely attempted to be faithful to Jesus according to their understanding" (Klaassen, *Anabaptism: Neither Catholic nor Protestant* (Waterloo: Conrad Press, 1973), 77).
[5] Chapter 10 above.
[6] Robert Friedmann, *The Theology of Anabaptism* (Scottdale, PA: Herald Press, 1973), 21.
[7] Gordon D. Kaufman, *Systematic Theology: A Historicist Perspective* (New York: Charles Scribner's Sons, 1968), 73.
[8] Ernst Troeltsch, *The Social Teaching of the Christian Churches and the Culture of Pluralism*, vol. 1, trans. Olive Wyon (New York: Harper & Row, 1960), 331.
[9] David Tracy, *The Analogical Imagination: Christian Theology and the Culture of Pluralism* (New York: Crossroad, 1981), 204.
[10] Stephen W. Sykes, *The Integrity of Anglicanism* (London A.R.: Mowbray, 1978), 68.

Chapter 12

¹ Later published in *Explorations of Systematic Theology: From Mennonite Perspectives*, Occasional Papers No. 7, ed. Willard Swartley (Elkhart: Institute of Mennonite Studies, 1984).
² Wolfhart Pannenberg, *Systematic Theology*, vols.1-3 (Grand Rapids: Eerdmans, 1991-1998).
³ Owen C. Thomas, *Introduction to Theology* (Cambridge, GB: Greeno, Hadden & Co., 1978), 1.
⁴ *Ibid.*, 4
⁵ *Ibid.*
⁶ Describing his own "conversion" to the sociological method, Roman Catholic theologian Gregory Baum states: "I found that the sociological tradition contains basic truth absent from philosophical and theological thought, truth that actually modifies the very meaning of philosophy and theology. I am thinking here especially of the relationship between mind and society. While sociologists may differ in their understanding of this relationship, all of them in one way or another acknowledge that society (the institutions in which we live) affects our consciousness (the way we perceive reality and think about it). Thought, in other words, is socially grounded" (Baum, *Religion and Alienation: A Theological Reading of Sociology* [Toronto: Paulist Press, 1975], 1).

Baum's emphasis on the social rootedness of all thought, and the indispensability of an awareness of the "sociology of knowledge" for all theological work, provides an important corrective to the rather one-sided alliance of theology and philosophy in Thomas. Nevertheless, there is in modern theology the reductionist tendency to bracket the question of truth and verifiability in favour of the social function and utility of religion—the breaking of all ties with philosophy in the classical sense in favour of a social-scientific orientation. While the sociological perspective reminds theology of the importance of the relativity and critique of all ideology, philosophy and literature remind theology of its claim to truth apart from any pragmatic or utilitarian value or function in maintaining the *status quo* or motivating social change.
⁷ David Tracy, *The Analogical Imagination: Christian Theology and the Culture of Pluralism* (New York: Crossroad, 1981), 405.
⁸ Gordon Kaufman, *Systematic Theology: A Historicist Perspective* (New York: Charles Scribner's Sons, 1968), 69.
⁹ *Ibid.*, 73.
¹⁰ Gordon Kaufman, "Nuclear Eschatology and the Study of Religion," *Journal of the American Academy of Religion* 51:1 (March 1983): 3-14, 3.
¹¹ *Ibid.*, 13
¹² Kaufman, *Systematic Theology: A Historicist Perspective* (New York: Charles Scribner's Sons, 1968); while remaining in line with his earlier position, Kaufman is espousing an increasingly more radical historicism.
¹³ According to the classical view, the objective reality of God, and the objective reality of meaning and purpose at the heart of creation is not contingent upon the continuation of time as history nor dependent upon our perception of that reality.

[14] What separates Tracy and Kaufman, in spite of their theological similarities, is that the Roman Catholic theologian Tracy is much more deeply rooted in the classical theological and ecclesiastical tradition than is the Mennonite Kaufman. Like his mentor, Bernard Lonergan, Tracy is constantly engaged not so much in deconstructing but in bridging the gap between the classical and the modern world.

This "bridging" concern of Lonergan's is strikingly apparent in his *The Way to Nicea* (London: Darton, Longman & Todd, 1976) and *Method in Theology* (New York: Herder and Herder, 1972). On the one hand, Lonergan rejects the notion that religion is "some eternal and immutable Platonic form" (*Nicea*, 7) and the classicist understanding of culture as universally normative, in which "at least *de jure* there was but one culture that was both universal and permanent" (*Method*, xi). Instead he contends that "As consciousness develops so too does religion, and so it is fallacious to infer that what is appropriate for children and for primitives constitutes the very essence of religion, always and everywhere the same" (*Nicea*, 7), and a modern empirical view of culture which "may remain unchanged for ages" but may also "be in process of slow development or rapid dissolution." (*Method*, xi). On the other hand, Lonergan argues that the trinitarian and christological developments of the classical period occurred precisely because of the early church's concern with *what is true*: "Dogma emerges from the revealed word of God, carried forward by the tradition of the Church; it does so, however, only to the extent that, prescinding from all other riches contained in the word of God, one concentrates on it precisely *as true*" (*Nicea*, 8). Or, put another way:

> . . . from the beginning the word of God contained within it an implicit epistemology and ontology, but what was there implicitly became known explicitly only through dialectical process that was spread over time; and this dialectic process was all the more complex, as the real roots of the problem were touched only indirectly (*Nicea*, 133).

In his *Method* which, unknown to many, grew out of his much earlier preoccupation with trinitarian and christological questions, what is espoused by Lonergan as firm, unchanging, universally true, "the rock on which one can build," is the transcendental method, the "dynamic structure of human consciousness" by which we can attain to knowledge, "the subject in his conscious, unobjectified attentiveness, intelligence, reasonableness, . . . responsibility" (*Method*, 19-20).While I have some serious difficulties with Lonergan's whole notion of the development of human consciousness from a lower more primitive level of differentiation to a higher, differentiated level, I find myself much closer to Lonergan's and Tracy's concern for fidelity to the classical tradition than to Kaufman's almost total rejection of the classical model of thinking.

[15] Tracy, *Analogical Imagination*, 68.
[16] *Ibid.*, 92, n 77
[17] *Ibid.*, 64.
[18] *Ibid.*, 108
[19] *Ibid.*, 248

[20] *Ibid.*, xi.

[21] Ernst Troeltsch, *The Social Teaching of the Christian Churches*, vol. 1, trans., Olive Wyon (New York: Harper & Row, 1960), 331.

[22] *Ibid.*, 339.

[23] *Ibid.*, 335

[24] For a comprehensive overview of the Frankfurt School of Critical Theory and Social Research—represented by thinkers such as Max Horkheimer, Theodor Adorno, Herbert Marcuse, Erich Fromm, Franz Newman, Leo Löwenthal and Friedrich Pollock—see Martin Jay's *The Dialectical Imagination* (Toronto: Little, Brown & Co., 1973). These critical Neo-Marxist thinkers are deeply indebted to the Jewish-prophetic tradition as well as to the Hegelian-Marxist tradition in their critique of modern ideology and the negativities of modern culture. But they are also profoundly critical of doctrinaire Marxism and the loss of the "transcendent" and the "subjective" in modern western thought and culture. They are keenly aware of the dialectical nature of the Enlightenment, rejecting the technocratization and bureaucratization of modern culture and supporting the Enlightenment notions of freedom, equality, and justice. One might say, they criticize the Enlightenment from within the Enlightenment and the left from within a commitment to the left.

[25] Not all modern eschatological thought is activistic, to be sure. There is a kind of quietistic eschatology which de-emphasizes the importance of history and human responsibility for society in anticipation of an apocalyptic end. I am not referring here to this passive-type of eschatology but rather to the Troeltschian prophetic-eschatological model which sees the ideal of the kingdom of God as in some sense continuous with the present and thus makes the eschatological future to a large extent contingent on human action and the human management of history.

[26] I want to emphasize strongly that in Western philosophical and theological thought we need to recover a sense of that which can be loosely referred to as "timeless" or "eternal"—namely, that the essence of which cannot be defined exhaustively in historical terms. For instance: the recent birth of my third child cannot be explained wholly in terms of the movement of past to present to future, or in terms of genetic-biological factors, or in terms of the sexual intercourse between two human beings. Not everything has been said when these important factors are accounted for. Here there is some reality which cuts diagonally across historical-chronology. I would say: Here is incarnation of that which is timeless or eternal—the historical incarnation or something which is not essentially or exclusively historical.

[27] Although there were fundamental differences between the Greeks and the Hebrews, according to Lonergan—the former broke the power of myth and magic through theory (literature, philosophy, and science), while the latter was more practical and broke it through faith in divine revelation and a view of God as personal, and had a truer knowledge of God than did the Greeks—it was Hellenistic thought "whereby the Christian religion was enabled to make explicit what from the beginning was contained implicitly in the word of God itself" (*Nicea*, 130).

[28] Chapter 19 above. I basically accept George Grant's definitions of these assumptions: modern humanity defines its essence as the unlimited freedom to shape human and nonhuman nature because it perceives itself as alone in the cosmos. "Historicism" is the fundamental rejection of universal and eternal verities in the Greek-philosophical sense and the belief that one cannot transcend the historical epoch of which one is a part, let alone history as such.

[29] Howard John Loewen, "Response to A. James Reimer," *The Conrad Grebel Review* 1.2 (Spring 1983), 56-58.

[30] Tracy, *Analogical Imagination*, 203.

[31] *Ibid.*, 204

[32] *Ibid.*, 211

[33] *Ibid.*, 215

[34] *Ibid.*, 217

[35] I think it could be convincingly argued that, similar to Max Weber's thesis that Calvinism and the spirit of capitalism were not connected in any simplistic causal way but made rather congenial partners, the leftwing of the Reformation—with its radical rejection of sacramentalism, its profound voluntarism (its emphasis on the right of the individual to leave the medieval church and to establish and join the church of his or her choice), and its strong belief in the separation of church and state, thus leaving secular society truly secular or on its own—has fundamental affinities with the modern spirit.

[36] I am not suggesting that we adopt a quietistic eschatology which ends up retreating religiously into the inward "spiritual" realm and supporting politically rightwing, even reactionary historical action. What I am suggesting is that the prophetic-eschatological emphasis remain primary precisely because of its taking history and human social responsibility seriously, but also that the inadequacies of a purely historicist model be recognized and supplemented with a more sacramental-priestly understanding of life.

[37] Here I agree with Karl Barth who, while belonging to the left-wing Social Democratic Party in the 1930s, maintained that theology as such, although never apolitical, must always in some sense remain prior to politics and thus maintain its ability to criticize ideologies both of the left and the right as well as those of the centre.

[38] Stephen W. Sykes, *The Integrity of Anglicanism* (London, GB: Mowbray, 1978), x.

[39] *Ibid.*, ix-x

[40] *Ibid.*, 5

[41] *Ibid.*, 69

[42] *Ibid.*, 43

[43] *Ibid.*, 49

[44] *Ibid.*, 68

[45] *Ibid.*, 93

[46] Chapter 3 above.

[47] I agree with David Tracy's concern to take seriously the diversity within the biblical emphasis: the narrative genre of the synoptics, which keeps alive the "dangerous and subversive Jesus of Nazareth" (*Analogical Imagination*, 28), the dialectical mode of Paul's thinking in which "grace is disclosed as the *power* of

the proclaimed word of the cross to confront and expose the radical negativities of each and all . . . ." (285), and the more meditative and ontological thought of John, which is more "appropriate to his emphasis on the manifestation of the Logos" (284) and in which "grace is disclosed as the gift of manifestation, the glory, of the Word who is Love" (285). Yet it seems to me that not all theological and church traditions can stress equally and in a balanced way all three modes of understanding Jesus. While recognizing the importance of all three—the dangerous apocalyptic Jesus, the proclaimed Jesus, and the mystical Jesus—each tradition may in actual fact be called in its own way to put the weight of its theology in one area without losing sight of the others. As the Catholics and Orthodox have tended to put the weight on the sacramental and mystical Jesus, and the Lutherans on the proclaimed Jesus, so the Anabaptists may be called to place the weight on the dangerous, historical, eschatological, and apocalyptic Jesus.

Chapter 13

[1] Originally published as "Mennonite Theological Self-Understanding, the Crisis of Modern Anthropocentricity and the Challenge of the Third Millennium" in *Mennonite Identity: Historical and Contemporary Perspectives,* eds. Calvin Wall Redekop and Samuel J. Steiner (Lanham, MD: University Press of America, 1988), 13-38.

[2] Steven Seidman makes much of this distinction in his "Modernity and the Problem of Meaning: The Durkheim Tradition," *Sociological Analysis* 46: 2 (1985), 109-30. According to Seidman:

> The Durkheimians take issue with the Weberian claim of the dissolution of sociocultural unity and the thesis of the secularization, segmentation, and privatization of moral and existential meanings. The Durkheimians (like Bellah and Parsons) argue that every society rests upon a religiously based set of shared moral understandings which by virtue of integrating the personal and social system provide a basis for identity and social community as well as a transcendent standard of understanding (111).

[3] For instance, in the words of Seidman:

> Against modernists, Durkheim asserts that modernity does not entail the extinction of religiously resonant collective representations but their transformation, especially the transmutation of Christianity into the religion of humanity. Although Durkheim shares with traditionalists their sense of the permanence of religion, he actually turns against them with what in the conservative tradition is a reactionary idea. He does this by first arguing that the essence of religion does not lie in a notion of the supernatural or a transcendent god, but in collectively empowered movements and ideals which assume diverse symbolic or representational forms. Second,

Durkheim suggests that today it is the Principles of 1789 (moral individualism, equality, social justice, democracy) which are considered sacred. It is therefore precisely the much-despised ideas of the modernists that function as the transcendent ideals, ethical imperatives, and unifying moral forces in modernity (117).

[4] I am referring here to the demise of traditional theism in the face of the methodological, epistemological, metaphysical, and cultural difficulties of speaking about God as ultimate or transcendent reality in the modern and postmodern theological context, especially in the light of overwhelming evil. See Gordon D. Kaufman, *God The Problem* (Cambridge, MA: Harvard University Press, 1972), 3-16; John J. O'Donnell, *Trinity and Temporality: The Christian Doctrine of God in the Light of Process Theology and the Theology of Hope* (Oxford: Oxford University Press, 1983), 1-25; and Jim Garrison, *The Darkness of God: Theology After Hiroshima* (Grand Rapids: Eerdmans, 1982), 9-21.

[5] This is a thesis I proposed in "The Nature and Possibility of a Mennonite Theology" (Chapter 10 above). It is also argued in a somewhat different more social-historical form by Hans-Jürgen Goertz in his "Das Täufertum—ein Weg in Die Moderne?" in *Zwingli und Europa. Referate und Protokolle des internationalen Kongresses aus Anlaß des 500. Geburtstages von Huldrich Zwingli 1984* (Göttingen: Vandenhoeck & Ruprecht, 1985), 165-81.

[6] The modern rejection of traditional theism in favour of an anthropocentrism must be seen not only in terms of "methodological atheism, which argues that God must be rejected as a meaningless term, a reality unverifiable in principle because outside the scope of our experience," but much more powerfully in terms of "protest atheism," which "rejects God in the name of man" and "either sees the divine and the human as necessarily opposed or rejects God in the name of suffering in the world" (O'Donnell, *Trinity and Temporality*, 2). The power and importance of the modern anthropocentric turn lies in its taking seriously human suffering and historical human emancipation. For Christian theology and the Christian church, any theocentric-theology which is to have meaning in the face of Auschwitz and Hiroshima, as well as massive inequality and injustice, must assert more aggressively than much traditional theology does human freedom and responsibility for overcoming evil, and must understand God himself as identifying with and involved in human suffering.

[7] While the concerns of modern anthropocentrism— human freedom, equality, social justice, and human responsibility for overcoming historical suffering and evil—are to be taken seriously, it is my strong conviction that unless the modern vision is seen in terms of obedience and faithfulness to God as transcendent and absolute reality (who, traditionally speaking, reveals or discloses his will to us), our very commitment to human emancipation is bound to turn into its opposite: narcissism and ultimate self-destruction, of which the specter of a nuclear holocaust is simply the most logical outcome.

[8] Werner O. Packull, "Some Reflections on the State of Anabaptist History: The Demise of Normative Vision," *Studies in Religion/Sciences Religieuses* 8:3 (1979), 313-23.

[9] Leonard Gross, "The Doctrinal Era of the Mennonite Church," *The Mennonite*

Quarterly Review 60.1 (1986), 88, 92.

[10] *Ibid.*, 101

[11] *Ibid.*

[12] Packull, "Some Reflections on the State of Anabaptist History," 321-22.

[13] *Ibid.*, 323

[14] Goertz, "Das Täufertum—Ein Weg in die Moderne?," *Zwingli und Europa*, 168.

[15] *Ibid.*, 169-70

[16] *Ibid.*, 171, 173

[17] *Ibid.*, 178

[18] *Ibid.*, 180

[19] What it shares with the Bender school of Anabaptist-Mennonite historiography, it seems to me, are certain assumptions about a) Anabaptists being precursors of modernity in some sense, and b) the essentially social-ethical core of Anabaptism in contrast to a doctrinal interpretation of the heart of the movement.

[20] It could be persuasively argued that the modern scientific crises (environmental, technological, and bureaucratic administration of every facet of life, genetic experimentation, nuclear accidents and war, and so on) are the ironic result of the anthropocentric turn which initially turned against traditional theism for emancipatory purposes.

[21] J. Denny Weaver, "The Work of Christ: On the Difficulty of Identifying an Anabaptist Perspective," *The Mennonite Quarterly Review* 59. 2 (1985): 107-29.

[22] Howard John Loewen, *One Lord, One Church, One Hope, and One God: Mennonite Confessions of Faith* (Elkhart, IN: Institute of Mennonite Studies, 1985).

[23] Denis Janz, *Three Reformation Catechisms: Catholic, Anabaptist, Lutheran* (Lewiston, NY: The Edwin Mellen Press, 1982), 5.

[24] *Ibid*

[25] *Ibid.*, 8, 13, 14, 21.

[26] For example, in his "A Christian Catechism Which Every Person, Before He is Baptized in Water, Should be Able to Recite," Hubmaier has Leon ask: "How many articles of the Christian creed are there?" To this Hans answers "Twelve" and proceeds to list the twelve articles of the Apostles' Creed. It is obvious that Hubmaier's strong emphasis on a "living faith" which results in "works of mercy" are placed within the context of the Credo (Janz, *Three Reformation Catechisms*, 147).

[27] The weight Menno Simons places on proper trinitarian-theological formulation can be seen from his 1550 "A Solemn Confession of the Triune, Eternal, and True God, Father, Son, and Holy Ghost," *The Complete Writings of Menno Simons*, ed. J.C. Wenger (Scottdale: Herald Press, 1974), 487-98. Peter Riedemann begins his 1545 *Account of Our Religion, Doctrine and Faith* (Suffolk, England: Hodder and Stoughton, in conjunction with The Plough Publishing House, 1950) with an extensive commentary on the various parts of the Apostles' Creed, each interpreted in light of a strong ethical concern.

[28] John C. Wenger, *The Doctrines of the Mennonites* (Scottdale, PA: Mennonite Publishing House, 1952), 23.

[29] Thus Peter Riedemann, in interpreting the first article of the Apostles' Creed, for instance, draws the following inference: "Therefore is this one, eternal, almighty God the one eternal and unchanging truth, which hath being in itself and remaineth eternally unchanged; which poureth itself into believing souls, maketh us like, similar and conformable to itself, that we may live and walk in it and testify to the truth within us and in word and life" (*Account of Our Religion*, 16).

[30] Loewen, *One Lord, One Church*, 46.

[31] *Ibid.*

[32] *Ibid.*, 15-16. There is some truth to this distinction, although it tends to blur the fact that the ancient ecumenical creeds were themselves formulated in the light of very particular, concrete, existential needs of the church and had from the start a confessional and liturgical function.

[33] *Ibid.*, 17

[34] *Ibid.*, 24. Commenting on the Dordrecht-Mennonite Church tradition, Loewen states the following: "Having its origins in the seventeenth century (1632), this confessional tradition has ruled the longest. The mother among Mennonite confessions, Dordrecht has functioned more powerfully than any other confession within a particular tradition. It has been the more conservative tradition in that it probably reflects the fewest external influences."

[35] *Ibid.*

[36] *Ibid.*, 24-5

[37] *Ibid.*, 25-6

[38] The influence of the larger social-historical environment is evident throughout but particularly in the context of the twentieth century, where the influences of Fundamentalism, denominationalism, and pluralism are especially strong (cf. Loewen, 31). One of the weaknesses of Loewen's compendium of Mennonite confessions is that the author does not give a sufficient social, political, and historical context for each of the confessions.

[39] *Ibid.*, 34

[40] *Ibid.*, 34-35

[41] Weaver, "The Work of Christ," 127-28. According to Weaver, "[w]hile the circumstances of their encounters in Strasbourg may have concealed it from them and also from Bucer and Capito, Sattler and Denck did have a very important ethical principle in common. Even though they began with differing and contradictory views of the work of Christ, they agreed that it was the early Jesus who supplied immediately—not expressed in various forms through an office—the norm for ethics and Christian behaviour. They possessed a common perspective not accounted for by Bucer's declaration of Sattler's orthodoxy and Denck's heterodoxy on the work of Christ. From quite different perspectives, Sattler and Denck arrived at the same ethical norm."

[42] Loewen, *One Lord, One Church*, 36.

[43] *Ibid.*, 40

[44] *Ibid.*, 44

[45] Catholic theologian Bernard Lonergan, for instance, divides the various theologically-related disciplines eight "functional specialities in theology":

research, interpretation, history, dialectic, foundations, doctrines, systematics, and communications. According to Lonergan, "[I]t is to be noted that such functional specialities are intrinsically related to one another. They are successive parts of one and the same process. The earlier parts are incomplete without the later" (*Method in Theology* [New York: Herder and Herder, 1972], 126, 127). In this paper I argue together with Lonergan for the distinctive but related tasks of the social-historian and the doctrinal-systematic theologian.

[46] Walter Klaassen says of the early Anabaptists' approach to biblical interpretation, "[i]t is therefore not the hierarchy as in Roman Catholicism, nor the scholar-teacher as in Protestantism who decides what the Word means in any given instance, but the gathered community under the guidance of the Spirit" ("Anabaptist Hermeneutics: Presuppositions, Principles and Practice," *Essays on Biblical Interpretation: Anabaptist-Mennonite Perspectives*, ed. Willard Swartley [Elkhart: Institute of Mennonite Studies, 1984], 10). Similarly, John Howard Yoder states,

> The first implication of this conception of the congregation listening to the Word of God is that the common man becomes a full member of the church. Now that the Bible is available in the language of the people, it is the entire congregation, and thus primarily simple people responding to the obvious meaning of the text, who will make the decision as to what God says for today. This implication of congregationalism found its most widespread realization in the Anabaptist movement, but it as well had begun with Huldrych Zwingli. One continues to find among later Anabaptists a serious suspicion of formal learning and of tools of the scholar. It seemed to them almost unavoidable that such learning would be used as a means of evading the greater meaning of Scripture ("The Hermeneutics of the Anabaptists" in *Essays on Biblical Interpretation*, 21).

The danger of extreme congregationalism when applied to biblical interpretation is that the universality of Christian truths revealed in the Scriptures, which transcends any particular congregation and any given time period, tends to be overshadowed by the concerns of a particular group of people and their experiences.

[47] Gross, "The Doctrinal Era of the Mennonite Church," 101.

[48] *Ibid.*, 83

[49] *Catechism: or A Brief Instruction for Young People from the Holy Scriptures in the Form of Questions and Answers*. New revised German-English edition including the Articles of Faith of the Evangelical Mennonite Church (*Kleine Gemeinde*) of Canada (Altona, MB: D.W. Friesen & Sons, 1954, 1957).

[50] The clinical-pastoral orientation is particularly well represented by the growing number of popular books authored by David W. Augsburger, such as *Anger and Assertiveness in Pastoral Care* (Philadelphia: Fortress Press, 1979); *Caring Enough to Forgive* (Scottdale: Herald Press, 1981); and *Beyond Assertiveness*, co-authored together with John Faul (Waco, TX: Caliber Books, 1980).

[51] The *Christian Peacemaker Teams* study document, a concept growing out of

Ron Sider's proposal made at the Mennonite World Conference in Strasbourg in July 1984, and approved in principle by the Council of Moderators and Secretaries of the Mennonite and Brethren in Christ Churches in October 1985, reflects such an orientation. Some of the writings of John H. Yoder, such as *The Politics of Jesus: Vicit Agnus Noster*, 2nd ed. (Grand Rapids: Eerdmans, 1994) also represent this genre of theological thinking.

[52] The first such General Conference meeting at Camp Lake, Wisconsin was entitled "Dialogue on Faith," and took place October 26, 1984; the second, "Dialogue on Biblical Interpretation and Practice," occurred November 15-7, 1985. I was present at the second conference and experienced first-hand the tension between these two approaches.

[53] This orientation is the predominant one in contemporary biblical scholarship and has been so ever since the rise of the modern historical-critical-contextual method. I think it would be fair to say that J. Denny Weaver represents this orientation when he states:

> If the search for Mennonite truth depends in a significant way on the process, then the locus of authority resides more with the ongoing people of God as a whole than in a particular institution or law code or absolutized biblical proposition. Authority is a dynamic process which maintains and preserves truth through the interaction of God's people and their perpetual asking. Truth emerges and is preserved in living form. It is always more than the proclamation of one person or institution, more than a cross section of any epoch—biblical or otherwise—frozen in its development. It emerges contextually from the living tradition of the church in conversation with the biblical materials and the church's core presuppositions. None of these statements—biblical or otherwise—is an absolute formulation. Therefore neither truth nor the Christian faith nor the existence of God's people is threatened by doubts or critique of any given theological formulation or the practice of historical scholarship on the Bible or any other part of the historical tradition ("Perspectives on a Mennonite Theology," *The Conrad Grebel Review* 2.3 [1984]: 193-94).

[54] This orientation is represented clearly by the recent polemical writings of George R. Brunk II, such as *A Crisis Among Mennonites* (Harrisonburg, VA: The Sword and Trumpet, 1983). It is also the position of Ted VanderEnde—although held somewhat more moderately—who makes the following claim:

> In this historic Mennonite position the Scriptures are never treated as the product of the community, as tradition in the modern sense of the word, but rather as the supreme God-given standard. The task of the community of faith is not to make a restatement of faith in Christ and his gospel to a new complex historical situation, but to re-live and re-apply dynamically and obediently this divine guide for faith and practice. Thus in each age since the apostolic age, in different cultural settings, believers have sought to live out the propositional principles of God's Word. ("Apostolic Versus Process

Hermeneutics: A Mennonite Dilemma" [paper presented at the "Dialogue on Faith" conference at Camp Wonderland, Camp Lake, WS, October 26-8, 1984]).

[55] John J. O'Donnell, for instance, in his use of Bernard Lonergan's interpretation of Nicea to understand Patristic doctrinal thought, makes the following crucial observation:

> In other words the language of Nicea must be understood heuristically. Lonergan writes, "It offers an open structure: it does not determine what attributes are to be assigned to the Father in scriptural, patristic, medieval or modern terms; of course, contemporary consciousness, which is historically minded, will be at home in all four." Nicea therefore leaves a great deal open and a great deal unsettled. But it does make a judgement and so provides a bare minimum which must be taken into account in any subsequent endeavour to formulate a Christian doctrine of God (*Trinity and Temporality*, 38-39).

What occurred in the first few centuries of orthodox theological formulation was not the fixation of doctrinal belief itself. This thesis is central to my own theological proposal at the end of this paper. In his profound study of the development that occurred from the multiplicity of the New Testament to the uniformity of the early creeds, which he considers the clarification of the truth of the consciousness, Bernard Lonergan makes the following statement: "Dogma emerges from the revealed word of God, carried forward by the tradition of the Church; it does so, however, only to the extent that, prescinding from all other riches contained in that word of God, one concentrates on it precisely *as true*." Further, "In the first place, within the ante-Nicene movement we have to recognize two distinct, though related, developments. There is no doubt that those early Christian centuries produced a development in trinitarian and christological doctrine but this doctrinal development contained within it another, more profound development: the development of the very notion of Dogma" (*The Way to Nicea* [London: Darton, Longman & Todd, 1976], 8, 13).

[56] See the article by Lydia Penner, "Urges New Confession of Faith as Basis for Mission," *Mennonite Reporter* (January 6, 1986): 5.

[57] Thomas Finger writes:

> Since discipleship is at the heart of the Mennonite existence, we will be deeply concerned about what the Nicene Creed, which is largely a doctrinal affirmation, does not say. We will probably insist that any adequate confession of faith must indicate what it means to follow Christ in the contemporary world. Such following will almost certainly involve suffering in conflict with the powers that be. Consequently, when we study the creeds of the past we will be on the lookout for what they do *not say*, and *why*. To discover this, we will probably seek to understand the ecclesiastical, social, and political *functions* of the creeds. We will also likely want to determine what groups excluded by the creeds and by the dominant church

were trying to say, and whether some of that might belong in adequate confessions ("The Way to Nicea: Reflections from a Mennonite Perspective," *The Conrad Grebel Review* 3. 3 [1985]: 247-48).

In his response to Finger's article, Sjouke Voolstra suggests that the time may have come for a new common Mennonite confession which would represent not only a *"consensus mennoniticus"* but also the *"consensus apostolicus* (Apostles' Creed)."* He agrees that the problems of early creeds for Mennonites which Finger raises—namely, what they do not say about discipleship and ethics and how they functioned sociologically and politically—need to be taken seriously. Nevertheless, Voolstra critically questions "whether ethical views belong in a creed, no matter how generally and non-specifically they may be stated, without incurring the danger of particularizing it and turning it into a denomination confession" (*The Conrad Grebel Review* 4. 1 [1986]: 59).

[58] For Yoder, "middle axioms" are those natural norms (liberty, equality, fraternity, democracy, human rights, social justice) which the Christian church may use in its witness to the state. These norms can be understood by the statesman even though he may not understand or profess Christian belief or discipleship. For the Christian, however, these norms do not have their origin outside of Christ—that is, in natural law or reason—but have their ultimate source and ground in *agape* or the "love of Christ" (*The Christian Witness to the State* [Newton, KS: Faith and Life Press, 1964], 72-3). What I am suggesting is that as Yoder's middle axioms are mediating principles between the church and the state, so "doctrines" as I am espousing them here are "mediating principles" between disparate parts of the Bible, as well as between the Bible and ever new ambiguous historical situations.

[59] In his *Anatomy of Criticism* (Princeton: Princeton University Press, 1957, 1971) Northrop Frye defines "archetype" as follows: "The symbol in this phase is the communicable unit, to which I give the name archetype: that is, a typical or recurring image. I mean by an archetype a symbol which connects one poem with another and thereby helps to unify and integrate our literary experience" (99). In his *The Great Code: The Bible and Literature* (Toronto: Academic Press, 1981), Frye defines the related concepts of "Type" and "Antitype" in the following way: "Typology is a figure of speech that moves in time: the type exists in the present and the antitype in the future. What typology really is is a mode of thought, what it both assumes and leads to, is a theory of history, or more accurately of historical process: an assumption that there is some meaning and point to history, and that sooner or later some event or events will occur which will indicate what that meaning is, and so become an antitype of what has happened previously" (80-1).

[60] Vander Goot advances the thesis that "prior to and outside of the scientific study of the Bible in the Christian community of faith, interpretation and immediate confessional response to the Bible is what should fund the theoretical enterprise of theology and biblical studies." He calls for a direct reading of the Bible as a whole in order to get a *"literal sense of the canon* (in contradistinction to a wooden literalistic sense)." For Vander Goot, "canon is the idea that there is an authoritative whole and that this authoritative whole is the conventional Christian

understanding of the Bible's overall message as a creation-fall-restoration-consummation story, which should be the controlling ingredient in the interpretation of the Bible's various parts" (*Interpreting the Bible in Theology and the Church* [Lewiston, NY: The Edwin Mellen Press, 1984], 1, 2, 3).

[61] This triadic structure is fundamental to the early church's *kerygma* as amply evident in the first few chapters of Acts. See, for example, Acts 2: 32-33: "This Jesus God raised up, and of that all of us are witnesses. Being therefore exalted at the right hand of God, and having received from the Father the promise of the Holy Spirit, he has poured out this that you both see and hear" (NRSV). The trinitarian formulation of Nicea-Constantinople was a further development of what was already implicit in the earliest confession about Jesus as Lord.

[62] The summary statement on *Leadership and Authority in the Life of the Church*, adopted by the Mennonite Church General Assembly at Bowling Green, Ohio, August 11-16, 1981, takes a comprehensive look at the questions of church polity, leadership, authority, and ordination as addressed by the New Testament, as understood in Anabaptist and Mennonite history, and as perceived in the present social-historical context. The strength of the document is that it recognizes the diversity of interpretations of the biblical texts on these matters and the need for the church to adapt itself to changing circumstances without selling out to dominant fads. Its weakness is that it does not provide the Mennonite church with a clear enough direction for the future. This, in my view, is at least partly because it does not develop a *doctrine of the church* in the context of the other major doctrines of the Christian church. Thus, while it refers briefly to the Schleitheim Confession of 1527 and the Dordrecht Confession of 1632, it does not place ecclesiology in the context of creation, fall, and reconciliation, and consummation (eschatology).

[63] The Bowling Green statement moves in this direction when it says:

> Some interpretations find in Galatians 3:27ff, a higher expression of *equality* between women and men in Christ than in the passages which speak about husbands' headship and about women's remaining silent in the church. Different passages may in fact have different emphases. The New Testament, however, points both to a new and liberating unity between men and women in Christ, and to distinctive roles of each in relation to the other. We should also stop reading many traditional understandings of social roles for women and men back into the biblical vision of how they relate to each other in their distinctiveness (23).

The document leaves us with a diversity of passages on this question, some more conservative passages stressing the "headship of husbands in relation to wives" (1 Corinthians 11 and Ephesians 5) and other passages stressing the radical equality of men and women in Christ (Galatians 3:27ff.), without providing us with a hermeneutical-doctrinal key by which to mediate these diverse passages into a consistent position for the church of the future.

[64] An excellent example of how the church might begin to address moral questions that it faces from within a doctrinal perspective is the recent "Statement

on Marriage, Divorce and Remarriage" submitted for consideration by the joint annual conference of the Mennonite Conference of Ontario and Quebec, Western Ontario Mennonite Conference, and United Mennonite Conference in March 1986. Where God's intent in creation, the reality of the fall, and possibilities for reconciliation and redemption are discussed and applied to the question of divorce and remarriage. The document concludes with this challenging statement:

> The work of the committee in preparing this document brought to light the unfinished theological tasks which face the Mennonite church. The committee struggled with the lack of clarity in matters of theology and polity in the Mennonite church, and had to spend much time defining theological assumptions before proceeding with the assignment. We suggest that the participating conferences take seriously the need to define our understandings of central doctrines such as Creation, the Fall and Redemption. Our understanding of these doctrines determines how we deal with moral issues like divorce and remarriage.

[65] *Leadership and Authority in the Life of the Church*, 32.

Chapter 14

[1] Originally published as "Toward Christian Theology From a Diversity of Mennonite Perspectives," *The Conrad Grebel Review* 6.2 (Spring 1988), 147-59.

[2] *The Conrad Grebel Review* 3.1 (Winter 1985): 100, 101.

[3] David Tracy, *Plurality and Ambiguity: Hermeneutics, Religion, Hope* (San Francisco: Harper & Row, 1987), 112.

[4] Carl S. Keener, "The Darwinian Revolution and its Implications for a Modern Anabaptist Theology," *The Conrad Grebel Review* 1.1 (Winter 1983): 29.

[5] Perry B. Yoder, "Toward a Shalom Biblical Theology," *The Conrad Grebel Review* 1.3 (Fall 1983): 42.

[6] C. Arnold Snyder, "The Relevance of Anabaptist Nonviolence for Nicaragua Today," *The Conrad Grebel Review* 2.2 (Spring 1984): 129.

[7] *Ibid.*, 130-31

[8] J. Denny Weaver, "Perspectives on a Mennonite Theology," *The Conrad Grebel Review* 2.3 (Fall 1984): 193.

[9] *Ibid.*

[10] *Ibid.*, 194

[11] *Ibid.*, 207

[12] Gayle Gerber Koontz, "The Trajectory of Scripture and Feminist Conviction," *The Conrad Grebel Review* 5.3 (Fall 1987): 219.

[13] *Ibid.*, 207

[14] *Ibid.*, 219

[15] Mitchell Brown, "Jesus: Messiah not God," *The Conrad Grebel Review* 5 (Fall

1987): 233-52.

[16] Howard J. Loewen, *One Lord, One Church, One Hope, and One God: Mennonite Confessions of Faith* (Elkhart, IN: Institute of Mennonite Studies, 1983): 15-16.

[17] George A. Lindbeck, *The Nature of Doctrine: Religion and Theology in a Postliberal Age* (Philadelphia, PA: Westminster Press, 1984).

[18] William A. Christian, Sr., *Doctrines of Religious Communities: A Philosophical Study* (New Haven: Yale University Press, 1987).

[19] Loewen, *One Lord, One Church*, 269.

[20] Ibid., 36

[21] Krister Stendahl, *Meanings: The Bible as Document and as Guide* (Philadelphia: Fortress Press, 1984), 1.

Chapter 15

[1] *The Conrad Grebel Review* became one of the forums for an ongoing debate about the role of the classical creeds in Mennonite theologizing: cf. Reimer, "The Nature and Possibility of a Mennonite Theology," *CGR* 1.1 (Winter 1983): 33-55; Howard John Loewen, "Reader Response [to Reimer]," *CGR* 1.2 (Spring 1983): 56-8; Reimer, "Reader Response [to Loewen]," *CGR* 1.3 (Fall 1983): 51-4; J. Denny Weaver, "Perspectives on a Mennonite Theology," *CGR* 2.3 (Fall 1984): 189-210; Darrol Bryant, "Reader Response [to Weaver]," *CGR* 3.2 (Spring 1985): 189-93; Thomas N. Finger, "The Way to Nicea: Reflections from a Mennonite Perspective," *CGR* 3.3 (Fall 1985): 231-49. The debate continued in other settings as well: cf. *Explorations of Systematic Theology From Mennonite Perspectives*, Occasional Papers No. 7, ed. Willard Swartley (Elkhart: Institute of Mennonite Studies, 1984); Ben C. Ollenburger, "Mennonite Theology: A Conversation around the Creeds," *The Mennonite Quarterly Review* 66.1 (1992): 57-89.

[2] Published as "Trinitarian Orthodoxy, Constantinianism and Theology from a Radical Protestant Perspective," in *Faith to Creed: Ecumenical Perspectives on the Affirmation of the Apostolic Faith in the Fourth Century*, ed. S. Mark Heim (Grand Rapids: Eerdmans, 1991), 129-61.

[3] An ecclesiology premised on the notion that the church is a visible social entity constituted only of individuals who have expressed their personal faith by means of adult baptism and committed themselves to a life of discipleship and nonconformity to the world. I prefer the designation of "Radical Protestantism" for those groups who have their historical and spiritual origins in the "leftwing" groups of the Reformation.

[4] Of Yoder's many books, including *Nevertheless* (1971), *The Original Revolution* (1972), *The Politics of Jesus* (1972), *What Would You Do?* (1983), and *When War is Unjust* (1984), his *The Christian Witness to the State* (1964) is in my opinion still one of the best. A whole generation of young educated Mennonites who have been interested in their Anabaptist heritage have read Yoder's books and taken him as the definitive interpreter of what it means to be an Anabaptist in the contemporary situation.

[5] Dennis D. Martin wrongly charges Yoder with portraying the

"Constantinian reversal as an overnight occurrence" ("Nothing New Under the Sun? Mennonites and History," *The Conrad Grebel Review* 5 [Winter 1987]: 8, n. 21).

[6] Yoder, "Radical Reformation Ethics in Ecumenical Perspective," *The Priestly Kingdom: Social Ethics as Gospel* (Notre Dame: University of Notre Dame Press, 1984), 108.

[7] Yoder, "Anabaptism and History," *The Priestly Kingdom*, 129.

[8] *Ibid.*, 208, n 25

[9] Yoder, "The Constantinian Sources of Western Social Ethics," *The Priestly Kingdom*, 140.

[10] *Ibid.*, 145

[11] Yoder, *Christian Attitudes To War, Peace, and Revolution: A Companion to Bainton* (Elkhart: Co-op Bookstore, 1983), 23-66.

[12] Yoder, *Preface to Theology: Christology and Theological Method* (Elkhart: Co-op Bookstore, 1981). Like *Christian Attitudes to War, Peace, and Revolution*, this volume is a collection of Yoder's lecture and seminar notes gathered over a twenty-year period (from the early 1960s to 1981).

[13] Yoder, *Preface to Theology*, 104.

[14] *Ibid.*, 123-26

[15] *Ibid.*, 133

[16] *Ibid.*, 136

[17] *Ibid.*, 138

[18] *Ibid.*, 139

[19] *Ibid.*, 140

[20] *Ibid.*

[21] *Ibid.*; italics mine. Yoder here manifests the kind of suspicion of Hellenistic influences on Christian sources that is so prevalent in modern theology, and implicitly suggests a connection between the biblical, Hebraic, and modern mind. The reference to the "modern reader" not being able to accept the Nicene wording is noteworthy. It implies that Yoder sees the Anabaptist-Mennonite reading of the Bible (biblical realism) as more palatable to the modern mind than the classical orthodox reading.

[22] *Ibid.*, 141

[23] J. Denny Weaver, "Christology in Historical Perspective," *Jesus Christ and the Mission of the Church: Contemporary Anabaptist Perspectives*, ed. Erland Waltner (Newton, KS: Faith and Life Press, 1990), 95, n. 12.

[24] *Ibid.*, 90

[25] *Ibid.*, 92

[26] Aloys Grillmeier, *Christ in Christian Tradition*, vol. 1, *From the Apostolic Age to Chalcedon (451)* (Atlanta: John Knox Press, 1975), 270.

[27] Weaver, "Christology in Historical Perspective," 93.

[28] *Ibid.*, 98

[29] See Donald F. Durnbaugh, *The Believers' Church: The History and Character of Radical Protestantism* (Scottdale, PA: Herald Press, 1968), 212-16.

[30] John E. Toews, *Jesus Christ the Convener of the Church* (Elkhart, IN: Mennonite

Church, 1989), 5. Although Ben C. Ollenburger is much more open to the importance of creeds than Toews here is, he makes the same point about creeds not offering a christology but just rules for christology. See Ollenburger, "Christology and Creeds," *AMBS Bulletin* 52 (May 1989): 2. One could say this if christology is defined exclusively in terms of the work of Christ and not his Being. If the being of Christ is considered to be part of christology, which surely it is, then the Nicene Creed provides us with a substantive christology and not just a rule for christology.

[31] Martin, "Nothing New Under the Sun? Mennonites and History," *The Conrad Grebel Review* 5.1 (Winter 1987): 4-5.

[32] *Ibid.*, 7

[33] *Ibid.*, 8

[34] *Ibid.*, 11

[35] Ollenburger, "Christology and Creeds," *AMBS Bulletin* 52 (May 1989): 1-3; Cornelius J. Dyck, "C. Norman Kraus's *Jesus Christ Our Lord* in Historical Anabaptist Perspective," *AMBS Bulletin* 52 (May 1989): 4-7; Marlin E. Miller, "Christological Concepts of the Classical Creeds and Mennonite Confessions of Faith," *AMBS Bulletin* 52 (May, 1989): 7-11.

[36] Howard Loewen, *One Lord, One Church, One Hope, And One God: Mennonite Confessions of Faith* (Elkhart: Institute of Mennonite Studies, 1985).

[37] Yoder, *Preface to Theology*, 123-25.

[38] *Ibid.*, 139.

[39] Rusch, *The Trinitarian Controversy*, ed. William G. Rusch (Philadelphia: Fortress Press, 1980), 2.

[40] See Rusch, *The Trinitarian Controversy*, 17.

[41] R.P.C. Hanson, *Studies in Christian Antiquity* (Edinburgh: T. & T. Clark, 1985), 239.

[42] *Ibid.*, 240

[43] *Ibid.*

[44] *Ibid.*, 244

[45] See Grillmeier, *Christ in Christian Tradition*, vol. 1, 228ff.

[46] Hanson, *Studies in Christian Antiquity*, 244.

[47] *Ibid.*, 247

[48] *Ibid.*, 248

[49] Cochrane, *Christianity and Classical Culture: A Study of Thought and Action from Augustus to Augustine* (London: Oxford University Press, 1940, 1974).

[50] Hanson, *Studies in Christian Antiquity*, 248.

[51] *Ibid.*, 260

[52] *Ibid.*, 250-51

[53] *Ibid.*, 276

[54] *Ibid.*, 276-77

[55] Grillmeier, *Christ in Christian Tradition*, vol. 1, 249-50.

[56] *Ibid.*, 251

[57] *Ibid.*, 257

[58] *Ibid.*, 260

[59] Hanson, *Studies in Christian Antiquity*, 239.

⁶⁰ I'm not denying that religion, including Christianity, ought to have a priestly-sacramental function, only that the prophetic-eschatological role ought to be stronger and the sacramental role subordinate.

⁶¹ Roberta C..Bondi, "The Fourth-Century Church: The Monastic Contribution," in *Faith to Creed: Ecumenical Perspectives on the Affirmation of the Apostolic Faith in the Fourth Century*, ed. Mark S. Heim (Grand Rapids: Eerdmans, 1991), 60-82

Chapter 16

¹ Wolfhart Pannenberg, *Systematic Theology: Volume 3* (Grand Rapids: Eerdmans, 1993, 1998), 129. According to Pannenberg, "For as the origin of all life the Spirit of God pledges to believers, to whom he is given as a lasting gift, participation in the eternal life of God and the resurrection from the dead (Rom. 8:11)."

² Originally published in *The Limits of Perfection: A Conversation with J. Lawrence Burkholder*, ed. Rodney J. Sawatsky and Scott Holland (Conrad Grebel College: Institute of Anabaptist and Mennonite Studies, 1993), 95-109.

³ John H. Yoder, *The Christian Witness to the State* (Newton, KS: Faith and Life Press, 1964), 23.

⁴ Gordon D. Kaufman, "The Church and the World," *Nonresistance and Responsibility and Other Mennonite Essays* (Newton,KS: Faith and Life Press, 1979), 47-48. This essay is a reprint from *The Context of Decision* (New York: Abingdon Press, 1964).

⁵ *Ibid.*, 53

⁶ Kaufman, "Nonresistance and Responsibility," *Nonresistance and Responsibility*, 65. This essay was originally published in *Concern* 6: A Pamphlet Series for Questions of Christian Renewal (Scottdale: Herald Press, 1958).

⁷ *Ibid.*, 71

⁸ *Ibid.*, 78

⁹ J. Lawrence Burkholder, *The Problem of Social Responsibility from the Perspective of the Mennonite Church* (Elkhart: Institute of Mennonite Studies, 1989), 223.

¹⁰ J. Lawrence Burkholder, "The Limits of Perfection: Autobiographical Reflections," in *The Limits of Perfection: A Conversation with J. Lawrence Burkholder*, 1-54.

¹¹ *Ibid.*, 40

¹² *Ibid.*, 42

¹³ *Ibid.*

¹⁴ *Ibid.*, 41

¹⁵ *Ibid.*, 9

¹⁶ *Ibid.*, 19

¹⁷ *Ibid.*, 30

¹⁸ Chapter 15 above

¹⁹ Ramsey MacMullen, *Christianizing the Roman Empire A.D. 100-400* (New Haven: Yale University Press, 1984).

²⁰ Elizabeth Allo Isichei, *Political Thinking and Social Experience: Some Christian*

Interpretations of the Roman Empire from Tertullian to Salvian (Christchurch, New Zealand: University of Canterbury, 1964), 27-40.

²¹ *Ibid.*, 41-57
²² *Ibid.*, 58-71
²³ *Ibid.*, 72-89
²⁴ *Ibid.*, 98-108
²⁵ Werner Packull, "Between Paradigms: Anabaptist Studies at the Crossroads," *The Conrad Grebel Review* 8.1 (Winter 1990): 1-22.
²⁶ *Ibid.*, 21
²⁷ *Ibid.*, 15
²⁸ *Ibid.*, 21

Chapter 17

¹ For my reflection on the funeral see "John Howard Yoder: A Tribute," *Anabaptist-Mennonite Scholars Network* 1.1 (May, 1998): 3, published by Toronto Mennonite Theological Centre.

² Originally published in *Essays & Tributes: John Howard Yoder 1927-1997* in *The Conrad Grebel Review* 16.2 (Spring, 1998). Reprinted in *What Mennonites Are Thinking*. Ed. Merle Good and Phyllis Pellman Good (Intercourse, PA.: Good Books, 1999): 151-65.

³ The new biography of Harold S. Bender tells the story of this generation of scholars: Albert N. Keim, *Harold S. Bender 1897-1962* (Scottdale: Herald Press, 1998) .

⁴ In the Winter of 1990 *The Conrad Grebel Review* collaborated with the Laurelville Mennonite Church Centre in sponsoring a seminar on "A Concern Retrospective: Myths and Realities," at Laurelville, Pennsylvania. All of the seven members of the original Concern group, with the exception of John Howard Yoder, accepted an invitation to reflect on their post-World War II European experience, concerns, and writings. These retrospectives were published in a special issue of *The Conrad Grebel Review* 8.2 (Spring 1990), together with a substantive historical introduction by Paul Toews, "The Concern Movement: Its Origins and Early History."

⁵ Cf. David A. Shank, "Reflections," *The Conrad Grebel Review* 16.2 (Spring 1998): 103-105.

⁶ C. Arnold Snyder, *Anabaptist History and Theology: An Introduction* (Kitchener, ON: Pandora Press, 1995).

⁷ Illustrative of this is the range of disciplines and methodologies applied to examining the Mennonite heritage in the light of postmodernity at the August 6-8, 1998 conference on "Anabaptists & Postmodernity" hosted by Bluffton College.

⁸ The latter an overview of Yoder's peace theology written for the special issue of *The Conrad Grebel Review* on John Howard Yoder (Spring, 1998). Another longer essay, entitled "Theological Orthodoxy and Jewish Christianity: A Personal Tribute to John Howard Yoder," appeared in *The Wisdom of the Cross:*

Essays in Honor of John Howard Yoder, ed. Stanley Hauerwas, Chris K. Huebner, Harry J. Huebner and Mark Thiessen Nation (Grand Rapids: Eerdmanns, 1999), 430-48.

Chapter 18

[1] Craig A. Carter, *The Pacifism of the Messianic Community: The Christological Social Ethics of John Howard Yoder* (a thesis submitted to the Faculty of Theology of the University of St. Michael's College, Toronto School of Theology: Toronto, 1999).

[2] *The Wisdom of the Cross: Essays in Honor of John Howard Yoder* eds., Stanley Hauerwas, Chris K. Huebner, Harry J. Huebner, and Mark Thiessen Nation (Grand Rapids: Eerdmans, 1999), 430-48

[3] John H. Yoder, *Nevertheless: The Varieties of Religious Pacifism* (Scottdale: Herald Press, 1971).

[4] Frantz Fanon, *The Wretched of the Earth* (New York: Grove Press, Inc., 1963).

[5] Personal letter, Reimer to Yoder, 26 February 1972.

[6] Personal letter, Yoder to Reimer, 3 March 1972.

[7] Karl Barth, "How I Have Changed My Mind: 1928-38; "How I Have Changed My Mind: 1938-48;" "How I Have Changed My Mind: 1948-58." Collected and reprinted in *Karl Barth: How I Changed My Mind,* introduction and epilogue by John D. Godsey (Richmond: John Knox Press, 1966).

[8] Yoder, *When War is Unjust: Honesty in Just War Thinking* (Minneapolis: Augsburg Publishing House, 1984).

[9] Yoder, *The Christian Witness to the State* (Newton, KS: Faith and Life Press, 1964).

[10] *Ibid.*, 60-73

[11] *Ibid.*, 66, 72

[12] Yoder, *Nevertheless: The Varieties of Religious Pacifism* (Scottdale: Herald Press, 1992).

[13] *Ibid.*, 135-36. On one of my car trips with Yoder in October, 1996, I asked him about this addition to the "Messianic Community" chapter. He expressed amazement at how carefully I had read him but did not really shed further light on the issue.

[14] *Ibid.*, 136.

[15] Reimer, "The Nature and Possibility of a Mennonite Theology," *The Conrad Grebel Review* 1.1 (Winter 1983): 33-55 (Chapter 10 above).

[16] *Ibid.*, 40-46.

[17] Yoder, *The Politics of Jesus* (Grand Rapids: Eerdmans, 1972).

[18] Yoder, *Preface to Theology: Christology and Theological Method* (Goshen, IN: Goshen Biblical Seminary). At his lecture on "The Politics of Jesus Revisited" (March 14, 1997), I asked him how existential questions of meaning figure in his social-political perspective on Jesus' theology. While not excluding the existential dimension, he made light of it by suggesting that I and Woody Allen had time to indulge in such preoccupations but most people in the world do not have that luxury.

[19] Yoder, *The Priestly Kingdom: Social Ethics as Gospel* (Notre Dame: University of Notre Dame Press, 1984); *Christian Attitudes to War, Peace, and Revolution: A Companion to Bainton* (Goshen, IN: Goshen Biblical Seminary, 1983); *Preface to Theology: Christology and Theological Method* (Goshen, IN: Goshen Biblical Seminary).

[20] Reimer, "Trinitarian Orthodoxy, Constantinianism, and Theology from a Radical Protestant Perspective," *Faith to Creed: Ecumenical Perspectives on the Affirmation of the Apostolic Faith in the Fourth Century*, edited by S. Mark Heim (Grand Rapids: Eerdmans, 1992), 129-61 (Chapter 15 above).

[21] Yoder, *Preface to Theology*, 140 (italics mine), as cited in "Trinitarian Orthodoxy, Constantinianism, and Theology from a Radical Protestant Perspective," 139. I am more and more of the view that we make too much of the difference between the Hebraic-biblical view and the Hellenistic-biblical-postbiblical view. They have much in common with each other, more than either has with modern and postmodern worldviews.

[22] Reimer, "Trinitarian Orthodoxy," 148.

[23] Reimer, "Towards a Theocentric Christology: Christ for the World," *The Limits of Perfection: A Conversation with J. Lawrence Burkholder*, eds., Rodney J. Sawatsky and Scott Holland (Waterloo, ON: Institute of Anabaptist-Mennonite Studies, 1993), 95-109 (Chapter 16 above).

[24] *Ibid.*, 103-7.

[25] Yoder gave the following presentations: March 12: a lecture on Tolstoy to my "Modern Christian Thought" class; March 13: a public lecture on "The Politics of Jesus Revisited" at Emmanuel College, Toronto School of Theology; a conversation with Mennonite doctoral students and friends on "The Jewishness of the Free Church Vision" at the Toronto Mennonite Theological Centre; March 14: a faculty forum on "Judaism as a Non-non Christian Religion," at Conrad Grebel College, to which faculty of the University of Waterloo Religious Studies Department were invited; and another public lecture on "The Politics of Jesus Revisited" in the Conrad Grebel College chapel.

[26] Yoder, "Judaism as a Non-non-Christian Religion" (Shalom Desktop Publishing, 1996).

[27] *Ibid.*, 118

[28] *Ibid.*, 121

[29] *Ibid.*, 119

[30] Yoder, "The Jewishness of the Free Church Vision," a lecture given at Toronto Mennonite Theological Centre, Toronto School of Theology, on March 13, 1997. First presented as the third lecture in the Bethel/Earlham series, Richmond, VA on April 30, 1985. Minimally revised as of May 1996. Some of my comments are taken from notes I made on Yoder's oral comments that went beyond the written text itself.

[31] *Ibid.*, 13, 22n.

[32] *Ibid.*, 3

[33] *Ibid.*, 4

[34] *Ibid.*, 4-6. Yoder goes on in his text to identify more specifically some sociological similarities between the historic Mennonite and Jewish experience

which are interesting but not relevant for my purposes here. One interesting thing he does say is that "Mennonites have seldom been thoroughly or riskily pacifist. Certainly their peace position does not enter as deeply into their spirituality and self-understanding as is the case for Friends," 6.

[35] *Ibid.*, 8-9

[36] *Ibid.*, 12

[37] *Ibid.*, 10

[38] Yoder, "See How They Go with Their Face to the Sun," *For the Nations: Essays Public and Evangelical* (Grand Rapids: Eerdmans, 1997). While the other two Jewish essays considered above stem from an earlier period in Yoder's thinking, this one was first presented on September 23, 1995, at Loyola Marymount University, Los Angeles.

[39] The title appears to be a conscious contrast to that of Stanley Hauerwas's book, *Against the Nations: War and Survival in a Liberal Society* (Minneapolis: Winston Press, 1985).

[40] Yoder, *For the Nations*, 6.

[41] *Ibid.*, 3

[42] Yoder, "See How They Go with Their Face to the Son," *For the Nations*, 53. Subsequent citations of this essay are inserted into the body of the text.

[43] A few of his publications are *Jesus at Thirty: A Psychological and Historical Portrait* (Minneapolis: Fortress Press, 1997); *The Origins of the Bible: Rethinking Canon History* (New York: Paulist Press, 1994); *Reading Israel's Story: A Canon-history Approach to the Narrative and Message of the Christian Bible*, Background Essays for Teachers in the Blenheim Bible Study Program (Kitchener, ON, n.d.).

[44] For a recent history and dialogue with members of this group, see *The Conrad Grebel Review* 8.2 (Spring, 1990). I was involved in the special event to which all seven original members of the 'Concern Group' were invited for conversation and reflection. Interestingly, Yoder decided not to attend. All those in attendance agreed that Yoder had probably been the most influential figure in articulating the concerns of this group of seven. John Miller has openly acknowledged his 'change of mind' on a number of issues since that time, including his critical distancing of himself from the position maintained by Yoder at a number of significant points.

[45] John W. Miller, Letter to Herbert C. Klassen, 3 March 1998.

[46] Personal letter, Miller to Klassen, 3 March 1998.

[47] Personal letter, Miller to Klassen, 3 March 20, 1998.

[48] *Ibid.*

[49] Yoder, *The Politics of Jesus*, 105.

[50] Wolfhart Pannenberg, who laments the avoidable divisions that occurred in Christian history as a result of Chalcedon in 451, the East-West split in the eleventh century, and the Reformation, says, "Some divisions are certainly necessary, i.e., in cases of apostasy from faith in Jesus Christ. Primitive Christianity had to separate itself from Judaizing and Gnostic errors, and the early church from Arianism." *Systematic Theology: Volume 3* (Grand Rapids: Eerdmans, 1998), 411.

[51] For a critical look at the influence of nominalism on Balthasar Hubmaier's

anthropology see my chapter, "The Adequacy of a Voluntary Theology for a Voluntaristic Age," *The Believers Church: A Voluntary Church*, Studies in the Believers Church Tradition, ed. William H. Brackney (Kitchener, ON and Scottdale, PA: Pandora Press and Herald Press, 1998), 135-48. Reprinted below.

Chapter 19

[1] Published as "Lost Horizons: Whatever Happened to Classical Theology?" in *CMBC Alumni Bulletin* (Fall 1983): 3-12.
[2] Robert Friedman, *The Theology of Anabaptism* (Scottale: Herald Press, 1973), 29
[3] *Ibid.*
[4] J.C. Wenger, *The Doctrine of the Mennonites* (Scottdale: Mennonite Publishing House, 1952), 2.
[5] Cited by David Tracy in *The Achievement of Bernard Lonergan* (New York: Herder & Herder, 1970), 12
[6] George P. Grant, *English-Speaking Justice* (Sackville: Mount Allison University, 1974), 89
[7] Gordon D. Kaufman, "Nuclear Eschatology and the Study of Religion," *Journal of the American Academy of Religion* 51.1 (March 1983): 4.
[8] *Ibid.*, 13
[9] *Ibid.*, 12-13
[10] *Ibid.*, 13
[11] Kaufman, "Biblical Authority in a World of Power," *Nonresistance and Responsibility and Other Mennonites Essays* (Newton, KS: Faith and Life Press, 1979), 22-23.
[12] Reimer, "Theological Method, Modernity, and the Role of Tradition," *Prophetic Vision Applied to One's Academic Discipline: 1978 Mennonite Graduate Seminar* (Elkhart, IN: Mennonite Board of Missions, 1978), 119 (Chapter 1 above).

Chapter 20

[1] I have described these moments in Peter's life, from existential faith to mature thinker, in "Passing on faith: Peter provides a model," *Canadian Mennonite* 2.16 (August 17, 1998): 8-9.
[2] *The Conrad Grebel Review* 4.2 (Spring 1986): 125-40; see also: "Further Reflections on 'The Theological Framework for the Authority of the Scriptures.' A. James Reimer responds to Glenn Brubacher," *CGR* 5.1 (Winter 1987): 71-5.
[3] According to Robert Friedmann, noted historian of Anabaptist sources, the special strength of early Anabaptism was that it was opposed to system building and opted rather for "existential," lived theology in which there was no "split between faith and life" (*The Theology of Anabaptism* [Scottdale: Herald Press, 1973], 27). I find totally unacceptable Friedmann's implied suggestion that a systematic theology and a lived Christianity are incompatible.
[4] Evangelical theologian John Jefferson Davis makes a distinction between

"doctrine" and "theology." According to Davis, "*Doctrine* . . . refers to scriptural teachings on the foundations of the faith—e.g., the deity of Christ, his substitutionary atonement, bodily resurrection, second coming, and so forth. *Theology* refers to the more developed ecclesiastical articulations, defences, and applications of those doctrines—e.g., the Chalcedonian formulation concerning the two natures of Christ" (*Foundations of Evangelical Theology* [Grand Rapids: Baker Book House, 1984], 44). While recognizing the importance of the distinction in this paper I will be using the two interchangeably.

⁵ George R. Brunk II, *A Crisis Among Mennonites* (Harrisonburg, VA: The Sword and Trumpet, and Johnstown, PA: Guidelines for Today, 1983), 1, 4, 8, 15, 18.

⁶ *Ibid.*, 1, 5, 6, 7, 11, 12, 13, 14, 16

⁷ *Ibid.*, 4, 7, 10, 16

⁸ *Ibid.*, 7. This is an interesting charge made by Brunk against the "liberals" in the church, since ordinarily one would think of evangelicals as being prone to allegorizing the biblical text. It simply demonstrates that Brunk's concern, like that of those who use the historical-critical method, is with maintaining the objective integrity of the biblical text.

⁹ *Ibid.*, 9

¹⁰ *Ibid.*, 13

¹¹ *Ibid.*, 10, 15, 19

¹² *Ibid.*, 8, 17

¹³ *Ibid.*, 18, 19

¹⁴ *Ibid.*, 14

¹⁵ *Ibid.*, 9

¹⁶ It was precisely in its militancy that classical fundamentalism of the 1920s was distinguished from early forms of evangelicalism and fundamentalism. In the words of George M. Marsden, "Fundamentalists were evangelical Christians, close to the traditions of the dominant American revivalist establishment of the nineteenth century, who in the twentieth century militantly opposed both modernism in theology and the cultural changes that modernism endorsed. Militant opposition to modernism was what most clearly set off fundamentalism from a number of closely related traditions, such as evangelicalism, revivalism, pietism, the holiness movements, millenarianism, Reformed confessionalism, Baptist traditionalism, and other denominational orthodoxies" (*Fundamentalism and American Culture: The Shaping of Twentieth-Century Evangelicalism 1870-1925* [Oxford: Oxford University Press, 1980], 4).

¹⁷ Here Mennonites simply reflect the low-church orientation of the larger "Free Church" or "Believers' Church" tradition, of which Donald Durnbaugh says: "With minor exceptions, these movements were not heretical in the technical sense of espousing doctrines formally condemned by Classical Protestantism nor did they denounce elements of faith usually considered essential. They were generally noncreedal in posture, but they did not so much reject the teachings contained in the ancient creeds as resist the demand for rigid adherence to them. This was for two reasons: first, they believed that creedalism had become a substitute for living faith; and secondly, they wished to remain open for new

insight from the scriptures" (*The Believers' Church: The History and Character of Radical Protestantism* [New York: The Macmillan Company, 1968], 207).

[18] Howard John Loewen, *One Lord, One Church, One Hope, and One God: Mennonite Confessions of Faith* (Elkhart: Institute of Mennonite Studies, 1985).

[19] Doctrinal systematization as expressed in the early church creeds, in late medieval scholasticism, and in sixteenth- and seventeenth-century Protestant orthodoxy by its very nature consisted of a second order of intellectual reflection, and because of its concern for order, balance, harmony, and universal truth tended to ignore the genuine diversity of the biblical materials, to ride roughshod over the concrete particularity of Jesus' life and teachings, and to ignore the genuine and legitimate diversity of life and thought within the Christian communities. These are the dangers of all doctrinal and systematic theologies.

[20] Ted VanderEnde, ed., *Consultation: A Hermeneutical Newsletter for Concerned Mennonites* (self-published at St. John Mennonite Church, Pandora, OH; first issue, Fall 1984, 2).

[21] *Ibid.*, 3

[22] VanderEnde is referring here to two recent publications by the Institute of Mennonite Studies: Willard Swartley, ed., *Explorations of Systemic Theology from Mennonite Perspectives,* Occasional Papers No. 7 (Elkhart: Institute of Mennonite Studies, 1984), and Willard Swartley, ed., *Essays on Biblical Interpretation: Anabaptist-Mennonite Perspectives* (Elkhart: Institute of Mennonite Studies, 1984).

[23] Ted VanderEnde, "Apostolic Versus Process Hermeneutics: A Mennonite Dilemma" (paper presented at the October 1984 "Dialogue on Faith," constituting also the second issue of *Consultation*, 3).

[24] *Ibid.*, 5

[25] According to Peter Stuhlmacher, "Due to the obduracy of Orthodoxy as sketched above, Pietism and Christian Free Thought together emerged to assert the possibility of a free new encounter and occupation with the Bible. In making common cause against Orthodoxy, the fixing of goals—vastly different in the two camps—was for a time postponed and the way paved for what we today call the historical-critical research of the Bible . . . . Pietism's bold, critical research into the original biblical text; the revival of knowledge of the biblical languages, Hebrew and Greek; and the equally daring move toward scientific discussion of the original meaning of the Old and New Testament writings served—as the examples of August Hermann Francke and Johann Albrecht Bengel indicate—this encounter with scripture in its pure originality, an encounter which revived the insight and missionary courage of faith" (*Historical Criticism and Theological Interpretation of Scripture,* trans. Roy A. Harrisville [Philadelphia: Fortress Press, 1977], 36-37).

[26] Marsden, *Fundamentalism,* 7.

[27] *Ibid.*, 20

[28] *Ibid.*, 107

[29] *Ibid.*, 117

[30] I am not thinking here only of such one-sided attacks on the method as that by Gerhard Maier, *The End of the Historical-Critical Method* (St. Louis: Concordia Publishing House, 1977), but also of such reputable scholars as Walter

Wink, who states quite forthrightly "Historical biblical criticism is bankrupt.... Biblical criticism is not bankrupt because it has run out of things to say or new ground to explore. It is bankrupt solely because it is incapable of achieving what most of its practitioners considered its purpose to be: so to interpret the Scriptures that the past becomes alive and illumines our present with new possibilities for personal and social transformation" (*The Bible in Human Transformation: Toward a New Paradigm for Biblical Study* [Philadelphia: Fortress Press, 1973], 1-2).

[31] Stuhlmacher, *Historical Criticism*, 86.
[32] *Ibid.*, 75
[33] *Ibid.*, 85
[34] *Ibid.*, 76-77
[35] Henry Vander Goot, *Interpreting the Bible in Theology and the Church* (Toronto and New York: The Edwin Mellen Press, 1984), 1.
[36] *Ibid.*, 2
[37] *Ibid.*
[38] *Ibid.*
[39] *Ibid.*
[40] *Ibid.*, 3
[41] *Ibid.*, 7-8
[42] *Ibid.*, 3
[43] *Ibid.*, 8
[44] *Ibid.*
[45] *Ibid.*, 9
[46] *Ibid.*, 16
[47] *Ibid.*, 27
[48] Walter Klaassen, "Anabaptist Hermeneutics: Presuppositions, Principles and Practice" in Swartley, *Swartley, Essays on Biblical Interpretation*, 5.
[49] *Ibid.*, 10.
[50] According to John H. Yoder, "It is a basic novelty in the discussion of hermeneutics to say that a text is best understood in a congregation.... The first implication of this conception of the congregation listening to the Word of God is that the common man becomes a full member of the church. Now that the Bible is available in the language of the people, it is the entire congregation, and thus primarily simple people responding to the obvious meaning of the text, who will make the decision as to what God says for today" ("The Hermeneutics of the Anabaptists" in Swartley, *Essays on Biblical Interpretation*, 21).

Chapter 21

[1] Johnson's use of the phrase "disciplined theological imagination" was brought to my attention by Kathy Brouwer, a graduate theology student of mine at Conrad Grebel College, in her unpublished essay, "The Trinity: A Feminist Articulation."

[2] The present form of the essay is a revised version of what appeared in *The Conrad Grebel Review* as "Doctrines: What are They, How do They Function, and Why do We Need Them?," 11.1 (Winter 1993): 21-36.

³ *Confession of Faith in a Mennonite Perspective* (Scottdale/ Waterloo: Herald Press, 1995), published by arrangement with the General Board of the General Conference Mennonite Church and the Mennonite Church General Board, and adopted at the delegate sessions of the two conferences at Wichita, KS on July 25-30, 1995.

⁴ Jaroslav Pelikan, *The Christian Tradition*, vol. 1, *The Emergence of the Catholic Tradition (100-600)* (Chicago: University of Chicago Press, 1971), 1.

⁵ Don S. Browning, *Religious Thought and the Modern Psychologies: A Critical Conversation in the Theology of Culture* (Philadelphia: Fortress Press, 1987), 18-20.

⁶ *Ibid.*, 20

⁷ Thomas N. Finger, *Christian Theology: An Eschatological Approach*, vol. 1 (Scottdale: Herald Press, 1985), 13.

⁸ This concept first impressed itself upon me in the 1970s when reading John Henry Newman's [1845] *An Essay in the Development of Christian Doctrine* (Middlesex, England: Penguin Books Ltd., 1974), and Bernard Lonergan's *The Way to Nicea: The Dialectical Development of Trinitarian Theology* (London: Darton, Longman & Todd, 1976).

⁹ A. James Reimer, "Trinitarian Orthodoxy, Constantinianism, and Theology from a Radical Protestant Perspective." Reprinted above (Chapter 15) as "Trinitarian Orthodoxy, Constantinianism, and Radical Protestant Theology."

¹⁰ I consider the first scientific revolution as bringing about the perception of a static, mechanistic universe constituted by a comprehensive and self-sufficient set of laws open to empirical investigation; the second to be represented by evolutionary theories culminating in the discoveries of Charles Darwin (1809-1882), which replace a static, mechanistic universe with a linear, developmental, and evolutionary paradigm. The third and most recent revolution is that initiated by Albert Einstein (1879-1955) which looks at reality not in mechanistic nor in linear, evolutionary terms but in a cyclical, curved, and multidimensional way, allowing for the interchangeability of matter and energy, in some ways akin to the ancient cosmologies.

¹¹ Margaret Loewen Reimer, *One Quilt Many Pieces: A Reference Guide to Mennonite Groups in Canada*, 3rd ed. (Waterloo, ON: Mennonite Publishing Service, 1983).

¹² John H. Redekop, *People Apart* (Hillsboro, KS: Kindred Press, 1987).

¹³ A. James Reimer, "Toward Christian Theology From a Diversity of Mennonite Perspectives" (Chapter 14 above).

¹⁴ *Confession of Faith in a Mennonite Perspective* (Scottdale/Waterloo: Herald Press, 1995).

¹⁵ Helmut Harder, *Guide to Faith* (Newton, KS: Faith and Life Press, 1979).

¹⁶ Cf. Howard John Loewen, *One Word, One Church, One Hope, and One God: Mennonite Confessions of Faith* (Elkhart: Institute of Mennonite Studies, 1985), 63-70.

¹⁷ Browning, *Religious Thought and the Modern Psychologies*, 20.

¹⁸ Finger, *Christian Theology* 1, 40.

¹⁹ Gayle Gerber Koontz, "The Trajectory of Scripture and Feminist Conviction," *The Conrad Grebel Review* 5.1 (1987): 201-20.

Chapter 22

¹ Taken from *Readings in Christian Thought*, ed. Hugh T. Kerr, 2nd edition (Nashville: Abingdon Press, 1990), 41.

² Published as "Biblical and Systematic Theology as Functional Specialties: Their Distinction and Relation," in *So Wide a Sea: Essays on Biblical and Systematic Theology*, ed. Ben C. Ollenburger (Elkhart: Institute of Mennonite Studies, 1991), 37-58. The same volume published a response to my essay by Gordon D. Kaufman, "Critical Theology and the Bible: A Response to A. James Reimer," 59-64, in which he criticizes me for ignoring the critical function of theology.

³Bernard Lonergan, for instance, to whom I am indebted for my notion of systematic theology as a "functional specialty," divides theology into eight functional specialties: research, interpretation, history, dialectic, foundations, doctrines, systematics, and communication (*Method in Theology* [New York: Herder and Herder, 1972], 127). David Tracy, strongly influenced by Lonergan, works with a tripartite schema: fundamental theology related primarily to the public of the academy; systematic theology linked primarily to the public of the church; and practical theology, focused primarily on society. "Theology, in fact," he says, "is a generic name not for a single discipline but for three: fundamental, systematic and practical theologies. Each of these disciplines needs explicit criteria of adequacy" (*The Analogical Imagination*. New York: Crossroad, 1981], 31). While most seminary programmes divide their curriculae into biblical, historical, systematic, practical (or pastoral) theology, some graduate theological programmes experiment with different classifications, like the new Conrad Grebel College Master of Theological Studies programme which has four subject areas: Scripture; Theology, Philosophy; History, Society, Culture; and Ethics, Mission, Ministry.

⁴ I am using "conversion" here similarly to the way Lonergan uses it when he says, "By conversion is understood a transformation of the subject and his world. Normally it is a prolonged process though its explicit acknowledgement may be concentrated in a few momentous judgments and decisions. Still it is not just a development or even a series of developments. Rather it is a resultant change of course and direction. . . . Conversion, as lived, affects all of a man's conscious and intentional operations. It directs his gaze, pervades his imagination, releases the symbols that penetrate to the depths of his psyche" (*Method in Theology*, 130-131). Conversion, for Mennonites theologically a condition for church membership, profoundly affects the way one goes about studying the Bible, church history, systematics and doctrine, and the practical life of the church.

⁵ *Catechism: German & English*, tr. P. J. B. Reimer (Altona, MB: D.W. Friesen & Sons, Ltd., 1954, 1957).

⁶ *Ibid.*, IV

⁷ George A. Lindbeck, *The Nature of Doctrine: Religion and Theology in a Postliberal Age* (Philadelphia: Westminster Press, 1984).

⁸ Cf. *Ibid.*, 94

⁹ *Ibid.*, 132

[10] *Ibid.*, 113

[11] *Ibid.*, 74.

[12] The problem with Lindbeck's schematization is that everything traditional—that is, pre-modern—is classified as "propositional," in contrast to modern (or nineteenth-century liberal) experientialism and postmodern cultural-linguisticism. This is an unfair caricature of the ancients' understanding of theology. Lindbeck seems to recognize this when he says quite correctly, "Both the Protestant who insists on scriptural inerrancy and the Roman Catholic traditionalist counterpart are likely to be suffering from vulgarized forms of a rationalism descended from Greek philosophy by way of Cartesian and post-Cartesian rationalism reinforced by Newtonian science; but in the early centuries of the church, ontological truth by correspondence had not yet been limited to propositionalism. Fundamentalist liberalism, like experiential-expressivism, is a product of modernity" (*ibid.*, 51). So is Lindbeck's own cultural-linguistic model a product of modernity, one might add. The point is, however, that while Lindbeck at points acknowledges that his so-called "traditional 'propositionalist'" category does not fit the ancients, he seems again and again to include the classical theological tradition under this category. I would suggest that classical theology, as represented by the church fathers during the classical period of orthodoxy, did not view doctrine either propositionally in the fundamentalist mode, experientially in the nineteenth-century liberal mode, or cultural-linguistically in the postmodern mode but confessionally with propositional-ontological, "experiential-expressive," and "cultural-linguistic" components. Absolutely essential to the classical way of thinking and confessing was a trinitarian understanding and experience of reality, giving it both a continuity and a discontinuity with the Greco-Roman tradition on the one hand, and the Hebraic world on the other. Charles Norris Cochrane's *Christianity and Classical Culture* (London: Oxford University Press, 1940) still remains a classic on this topic.

[13] Lindbeck, *The Nature of Doctrine*, 77ff.

[14] *Ibid.*, 78

[15] A. James Reimer, "Mennonite Theological Self-Understanding and Doctrinally Structured Systematic Theology" (Chapter 13 above).

[16] Karl Barth, *Learning Jesus Christ Through the Heidelberg Catechism* (Grand Rapids: Eerdmans, 1981), 17.

[17] Karl Barth, *Dogmatics in Outline* (New York: Harper & Brothers, 1959), 12, 13.

[18] *Ibid.*, 10, 11

[19] Karl Barth, *Church Dogmatics*, I/1 (Edinburgh: T. & T. Clark, 1936, 1969), 431-40.

[20] Barth, *Outline*, 13.

[21] Ben C. Ollenburger, "What Krister Stendahl 'Meant'—A Normative Critique of 'Descriptive Biblical Theology,'" in *Horizons in Biblical Theology* 8 (1986): 61-98.

[22] Krister Stendahl, "Biblical Theology: A Program," in *Meanings: The Bible as Document and as Guide* (Philadelphia: Fortress Press, 1984). First published as "Biblical Theology, Contemporary" in the *Interpreter's Dictionary of the Bible*, vol.

1 (Nashville: Abingdon Press, 1962). My own reading was based on the 1984 reprint. Ollenburger bases his critique on a 1965 article of Stendahl's, "Methodology in the Study of Biblical Theology," written for the Society of Biblical Literature.

[23] Ollenburger, "What Krister Stendahl 'Meant'—A Normative Critique," 69.

[24] Ibid., 74

[25] Ibid., 77

[26] Ibid.

[27] Ibid., 61-62

[28] Ibid., 78

[29] Ibid.

[30] Stendahl, "Meanings," *Meanings: The Bible as Document and as Guide*, 1.

[31] Kant: "I have therefore found it necessary to deny *knowledge* in order to make room for *faith*" (*Critique of Pure Reason*, trans. Norman Kemp Smith [Toronto: MacMillan, 1929], 29). The choice of the comparison is not solely arbitrary, for biblical theologians as historians claim to be dealing with *knowledge* in the historical-critical sense, while biblical and systematic theologians as theologians deal with the same material from a stance of faith.

[32] Stendahl, "Biblical Theology," 29.

[33] Ibid., 25

[34] Ibid., 30

[35] This depends, of course, on how loosely one defines what constitutes a "discipline." David Tracy, for example, goes into an extensive discussion of theology as a legitimate academic discipline with certain criteria of adequacy, warrants, and backing (or publicness) like every other discipline in the university. Tracy argues against the view that theology, generically speaking, is one separate discipline, and maintains that theology consists of three disciplines: fundamental, systematic, and practical, each making its own truth- and meaning-claims and needing separate criteria of adequacy (*The Analogical Imagination*, 14-31). It is not clear where in Tracy's whole scheme of things biblical theology or biblical studies as a separate focus fits, although it appears to belong most comfortably in his discipline of systematic theology. I am more inclined than is Tracy to give biblical theology a distinct place in the theological enterprise, but to argue for the generic methodological unity of all types of theological studies whether biblical, historical, systematic or practical. To define biblical theology and systematic theology as distinct disciplines, with separate methodologies, separate truth claims, and separate criteria of adequacy strikes me as undermining the unity of Christian theology itself. That is why Lonergan's notion of distinct but interdependent "functional specialties" within theology as a unified method appeals to me. It allows for the separateness of the tasks but assumes certain common assumptions concerning the reality of God and God's presence within history and the church.

[36] I am not suggesting that the Bible and the creeds have equal authority for the Christian church, merely that the selection of the biblical writings and the defining of orthodoxy in the creeds took place more or less during the same time (creedalization extending beyond canonization in time) and for similar

reasons. The apostolic witness to Christ as recorded in the biblical writings themselves is prior (both in authority and in chronology) to the formulation of the creeds. On the other hand, the confession-content of the creeds (e.g., Jesus is Lord) reaches back further than the written content of the biblical materials themselves and thus is more primal or primary.

[37] I am using the term "translation" deliberately here to describe the work of the biblical theologian, in contrast to "mediation" as the work of the systematic theologian. Translation is what the biblical scholar, like Paul Minear, is doing when he is preparing a new, updated Revised Standard Version of the Bible. His primary goal is to present the original as accurately as possible. Because the meaning of words and concepts changes, he needs to make changes here and there; he tries, for instance, to use more inclusive language wherever the original warrants it. The biblical theologian does more than simply translate, she also elucidates, interprets, analyzes, and synthesizes, enters into and engages herself with the assumptions of the biblical world. Nevertheless, I think the work of the Bible translator is a kind of paradigm for what the biblical theologian does or ought to do: focus on the world of the Bible and present that world as faithfully as possible to us in our world. At the point where the biblical theologian begins consciously to move beyond the biblical world in order to "mediate" or "bridge" these two worlds, the line between the task of biblical theology and systematic theology becomes increasingly more fuzzy. One and the same person can of course be both biblical theologian and systematic theologian.

[38] In the words of Raymond B. Williams, "Thus, the Bible is not a captive of one methodology; rather, literary, historical, sociological, archeological and philosophical analyses complement the study of the Bible. Genealogical relationships of disciplines and methods exist so that the study of the Bible applies a wide range of critical methods developed in the Western intellectual tradition to the central text of that tradition" (Foreword *The Bible and the Liberal Arts*. Papers from a Conference, October 16-17, 1986 [Crawfordsville, IN: Wabash College, 1986]). All these different methodologies are devoted to the study of the biblical texts themselves. The systematician also is an interdisciplinarian, but is more directly engaged in conversing with and addressing the various disciplines as bearers of the assumptions of contemporary culture, intent both on mediation and on confrontation.

[39] At the point of this faith bias the biblical theologian and the systematic theologian are united in their methodologies. Here both of them are Christian theologians.

[40] See Chapter 13 above.

[41] Chapter 34 below.

[42] Because the biblical theologian is not simply a historian but also a theologian—that is, she considers the biblical writings to have authority and normativity as the "Word of God" for herself and for the Christian community—the primary motive for specializing in the biblical texts and the biblical world is to discover in what sense that world has authority over us and how it can be made accessible to the believing community. Here again the biblical theologian and the systematic theologian overlap in their specialties.

[43] Culture (e.g., language, art, science, politics, economics, and so on) is that which makes us human. One cannot throw off culture without losing one's own humanity. Contemporary culture (whether one views it on the superficial level of its diversity or on the deeper level of its homogeneity) is the culture within which our own humanity is being expressed; it is a culture from which we cannot extricate ourselves. There are, of course both positive (divine?) and negative (demonic?) elements in every culture. It is the task of systematic theology to analyze modern culture and to determine which aspects are to be affirmed (as supportive of our own humanity and universal humanity) and which are to be rejected (as destructive of humanity). For the Christian, what it means to be human receives its primary definition from God's Word in Jesus Christ.

[44] The uniqueness of modern technology, and the assumptions behind this technology, particularly its presuppositions concerning human freedom, the domination of human and nonhuman nature, its reduction of reason to technical or analytical reason, and its homogenizing effect on modern world culture, finds its most penetrating articulation in the writings of Martin Heidegger, Hans Jonas, George Grant, and Jacques Ellul, among others. At the very heart of modern technology, it would appear, is a denial of any accountability to a transcendent reality.

[45] Cf. Philip Rieff, *The Triumph of the Therapeutic: Uses of Faith After Freud* (Chicago: University of Chicago Press, 1966, 1987); and Paul C. Vitz, *Psychology As Religion: The Cult of Self-worship* (Grand Rapids: Eerdmans, 1977).

[46] Lindbeck, *The Nature of Doctrine*, 118.

[47] *Ibid.*, 34

[48] *Ibid.*, 7-8

[49] *Ibid.*, 65 To his credit Lindbeck seriously addresses the problem of truth claims and admits that the great advantage of the cognitive-propositional view of religion (in contrast to the experiential-expressive view) is that it can allow for such truth claims, and that it is the burden of the cultural-linguistic approach to show that it too can do so. But despite his valiant attempts to demonstrate through his intrasystematic notion of truth, and even a certain kind of propositional-correspondence view of truth (in which the entire system can be described as a giant proposition corresponding to what it considers to be "Most Important" and "Ultimately Real"), truth is in the end still described in terms of practice—living out one's story. The question which remains is this: Is there such a thing as a wrong story, or are there right and wrong parts to a story, and how (by what criteria) does one determine when a story is right and when it is wrong?

[50] *Ibid.*, 69

Chapter 23

[1] "God (Trinity), Doctrine of," *The Mennonite Encyclopedia*, vol. 5 (Scottdale: Herald Press, 1990), 342-48.

[2] Wolfhart Pannenberg, *Systematic Theology*, vol. 2 (Grand Rapids: Eerdmans, 1994), 1-9.

[3] Karl Rahner, ed., *Encyclopedia of Theology: The Concise Sacramentum Mundi* (New York: Crossroad, 1986), 564-66.

[4] Werner O. Packull, *Mysticism and the Early South German-Austrian Anabaptist Movement 1525-1531* (Scottdale: Herald Press, 1977), 17-34.

[5] Robert Friedmann, *The Theology of Anabaptism* (Scottdale: Herald Press, 1973), 53-57; idem, "The Encounter of Anabaptists and Mennonites with Anti-Trinitarianism," *Mennonite Quarterly Review* 22 (1948): 139-162; John C. Wenger, *The Doctrines of the Mennonites* (Scottdale: Herald Press, 1952), 1ff.

[6] Packull, *Mysticism*, 25-7.

[7] *Ibid.*, 31ff.

[8] Peter Riedemann, *Account of Our Religion, Doctrine and Faith* (London: Hodder and Stoughton, in conjunction with Plough Publishing House, 1938, 1970).

[9] *Ibid.*, 43

[10] Menno Simons, *The Complete Writings*, trans. L. Verduin, ed. J. C. Wenger (Scottdale: Herald Press, 1984), 491-92, 496.

[11] *Ibid.*, 496

[12] John R. Loeschen, *The Divine Community: Trinity, Church, and Ethics in Reformation Theologies* (Kirksville, MO: The Sixteenth Century Journal Publishers, 1981), 97.

[13] *Ibid.*, 73

[14] *Ibid.*, 75

[15] *Ibid.*, 80-1

[16] *Ibid.*, 101-102

[17] Hans-Jürgen Goertz, "Zwischen Zwietracht und Eintracht: Zur Zweideutigkeit täuferischer und mennonitischer Bekenntnisse," *Mennonitische Geschichtsblätter* 43.44 (1986-87): 16-46.

[18] The best source book for studying Mennonite confessions of faith from the time of the Dordrecht Confession, the mother of all later North American confessions, to the present is Howard John Loewen's *One Lord, One Church, One Hope, and One God: Mennonite Confessions of Faith in North America* (Elkhart: Institute of Mennonite Studies, 1985).

[19] *Ibid.*, 36

[20] Friedmann, "The Encounter of Anabaptists and Mennonites with Anti-Trinitarianism," 152-3.

[21] Daniel Kauffman, *Doctrines of the Bible: A Brief Discussion of the Teachings of God's Word* (Scottdale: Mennonite Publishing House, 1929).

[22] Cf. Kaufman, *God the Problem* (Cambridge, MA: Harvard University Press, 1972).

[23] Kaufman, *Systematic Theology: A Historicist Approach* (New York: Charles Scribner's Sons, 1968).

²⁴ Cf. Kaufman, *The Theological Imagination: Constructing the Concept of God* (Philadelphia: Westminster Press, 1981); *Theology for a Nuclear Age* (Philadelphia: Westminster Press, 1985).

²⁵ H. Victor Froese has recently provided a valuable summary and critical evaluation of Kaufman's thought in an article entitled "Gordon D. Kaufman's Theology 'Within the Limits of Reason Alone': A Review," *The Conrad Grebel Review* 6 (1988): 1-26.

²⁶ Thomas N. Finger, *Christian Theology: An Eschatological Perspective*, 2 vols. (Scottdale: Herald Press, 1985, 1989); also *idem*, "The Way to Nicea: Reflections from a Mennonite Perspective," *The Conrad Grebel Review* 3.3 (1985): 231-49.

²⁷ Cf. my article, "The Nature and Possibility of Mennonite Theology" (Chapter 10 above).

²⁸ Carl S. Keener, "The Darwinian Revolution and its Implications for a Modern Anabaptist Theology," *The Conrad Grebel Review* 1.1 (1983): 13-32.

²⁹ Mitchell Brown, "Jesus: Messiah not God," *The Conrad Grebel Review* 5.3 (1987): 233-52.

³⁰ Gayle Gerber Koontz, "The Trajectory of Scripture and Feminist Conviction," *The Conrad Grebel Review* 5.3 (1987): 201-20.

³¹ Cf. Chapter 13 above; also J. Denny Weaver, "Mennonite Theological Self-Understanding: A Response to A. James Reimer" in *Mennonite Identity: Historical and Contemporary Perspectives*, ed. Calvin Wall Redekop and Samuel J. Steiner (Lanham, MD: University of America Press, 1988), 39-61.

*For additional bibliographical sources see *Explorations of Systematic Theology: From Mennonite Perspectives*, ed. Willard Swartley (Elkhart: Institute of Mennonite Studies, 1984). This collection includes essays by Marlin E. Miller, Marlin Jeschke, J. Denny Weaver, Thomas Finger, A. James Reimer, and Howard J. Loewen; A. James Reimer, "Theological Method, Modernity and the Role of Tradition" Chapter 1 above; J. Denny Weaver, "Perspectives on a Mennonite Theology," *The Conrad Grebel Review* 2.3 (1984): 189-210.

Chapter 24

¹ Published as "Tillich's Christology in Light of Chalcedon," in *The Theological Paradox/Das Theologische Paradox* (Berlin: Walter de Gruyter, 1995), 122-40.

² Tillich, "Um was es geht: Antwort an Emanuel Hirsch," *Theologische Blätter* 14, 5 (May 1935): 119. See my reference to this in "Tillich, Hirsch and Barth: Three Different Paradigms of Theology and its Relation to the Sciences," *Natural Theology Versus Theology of Nature?* ed. Gert Hummel (Berlin: Walter de Gruyter, 1994), 101-124.

³ Paul Tillich,*Systematic Theology* II (Chicago: University of Chicago Press, 1957), 140.

⁴ R.P.C. Hanson, *Studies in Christian Antiquity* (Edinburgh: T. & T. Clark, 1985), 244-45.

⁵ *Ibid.*, 269.

⁶ A. James Reimer, "Trinitarian Orthodoxy, Constantinianism, and Theology from a Radical Protestant Perspective" in *Faith to Creed: Ecumenical Perspectives*

on the Affirmation of the Apostolic Faith in the Fourth Century, ed. S. Mark Heim (Grand Rapids: Eerdmans, 1991), 129-61.
   7 Aloys Grillmeier, S.J., *Christ in Christian Tradition* I (Atlanta: John Knox Press, 1965, 1975), 544-45.
   8 Grillmeier, *Christ in the Christian Tradition* II, 4.
   9 *Ibid.*, 5, 156, 165.
   10 Bernard Lonergan, *The Way to Nicea* (London: Darton, Longman & Todd, 1976).
   11 Grillmeier, *Christ in the Christian Tradition* II, 10.
   12 Charles Norris Cochrane, *Christianity and Classical Culture: A Study of Thought and Action From Augustus to Augustine* (London: Oxford University Press, 1940, 1974).
   13 Grillmeier, *Christ in the Christian Tradition* II, 188.
   14 *Ibid.*
   15 *Ibid.*, 9.
   16 In the words of Tillich: "Denn Kirche ist die Verwirklichung der Heilkräfte in der Welt, die dem neuen Sein zugehören in der sozialen Sphäre. Sie machen erst die gesammte Kultur möglich. Kirche ist nicht etwas, wozu man 'auch noch' geht. Innerhalb des Sozialen, des Wirtschaftlichen, des Wissenschaftlichen und der Politik muß sie verwirklicht werden. Kirche ist Repräsentation und Ziel dessen, was als heilende Kraft in der Welt und allem Leben steht" (*Christus und unsere Wirklichkeit*, 6). This was a lecture by Tillich given in the Gmelin-Institut in Clausthal on August 11, 1948, which is in typewritten manuscript form and as far as I know remains unpublished.
   17 Grillmeier, *Christ in the Christian Tradition* II, 108.
   18 *Ibid.*, 147.
   19 *Ibid.*, 556-57.
   20 R.P.C. Hanson, *Studies in Christian Antiquity*, 247.
   21 Grillmeier, *Christ in the Christian Tradition* I, 555.
   22 *Ibid.*, 553.
   23 Tillich, "What is Wrong with the 'Dialectical Theology'?" *The Journal of Religion* 15.2 (1935): 127-145.
   24 Tillich, *On the Boundary: An Autobiographical Sketch* (New York: Charles Scribner's Sons, 1936), 13.
   25 See Tillich, "Das Wohnen, der Raum und die Zeit," *Die Form* (1933): 11-12.
   26 Tillich, "History as the Problem of our Period," *Hauptwerke/Main Works*, vol. 6, ed. Gert Hummel (Berlin/New York: De Gruyter, 1992), 225-34, 226.
   27 Gordon D. Kaufman, *In Face of Mystery: A Constructive Theology* (Cambridge, MA: Harvard University Press, 1993), 97ff.
   28 Cf. George Grant, *Time as History* (Toronto: Canadian Broadcasting Corporation, 1969); Hans Jonas, *The Imperative of Responsibility: In Search of an Ethics for the Technological Age* (Chicago: University of Chicago Press, 1984).
   29 Tillich, "Christologie und Geschichtsdeutung," *Hauptwerke/Main Works*, vol. 6, 189-212.
   30 Tillich, "The Interpretation of History and the Idea of Christ," *The Interpretation of History* (New York/London: Scribner, 1936), 210-11.

Chapter 25

[1] Michael Welker, *God the Spirit* (Minneapolis: Fortress, 1994); translation from the German, *Gottes Geist: Theologie des Heiligen Geistes* (Neukirchener Verlag, Neukirchen-Vluyn, 1992); Harvey Cox, *Fire from Heaven: The Rise of Pentecostal Spirituality and the Reshaping of Religion in the Twenty-first Century* (New York: Addison-Wesley, 1995).

[2] "Angels and Demons and the Holy Spirit," *Mennonite Reporter* 27.10 (May 12, 1997): 8. At the annual meetings of Canadian Church Press, June 1998, this article received an Award of Merit ("Honorable Mention") in the "Theological Reflection—Doctrinal" category.

[3] Personal letter, Reimer to Welker, December 10, 1999.

[4] Personal letter, Welker to Reimer, January 12, 2000. My translation.

[5] *The Secular City: Secularization and Urbanization in Theological Perspective* (London: SCM Press, 1965)

[6] C. Peter Wagner, *Wrestling with Dark Angels: Toward a Deeper Understanding of the Supernatural Forces in Spiritual Warfare* (Ventura, CA: Regal Books, 1990)

[7] "Deliverance from Demons," *Canadian Mennonite* 1.5 (March 2000): 8. Burkholder is a minister in the Mennonite Conference of Eastern Canada, and holds graduate degrees in history from University of Toronto and theology from Conrad Grebel College. His book *A Mennonite Theology of Deliverance Healing* is to be published in Fall 2000.

[8] Cited by Cox, *Fire from Heaven*, 285.

[9] *Church Dogmatics*, vol. 3, Part 1 (Edinburgh, T. & T. Clark, 1958), 84-5.

Chapter 26

[1] The original title of the sermon was "Apocalypse: the curtain tore, the earth shook, rocks split, tombs opened, saints rose and went into the holy city (Mt. 27: 51-3)."

[2] Walter Klaassen, *Armageddon and the Peaceable Kingdom: Prophecy and Mystery True to the Gospel* (Scottdale: Herald Press, 1999), 9.

Chapter 27

[1] See Hugh T. Kerr, ed., *Readings in Christian Thought*, 2nd edition (Nashville: Abingdon Press, 1966, 1990), 24-8.

[2] Cf. *Glamorous Powers* (New York: Alfred A. Knopf, 1988) and *Mystical Paths* (New York: Alfred A. Knopf, 1992). These are two of a series of six novels by Susan Howatch on the lives of English clergy.

[3] First published as "Medugorje: The Virgin Mary Appears in Yugoslavia," in *IRF: A Newsletter of the International Religious Foundation, Inc.* 2.6 (Nov.-Dec. 1987): 1-2, 11.

[4] Michael P. Carroll, *The Cult of the Virgin Mary: Psychological Origins* (Princeton: Princeton University Press, 1986), 221, 222.

Chapter 28

[1] What started as a paper in a graduate course was later published as "Chiliastic Imagination and Social Change: Bloch's Interpretation of Müntzer," in *CLIO: A Journal of Literature, History and the Philosopher of History* 9.2 (Winter 1980): 253-67.

[2] John Henry Newman, *Selected Sermons, Prayers, and Devotions* (New York: Vintage Books, 1999), 89.

[3] Ernst Bloch, *Thomas Müntzer als Theologe der Revolution* (Frankfurt am Main: Suhrkamp Verlag, 1976).

[4] The Catholic theologian Gregory Baum devotes substantial space to Bloch's book on Müntzer in his *Religion and Alienation: A Theological Reading of Sociology* (Toronto: Paulist Press, 1975). See also Harvey Cox's foreword and Jürgen Moltmann's introduction to Ernst Bloch's *Man On His Own* (New York: Herder and Herder, 1971). Cox points out that nearly half of the contributors to a *Festschrift* for Bloch's eightieth birthday in 1965 were theologians.

In contrast stands the seeming lack of interest by historians. Harold S. Bender, in his article "The Zwickau Prophets, Thomas Müntzer, and the Anabaptists," *Mennonite Quarterly Review* 27.1 (January 1953): 3-16, never refers to Bloch. Robert Freidmann does not mention Bloch in his "Thomas Muentzer's Relation to Anabaptism," *MQR* 31. 2 (April 1957): 75-87, even though he has a bibliographical note listing numerous Marxist works on the subject. Abraham Friesen's "Thomas Müntzer in Marxist Thought," *Church History* 34.3 (September 1965): 306-27, devotes some space to Bloch, comparing the latter's chiliastic ideas to Sorel's notion of myth. However, in "Thomas Müntzer Between Marxist-Christian Diatribe and Dialogue," *Historical Reflections* 4.1 (Summer 1977): 67-89, Werner O. Packull gives a rather comprehensive overview of Marxist-Christian scholarship on Müntzer, but refers to Bloch only in passing, saying: "Such neo-Marxist historians as Ernst Bloch, who were willing to ascribe to the power of religious myth an almost autonomous motivating force, have been disowned by their more orthodox comrades" (74). It is of significance that in a collection of ten essays coming from Christian Democrats of the German Democratic Republic, written from a Marxian orientation, no mention is made of Bloch. See *Prophet einer neuen Welt: Thomas Müntzer in Seiner Zeit* (Berlin: Union Verlag, 1975).

[5] Abraham Friesen accuses Bloch of too hastily identifying Müntzer as an Anabaptist, not differentiating adequately within the original Anabaptist movement, and erroneously assuming that the major leaders of the early Anabaptists, including those of Swiss origin, were influenced by the revolutionary and communist ideas of Müntzer. See A. Friesen, "The Marxist Interpretation of Anabaptism," *Sixteenth Century Essays and Studies* 1 (June 1970): 17-34.

[6] See Hans-Jürgen Goertz, "The Mystic with the Hammer: Thomas Müntzer's Theological Basis for Revolution," *Mennonite Quarterly Review* 50 (April 1976): 83-113. See also Werner O. Packull, "Thomas Müntzer between Marxist-Christian Diatribe and Dialogue," 89.

[7] See Jürgen Busche, "Ein Denker und Erzähler, ein philosophischer Lehrer," *Frankfurter Allegemeine Zeitung* (August 5, 1977), 20. According to Jürgen

Moltmann, Bloch never officially joined the communist party as such (Introduction to *Man On His Own*, 23).

[8] Ernst Bloch, "Blick in den Chiliasmus des Bauernkriegs und Wiedertäufertums," *Genius: Zeitschrift für Werdende und alte Kunst* 2. 2 (München: Kurt Wolff Verlag, 1920): 310-13.

[9] Ernst Bloch, *Das Prinzip Hoffnung* (Frankfurt am Main: Suhrkamp Verlag, 1959), V, 1628.

[10] See Friesen, "The Marxist Interpretation of Anabaptists," 18. Friesen here refers to the "related problems which the imposition of a theoretical structure upon the historical evidence has created for the Marxists..."

[11] For Bloch, humanity and the cosmos remain always unfinished. He rejects all ideological distortion of the truth, Marxist as well as non-Marxist. See Moltmann on the notion of provisionality in Bloch's thought, "Introduction" to *Man On His Own*, 20.

[12] See A. James Reimer, "Theological Debate in Yugoslavia," *The Ecumenist* 15.6 (September-October 1977): 90.

[13] Moltmann, "Introduction," 22.

[14] Bloch, "Karl Marx, Death and the Apocalypse," *Man On His Own*, 39.

[15] *Ibid.*, 39.

[16] Hans-Jürgen Goertz, "The Mystic with the Hammer," 84.

[17] See Friesen, "Thomas Müntzer in Marxist Thought," 306. See also Packull, "Thomas Müntzer Between Marxist-Christian Diatribe and Dialogue," 75, where he remarks that "Closely linked with the above has been the concern to debunk the tradition shaped by Luther which pictured Müntzer as the *incarnatus diabolus*."

[18] James M. Stayer, "Thomas Müntzer's Theology and Revolution in Recent Non-Marxist Interpretations," *MQR* 43 (April 1969): 143.

[19] Friesen, "Thomas Müntzer in Marxist Thought," 306.

[20] *Ibid.*, 306. See also Bender, "The Zwickau Prophets, Thomas Müntzer, and the Anabaptists," in which the author argues that "the continued designation of Müntzer as an Anabaptist is historically completely untenable. Müntzer was in no sense an Anabaptist" (6). Note also Friedmann's assertion about Müntzer: "That he was a 'beginner of Anabaptism' in any sense whatsoever is, however, just as incorrect as the popular opposite claim which sees in him a forerunner of modern socialism," in "Thomas Müntzer's Relation to Anabaptism," 86.

[21] See James M. Stayer, "Thomas Müntzer's Theology and Revolution in Recent Non-Marxist Interpretations," 142. Stayer talks about a "Müntzer Renaissance" since World War II.

[22] Engels, "The Peasant War in Germany (Chapter 2)," *Marx & Engels on Religion* (New York: Schocken Books, Inc., 1964), 97.

[23] Modern Anabaptist scholarship has convincingly demonstrated the heterogeneous nature of early Anabaptism.

[24] Friedrich Engels, "The Peasant War in Germany," 98.

[25] Ernst Bloch, *Thomas Müntzer*, 9. The translations from the German edition throughout the essay are the author's. In subsequent pages citations of this work are incorporated into the body of the text.

[26] Packull, "Thomas Müntzer Between Marxist-Christian Diatribe and

Dialogue," 88.

²⁷ Ibid.

²⁸ See for instance Willis M. Stoesz, *At The Foundations of Anabaptism: A Study of Thomas Müntzer, Hans Denk and Hans Hut* (unpublished Ph.D. dissertation, Union Theological Seminary and Columbia University, 1964), 77ff.

²⁹ Max Steinmetz, "Thomas Müntzer in der Forschung der Gegenwart," *Zeitschrift für Geschichtswissenschaft* 23 (1975): 675.

³⁰ Goertz, "The Mystic with the Hammer," 87.

³¹ Ibid., 112.

³² Ernst Bloch, "Blick in den Chiliasmus des Bauernkriegs and Wiedertäufertums," 310. See also Bloch, *Thomas Müntzer*, 56.

³³ Bloch, "Blick in den Chiliasmus," 313; *Thomas Müntzer*, 64.

³⁴ Goertz, "The Mystic with the Hammer," 112.

³⁵ Packull, "Thomas Müntzer Between Marxist-Christian Diatribe and Dialogue," 87.

³⁶ Bloch, *Thomas Müntzer*, 228. See also Moltmann, "Introduction," 22-23.

³⁷ Karl Mannheim, *Ideology and Utopia* (New York: Harcourt, Brace, World, 1936), 192-93.

Chapter 29

¹ Originally published as "Theology and Nationalism," in *Canadian Mennonites and the Challenge of Nationalism*, ed. Abe J. Dueck (Winnipeg: Manitoba Mennonite Historical Society, 1994), 1-20; and "Mennonites, Theology and Nationalism," in *Journal of Mennonite Studies* 12 (1994): 89-103.

² Karl Barth, *Church Dogmatics: The Doctrine of Creation*, vol. 3, Part 1 (Edinburgh: T. & T. Clark, 1958), 337ff, 350ff, 388ff.

³ Miroslav Volf, *Exclusion and Embrace: A Theological Exploration of Identity, Otherness and Reconciliation* (Nashville: Abingdon Press, 1996).

⁴ Cf. A. James Reimer, "Nation and the Myth of Origin in Paul Tillich's Radical Social Thought," in Reimer, ed., *The Influence of the Frankfurt School on Contemporary Theology: Critical Theory and the Future of Religion; Dubrovnik Papers in Honour of Rudolf J. Siebert* (Lewiston, NY: The Edwin Mellen Press, 1992), 283-95.

⁵ It is said of Karl Barth, that when a student asked him what role reason played in his theological system, he is to have answered: "I use it." A story about Barth told in a dinner address by John Godsey of Wesley Theological Seminary, at a conference sponsored by the Center for Barth Studies at Princeton Theological Seminary, June 17-19, 1999. This response by Barth illustrates perfectly his understanding of reason within theology—it was purely an instrument, never intrinsic to the theological task. This differs generally from Catholic theology in which reason, in the form of 'natural theology' is much more foundational.

⁶ A. James Reimer, The *Emanuel Hirsch and Paul Tillich Debate: A Study in the Political Ramifications of Theology* (Lewiston, NY: The Edwin Mellen Press, 1989).

Later translated into the German by Doris Lax and published as *Emanuel Hirsch und Paul Tillich: Theologie und Politik in einer Zeit der Krise* (Berlin: Walter de Gruyter, 1995).

[7] Hirsch, "Die Liebe zum Vaterlande," *Pädagogisches Magazine*, Heft 975 (Langensalza, 1924): 9-12.

[8] See Hirsch, "Ein christliches Volk," *Der Geisteskampf der Gegenwart* 54.7 (1918): 163-66.

[9] Hirsch, "Theologisches Gutachten in der Nichtarierfrage," *Deutsche Theologie* 1 (May 1934): 182-99.

[10] Cf. Tillich, "Christentum, Sozialismus, und Nationalismus," *Wingolfs-Blätter* 53 (1924): 78-80.

[11] Tillich, *The Socialist Decision*, trans. Franklin Shermon with an introduction by John R. Stumme (New York: Harper & Row, 1977): 3ff.

[12] Tillich, "Christentum und Emigration," *Gesammelte Werke*, vol. 8, ed. Renate Albrecht (Stuttgart: Evangelisches Verlagswerk, 1959-1972), 190.

[13] See Tillich, *On the Boundary: An Autobiographical Sketch* (New York: Charles Scribner's Sons, 1936).

[14] Tillich, "Das Wohnen, der Raum und die Zeit," *Die Form* 8 (1933): 11-12.

[15] Reimer, ed., *The Influence of the Frankfurt School on Contemporary Theology* See note 4 above.

[16] Srdjan Vrcan, "Religion, Nation, and Class in Contemporary Yugoslavia," *The Influence of the Frankfurt School on Contemporary Theology*, 91.

[17] Paul Mojzes, "Religion and the Left in Yugoslavia," *The Influence of the Frankfurt School on Contemporary Theology*, 83ff.

[18] Ibid., 81

[19] Shenk, "The Protestant Experience in Yugoslavia: Response to Modernity," *The Influence of the Frankfurt School on Contemporary Theology*, 142.

[20] Ibid., 143-44

[21] See Peter J. Dyck, "Are They Dutch, German or Mennonite?," *Festival Quarterly* 19.3 (Fall 1992): 33.

[22] See "Quebecker Stirs Strong Emotions at Mennonite Schools," *Mennonite Reporter* (October 19, 1992): 1-2; and "MCC Hears Moving Stories: Quebecker Explains her Faith and Politics," by Wilma Derksen, *Mennonite Reporter* (February 10, 1992).

[23] Cf. Mario Liverani, "Nationality and Political Identity," in *The Anchor Bible Dictionary*, Vol. 4 (New York: Doubleday, 1992), 1031-37.

[24] Ibid., 4: 1039

[25] Ibid., 4, 1037-48, "Nations."

[26] Ibid., 4: 1037

[27] Yoder, "See How They Go with Their Faces to the Sun," *For the Nations: Essays Public and Evangelical* (Grand Rapids: Eerdmans, 1997), 51-78.

[28] Published as John W. Miller, *The Origins of the Bible: Rethinking Canon History* (New York: Paulist Press, 1994), see especially 123-26.

Chapter 30

¹I distinctly remember sitting in Paul Layman's apartment, listening to him describe the night in 1939 when he tried to persuade Bonhoeffer to stay in North America, not realizing at the time that Bonhoeffer was already deeply involved in the conspiracy against Hitler.

² A. James Reimer, *The Emanuel Hirsch and Paul Tillich Debate: The Political Ramifications of Theology* (Lewiston, NY: The Edwin Mellen Press, 1989), xi.

³ See Diether Götz Lichdi, *Mennoniten im Dritten Reich: Dokumenten und Deutung*. Schriften des Mennonitsche Geschictsvereins Nr. 9 (Weierhof/Pfalz, 1977), and John D. Thiessen, "The Mennonite Encounter with National Socialism in Latin America, 1933-1944, *Journal of Mennonite Studies*, vol. 12 (1991): 104-17

⁴ Cf. Yoder, *Karl Barth and the Problem of War* (Nashville: Abingdon Press, 1970), 64ff.

⁵ Cf. Hans Frei, *Types of Christian Theology* (New Haven: Yale University Press, 1992)

⁶A recent conference on the thought of Karl Barth, in June, 1999, sponsored by the newly established Center for Barth Studies at Princeton Seminary, drew some 300 participants, considerably beyond expectations.

⁷ For a nuanced recent discussion of the 'Athens-Jerusalem debate' see Nicholas Wolterstorff, "Tertullian's Enduring Question," in *The Cresset* 62.7 (June/July, 1999): 5-16.

⁸ Reimer, *The Emanuel Hirsch and Paul Tillich Debate*, 356.

⁹ Karin Schäfer, *Die Theologie des Politischen bei Paul Tillich unter besonderer Berücksichtigung der Zeit von 1933 bis 1945* (Frankfurt am Main: Peter Lang, 1988). Hereafter cited in the body of the text.

¹⁰Emanuel Hirsch, "Unsere Frage an Gott," *Evangelische Wahrheit* 5. 22 (1914): 370-72.

¹¹ Hirsch, "Luthers Gedanken über Staat und Krieg," Sonderabdruck aus den *Wingolf-Blättern* 46, 7 (January, 1917), 175-79; "Ein christliches Volk," *Der Geisteskampf der Gegenwart* 54. 7 (1918): 163-66; "Der Pazifismus," Sonderabdruck aus den *Wingolf-Blättern* (Mühlhausen: Paul Fischer, 1918), 1-16.

¹² One should be careful not to attribute to Luther and early Lutherans too systematic an understanding of a two kingdom doctrine. James M. Stayer, for instance, has recently argued against me that the doctrine of the two kingdoms did not really come into currency until the late 1920s. He believes that Hirsch did not use the phrase "two kingdoms" until 1929, although Hirsch does to be sure distinguish between the kingdom of the world and the invisible kingdom of God (Stayer, *Martin Luther: German Saviour* [Montreal and Kingston: McGill - Queen's University Press, 2000], 155 n58). I would continue to hold that the two-kingdom doctrine was there implicitly if not explicitly.

¹³ "Der Pazifismus," 15. For Hirsch, justice as righteousness (*Gerechtigkeit*) appears to be understood somewhat differently from the way Tillich views it. For Tillich justice is understood more in socialist egalitarian terms; for Hirsch it has to do with a nation's proper understanding of itself before God and the

conduct of its affairs accordingly.

[14] Tillich, "Autobiographical Reflections" in *The Theology of Paul Tillich*, ed. Charles W. Kegley and Robert W. Bretail (New York: Macmillan, 1964), 12.

[15] The Greek term *kairos*, meaning "fulfilled time," plays a central role in Tillich's early political writings, in which he tries to bring together socialist thought and Christian thinking about history. *Kairos* becomes for him the bridging concept between socialism and Christianity—the socialist movement is the *kairos* moment in history, when through the proletariat (representing the new humanity) the divine is enters history in a unique way.

[16] Tillich, *Love, Power and Justice* (New York: Oxford University Press, 1954, 1960), 100.

[17] *Ibid.*, 123-24.

[18] Cf. John Howard Yoder, *Karl Barth and War* (Nashville: Abingdon Press, 1970), 37ff.

[19] "Truth and Revelation in Tillich's 1925 Dogmatics," *Truth and History—A Dialogue with Paul Tillich / Wahrheit und Geschichte—Ein Dialog mit Paul Tillich* (Berlin: Walter de Gruyter, 1998), 227-38; "A Postliberal Metaphysics for Christian Ethics: The 1925 Dogmatics of Karl Barth and Paul Tillich," a chapter in a soon-to-be published book edited by Jean Richard.

[20] Because this paper was presented to an audience that had come to hear a panel on Tillich's thought on the subject of war and peace, I concentrated on Tillich's pespective on Barth's views rather than analyzing Barth's own position on war.

[21] See Schäfer, *Die Theologie*, 94-125, for an analysis of these texts.

[22] Bishop Ludwig Müller, a former army chaplain, personal friend, and confidante of Hitler, was the controversial, newly-elected head of the "German-Christian" controlled national German Evangelical Church. Martin Niemöller, the leader of the Pastors' Emergency League and symbol of the Confessing Church's opposition to the German Christians, became the personal prisoner of Hitler in the Dachau concentration camp in 1937.

Chapter 31

[1] "God is not a Pacifist," *Canadian Mennonite* 3.15 (July 26, 1999): 8-9. The biblical texts for the sermon were Deut. 32:18-34 and Rom. 12:9-21.

[2] Miroslav Volf, *Exlcusion and Embrace: A Theological Exploration of Identity, Otherness, and Reconciliation* (Nashville: Abingdon Press, 1996). See especially 275-306. In the end, Volf compromises his own powerful critique of the human use of violence by slipping back into a Niebuhrian type of political realism: "It may be that consistent nonretaliation and nonviolence will be impossible in the world of violence. Tyrants may need to be taken down from their thrones and the madmen stopped from sowing desolation" (306).

Chapter 32

[1] Previously published as "Christians and the Civil Order" in *The Grebel Scholar*2.1 (August 1999): 5-7 and in a shortened and modified form in *Canadian Mennonite* 3.17 (August 30, 1999): 6-7.

[2] The concept of "orders of creation" has received a bad name ever since German Christians during the Hitler period applied this notion to race. It is for this reason that Dietrich Bonhoeffer preferred to talk about 'mandates'—the tasks that Christians have in the world. I believe that it may be possible to rehabilitate the notion of 'orders'—in the sense of divinely ordained institutions intended by God for the preservation of individual and social life, if these are not given too fixed and rigid a form, are subject to prophetic critique in the light of God's revelation in Christ, not used as a form of domination and exploitation, and open to change and reformation.

[3] Karl Barth in his *The Göttingen Dogmatics* [1925] (Grand Rapids: Eerdmans, 1991), says that even in Christ God is revealed as hidden. See my "Truth and Revelation: Epistemological Presuppositions in Tillich's 1925 *Dogmatik*," in *Truth and History—a Dialogue with Paul Tillich/Wahrheit und Geschichte—Ein Dialog mit Paul Tillich* (Berlin: Walter de Gruyter, 1998), 232.

[4] John Howard Yoder, in his *The Christian Witness to the State* (Newton, KS: Faith and Life Press, 1964) identifies seven classical options: Medieval Catholic, Lutheran, Calvinist, Liberal Pacifist/Niebuhrian, Jehovah's Witness, Traditional Amish-Mennonite, and his own (60-73). For my purposes these can be collapsed into four.

[5] Ernie Regehr, "Defence and human security," *The Ploughshares Monitor* (December 1999): 2-6. See also Margaret Loewen Reimer's interview with Regehr, "'Premier' peacemaker focuses on reducing violence," *Canadian Mennonite* 4.8 (April 17, 2000): 18-19.

[6] The CGC Council in the end voted against applying for such funding from DND, believing that it would compromise our peace witness.

Chapter 33

[1] The original title was "Virtue, Justice and the Moral Community: A Mennonite Theological Appraisal of Alasdair MacIntyre."

[2] Chris Huebner, for instance, has concentrated in his doctoral work on MacIntyre, Hauerwas, Yoder, and the narrative school. Cf. Chris K. Huebner, "Mennonites and Narrative Theology: The Case of John Howard Yoder," *The Conrad Grebel Review* 16.2 (Spring 1998): 15-38. See also Harry Huebner and David Schroeder, *Church as Parable: Whatever Happened to Ethics?* (Winnipeg: CMBC Publications, 1993).

[3] A special issue of *The Conrad Grebel Review* (13.2 [Spring 1995]) was devoted to this "Dialogue with Stanley Hauerwas."

[4] Reimer, "Dialogue with Stanley Hauerwas: Introduction," *The Conrad Grebel*

Review 13.2 (Spring 1995): 134.

[5] Personal letter, Hauerwas to Reimer, April 20, 1998.

[6] Alasdair MacIntyre, *After Virtue: A Study in Moral Theory*, 2nd ed. (Notre Dame: University of Notre Dame Press, 1984), 225.

[7] *Ibid.*, 252

[8] Ted Koontz, "Mennonites and 'Postmodernity'," *The Mennonite Quarterly Review* 63. 4 (October 1989): 427.

[9] Koontz's paraphrase of John Rawls's position, "Mennonites and 'Postmodernity,'" 409-10.

[10] Communitarianism must surely be considered as one option among many but not as a defining characteristic of modernity, for most would characterize postmodernity as the *total* absence of consensus and community.

[11] *Ibid.*, 414

[12] Cf. George A Lindbeck, *The Nature of Doctrine: Religion and Theology in a Postliberal Age* (Philadelphia: Westminster Press, 1984), 113-15.

[13] Scott Holland, "The Problems and Prospects of a 'Sectarian Ethic': A Critique of the Hauerwas Reading of the Jesus Story," *The Conrad Grebel Review* 10.2 (Spring 1992): 157-68, 160.

[14] *Ibid.*, 162

[15] *Ibid.*

[16] *Ibid.*, 166

[17] *Ibid.*, 167

[18] Cf. Margaret Loewen Reimer, *One Quilt Many Pieces: A Reference Guide to Mennonite Groups in Canada* (Waterloo: Mennonite Publishing Service, 1990).

[19] John Richard Burkholder and Barbara Nelson Gingerich, eds., *Mennonite Peace Theology: A Panorama of Types*. Printed by Mennonite Central Committee Peace Office, Akron, PA (January 1991).

[20] MacIntyre, *After Virtue*, 19.

[21] *Ibid.*, 216

[22] Cf. *ibid.*, 220-21

[23] MacIntyre, *Whose Justice? Which Rationality?* (Notre Dame: University of Notre Dame Press, 1988).

[24] MacIntyre, *Three Rival Versions of Moral Enquiry: Encyclopaedia Genealogy and Tradition* (Notre Dame: University of Notre Dame Press, 1990), 226.

[25] *Ibid.*, 230-31 Cf. also Chapter 6 above.

[26] Cf. MacIntyre, *After Virtue*, 162ff.

[27] *Ibid.*, 266

[28] Hans Jonas, *The Imperative of Responsibility: In Search of an Ethic for the Technological Age* (Chicago: University of Chicago Press, 1984), 45-6.

[29] Hutterites, modern descendants of sixteenthth-century Anabaptists, for instance, live in strict communitarian colonies but use the most advanced technological machinery and computers.

Chapter 34

[1] Reimer, "A forum on homosexuality," in *Mennonite Reporter*, 17.13 (June 22, 1987), 7-9. This essay was later that year discussed at a Conrad Grebel College Faculty Forum.

[2] An open lecture to students at Conrad Grebel College, November 12, 1986.

[3] My talk, entitled "Theological Perspectives on Homosexuality," was given upon invitation at the International Convention (with the theme "Journey Toward Wholeness") of the Brethren/Mennonite Council for Lesbian and Gay Concerns in Toronto, Ontario, October 7-9, 1988.

[4] The occasion was a discussion of "homosexuality" as part of the Lakeside, OH Peace and Justice Week on August 3, 1999, a session chaired by Rev. Grayson Atha, pastor of King Avenue United Methodist Church in Columbus, OH.

[5] Yoder, "Radical Reformation Ethics in Ecumenical Perspective" in *The Priestly Kingdom: Social Ethics as Gospel* (Notre Dame: University of Notre Dame Press, 1984), 117.

[6] *The Challenge of Peace: God's Promise and Our Response: A Pastoral Letter on War and Peace*. May 3, 1983. National Conference of Catholic Bishops (Washington: United States Catholic Conference, 1983), i.

[7] For the following categories, the various approaches to homosexuality, and their representatives, particularly the views of Karl Barth, Helmut Thielicke, and Gregory Baum, I am indebted to the work of Edward Batchelor, who in his helpful book *Homosexuality and Ethics* (New York: The Pilgrim Press, 1980) gathers the writings of numerous theologians on the subject. See especially Roger L. Shinn's opening essay, "Homosexuality: Christian Conviction and Inquiry," 11-13.

[8] Karl Barth, "Church Dogmatics," in Batchelor, *Homosexuality and Ethics*, 49.

[9] Helmut Thielicke, "The Theologicalethical Aspect of Homosexuality," in *Homosexuality and Ethics*, 100.

[10] Gregory Baum, "Catholic Homosexuals," in *Homosexuality and Ethics*, 23. [I take this to be the position taken by Mennonite academics, church leaders and others who signed or endorsed the recent statement, "A welcoming open letter on homosexuality," *Mennonite Weekly Review* (February 17, 2000): 7. My own approach to and position on the delicate issue of heterosexual, homosexual, and lesbian sexuality differs in significant ways from this most recent statement by sizeable group of Mennonites.]

Chapter 35

[1] Later published as "The Adequacy of a Voluntaristic Theology for a Voluntaristic Age," in *The Believers Church: A Voluntary Church* , ed. William H. Brackney (Kichener and Scottdale: Pandora Press, co-published with Herald Press, 1998), 135-48.

[2] For helpful discussion of late medieval voluntarism and nominalism, see William C. Placher, *A History of Christian Theology: An Introduction* (Philadelphia: Westminster Press, 1983), 162ff.

[3] Her first book was *George Grant and the Twilight of Justice* (Toronto: University of Toronto Press, 1984). More recently she has authored *Theology of Law and*

Authority in the English Reformation (Atlanta: Scholars Press, 1991).

[4] Joan Lockwood O'Donovan, "Subsidiarity and Political Authority in Theological Perspective," *Studies in Christian Ethics* 6.1: 19.

[5] *Ibid.*, 26-27

[6] *Ibid.*, 29

[7] *Ibid.*, 28

[8] *Ibid.*, 30

[9] *Ibid.*, 33

[10] Joan E. O'Donovan, "Man in the Image of God: The Disagreement between Barth and Brunner Reconsidered," *Scottish Journal of Theology* 39: 437.

[11] *Ibid.*, 439

[12] *Ibid.*, 457, 459

[13] *Ibid.*, 435

[14] *Ibid.*, 456-57

[15] Balthasar Hubmaier, "Freedom of the Will, I," in *Balthasar Hubmaier: Theologian of Anabaptism*, tr. and ed. H. Wayne Pipkin and John H. Yoder (Scottdale: Herald Press, 1989), 426-48.

[16] Hubmaier, "Freedom of the Will, II," in *Balthasar Hubmaier: Theologian of Anabaptism*, 449-91.

[17] *Ibid.*, 473.

[18] Hubmaier, "A Christian Catechism," *Balthasar Hubmaier: Theologian of Anabaptism*, 359.

[19] Hubmaier, "Freedom of the Will, I," 429.

[20] *Ibid.*, 430

[21] *Ibid.*, 432

[22] *Ibid.*, 438

[23] *Ibid.*, 438

[24] *Ibid.*, 442

[25] *Ibid.*, 443

[26] Hubmaier, "Freedom of the Will, II," 454.

[27] *Ibid.*, 456

[28] *Ibid.*, 467

[29] *Ibid.*, 472

[30] "Pilgram Marpeck's Confession of 1523," *The Writings of Pilgram Marpeck*, trans. and ed. William Klassen and Walter Klaassen (Scottdale: Herald Press, 1978), 127.

[31] *Ibid.*, 128

[32] *Ibid.*, 129

[33] *Ibid.*, 131

Chapter 36

[1] The venue was a conference on ecclesiology for scholars, church leaders and students of theology hosted by the Institute of Mennonite Studies, at Associated Mennonite Biblical Seminary, Elkhart, Indiana on February 5, 2000. The theme was "Without Spot or Wrinkle: Reflecting Theologically on the Nature of the Church." The proceedings have been published recently: Karl Koop and Mary H. Schertz, eds., *Without Spot or Wrinkle: Reflecting Theologically on the Nature of the Church*, Occasional Papers 21 (Elkhart: Institute of Mennonite Studies, 2000).

[2] Privately Volf told me he considered Yoder one of the most important theologians of the second half of the twentieth century.

[3] On March 16 and 17, 2000, Conrad Grebel College and Toronto Mennonite Theological Centre sponsored a series of lectures and conversations by Volf on topics related to his books *Exclusion and Embrace* and *After Our Likeness*.

[4] The gender specific component of the affirmation "I believe in God the 'Father' almighty" is relative to the ancient identification of transcendence with the male. What is not relative is the notion behind this gender specific language—namely the firm belief that the first person of the Trinity refers to the God who is separate from the created order, in contrast to the deities of the pagan nature religions. Because language is dynamic, and because sexuality itself evolves, there is no guarantee that "fatherhood" continues to represent transcendence as it did for the ancients. It is logically conceivable, for instance, that in the future the "father" image might have an immanentist connotation and "mother" represent transcendence. Consequently, it is theologically unsound to absolutize the "father" image in the first article. Not only is it unwise to do so, it is idolatrous contravening the Hebraic conviction that God is beyond all form.

[5] While Jesus of Nazareth was of male gender, the eternal Christ that was manifest in him is not gender exclusive.

[6] Miroslav Volf, *After Our Likeness: The Church as the Image of the Trinity* (Grand Rapids: William B. Eerdmans Publishing Company, 1998).

[7] Joseph Cardinal Ratzinger with Vittorio Messori, *The Ratzinger Report: An Exclusive Interview on the State of the Church* (San Francisco: Ignatius Press, 1985), 46.

[8] Volf in his book, *After Our Likeness*, refers to the Anabaptists only once in a footnote and names them together with the English Separatists (Volf, 132, n.19). The name of John Howard Yoder also appears only once together with James W. McClendon, Jr., and others who seek "to reclaim the communal dimensions of the believers' church heritage" (Volf, 3). This astonishing oversight on the part of Volf is unforgivable academically, since his own subsequent proposal bears such a remarkable similarity to what Anabaptists had said much earlier and his older contemporary John H. Yoder made his life-long preoccupation. Had he taken the Anabaptist tradition more seriously, his own claims would seem less novel and would have been modified at a number of important points. More of this below.

[9] Peter Rideman quite explicitly grounds the notion of Christian communalism in the divine Trinitarian community: "Community, however, is naught else than

that those who have fellowship have all things in common together, none having aught for himself, but each having all things with the others, even as the Father hath nothing for himself, but all that he hath he hath with the Son, and again, the Son hath nothing for himself, but all that he hath, he hath with the Father and all who have fellowship with him. Thus all those who have fellowship with him likewise have nothing for themselves, but have all things with their Master and with all those who have fellowship with them, that they might be one in the son as the Son is in the Father." *Confession of Faith* (Bungay, Suffolk: Hodder and Stoughton in conjunction with The Plough Publishing House, 1938), 43. Had Volf known about some of these early 16th century writers, and had he located the origins of the Free Church tradition not in the 16th c. English dissenting tradition but in continental Anabaptism, his criticisms of the Free Church would have been different.

[10] Although Volf does not make this point, it is clear that Ratzinger falls into the ancient Realist camp in this regard, as opposed to the Nominalists; that is, invisible universals are real and the reality of the particulars/individuals lies in their participation in the universal. In contrast, the Free Church tradition, including Volf (something which he does not explicitly acknowledge in this particular work) falls in the voluntaristic/nominalist tradition, where the individual/particular acting subject is more real than the universal. In this latter nominalistic tradition God, and the three divine persons within God, tend to be viewed as individual acting agents. In my own thinking I have in recent years sought to retrieve some modified forms of Realism. Volf's theology is too nominalistic in my view, and as such reflects most contemporary theology.

[11] One is reminded here of Bonhoeffer's famous understanding of the church as Christ present. Although Volf refers to Bonhoeffer a number of times, it is surprising that he does not make this comparison more explicitly. In Bonhoeffer's thought the identity between Christ and the Church is less mystical and ontological, and more concrete, sociological, and historical.

[12] I might observe here that in the West the Mass is understood as a repeated reinactment of the sacrifice of Christ. The East understands the Eucharist much more broadly as the celebration of the incarnation as such—including the whole Christ-event—in which the created order is taken up into the very Trinitarian life of God.

[13] Volf describes the Eastern celebration of the Eucharist, paraphrasing and quoting Zizioulas, in these terms:

> Since the eucharistic celebration and the (eschatological) heavenly liturgy represent an identical reality, the structure of the heavenly congregation as described in the Apocalypse—the throne of God and of the Lamb, surrounded by the elders with 'seven spirits' and, before the throne, the 'sea of glass' (Rev. 4: 2-6)—serves as the model for the structure of the local church. 'The "place (or throne) of God" in the eucharistic synaxis is occupied in reality by the bishop . . . who is surrounded by the thrones of the "presbyters" and assisted by deacons, with the people facing him.' The Spirit constitutes the church through the bishop, the presbyters and deacons, and the

people in their structured relationships." (Volf, 108)

Volf agrees with those who charge Zizioulas with having an "overrealized eschatology" (Volf, 101).

[14] Cf. Donald Durnbaugh, *The Believers' Church: The History and Character of Radical Protestantism* (Scottdale: Herald Press, 1968), 8-22. Durnbaugh discusses the three different views of the origins of the Believers' Church: sectarian, Puritan, Anabaptist, and makes a persuasive case for the Anabaptists as the true progenitors of the Free Church movement.

[15] Robert Friedmann, *The Theology of Anabaptism* (Scottdale: Herald Press, 1973), 78-87.

[16] In a January 25 e-mail/letter to Volf I made the following observations:

> There are a number of initial observations I have about your book. I like very much your Trinitarian approach; I have since the early 1980s argued in various publications that Mennonites need to ground their concern for social ethics in Trinitarian theology. I also think the distinction/connectedness between the Immanent and Economic Trinity is very important. But, I wonder, whether one can know as much about the Immanent Trinity as you seem to assume. I find also with Barth (I'm just ploughing through his Vol. III/1) that, despite his suspicion of all speculative thought, he seems to know a lot about the intrinsic nature of God. Also, I think you rightly critique the feminist (in your 'Embrace' book) grounding of gender identity in God, as really first a projection and then a reappropriation. But don't you do the same when you understand the inner relational-personal sociality of the Trinity as the basis of gender identity and relationships? Most mystifying I found (in your ecclesiology book) why you take John Smyth as *the* representative of Free Church ecclesiology without any reference whatsoever to the Continental Anabaptists, who came almost 100 years earlier and, I would argue, are the real progenitors of the Free Church tradition. If you had done so, your critique of the Free Church tradition (as being too individualistic) would have had to be modified. Early Anabaptists had a non-individualistic ecclesiology very similar to the one you yourself espouse in the second part of your book. It's interesting that Ridemann, the early 16th c. Hutterite theologian grounds Hutterian communalism on the Trinity: as all three persons of the Trinity have everything in common so ought we to have everything in common.

[17] I have elsewhere discussed the Realist critique of a Nominalist/Voluntarist understanding of Church. Cf. "The Adequacy of Voluntarism in a Voluntaristic Age," *The Believers Church: A Voluntary Church* (Kitchener, ON: Pandora Press, co-published with Herald Press, 1998), 135-48. Also reprinted as Chapter 35 above.

[18] "Apologia," *Balthasar Hubmaier: Theologian of Anabaptism*, tr. and ed. H. Wayne Pipkin and John H. Yoder (Scottdale and Waterloo: Herald Press, 1989), 546-547.

¹⁹ For this observation I am indebted to John Toews, Romans scholar and President of Conrad Grebel College.

Chapter 37

¹ Thomas C. Oden, *Agenda For Theology: After Modernity . . . What?* (Grand Rapids: Zondervan, 1990)
² *The Living God: Systematic Theology: Volume One* (San Francisco: HarperSanFrancisco, 1987); *The Word of Life: Systematic Theology: Volume Two* (San Francisco: Harper SanFrancisco, 1989); *Life in the Spirit: Systematic Theology: Volume Three* (San Francisco: HarperSanFrancisco, 1992).
³ For a critical review of one of the volumes in this series of *Ancient Christian Commentary on Scripture*, see *First Things* No. 91 (March 1999): 40-3.
⁴ See Oden's response to Robin Darling Young of Catholic University of America in *First Things* No. 94 (June/July 1999): 3.
⁵ In his response to a critical review of his biblical commentary series by Robin Darling Young, Oden is more careful in the way he understands the diversity within the ecumenical consensus, denying a univocal patristic biblical understanding. "Fighting About the Fathers," *First Things* No. 94 (June/July 1999): 2.
⁶ Wolfart Pannenberg, *Systematic Theology: Volume 1* (Grand Rapids: Eerdmans, 1991); *Systematic Theology: Volume 2* (Grand Rapids: Eerdmans, 1994); *Systematic Theology: Volume 3* (Grand Rapids: Eerdmans, 1998).
⁷ John H. Yoder, "Radical Reformation Ethics in Ecumenical Perspective," *The Priestly Kingdom* (Notre Dame: University of Notre Dame Press, 1984), 117
⁸ Thomas C. Oden, *After Modernity . . . What? Agenda for Theology* (Grand Rapids: Zondervan, 1990).
⁹ Daniel Liechty, *Theology in Postliberal Perspective* (London and Philadelphia: SCM Press and Trinity International Press, 1990).
¹⁰ *Conrad Grebel Review*, 10.2 (Spring 1992): 232.
¹¹ Miroslav Volf, *After Our Likeness: The Church as the Image of the Trinity* (Grand Rapids:Eerdmans, 1998); *Exclusion and Embrace: A Theological Exploration of Identity, Otherness, and Reconciliation* (Nashville: Abingdon Press, 1996).

Index

A
Abortion: 89, 343, 349, 354.
Adorno, Theodor W.: 55, 583 n5.
  See also Frankfurt School.
Alston, Wallace: 23.
Anselm, St.: 30, 337.
Aquinas, Thomas: 525, 557.
Arendt, Hannah: 73.
Arianism: 243.
Aristotle: 94, 105, 109, 495, 509, 525, 528.
Arminius, Jacobus: 489.
Atheism: 23, 484, 558.
Augustine, St.: 307, 487, 490, 495, 605 n49.
Augustinian: 285, 395, 490, 495-06, 528.

B
Bach: 434.
Bacon, Francis: 79, 349, 363.
Barth, Karl: 34, 39, 43, 134-37, 140, 174, 190, 206, 270, 291 302, 307, 322, 364, 379-81; 407-08, 415-16, 423, 426, 457, 458, 476, 477-85, 521, 529-31, 539, 608 n7, 617 nn16-17, 629 n4, 631 n3.
Batchelor, Edward: 633 n7.
Baum, Gregory: 38, 54, 67, 80-84, 118, 126, 182, 443, 522, 574 n25, 579 n38, 586 n6, 625 n4.
Bender, Harold S.: 162, 164-65, 178, 304-06, 581n6, 584 nn7, 9, 588 n4, 595 n19, 607 n3, 625 n4, 626 n20.
Bible:
– and doctrinal thinking 244-45,
– and trinitarian orthodoxy: 252-62;
– and theocentric christology: 281-87; 323-24, 327, 334-35;
confessional reading of – : 340-54; 357-59, 367, 371;
– in biblical and systematic theology: 372-89;
and nationality: 470-73;
and homosexuality: 514-17; 597

n46, 598 n53, 604 n21, 613 n25, 616 n4, 618 n36.
Biblical hermeneutics: 225, 513 *see also* hermeneutics.
Biblical narrative: 84, 228, 229, 253, 262, 280, 307, 351.
Biblical realism: 168, 250, 602 n21.
Biblicism: 48-49.
Bloch, Ernst: 443, 444, 625 n3, 626 n18.
Blondel: 39.
Bloom, Allan: 101.
Bondi, Roberta C.: 270, 606 n61.
Bonino, José Míguez: 23.
Brackney, William H.: 524.
Brown, Mitchell: 237, 242, 602 n15, 624 n29.
Brubacher, Glen: 337, 611 n2.
Brunk, George R.H.: 304, 598 n54.
Burkholder, J. Lawrence: 182, 184, 272-86, 289, 295, 298, 426, 581 n2, 606 n9, 609 n23.
Burkholder, John Richard: 630 n19.
Busche, Jürgen: 625 n7.

C
Canon, biblical: 346, 352, 362, 490.
Capitalism: 25, 33, 214, 463, 592 n35.
Carter, Craig: 300, 608 n1.
Catholic
– ecclesiology: 559-62
Catholic, Roman: 63, 81, 304, 329, 339, 353, 363, 428, 438, 467, 517, 537, 539, 546, 550, 559-62, 573 n8, 589 n6, 590 n14, 597 n16, 617 n12.
Celibacy: 523.
Chalcedon: 307, 315-6, 392, 407-20.
Christocentrism: 116, 246, 281, 370
Christology: 82, 87, 142, 192, 200, 222, 233, 236, 272, 273, 307, 322, 406-20, 581 n9, 585 n34, 604 nn23, 30, 605 n35, 622 n1.
Classical consciousness: 328.
Classical imagination: 139-41, 306, 319, 323.

Classical Orthodoxy: 226, 239, 249, 264-7, 269, 316, 317.
Cochrane, Charles Norris: 266, 617 n12, 623 n12.
Collingwood, R.G.: 42.
Community: 16, 34, 44, 78, 102-03, 109-110, 116-18, 129, 131, 158, 170, 337, 338, 423, 441, 453, 457, 517, 527-8, 573 n8, 580 n4, 587n52, 593 n2, 597 n46, 598 n54, 619 n42, 632 n18. Christian– : 180-81, 211, 229, 249-50, 260, 273, 280-85, 305, 339, 360, 368, 375-80, 386, 409-13, 491, 501, 538-41, 548-50, 560-62;
Gordon D. Kaufman on – : 142-43, 152-53, 274-5;
Hutterian Anabaptist – : 398;
John Howard Yoder on – : 293-317;
Mennonite – : 210, 216-30, 233-43, 289-90, 340-53, 355-56, 400-405, 430, 501-11, 514-21;
Messianic – 189, 199-200, 207, 69 n13;
Nationalism and – : 461-73, 475-80;
Peter Rideman on – :398, 633 n9;
Puralism and the religious – 82-87.
Concern group: 277, 278, 289, 291, 298, 604 n4, 610 n 44.
Confessing Church: 226, 387, 457, 478, 483-85, 498, 630 n22.
Confession, Dordrecht: 220, 283, 358, 363, 401, 621 n18.
Confession, Mennonite: 210, 220-24, 229, 239, 244, 363, 365, 368, 400-401, 405, 456, 596 n34, 619 n18.
Congregationalism: 547, 595 n46.
Conrad Grebel College: 21, 36, 101, 117, 121, 133, 154, 209, 272, 290, 291, 307, 308, 469, 486, 493, 494, 499, 508, 513, 514, 516, 538, 606 n2, 609 n25, 616 n3, 624 n7, 633 n1, 635 n3.
Constantine: 309-12.
Constantinian: 273, 307, 308, 312;
Constantinianism: 307.

Consumerism: 27, 37, 434.
Conversion: 22, 34, 79, 110, 116, 136, 141, 210, 222, 241 122, 165-66, 335-36, 344, 376, 390, 402, 461, 510, 589 n6, 616 n4, ;
of Constantine 268-69, 293-94;
Copleston, Frederick: 15, 567 n1.
Creed, eccumenical: 125, 210, 227-29, 239, 248, 259, 306, 339, 388, 596 n32.
Creed, Nicene: 240, 253-5, 333, 361, 604 n30.
Cross: 169-171, 491, 562-63;
ethic of the 192;
way of the 179, 292-94, 492, 495.

D
Darwin, Charles: 615 n10.
Davis, Charles: 117-19, 579 n34, 580 n46, 583 n5.
Deleuze, Gilles: 562.

Dewart, Leslie: 38.
Dilthey, Wilhelm: 42.
Dixon, John W. Jr.: 120, 580 n48.
Docetism: 233, 243.
Doctrine of creation: 86, 322, 457, 472, 495.
Doctrine of God:14, 87, 152-53, 232, 241-45, 248, 257, 261-71, 286-87, 290, 296, 298, 306, 317, 322, 361, 367-69, 392-405, 407, 409, 415, 457, 486, 493, 495, 538, 551, 554, 558, 564.
Doctrine of the Church: 205, 230, 241, 244, 250, 259, 501, 539, 543, 561.
Doctrine of the Holy Spirit: 87, 222, 244, 322, 347, 371, 422, 424-8.
Doctrine of the Trinity: 142, 243, 255, 263-64, 356, 400, 409, 422, 490-91, 541.
Driver, Tom F.: 24.

E
Eckhardt, Meister: 395.

Ecumenical:
– body: 428;
– Christianity: 14-15, 233;
– confessions: 352;
– consensus: 558-60, 638 n5;
– councils: 296, 353, 363, 556-57;
– Credo: 393;
– Gifts of the Spirit: 537-552
Ellul, Jacques: 67.
Engels, Freidrich: 448, 626 n22, 24.
Enlightenment: 36, 82, 101, 109, 113-14, 119-20, 123, 172, 206-07, 210, 230, 245, 286, 367, 394, 509-11.
"dialectic of – ": 37, 54-66;
Immanuel Kant and –:107-08, 402;
George Grant and – : 22, 31, 90;
Gordon D. Kaufman and – : 37-41, 48, 174-77;
modernity and – : 69-74, 161-64, 198, 214-17;
– and nationalism: 460-62;
post- – : 16, 151-52, 201-02, 208, 211, 238;
Robert Friedmann and – : 164-67.
Environment(al): 71-72, 79, 83, 136, 196, 202, 271, 286, 341, 356, 368-69, 402, 404-05, 418, 424, 511.

F
Fall, the: 119, 294, 366, 377, 497, 516, 520, 527-33, 542;
fallenness: 79, 298, 305, 495, 521.
Fanon, Frantz: 302
Fascism: 43, 72, 464.
Feminism: 114, 237.
Feuerbach, Ludwig: 141.
Finger, Thomas N.: 183, 192, 228, 237, 247, 360, 367, 404, 573 n33, 586 n2, 601 n1, 613 n28, 620 n31.
Foundational: 78, 117, 230, 476.
Foundationalism: 16, 302, 315, 507;
anti – : 15-17, 315, 506;
non – : 191, 290, 293, 457.
Frankfurt School (of Critical Theory): 30, 54, 84, 183, 200, 443, 446, 570 n2, 574 n26, 593 n24.

Free church ecclesiology: 539-45, 562.
Free will: 210, 22, 241-42, 245, 396, 402, 489, 526, 534-36.
Frei, Hans: 142, 584 n9.
Freud, Sigmund: 437.
Freidmann, Robert: 162-81, 237, 305, 584 n12, 611 n3.
Fundamentalism: 64, 134, 210, 241, 344, 348, 363, 403, 596 n38, 612 n16.

G
Gadamer, Hans-Georg: 112, 579 n24.
General Conference Mennonite Church: 225, 343, 345, 355, 365, 598 n52, 615 n3.
Gilkey, Langdon: 38, 588 n40.
Goertz, Hans-Jürgen: 210, 213-18, 447, 452, 595 n14, 625 n6.
Grant, George: 21-25, 38, 41, 55, 64, 67, 88-100, 132, 141, 150, 321, 567 n3, 569 n1, 575 n1, 576 nn3-7, 15, 21, 40, 581 n5.
Grillmeier, Aloys: 257, 268, 407, 410, 604 n26.
Gross, Leonard: 212, 217, 224, 596 n9.
Grote, Jim: 77, 574 n21.
Gurion, Ben: 311.

H
Habermas, Jürgen: 83-84, 571 n3.
Hanson, R. P. C.: 265-69, 407,409,414, 605 n41, 622 n4.
Harder, Helmut: 366, 615 n15.
Harvey, Van A.: 23, 38.
Haskins, Charles Homer: 105-07, 578 n3.
Hauerwas, Stanley: 300, 500-03, 504-07, 630-31 nn3-5, 631-32 n4.
Hawking, Stephen: 147, 153, 582 n10.
Hegel, G. W. F.: 39, 43, 145, 570 n19.

Heidegger, Martin: 25, 88-100, 577 nn42-57, n59.
Henry, John Newman: 363, 371, 444, 615 n8, 625 n2.
Hermeneutics: 113, 122, 225, 339, 347, 353, 380, 506-07, 513-14, 597 n46, 598 n54, 602 n3, 611 n51, 613 n23, 614 n50.
Hershberger, Frederick: 277, 278, 288.
Herzog, Frederick: 23.
Heterogeneity: 216, 220, 232-38, 317, 347, 364, 377, 401, 405, 615 n11, 622 n31. *See also* polygenesis.
Hirsch, Emanuel: 47, 88-89, 328,407, 444, 475-86, 570 n41, 622 n2, 627 nn6-9, 629 nn2, 10, 13.
Historicism: 77-78, 89-93, 148-79, 502-11, 582 n3.
Hitler, Adolf: 99, 226, 270, 277, 408, 460, 464, 475, 485, 498, 508, 629 n1.
Hobbes, Thomas: 132, 136.
Holland, Scott: 272, 506-08, 606 n2, 632 n13.
Holmer, Paul: 506.
Holy Spirit: 78, 87, 124, 135, 153, 175, 180, 184, 219, 222, 231, 241, 243-44, 280, 287, 322, 338, 347, 351, 431, 459, 473, 497, 513, 516, 521, 538, 542, 547, 557-62, 585 n24.
doctrine of – : 255-71, 361-71, 421-28;
– and trinitarian God: 333-35, 487-92.
Homosexuality: 343, 345, 349, 354, 371, 388, 513-23, 551, 633 nn1, 3, 4, 7-10.
Horkheimer, Max: 55, 64, 571 n2.
Hubmaier, Balthasar: 219, 524, 534-36, 595 n26, 634 n15, 637 n18.

I
Idealism: 273, 277; German – 56, 571 n3.
Idolatry: 31, 52, 119, 146, 156, 229, 258, 270, 272, 415, 475, 538, 580 n46.

Immanent Trinity: 89, 140, 157, 192, 393, 395, 400, 487, 539, 546, 559, 621 n1-2, 637 n16.

Individualism: 27, 69, 143, 216, 275, 460-61, 505, 525, 541-44, 593 n3, 635 n8-9.

Irving, John: 488.

J
Janz, Denis: 218, 595 n23.
Joachim, of Fiore: 453.
Jonas, Hans: 67, 71-80, 150-51, 418, 510-11, 572 n9,11; 574 n12; 582 n11; 620 n44.
Joyce, James: 67.
Judaism: 92, 111, 124, 148, 251, 265, 610 n50;
John Howard Yoder and – : 291-97, 300-317, 609 n 25, 30, 34, 610 n38.

K
Kahane, Meir: 311, 610 n36.
Kant, Immanuel: 21, 33-35, 42, 92, 107-08, 141, 155, 174, 334, 366, 384, 402-03, 510, 573 n6.
Kauffman, Daniel: 212, 224, 403-04, 424, 621 n21.
Kaufman, Gordon D.: 21, 22-34, 36-53, 60, 64, 121, 138-58, 161-81, 182, 188, 191-202, 234, 237, 273-87, 289, 298, 305-06, 321-34, 327-73, 403-04, 418, 560, 567 n4, 569 n16, 570 n42, 581 nn3-4, 8, 583 n6, 589 nn10, 12, 14, 606 n4, 621 n22
Kaufman, Eduard G.: 288.
Keener, Carl S.: 235-36, 622 n28.
Kerr, Hugh T.: 580 n2.
Kerygma: 117, 168-69, 203, 226, 229, 253-79, 293, 338-39, 360, 372-73, 389, 404, 407-11, 471, 601 n61.
Klaassen, Walter: 289, 353, 433, 574 n24, 588 n4, 597 n46, 614 n48, 624 n2 (chap. 26), 634 n30.
Klassen, William: 289, 634 n30.

Koontz, Gayle Gerber: 237, 371, 405, 602 n12, 615 n19, 622 n30.
Koontz, Ted: 504-06, 632 n8.
Kuhn, Thomas S.: 573 n8.
Küng, Hans: 67, 85, 573 n8.

L
Lactantius: 307.
Lampert, Laurence: 93-94, 576 n8.
Leibniz, Gottfried: 91.
Lewis, C. S.: 54, 88.
Liberalism: 22-35, 39-40, 55-62, 90-92, 99, 205-07, 234, 342, 344, 463, 478, 484, 489, 504-07, 568 n51, 569 n1, 576 n6, 583 n5, 617 n12.
Lichdi, Diether Götz: 629 n3.
Liechty, Daniel: 560, 638 n9.
Lindbeck, George: 85, 121, 240, 389; 476, 504-06, 574 n28, 603 n17, 617 nn7, 12, 620 n49.
Lindsey, Hal: 432.
Liverani, Mario: 471, 628 n23.
Lockwood O'Donovan, Joan: 77-78, 524, 527-31, 574 n22, 634 n4.
Loeschen, John R.: 393, 399-400, 621 n12.
Loewen, Howard John: 202, 210, 218-23, 239, 582 n1, 592 n29, 595 n22, 596 n34.
Lonergan, Bernard: 121, 192, 196, 201, 324, 580 nn49-50, 590 n14, 591 n27, 596 n45, 599 n55, 610 n5, 615 n8, 616 nn3-4, 623 n10.
Lovitt, William: 577 n42.
Luther, Martin: 149, 166, 185, 214-15, 219, 242, 325, 396-98, 479, 626 n27, 629 n12.

M
MacIntyre, Alasdair: 501-12, 579 n32, 632 n6.
MacMullen, Ramsay: 282, 606 n 19.
Mannheim, Karl: 455, 627 n37.
Marcion: 362, 455, 490.
Marcuse, Herbert: 571 n2, 591 n24.
Marpeck, Pilgram: 494, 499, 582 n2,

634 n30.
Marquardt, Friedrich-Wilhelm: 568 n53
Marsden, George M.: 348-49.
Martin, Dennis D.: 260-61, 605 n31.
Marx, Karl: 21, 35, 39, 42, 417, 448.
Marxism: 25, 47, 78, 92, 148, 443-55, 463, 484, 591 n24.
Mary, Virgin: 373, 347-442, 624 n3, 624 n4.
Materialism: 75, 151, 200, 430, 433-34.
Maurice, F. D.: 59-60.
Meagher, John: 124, 580 n53.
Meir, Golda: 311.
Mennonite Church: 183-84, 286-87, 292, 400-02, 468-70, 508-09;
– and Biblical Interpretation: 337-54;
– and Doctrine: 364-67;
– and Systematic Theology: 191-208, 209-31, 402-05.
Metz, Johann Baptist: 84, 139, 157, 192.
Miller, John W.: 289, 298, 313-15, 472.
Miller, Marlin E.: 261.
Mitcham, Carl: 77, 574 n21.
Mojzes, Paul: 467, 628 n17.
Moltmann, Jürgen: 139, 157, 183, 192, 322, 422, 443, 539, 544.
Monasticism: 270, 284.
Mozart, Wolfgang A.: 144.
Münster (Westphalia): 215, 422, 450-51.
Müntzer, Thomas: 170, 186, 397-98, 443-55, 491, 625 nn3-6, 626 nn17-21, 627 nn28-29.
Murphy, Nancey: 132-37, 581 n1.
Mysticism: 23, 327, 397-98, 424, 445.

N
National Socialism: 47, 89, 99, 457, 459-62, 474-85.
Nationalism: 26-28, 456-73, 478, 484, 577 n38.
Natural Law: 15, 50, 329, 396, 517-519, 526, 528.
Neo-orthodoxy: 39-40, 58, 235, 361-64, 368.
Nestorians: 410.
Neufeldt, Ron: 578 n2.
Newman, John Henry: 363, 371, 444.
Nicea: 124, 226, 229, 258, 268-69.
Niebuhr, Reinhold: 39, 278, 292, 301-02, 304.
Niebuhrian Political Realism: 278-79, 304, 306, 508, 563, 630 n2.
Nietzsche, Friedrich: 25, 39, 69, 90-100, 417, 509, 526, 569 n1, 572 n3, 578 n43.
Non-resistance and/or Non-violence: 36, 48-53, 87, 136-37, 164, 174, 177, 185, 210, 222, 242-44, 251-52, 274, 276-77, 292, 295, 297, 301-02, 305, 309, 343, 377, 402-03, 477, 486-500, 508-09, 552, 554, 564.
Nonfoundationalism: 290, 457.
Novak, Michael: 38.

O
Oden, Thomas: 17, 322, 537, 554-61, 638 nn1-5, 638 n8.
Ogden, Schubert: 121.
Ollenburger, Ben C.: 247, 261, 372, 380-86, 603 n1, 605 n30, 605 n35, 616 n2, 617 n21.
Orders of Creation: 50, 456-73, 633 n2.
Ordinances: 222, 243-44, 327 – See also Sacraments
Orthodoxy (Classical, Theological, Trinitarian): 15, 22, 64, 86, 107, 125, 187, 210, 226, 234-37, 239, 247-71, 281-85, 300-17, 326, 340, 344, 350-54, 361, 392-405, 408-09, 411, 413, 415, 526, 560
Orthodoxy, Protestant: 226, 361, 363, 408, 415, 460, 485.
Orthodoxy, Eastern: 249, 363, 428,

467, 550.
Orthopraxis: 187, 189, 200, 204, 236, 239, 326, 367, 583, 587 n25.

P
Pacifism: see Non-resistance
Packull, Werner: 212, 285-86, 289, 447, 449, 454, 469, 499, 594 n8, 607 n25, 621 n4, 625 n4, 625 n6, 626 nn17, 26, 627, n35.
Pannenberg, Wolfhart: 17, 89, 139, 157, 183, 192, 273, 322-23, 393, 537, 539, 554, 558-60, 585 n2, 606 n1, 610 n50, 621 n1, 638 n6.
Peace Witness: 14-15, 248, 290, 292, 305, 370, 428, 457, 486, 494, 550-52. *See also* Non-resistance.
Peachey, Paul: 289.
Pelikan, Jaroslav: 124, 357, 580 n52, 615 n4.
Pentecostalism: 421-28, 550.
Pietism: 215, 348, 350, 389,
Plato/Platonic thought: 68-9, 76, 92-100, 109, 130, 151, 157, 171, 265, 296, 395, 418, 495, 525, 577 n22, 581 n4, 582 n3, 590 n14.
Pneumatology: 290, 296, 322, 421-22, 554.
Polygenesis: 220, 232, 238, 289. *See also* heterogeneity.
Positivism: 56, 82, 131, 179, 507, 568 n37, 583 n5.
Predestination: 167, 242, 396, 488-89, 526-27, 534.
Progressivism: 77, 192, 497, 528.

R
Rahner, Karl: 39, 190, 206, 329 621 n3.
Ratzinger, Joseph: 537, 539-46, 635 n7, 636 n10.
Realism: 349, 524-36, 549, 636 n10.
Biblical – : 168, 250, 604 n21;
Niebuhrian – : 508, 563, 630 n2.
Reason: 15-17, 26, 55, 58, 64-66, 68-70, 77, 198, 573 n6, 577 n21, 583 n5, 600 n58, 627 n5.
Instrumental – : 90, 100;
Technical – : 14, 37, 114, 127, 130, 163, 176, 198, 202, 334, 465, 620 n44.
Redekop, Calvin Wall: 209, 289, 574 n27, 593 n1, 622 n31.
Redekop, John: 365, 615 n12.
Reform, Magisterial/Protestant: 164, 310, 327, 573 n8, 592 n35.
Reform, Radical: 14, 132-33, 164, 250-51, 289, 308-11, 444, 524, 588 n4, 592 n35, 603 n3.
Reimer, A. James: 154, 247, 337, 372, 568 n37, 569 nn13, 15, 570 n41, 575 n33, 34, 576 n18, 580 n55, 592 n29, 603 n1, 608 nn5, 6, 15, 609 nn20, 23, 611 n12, 611 n2, 615 n9, 13, 616 n2, 617 n15, 622 n31, 622 n6, 624 nn3, 4, 626 n12, 627 nn4,6, 628 n15, 629 n2, 8, 631 n4, 5, 633 n1
– Correspondence with Gordon Kaufman: 154-58.
Reimer, Margaret Loewen: 291, 615 n11, 631 n5.
Reimer, P. J. B.: 616 n5.
Resurrection: 84, 172, 222, 241, 243, 245, 262, 266, 272, 280, 287, 293, 333, 344, 360-61, 366, 373, 377, 404, 427, 432, 434-35, 451, 497-98, 522, 532-34, 538, 552, 606 n1, 612 n4.
Revolution, Scientific: 167, 349, 363, 615 n10.
Ritual: 201, 473.
Rotstein, Abraham: 567 n14, 568 n52, 577 n26.
Ruether, Rosemay Radford: 23.
Rusch, William G.: 263, 605 n39.

S
Sacramentalism: 162, 178, 253, 328, 542, 592 n35.
Sacraments: 172, 310, 327, 428, 550.
Salvation: 77, 82, 219, 222, 229, 241, 244, 264, 272, 282, 293, 310, 325-26, 340-41, 344, 353, 358, 362, 366, 385,

394, 402, 411-415, 420, 438, 451, 453, 470, 485, 487, 516, 542, 545-46, 548.
Sawatsky, Rodney: 116, 579, n33, 606 n2, 609 n23.
Schäfer, Karin: 477, 481-85, 625 n9.
Schleiermacher, Friedrich: 39, 307, 385, 568 n54.
Schleitheim: 214-15, 223, 273-74, 286, 304, 397, 495-96, 499, 601 n62.
Scholasticism: 363, 412, 613 n19.
Scholasticism, Protestant: 350, 363.
Scholder, Klaus: 481.
Schroeder, David: 67, 572 n1, 631 n2.
Scotus, Duns: 525.
Sectarianism: 193-200, 281, 291, 469.
Secularism: 424, 434, 484.
Sermon on the Mount: 50, 136, 221, 241, 243, 273, 278-81, 428, 479, 491.
Sexuality: 230, 244, 343, 345, 349, 354, 371, 388, 472, 513-24, 551, 633 nn1-10, 635 n4.
Seymour, William Joseph: 425.
Shank, David: 289, 607 n5.
Shinn, Roger L.: 23, 302, 633 n7.
Siebert, Rudolf J.: 54, 67, 83-4, 568 n37, 574 n26, 627 n4.
Simons, Menno: 219, 397, 399-400, 451, 557, 595 n27, 621 n10.
Smyth, John: 539, 544, 637 n16.
Snyder, C. Arnold: 12, 162, 236, 289, 499, 582 n2, 602 n6, 607 n6.
Social Justice: 67-87, 103, 344-45, 438, 506, 513, 594 n3, 594 n7, 600 n58.
Socrates: 15.
Sorensen, Andrew A.: 580 n4.
Sovereignty of God: 196, 242, 330, 332, 396, 550.
Spender, Stephen: 68, 572 n2, 576 n5.
Spiritual Warfare: 421-36, 444, 623 n6.

Stayer, James: 289, 447, 626 n18, 626 n21, 629 n12.
Steiner, George: 577 n22.
Steiner, Samuel J.: 209, 574 n27, 592 n1, 622 n31.
Stendahl, Krister: 242, 380-86, 603 n21, 617 nn21-22.
Stoesz, Willis: 447, 627 n28.
Storch, Nicholas: 447.
Strong, August H.: 349.
Stuhlmacher, Peter: 349, 613 n25.
Swartley, Willard M.: 191, 247, 589 n1, 597 n46, 603 n1, 613 n22, 614 nn48, 50, 622 n31.
Swartzentruber, A. Orley: 289.
Sykes, Stephen: 54-66, 182, 190, 205-07, 568 n54, 571 n7, 588 n10, 592 n38.
Syncretism: 60, 64.

T
Temple, William: 59.
Tennyson, Alfred Lord: 132, 136.
Tertullian: 306-07.
Theology:
Anabaptist – : 164-73, 186, 304, 583-84 nn6-8, 584 nn12-13, 588 nn1-6;
Anglican – : 56, 61, 205-06, 592 n38;
Classical – : 36, 70, 86, 162, 208, 321-36, 555, 617 n12;
doctrinal – : 61-62, 166, 185-90, 205-06, 359, 367;
evangelical – :235, 612 n4;
liberation – 81-82, 84, 189, 200, 234-36, 402, 558;
Mennonite – : 77-79, 87, 161-80, 182-90, 191-208, 209-10, 220, 232-44, 248-49, 261, 272, 282, 287, 402, 444, 501, 504, 514, 582 n2, 586 n41, 588 n3, 593 n1, 595 n27, 596 n29;
narrative – : 235-36, 501-512, 632 nn3, 6, 23-24;
negative – : 30, 32;
radical – :40, 58, 81, 586 n40;
systematic – : 22, 54, 57, 61-65, 118,

133, 166-81, 182-90, 191-208, 209-31, 292, 322-28, 343, 350, 360, 373-91, 611 n3, 616 n3, 619 n37, 620 n43.
Tillich, Paul: 42, 47, 132, 134, 475-86, 628 nn10-14, 629 n2, 630 n14, 18.
Toews, John E.: 259, 604 n30.
Toews, Paul: 289, 606 n4.
Tracy, David: 24, 36-38, 58, 60, 64-67, 121, 172-77, 182, 190, 192, 194, 234, 507, 569 n4, 585 n22, 588 n9, 592 n47, 603 n3, 616 n3, 618 n35.
Trudeau, Pierre Elliot: 27.

U
Utopianism: 42, 72-77, 152, 446-48, 455.

V
Van Braght, Thieleman: 346.
Vander Goot, Henry: 229, 351-54, 600 n60, 614 n35.
VanderEnde, Ted: 237, 343, 345, 598 n54, 613 n20.
Vincent of Lerins: 555-56, 638 n2.
Volf, Miroslav: 323, 458, 537-52, 627 n3, 630 n2, 635 nn6, 8-11, 13,16.
Voluntarism: 164, 173, 209, 211, 524-36, 633 n2, 634 nn16, 30.
Voolstra, Sjouke: 226, 599 n57.
Vrcan, Srdjan: 628 n16.

W
Wagner, C. Peter: 426, 624 n6.
Weaver, Alain Epp: 138, 581 n1
Weaver, J. Denny: 87, 138, 217, 247-49, 256-69, 282, 575 n33, 595 n21, 598 n53, 602 n8, 603 n1, 604 n23, 622 n31.
Welch, Claudel: 573 n7.
Welker, Michael: 421-22, 428, 624 n1.
Wenger, John C.: 182-87, 219, 288, 326, 396-97, 588 n3, 595 n27, 621 n10.

Whillier, Wayne: 88, 575 n1.
Wiebe, Donald: 117-19, 579 n40.
William of Ocham: 525.
Wittgenstein, Ludwig: 390.
Wolf, Arnold: 311.
Woolf, Virginia: 68.

Y
Yoder, John Howard: 48, 52, 125, 162-63, 168-78, 182, 186, 202, 228, 236-37, 273-76, 282, 322, 353, 471, 476, 494, 502, 506-07, 514, 538, 560, 580 n56, 581 nn2,6, 585 nn22-23, 26, 34, 596 n46, 598 n51, 600 n58, 603 n4-22, 605 n37, 607 nn1-2, 4, 8, 608 n1, 609 nn21, 34, 614 n50, 629 n4, 631 n2, 634 n15, 635 nn2, 8.
– and trinitarian orthodoxy: 247-70;
legacy of – : 288-99;
– on Jewish Christianity: 300-17.
Yoder, Perry B.: 236, 605 n5.

Z
Zionism: 309-10, 609 n26.
Zizioulas, Metropolitan John D.: 537-46, 636 n13.
Zwingli, Huldryuch: 185, 452, 531, 594 n5, 595 n14, 597 n46.
Zylstra, Bernard: 568 n28.

The Author

A. James Reimer was born in Morris, Manitoba, the eldest of five children. He grew up in Altona, Manitoba, where he attended elementary and high school, and was baptized into the Altona Bergthaler Mennonite Church in 1958. In 1960, he enrolled in the Canadian Mennonite Bible College in Winnipeg, graduating in 1963 with a Bachelor of Christian Education degree. After two years as a news reporter for the *Red River Valley Echo*, Reimer taught at Elim Bible School in Altona for two years. He also directed Camp Assiniboia outside of Winnipeg from 1965 to 1971.

In 1967, Reimer began an Honours B.A. in History and Philosophy at the University of Manitoba, graduating in 1971. He was awarded a Rockefeller Theological Fellowship which led him to Union Theological Seminary in New York City for a year of studies in the Master of Divinity program. In 1972, Reimer moved back to Canada to begin a Master's degree in History at the University of Toronto, concentrating on European intellectual history. His major research work was on the philosopher Ludwig Feuerbach. While engaged in graduate studies, he was Student Services coordinator for the United Mennonite Conference of Ontario (now part of the Mennonite Conference of Eastern Canada), working with Mennonite students on university campuses.

In 1975, Reimer began Ph.D. studies at the University of St. Michael's College, affiliated with the University of Toronto. He graduated in 1983 with a dissertation on the topic, "Theological Method and Political Ethics: The Paul Tillich-Emanuel Hirsch Debate of 1934-35."

In 1978, Reimer began his teaching career at Conrad Grebel College, University of Waterloo, where he continues to teach in the areas of modern theology, Mennonite theology and ethics, and religion. For many years he was director of the Conrad Grebel College graduate program in theology (Master of Theological Studies). In 1990, he became the founding director of the Toronto Mennonite Theological Centre, a research and teaching centre at the Toronto School of Theology (TST). He has taught courses at TST since the early 1980s in Anabaptist-Mennonite history and theology, as well as in his area of specialty: German theology in the Hitler period, concentrating especially on Dietrich Bonhoeffer and the Confessing Church. Reimer has published many articles in academic journals and popular periodicals and is the author/editor of several books, including *The Emanuel Hirsch and Paul Tillich Debate: A Study in the Political Ramifications of Theology* (Edwin Mellen, 1989), translated into German as *Emanuel Hirsh und Paul Tillich: Theologie und Politik in einer Zeit der Krise* (Walter de Gruyter, 1995); and *The Influence of the Frankfurt School on Contemporary Theology: Critical Theory and the Future of Religion* (Edwin Mellen, 1992).

Reimer is a member of the Rockway Mennonite Church and is engaged frequently in teaching and preaching in the Mennonite community. Choral music has been an avocational interest of Reimer's since he directed the church choir in Altona, Manitoba. From 1967 to 1971, Reimer was the leader of a religious folk group in Manitoba, "The Faith and Life Singers." Since 1995, he has been singing bluegrass gospel music with a band named "Five-on-the-Floor." He is married to Margaret Loewen Reimer. They have three children: Christina, born 1975; Thomas, 1980; and Micah, 1983.

About Pandora Press

Pandora Press is a small, independently owned press dedicated to making available modestly priced books that deal with Anabaptist, Mennonite, and Believers Church topics, both historical and theological. We welcome comments from our readers.

Visit our full-service online Bookstore:
www.pandorapress.com

Esther and Malcolm Wenger, poetry by Ann Wenger, *Healing the Wounds* (Kitchener: Pandora Press, 2001; co-published with Herald Press).
  Softcover, 210 pp. ISBN 1-894710-09-6.
  $18.50 US/$21.00 Canadian. Postage $5.00 US/$7.00 Canadian
[Experiences of Mennonite missionaries with the Cheyenne people]

Pedro A. Sandín-Fremaint, *Cuentos y Encuentros: Hacia una Educación Transformadora* (Kitchener: Pandora Press, 2001).
  Softcover 163 pp ISBN 1-894710-08-8.
  $12.00 US/ $16.00 Canadian. Postage $5.00 US/$7.00 Canadian.
[Spanish. Stories and discussion questions for Christian education]

A. James Reimer, *Mennonites and Classical Theology: Dogmatic Foundations for Christian Ethics* (Kitchener: Pandora Press, 2001; co-published with Herald Press)
  Softcover, 650pp. ISBN 0-9685543-7-7
  $52.00 U.S./$65.00 Canadian. Postage: $5.00 U.S./$7.00 Can.
[A theological interpretation of Mennonite experience in 20th C.]

Walter Klaassen, *Anabaptism: Neither Catholic nor Protestant*, 3rd ed (Kitchener: Pandora Press, 2001; co-pub. Herald Press)
  Softcover, 122pp. ISBN 1-894710-01-0
  $12.00 U.S./$15.00 Can. Postage: $3.00 U.S./$4.00 Can.
[A classic interpretation and study guide, now available again]

Dale Schrag & James Juhnke, eds., *Anabaptist Visions for the new Millennium: A search for identity* (Kitchener: Pandora Press, 2001; co-published with Herald Press)
  Softcover, 242 pp. ISBN 1-894710-00-2
  $18.00 U.S./$24.00 Canadian. Postage $4.00 U.S./$5.00 Can.
  [Twenty-eight essays presented at Bethel College, June, 2000]

Harry Loewen, ed., *Road to Freedom: Mennonites Escape the Land of Suffering* (Kitchener: Pandora Press, 2000; co-published with Herald Press)
  Hardcover, large format, 302pp. ISBN 0-9685543-5-0
  $35.00 U.S./$39.50 Canadian. Postage: $7.00 U.S./$8.00 Can.
  [Life experiences documented with personal stories and photos]

Alan Kreider and Stuart Murray, eds., *Coming Home: Stories of Anabaptists in Britain and Ireland* (Kitchener: Pandora Press, 2000; co-published with Herald Press)
  Softcover, 220pp. ISBN 0-9685543-6-9
  $22.00 U.S./$25.00 Canadian. Postage: $4.00 U.S./$5.00 Can.
  [Anabaptist encounters in the U.K.; personal stories/articles]

Edna Schroeder Thiessen and Angela Showalter, *A Life Displaced: A Mennonite Woman's Flight from War-Torn Poland*
(Kitchener: Pandora Press, 2000; co-published with Herald Press)
  Softcover, xii, 218pp. ISBN 0-9685543-2-6
  $20.00 U.S./$24.00 Canadian. Postage: $4.00 U.S./$5.00 Can.
  [A true story: moving, richly-detailed, told with candor and courage]

Stuart Murray, *Biblical Interpretation in the Anabaptist Tradition*
(Kitchener: Pandora Press, 2000; co-published with Herald Press)
  Softcover, 310pp. ISBN 0-9685543-3-4
  $28.00 U.S./$32.00 Canadian. Postage: $4.00 U.S./$5.00 Can.
  [How Anabaptists read the Bible; considerations for today's church]

Apocalypticism and Millennialism, ed. by Loren L. Johns
(Kitchener: Pandora Press, 2000; co-published with Herald Press)
  Softcover, 419pp; Scripture and name indeces
  ISBN 0-9683462-9-4
  $37.50 U.S./$44.00 Canadian. Postage: $5.00 U.S./$6.00 Can.
  [A clear, careful, and balanced collection: pastoral and scholarly]

Later Writings by Pilgram Marpeck and his Circle. Volume 1: The Exposé, A Dialogue and Marpeck's Response to Caspar Schwenckfeld
Translated by Walter Klaassen, Werner Packull, and John Rempel
(Kitchener: Pandora Press, 1999; co-published with Herald Press)
Softcover, 157pp. ISBN 0-9683462-6-X
$20.00 U.S./$23.00 Canadian. Postage: $4.00 U.S./$5.00 Can.
[Previously untranslated writings by Marpeck and his Circle]

John Driver, *Radical Faith. An Alternative History of the Christian Church*, edited by Carrie Snyder.
(Kitchener: Pandora Press, 1999; co-published with Herald Press)
Softcover, 334pp. ISBN 0-9683462-8-6
$32.00 U.S./$35.00 Canadian. Postage: $5.00 U.S./$6.00 Can.
[A history of the church as it is seldom told – from the margins]

C. Arnold Snyder, *From Anabaptist Seed. The Historical Core of Anabaptist-Related Identity*
(Kitchener: Pandora Press, 1999; co-published with Herald Press)
Softcover, 53pp.; discussion questions. ISBN 0-9685543-0-X
$5.00 U.S./$6.25 Canadian. Postage: $2.00 U.S./$2.50 Can.
[Ideal for group study, commissioned by Mennonite World Conf.]
Also available in Spanish translation: *De Semilla Anabautista*, from Pandora Press only.

John D. Thiesen, *Mennonite and Nazi? Attitudes Among Mennonite Colonists in Latin America, 1933-1945.*
(Kitchener: Pandora Press, 1999; co-published with Herald Press)
Softcover, 330pp., 2 maps, 24 b/w illustrations, bibliography, index. ISBN 0-9683462-5-1
$25.00 U.S./$28.00 Canadian. Postage: $4.00 U.S./$5.00 Can.
[Careful and objective study of an explosive topic]

Lifting the Veil, a translation of *Aus meinem Leben: Erinnerungen von J.H. Janzen*. Ed. by Leonard Friesen; trans. by Walter Klaassen
(Kitchener: Pandora Press, 1998; co-pub. with Herald Press).
Softcover, 128pp.; 4pp. of illustrations. ISBN 0-9683462-1-9
$12.50 U.S./$14.00 Canadian. Postage: $4.00 U.S. and Can.
[Memoir, confession, critical observation of Mennonite life in Russia]

Leonard Gross, *The Golden Years of the Hutterites*, rev. ed.
(Kitchener: Pandora Press, 1998; co-pub. with Herald Press).
  Softcover, 280pp., index. ISBN 0-9683462-3-5
  $22.00 U.S./$25.00 Canadian. Postage: $4.00 U.S./$5.00 Can.
  [Classic study of early Hutterite movement, now available again]

The Believers Church: A Voluntary Church, ed. by William H. Brackney
(Kitchener: Pandora Press, 1998; co-published with Herald Press).
  Softcover, viii, 237pp., index. ISBN 0-9683462-0-0
  $25.00 U.S./$27.50 Canadian. Postage: $4.00 U.S./$5.00 Can.
  [Papers from the 12th Believers Church Conference, Hamilton, ON]

An Annotated Hutterite Bibliography, compiled by Maria H.
Krisztinkovich, ed. by Peter C. Erb (Kitchener, Ont.: Pandora Press, 1998).
(Ca. 2,700 entries) 312pp., cerlox bound, electronic, or both.
  ISBN (paper) 0-9698762-8-9/(disk) 0-9698762-9-7
  $15.00 each, U.S. and Canadian. Postage: $6.00 U.S. and Can.
  [The most extensive bibliography on Hutterite literature available]

Jacobus ten Doornkaat Koolman, *Dirk Philips. Friend and Colleague of Menno Simons*, trans. W. E. Keeney, ed. C. A. Snyder
(Kitchener: Pandora Press, 1998; co-pub. with Herald Press).
  Softcover, xviii, 236pp., index. ISBN: 0-9698762-3-8
  $23.50 U.S./$28.50 Canadian. Postage: $4.00 U.S./$5.00 Can.
  [The definitive biography of Dirk Philips, now available in English]

Sarah Dyck, ed./tr., *The Silence Echoes: Memoirs of Trauma & Tears*
(Kitchener: Pandora Press, 1997; co-published with Herald Press).
  Softcover, xii, 236pp., 2 maps. ISBN: 0-9698762-7-0
  $17.50 U.S./$19.50 Canadian. Postage: $4.00 U.S./$5.00 Can.
  [First person accounts of life in the Soviet Union, trans. from German]

Wes Harrison, *Andreas Ehrenpreis and Hutterite Faith and Practice*
(Kitchener: Pandora Press, 1997; co-published with Herald Press).
  Softcover, xxiv, 274pp., 2 maps, index. ISBN 0-9698762-6-2
  $26.50 U.S./$32.00 Canadian. Postage: $4.00 U.S./$5.00 Can.
  [First biography of this important seventeenth century Hutterite leader]

C. Arnold Snyder, *Anabaptist History and Theology: Revised Student Edition* (Kitchener: Pandora Press, 1997; co-pub. Herald Press).
  Softcover, xiv, 466pp., 7 maps, 28 illustrations, index, bibliography. ISBN 0-9698762-5-4
  $35.00 U.S./$38.00 Canadian. Postage: $5.00 U.S./$6.00 Can.
[Abridged, rewritten edition for undergraduates and the non-specialist]

Nancey Murphy, *Reconciling Theology and Science: A Radical Reformation Perspective* (Kitchener, Ont.: Pandora Press, 1997; co-pub. Herald Press).
  Softcover, x, 103pp., index. ISBN 0-9698762-4-6
  $14.50 U.S./$17.50 Canadian. Postage: $3.50 U.S./$4.00 Can.
[Exploration of the supposed conflict between Christianity and Science]

C. Arnold Snyder and Linda A. Huebert Hecht, eds, *Profiles of Anabaptist Women: Sixteenth Century Reforming Pioneers* (Waterloo, Ont.: Wilfrid Laurier University Press, 1996).
  Softcover, xxii, 442pp. ISBN: 0-88920-277-X
  $28.95 U.S. or Canadian. Postage: $5.00 U.S./$6.00 Can.
[Biographical sketches of more than 50 Anabaptist women; a first]

The Limits of Perfection: A Conversation with J. Lawrence Burkholder 2nd ed., with a new epilogue by J. Lawrence Burkholder, Rodney Sawatsky and Scott Holland, eds.
(Kitchener: Pandora Press, 1996).
  Softcover, x, 154pp. ISBN 0-9698762-2-X
  $10.00 U.S./$13.00 Canadian. Postage: $2.00 U.S./$3.00 Can.
[J.L. Burkholder on his life experiences; eight Mennonites respond]

C. Arnold Snyder, *Anabaptist History and Theology: An Introduction* (Kitchener: Pandora Press, 1995).   ISBN 0-9698762-0-3
  Softcover, x, 434pp., 6 maps, 29 illustrations, index, bibliography.
  $35.00 U.S./$38.00 Canadian. Postage: $5.00 U.S./$6.00 Can.
[Comprehensive survey; unabridged version, fully documented]

C. Arnold Snyder, *The Life and Thought of Michael Sattler* (Scottdale: Herald Press, 1984).
   Hardcover, viii, 260pp. ISBN 0-8361-1264-4
   $10.00 U.S./$12.00 Canadian. Postage: $4.00 U.S./$5.00 Can.
[**First full-length biography of this Anabaptist leader and martyr**]

Pandora Press	**Herald Press**
33 Kent Avenue	616 Walnut Avenue
Kitchener, Ontario	Scottdale, PA
Canada N2G 3R2	U.S.A. 15683
Tel./Fax: (519) 578-2381	Orders: (800) 245-7894
E-mail:	E-mail:
info@pandorapress.com	hp@mph.org
Web site:	Web site:
www.pandorapress.com	www.mph.org